PHILIPPIKA

Altertumswissenschaftliche Abhandlungen
Contributions to the Study
of Ancient World Cultures

Herausgegeben von / Edited by
Joachim Hengstl, Elizabeth Irwin,
Andrea Jördens, Torsten Mattern,
Robert Rollinger, Kai Ruffing, Orell Witthuhn

55,2

2020
Harrassowitz Verlag · Wiesbaden

Legal Documents in Ancient Societies (LDAS) 8

Legal Documents in Ancient Societies

Accounts and Bookkeeping in the Ancient World

Edited by
Andrea Jördens and Uri Yiftach

2020
Harrassowitz Verlag · Wiesbaden

Gedruckt mit Unterstützung der German-Israeli Foundation.

Steering Committee of "Legal Documents in Ancient Societies":
Sophie Démare-Lafont, Mark Depauw, Michele Faraguna, Éva Jakab,
Dennis P. Kehoe, Uri Yiftach.

Bibliografische Information der Deutschen Nationalbibliothek
Die Deutsche Nationalbibliothek verzeichnet diese Publikation in der Deutschen
Nationalbibliografie; detaillierte bibliografische Daten sind im Internet
über http://dnb.dnb.de abrufbar.

Bibliographic information published by the Deutsche Nationalbibliothek
The Deutsche Nationalbibliothek lists this publication in the Deutsche
Nationalbibliografie; detailed bibliographic data are available in the internet
at http://dnb.dnb.de.

For further information about our publishing program consult our
website http://www.harrassowitz-verlag.de

Satz & Layout: Elke Fuchs
Printed on permanent/durable paper.
Printing and binding: Hubert & Co., Göttingen
Printed in Germany

ISSN 1613-5628
ISBN 978-3-447-11198-0

Contents

Graeco-Roman Egypt

Rome and the Empire

Vorwort

„Running a state is based on absorbing, processing and safekeeping information on its population and territory. The said operations are conducted by a series of officials and a range of bureaus whose cooperation is indispensable for the effective performance of these tasks. One mode of cooperation is vertical. A lower instance collects information on site and then forwards it to a higher instance, where the information is used to verify that past decisions were put into practice and as a basis for taking future ones. Still, bureaucratic apparatuses are pyramid-shaped, meaning that the higher instance is expected to receive information from more than one subordinated instance. Consequently, were the higher instance to receive the mass of raw information as collected by each and every subordinated instance on site, it would simply not possess the intellectual capacity of internalizing or deploying the data for its purposes. Accordingly, one of the key tasks facing the lower instances would be to convert the data of its operations in a new, handy format that could be feasibly processed and applied by its superiors."[1]

Mit diesen wenigen Sätzen ist die Problemstellung umrissen, die am Ausgang unser gemeinsamen Forschungen zum Thema *Synopsis: Data Processing and State Management in Roman Egypt (150 BCE-300 CE)* stand. Den Abschluß des mehrjährigen Gemeinschaftsprojektes, das von 2013 bis 2016 von der German-Israeli Foundation gefördert wurde,[2] bildete eine vom 22. bis 24. September 2016 in Schwetzingen nahe Heidelberg veranstaltete Tagung, deren Akten nunmehr hiermit publiziert werden. Unter dem Titel *Accounts and Bookkeeping in the Ancient World: Question of Structure* wurde sie zugleich als achtes Treffen der von Uri Yiftach mitbegründeten Arbeitsgruppe *Legal Documents in Ancient Societies* durchgeführt.

Diese Entscheidung erwies sich als überaus glücklich, erlaubte dies doch, die von uns erarbeiteten Ergebnisse, die vornehmlich an den aus dem griechisch-römischen Ägypten überlieferten Papyri gewonnen wurden, mit verwandtem Quellenmaterial anderer antiker Kulturen abzugleichen. Während dreier intensiver Tage wurde nicht nur immer wieder vor Augen geführt, welch großes Potential das stets unterschätzte und nur scheinbar unattraktive Format der Listen und Verzeichnisse besitzt, sondern auch, welch hoher Erkenntnisgewinn gerade aus einer solchen vergleichenden Betrachtung erwachsen kann. Die jetzt in gedruckter Form vorgelegten Beiträge haben die in sie gesetzten Erwartungen jedenfalls auf das schönste bestätigt. Der daraus zusammengestellte Band sieht sein Ziel erfüllt, wenn es ihm gelingt, zu weiterer Diskussion dieser oft zu unrecht vernachlässigten Textgattung anzuregen und im Idealfall das auf den ersten Blick recht sperrig wirkende Thema *Accounts*

---

1 So die Einleitung unseres gemeinsam bei der German-Israeli Foundation gestellten Antrags; vgl. die folgende Anm.

2 GIF Grant No: G-38-111.4/2011, Laufzeit 01/2013-12/2016; Principal Investigators: Prof. Dr. Andrea Jördens (Universität Heidelberg), Prof. Uri Yiftach-Firanko (Hebrew University, Jerusalem, ab 10/2014 Tel Aviv University); Mitarbeiter: Dr. Shimon Epstein (Jerusalem), Nikolaos Theodorakopoulos und besonders Dr. Nicola Reggiani (beide Heidelberg).

and Bookkeeping womöglich sogar auf längere Sicht vom Ruch gepflegter Langeweile zu befreien.

Den Teilnehmern an der ertragreichen Tagung gilt für ihre Beiträge und ihre Diskussionsbereitschaft nochmals unser herzlichster Dank, ebenso Susanne Rein und vor allem Nicola Reggiani für die unermüdliche Hilfe in der Organisation. Dank schulden wir überdies der German-Israeli Foundation, und zwar sowohl für die großzügige Finanzierung der Tagung wie auch des Projektes als ganzen. Durch den freundlicherweise gewährten Druckkostenzuschuß wurde zudem die Publikation der Akten in derselben Reihe ermöglicht, in der auch schon der erste Band der Reihe *Legal Documents in Ancient Societies* erschienen war. Sehr zu danken haben wir schließlich erneut vor allem Elke Fuchs, die sich durch ihr nun schon bewährtes Engagement in Sachen Satz und Layout ein weiteres Mal allergrößte Verdienste erworben hat.

Heidelberg, im November 2019 Andrea Jördens – Uri Yiftach

Ten Years LDAS: Summary of Activities and Results

The research group *Legal Documents in Ancient Societies* was founded in 2007 on the initiative of Roger S. Bagnall, then the head of the newly founded *Institute for the Study of the Ancient World at New York University*. The main objective of the group was to overcome academic compartmentalization in bringing together, and facilitating scientific exchange between students of everyday, legal and administrative documentation in different ancient civilizations and societies. To enable this, a six-headed steering committee was formed, each member representing one field of research. Sophie Démare Lafont (Paris): The Ancient Near East; Mark Depauw (Leuven), later substituted by Katelijn Vandorpe (Leuven): Ancient Egypt; Michele Faraguna (then Trieste): The Greek World; Éva Jakab (Szeged): Rome and Roman Law; Dennis Kehoe (Tulane): Law and Economics; Uri Yiftach (then Jerusalem): Greco-Roman Egypt.

Thanks to the generous support of the *Institute for the Study of the Ancient World at New York University*, lasting through the group's fourth meeting, and the friendly collaboration of the members of the steering committee it was possible to hold, in the period 2007-2016 eight meetings, each dedicated to a specific subject. In seeking overarching themes, whose discussion could open new horizons for the study of ancient documentation from hitherto unsought perspectives, *Legal Documents in Ancient Societies* has discussed in its meetings (each followed by a publication), media of documentation ("The Letter", Rome 2008), the selection, collection and organization of recorded data ("Identifiers", Leuven 2010), preservation and authentication methods of legal and administrative documents ("Archives", Trieste 2011; "Accounts", Schwetzingen 2016), the economic context of, and stimulus for the documentation of legal acts ("Transaction Costs", Washington, DC 2009). Other meetings were dedicated to more 'traditional' themes: Sale (Budapest, 2012), Guardianship (Jerusalem, 2013), and Loan (Paris, 2015). Even here, however, the analysis in the unique framework of cross departmental and doctrinal exchange has yielded new recognitions, which will certainly elicit discussion in years to come.

In the eighth meeting, taking place in Schwetzingen 22.-24.9.2016, was also for me the concluding meeting of ten years of highly intensive and productive collaboration. Taking place under, and funded by the *German Israel Foundation for Scientific Research and Development* in connection with the project *Synopsis: Data Processing and State Management in Roman Egypt* (30 BCE-300 CE) (G-38-111.4/2011), we aimed at applying the methodology and discourse slowly developed in the course of the preceding seven meetings, for the study of a genre frequently neglected by students of ancient diplomatics: reports and accounts. As such, it was a worthy conclusion, embodying the innovative and inquisitive spirit that guided *Legal Documents in Ancient Societies* since its foundation. Particular thanks are due to Andrea Jördens, who generously hosted the meeting in Schwetzingen, and is coeditor of the present volume, and Michele Faraguna, who as chief editor of Edizioni Università di Trieste made the publication of three of the seven volumes listed below possible, and the editors of the series *PHILIPPIKA* —then *Marburger altertumskundliche Abhandlungen,* now *Altertumswissenschaftliche Abhandlungen / Contribu-*

tions to the Study of Ancient World Cultures— who have thus assumed the publication of both the first, and so-far concluding publication of *Legal Documents in Ancient Societies*.

Tel Aviv, July 2019 Uri Yiftach

U. Yiftach-Firanko (ed.), *The Letter: Law, State, Society and the Epistolary Format in the Ancient World (Legal Documents in Ancient Societies I: Rome, 28-30.9.2008)* (PHILIPPIKA: Marburger altertumskundliche Abhandlungen 55,1) (Harrassowitz Verlag, Wiesbaden 2013). ISBN: 978-34-4706-764-5.

D.P. Kehoe, D. Ratzan, U. Yiftach, *Law and Transaction Costs in the Ancient Economy (Legal Documents in Ancient Societies II: Washington, D.C., 27-28.7.2009)* (University of Michigan Press, Ann Arbor 2015). ISBN: 978-0-472-11960-8.

M. Depauw, S. Coussement (eds.), Identifiers and Identification Methods in the Ancient World (Legal Documents in Ancient Societies III: Leuven and Brussels, 23-25.9.2010) (Peeters, Leuven 2014). ISBN : 978-90-4292-983-8.

M. Faraguna (ed.), Archives and Archival Documents in Ancient Societies (Legal Documents in Ancient Societies IV: Trieste, 30.9-1.10.2011) (EUT Edizioni Università di Trieste, Trieste 2013). ISBN: 978-88-8303-813-6, eISBN: 978-88-8303-814-3.

É. Jakab (ed.), Sale and Community Documents from the Ancient World. Individuals' Autonomy and State Interference in the Ancient World (Legal Documents in Ancient Societies V: Budapest, 5-8.10.2012) (EUT Edizioni Università di Trieste, Trieste 2015). ISBN: 978-88-8303-685-9.

U. Yiftach, M. Faraguna (eds.), Ancient Guardianship: Legal Incapacities in the Ancient World (Legal Documents in Ancient Societies VI: Jerusalem, 3-5.11.2013) (EUT Edizioni Università di Trieste, Trieste 2017). ISBN: 978-88-8303-813-6, eISBN: 978-88-8303-814-3.

S. Démare-Lafont (ed.), Debt in Ancient Mediterranean Societies. A Documentary Approach (Legal Documents in Ancient Societies VII: Paris, 27-29.8.2015) (Hautes Études orientales 56, Moyen et Proche-Orient 8) (Droz, Geneva 2019). ISBN : 978-2-600-05741-7. ISBN PDF : 978-2-600-15741-4.

A. Jördens, U. Yiftach (eds.), Accounts and Bookkeeping in the Ancient World: Question of Structure (Legal Documents in Ancient Societies VIII: Schwetzingen, 24-26.9.2016) (Philippika: Altertumswissenschaftliche Abhandlungen / Contributions to the Study of Ancient World Culture 55,2) (Harrassowitz Verlag, Wiesbaden 2020). ISBN: 978-3-447-11198-0.

Contributors

Cristina Carusi is Associate Professor of Greek History at the University of Parma. Previously, she held research and teaching appointments at the Center for Hellenic Studies (Washington, DC), the University of Texas at Austin, and the Institute for Advanced Study (Princeton). Her research interests center on Greek history and epigraphy, with special attention to the institutions, law, and economy of Greek city-states. In addition to several articles in international volumes and journals, she authored a book on the production, commerce and taxation of salt in the Greek world and co-edited a volume on the Athenian grain-tax law of 374/3.

Véronique Chankowski is Director of the French School of Athens and Professor of Ancient Economy and Aegean History in the University Lyon 2. As an epigraphist working also with archaeological sources, she has published several studies on ancient Greek economy. She worked on Delos where she studied the rich epigraphic corpus of the sanctuary's accounts, from a financial and monetary history perspective. She also addressed the issue of commercial relations through the study of warehouses and distribution channels in the Mediterranean. Her last book is *Parasites du dieu. Comptables, financiers et commerçants dans la Délos hellénistique*, Athens, 2019.

Willy Clarysse taught Greek, Coptic and Ancient History including papyrology at the KULeuven. He is a member of the Royal Flemish Academy of Belgium. He published Greek and demotic papyri and ostraca and numerous studies on prosopography, onomastics, institutions, religions and languages of Greco-Roman Egypt. His main projects concern the bilingual documentation of Egypt between Alexander the Great and Mohammed, with books on Fayum villages, papyrus archives and tax lists. He is a collaborator at the database Trismegistos, where he is responsible for the Leuven Database of Ancient Books (LDAB).

Daniel E. Fleming is the Edelman Professor of Hebrew and Judaic Studies at New York University. His range of study spans pre-Classical Mesopotamia, Syria, and Israel through the second and early first millennia BCE. After two early books on the Late Bronze Age Syrian city of Emar (*The Installation of Baal's High Priestess at Emar*, 1992; *Time at Emar*, 2000), he has returned to work on the site in collaboration with Sophie Démare-Lafont (especially "Emar Chronology and Scribal Streams: Cosmopolitanism and Legal Diversity," *Revue d'Assyriologie* 109 [2015] 45-77).

Melanie Groß acquired her PhD in Assyriology in 2014 at the University of Vienna and is currently working as a researcher in the project "Persia & Babylonia" at Leiden University. Her research focuses on the socio-economic history of 1st millennium BCE Mesopotamia and is based on the cuneiform archival documentation from this time period. Among her primary interests are ancient state structures and the institutions of palace and temple in ancient Assyria as well as Babylonia.

Éva Jakab is Professor of Roman Law and head of the Doctoral School of the Károli University Budapest, teaching also at the University of Szeged. She is corresponding member of the Austrian Academy of Sciences; member of the international Jury "Consorzio Interuniversitario Gérard Boulvert" (Naples). She completed her studies in Legal History at the LMU Munich as a DAAD and Humboldt fellow; recently she spent two terms in Oxford as Visiting Fellow at All Souls College. Since 2008 she is member of the Steering Committee of the international research group "Legal Documents in Ancient Societies (LDAS)", engaged with comparative studies. Her main research field is Roman law, with a strong comparative aspect regarding the law of the provinces, focused on everyday practice as mirrored in documentary texts. She published several books and articles in German, English, Italian, French, and of course in Hungarian.

Andrea Jördens is Professor of Papyrology at Ruprecht-Karls-Universität Heidelberg, director of the Heidelberg papyrus collection and chief editor of *Sammelbuch* und *Berichtigungsliste der griechischen Papyrusurkunden*. Apart from editions of Greek documentary papyri, she has published numerous studies on the economic and social history of the "Greek Millennium" in Egypt. In addition to her focus on administrative and legal history, her recent work has concentrated on topics in culture and religious history.

Miklós Könczöl is associate professor at Pázmány Péter Catholic University, and research fellow at the Institute for Legal Studies, Centre for Social Sciences, Budapest. His research focuses on the history of legal rhetoric, theory of argumentation, and political philosophy.

Thomas Kruse gained his PhD in 2002 at Heidelberg. He has held several positions at the Institute for Papyrology of the University of Heidelberg, and was appointed Senior Lecturer in Ancient History in 2004. Since 2009 he works as a Senior Researcher at the Austrian Academy of Sciences, where he currently heads the working group for Ancient Legal History and Papyrology at the Institute for the Study of Ancient Culture. The focus of his research is on the history and the administrative institutions of Ptolemaic and Roman Egypt.

David Lewis is Lecturer in Greek History and Culture at the University of Edinburgh, Scotland. He works on the history of labour in ancient Greece, with a particular focus on slavery. He is co-editor (with E. M. Harris & M. Woolmer) of *The Ancient Greek Economy: Markets, Households and City-States* (Cambridge University Press, 2016), co-editor (with E. Stewart & E. M. Harris) of *Professionals and Skilled Labour in the Greco-Roman World* (Cambridge University Press, 2020), and author of *Greek Slave Systems in their Eastern Mediterranean Context, c. 800-146 BC* (Oxford University Press, 2018).

Sandra Lippert is *Directrice de recherche* at the French National Center for Scientific Research (CNRS) and a member of the research team "Archéologie, Philologie, Histoire d'Orient et d'occident" (UMR 8546 – CNRS, EPHE, ENS, PSL) at Paris. Her work focuses on Demotic studies, ancient Egyptian law, and the economy of Egyptian temples in the Graeco-Roman period. Since 2000, she collaborates with Karl-Theodor Zauzich and Maren Schentuleit on the edition of Demotic texts of the Roman period from Soknopaiou Nesos in the Fayum.

Julia Lougovaya is since 2010 a research and teaching fellow in Ancient History and Papyrology at the Ruprecht-Karls-Universität Heidelberg. She works mainly in the area of Greek epigraphy and papyrology. Her current research is concerned with material aspects of writing practices in the ancient world, ancient education, and institutions in archaic Greek poleis.

Manuel Molina is Research Professor at the Spanish National Research Council (CSIC, Madrid) since 2008. He has published numerous editions of Sumerian legal and administrative documents, currently kept in the British Museum and in other collections. He has also written on administrative, social and economic topics in IIIrd millennium Mesopotamian history. He is the editor of the online resource Database of Neo-Sumerian Texts (BDTNS, http://bdtns.filol.csic.es), which makes available to scholars a corpus of nearly 100,000 Sumerian and Akkadian administrative cuneiform tablets dated to the Neo-Sumerian period (c. 2110-2003 BC).

Nicola Reggiani is research fellow in Papyrology at the University of Parma, where he focuses mostly on Greek medical papyri and digital papyrology. His post-doc within the project Synopsis at the Heidelberg Istitute of Papyrology dealt with the administrative and writing mechanics of official reports in Graeco-Roman Egypt.

Patrick Sänger is Professor of Ancient History at the university of Münster. His main interests are the administrative, legal and social history of the Eastern Mediterranean, especially of Egypt from Hellenistic till the Late Antique period. He also devoted himself to the editing of documentary papyri and of Ephesian inscriptions. His most recent book is on the Ptolemaic form of organization "*politeuma*" (2019).

Ornella Salati received her D.Phil. in Ancient History from Scuola Normale Superiore in Pisa in 2015. She is currently a Post-Doc Researcher at the University of Naples 'Federico II' as a member of the ERC-project PLATINUM. Her research interests include Roman military history, especially in the Eastern empire, and papyrology.

Maren Schentuleit is Associate Professor for Egyptology and Coptic Studies at Oxford University and Lady Wallis Budge Fellow of University College. She has been researching Greek and Demotic sources from Soknopaiou Nesos for almost two decades and collaborates with Karl-Theodor Zauzich, Sandra Lippert, Martin Stadler and Marie-Pierre Chaufray on the edition of Demotic texts from this site.

Katelijn Vandorpe is Professor of Papyrology and Ancient History at the KU Leuven University, Belgium, and a member of the Royal Flemish Academy of Belgium. Her main research field is Greco-Roman Egypt, and her publications include archival research, studies on seals, onomastics, institutions, socioeconomic aspects of this multicultural society and text editions (e.g. with T. Christensen and D.J. Thompson: P. Haun. IV 70).

Nick Vaneerdewegh graduated in Ancient History and Policy Economics, and is currently a PhD student who is part of a project on tax burden in Ptolemaic Egypt at the KU Leuven, directed by K. Vandorpe.

Uri Yiftach is Professor at Tel-Aviv University, and he is an Ancient Historian, Classical Philologist and Papyrologist. He has extensively studied scribal traditions, legal institutions, and administrative practices in Ptolemaic and Roman Egypt. His current interest is primarily linguistic.

Ancient Near East

Who watches the watchers?
New evidence on the role of foremen in the Ur III administration*

Manuel Molina, Madrid

The administration of the Ur III state (c. 2110–2003 BC) is well known for the enormous mass of documentation it has left behind: more than 97,000 Sumerian cuneiform tablets are currently catalogued in BDTNS, and many others remain unpublished in museums and private collections all over the world.[1]

The feeling of someone who approaches this documentation might be that large administrations, at least, kept a record of everything, even the most insignificant issues. But this was obviously not true. Like any other administration, no matter how complex it is or tends to be, the Ur III administrative apparatus relied on written documentation, but also on oral communication, personal decisions and on trust. However, trust could be betrayed, and mechanisms to avoid it needed to be implemented. The present contribution deals with some of these procedures put into practice by the administration in the management of manpower.

§ 1. In large administrations like those of Umma or Girsu, foremen had at their disposal gangs of men and women of different ages and social conditions. With them under their responsibility, foremen were entitled to fulfil a fixed amount of work per year through various types of tasks, most frequently agricultural activities, irrigation, transportation, craft production, milling and textile works. When a work-gang performed one of these tasks, an official sealed a tablet recording its completion and delivered it to the foreman. One example of these labour accounts shall suffice:

USC 6513 = CDLI P235328

330 sar al aka 4 sar-ta, a_2-bi u_4 82½ ĝuruš, 350 sar al aka 5 sar-ta, a_2-bi u_4 70 ĝuruš, 96 ĝuruš u_4 1-$še_3$, KA-us_2-sa_2 ĝar-ra, a_2 $ša_3$-gu_4-ka, a-$ša_3$ [Me]-en-kar_2, **ugula Lu_2-du_{10}-ga, kišib Šeš-kal-la**, mu us_2-sa bad_3 mar-tu ba-du_3 (ŠS5). *Seal:* Šeš-kal-la, dub-sar, dumu Na-DI.

330 *sar* (1 *sar* = 35 m^2) of hoeing at 4 *sar* each (man-day), its work is 82½ workdays; 350 *sar* of hoeing at 5 *sar* each (man-day), its work is 70 workdays; 96 men during one day

* This research has been made possible thanks to the financial support granted by the Spanish Ministerio de Economía, Industria y Competitividad through the project FFI2015-66790-P. Text 1 (BM 21411) and Text 2 (BM 22859) are here published by kind permission of the Trustees of the British Museum. I am very grateful to Piotr Steinkeller, who read the manuscript and offered valuable comments and suggestions. All abbreviations used are those of BDTNS (http://bdtns.filol.csic.es).

1 See Molina 2008.

(= 96 workdays) have put ... Work (carried out by) oxdrivers. At the Menkar-field. Foreman: Luduga. Seal of Šeškala. Year /following that in which the wall of the Amorites was built (Šu-Suen 5). *Seal:* Šeškala, scribe, son of NaDI.

One of the numerous issues these texts raise concerns the way these calculations were made and who was responsible for them. Was it the foreman who was in charge of the work-gangs, or was it the sealing official who gave the final approval to the workdays[2] said to have been necessary for the works? Or was it someone else? Were inspections carried out in situ, while the works were performed, or immediately afterwards?

There is actually in the Ur III corpus a large amount of tablets recording inspections (gurum$_2$ aka),[3] which were essentially of two types: a) those apparently made on the ground, carried out to have control over the works and the workforce employed in them; b) those made on workers in service in certain sectors of the provincial economy, establishments or households, which also provided detailed information about the condition of the workers.

The most numerous are those belonging to the first category: there are, for example, more than 300 texts of this type preserved for the Umma province. A comprehensive study of them, and of their relationships with single labour accounts of foremen, like the preceding text, has yet to be made. Basically, they presented very similar contents to labour accounts: they recorded either the number of workers belonging to one or more gangs, or the workdays completed, together with the name of the foremen; most frequently, the type of task carried out and the place where it was performed; the day, month and year when the inspection (gurum$_2$ aka) took place; and eventually a sealing official or his name preceded by ĝiri$_3$ "under the responsibility of".

Some of them can be grouped together chronologically in the span of a few weeks, showing that certain tasks in certain places were inspected daily, until the job was completed, and also that inspections could be repeated year after year.

An example of these texts, a group constituted by twenty-seven tablets, follows, although many others could be provided. It has been chosen because some of the texts record work-gangs under the supervision of the foreman Luduga, while others mention Šeškala, the official under whose responsibility the inspections were carried out; both Luduga and Šeškala were probably the same officials recorded in the preceding labour account (USC 6513). The tablets record works intended for the preparation of the Menkar-field for cultivation, namely hoeing and weeding, performed between the fifth and the eighth months of the year. They always follow the same pattern:

n hired workers (ĝuruš huĝ-ĝa$_2$) have cut weeds (kiši$_{17}$ or dih$_3$), *n sar* each (1 *sar* = 35 m^2) // *n* hired workers (guruš huĝ-ĝa$_2$), at a salary of *n* liters of barley each (a$_2$ še *n* sila$_3$-ta), have hoed *n sar* each (al *n* sar-ta).

---

2 "Workdays", or "man-days", is an abstract notation, which means that the days recorded in the text are not real days of work but accounting units: 10 guruš u$_4$ 1-še$_3$ does not mean that "10 workers (worked) during 1 day", but that 10 workdays were performed by *n* workers during *n* days (e.g. 4 workers during 2.5 days, or 20 workers during 0.5 days).

3 For gurum$_2$ aka "inspection made", see Steinkeller 1982; de Maaijer and Jagersma 2003/04: 353; Attinger 2005: 226.

Their foreman (ugula) is PN_1. Under the responsibility of (ĝiri$_3$) PN_2. Inspection performed on the *n*th day (gurum$_2$ ak u$_4$ *n*-kam). At the field of Menkar. Month and year name.

ŠS1/[x]/6: 10 ĝuruš huĝ-ĝa$_2$, ugula Kal-la, 11 ĝuruš huĝ-ĝa$_2$, **ugula Lu$_2$-du$_{10}$-ga**, al 6 sar-ta, a-ša$_3$ Me-en-kar$_2$, ĝiri$_3$ Šeš-kal-la, gurum$_2$ aka u$_4$ 6-kam (MVN 14 492)

ŠS1/v/3: 10 ĝuruš huĝ-ĝa$_2$, ugula Kal-la, 10 ĝuruš huĝ-ĝa$_2$, **ugula Lu$_2$-du$_{10}$-ga**, al aka 5 sar-ta, gurum$_2$ aka u$_4$ 3-kam, a-ša$_3$ Me-en-kar$_2$ (MVN 14 281)

ŠS1/v/11: 2 ĝuruš, ugula Kal-la, 10 ĝuruš, **ugula Lu$_2$-du$_{10}$-ga**, a$_2$ [5] sila$_3$-ta, al 5 [sar]-ta, gurum$_2$ aka u$_4$ 11-kam, a-ša$_3$ Me-en-kar$_2$, (UTI 5 3204)

ŠS1/v/20: 23½ ĝuruš a$_2$ 6 sila$_3$-ta, al 5 sar-ta, gurum$_2$ aka u$_4$ 20-kam, a-ša$_3$ Me-en-kar$_2$ (UTI 3 2034)

ŠS1/v/21: 24 ĝuruš huĝ-ĝa$_2$, a$_2$ 6 sila$_3$-ta, al 4 sar-ta, u$_4$ 21-kam, 32 ĝuruš huĝ-ĝa$_2$, a$_2$ 6 sila$_3$-ta, al 3 sar-ta, gurum$_2$ aka u$_4$ 22-kam, a-ša$_3$ Me-en-kar$_2$ (Farmer's Instructions 3.09)

ŠS1/vi/4: 13 ĝuruš huĝ-ĝa$_2$, a$_2$ 6 sila$_3$-ta, al 5 sar-ta, gurum$_2$ aka u$_4$ 4-kam, a-ša$_3$ Me-en-kar$_2$, **ĝiri$_3$ Šeš-kal-la** (MVN 16 642)

ŠS1/vi/5: 13 ĝuruš-[huĝ]-ĝa$_2$, a$_2$ 6 [sila$_3$]-ta, al 6 sar-ta, gurum$_2$ aka u$_4$ 5-kam, a-ša$_3$ Me-en-kar$_2$, **ĝiri$_3$ Šeš-kal-la** (UTI 5 3183)

ŠS1/vi/10: 15 ĝuruš huĝ-ĝa$_2$, a$_2$ 7 sila$_3$-ta, al 7 sar-ta, gurum$_2$ aka u$_4$ 10-kam, a-ša$_3$ Me-en-kar$_2$, **ĝiri$_3$ Šeš-kal-la** (Nisaba 9 107)

Other texts belonging to this dossier and dated to Amar-Suen 7 or to the following days of Šu-Suen 1 are:

AS7/vii/2: SACT 2 60
AS7/vii/3: ŠA 80, pl. 111
AS7/vii/7: NYPL 232
AS7/vii/10: SACT 2 56
AS7/vii/12: TCS 36
ŠS1/vi/12: BPOA 6 124
ŠS1/vi/14: MVN 16 946
ŠS1/vi/15: MVN 14 548
ŠS1/vi/16: MVN 16 631
ŠS1/vi/19?: UTI 5 3201
ŠS1/vi/20: MVN 18 275
ŠS1/vi/23: BPOA 6 1405
ŠS1/vi/24: Nisaba 9 254
ŠS1/vi/26: UTI 3 2178
ŠS1/vi/28: MCS 3, p. 88
ŠS1/vi/29: UTI 5 3305
ŠS1/8/10: MVN 16 941
ŠS1/8/13: BIN 5 218
ŠS1/8/14: BPOA 6 1338

§ 2. The administrative connection of daily inspections with single labour accounts of foremen will be better understood with the group of tablets schematized below in Table 1. They are all dated to the first regnal year of Šu-Suen, "during the harvest" (ša$_3$ buru$_{14}$), sealed by the same official (Ur-lugal), and record exactly the same tasks by several work-gangs supervised by different foremen. Interestingly, two (or three) of them record also the expression gurum$_2$ aka u$_4$ 18-kam "inspection belonging to the 18th day", an inspection that most probably was also carried out in the rest of cases (cf. the inspection digests discussed below). Therefore, the approval of the labour account by the Umma official who sealed the tablet for the foreman seems to have been confirmed by an inspection on the ground. I cannot say whether these inspections were carried out every day on every work-gang all over the Umma province, or whether they were randomly made, an issue that a thorough study of inspection texts will perhaps clarify.

	BPOA 1 752	BPOA 7 2392	UTI 5 3146	BPOA 1 673	BPOA 6 53	BPOA 6 1139
n ĝuruš u$_4$ 1-še$_3$ še gur$_{10}$-a zar$_3$ tab-ba	198 ĝuruš	233 ĝuruš	217 ĝuruš	28 ĝuruš	236 ĝuruš	72 ĝuruš
n ĝuruš u$_4$ 1-še$_3$ gu$_4$-e us$_2$-sa-(a) a-ša$_3$ Ka-ma-ri$_2$	12 ĝuruš	18 ĝuruš	30+1$^?$ ĝuruš	36 ĝuruš	18 ĝuruš	18 ĝuruš
n ĝuruš u$_4$ 1-še$_3$ KA.GIR$_3$-da e Ki-sur-ra-(ka) ad aka	80 ĝuruš	74 ĝuruš	80 ĝuruš	96 ĝuruš	92 ĝuruš	–
gurum$_2$ aka u$_4$ 18-kam	√	√	[√?]	–	–	–
ugula PN	**Da-DU-mu**	**Ba-sa$_6$**	**Ur-^{d}En-lil$_2$-la$_2$**	**Lugal-ku$_3$-zu**	**Da-a-gi**	**Ur-^{ĝiš}gigir**
kišib Ur-lugal ša$_3$ buru$_{14}$ mu ^{d}Šu-^{d}Suen lugal *Seal*: Ur-lugal dub-sar dumu Da-a-gi$_4$	√ √ √ √	√ √ √ √	√ √ √ √	√ √ √ √	√ √ √ √	√ √ √ √
Translation: n workers during 1 day (= *n* workdays) have reaped grain and have piled up sheaves, *n* workers during 1 day (= *n* workdays) have driven oxen (lit. "have followed upon the oxen"), at the field of Kamari; *n* workers during 1 day (= *n* workdays) have performed matting work on the path$^?$ of the embankment of Kisura. Inspection belonging to the 18th day. Foreman: PN. Seal of Ur-lugal. During the harvest. Year: Šu-Suen 1. *Seal:* Ur-lugal, scribe, son of Da'agi.						

Table 1

These daily inspections on the ground were later summarized in other texts listing the name of the foremen, the number of workers under their responsibility, and the tasks performed. The names of foremen given above are collected together in a group of texts of this kind dated to the third month of Amar-Suen's seventh regnal year. Even if not expressed in the text, the connecting link was certainly the sealing official of their labour accounts. An example of the texts from this dossier is the following:

PPAC 4 173

	1	3 ĝuruš ugula **Ba-sa$_6$**
	2	3 ugula Ur-mes
	3	3 ugula Unken-ne$_2$
	4	3 ugula I$_7$-pa-e$_3$
	5	3 ugula **Ur-^{d}En-lil$_2$-la$_2$**
	6	**3 ugula Lugal-ku$_3$-zu**
	7	3 ugula **Da-du-mu**
	8	3 ugula Lugal-e$_2$-mah-e
rev.	1	3 ugula **Ur-^{ĝiš}gigir**
	2	3 ugula Ur-^{ĝiš}gigir šabra
	3	tug$_2$-sag$_x$ (ŠE.KIN) 0.0.1^{gana2}-ta
	4	gurum$_2$ u$_4$ 17-kam

5 a-ša$_3$ ušur$_3^!$ (<LAL$_2$>×LAGAB) Da-ur$_4$
6 iti še-kar-ra-ĝal$_2$
7 mu Hu-hu-nu-ri^{ki} ba-hul

Three workers, (their) foreman is Basa; three (workers, their) foreman is Urmes; three (workers, their) foreman is Unkenne; three (workers, their) foreman is Ipa'e; three (workers, their) foreman is Ur-Enlila; three (workers, their) foreman is Lugal-kuzu; three (workers, their) foreman is DaDUmu; three (workers, their) foreman is Lugal-emahe; three (workers, their) foreman is Ur-gigir; three (workers, their) foreman is Ur-gigir, the prefect. (They have done) ploughing work, at 1 *iku* (= 0.35 ha.) each (per day).
Inspection belonging to the 17th day.
At the neighbouring field of Da'ur.
The month of "barley is on the quay" (iii). The year in which Huhnuri was destroyed (Amar Suen 7).

The whole dossier, with slight differences in the number of workers, foremen and tasks is constituted by the following texts:

AS7/iii/3: MVN 4 17
AS7/iii/7$^?$: Ebay WWW20021221-01 (= BDTNS 167911)
AS7/iii/15: TJAMC IOS 13 (pl. 51)
AS7/iii/17: PPAC 4 173
AS7/iii/19: Bull. Buffalo SNS 11-2, p. 141 10
AS7/iii/22: BPOA 1 1210
AS7/iii/24: MVN 4 18

§ 3. The second type of inspection mentioned above is the "inspection list",[4] also called "gurum$_2$ aka roster", but its administrative connection with daily inspections on the ground is not obvious. The inspection lists are long records of workers listed by name and classified according to the wages they received, their social status, age, and family relationships. They also included information on the reasons for the absence of certain workers, i.e. sickness, death, absenteeism or transfer to other gangs. This sort of information, which is not usually found in daily inspection texts, means that these were not used to compile the inspection lists. Nevertheless, it is important to know who was behind the compilation of these inspection lists, since they were used to calculate the wages needed for the work-gangs, and also to calculate the capital section of a foreman's balanced-account[5] (see below).

To try to answer to this question we will turn our attention now to the Girsu provincial archive. The composition of this corpus with respect to inspection texts is somewhat different: there are not as many daily inspection texts as there are in the Umma corpus, but it includes some fifty labels (pisaĝ dub-ba) that were hung from baskets holding

4 Inspection lists from Umma have been studied by Steinkeller (1987) and Koslova (2004; 2008: 165–173 and Texts 13–21). Texts of this type from Umma are the following (after Koslova 2008: 175): Torino 2 703, OrSP 47–49 324, YOS 4 232, BM 106132, BCT 2 288, OrSP 47–49 382, OrSP 47–49 483, RA 73, pp. 115–120 and YOS 18 115.
5 See Steinkeller 1987: 76, 2003: 47, and Koslova 2013: 318.

inspection tablets, and many of these inspections were carried out on personnel working at the temple households of the province, for example:[6]

TCTI 2 3687
pisaĝ dub-ba, gurum$_2$ aka, ĝiri$_3$-se$_3$-ga, eren$_2$ saĝ-apin, e$_2$ ^{d}Nanše, ĝiri$_3$ Ur-e$_2$-ninnu, dumu Al-la-mu, i$_3$-ĝal$_2$, mu Ša-aš-ru-um^{ki} ba-hul
Tablet-basket: it contains (tablets of) inspections of personnel, (concerning) *eren*-workers (working as) chief ploughmen at the household of Nanše. Year in which Šašrum was destroyed (Amar-Suen 6).

These baskets would have contained inspection lists,[7] like the one published in MVN 13 346, which recorded workers under the responsibility of the foreman Ur-Ninpiriĝ. The workers, listed by their personal names, were classified according to their category, age, profession and the wages they received, indicating also whether they were absent because they had died. The last lines of this tablet read as follows:

(...) gurum$_2$ aka dib-ba, eren$_2$ saĝ-apin, ugula Ur-^{d}Nin-piriĝ, e$_2$ ^{d}Nanše, mu Ša-aš-ru^{ki} ba-hul
(...) (Tablet of) inspection transferred (concerning) *eren*-workers (working as) chief ploughmen, (their) foreman (being) Ur-Ninpiriĝ, at the household of Nanše. Year in which Šašrum was destroyed (Amar-Suen 6).

§ 4. Some insights on how these inspection lists were compiled, and who was responsible for the information written down on them, may be provided by two unpublished texts kept in the British Museum, here edited for the first time.

Text 1. BM 21411. 1896-330-77
Copy: Fig. 1. Photo: Fig. 2 and BDTNS 041983
Date: Šulgi 47. 82×48×27

1	1 Ur-sa$_6$-ga
2	1 Ur-^{d}Ba-u$_2$
3	1 Lu$_2$-kal-la
4	1 Ab-ba
5	1 Ur-Ba-gara$_2$
6	1 A-hu-ma
7	1 Ur-ki-la$_2$-a
8	*Blank line*
9	ugula eren$_2$-na e$_2$ eš$_3$

6 See Maekawa 1999: 77.

7 Inspection lists from Girsu are, for example: HLC 2 10 (pl. 53) (Š41/vii); UDT 58 (Š43); CT 1, pl. 6 94-10–15 5 (Š43/viii); Orient 16, p. 91 135 (Š46/ix/7); CT 7, pl. 13 BM 12939 (Š47); HLC 1 26 (pl. 22) (Š47/v); ASJ 11, p. 129 59 (Š48); PPAC 5 324 (Š48/v); MVN 2 176 (Š48/vii); MVN 17 54 (Š48/xii); PPAC 5 1552 (AS1); TUT 159 (AS1/v); HLC 1 253 (pl. 46) (AS2); MVN 6 290 (AS2); MVN 6 298 (AS2); SAT 1 417 (AS2); ASJ 18, p. 157 2 (AS2/vii); MVN 17 55 (AS4); CTNMC 54 (AS4/i); MVN 13 346 (AS6); TCTI 1 736 (ŠS1/xii); PPAC 5 286 (-/v); HLC 2 25 (pl. 63) (date lost); HLC 3 238 (pl. 113) (date lost); MVN 22 24 (date lost); PPAC 5 1 (date lost).

10 lu$_2$ gub-ba ba-zah$_3$-še$_3$ nu-mu-sar-a
11 lu$_2$ ti-la ba-uš$_2$-še$_3$ nu-mu-sar-a
12 mu lugal-bi in-pa$_3$-eš$_2$
rev. *Blank space*
1 mu us$_2$-sa
2 Ki-maš^{ki} ba-hul
Blank space

Ursaga, Ur-Ba'u, Lukala, Abba, Ur-Bagara, Ahuma, Ur-kila'a.
(They are) foremen of *eren*-workers (working at) the temple household(s) and sanctuaries. They swore by the name of the king that they will not have inscribed a man in service as an absentee, that they will not have inscribed a living man as a dead one.
Year following that in which Kimaš was destroyed (Šulgi 47).

§ 5. The first issue raised by this text is the interpretation of e$_2$-AB in line 9, a term that is most frequently understood by text editors as e$_2$-kurušda "fattening house". In fact, in Ur III texts, most of the time kurušda is written with the sign AB (KWU 821),[8] which might also be read as eš$_3$ "shrine, sanctuary". Although the interpretation e$_2$-kurušda "fattening house" cannot be completely ruled out, here I prefer the reading e$_2$ eš$_3$ "temple household (and) sanctuaries" because of the –in my view– clear relationship of the oath recorded in the text with inspection lists and balanced-accounts that are well attested for temple households, but not for a fattening house in the Girsu/Lagaš province (see below).

Unfortunately, I cannot say which household(s) and sanctuaries are being referred to in our text, since I have not been able to identify the foremen recorded in it. With regard to the sanctuaries, it would be tempting to identify the *eren*-workers of Text 1 and their foremen with those mentioned in a group of fifty texts, dating between Šulgi 46 and Šu-Suen 4, which deal with complementary tasks assigned to eren$_2$ eš$_3$ didli "*eren*-workers of various sanctuaries".[9] Nevertheless, despite the accurate recording of the overseers' and foremen's personal names in this dossier, no prosopographical links can be established with our text. This could be due, of course, to the function of these accounts, which were specifically meant to record the reallocation of workers to different tasks and establishments of the provincial and royal sectors. The numerous sanctuaries or chapels disseminated all over the province and the administrative relationship frequently shown with temple households make it perfectly plausible that one or more temple households and sanctuaries were meant in Text 1 with e$_2$ eš$_3$.

8 KWU 822 for kurušda is rarely used: see for example ASJ 19, p. 138 122 (BM 109149): i 19; Borrelli 2013: T 11 (BM 18073) rev. 2 and 4; on seal legends it is found for example in Torino 2 645: Ur-^{d}Dumu-zi-da, dub-sar, dumu Ur-niĝar$_x$^{ĝar} kurušda (photo CDLI P135491).

9 See Uchitel 1992; Lafont 1994: 107–110; Uchitel 1996; Sallaberger 1999: 311–313; Sharlach 2004: 95–98; Allred 2008 and 2014. A list of 38 texts of this group was provided by Allred 2008: 11. The following tablets should be added to that list: Studies Owen, p. 169 L. 6429 (AS8/v/10+); AnOr 1 192 (ŠS4); SM 1899.02.314 = CDLI P406048 (-/ii/8); LB 586 = CDLI P389069 (-/iv/15); NBTS 4 = CDLI P423352 (-/iv/18); UC CSC 1946 = CDLI P479897 (-/iv/19); PPAC 5 173 (-/iv/25); PPAC 5 1637 (-/iv/26); MVN 22 56 (date lost); LB 473 = CDLI P388990 (date lost); AAICAB 1/3, Bod. A 022b (date lost); Studies Owen, p. 168 L. 5652 (date lost).

Note in this regard, for example, the expressions e$_2$ ^{d}Ba-u$_2$ 3-a-bi, e$_2$ ^{d}Nin-ĝir$_2$-su 2-a-bi, u$_3$ eš$_3$ didli-bi "the three temple households of Ba'u, the two temple households of Ninĝirsu, and their various respective sanctuaries" (HLC 2 28 [pl. 66]: rev. iii 8-10; PPAC 5 3: i 2, ii 3, ii 8-9), which are detailed in HLC 2 2 (pl. 52), a list of deliveries of goats. Similarly, an inspection (UDT 58) of the personnel of the sanctuaries of Nanše at Niĝin is resumed at the end of the text as gurum$_2$ aka eš$_3$ didli e$_2$ ^{d}Nanše "inspection of the various sanctuaries of the temple household of Nanše", and a basket label (OBTR 162) recorded inspections of the personnel of the temple household and the sanctuaries of Girsu (e$_2$ eš$_3$ Ĝir$_2$-su^{ki}) and of the goddess Nanše (e$_2$ ^{d}Nanše, eš$_3$ didli-bi).

If this interpretation is correct, then foremen and *eren*-workers of Text 1 could well be identified with those recorded in the "inspection lists" like MVN 13 346, cited above (§3), and with those recorded in the "staff lists" of temple households,[10] the kind of tablets that were also kept in the baskets mentioned in §3. These "staff lists" constitute a very interesting group of texts that recorded the personnel of temple households in the Girsu/Lagaš province.[11] Among this personnel, a number of foremen (ugula eren$_2$-na) and their *eren*-workers, mainly assigned to cultivation and irrigations tasks,[12] was recorded.[13] An example of these texts follows:

ITT 3 5270

1	1 saĝĝa 5 aga$_3$-us$_2$
2	1 pisaĝ-dub-ba 1 šeš-tab-ba
3	1 saĝ-du$_5$ 1 šeš-tab-ba
4	1 ka-guru$_7$ 1 šeš-tab-ba
5	1 šar$_2$-ra-ab-du
6	3 dub-sar gu4 10
7	3 šeš-tab-ba
8	15 nu-banda$_3$
9	1 šeš-tab-ba

10 The "staff lists" have been studied by Gelb 1979: 12–24; Lafont 1994: 104–106; Maekawa 1999: 76–82; Studevent-Hickman 2006: passim. The following "staff lists" are currently known: MVN 17 3 = Priests and Officials, p. 99 App. 3 (e$_2$ ^{d}Nin-dar-a, balanced-account, Š37); Priests and Officials, p. 96 App. 1 (e$_2$ Urub$_x$^{ki}, Š43); HSS 4 4 (various temple households, AS2/i); MVN 18 607 (e$_2$ ^{d}Nin-dar-a and others, AS7); ITT 2 865 (e$_2$ ^{d}Hendur-saĝ, AS8/iv); ITT 2 907 (e$_2$ Ba-gara$_2$, AS8/iv); ITT 2 4192 (e$_2$ ^{d}Ig-alim, AS8/vii); ITT 3 5270 (e$_2$ ^{d}Nin-ĝiš-zi-da, AS8$^{?}$); ITT 2 3536 (e$_2$ Urub$_x$^{ki}, ŠS1/iv); MVN 13 319 (household name lost, -/iii/20); ASJ 20, p. 103 4 (e$_2$ ^{d}Lugal-Urub$_x$^{ki} u$_3$ e$_2$ ^{d}[...], undated); ASJ 20, p. 101 3 (e$_2$ ^{d}Nin-ĝir$_2$-su, e$_2$-babbar, e$_2$ ^{d}Ĝiš-bar-e$_3$, e$_2$ ^{d}Pa-bil$_3$-saĝ, e$_2$ Ba-gara$_2$, undated); Priests and Officials, p. 101 App. 4 (e$_2$ ^{d}Nin-MAR.KI, e$_2$ ^{d}Na-du$_3$-a, e$_2$ ^{d}En-ki, e$_2$ ^{d}Inanna, undated); TÉL 34a (e$_2$ ^{d}Nin-ĝiš-zi-da, undated); MVN 6 279 (e$_2$ Šul-gi, undated); Priests and Officials, p. 98 App. 2 (e$_2$ ^{d}Nin-dar-a and others, date lost).

11 For an overview of the different temple households in the three districts of the province, see Studevent-Hickman 2006: 106 Table 3.1.

12 See Maekawa 1999: 81, with previous literature; Studevent-Hickman 2006: 108.

13 Staff lists recording foremen and *eren*-workers are the following: Priests and Officials, p. 96 App. 1 (Š43); ITT 2 865 (AS8/iv); ITT 2 907 (AS8/iv); ITT 2 4192 (AS8/vii); ITT 3 5270 (AS8$^{?}$); ITT 2 3536 (ŠS1/iv); ASJ 20, p. 103 4 (undated); ASJ 20, p. 101 3 (undated); Priests and Officials, p. 98 App. 2 (date lost).

	10	30 engar
	11	90 gu$_4$-da-ri-a
	12	1 gu-za-la$_2$
	13	1 a-igi-du$_8$
	14	1 lu$_2$-nisig
rev.	1	1 naĝar
	2	1 ašgab
	3	1 tug$_2$-du8
	4	1 i$_7^!$-da gub-ba
	5	2 ugula eren$_2$-na 48 eren$_2$
	6	[x] ½ UN-ga$_6$
	7	1 ugula ša$_3$-gu$_4$
	8	[gur]um$_2$ ĝiri$_3$-se$_3$-ga
	9	[e$_2$ ^{d}]Nin-ĝiš-zi-da
	10	[ugula Du$_{11}$]-[ga]-zi-da
	11	[mu en Eridu (?)]^{ki} / [ba-huĝ (?)]

1 administrator (and his) 5 guards, 1 archivist (and his) assistant, 1 land surveyor (and his) assistant, 1 granary manager (and his) assistant, 1 *šarabdu*-official, 3 scribes of 10 plough-teams (and) 3 assistants, 15 supervisors (of plough-teams) (and) 1 assistant, 30 ploughmen, 90 ox drivers, 1 throne-carrier, 1 canal-worker, 1 vegetable-grower, 1 carpenter, 1 leather-worker, 1 felter, 1 man in service at the canal, 2 foremen of *eren*-workers (and) 48 *eren*-workers, [x]+½ menials, 1 foreman of ox drivers.
Inspection of personnel of the household of god Ninĝišzida.
[Under the supervision of Du]gazida.
[The year in which the high priest of Eridu was installed (?)] (Amar-Suen 8).

§ 6. The uniqueness of Text 1 is based on the oath taken by the foremen, who swore that "they will not have inscribed a man in service as an absentee, that they will not have inscribed a living man as a dead one". This was an oath taken in the name of the king, commonly known as a "promissory oath".[14] This sort of oath is ubiquitous in Ur III documents: more than 700 texts recording them are preserved. In the vast majority of cases, they are taken in the context of judicial procedures or, much more frequently, in the context of agreements (loans, sales, leases, security arrangements, *šuku*-allotments), in connection with goods that have to be returned, or with the repayment of arrears (la$_2$-i$_3$).

14 I am grateful to Walther Sallaberger for having shared with me his thoughts on the oath recorded in Texts 1 and 2. On the "promissory oath", see Sallaberger 2008; a different view was expressed by Steinkeller 1989: 75–80.

"Promissory oaths" dealing with workforce are much rarer, although some can be found:[15]

- MVN 6 117 (Girsu, undated): oath (probably taken by a foreman) on the transfer and death of workers.
- TLB 3 171 (Girsu, undated): oath taken by a foreman on the work, absence and transfer of workers.
- MVN 22 24 (Girsu, date lost): oath taken by two foremen (rev. i 24–26) on the transfer and death of workers.
- TLB 3 64 (Girsu, undated): oath taken by foremen and scribes for unknown purpose.
- BPOA 2 2619 (Umma, AS1): oath taken by a foreman on the sickness of a worker.

The grounds for these oaths can now be understood more clearly, thanks to Texts 1 and 2. In fact, it could happen that foremen might have altered the real situation of workers, making them appear as dead when they were alive, as absent when they were in service, or (according to Text 2) as youths when they were adults. In what sort of documents and circumstances would they have done so? Certainly, it would have been absurd to do it in the context of daily works, first because inspections were carried out by other officials, as was seen above in §1–2; and second, because to protect their own interests they needed to demonstrate that work was being performed, not the opposite.

More reasonably, inspection lists, such as those discussed in §3, were the records where they would have falsified the information. As was said above (§3 and fn. 5), inspection lists were used to calculate the capital section of a foreman's balanced-account.[16] In this section, the workers at the disposal of the foreman, mainly calculated from the inspection lists,[17] plus the result of the previous year's balance, were added up, thus constituting the "capital" (saĝ-niĝ$_2$-gur$_{11}$-ra, also known as "debits") of the foreman. The "capital" was then compared with the "withdrawals" (zi-ga, also known as "credits"), justified by means of the receipts provided by the foreman and validated by his supervisor (see §1–2). As a result, a balance indicating whether there was a "deficit" (la$_2$-i$_3$) or a "surplus" (diri) in the amount of work expected from the foreman and his workers was calculated. This result, whether positive or negative, was carried forward (si-i$_3$-tum) to the balanced-account of the following year, where it was added to the work expected from him, thus again constituting the capital of the foreman for that new year. The balanced-accounts concerning the foreman were archived and kept in a tablet-basket.[18]

---

15 The few examples of "assertory oaths" (nam-erim$_2$ ku$_5$) in the Girsu corpus, taken by foremen on the status of workers, have been collected by Notizia and Verderame 2017: 61.

16 Some examples of balanced-accounts of workforce from Girsu are the following: MVN 17 3 = Priests and Officials, p. 99 App. 3 (Š37); CT 9, pl. 46 BM 21348 (Š46/v); TCTI 1 896 (date lost); NATN 674 (undated).

17 Cf. in this regard the expression ša$_3$ gurum$_2$ "in the inspection", referring to workdays recorded in the capital section of balanced-accounts: CT 9, pl. 46 BM 21348: rev. i 5 (Girsu, Š46); OBTR 258 = CUSAS 16 63: ii. 3 (Girsu, AS1); NATN 674: 1 (Girsu, undated); TCTI 1 896: i 5 (Girsu, date lost). It most probably indicated that the amount of workdays had been taken from inspection lists.

18 For the case of the aforementioned Luduga (§1), we have a label of a tablet-basket plausibly connected with him and dated to Šu-Suen 9 (BPOA 1 1069):
pisaĝ dub-ba, niĝ-kas$_7$-aka, Lu$_2$-du$_{10}$-ga ugula, mu e$_2$ ^{d}Šara$_2$ ba-du$_3$
Tablet-basket (containing) balanced-accounts of Luduga, the foreman. The year in which the temple of Šara was built (Šu-Suen 9).

Nevertheless, this system of accounting had some weaknesses. The first one was the exaggerated demands of work made on foremen, who were always in debt with the administration, accumulating deficits of work performance year after year. Secondly, workers did not constitute a stable workforce, since people frequently fled, died, became unwell or were transferred to other gangs. To reduce the pressure on them, and taking advantage of the unpredictability of available manpower, the foremen, who were responsible for the information and details in the inspection lists, sometimes decided to manipulate them.

They thus registered people who actually were in regular service as absent from work or dead, or adults as younger workers. By altering the inspection lists in this way, they could reduce, to some extent, the amount of work expected from their work-gangs and relieve their liability. Making foremen take an oath swearing that they would not do so was the way the administration tried to prevent them from manipulating inspection lists and therefore altering work plans.

§ 7. This was a problem that not only affected the management of workforces in temple households, but also in other areas of the provincial economy, as is shown by Text 2.

Text 2. BM 22859. 1897-511-5
Copy: Figs. 3–4. Photo: Fig. 5–6 and BDTNS 042909
Undated. 82×48×27

i	1	1 Lu$_2$-uš-ge-na dumu x-da
	2	1 Ur-^{d}Da-mu dumu A-tu
	3	1 Ba-la-la
	4	————
	5	nu-banda$_3$ Na-ba-sa$_6$
	6	1 Ur-sa$_6$-ga dumu Lugal-igi
	7	1 Lu$_2$-^{d}Ba-u$_2$
	8	1 Ur-e$_2$-ninnu
	9	dumu Ur-sa$_6$-ga
	10	nu-banda$_3$ Lugal-igi
	11	1 Ur-niĝar$_{x}^{\text{ĝar}}$
	12	1 Lugal-da-ga dumu Lu$_2$-ba
	13	1 Ur-Šu-ga-lam-/ma
	14	dumu Du$_{11}$-[ga-zi]-da
ii	1	1 Lu$_2$-^{d}Inanna
	2	dumu Ĝiš-sa$_6$
	3	nu-banda$_3$ UN-ga$_6$
	4	1 Ur-ki-gu-la dumu Zi-NE-sa$_6$
	5	1 Lu$_2$-^{d}Ba-u$_2$
	6	dumu Ur-^{ĝiš}gigir
	7	1 Šeš-kal-la

		8	dumu Lu$_2$-^{d}Ba-u$_2$
		9	nu-banda$_3$ Ur-^{d}Nanše dumu Ur-DUN
		10	1 Lu$_2$-diĝir-ra
		11	dumu Ur-DUB.MI
		12	1 Lu$_2$-^{d}Ba-u$_2$ dumu Ur-^{ĝiš}gigir
		13	1 Lu$_2$-eb
		14	1 Ur-lugal
		15	dumu Gu$_2$-⌈x⌉-gi-me (*or* Gu$_2$-[g]i$_4$)
		16	nu-banda$_3$ Ur-^{d}Utu
rev.	i	1	1 Ur-^{d}Ba-u$_2$
		2	dumu He$_2$-ti
		3	1 Ur-mes
		4	dumu Za-a
		5	nu-banda$_3$ Lu$_2$-kal-la šeš saĝ-du$_5$
		6	————————
		7	1 Inim-^{d}Inanna
		8	1 Lu$_2$-diĝir-ra dumu ⌈x-(x)-NI$^{?}$⌉
		9	1 Ur-ĝar
		10	1 Ur-^{d}Ba-u$_2$ dumu Za-ga-la$_2$
		11	1 Ur-sukkal
		12	1 Ur-^{d}Ba-u$_2$ dumu Na-DI
		13	1 Ur-^{d}Ba-u$_2$ dumu Lu$_2$-kal-la
		14	1 Ur-^{d}Lamma
		15	1 Niĝ$_2$-^{d}Ba-u$_2$
		16	1 Ur-^{d}Šul-pa-e$_3$ dumu Ur-^{d}Da-mu
		17	1 Ur-sa$_6$-ga
		18	1 Lugal-ur$_2$-ra-ni
		19	1 Ur-^{d}Ba-u$_2$ dumu Ur-LI
		20	1 He$_2$-na-ti
		21	1 Lu$_2$-^{d}Ba-u$_2$ <dumu> A-hu-a
		22	1 Lugal-a-ma-ru
		23	1 Ba-za-mu
		24	1 Lu$_2$-^{d}[Ba]-⌈u$_2$⌉ dumu Šeš-šeš
		25	1 Ab-ba-ge-na
		26	1 Lu$_2$-^{d}Na-du$_3$-a mu Ur-^{d}Lamma-še$_3$
	ii	1	1 Ur-^{d}Asar dumu Na-DI
		2	1 Ur-^{d}Asar dumu Al-la
		3	1 I-ti-a
		4	1 Lu$_2$-^{d}Ba-u$_2$ dumu Ur-^{d}Suen
		5	1 Lu$_2$-^{d}Inanna
		6	1 Ur-^{d}Šul-pa-e$_3$ dumu Ur-^{d}Suen
		7	1 Lugal-pa-e$_3$ mu Ur-sa$_6$-ga-še$_3$
		8	1 Niĝ$_2$-ša$_3$-ge mu Ur-gu-la-še$_3$
		9	1 Ur-^{ĝiš}gigir mu Ur-^{d}⌈Utu$^{?}$-še$_3$⌉
		10	*Erased line*

11 ti-la ba-uš$_2$-še$_3$ buluĝ-ĝa$_2$ tur-ra-še$_3$ nu-u$_3$-ši-gid$_2$-da
12 mu lugal-bi in-pa$_3$-de$_3$

Lu-ušgena, son of x-da; Ur-Damu, son of Atu; Balala. (Their) overseer is Nabasa.
Ursaga, son of Lugal-igi; Lu-Ba'u; Ur-eninnu, son of Ursaga. (Their) overseer is Lugal-igi.
Ur-niĝar; Lugal-daga, son of Luba; Ur-Šugalama, son of Dugazida; Lu-Inanna, son of Ĝišsa. (Their) overseer is UNga.
Ur-kigula, son of ZiNEsa; Lu-Ba'u, son of Ur-gigir; Šeškala, son of Lu-Ba'u. (Their) overseer is Ur-Nanše, son of Ur-DUN.
Lu-diĝira, son of Ur-DUB.MI; Lu-Ba'u, son of Ur-gigir; Lu-eb (and) Ur-lugal, they are sons of Gu(...)gi. (Their) overseer is Ur-Utu.
Ur-Ba'u, son of Heti; Urmes, son of Za'a. (Their) overseer is Lukala, brother of the field registrar.
Inim-Inanna; Lu-diĝira, son of ...; Urĝar; Ur-Ba'u, son of Zagala; Ur-sukkal; Ur-Ba'u, son of NaDI; Ur-Ba'u, son of Lukala; Ur-Lamma; Niĝ-Ba'u; Ur-Šulpa'e, son of Ur-Damu; Ursaga, Lugal-urani; Ur-Ba'u, son of Ur-LI; Henati; Lu-Ba'u, <son of> Ahu'a; Lugal-amaru; Bazamu; Lu-Ba'u, son of Ur-Suen; Lugal-pa'e, on behalf of Ursaga; Niĝ-šage, on behalf of Urgula; Ur-gigir, on behalf of Ur-Utu$^?$.
They swore by the name of the king that they will not have recorded a living man as a dead one, a grown-up one as a young one.

The foremen and overseers recorded in this text worked at a large brewery-mill complex, probably located in Girsu, which is suggested by the identification of the last group of them as brewers, and of two more as millers, in Orient 16, p. 85 127 (Text A in Table 2). This long text, dated to Šulgi 35, is a balanced-account of workdays performed under the responsibility of foremen of *eren*-workers working at the mill (iii 6) and the brewery (rev. I 6). The foremen of brewers can also be identified in MVN 2 175 (Text B), a long list of workers on duty at the brewery, dated to Šulgi 46. Some of the overseers (nu-banda$_3$) of Text 2 are also mentioned as supervisors of works performed at a canal in PPAC 5 1257 (Text C).

Here follows a concordance of foremen and overseers recorded in Text 2 with their occurrences in the above mentioned texts:

Mill section (i 1, probably until rev. i 5)	
Lu$_2$-uš-ge-na dumu x-da	
Ur-^{d}Da-mu dumu A-tu	A i 21
Ba-la-la	
nu-banda$_3$ Na-ba-sa$_6$	A ii 4
Ur-sa$_6$-ga dumu Lugal-igi[19]	
Lu$_2$-^{d}Ba-u$_2$	
Ur-e$_2$-ninnu dumu Ur-sa$_6$-ga	

19 Ursaga, son of Lugal-igi, is recorded taking an "assertory oath" (nam-erim$_2$ ku$_5$) on the filling of the granary of the field "Ninĝirsu-azida-Nanše", in CT 3, pl. 21 BM 18957: iii 1–5 (Girsu, Š46).

nu-banda$_3$ Lugal-igi	C ii 8
Ur-niĝar$_x^{ĝar}$	
Lugal-da-ga dumu Lu$_2$-ba	
Ur-Šu-ga-lam-ma dumu Du$_{11}$-ga-zi-da	
Lu$_2$-^{d}Inanna dumu Ĝiš-sa$_6$	
nu-banda$_3$ UN-ga$_6$	C ii 3
Ur-ki-gu-la dumu Zi-NE-sa$_6$	
Lu$_2$-^{d}Ba-u$_2$ dumu Ur-^{ĝiš}gigir	
Šeš-kal-la dumu Lu$_2$-^{d}Ba-u$_2$	
nu-banda$_3$ Ur-^{d}Nanše dumu Ur-DUN	
Lu$_2$-diĝir-ra dumu Ur-DUB.MI	
Lu$_2$-^{d}Ba-u$_2$ dumu Ur-^{ĝiš}gigir	
Lu$_2$-eb	
Ur-lugal	
dumu Gu$_2$-[x]-gi-me (*or* Gu$_2$-[g]i$_4$)	
nu-banda$_3$ Ur-^{d}Utu	
Ur-^{d}Ba-u$_2$ dumu He$_2$-ti	
Ur-mes dumu Za-a	
nu-banda$_3$ Lu$_2$-kal-la šeš saĝ-du$_5$	C i 18
Brewery section (rev. i 7 – ii 9)	
Inim-^{d}Inanna	A iii 27
Lu$_2$-diĝir-ra dumu ⌈x-(x)-NI$^?$⌉	A iii 21
Ur-ĝar	A iii 14
Ur-^{d}Ba-u$_2$ dumu Za-ga-la$_2$	
Ur-sukkal	
Ur-^{d}Ba-u$_2$ dumu Na-DI	
Ur-^{d}Ba-u$_2$ dumu Lu$_2$-kal-la	
Ur-^{d}Lamma	B iii 18
Niĝ$_2$-^{d}Ba-u$_2$	B v 10, vi 9
Ur-^{d}Šul-pa-e$_3$ dumu Ur-^{d}Da-mu	A iii 20
Ur-sa$_6$-ga	A iii 9; B rev. iv 16
Lugal-ur$_2$-ra-ni	A iii 18; B i 16
Ur-^{d}Ba-u$_2$ dumu Ur-LI	A iii 10; B ii 34, v 28
He$_2$-na-ti	B iv 7, v 33
Lu$_2$-^{d}Ba-u$_2$ <dumu> A-hu-a	B rev. iv 37
Lugal-a-ma-ru	A iii 11
Ba-za-mu	A iii 17
Lu$_2$-^{d}[Ba]-u$_2$ dumu Šeš-šeš	A iii 26
Ab-ba-ge-na	A rev. i 2

Lu$_2$-^{d}Na-du$_3$-a mu Ur-^{d}Lamma-še$_3$	A iii 15
Ur-^{d}Asar dumu Na-DI	A iii 13
Ur-^{d}Asar dumu Al-la	A iii 29 ; B iii 28
I-ti-a	A iii 19
Lu$_2$-^{d}Ba-u$_2$ dumu Ur-^{d}Suen	
Lu$_2$-^{d}Inanna	B iv 38, v 36
Ur-^{d}Šul-pa-e$_3$ dumu Ur-^{d}Suen	
Lugal-pa-e$_3$ mu Ur-sa$_6$-ga-še$_3$	A iii 24
Niĝ$_2$-ša$_3$-ge mu Ur-gu-la-še$_3$	
Ur-^{ĝiš}gigir mu Ur-^{d}[Utu$^?$-še$_3$]	B ii 7, vi 13

Table 2

§ 8. To sum up, foremen had at their disposal work-gangs of men and women to perform different tasks in agriculture, irrigation, transportation, crafts production, milling and textile production. Generally depending on their age, sex and social status, workers received different wages and were supposed to perform varying amounts of work. The work expected from these gangs also varied through the years, due, among other reasons, to the death of workers, long illnesses, absence from work, or transfer to other gangs. All these details were gathered in inspection lists, texts that were presumably written down on the basis of the information provided by foremen. These inspection lists were crucial to planning the wages needed, and to fixing the amount of work expected for certain periods of time from the work-gangs under the responsibility of the foremen. Expectations of work were nevertheless overestimated by the administration, so foremen put in place a mechanism of manipulation of data dealing with the situation of their workers, in order to reduce the pressure on them: they registered workers on duty as if they were dead or absent, and adults as if they were young men and women.[20] In this way, the calculations of the amount of work expected from the gangs for the coming year would be appreciably lower. Other alterations of reality at other stages of the relationship of foremen with the administration would be more problematic, since inspections on the ground by other officials could be made during or right after the works were performed. To avoid the frauds, the administration made foremen to take an oath by the name of the king, as is attested in Texts 1 and 2. We do not know how frequent and widespread within the Ur III state these practices were, and whether oaths to avoid them were regularly or exceptionally required from foremen. The very few testimonies we have are concentrated in the Girsu/Lagaš province and during the last years of Šulgi's reign. Beyond this, further explanations for the manipulations implemented by foremen, possibly based on the difficulties of the deep administrative and economic reorganization of the Girsu/Lagaš province put into effect by king Šulgi, would be a matter of speculation.

20 Manipulation of data in administrative texts has also been demonstrated, for example, for the so-called *naptan šarrim* documents of Mari (Sasson 1982).

Text 1
BM 21411

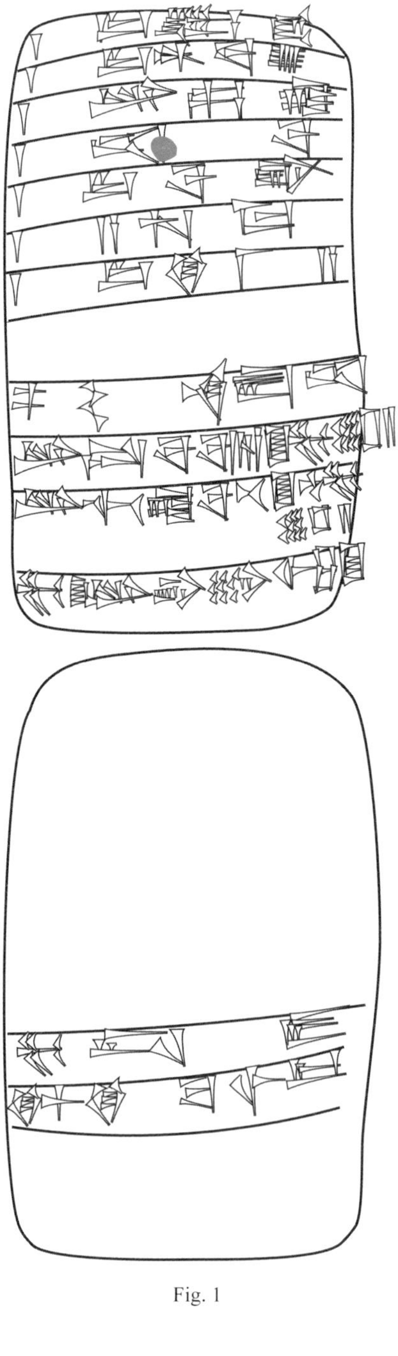

Fig. 1

Text 1
BM 21411

Fig. 2

Text 2
BM 22859
obv.

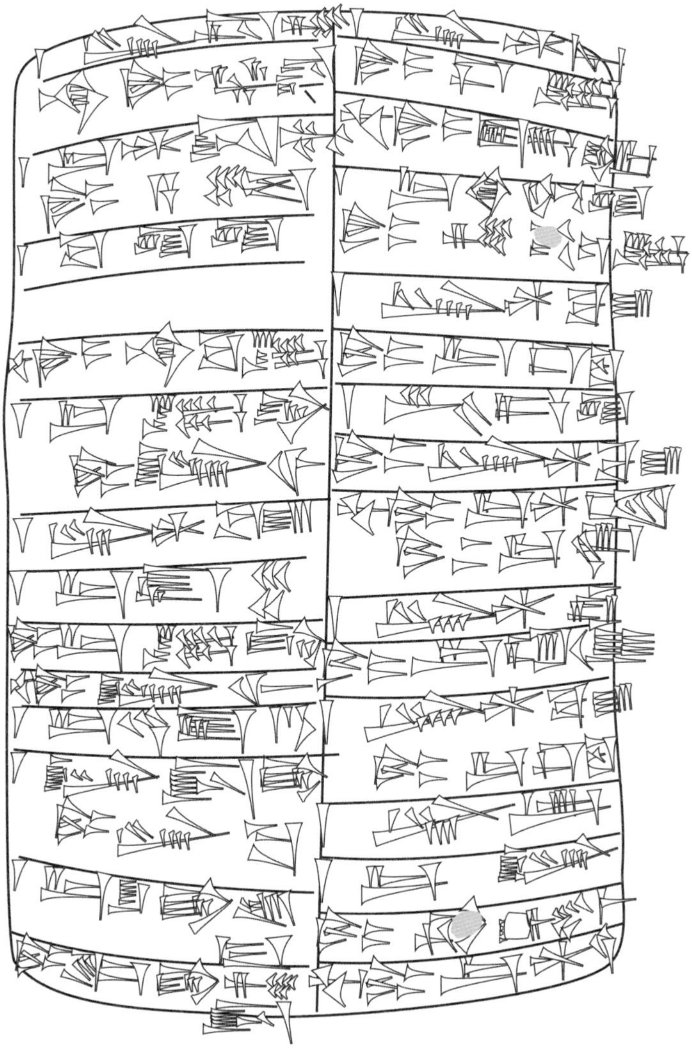

Fig. 3

Text 2
BM 22859
rev.

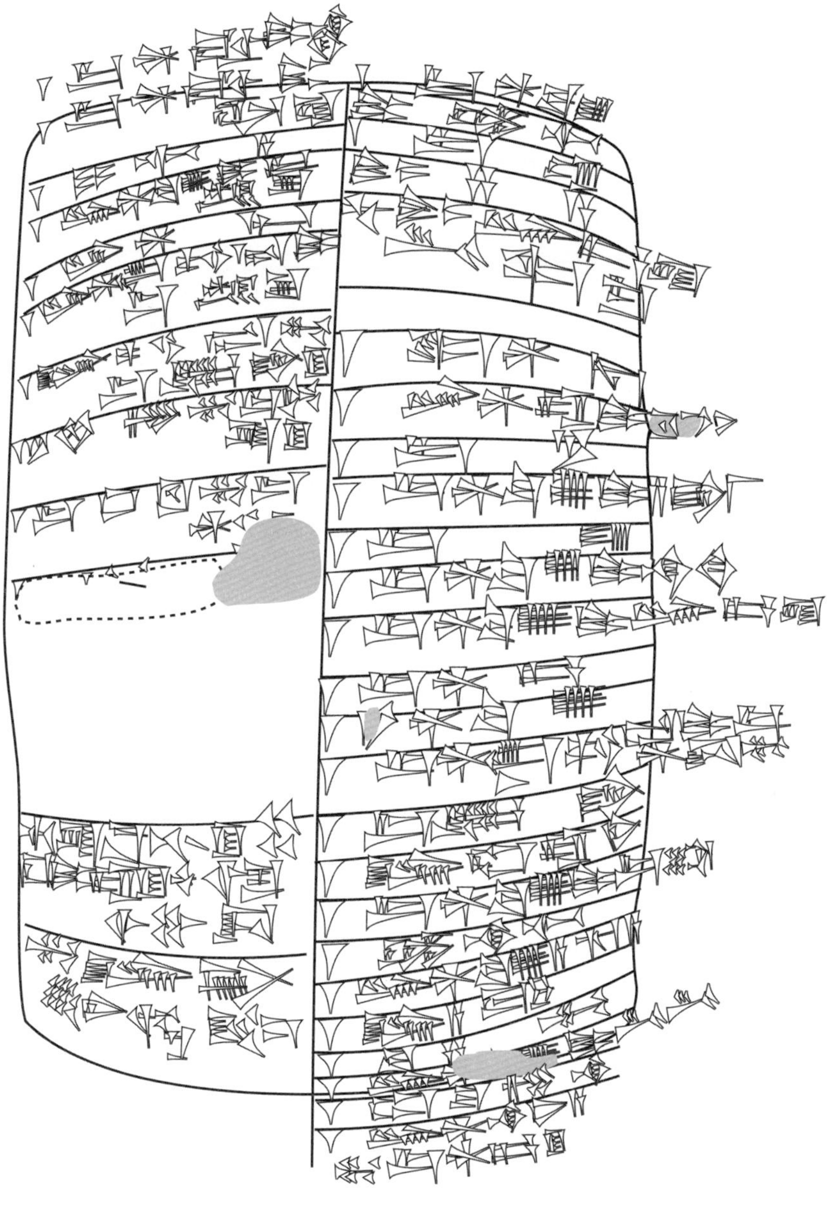

Fig. 4

Text 2
BM 22859
obv.

Fig. 5

Text 2
BM 22859
rev.

Fig. 6

Bibliography

Allred, L. B. 2008. "Labour Assignments from the City of Girsu", in P. Michalowski (ed.), *On the Third Dynasty of Ur. Studies in Honor of Marcel Sigrist.* Journal of Cuneiform Studies – Supplemental Series 1. Boston, pp. 11–19.

Allred, L. B. 2014. "Girsu Labour Assignments Revisited". *Cuneiform Digital Library Notes* 2014: 12, 4 pp.

Attinger, P. 2005. "A propos de AK 'faire' (II)". *Zeitschrift für Assyriologie* 95, pp. 208–275.

Borrelli, N. 2013. *Managing the Land: Agricultural Administration in the Province of Ĝirsu/Lagaš During the Ur III Period.* Ph. D. Diss. Università degli Studi di Napoli "L'Orientale".

Gelb, I. J. 1979. "Household and Family in Early Mesopotamia", in E. Lipiński (ed.), *State and Temple Economy in the Ancient Near East.* I. Orientalia Lovanensia Analecta 5. Leuven, pp. 1–97.

Koslova, N. 2004. "Fluktuation der Arbeitskrafte im Umma der Ur III-Zeit: Santag 6: 384". *Babel und Bibel* 1, pp. 23–82.

Koslova, N. 2008. "Bezeichnungen der Arbeitskräfte in Umma der Ur III-Zeit", in S. Garfinkle and J. C. Johnson (eds.), *The Growth of an Early State in Mesopotamia: Studies in Ur III Administration.* Biblioteca del Próximo Oriente Antiguo 5. Madrid, pp. 149–206.

Koslova, N. 2013. "Absence from Work in Ur III Umma: Reasons and Terminology", in S. Garfinkle and M. Molina (eds.), *From the 21st Century BC to the 21st Century AD. Proceedings of the International Conference on Neo-Sumerian Studies Held in Madrid, July 22-24, 2010.* Winona Lake, pp. 313–332.

Lafont, B. 1994. "L'avènement de Šu-Sîn". *Revue d'Assyriologie et d'Archéologie Orientale* 88, pp. 97–119.

Maaijer, R. de, and B. Jagersma. 2003/04. "[Review of] Å.W. Sjöberg *et al.*, The Sumerian Dictionary of the University Museum of the University of Pennsylvania. A/3. Philadelphia 1998". *Archiv für Orientforschung* 50, pp. 350–355.

Maekawa, K. 1999. "The 'Temples' and the 'Temple Personnel' of Ur III Girsu-Lagash", in K. Watanabe (ed.), *Priests and Officials in the Ancient Near East. Papers of the Second Colloquium on the Ancient Near East – The City and its Life, held at the Middle Eastern Culture Center in Japan (Mitaka, Tokyo. March 22-24, 1996).* Heidelberg, pp. 61–102.

Molina, M. 2008. "The Corpus of Neo-Sumerian Tablets: An Overview", in S. Garfinkle and J. C. Johnson (eds.), *The Growth of an Early State in Mesopotamia: Studies in Ur III Administration.* Biblioteca del Próximo Oriente Antiguo 5. Madrid, pp. 19–53.

Notizia, P. and L. Verderame. 2017. "Nuove letter-order neo-sumeriche da Ĝirsu-Lagaš nel British Museum". *Rivista degli Studi Orientali* 89, pp. 59–73.

Sallaberger, W. 1999. "Ur III-Zeit", in *Mesopotamien. Akkade-Zeit und Ur III-Zeit.* Annäherungen 3. Orbis Biblicus et Orientalis 160/3. Freiburg/Göttingen, pp. 119–390.

Sallaberger, W. 2008. "Der Eid im Gerichtsverfahren im neusumerischen Umma", in P. Michalowski (ed.), *On the Third Dynasty of Ur. Studies in Honor of Marcel Sigrist.* Journal of Cuneiform Studies – Supplemental Series 1. Boston, pp. 159–176.

Sasson, J.M. 1982. "Accounting Discrepancies in the Mari NÌ.GUB [NÍG.DU] Texts", in G. van Driel and Th. J. H. Krispijn, M. Stol and K. R. Veenhof (eds.), *Zikir Šumim: Assyriological Studies Presented to F. R. Kraus on the Occasion of his Seventieth Birthday.* Leiden, pp. 326–341.

Sharlach, T. 2004. *Provincial Taxation and the Ur III State.* Cuneiform Monographs 26. Leiden.

Steinkeller, P. 1982. "On the Reding and Meaning of igi-kár and gúrum (IGI.GAR)". *Acta Sumerologica* 4, pp. 149–151.

Steinkeller, P. 1987. "The Foresters of Umma: Toward a Definition of Ur III Labour", in M. Powell (ed.), *Labour in the Ancient Near East.* American Oriental Series 68. New Haven, pp. 73–115.

Steinkeller, P. 1989. *Sale Documents of the Ur-III-Period.* Freiburger Altorientalische Studien 17. Stuttgart.
Steinkeller, P. 2003. "Archival Practices at Babylonia in the Third Millennium", in M. Brosius (ed.), *Ancient Archives and Archival Traditions. Concepts of Record-Keeping in the Ancient World.* Oxford, pp. 37–58.
Studevent-Hickman, B. 2006. *The Organization of Manual Labour in Ur III Babylonia.* Ph. D. Diss. Harvard University.
Uchitel, A. 1992. "Erín-èš-didli". *Acta Sumerologica* 14, pp. 317–338.
Uchitel, A. 1996. "Erín-èš-didli (II): Patterns of Conscription and Works Assignment During the Years AS 8 – ŠS 1". *Acta Sumerologica* 18, pp. 217–228.

Writing as Administrative Option: The Diviner of the Gods at Late Bronze Age Emar

Daniel E. Fleming, New York[1]

At a meeting defined by "Accounts and Bookkeeping in the Ancient World," Julia Lougovaya offered a contribution defined by the possibility of non-written administration, financial oversight in early Greece by *tamiai* "treasurers" whose responsibilities appear to have been carried out without reliance on texts. The conference title invokes terms that are difficult to imagine without written record-keeping: literally so with "bookkeeping" and nearly as restrictively with "accounts." Yet it is possible for the development of written frameworks for administration to lure us into thinking that financial oversight of institutions requires writing, and then into interpreting all written remains from such oversight as elements of systematic record-keeping that we can only imagine in textual terms.

As a complement to Lougovaya's contribution, I offer these reflections on a modest collection of administrative documents from the workplace of an official who called himself "the diviner of the gods" at a small city named Emar, on the great bend of the Euphrates River in northwestern Syria. The documents span two generations of the diviners in the 13th and early 12th centuries. As part of larger research on the site, Sophie Démare-Lafont and I have published an extended study of this material, as "Ad Hoc Administration and Archiving at Emar: Free Format and Free Composition in the Diviner's Text Collection," *Aula Orientalis* 36 (2018) 29-63. Against what may be expected of administrative writing, we concluded that every such text from this diviner's archive was conceived independently, not by any repeated template, so that each one takes distinct form, even when the recorded inventories or transfers involved comparable administrative acts. A corollary to this conclusion is that the texts were not essential to the oversight reflected in them; inventory could be conducted without writing down the results, and the diviner could oversee transfers of various goods and valuables without documentary record. With the present article, I pursue the character of this administrative writing as optional, each choice as individual as the texts themselves, in a structure of authority and accountability that is not ultimately defined by the creation of a textual corpus of reference.

---

1 My contribution to the Schwetzingen meeting was composed as a collaboration with my colleague Sophie Démare-Lafont, with whom I have been working on questions of Emar society and law for more than ten years. Although this article is attached to my name alone, it is as much a product of that collaboration as the pieces published under both names together. Her ideas about the individuality of the diviner's administrative writing, the limited time horizon for any such texts, and the priority of oral transactions to writing in ancient Near Eastern law suffuse my own approach to this material, and she has of course read and responded to the article before it reached its finished form. By accepting to limit authorship to my name, I acknowledge final responsibility for the ideas therein.

As "diviner of the gods," the building M-1 diviner was charged to supervise the operation of sacred places and their rites for a range of sites identified with the city of Emar as a body.[2] The family of the diviners who inhabited this edifice and who bore this title can be traced through three generations:

Zu-Baʿla (son of Šuršu) – appointed by the Hittites
Baʿlu-qarrad son of Zu-Baʿla
Šaggar-abu son of Baʿlu-qarrad
Baʿlu-malik son of Baʿlu-qarrad[3]

There is no evidence for written reflection of this cultic oversight until the term of Baʿlu-qarrad, a fact that by itself suggests that responsibility for financial and ritual supervision of sacred affairs could be maintained without textual "bookkeeping."[4] We only know about the diviners' work, however, because of the texts that survived and were excavated in area M at Emar (modern Meskeneh), ranging from long accounts of public ritual performance to lists of names or objects to diverse sketches of transfers involving animals, grain, precious objects and more.[5]

---

2 This is evident in the oldest ritual text preserved from the building M-1, which records six months of public celebrations under the heading, "rites of the city" ([*pár-ṣ*]*i ša* URU.KI, E446:1) and then makes repeated reference to the diviner's interest (lines [26], 28, 39, 26*, 44, 51, 53, 64, 65, 82, 95, 102, 105, and 116). For systematic treatment of the text and a collated edition, see Daniel Fleming, *Time at Emar: The Cultic Calendar and the Rituals from the Diviner's Archive* (Winona Lake, Ind.: Eisenbrauns, 2000) 143-73, 268-80. The texts from Emar's building M-1 have been examined as a securely provenanced whole by Matthew Rutz, *Bodies of Knowledge in Ancient Mesopotamia: The Diviners of Late Bronze Age Emar and Their Tablet Collection* (Leiden: Brill, 2013).

3 For the filiation of Zu-Baʿla see Yoram Cohen, "Problems in the History and Chronology of Emar," *Kaskal* 10 (2013) 291-92 (281-94), in response to Masamichi Yamada, "The Chronology of the Emar Texts Reassessed," *Orient* 48 (2013) 125-56. In our own extended reevaluation of the chronology and textual production of Emar, Démare-Lafont and I estimate that Zu-Baʿla was active from the 1260s to the 1250s, Baʿlu-qarrad from the 1240s to the 1220s, and Baʿlu-malik from the 1200s to the 1180s, after his older brother died without extended service; see Sophie Démare-Lafont and Daniel Fleming, "Emar Chronology and Scribal Streams: Cosmopolitanism and Legal Diversity," *Revue d'Assyriologie* 109 (2015) 45-77.

4 The important alignment of the written texts with the last two generations of building M-1 diviners was worked out by Yoram Cohen, *The Scribes and Scholars of the City of Emar in the Late Bronze Age* (Winona Lake, Ind.: Eisenbrauns, 2009) 147-83.

5 In his publication of the Akkadian texts from daily life, Daniel Arnaud divides the cultic and administrative materials into various groups of records (especially E274 – E368) and of rituals (E369 – E535); *Recherches au pays d'Aštata: Emar VI/3* (Paris: Éditions Recherche sur les Civilisations, 1986). While the distinct text numbers suggest more than 250 documents, more than half of these are fragments that probably reflect a much smaller number of original tablets, now impossible to reconstruct in most cases. It is likely that beyond the French excavations, further looting of the site took tablets from the building M-1, as seen in the testament of the diviner Baʿlu-qarrad published as no.7 in Arnaud, "Tablettes de genres divers au Moyen-Euphrate," *Studi micenei ed egeo-anatolici* 30 (1992) 195-245. Many of the "lists" published as BLM 16-30 could only have been composed as part of the same cultic supervision, an impression most unavoidable in the dedication of offerings by (the diviner) Baʿlu-malik in BLM 24, which includes reference to his two sons, elsewhere known as Zuzu and Ipqi-Dagan; Joan Goodnick Westenholz, *Cuneiform Inscriptions in the Collection of the Bible Lands Museum Jerusalem: The Emar Tablets* (Groningen: Styx, 2000). Among the various texts published from the antiquities market, these are not the only probable examples, but there is benefit to working from a text base

Especially in light of the individuality of the diviner's textual accounting, it is extremely difficult to reconstruct the purpose of his writing, which certainly varied. We must keep in mind that written accounting has a natural time horizon beyond which records would be discarded as irrelevant. Even where the work relied heavily on systematic text production in a mode that evokes bureaucracy – which is not true of Emar – the interest would generally have been short-term. At the same time, the point of writing appears to be to look at something again, whether in an hour, the next day, or later. We cannot be sure whether return to a text was planned or merely potential; whether a text would be viewed more than once; or how long the horizon of its potential usefulness may have been. The disposal of a written text, in contrast, would mean that both planned and potential reference to it were dropped with finality. No one would ever again check the text, and any memory of the transaction it recorded would be only in the mind of the person who oversaw it. The decision to abandon all possibility of return to a text may have been driven by diverse intents: a systematic housecleaning of documents; or attached to the individual text in hand and a particular moment of decision. Also, while texts would only be jettisoned consciously, as we know too well, they may overstay their usefulness, like our own.[6]

The question is then what the diviner's texts from Emar could reveal about this expectation of planned or potential return to them. Although we have only limited ability to penetrate the mindset behind their composition and reuse, there are features that Démare-Lafont and I did not pursue with our primary analysis of the collection.

Signed with Seals

Some of the surviving administrative texts were sealed.[7] All writing suggests at least the possibility of return to the text, but sealing indicates a return that concerns the legitimacy of and specific authority behind the given transaction. With the seal, it is not just the details of objects, persons, gods, and occasions that are recalled; it is the character of the administrative act. Even as some texts were sealed, in keeping with the larger pattern of this textual assemblage, sealing was in no way systematic. Among the excavated tablets, ten bear seals, all but two of which (E279 and E285) exhibit some association with sacred affairs.[8]

Texts are sealed by widely different people, with different seals. E363, E364, and E366 were all sealed by the diviner Ba'lu-qarrad, who used a cylinder seal bearing the name of

---

limited to the excavated tablets from the building M-1, the identification of which has no element of guesswork.

6 These ruminations reflect a particular conversation with Sophie Démare-Lafont regarding what she finds surprising in any survival of accounting texts, which would naturally not have been kept long-term in any systematic way.

7 Beyond the primary publication of the Emar seals by Dominique Beyer, *Emar IV: Les sceaux* (Göttingen: Vandenhoeck & Ruprecht, 2001), see also Maria Elena Balza, *Sigilli e modalità di sigillatura a Emar nel Tardo Bronzo (XIV – XIII sec. a.C.)* (Lugano: Italian University Press, 2009).

8 This set could be extended in two directions by inclusion of texts without provenance but with contents and seal impressions that align with the building M-1 tablets, as well as by considering some of the documents from the storm god temple in area E, which display seals from the diviner's family (E43, E56, and E61); see the chart in Balza (2009: 26). It is not clear what texts beyond those with seals can be identified with the diviner's supervisory work.

Dagan-aẖu, found also on Ba'lu-qarrad's personal testament (SMEA 30 no.7).[9] E285, E287, and E305 all have the diviner Ba'lu-malik's seal, and the first two of these include a second seal to represent some authority outside the diviner's office: E285 with an unknown but evidently external character named Punu; and E287 with a Hittite/Carchemish official named Kili-Šarruma.[10] Four more texts have a single seal each, all with different people, none of whom belongs to the diviner's workplace. E275 has a stamp seal belonging to a probable outsider of uncertain name;[11] E279 preserves only a damaged impression without identification;[12] E290 has a ring seal inscribed in Anatolian hieroglyphs only with the divine name ^{d}Teššub-*ba*;[13] and the Mittani-type seal on E309 resembles the unidentified example with E279.[14]

The sealed texts as a group do not reflect a single framework of authority or oversight. The repeated use of the diviner's seals is a natural extension of composition in this setting, even as the occasional rather than systematic use raises the question of what transactions warranted special attention to the resulting document. Most of the texts with the diviner's seal deal with transfer of goods for ritual (287, 305, 363, 364, 366), with one text (285) suggesting the personal affairs of the diviner and his family.[15] That last text is one with a second seal, indicating concern to confirm a second authority. While the small set of what Démare-Lafont and I call "inventories" is not generally associated with sealing, a unique list of "jewels" (*šukuttu*) found in the storm god temple of area E is signed on the reverse with four seals, led by Ba'lu-qarrad's brother Kapi-Dagan as "diviner" (^{lú}ẖal) and concluded by his son Ba'lu-malik. The occasion for such unusual oversight is not clear, with

9 See A.62, in Beyer 2001: 84.

10 Ba'lu-malik's seal is A.69 in Beyer (2001: 88), and it appears with an impressive range: on these three texts from the building M-1; on three administrative texts from the storm god's temple in area E (E43, E56, and E61); on two cult inventories published by Westenholz (BLM 28 and 29), identified by Cohen (2009: 170-71); and on TBR 70, a private legal document without excavated provenance (Arnaud, *Textes syriens de l'Âge du Bronze Récent* [Barcelona: Editorial AUSA, 1991]). Westenholz (2000: 70) observes that BLM 28 and 29 "refer to similar items, people and gods" as E287, which is also sealed by Kili-Šarruma, whom Cohen (2009: 114) considers "a Hittite official of a high rank," since he is the son of the "Overseer of the Land" (ugula.kalam.ma) Mutri-Teššub. He has three different seals (B33, B63, and B64 in Beyer 2001), found also on ASJ 14 no.48; TBR 20, 97; BLM 28, 29; and E61. For ASJ 14 texts, see Akio Tsukimoto, "Akkadian Texts in the Hirayama Collection III," *Acta Sumerologica* 14 (1992) 289-310. Because of the connection in E61, Cohen (2009: 171) guesses that BLM 28 and 29 may have come from the storm god temple, but given the larger number of unprovenanced Emar texts clearly from the building M-1 and the similar conjunction of names in E287, this origin may be more likely.

11 Beyer (2001: 153) reads Kutumilia(?), as C3, only here; Balza (2009: 100 n.122) has *Ku-tu/tú-x-x-i*[*a*].

12 Beyer (2001: 242), E71, of Mittani type, only here.

13 Beyer (2001: 137), B49, only here.

14 Beyer (2001: 245), E79, only here.

15 With their resemblance to E287, BLM 28 and 29 appear to reflect transfer of precious objects rather than simple inventory of items on hand. Westenholz observes for BLM 28 that Kili-Šarruma "has the responsibility for sealing incoming and outgoing materials for various deities in several localities" (2000: 90). ASJ 14 no.48 records the transfer of metal objects, evidently into (rather than out of) the domains of two gods identified with the nearby town of Ešši, sealed only by Kili-Šarruma. The small tablet E61 simply records a basket of special stones, also perhaps as an arrival or departure from the storm god temple.

two of the building M-1 diviners joining two outsiders to account for valuables identified with "Aštartu of the City" though the text was found in the male storm god's temple.[16]

Ba'lu-qarrad's seal only appears on accounting texts alone, without need of or benefit from any further authority (E363, E364, and E366).[17] Stated differently, the need to join the diviner's authority to some other figure only arises in the last generation of building M-1 diviners. The political conditions for such a shift are intriguingly complex. It is almost certain that Emar's local monarchy collapsed before the fall of the city.[18] The period after that collapse coincided roughly with the activity of the diviner Ba'lu-malik and a time of less direct involvement of the Carchemish sovereign at Emar. This was a time when conditions at Emar may have depended more on factors in the immediate region, still perhaps outside the city itself, than on imposition from an imperial hierarchy going up the chain of authority by way of Carchemish and the Hittite capital.

Unsealed Texts

It is as important to emphasize what was not sealed as what carries one or more seals. In the diviner's archive itself, ten texts bear seal impressions and roughly thirty do not, if we exclude small fragments that cannot be evaluated and probably connect to larger tablets. The non-sealed texts cover a wide range of types, including the inventories as well as all the types that could be sealed – so far as any "type" exists in the archive, since the text assemblage is so completely individual. The following list reflects the categories from Fleming and Démare-Lafont (2018), which includes an appendix with individual text summaries:

Sealed:

E275: transfer with ritual association
(reverse mostly uninscribed)
E279: transfer without evident sacred association – support for hostages at distance?
(fully inscribed)

16 The placement of Ba'lu-malik's seal sets it apart from the other three: the seals of Kapi-Dagan the diviner, Abunnu, and Ari-Šarruma each follow the cuneiform description on the reverse and lower edge of the tablet. Ba'lu-malik's name and seal are found on the right edge, in uncertain relation to the others (Beyer 2001: 88, 139). Cohen (2009: 171-73) suggests that Ba'lu-malik and his uncle Kapi-Dagan may have competed for the office after the death of Ba'lu-qarrad, so the appearance of their seals on the same tablet does not necessarily demonstrate collaboration. It is even possible that the seal of Ba'lu-malik was added later, since the arrangement appears to depend on the other three.

17 One building M-1 administrative text is sealed by Ba'lu-malik alone: E305, involving ritual vessels assigned to named men. Two of the three texts sealed by Ba'lu-qarrad also involve the transfer of the same kind of ritual vessels (E363 and E364). The third Ba'lu-qarrad text (E366) describes bronze assigned to men associated with the *kubadu* rite; note also one more text sealed only by the diviner Ba'lu-malik, found in the storm god temple, involving the transfer of silver (E56).

18 See our engagement in Démare-Lafont and Fleming (2015) with the historical reconstruction of Yoram Cohen and Lorenzo d'Alfonso, "The Duration of the Emar Archives and the Relative and Absolute Chronology of the City," in d'Alfonso, Cohen, and Dietrich Sürenhagen eds., *Emar among the Late Bronze Age Empires: Chronology, Environment, Society* (Münster: Ugarit-Verlag, 2008) 1-23. We agree that the monarchy fell before the end of the Late Bronze Age city, though roughly one generation before it instead of two.

E285: transfer for the diviner's household
(bottom half of reverse uninscribed)
E287: transfer for temples and shrines
(reverse uninscribed)
E290: transfer with general link to sacred stores
(bottom half of reverse uninscribed)
E305: transfer with ritual association
(reverse uninscribed)
E309: transfer with general link to sacred stores
(bottom half of obverse and entire reverse uninscribed)
E363: transfer with ritual association
(reverse uninscribed)
E364: transfer with ritual association
(reverse uninscribed)
E366: transfer with ritual association
(reverse uninscribed)

Unsealed:

E274?: inventory not as "jewels" (*šukuttu*) with other religious interest
(fully inscribed)
E276: transfer with ritual association
(uncertain sealing)
E277: transfer without evident sacred association
(uncertain sealing)
E278: transfer without evident sacred association
(reverse uninscribed)
E282: inventory as "jewels" (*šukuttu*)
(reverse uninscribed?)
E283: inventory not as "jewels" (*šukuttu*) with other religious interest
(fully inscribed)
E284?: transfer for temples and shrines
(reverse covered by writing overlapping from obverse)
E286: transfer for temples and shrines
(reverse uninscribed)
E288?: inventory as "jewels" (*šukuttu*)
(reverse uninscribed?)
E289: transfer for temples and shrines
(reverse uninscribed?)
E296: transfer with general link to sacred stores
(reverse partly uninscribed)
E300?: transfer with ritual association
(reverse partly uninscribed)
E303?: possible inventory
(fully inscribed)

E304?: (not definitely administrative)
(large left margin)
E306: transfer with ritual association
(fully inscribed)
E307: transfer with ritual association
(reverse partly uninscribed)
E311: transfer without evident sacred association
(reverse uninscribed)
E312: transfer for the diviner's household
(reverse uninscribed)
E316: transfer without evident sacred association?
(reverse uninscribed – only three lines on the obverse)
E317?: transfer without evident sacred association
(reverse uninscribed)
E318: transfer without evident sacred association
(reverse partly uninscribed)
E319: transfer without evident sacred association (extract from E279)
(reverse uninscribed with some lines extending from obverse)
E320: transfer without evident sacred association
(reverse partly uninscribed)
E321: transfer without evident sacred association
(fully inscribed)
E323: transfer with general link to sacred stores?
(reverse uninscribed?)
E325?: transfer with general link to sacred stores
(apparently fully inscribed)
E327: transfer with general link to sacred stores?
(fully inscribed)
E331: transfer with general link to sacred stores?
(reverse uninscribed)
E336: list of personal names
(four-column tablet with two and a half columns inscribed – the only multi-column tablet associated with administration, outside the ritual texts)
E338: list of personal names
(fully inscribed)
E361: transfer without evident sacred association
(fully inscribed)
E365?: transfer with ritual association
(fully inscribed?)
E367: transfer for the diviner's household
(fully inscribed)

Sealing seems mainly to have been reserved for affairs in the sacred sphere, the primary domain of the diviner's supervisory role. Likewise, transfers not involving the gods, their sanctuaries, and their rites were not generally sealed. In the above group of unsealed administrative texts, ten are transfers "without evident sacred association" and two are transfers "for the diviner's household." This pattern nevertheless leaves a substantial number of texts with some connection to the diviner's oversight of Emar's cultic establishments.

It does not appear to have been necessary to prove a count of sacred items by showing who made the count or confirmed it. Equally, most transfer texts – not to mention the transfers never recorded in texts – did not require a seal. It appears that the seal demonstrates supervision by the signing authorities, yet the same diviner would have recorded similar transactions without seal. For example, the precious items in E287 were sealed by the diviner, but the similar account in E286 lacks the seal; a transfer of vessels is sealed in E305 but not in E307, a less elaborate text with concern for assignment of the same items. There should be some added value to sealing, when it was done, even if sealing was not necessary.

Each of the sealed documents reflects the need of a single moment, not a systematic, repeated process and its recording. There is no sign that the creation of sealed texts was ever part of a larger accounting or checking of records; the authority was needed for any future check on the transaction in itself. Most often, the sealed texts are fairly short, inscribed only on the obverse of tablets – another reflection of the focus on individual transactions rather than complex accounting. Two exceptions are E275 and E279, both sealed by outsiders to the diviner's office. Whatever provoked the need for a seal, these do not depend on the diviner's own authority.

For the purposes of my reflection on written administrative texts from the diviner's archive at Emar, the most important feature of sealing practice is its unsystematic character. Sealing suggests the possibility of a check by some accounting authority beyond the diviner himself, but attention to such authority depended on the (unknown) occasion and the availability of high-status persons who had no demonstrable relationship to the diviner, public religious practice at Emar, or any of its sacred sites. We cannot know whether a sealed text was kept longer than an unsealed one, and with what expectations. Sealing was an extension of writing itself, as a check on the diviner's accounting, even as writing appears to have been an extension of oversight that did not generally require a written record.

Tablet Preparation

In our investigation of the Emar diviner's administrative collection as a whole, Démare-Lafont and I observed that no two texts are iterations of the same accounting operation, drawn up according to a predetermined template. One example is the inventory of *šukuttu* "jewels": the storm god temple text E43 is sealed by four authorities for a single sacred store, belonging to Aštartu of the City, whereas E282 is unsealed and combines lists of jewels for three different deities. Several of the transfer texts involve grain, flour, or bread, and all take different form. For example:

- E312 simply presents some matching quantity of flour for seven individuals, five of whom are women.
- E316 has only three lines, noting quantities of grain and a milled product "into the hand of Ipqi-Dagan."

- E317 is likewise short: in four lines, the text identifies barley rendered as "porridge" (*pappāsu*-meal), then abruptly switches to donkeys and silver that a man must "now" give – for that grain?
- E318 offers a longer selection of different quantities of different bread type, without identifying the recipients by the names of humans or gods.
- E320 lists nine men who did not "give" grain, concluded by a "total" counted by 34 "houses."

While the construction of each administrative text is unique, whether short or long, there is another aspect of what I have labeled "tablet preparation" that suggests patterns that appear to be related to intended use. These patterns warrant comparison with cuneiform administration outside Emar that I do not undertake here. The primary observation is that the diviner's administrative writing relates in very different ways to the capacity of each tablet. Many of the texts leave all or a large part of the reverse uninscribed, whether or not they are sealed. In contrast, a smaller selection of the texts fill the tablet entirely, suggesting that the relationship between tablet and written product was more carefully planned. This in turn raises the possibility that such texts may have accompanied a different expectation of future reference or may have been disposed of less quickly.

A substantial majority of both the sealed and unsealed texts was composed by leaving some portion of the tablet uninscribed. Of the six texts sealed by one of the diviners, all but E285 are written with the entire reverse left uninscribed, and E285 leaves a space at the end for sealing. Because so many unsealed texts were written in the same way, the failure to use the whole tablet cannot be explained by the need to accommodate a seal. The fact that such tablets could be sealed shows that they cannot all be regarded as reminders to use and then discard immediately. And yet we also find similar tablets that seem more ephemeral; Arnaud considers the three-line E316 to be written with "negligence," and this could be no more than a short-term personal reminder. Overall, these small tablets are adaptable, prepared without commitment to any specific application.

In contrast to the texts that do not fill their tablets, another group of texts fill the obverse and reverse. From the list presented above, the "fully inscribed" tablets include the following:

E274: at least 27 lines; inventory of vessels identified with various deities
E279: 50 lines; grain allotments without sacred association (related to E319) – sealed[19]
E283: 25 lines; inventory of bronze objects as *unūtu* ("items") with concern for weight
E303: more than 6 lines; possible inventory of silver, furniture, textiles
E306: 19 lines; vessels for "men of battle," "men of the goddesses"
E321: 20 lines; animals, garments, etc. "received" by various persons or groups
E327: 16 lines; mostly sheep for transfer – sacred context?
E338: 24 lines; list of personal names
E361: 12 lines; provision for the move of a queen from Kinza (Qadesh) to Šatappi

19 For discussion of this pair of texts, see Fleming and Démare-Lafont (2018: 40-1). E319 represents an extract from E279, but the shorter text offers more detail regarding the transfer, which is described as a *ḫubtētu*, which we suggest could be interpreted as an abstract form of the noun *ḫubtu*, that which is taken by force, possibly referring to captives who receive financial support from their city of origin.

E365: at least 10 line; transfer of sheep to gods and humans
E367: 9 lines; flour, partly for the diviner's household

All of these but E279 are unsealed, so their basis for reexamination does not derived from recording the formal authority by which the transaction was witnessed. Three inventories are drawn up in this manner. Transfers involve both cultic and evidently non-cultic affairs. Although the texts tend to be longer than those with uninscribed or partially inscribed reverse, their scale varies vastly.

Another notable group is recorded with a horizontal dividing line between every entry, a degree of effort that appears superfluous for a short-lived memorandum. These are concentrated among the transfers of grain or bread for purposes not evidently associated with cultic affairs (E315 and E318), and of sheep for what may be sacred use (E324, E325, and E329).

Conclusion

I return to where we began: no two texts from the diviner's administrative corpus follow the same structure, even when the transactions belong to the same type. This means that the relationship of writing or text production to administrative act is individual, by convenience, rather than by standard. Further, the writing does not reflect accountability to any higher or external authority; the appearance of outsiders in seals is by convenience. Rather, these texts serve only the writers, the diviners of the M-1 building. The diviner himself serves both the city of Emar and the sovereign external power of the Hittites as manifest at Carchemish, but he runs the practical operation of his supervisory role on his own terms.

Therefore, the administrative authority of the diviner does not lie in the creation of a textual record but in the oversight itself. The individuality of the texts suggests also that the connection between writing and administrative acts is partial, not systematic or complete. It is likely that a minority, even a small minority, of all the administrative acts of the diviner are preserved in the documentation preserved in the M-1 building. It is not just that the rest of the texts were lost or discarded. The individuality and ad hoc character of the texts and their sealing suggests that writing was only used according to perceived need. In his responsibility for the oversight of sacred affairs defined by the city of Emar, the diviner of the building M-1 thus partook of an authority and process that overlaps with and in broad historical terms anticipates what is suggested for early Greece in the old narrative texts cited by Lougovaya.

“The total of the crown prince’s revenues” – Record-keeping in the Neo-Assyrian palaces

Melanie Groß, Leiden[1]

The origins of the Assyrian Empire go back to the early second millennium BCE. After a period of decline, it began to arise from the northern part of modern Iraq in the late 10th century and grew considerably larger under its powerful kings Aššurnaṣirpal II (883–859 BCE) and Shalmaneser III (858–824 BCE). While in the later 8th century the kings Tiglath-pileser III and Sargon II pushed its borders further outwards, it obtained its maximum extent in the succeeding phase which is associated with the reigns of Sennacherib, Esarhaddon and Assurbanipal. Finally, its borders reached from the Mediterranean Sea into the Zagros Mountains and from the foothills of the Taurus Mountains to the Arabian Desert and the Persian Golf. The Empire prospered, but at the same time it was threatened by internal crisis and foreign affairs. It finally collapsed when a coalition of Babylonian and Median forces subsequently conquered the most important centres in the Assyrian heart-land: the religious centre Assur in 614 BCE and, two years later, in 612 BCE, the imperial capital Nineveh.

While the Bible and the classical sources provide an external and somewhat distorted view-point of an oppressing Empire and its decadent kings, we are fortunate to have available from 1st-millennium Assyria up to 50,000 cuneiform clay tablets written in the Akkadian language. The corpus covers a broad range of different text genres. On the one hand, it includes literary compositions, ritual texts and omen series which are attributed to the well-known “Library of Assurbanipal” from Nineveh (Kuyunjik). On the other, a considerable number of royal inscriptions and treaties are preserved. Another important text group are the archival documents, which comprise letters – that is, especially the state correspondence from Nineveh – legal records and administrative texts.

The archival documents mainly date to the last 150 years of the Empire’s existence and comprise less than 10,000 texts. From this figure we count approximately 1,000 adminis-trative records. In accordance with the written sources in general, most of these texts origi-nate from Nineveh and are kept in the British Museum. A smaller portion was found in Kalhu and some more administrative records come from Assur and the provincial capitals Šibanība, Tušhan, Gūzāna and Til-Barsip as well as the cities Bīt-Adad-erība, Dūr-Katlimmu and Tarzi.

1 This article has been written in the framework of IAP VII “Greater Mesopotamia” and the ERC-CoG-2015 – ERC Consolidator Grant Project “Persia and Babylonia” (ID 682241). Compare the citation in the heading with SAA 7 59 ii 1.

In addition to text editions, only selected groups among the administrative documents have ever been examined in more detail. In the introductions to their editions of administrative texts from Nineveh, Fales and Postgate (1992 and 1995) provide a somewhat broader discussion about this text type. And more recently has Gaspa (2012) examined the format and layout of Neo-Assyrian administrative records.[2] Unlike other text corpora, such as the royal correspondence, these records have been largely left untouched, also because they are particularly enigmatic and ephemeral in nature.

This article represents another step to shed light on these not easily accessible but not less fascinating remnants of Assyrian state and its administration. I will focus on the typology and background of administrative documentation originating from the royal palaces of the two major cities Kalhu and Nineveh. Both cities functioned as capitals of the Neo-Assyrian Empire. In the 9th century Aššurnaṣirpal II was the first among the Assyrian kings to give up on Assur as the traditional capital city and established Kalhu as the imperial centre instead. Kalhu retained its central role until Dūr-Šarrukīn was completed and inaugurated as the new capital towards the end of the reign of Sargon II (707/706 BCE). Before Dūr-Šarrukīn was ever properly used as capital city, Sargon's son and successor Sennacherib abandoned the city in favour of Nineveh which not only remained capital city until the end of the Assyrian Empire but also grew to the biggest among the Assyrian capitals.

1. The remnants of administrative documentation in the palaces of Kalhu and Nineveh

1.1 The administrative documentation of Kalhu

The two buildings that held written remnants of the palace administration in Kalhu are the North-West Palace on the main citadel and Fort Shalmaneser, which was located more than 1 km east of the citadel.[3] Both were built during the 9th century – the North-West Palace as main royal residence in the reign of Aššurnaṣirpal II and Fort Shalmaneser as military headquarters during the reign of Shalmaneser III. Both kept their original function until Sargon II moved (albeit for only a very short interim) the imperial capital to Dūr-Šarrukīn. These palaces certainly lost their initial purpose when Sennacherib established Nineveh as the administrative, political and ideological centre of the Empire, but were maintained as royal establishments until the end of the Empire's existence.

In the North-West Palace c. 80 administrative records have been found scattered in storage rooms which were situated on the north side of the courtyard leading to the throne-room.[4] They were left behind along with part of the state correspondence dating to the reigns of Tiglath-pileser III and Sargon (in Room ZT 4) and, in a few cases, along with legal records from the 7th century (in Rooms ZT 14, 16 and 17). It is likely that these rooms and the tablets therein were affiliated with the suite in the north-eastern corner of that courtyard

2 Fales and Postgate 1992 and 1995; Gaspa 2012.

3 For floor planes see Oates and Oates 2001: Fig. 15 and Fig. 33 on pp. 37 and 61 (North-West Palace) and Fig. 91 on pp. 146–147 (Fort Shalmaneser). See also Kertai 2015, Plates: Figs. 4 and 9.

4 The principal edition for these texts is still Parker 1961.

which might have been the office of the palace scribe (*ṭupšar ekalli*).[5] Such a reconstruction of the spatial organisation of the palace is especially intriguing in view of Room ZT 4 where installations of baked bricks were discovered which were probably used for filing the tablets. Based on the fact that the bulk of the administrative records was found in ZT 4 and, hence, contextualised with the state correspondence from the second half of the 8th century, we are mostly dealing here with the administrative documentation from the same period when the imperial capital was about to be moved to Dūr-Šarrukīn. While most of these tablets do not bear a date, this is supported by their content, including prosopographical connections to other texts.[6]

The administrative tablets (c. 110 tablets) from Fort Shalmaneser also mostly date to the 8th century.[7] The bulk of these tablets (c. 80 tablets) was found in storage rooms next to the northern entrance of the palace and accessible via the North-East Courtyard (Rooms NE 48, 49 and 50). Some more tablets originate from storage rooms located immediately next to these rooms, but accessible from the North-West Courtyard instead (Rooms NW 20 and 21). All these tablets were possibly connected to the office situated in the north-eastern corner of the South-East Courtyard where a few more tablets have been found (NE 55, NW 3). There is reason to assume that the office in question was the one of the palace manager (*rab ekalli*).[8] A smaller number of tablets (c. 10 tablets) originates from Room SW 6 in the north-eastern corner of the South-West Courtyard which, fittingly to the content of these tablets (lists of wine rations), contained a number of large storage jars. In close vicinity to this group a few tablets (c. 7 tablets) were found in Rooms SE 10 and 1 in the north-western corner of the South-East Courtyard. They belong to the dossier (comprising legal records, administrative documents and letters) of palace managers who administered this palace in the 7th century and are the only remnants of administrative documents from this palace which date to the late Neo-Assyrian period. A few more tablets were found in other rooms including Room SE 14 which is accessible from the South-East Courtyard, Room N2 which is close to Rooms SE 10 and 1 but accessible from North-East Courtyard, and Room C1 which is accessible from the South-West Courtyard. At least with Rooms NE 48-50 we can identify a distinct area which was used to keep the administrative documentation. Among other administrative documents, they contained comparatively many dealing with the distribution of wine rations as well as the muster and allocation of horses.[9]

1.2 The administrative documentation of Nineveh

In Nineveh the majority of the c. 450 administrative texts originates from the South-West Palace and the North Palace on the main citadel.[10] Due to in-accurate or rather non-existent documentation in the pioneering days of Near Eastern archaeology in the 19th century, only

5 See the detailed discussion in Groß and Kertai 2019: 12–14.

6 See, for instance, Zadok 2013.

7 The principal editions for these texts are in Kinnier Wilson 1972 and Dalley and Postgate 1984.

8 Again, see the detailed discussion in Groß und Kertai 2019: 8–12.

9 For the text contents and find spots see Dalley and Postgate 1984 *passim*, and especially the catalogue on pp. 261–265.

10 The principal editions of the administrative documentation from Nineveh are Fales and Postgate 1992 and 1995.

for exceptional tablets do we know in which of the two palaces or even in which room from within one of the two palaces they were found. Museo-archaeological studies have revealed though that administrative documents dating to the reign of Sargon II originate from the North Palace and those dating to the reigns of succeeding kings in the 7th century originate from the South-West Palace. These later records represent the majority of the texts and presumably originate primarily from Room LIV (and surroundings) situated in the north-western part of the palace which, according to this reconstruction, also contained letters and astrological reports, queries to the sun-god Šamaš and legal records.[11] This proposed distribution of the textual findings on chronological grounds corresponds with the likelihood that the South-West Palace – built as "Palace without a Rival" by Sennacherib and not encompassed in size by any other Assyrian palace – maintained its role as principal royal palace into Assurbanipal's reign and possibly even until the end of the Empire's existence.[12] The North Palace for its part served as "Succession House" (*bet redûti*) since the reign of Sargon II where Sennacherib and his successors – as designated crown princes – resided and from where they carried out their governmental duties.

For the reign of Sargon we have, hence, royal administrative documentation (administrative documents, letters) originating from both Kalhu and Nineveh. This is due to the fact that for the greater part of Sargon's reign Dūr-Šarrukīn was established and completed while Kalhu was meanwhile still functioning as imperial capital and shortly before the imperial capital was moved to Nineveh. This move might have entailed the transfer of relevant administrative documentation from Kalhu and/or Dūr-Šarrukīn.[13]

Albeit we have to count in the fact that the original storage spaces were already disturbed in antiquity – either due to hostile attacks or the gradual decay of buildings (and therewith the destruction of an upper storey)[14] – and notwithstanding the partly lack of archaeological documentation and the limited possibilities of modern reconstructions, distinct rooms or room clusters were designated to accommodate the administrative documentation along with other text groups such as the state correspondence. A somewhat systematic organisation of this documentation is furthermore indicated by the offices or bureaus which in the case of the two palaces in Kalhu can be tentatively associated with larger collections of administrative tablets in certain palace areas. It is clear from this close association of specific text genres connected to state administration (administrative records, state letters) and the usage history of the particular palace buildings in question that we are dealing here with the administration from the imperial centres of Assyria in their heyday.

11 See Reade 1986 and Parpola 1986.

12 Parpola 1986: 232–233, fn. 48 and Kertai 2013: 21–22.

13 Alternatively, the presence of the correspondence of Sargon in the North Palace of Nineveh might be the result of the fact that crown prince Sennacherib was involved in the government affairs (incl. the establishment of Dūr-Šarrukīn, aspects of which are discussed in numerous state letters from Nineveh) and conducted his governmental tasks on behalf of his father (who was absent from Assyria also because of his stay in Babylonia).

14 Note, however, the critical viewpoint of Kertai (2015: 205–210) towards the possible existence of a (continuous) upper storey.

The administrative records (along with the state correspondence) from the royal palaces in Nineveh and Kalhu are the core group among the remnants of written testimony for the Neo-Assyrian palace administration. At the same time, they represent only a fraction of the original amount of administrative palace documentation.

Except for the fact that not everything has been unearthed, this is due to the dumping or re-cycling of tablets in antiquity and, in particular, due to the bilingual administrative system of the Assyrians. Along with the application of the Aramaic language and script they in-creasingly used perishable writing material such as parchment and writing boards made of wood and ivory. While a few such writing boards have been found in Nimrud and Assur and several references can be found in the cuneiform sources,[15] we can only speculate about the amount of data once recorded on perishable writing materials. All this is aggra-vated by the likelihood that the Assyrians did not document every step of their administra-tive procedures and, also, by the fact that what is documented is not necessarily intelligible for the modern scholar.[16] As a consequence, the Neo-Assyrian administration can only be reconstructed to a limited extent and with several question marks, a fact which, however, should not prevent us from studying this essential component of the Assyrian Empire.

In accordance with the double function of the royal palace as residence of the king and his family as well as governmental centre of state, also the administrative records deal with both: the palace administration proper and the management of the Empire via the provinces and their governors. Like the two spheres were intermingled in the everyday routine, also the documentation does not necessarily and in each case distinguish between the two spheres.

2. A typology of Neo-Assyrian imperial administrative documents

Administrative documents are a fundamental tool for the management of a household or an institution. While they can relate to other types of documents such as legal records and royal decrees, administrative documents are usually not legally binding and do not bear an official character. The range of information given on administrative tablets from Assyrian palaces includes:

1. type and amount of commodity
2. party/parties involved
3. type of transaction
4. date (and place)[17]

The type and the amount of the commodity is a constant and obvious element of each Assyrian administrative record. Also the parties which are directly involved in the trans-action are usually indicated. For instance, a document lists amounts of barley along with representatives of the palace personnel. The other details, however, are not necessarily pro-

15 Wiseman 1955.

16 Postgate 2007.

17 Cf. Jursa (2004: 150) who discussed in detail the Neo-Babylonian administrative documentation (of temples).

vided or not provided in an (for modern scholars) intelligible way. The type of transaction is either not specified at all or indicated only on the basis of short keywords. While the date is occasionally given, the official or department who controlled the transaction on behalf of the palace often remains invisible. Hence, in the worst case we do not get to know whether the palace servant received a ration of barley from the palace or whether he delivered barley to the palace, though we might have good reasons to assume the first scenario. Neither might we learn about the time and place nor about the palace office responsible for the transaction. Despite the fact that this information was simply not recorded, some of the details are often also just lost because they were only given at the beginning or at the end of a tablet, those two parts of a clay tablet which are most vulnerable to damages.

Based on the range of details potentially given in administrative records, three categories emerge along which the administrative system may have worked:

a. type of commodity
b. type of transaction
c. responsible office or department[18]

In the following I will briefly discuss these three categories and whether the administration and its documentation was organised along with them.

2.a. Type of commodity

The classification according to the type of commodity is the most obvious way and indeed usually we can distinguish clearly between tablets dealing with either

- edibles or
- domestic animals[19] or
- wool, cloth and clothing or
- precious materials and items or
- raw materials or building materials or
- horses and mules or
- people or
- land

Many of these categories count in a wide range of sub-categories. Administrative documents dealing with edibles do usually either deal with raw ingredients (including animals or raw meat, corn, vegetables and fruit) or with processed ingredients and finished food and drink (including soup, roasted meat, sweets, beer and wine). On the one hand, these texts are ration lists which record the distribution of wine, beer or bread to, for instance, palace personnel. On the other, a number of administrative records are preserved which deal with domestic animals (mostly sheep but also oxen) and barley as they were due from the provinces (and other administrative units). Furthermore, a comparatively large amount of

18 Cf. Jursa (2004: 149) and his classifications of the Neo-Babylonian administrative text material.

19 Due to their manifold use, domestic animals occur *inter alia* in association with food, wool and leather and as well as a means of transport.

texts deals with edibles in the context of processing of offerings at the temples (and the palaces).

In connection with cloths and clothing, labels were found in the palaces of Nineveh which were originally attached to the goods in question and record the delivery of special types of wool and garments to the palace. A few texts deal with the distribution of commodities like wool or flax to various palaces and palatial departments for further processing or consumption.

The category precious materials and items includes texts about silver as a means of payment. Here, we find texts which deal with silver indebted to the palace or labels which were attached to considerable amounts (1 talent = 30 kg) of silver delivered to the palace by officials and vassals. Furthermore, precious materials (such as gold and lapis lazuli, wood) and items made out of these precious materials (such as jewellery and other accessories, furniture) are recorded in administrative documents as gifts handed out by the palace to its visitors or handed in to the palace by visitors from within and from beyond the Empire's realm. Also lists of tablets and writing boards, which have been collected from all parts of the Empire (but especially Babylonia) for the library in Nineveh, can be counted among the documentation of precious items.

Furthermore, administrative records were found which deal with the building progress (in terms of layers of bricks) in Dūr-Šarrukīn. Every high official of state bore responsibility over a certain building section.

A larger number of texts (from Nineveh and Kalhu) deals with horses and mules which were delivered to the palace or which were assigned to members of the Assyrian army.

Also a larger group of administrative texts deals with people, either with people (or entire families) deported from conquered territories and/or people (or entire families) working the fields and gardens in the Assyrian Empire. Furthermore, lists of another type of workforce (craftsmen such as weavers) as well as of military forces and military contingents are preserved. Furthermore, high-ranking state officials and palace personnel were recorded in administrative documents. They are either simply listed without any further information or occur in texts which record their assignment to specific residences (presumably in the context of a temporary stay in Nineveh).

Finally, land including landed properties (fields, gardens) as well as towns, cities and provinces are subject of administrative documentation. Cultivated land is recorded along with its location and the people who work on it as well as their equipment (as is the case with the so-called Harran Census).[20] Furthermore, estates or entire towns and cities are assigned (to look after) or granted to people. A few documents list provinces or administrative units in an overview.

In several administrative texts, however, different categories occur together. This is true for texts which deal with obligations involving a wider range of things. Payments of *ilku* obligations in kind involve edibles, clothing and silver (e.g. SAA 7 45, SAA 11 88, ND 3467). Also tribute (*maddattu*) payments and audience gifts (*nāmurtu*) involve different things such as horses, silver and clothing (e.g. SAA 11 104, SAA 7 128).

20 SAA 11 201–220. For a discussion see Fales and Postgate 1995: XXX–XXXIV.

Furthermore, a few administrative texts deal with different categories which are causally linked to each other. This might be the case with a text listing the places where *šakintu*s are positioned and continues with listing the distribution of in total 145 weavers (SAA 7 23).[21] It is clearly the case for a group of texts (SAA 7 148-154, 155-157) which are the remnant of accounts of banquets with presumably a cultic background. These texts first list the prepared dishes along with their amounts and continue with listing title-bearers or offices, mainly from the army and from among the scholars. These people were presumably the recipients or consumers of the meals.[22]

These observations in connection with the type of commodity give a first impression on the nature of the transactions. The fact that the majority of the documents keeps separate the different types or sub-types of commodities and distinguishes between their state of preparation or manufacture points to specialised administrative channels and well organised administrative procedures. Administrative documentation (like archival documentation in general) evolves from concrete situations and has a clear connection to time and space. For instance, it was recorded how many sheep were put on disposal for a certain offering which was about to take place in the temple of Aššur or, which army member receives how many horses in the course of military campaign preparations. Such a situative character of the sources makes clear why one administrative record usually deals with one type of commodity or related commodities.

This also leads to the question about the time of drafting of the document in relation to the time of transaction. It is clear that administrative records were not only drawn up at the time of the actual transfer but also *ante factum* and *post factum*. Furthermore, a transfer involves different stages and, hence, administrative records deal with the initial situation, with an interim state or with the finalisation of a transfer. Hence, we are not only dealing with primary records but also with records which were drawn up on the basis of other records. The different types of records can also hint to the stage of the documented procedure. For instance, a memorandum noting the pending incoming and outgoing payments of cloth and garments was drawn up before the actual transfer (SAA 7 112). On the other hand, a textile label from 7th-century Nineveh proves the actual delivery of wardrobe to the palace (SAA 7 94). And an account was apparently made after the actual income of red and black wool – perhaps on the basis of such labels – and already in connection with the re-distribution of the wool (SAA 7 115).

Neo-Assyrian administrative documents do not follow a standard format. They have varying sizes and shapes (portrait and landscape) and show varying ways of organising the text on the tablet (with or without columns, rulings, tables). Furthermore, due to the limited aesthetics, one gets the impression that these records were hastily written and usually not meant for the long-term use. This impression is supported by the fact that only about 15 % percent of the administrative records under discussion here do have a date whereas from

21 For the *šakintu* as the female manageress of the queen and the queen and her household being involved in textile production see Svärd 2015: 91–104, 126.

22 For a discussion of these texts see Mattila 1990 as well as Fales and Postgate 1992: XXXI–XXXIV.

among these only a fraction bears full dates allowing us to pin down the administrative action to a concrete year. Even if the dates might to some extent be broken off, it is safe to assume that dates were not a common feature. Despite the fact that administrative texts were drafted at different moments (before, at the time, or after) in relation to the transaction which was drafted on them, both the rudimentary appearance of the tablets and the type and organisation of the data thereon points to a tendency towards short-term drafting and short-term use of these texts.

2.b. Type of transaction

Although information about the type of transaction is not always available, we can distinguish between three types of actions recorded by administrative texts:

- income of commodities
- expenditure of commodities
- stock-taking

While inventory lists are comparatively low in number, the great majority are records of either incoming or outgoing goods.

Regardless of whether records deal with goods coming in or going out, we can distinguish between records of a single transaction, of multiple identical transactions and of multiple distinct transactions. As a separate group we can list here memoranda which are informal notes written by or by order of the official in charge of the movement of goods.[23]

Records of a single transaction are sealed labels once attached to the container of the transferred commodity or the commodity itself. The majority of the documents belongs to the second group of multiple identical transactions and are *de facto* lists of specific types of commodities either brought to or delivered by the palace. In several cases these lists contain a heading or a postscript or both with details about the nature of the transaction, the responsible office and the date. For instance, some lists from Fort Shalmaneser subsequently enumerate the amount and the recipient, while only from the heading it becomes clear that these are wine rations given out for consumption on a specific day towards the end of the year.[24] Some of these ration lists also have a postscript preserved, as is the case with other administrative records. This final section is often used to give the total of the amounts listed, sometimes on the basis of sub-totals given in sub-sections. In these cases we can usually talk about accounts. The tablet SAA 7 118 from Nineveh, for instance, includes two separate accounts: on the one hand, an account about the processing of stones and, on the other, an account about the income of horses. While the tablet bears no heading, two totals on the basis of sub-totals are established and a precise date is given at the end of the record.

In many of the administrative records keywords were used in order to specify the background of the transaction. Since the palace economy was geared towards consumption

23 Cf. these types of administrative documents with Jursa 2004: 150–154. For an example of administrative records recording multiple distinct transactions see SAA 7 148–154 (briefly discussed above).

24 For a discussion see Fales 1994.

rather than production, we especially find keywords for incoming goods which were levied by or on behalf of the palace. We can identify four main groups:

- taxes and dues from Assyrians
- audience gifts from Assyrians and vassals
- tribute from vassals
- booty from enemies

For audience gifts, tribute and booty the keywords *nāmurtu*, *maddattu* and *hubtu* were applied. For taxes and other dues we deal with a number of different terms, including those for specific taxes on corn (*nusāhu*), straw (*šibšu*) and domestic animals (*ṣibtu*). Sometimes people were indebted to the palace (for unsaid reasons) as outlined in a number of administrative records which record these debts (*hubullu*) in detail. In addition, there is the *ilku*-obligation which requires military service or corvée work and, alternatively, payments in kind for the army. Another important term to be mentioned here is *iškāru* which designates a system of production outsourced by the palace.[25] In connection with this system, both the raw materials given out by as well as the produced materials handed in to the palace are designated *iškāru*.[26]

In fact, the ambiguous use of these terms is a general phenomenon and closely related to or even provoked by the redistributive system of the centralised palace economy. For instance, tribute (*maddattu*), as it was received by the king from his vassals, was distributed to key members of the royal family and high-ranking state officials (SAA 1 34, SAA 11 36). The income of the palace, generated from the palace's own land and resources but especially from the four groups of external revenue, was not just kept but given out for the subsistence of palace residents and staff as well as the wider court of the king. Furthermore, the financing and supply of the Assyrian army was a central concern of the palace. The same is true for the maintenance of the temples and therewith their divine residents and affiliated personnel. Here the offering system and along with it the organisation of the great amounts of foodstuffs is a central issue. While gods were the primary consumers of the divine meal, the leftovers (*rēhu*, *rēhātu*) of these offerings were consumed by the temple personnel and the king and his court. On special occasions huge banquets were organised where these leftovers were consumed.[27] In addition to the re-distributive system, also the principle of reciprocity reinforced the ambiguity of the system and its documentation. This is, for instance, clear in connection with the audience gifts, *nāmurtu*. Based on the rules of gift-exchange, the term was used to refer to gifts given by the palace and gifts delivered to the palace.

In addition to these explicit keywords based on the tax system, technical terms were in use in order to describe the administrative transaction or at least hint to the background of the administrative action recorded. These terms include substantives, verbs and prepositions, whereas the substantives and the verbs can share the same root (*irbu* and *erēbu*). The most common substantives include:

---

25 See Groß 2018 *passim*.

26 For more details see Postgate 1974 and Radner 2007.

27 See, for instance, Milano 1998 and Joannès 2013.

- *akiltu* (consumption, > *akālu* = to consume)
- *irbu* (income, > *erēbu* = to enter)
- *nikkassu* (account), *nikkassu epēšu* (to make the account)
- *pahhurtu* (collection, > *puhhuru* = to collect, muster)
- *šazbussu* or *šuzbultu* (consignment, shipment, > *zabālu*)
- *za'uzzu* (distribution, > *zâzu* = to divide)

The verbs are (occasionally in other than the G-stem):

- *abālu* (to bring)
- *amāru* (to inspect)
- *erēbu* (to enter)
- *mahāru* (to receive)
- *leqû* (to take)
- *nadānu* (to give, deliver)
- *našû* (to transport)
- *zabālu* (to carry, transport)

The prepositions and prepositional phrases are:

- *ana* (to)
- *ina* (in, into)
- *ina libbi* (from, thereof)
- *ina* (*ana*) *qātē* (in the care of)
- *ina pāni* (before, at the disposal of)
- *issu pāni* (on account of, from)
- *piqit* (charge of)
- *qātē* (care of)
- *ša* (of)
- *ša qātē* (in the care of)

The majority of these terms indicates the direction of the goods traffic. Either goods were delivered to the palace or distributed by the palace. From among the prepositional phrases some (*ina qātē*, *ša qātē*, *qātē* and *piqit*) hint to the fact that a commodity is received not for consumption, but in order to take care of the further processing of this commodity. The person (or institution) in question does not receive a commodity, but the responsibility for the commodity. The verb *amāru* is especially applicable to inventories. From among all the expressions *ša* is more problematic since it does not clearly express whether goods were handed in or given out by the palace. For instance, when it is recorded in a document (SAA 7 133) that 10 jars of wine are "of" Aplāya, the palace herald (*nāgir ekalli*), and this document does not add any other information on this procedure, we cannot be certain whether this wine has been delivered by or to this high-ranking official. Moreover, it might even state that 10 jars of wine were not handed over to or by Aplāya, but that this is the amount of wine owned by Aplāya.

All in all, the keywords relating to the Assyrian tax system as well as the technical terms just described, if applied in the administrative records, do contribute significantly to the understanding of the text and its message. Unfortunately, while these expressions occur in other archival text genres,[28] only about 25 % of the administrative texts do mention them or have them preserved whereas the latter might have a greater impact in view of the high number of administrative texts whose beginning is not preserved.

If we examine the types of transaction and the types of commodities in combination, the inner logic or order, with the type of transaction as the main and the type of commodity as the second parameter, becomes apparent.[29] Based on the occasion and the purpose associated commodities were handled and recorded. For instance, on a record about the redistribution (*za'uzzu*) of income from the tax on domestic animals (*ṣibtu*), we find a homogeneous selection of groups of oxen and sheep (SAA 11 90). On the contrary, in connection with *ilku* payments for the supply and equipment of the army we come across various different commodities including grain, fat and garments in the very same tablet.

2.c. Responsible office or department

If we search the administrative texts for information about the office or department under whose responsibility the recorded administrative action has been performed and recorded, we hardly find any. In rare cases officials, who must have controlled or initiated the transaction, do appear in the texts. For instance, a chief of trade (*rab kāri*) (personal name broken) has been responsible for the collection of oxen and sheep as tribute (*maddattu*) (ND 2754, edited in Postgate 1974: 394–395). Or, in the fragment SAA 11 82 the chief confectioner (*rab karkadinni*) is mentioned in the postscript.

If we look at the administration of the Assyrian Empire as a whole and the palace administration in particular, it emerges that in addition to state officials (magnates, including provincial governors) a considerable number of specialized managers or officials (many of which were concerned with foodstuff, as was the case with the chief confectioner) have been active throughout the Empire in order to control and channel the various goods and commodities due from the provinces but also from beyond the borders (from conquered or subjugated territories) on behalf of the king.[30] Along with the fulfilment of their tasks, these officials were mobile and usually not constantly stationed at the royal palace in the capital city or any other of the royal palaces.

However, there are other officials who were positioned and active at the palaces where these texts have been found. In connection with the discussion about the findspots of the administrative palace documentation, bureaus were already mentioned which can be attributed to offices of the palace scribe (*ṭupšar ekalli*) and the palace manager (*rab ekalli*). These two officials were key figures of the palace administration proper: For the administration of the individual royal palace buildings a *rab ekalli* has been appointed to each of

28 It would be worth to look into the appearance of the same administrative keywords in these other text genres (mainly legal records and letters) on another occasion.

29 However, since vassals had to pay tribute and audience gifts, these two types of fees can occur together; e.g. SAA 7 45.

30 See Groß 2020 and Groß 2015.

them.[31] The palace scribe, on the other hand, was head of the chancery of the main royal palace and "secretary of state".[32] Do we find any references to these offices in our texts? In fact we do. In SAA 7 18 (lines i 14′–15′) the palace scribe (*ṭupšar ekalli*) Marduk-erība is mentioned towards the end of the text and the palace scribe Nabû-bēlšunu is mentioned at the end of the text SAA 11 140. Furthermore, according to ND 3467 (edited in Postgate 1974: 399–401) the palace manager (*rab ekalli*) controls the income of payments in kind of *ilku* tax. While such references remain scarce, they indicate that once commodities entered the palace realm proper or were of direct interest for the palace proper, these were the officials who supervised their administration and their documentation, while they must have been supported by others such as the other scribes of the chancery. On special occasions a specialized manager might have been present: for instance, the wine manager (*rab karāni*) is frequently listed in the so-called wine lists from Kalhu and was presumably also responsible for the wine rations given out on this occasion. Or, at the time of the drafting of the lists dealing with precious metal and precious items, the treasurer (*masennu*) might have been present.

What does all this say about the Assyrian royal administration and the palace departments responsible for the management of the traffic of goods? First, depending on the type of transaction or the background of the transfer, different channels were activated before goods came to or after goods left the palace. Of course, goods from foreign delegations handed over as audience gifts passed through other channels than the grain levied from the provinces under the control of the local tax masters and governors. Once they had entered the realm of the palace administration, however, only a handful of offices were in charge of the further treatment, that is, storage, processing or distribution.

31 Gross 2014 and Groß and Kertai 2019: 12–14.

32 Luukko 2007 and Groß 2020. The *rab ekalli* is not to be confused with the *ša-pān-ekalli* official who was one of the most important figures in the direct environment of the king and of his itinerant court (see Groß 2020).

Bibliography

Dalley, S. and J.N. Postgate 1984: *The Tablets from Fort Shalmaneser*. Cuneiform Texts from Nimrud 3. London: British School of Archaeology in Iraq.

Fales, F.M. 1994: "A Fresh Look at the Nimrud Wine Lists," in L. Milano (ed.), *Drinking in Ancient Societies. History and Culture of Drinks in the Ancient Near East*. Rome: Sargon srl, 361–380.

Fales, F.M. and J.N. Postgate 1992. *Imperial Administrative Records, Part I: Palace and Temple Administration*. State Archives of Assyria 7. Helsinki: Helsinki University Press.

Fales, F.M. and J.N. Postgate 1995. *Imperial Administrative Records, Part II. Provincial and Military Administration*. State Archives of Assyria 11. Helsinki: Helsinki University Press.

Gaspa, S. 2012: "The Accountant's Job: Professional Numeracy and Record-Keeping in the Assyrian Administrative Practice," in G.B. Lanfranchi, D. Morandi Bonacossi, C. Pappi and S. Ponchia (eds), *Leggo! Studies Presented to Frederick Mario Fales on the Occasion of His 65th Birthday*. Wiesbaden: Harrassowitz, 307–324.

Groß, M. 2015: "Food and drink for the palace: the management of foodstuffs in Neo-Assyrian times and beyond," *State Archives of Assyria Bulletin* 21, 21–45.

Groß, M. 2018: "Craftsmen in the Neo-Assyrian Empire," in A. Garcia-Ventura (ed.), *What's in a Name? Terminology Related to Work Force and Job Categories in the Ancient Near East*. Alter Orient und Altes Testament 440. Münster: Ugarit, 369–395.

Groß, M. 2020: "At the Heart of an Empire: The Royal Household in the Neo-Assyrian Period. Leuven: Peeters.

Groß, M. and D. Kertai 2019: "Becoming Empire. Neo-Assyrian palaces and the creation of courtly culture," *Journal of Ancient History* 7/1, 1–31.

Joannès, F. 2013: "Quand le roi mange comme un dieu ... Les transferts entre table divine et table royale en Assyrie et en Babylonie au Ier millénaire av. J.-C.," in C. Grandjean, C. Hugoniot, B. Lion (eds), *Le banquet du monarque dans le monde antique*. Tours – Rennes: PUR, 327–342.

Jursa, M. 2004: "Accounting in Neo-Babylonian Institutional Archives: Structure, Usage, Implications," in M. Hudson and C. Wunsch (eds), *Creating Economic Order. Record-Keeping, Standardization, and the Development of Accounting in the Ancient Near East IV*. Bethesda: CDL Press, 145–198.

Kertai, D. 2013: "The Multiplicity of Royal Palaces. How many Palaces did an Assyrian King Need?," in D. Kertai and P.A. Miglus (eds), *New Research on Late Assyrian Palaces. Conference at Heidelberg January 22nd, 2011*. Heidelberg: Heidelberger Orientverlag, 11–22, Pls. IV–VI.

Kertai, D. 2015: *The Architecture of Late Assyrian Royal Palaces*. Oxford: Oxford University Press.

Kinnier Wilson, J.V. 1972: *The Nimrud Wine Lists. A Study of Men and Administration at the Assyrian Capital in the Eighth Century B.C.* Cuneiform Texts from Nimrud 1. London: British School of Archaeology in Iraq.

Luukko, M. 2007: "The Administrative Roles of the 'Chief Scribe' and the 'Palace Scribe' in the Neo-Assyrian Period," *State Archives of Assyria Bulletin* 16, 227–256.

Mattila, R. 1990: "Balancing the Accounts of the Royal New Years's Reception," *State Archives of Assyria Bulletin* 4/1, 7–22.

Milano, L. 1998: "Aspects of Meat Consumption in Mesopotamia and the Food Paradigm of the Poor Man of Nippur," *State Archives of Assyria Bulletin* 12/2, 111–127.

Oates, J. and Oates, D. 2001: *Nimrud. An Assyrian Imperial City Revealed*. London: British School of Archaeology in Iraq.

Parker, B. 1961: "Administrative Tablets from the North-West Palace, Nimrud," *Iraq* 23/1, 15–67 and Pls. IX–XXX.

Parpola, S. 1986: "The Royal Archives of Niniveh," in K.R. Veenhof (ed.), *Cuneiform Archives and Libraries. Papers read at the 30[e] Rencontre Assyriologique Internationale, Leiden, 4–8 July 1983*. PIHANS 57. Istanbul: Nederlands historisch-archaeologisch instituut te Istanbul, 223–236.

Parpola, S. 1987: *The Correspondence of Sargon II, Part I: Letters from Assyria and the West*. State Archives of Assyria 1. Helsinki: Helsinki University Press.

Postgate, J.N. 1974: *Taxation and Conscription in the Assyrian Empire*. Studia Pohl, Series Maior 3. Rome: Pontifical Biblical Institute.

Postgate, J.N. 2007: "The invisible hierarchy: Assyrian military and civilian administration in the 8th and 7th centuries BC," in J.N. Postgate (ed.), *The Land of Assur & the Yoke of Assur. Studies on Assyria 1971–2005*. Oxford: Oxbow Books, 331–360.

Radner, K. 2007: "Abgaben an den König von Assyrien aus dem In- und Ausland," in H. Klinkott, S. Kubisch and R. Müller-Wollermann (eds), *Geschenke und Steuern, Zölle und Tribute. Antike Abgabenformen in Anspruch und Wirklichkeit*. Culture and History of the Ancient Near East 29. Leiden/Boston: Brill, 213–230.

Reade, J.E. 1986: "Archaeology and the Kuyunjik Archives," in K.R. Veenhof (ed.), *Cuneiform Archives and Libraries. Papers read at the 30e Rencontre Assyriologique Internationale. Leiden, 4–8 July 1983*. PIHANS 57. Istanbul: Nederlands historisch-archaeologisch instituut te Istanbul, 213–222.

Svärd, S. 2015: *Women and Power in Neo-Assyrian Palaces*. State Archives of Assyria Studies 23. Winona Lake: The Neo-Assyrian Text Corpus Project.

Wiseman, D.J. 1955: "Assyrian Writing-Boards," *Iraq* 17/1, 3–13.

Zadok, R. 2013: "The Archive of Šamaš-šarra-uṣur from Calah," in A.F. Botta (ed.), *In the Shadow of Bezalel. Aramaic, Biblical, and Ancient Near Eastern Studies in Honor of Bezalel Porten*. Culture and History of the Ancient Near East 60. Leiden/Boston: Brill, 387–407.

Ancient Greece

Tamiai in Homeric Epic

Julia Lougovaya, Heidelberg

This paper investigates the parameters of apparent managerial tasks associated with the words *tamias* or *tamia*, 'steward' or 'controller', in Greece of the Early Iron Age, archaeologically speaking, a society whose functioning, especially in respect to its basic economic organization, finds some reflection in Homeric epic.[1] Although there may have been no bookkeeping in the strict sense of the word in Greece in that period, for there were neither books nor writing at the time, keeping track of supplies—their acquisition, storage, and distribution—appears to have been perceived as a distinct duty discharged by a *tamias* or *tamia*. Since of all activities that entail movement, exchange, and consumption of goods in epic the most frequently described one is feasting, commensality being of paramount importance in Homeric society, *tamiai* are depicted as primarily associated with the distribution of victuals. Analysis of the passages in Homer in which they are described or even simply alluded to allows for some insight into their possible roles. It is hoped that this will also lay the groundwork for future investigation into possible continuity between the *tamiai*'s tasks in epic and an office related to a sanctuary supervision and administration attested from the late archaic period.[2]

The etymology of the word ταμίας has been traditionally seen in the aorist ταμεῖν, 'to cut', although its morphology remains unclear.[3] Male anthroponyms *ta-mi-je-u* and *ta-me-je-u* appear in two Linear B tablets originating in Pylos (Jn 310.3) and in Thebes (Av 106.6), respectively; presumably they denote an occupation, but its nature cannot be ascertained.[4] By the time it appears in epic, the word has a large spectrum of applications and

1 Cf. the fortuitous remark by Walter Donlan about Homeric society that, "[a]lthough it is not an 'historical society' in any sense of the word, we can, in a scientific manner, extract a real society from it. The basic economic situation is especially clear and consistent in the texts, and to some extent matches up with the archaeology of the period," W. Donlan, "The Homeric Economy," in I. Morris and B. Powell (eds), *A New Companion to Homer*, Leiden 1997, p. 649-667, at p. 649.

2 This is subordinate to a larger project that aims to investigate the emergence and working of magistracies in archaic Greece, an issue which is closely related to the tantalizing question of state formation. For an especially updated approach to the question of state formation in Early Iron Age Greece, see J.K. Davies, "State Formation in Early Iron Age Greece: The Operative Forces," in A. Duploy and R. Brock (eds), *Defining Citizenship in Archaic Greece*, Oxford 2017, p. 51–78.

3 P. Chantraine, *Dictionnaire étymologique de la langue grecque. Histoire des mots*, T. IV.1 (P-Y), Paris 1977, s.v.; R. Beekes, *Etymological Dictionary of Greek*, Leiden 2010, s.v. Somewhat misleadingly, LSJ states under ταμίας 'prop. *one who carves and distributes*'; given the association of *tamiai* in epic with food distribution, this may suggest their involvement in carving meat, for which, however, there is no evidence. Cf. also W. Bubelis, *Hallowed Stewards*, Ann Arbor 2016, p. 119 with n. 1.

4 V. Aravantinos, "Mycenaean Thebes: Old Questions, New Answers," in *Espace civil, espace religieux en Egée, Actes des Journées d'archéologie et de philologie mycéniennes, Lyon, 1er février et 1er mars 2007*, Lyon 2010, p. 51-72, at p. 60-61. For the edition of the Theban tablet, see V.L. Aravantinos,

tends to indicate an agent concerned with control, preservation, and dispensation of funds, which are normally not in his or her possession. Since the feminine form of the word, ταμίη or ταμία, occurs much more frequently in early epic than its masculine counterpart, it has been assumed that the form *tamias* was due to masculinization of the originally feminine form *tamia*.[5] The historical development has been correspondingly seen in the transference of housekeeping duties carried out by a female *tamia* in a palace to supervision and dispensation of communal funds by her male counterpart.[6] In order to reexamine this assumption, I will first give a brief survey of attestations of *tamiai* in Homeric epic and then contextualize transactions in which they are involved.[7]

1. Female *tamiai*

The word ταμίη appears in Homeric epic, often in a formulaic verse, to describe a servant who, for the lack of a more precise word, can perhaps be best rendered as 'housekeeper'. It can stand alone or in apposition to γυνή, 'woman', or ἀμφίπολος, 'attendant'. What distinguishes a woman referred to as ταμίη from other household personnel is that she is usually held in high honor and may be called αἰδοίη, 'venerable'. The *tamiai* are persons of particular trust: Eurynome and Eurycleia, the most loyal servants and once nurses of Penelope and Odysseus, respectively, are each called ταμίη. These women may have been in charge of provisions stored in the house of the ruler, usually a prince (*basileus*), though once a priest of Apollo, Maron, and would have had as good if not better knowledge of the owners' possessions. Although the word can be applied almost as a title with no immediate description of the associated tasks or duties (e.g. in *Od.* 17.495), in most occurrences *tamiai* are engaged in management or allocation of goods, often associated with feasts. Thus, there are seven passages in the *Odyssey* in which *tamiai* serve food at meals given by various hosts, such as Telemachus, Menelaus, Alcinous, or even Circe. Each time an unnamed housekeeper is referred to in the same formulaic verses:

σῖτον δ' αἰδοίη ταμίη παρέθηκε φέρουσα,
εἴδατα πόλλ' ἐπιθεῖσα, χαριζομένη παρεόντων

A venerable housekeeper brought and served bread, adding many dainties with it, giving generously of her store. (*Od.* 1.139-140 et al.[8])

L. Godart, and A. Sacconi (eds), *Thèbes. Fouilles de la Cadmée I. Les tablettes de l'Odos Pelopidou. Édition et commentaire*, Pise – Rome 2001, p. 31-32 and p. 176-178.

5 C.D. Buck and W. Petersen, *A Reverse Index of Greek Nouns and Adjectives Arranged by with Brief Historical Introductions*, Chicago 1945, p. 169.

6 Cf. perhaps the most influential expression of this supposition in G. Busolt, *Griechische Staatskunde*, 3. neugestaltete Auflage, Vol. 1, Munich 1920, p. 589-590, but see now Bubelis, *Hallowed Stewards*, esp. p. 17 with n. 39 and p. 121.

7 For the development of the office, in particular in archaic and classical Athens, see now Bubelis, *Hallowed Stewards*.

8 *Od.* 1.139-140, 4.55-56, 7.175-176, 10.371-372, 15.138-139, 17.94-95, and 17.259. Some of the occurrences are suspected interpolations from elsewhere in the poem, cf. A. Heubeck, S. West, and J.B. Hainsworth, *A Commentary on Homer's Odyssey*, Vol. 1, Oxford 1988, p. 94, but this is irrelevant for us here; the verse following 17.259 differs from that in other appearances of the formula.

The food that these *tamiai* bring is distinct from both wine and meat, which are served by other servants or even by the participants of the feast themselves; *sitos* in these passages refers to cereal in the form of bread, while the things described as 'many dainties' are never explained but perhaps included cheeses, honey, or produce.[9]

Although the female *tamiai* in these scenes and elsewhere never mix and serve wine, they can be in charge of its storage and dispensation,[10] as, for example, a *tamia* at Nestor's palace at Pylos is, who furnishes from the cellar the ten-year wine that her master mixes at the feast he gives for his guests.[11] And when Telemachus is about to leave Pylos, Nestor's sons bring and yoke horses under a chariot, "in which a woman, the housekeeper, put food and wine and dainties of the kind that Zeus-cherished kings eat."[12] The wine under a housekeeper's control could be of different quality, and she was the one to know the difference. Nestor's housekeeper must have kept track of the vintages to know which were 'ten-year' jars, while Eurycleia gets for Telemachus twelve jars of 'second best' wine, that is, after the one kept in the hope of Odysseus's return (*Od.* 2.349-352). One assumes that there were wines of lower grades in his cellar, too, from which the suitors were served, and the arrangement of the jars in the cellar must have helped differentiate them. Eurycleia is presented as having full control and knowledge of the stored victuals:

ἐν δὲ πίθοι οἴνοιο παλαιοῦ ἡδυπότοιο
ἕστασαν, ἄκρητον θεῖον ποτὸν ἐντὸς ἔχοντες,
ἑξείης ποτὶ τοῖχον ἀρηρότες, …
…
κληισταὶ δ' ἔπεσαν σανίδες πυκινῶς ἀραρυῖαι,
δικλίδες: ἐν δὲ γυνὴ ταμίη νύκτας τε καὶ ἦμαρ
ἔσχ', ἣ πάντ' ἐφύλασσε νόου πολυϊδρείῃσιν,
Εὐρύκλεα …

Storage jars of sweet old wine stood there, filled with the unmixed divine drink, in rows and fastened along the walls … And the double doors thereto were fastened tightly. The housekeeping woman was in charge day and night, Eurycleia, who kept track of everything there in her knowledgeable mind. (*Od.* 2.340-342, 344-347)

Another knowledgeable housekeeper was a member of the house of Maron, a priest of Apollo, whose shrine Odysseus and his men spared when plundering the Ciconian city of Ismarus. Maron made a gift of wine to Odysseus, which would prove crucial to his rescue from the Cyclops. The preciousness of the wine is emphasized by the fact than nobody in the household except thc host, his wife, and one housekeeper had access to it:

9 There is a vast amount of scholarly literature on Homeric feasting; for the kind of foods consumed by Homeric heroes, cf. above all S. Sherratt, "Feasting in Homeric Epic," *Hesperia* 73 (2004), p. 301-337, esp. p. 305-306 for what could be referred to by εἴδατα πόλλ(α).

10 *Tamiai* are never depicted drinking wine, but there is no apparent prohibition on women's consumption of wine as there seems to be one for meat, cf. Z. Papakonstantinou, "Wine and Wine Drinking in the Homeric World," in *L'antiquité classique* 78 (2009), p. 1-24, esp. p. 7-8.

11 τὸν ἑνδεκάτῳ ἐνιαυτῷ / ὤιξεν ταμίη καὶ ἀπὸ κρήδεμνον ἔλυσε, "in the eleventh year the housekeeper drew [the wine] after loosening the sealing string" (*Od.* 3.391-392).

12 ἐν δὲ γυνὴ ταμίη σῖτον καὶ οἶνον ἔθηκεν / ὄψα τε, οἷα ἔδουσι διοτρεφέες βασιλῆες, *Od.* 3.479-480.

οἶνον ἐν ἀμφιφορεῦσι δυώδεκα πᾶσιν ἀφύσσας
ἡδὺν ἀκηράσιον, θεῖον ποτόν: οὐδέ τις αὐτὸν
ἠείδη δμώων οὐδ' ἀμφιπόλων ἐνὶ οἴκῳ,
ἀλλ' αὐτὸς ἄλοχός τε φίλη ταμίη τε μί' οἴη.

He [sc. Maro] filled twelve jars in all, wine sweet and unmixed, a drink divine. Not one of his slaves nor of the maids in his halls knew thereof, but himself and his dear wife, and one housekeeper only. (*Od.* 9.204-207)

Besides dealing with various food supplies, a *tamia* might help arrange a bath for her master or for an important guest, a task that entailed access to such stored goods as valuable utensils, oils, and clothing.[13] Notably, *tamiai* are never involved in carving or serving meat. This could be done by a male 'divider', sc. 'carver', as, for example, at the meal in Odysseus's house cited earlier where a *tamia* served bread and other dainties, but "the carver raised and placed in front of them boards with various meats."[14] The fact that *tamiai* did not handle meat somewhat undermines the hypothesis that the feminine form of the word was the source for the masculine.[15] For, if the meaning of 'cutting' is inherit in the root, it is likelier to have been at some stage connected with the tasks of a male agent than a female one.

Since female *tamiai* are associated with a household, it is not surprising that in the *Iliad* they make but brief appearances and only on the Trojan side, in Priam's palace. One informs Hector, who comes home looking for his wife, that Andromache has gone to the wall overlooking the battle field (*Il.* 6.381 and 390), and another pours water over Priam's hands as the old man prepares to pray to Zeus before setting out for the camp of the Greeks (*Il.* 24.302-304). The two instances do not have to feature the same *tamia*—even in the much smaller household of Odysseus, at least two women, Eurycleia and Eurynome, are called *tamiai*, and thus the palace of Priam could presumably have many more. Unlike in the *Odyssey*, where *tamiai* are engaged mostly in the dispensation of stored provisions, in the *Iliad* they appear rather as a token feature of palace-life.[16] On the Greek side, where life of the military camp is managed mostly by men and all women are but prizes of war, there are no female *tamiai*.[17]

13 Cf. *Od.* 8.449-850, 23.154-155; *Il.* 24.302-304.

14 δαιτρὸς δὲ κρειῶν πίνακας παρέθηκεν ἀείρας / παντοίων, *Od.* 1.141.

15 The refraining from dealing with meat on the part of *tamiai* might not have been a special feature of their tasks, but a more general abstinence of women in epic from any kind of handling and eating meat. Cf. J. Rundin, "A Politics of Eating: Feasting in Early Greek Society," *American Journal of Philology* 117 (1996), p. 179-215, esp. p. 189-190; H. van Wees, "Princes at Dinner: Social Event and Social Structure in Homer," in J.P. Crielaard (ed.), *Homeric Questions,* Amsterdam, 1995, p. 147-182, esp. p. 154-163.

16 This is similar to the usage of the word in the *Homeric Hymn to Demeter*, where Demeter in her anguish for Persephone sits herself by the roadside in Eleusis and assumes the appearance of an old woman like those "who are nurses for the children of kings, ministers of justice, and housekeepers in their echoing palaces" (οἷαί τε τροφοί εἰσι θεμιστοπόλων βασιλήων / παίδων καὶ ταμίαι κατὰ δώματα ἠχήεντα, *Hom.Hymn.Dem.* 103-104).

17 Most women on the Greek side in the *Iliad* are acted upon rather than act and thus the tasks they might perform are not spoken of; Hecamede, Nestor's prize from Achilles' raid of Tenedos, is an apparent

2. Male *tamiai*

The masculine form ταμίης or ταμίας is, at first glance, associated with a wide range of subjects, from Zeus himself to unnamed army support personnel, but a closer look reveals some important similarities in the literal and metaphorical usages. In the *Odyssey*, the word appears only once, when Odysseus tells the Phaeacians about his month-long visit to Aeolus, "whom the son of Cronus made a keeper (ταμίην) of winds, to stop or set them in motion, whichever he wishes."[18] The mythical character, depicted as a mortal but dear to the gods somewhat like the Phaeacians, famously gives Odysseus a skin with winds, which his friends, presuming it contains treasures, secretly untie, thereby ruining their chance of reaching home. This description of Aeolus as a steward of winds, which he dispenses even though they are ultimately the gods' possession, is somewhat akin to those of the female housekeepers who dispense their master's possessions as gifts to foreign visitors.

In the *Iliad*, Zeus is twice described with the same formulaic verse as 'the dispenser (ταμίης) of battle', but it is instructive to examine the context of the verses. Its first appearance is in the scene of Athena's descent to Earth in the form of an exceptionally bright star. As she plunges between the two hosts brought to a temporary armistice, onlookers on both sides are bewildered:

> … θάμβος δ' ἔχεν εἰσορόωντας
> Τρῶάς θ' ἱπποδάμους καὶ ἐϋκνήμιδας Ἀχαιούς·
> ὧδε δέ τις εἴπεσκεν ἰδὼν ἐς πλησίον ἄλλον·
> ἦ ῥ' αὖτις πόλεμός τε κακὸς καὶ φύλοπις αἰνὴ
> ἔσσεται, ἢ φιλότητα μετ' ἀμφοτέροισι τίθησι
> Ζεύς, ὅς τ' ἀνθρώπων ταμίης πολέμοιο τέτυκται.
>
> Amazement seized the onlookers, both the Trojans, breakers of horses, and the Achaeans, wearers of beautiful gaiters, so that a man who saw it would say to the one next to him, "Really, there will be dreadful war and terrible fighting, or else Zeus is bringing about amity between both sides, he who is the dispenser of war among the mortals." (*Il.* 4.79-84)

The entire scene is presented as a metaphorical balance, with the Trojans and Greeks ready either to plunge into battle or to settle a peace, depending on what Zeus the dispenser sends forth. The second occurrence is in the context of Odysseus's insistence to Achilles that the army eat before launching into the fighting, for otherwise:

> αἶψά τε φυλόπιδος πέλεται κόρος ἀνθρώποισιν,
> ἧς τε πλείστην μὲν καλάμην χθονὶ χαλκὸς ἔχευεν,
> ἄμητος δ' ὀλίγιστος, ἐπὴν κλίνῃσι τάλαντα
> Ζεύς, ὅς τ' ἀνθρώπων ταμίης πολέμοιο τέτυκται.
> γαστέρι δ' οὔ πως ἔστι νέκυν πενθῆσαι Ἀχαιούς.

---

exception as she is depicted preparing and serving food and restorative drink in Nestor's tent (11.624-640) and making a bath for Machaon (14.5-8).

18 κεῖνον γὰρ ταμίην ἀνέμων ποίησε Κρονίων / ἠμὲν παυέμεναι ἠδ' ὀρνύμεν, ὅν κ' ἐθέλῃσι, *Od.* 10. 21-22.

Quickly will the men have their fill with fighting, as when the bronze cuts mostly straw to the ground, but the harvest is very small, whenever Zeus inclines his balance, he who is the dispenser of war among the mortals. It should not be that the Achaeans mourn the dead men with their bellies. (*Il.* 19.221-225)

The precise meaning of the metaphor in lines 222-223 has been much discussed already in antiquity, but, significantly, the image of harvested wheat brings to the fore the main issue at stake, namely, the meal for the soldiers that Odysseus is insisting on. In the context of the harvest and meal, Zeus as dispenser, as Mark Edwards observes, is holding his balance "like a steward weighing supplies from the commissariat."[19]

Curiously, both instances of Zeus being called ταμίης, 'dispenser', occur in reported speech, as if the speaker within the poem makes an allusion to an immediately familiar image. This familiarity is borne out by a brief and matter-of-fact reference to *tamiai* as support personnel in the Greek camp: at the beginning of the same book, which is devoted to Achilles' return to the battle after the death of Patroclus, Achilles calls a gathering of all the Achaeans. Walking along the sea shore, he utters a cry with the result that

καί ῥ' οἵ περ τὸ πάρος γε νεῶν ἐν ἀγῶνι μένεσκον
οἵ τε κυβερνῆται καὶ ἔχον οἰήϊα νηῶν
καὶ ταμίαι παρὰ νηυσὶν ἔσαν σίτοιο δοτῆρες,
καὶ μὴν οἳ τότε γ' εἰς ἀγορὴν ἴσαν …

even those who before stayed in the gathering place of the ships, those who were helmsmen and held the steering oars of the ships and those who were stewards by the ships, distributors of food, even they came then to the gathering … (*Il.* 19.42-45).

The phrasing of this passage along with similes discussed above suggest that ταμίαι, equated here with σίτοιο δοτῆρες, 'the distributors of food', must have been an ordinary feature of a military camp. While it is common sense that an army needs food, the question that presents itself is why the job of distributing victuals has a special designation and this designation is even befitting a god, even if metaphorically. This brings us to the issue of food allocation as reflected in the world presented by epic. Of interest are not the social aspects of food consumption, but rather the venues of food supply, which in turn affect the modes of its distribution.

3. Venues of food acquisition in Homeric epic

Feasting is the most frequent activity in the *Odyssey* and second—after fighting—in the *Iliad*, and the poems do give some, even if very brief, indications of how victuals were acquired and distributed, which varied depending on circumstances. Leaving aside undefined 'dainties', εἴδατα πόλλα, food in Homeric epic falls into three major categories: cereal in the form of bread (both wheat and barley), wine, and meat, the acquisition of which may vary in (a) a settled community in ordinary, or (b) in extraordinary circumstances, and (c) on a military campaign.

19 M. Edwards, *The Iliad: A Commentary*, Vol. V: Books 17-20, Cambridge 1991, 260-262.

(a) The sources of the main types of sustenance in a settled community in ordinary circumstances are exemplified by the scenes on Achilles' shield: the supply of cereal is indicated by the depiction of ploughing and harvesting, that of wine by grape-picking, while a herd of cattle and a sheep farm attest to meat and milk production (*Il.* 18.541-589). The estate is said to be that of a prince, *basileus* (τέμενος βασιλήϊον, *Il.*18.550), and is worked presumably by people who depend on him in various ways as well as by hired hands.[20] Except meat, which is never stored in Homeric epic but is consumed immediately after slaughter, victuals are stored at the owner's house, from where they can be distributed by a housekeeper upon the demand of an authorized person, such as the head of the household or his close relations.

A meal can be given by a host, be it Alcinous, who invites all the present Phaeacians to a feast (*Od.* 8.37-39) or the swineherd Eumaeus who makes a meal for his comrades and Odysseus (*Od.* 14.414-417). Telemachus's futile attempt to drive the suitors out of his house by appealing to them, "partake in other meals eating from your own possessions and taking turn at your houses!" shows that the duty of hosting a feast was expected to rotate.[21] Alternatively, participants could contribute to a common meal.[22] Thus, a festival of Poseidon, which is taking place in Pylos when Telemachus arrives, furnishes a picture of a communal feast at which nine companies of men, 500 each, contribute nine oxen each (*Od.* 3.5-8). The boundaries between the two types of feasts, however, are not strictly drawn. Non-contributors could be invited to join a communal meal and guests could bring contributions to a hosted feast, as do those arriving to the weddings held in the house of Menelaus and Helen in Sparta.[23]

(b) In extraordinary circumstances, such as, for example, hosting outsiders, whether as guests or allies, a community may be required to support more than its own immediate needs, be it in food or material supplies.[24] When Odysseus, pretending to be Aethon, a younger brother of prince Idomeneus of Cnossus, the leader of the Cretan contingent at Troy (cf. *Il.* 2.645-652), tells Penelope about Odysseus's stop at Crete on his way to Troy, he describes a meal that involved contributions from the collective. While he, that is, Aethon, entertained Odysseus from the stock of his own house, feeding his company called for contributions of provision—bread, wine, and meat—from the people, δημόθεν:

20 On hired workers in epic, see, for example, M. Finley, *The World of Odysseus*, New York 1982, p. 52-54; A. Brown, "Homeric Talents and the Ethics of Exchange," *The Journal of Hellenic Studies* 118 (1998), p. 165-172, esp. p. 167-168.

21 ἄλλας δ' ἀλεγύνετε δαῖτας,/ ὑμὰ κτήματ' ἔδοντες, ἀμειβόμενοι κατὰ οἴκους, *Od.* 1.373-375, cf. *Od.* 2.139-140.

22 Sherratt, "Feasting in Homeric Epic," p. 304; cf. M. Dietler, "Feasts and Commensal Politics in the Political Economy: Food, Power and Status in Prehistoric Europe," in P. Wiessner and W. Schiefenhövel (eds), *Food and the Status Quest: An Interdisciplinary Perspective*, Oxford 1996, pp. 87-125.

23 "They [sc. guests] drove sheep and brought wine, the joy of men, and their beautifully-veiled wives sent bread with them" (οἱ δ' ἦγον μὲν μῆλα, φέρον δ' εὐήνορα οἶνον·/ σῖτον δέ σφ' ἄλοχοι καλλικρήδεμνοι ἔπεμπον, *Od.* 4.621-623).

24 This is also the situation in besieged Troy: while the city seems to have enough to feed the Trojan contingent (*Il.* 8.505-507), Hector talks of wearing out his people by requisition of food and gifts for the allies (*Il.* 17.220-226) and laments that the wealth of Troy is not what it used to be (*Il.* 18.288-292).

τὸν μὲν ἐγὼ πρὸς δώματ᾽ ἄγων εὖ ἐξείνισσα,
ἐνδυκέως φιλέων, πολλῶν κατὰ οἶκον ἐόντων·
καί οἱ τοῖς ἄλλοισ᾽ ἑτάροισ᾽, οἳ ἅμ᾽ αὐτῷ ἕποντο,
δημόθεν ἄλφιτα δῶκα καὶ αἴθοπα οἶνον ἀγείρας
καὶ βοῦς ἱρεύσασθαι, ἵνα πλησαίατο θυμόν.

I led him [sc. Odysseus] to our home and entertained him well, treating him kindly from the plenty that was in the house. And to the others, his comrades, who followed him, I gave barley and dark wine, collecting it from the people, and cattle to sacrifice and eat so that they could satisfy their desires. (*Od.*19.194-198)

These contributions would have been immediately expendable: people contributed food for Odysseus's comrades to consume. In other instances of communal contributions, however, some additional transactions seem to have been implied. Thus, Alcinous asks the princes of the Phaeacians to contribute each a tripod and a cauldron as a gift to Odysseus when the latter is about to leave Scheria for Ithaca. While this would be an immediate transaction, Alcinous adds that the princes will collect from the community to repay themselves:

ἀλλ᾽ ἄγε οἱ δῶμεν τρίποδα μέγαν ἠδὲ λέβητα
ἀνδρακάς, ἡμεῖς δ᾽ αὖτε ἀγειρόμενοι κατὰ δῆμον
τεισόμεθ᾽· ἀργαλέον γὰρ ἕνα προικὸς χαρίσασθαι.

Let us each give him a great tripod and a cauldron, we will later collect from the people to repay ourselves, for it is hard to give from one's own store without being repaid. (*Od.* 13.13-15)

Whatever was to be collected from the people (ἀγειρόμενοι κατὰ δῆμον), it would *not* be tripods and cauldrons, but something that could be gathered and converted into wealth equal to that of cauldrons and tripods. When the suitors attempt to buy their lives, the proposed deal also entails collecting unspecified contributions from among the people and converting them into portable wealth. Eurymachus makes an offer to Odysseus:

… ἀτὰρ ἄμμες ὄπισθεν ἀρεσσάμενοι κατὰ δῆμον,
ὅσσα τοι ἐκπέποται καὶ ἐδήδοται ἐν μεγάροισι,
τιμὴν ἀμφὶς ἄγοντες ἐεικοσάβοιον ἕκαστος,
χαλκόν τε χρυσόν τ᾽ ἀποδώσομεν …

and we will collect from the people to pay you back whatever had been drunk and eaten in your house, each paying the price of twenty oxen, giving it in bronze and gold … (*Od.* 22.55-58)

Although there is no explanation of how this would be carried out, it seems plausible that the initial step involved collecting agricultural products, which would have to be stored and measured for eventual exchange. While epic provides some information on the comparative values of expensive objects,[25] the values of more mundane commodities, such as cereal, are

25 Cf., above all, A.L. Macrakis, "Comparative Economic Value: The Oxen-Worth," in K. Rigsby (ed.), *Studies Presented to Sterling Dow on his 80th Birthday*, Durham, N.C., 1984, pp. 211-215.

never given, probably because they were of no interest for the epic story.[26] Yet, measured and quantified they must have been, and since the *Odyssey* assigns a *tamia* to storage, it may have been her task, too, to keep track of the collected goods.

(c) On a campaign, the three main categories of food—cereal, wine, and meat—could not have been produced in the same way as they were in settled communities, but had to be supplied long-distance or acquired by some means of exchange or pillage, or both, on the spot.[27] Let us start with meat, which was consumed in great quantities and the distribution of which at a feast was of paramount significance.[28] Methods of its supply, however, can be gleaned only from fleeting allusions. Thus, before his duel with Achilles, Aeneas recalls his previous encounter with the Greek hero, "when he came after our cattle and sacked Lyrnessus and Pedasus."[29] The casualness with which the purpose of Achilles' forage is given suggests that this was the default method of acquiring meat on a campaign. Cattle, of course, was not the only object of the raids; when later in the duel Achilles recounts the same episode, he talks of capturing also the women of Lyrnessus (*Il.* 20.187-194), a common commodity in war. Captive women, cattle, and whatever else could be pillaged on such raids, constituted portable wealth that could be consumed or exchanged, providing a means for the acquisition of further provisions, such as wine. Bartering war booty for wine is depicted in the famous vignette:[30]

> νῆες δ' ἐκ Λήμνοιο παρέσταν οἶνον ἄγουσαι
> πολλαί, τὰς προέηκεν Ἰησονίδης Εὔνηος,
> τόν ῥ' ἔτεχ' Ὑψιπύλη ὑπ' Ἰήσονι ποιμένι λαῶν.
> χωρὶς δ' Ἀτρεΐδῃς Ἀγαμέμνονι καὶ Μενελάῳ
> δῶκεν Ἰησονίδης ἀγέμεν μέθυ χίλια μέτρα.
> ἔνθεν οἰνίζοντο κάρη κομόωντες Ἀχαιοί,
> ἄλλοι μὲν χαλκῷ, ἄλλοι δ' αἴθωνι σιδήρῳ,
> ἄλλοι δὲ ῥινοῖς, ἄλλοι δ' αὐτῇσι βόεσσιν,
> ἄλλοι δ' ἀνδραπόδεσσι· τίθεντο δὲ δαῖτα θάλειαν.

Numerous ships from Lemnos arrived carrying wine, which the son of Jason, Euneus, sent, whom Hypsipyle had borne to Jason, the shepherd of his people. A thousand measures of sweet wine gave the son of Jason separately to the sons of Atreus, Agamemnon and Menelaus, to take. From the ships the flowing-haired Achaeans

26 The smallest comparative value is perhaps that of a sheep, which seems to be a tenth of an ox, cf. *Il.*11.244-245, with Macrakis, "Comparative Economic Value," p. 212.

27 The problem of food supply of the Greek army has been famously discussed already by Thucydides (1.11).

28 See, for example, J. Rundin, "A Politics of Eating"; R. Seaford, *Money and the Early Greek Mind: Homer, Philosophy, Tragedy*, Cambridge 2004, p. 23-47.

29 ὅτε βουσὶν ἐπήλυθεν ἡμετέρῃσι,/ πέρσε δὲ Λυρνησσὸν καὶ Πήδασον, *Il.* 20. 91-92.

30 The scene is discussed in most treatments of trade in early Greece or Homer, and thus bibliography is abundant, cf., for example, W. Donlan, "The Homeric Economy," in I. Morris and B. Powell (eds), *A New Companion to Homer*, Leiden 1997, p. 649-667; D.W. *Tandy, Warriors Into Traders: The Power of the Market in Early Greece*, Berkeley – Los Angeles – London 1997, p. 72-75; W. G. Kopcke, *Handel* (ArchHom M), Göttingen 1990. What is of interest to us here, however, is not the items of trade, but the mechanism of collective participation in acquisition and distribution of supplies.

> supplied themselves with wine, some in exchange for bronze, others for shining iron, others for hides, others for whole oxen, and others for slaves taken in war. And they made a sumptuous feast. (Il. 7.467-475)

Agamemnon and Menelaus receive wine as a gift, but the rest—presumably including other heroes and leaders—have to barter, and at least some of the described transactions would have to be carried out by or on behalf of a collective. Indeed, it is rather unlikely that the poet wants us to imagine each man individually bringing something for the traders on the ships and leaving with his personal jar. Rather, a collective formed by those who had acquired the object of barter, for example, a company of men that carried out a successful raid, would carry out the transaction, whether through its leader or some other representative. Consumption of wine acquired in this way would presumably be shared by those who contributed to its acquisition, though a leader would enjoy privileged access, as it transpires in Menelaus's reference to the leaders of the Achaeans, as "those who beside Agamemnon and Menelaus, sons of Atreus, drink people's wine (δήμια πίνουσιν) and each give command to his people."[31]

Besides Lemnian, there is also wine from Thrace in the Greek camp, as we learn from Nestor, who reminds Agamemnon that "your tents are full of wine that the ships of the Achaeans carry every day from Thrace across the wide sea."[32] It is not clear whether this wine was sent as a gift, upon some mutually agreed conditions,[33] or in the hope of future advantages.[34] Whatever the nature of Agamemnon's transactions with the source of Thracian wine, its daily supply would hardly be intended for his personal consumption, but must have been distributed further.

The sources of supply of cereal for the Greek army at Troy is never mentioned, but we learn that *sitos*—which ought to have included grain but perhaps also wine—was distributed by *tamiai*, and since they are said to be 'by the ships' (*Il.* 19.44), it must have been supplied by ships, similar to, or along with, wine. And as with wine, it must have been acquired on behalf of a collective; whether it originated back at a military contingent's place of origin or it resulted from a transaction elsewhere, it would have needed to be regularly allotted since the demand for it would have been both constant and high. The role of those distributing it, the *tamiai*, perhaps with a balance or some device for measuring

31 οἵ τε παρ' Ἀτρεΐδῃς Ἀγαμέμνονι καὶ Μενελάῳ / δήμια πίνουσιν καὶ σημαίνουσιν ἕκαστος /λαοῖς, Il. 17.249-251. It seems somewhat misleading to interpret this as drinking at public expense (cf., e.g. van Wees, "Prince at Dinner," p. 165-166.), for the wine is not contributed by the king's subjects; rather, it is acquired on behalf and through the contributions of a collective, but with the prince, or princes, having a special entitlement to it.

32 πλεῖαί τοι οἴνου κλισίαι, τὸν νῆες Ἀχαιῶν / ἠμάτιαι Θρῄκηθεν ἐπ' εὐρέα πόντον ἄγουσι, *Il.* 9.71-72.

33 Seaford, *Money and the Early Greek Mind*, p. 23-26, outlines ten types of transaction in which goods or funds, including humans, are allocated in Homeric epic, which range from the acquisition by force with no recompense to a form of trade, which he defines as "the impersonal instantaneous exchange of goods equivalent in value" (p. 23).

34 Presumably gift-giving could help one access more lucrative deals, constantly offered by opportunities of war. Thus, Euneus, who sends wine as a gift to Agamemnon and Menelaus, on another occasion buys the captive Lycaon, one of Priam's sons, from Achilles for a silver bowl worth one hundred oxen, and then lets Eetion of Imbros ransom him for three times that (Il. 21.79-80; 23.746-747). On opportunistic trade in Homeric epic, see Donlan "The Homeric Economy," p. 652-654.

volume, would essentially have been to enable collective consumption in the form of communal meals. There is no reason then to suppose, that this function, which was performed by male *tamiai,* would have derived from their female counterparts in a prince's palace,[35] for the need for the constant distribution of resources, in particular, victuals, would be no smaller but likely bigger in any kind of collective undertaking, especially on a military campaign.

If the function of *tamiai* as depicted in Homeric epic was closely related to enabling and regulating commensality by keeping track of the supply and distribution of victuals, can any continuity be detected with a later office of temple attendants? Some recent studies of state formation in early archaic Greece stress the role of commensality in the emergence of political communities, for it helps explain "how Greek political communities could make up through participation what they lacked in administration."[36] Since commensality was intrinsic to religious celebration, the task of distribution of either collectively contributed supplies or those supplied on behalf of a collective, which initially may have been confined to victuals but within the 8th century came to include utensils and other equipment, would perhaps have been conceived of belonging to *tamiai.* With the monumentalization of shrines and their accumulation of wealth, these tasks would eventually crystallize into an office concerned with 'keeping-track of' or managing—widely understood—the sacred precinct, while also retaining from an earlier period the aspects of community trust and the authority for regulating matters under their guardianship.[37]

35 Cf. Buck – Petersen, *A Reverse Index*, p. 169: "ταμίης 'dispenser, steward' is clearly a masculinization of the fem. ταμίη 'house-wife, stewardess' … for it was she who dispensed the store of victuals in Homer."

36 J. Whitely, "Citizenship and Commensality in Archaic Crete. Searching for the Andreion," in A. Duploy and R. Brock (eds), *Defining Citizenship in Archaic Greece*, Oxford 2017, p. 227-248, at p. 227; cf. also J. Block, "Citizenship, the Citizen body and Its Assemblies," in H. Beck (ed.), *A Companion to Ancient Greek Government*, Malden – Oxford 2013, p. 161-175.

37 For the duties and social standing of archaic *tamiai*, cf. Bubelis, *Hallowed Stewards*, p. 118-146.

Greek Sanctuaries as Administrative Laboratories: Bookkeeping Experience on Delos, from Wood Tablets to Marble Steles

Véronique Chankowski, Lyon

Greek sanctuaries are places where administrative experience and innovations were possible, due to the amount of money involved in their chests and because of the visibility to be given to the administration of the gods properties. Sanctuaries were under the supervision of civic authorities in the communities within the boundaries of which they lie. Since it was the responsibility of public officials to administrate the god's properties, the sacred chest could become a kind of financial reserve for the city. Public financial surpluses were regularly dedicated to sanctuaries in the form of precious metallic vases in order to increase the fortune of gods. It could also happen that some monetary surpluses were consecrated by a city in the sanctuary of its auspicious god (apart from several specific situations as the consecration of foundation capitals). The financial reserves of the sanctuary may in turn provide loans to the city and to the citizens on advantageous terms, so that cities benefiting from a rich sanctuary would have an easy access to capital.[1] This situation, roughly described here in its main lines, explains why the so-called "sacred accounts" constitute the major part of our documents on Greek bookkeeping and accounting. Admittedly "city accounts" did exist too, since all the officials were submitted to strict accountabilities and reviews whether they had managed "public" or "sacred" funds.[2] But city accounts were usually not preserved on stone, contrary to the accounts of sanctuaries.[3] However, the distinction between "sacred" and "public" money is not completely clear, as shown in the numerous publications dedicated to this question, which concerns not only the vocabulary but also the institutions.[4] Since sanctuaries were often places where civic institutions and civic officials managed huge amounts of money, they also tended to be places where bookkeeping methods were experimented and sometimes spread to other entities.

This paper aims to shed light on some specificities of the Greek way of understanding accountancy. Former work about the Delian accounts, where detailed analysis is provided, will constitute the basis of the analysis.[5] On other documents, the masterful synthesis of Leopold Migeotte on the finances of Greek cities provides a very precise and detailed

1 Migeotte 2014, 20–25.
2 Fröhlich 2004.
3 See for instance in Argos the discovery of bronze tablets with public and sacred accounts : Kritzas 1992 et Kritzas 2006.
4 See recently Rousset 2013 and Rousset 2015; Dreher 2014.
5 Chankowski 2013 and Chankowski, to be published.

overview of the evidence and can be completed by comparisons with other periods and other contexts.[6]

1. The organization of the registers

As a case study for accounting methods, Delos offers an exceptional situation since about 500 steles (with various states of preservation) correspond to the engraving of annual accounts recording the detail of the financial activity of the sanctuary under the supervision of civic officials, from the end of the 5th to the middle of the 2nd century a.C.

One interesting but neglected aspect of those inscriptions is that they also mention expenses for bookkeeping during each year, among which several writing supports are mentioned. In many studies about ancient archives, these writing supports bought by the officials are usually interpreted as intended for drafts documents, used by the administrators when they were preparing the final text, which would be later on engraved on the stele.[7] But the situation is in fact more complicated. A hierarchy between those different documents can be shown through the study of the writing material bought by the annual officials. It is the more visible during the period named "Delian Independence" (314–167 BC), where the sanctuary of Apollon was under the administration of the city of Delos and no more under Athenian domination.

According to the testimony of the annual accounts, the officials (the *hieropoioi*) bought each year a *deltos*, a wooden panel of cypress (a high quality substrate), whose destination is clearly described: they paid a worker to write on the *deltos* a copy of the data already inscribed on the annual stele (*IG* XI 2, 287, A, 197 : τῶι εἰς τὴν δέλτον γράψαντι τὰ ἐκ τῆς στήλης). After that, the stone stele could be placed in the sanctuary and fixed with lead in its basis.

During their year of service, the *hieropoioi* also bought a *leukôma* (a wooden panel covered with white substance). Contrary to the *deltos*, the *leukôma* could probably be reused if painted again. It was explicitly intended for the display of the monthly accounts on the agora (*IG* XI 2, 161 A, 89: τοῖς κατὰ μῆνα λόγοις ἐκτιθεμένοις εἰς τὴν ἀγορὰν λεύκωμα). The Council indeed regularly examined monthly accounts, but the final text of the stele was not only the collection of the monthly accounts. So, the text of the *leukôma* was not a preliminary draft for the final account. The expression κατὰ μῆνα (for instance *ID* 442, A, 180: τάδε ἀνήλωται εἰς τὰ κατὰ μῆνα) refers to a specific chapter of the accounts which concerns current expenditure, like regular supplies from the market, for which the officials used a specific capital in the sanctuary, so that they did not need to ask each time for the authorization of the *ekklesia*, as they had to do for other expenses like the award of public contracts.

In the accounts as they are engraved on the steles, monthly expenses are always separated from other expenses, which were submitted to the decision of the *ekklesia* (τάδε ἀνήλωται εἰς τὰ κατὰ μῆνα / τάδε ἀνήλωται κατὰ νόμους καὶ ψηφίσματα).[8] Sometimes the officials even specified the total amount of the monthly expenses, showing that it was

6 Migeotte 2014 and the collection of articles in Chankowski, Rousset 2015.

7 Migeotte 2008, 62 and 73 ; Davies 2003 ; Faraguna 2013, 167 ; Epstein 2013, 132.

8 *IG* XI 2, 269, ab, 14; *IG* XI 2, 290, 105 ; *ID* 442, A, 180 ; *ID* 456, B, 4 ; *ID* 459, 43 ; *SEG* XXXV, 882, A, l. 2.

understood as a separate chapter in their accounting. Since other expenses were already controlled when submitted to the *ekklesia*, we may suppose that only the working capital used for the monthly expenses, and not all the financial activity of each month, was the subject of the public control done periodically by the *logistai* during the year of function of the officials in charge of the administration of the sanctuary.[9] This observation leads also to the conclusion that the *leukômata* were not drafts but the substrate of a specific element of the annual account. It is also supported by the existence of another writing substrate, the *peteura*, intended for awarding public contracts.

Nor are the *peteura* preliminary drafts of the final account on stone. The word πέτευρον means "plank". It was also bleached for writing (*IG* XI 2, 205, bc, l. 22: πέτευρον λευκ[ώσαντι]). As mentioned in the accounts, the *peteura* were registers for lists of cautions, contracts, offerings,[10] with the names of all the financial partners of the business of the sanctuary.

The administrators of the sanctuary bought regularly sheets of papyrus (χάρτη) which were probably used to produce first drafts. They needed them at the end of the year, when they were preparing their final account, because they always bought the χαρτία in the last months.[11] Their use is maybe connected with the constraints of the abacus. It is clear from the Delian accounts that the officials were currently doing the four mathematics operations, but the use of the acrophonic system, with tokens put on the abacus, makes it impossible to write directly the result of the operation, as we do with Arabic numerals.[12] It was necessary to report on a sheet of papyrus the different intermediate results in order to get a total.

Thus *leukômata* and *peteura* were the substrates of specific records hold separately during the administrative year. They could be kept separately in the sanctuary. Besides these registers, the administrators had also access to another type of documents: the public records of the treasurers of the city. The writing material for these records do not appear in the accounts of the sanctuary because it was not the responsibility of its administrators to buy it, but it is clear from the steles that the evidence from the records of the treasurers of the city is integrated in the annual account of the sanctuary: the account of the sanctuary is a mathematic annual synthesis of the sacred chest and of the public chest, as the unique balance of the accounts shows.[13]

Moreover, the accounts show that the elaboration of the text engraved finally on the stele benefited also from other evidence coming from banker's records. Bankers intervened in the redaction of the annual accounts by giving to the *hieropoioi* the exact amount of several sums according to the Attic standard. These amounts consisted in coins transferred

9 Contrary to the opinion of Vial 1984, 102 and 158; Fröhlich 2004, 271 and Migeotte 2008, 62–63.

10 For instance *IG* XI 2, 287, A, 42 and 71 ; *ID* 316, 70 ; *ID* 338, A, 19 and 54 ; *ID* 372, A, 75, 103 and 116 ; *ID* 442, A, 200 and 204.

11 *IG* XI 2, 161, A, 112 ; *IG* XI 2, 2013, A, 56 ; *IG* XI 2, 199, A, 22, etc. See Glotz 1929 for other references.

12 Schärlig 2014.

13 Chankowski 2013, but an erroneous view defended in Migeotte 2014, 595; cf. *ID* 399 A, l. 41 : ἀπὸ παντὸς τοῦ ἀργυρίου τοῦ τ[ε] ἱεροῦ καὶ τοῦ δημοσίου.

by several individuals to the banks for payment to the sanctuary: it means that Apollo had banking accounts in several banks, as did other gods in Cos, for instance.[14]

In the final accounts of the *hieropoioi* the involvement of the bankers appears in the description of the amounts contained in jars stored in the sacred chest (for instance, *ID* 442, A, l. 68–70 : στάμνου οὗ ἐπιγραφή· ἀπὸ τῆς Νυμφοδώρου καὶ Ἡρακλείδου, ἐπὶ Δημάρου Ποσιδεῶνος, ἔθεσαν ἱεροποιοὶ οἱ ἐπ᾽ ἄρχοντος Τελεσαρχίδου Εὐβοεὺς καὶ Παρμενί<u>ων</u> τὸ πραχθὲν ἐνηροσίων, ἐνοικίων, τελῶν, τόκων ⊢𐅈Χ𐅆ΗΗΗΗ𐅅ΔΔΔΓ⊢⊢IIIC(//)). This inscription on the jar is a copy from a banker's register listing the amount of several payments made to a bank account of Apollo.

All these different registers, whether they were elaborated by the administrators themselves (as the *peteura* and *leukômata*) or they were created by other financial partners of the sanctuary (as the public records of the city, or the registers of the bankers), were not drafts for the stele. They were independent series of documents and could have been stored as thematic registers (as the cautions and contracts for instance) or according to specific classification (individual accounts in the banks registers). The text of the annual account, as prepared with its own preliminary drafts on sheets of papyrus, engraved on the stele and copied on the *deltos*, was elaborated with the evidence recorded in these different registers, under the unique responsibility of the *hieropoioi* who were in charge of the final synthesis.[15] Although it is visible only through the diversity of writing material bought by the *hieropoioi*, it seems clear that the Delian accounts can be considered as a ledger, since it presents a comprehensive information elaborated from a panel of documents and registers. It is neither the result of a simple narrative logic, nor a selection of evidence from drafts of financial reports, but an exhaustive synthesis of capital movements. If we consider the system in its entirety, it is not so far away from the method of the double-entry book-keeping system as Pacioli theorized it during the 15th century AD.[16]

14 Parker & Obbink 2000, n°1. On the banks working for the Delian sanctuary, see Bogaert 1968, 170–187.

15 Chankowski 2013, 941–944 ; Chankowski 2008, 84–86.

16 De Roover 1956, 118–123; Minaud 2005, 32–44.

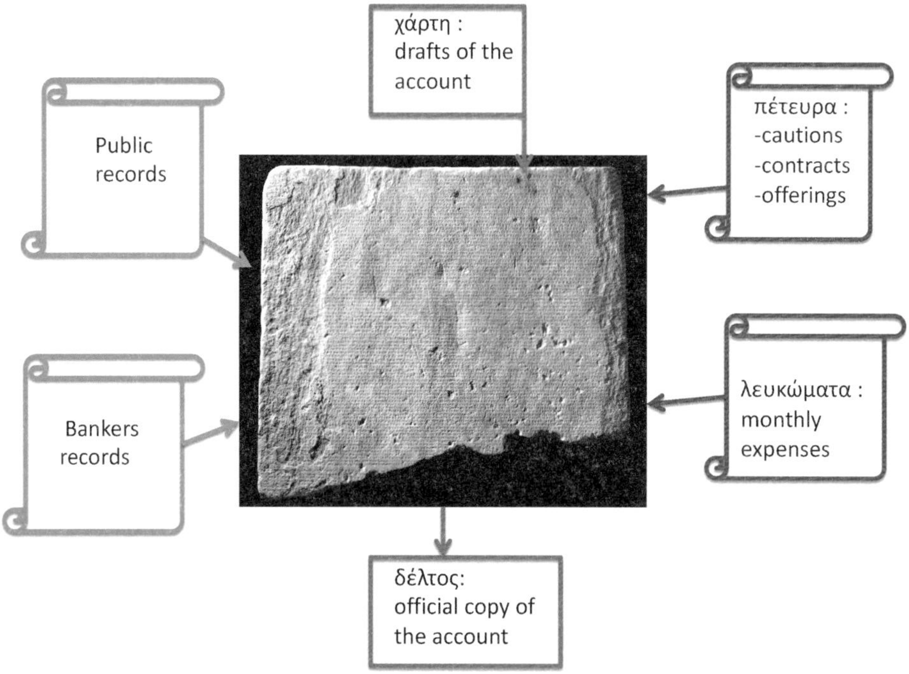

The organization of the registers in the production of the final account in the sanctuary of Apollo on Delos.

2. The legal status of the documents

For some scholars, the appearance of this accounting tends to demonstrate that the engraving of the accounts answers only symbolic reasons: the very small letters, the height of the stone, the messy aspect of the shaping, accredit the idea that the administrators had created monuments symbolizing their probity, more than readable documents on stone.[17] Some rare and slim pieces of information allow questioning this idea.

Moreover, the creation of such monuments for each year of administration was costly: according to the Delian accounts, about 300 drachmas per year for the supply of the stone, the engraving of the stele, its transport and its sealing with lead. It means that the sanctuary would have spend more than seven talents (at least half or the third of the cost of the building of a small temple[18]) to present its financial records during the 147 years of the period called "Independence", without mentioning the other periods of its administrative

17 de Ste. Croix 1956; Linders 1988; Epstein 2013, 132 : "The Parthenon inscriptions as we have them are hardly a convenient tool for democratic accountability". Concerning the inventories, see also Vial 1984, 222 reporting the opinion of Jacques Tréheux: "Selon lui, l'érection de la stèle et la publication de l'inventaire avaient une valeur principalement symbolique et étaient une manifestation de la piété des hiéropes et de la cité au nom de laquelle ils agissaient".

18 Burford 1969, 81–83: 10 talents (eginetic) for the building of the Propylaia of the sanctuary of Asklepios in Epidaurus.

activity. These numerous stones also occupied an important place in a sanctuary (but this archaeological aspect has received few investigation). The gratitude to the administrators of god's assets could have been shown by more simple dedications than meters of engraved sums and evidence.

On Delos again, but in an Athenian context since the inscription dates from the 4th century, when Athenian officials were in charge of the administration of the sanctuary, an epigraphic fragment found during the excavations in 1987 offers an interesting testimony.[19] This inscription constitutes the end of the account of Philistides, the secretary of a board of *naopoioi* in charge of some sacred money for a building program during the year 345/344 BC. It contains the fragmentary report of a trial against the unfortunate secretary, who was accused of stealing sacred money. He successfully applied the legal procedure of *paragraphe*, refuting the accusation and requesting the court to drop the charges. One of his arguments seemed to be connected with the information written by the former board of officials on the accounting stele: the secretary was probably able to prove that, contrary to the sums that they had declared on the stele (l. 48: [γ]ράφουσιν ἔχοντας εἰς τὴν στ[ήλην]), the former board of officials did not transmit the correct amount to their successors. It is worth to note that the account as presented on the stone served as a legal element of proof. Exactly as did the Roman *codex accepti et expensi* of the *paterfamilias* and the *codex rationum* of the bankers,[20] the text of the account as engraved on the stele could be presented to the court.

Later, during the Delian Independence, the document on stone is mentioned several times as a reference: debts, for instance, are listed according to the register of debtors written on the steles.[21] In the text inscribed on stone, the words "the stele" simply means sometimes the account itself, as a validated and open-accessed document (τὸ λοιπὸν τοῦ περιόντος ἐκ τῆς στήλης, *ID* 442, A, 35: "the rest of the balance of the stele").[22] As we have seen, the text of the account as engraved on the stone is the authoritative document to be copied on the *deltos*. It was probably a right way to avoid such problems as those who occurred in Paros, when some officials had erased some data and added others in the records placed under their responsibility.[23]

As legal documents, these engraved financial records appear to be part of the financial and legal system of the city. Another example from the *Tituli Camirenses* (110, l. 9–19) seems to point to the same direction. The inscription is dated between 225 and 180 BC. It shows how a citizen of Camiros named Philocrates reorganized, as a *hieropoios*, part of the archives of his city by ordering a copy of missing information from the originals records saved in a sealed box:

τῶν τε χρηματισμῶν τῶν ἐν τοῖς προχείροις διαφωνούντων ἐξ ἐτέων ἑβδομήκοντα καὶ ἑπτὰ ἐπεμελήθη ὅπως, λυθεισᾶν τᾶν κιβωτῶν, πάντες οἱ ἀπό<λ>ογοι ἀναγραφῶντι, ἐξ οὗ συνάντασε Καμιρεῦσι τούς τε αἱρουμένους ἐπὶ τὰς κο[ι]νὰς πράξεις ὑπ' αὐτῶν εὐχερῆ

19 This document, published in Chankowski 2001, should have been mentioned in Harris 2013. See also Chankowski 2008, n° 55, 515–518 (full text of the inscription and translation); *SEG* 51, 1001.

20 Andreau 1996.

21 *ID* 290, 11–12 ; *ID* 316, 19 ; *ID* 356 bis, A, 34 ; *ID* 371 l. 37.

22 Kahrstedt 1938 about the same habit in Athenian documents.

23 Lambrinoudakis & Wörrle 1983.

ποιεῖσθαι τὰν ἐπίσκεψιν περὶ ὧν κα χρήζωντι, ἐμ μηθενὶ καθυστεροῦντας, καὶ πλείονα χώραν ἀμφισβατηθεῖσαν ὑπό τινων ἀνακτήσασθαι, εὑρεθέντων τῶν περὶ αὐτᾶς χρηματισμῶν, καὶ διάφορον ἱκανὸν πετεῖν πραθέντων τῶν καρπῶν καὶ τᾶς χώρας·

The text of the decree creates an opposition between τὰ πρόχειρα and οἱ κιβωτοί, two different places for storing documents with two different levels of accessibility: the *kibôtoi* were probably sealed and had to be opened according to a complex procedure, when the *procheira* offered probably open-accessed data concerning the administration of the city.[24] Philocrates ordered a transcription of the records (οἱ ἀπό<λ>ογοι), and the decree insists on the fact that this transcription, whose substrate of writing is unknown, allowed the other officials to proceed quickly to urgent arbitrations for the city and the citizens.

The documents transcribed were probably not exactly missing since 77 years.[25] The verb διαφωνεῖν is to be understood here as a technical term of accounting. It has some epigraphic parallels on Delos and in Caria,[26] where it concerns some incoherence or inadequacy in the calculation of sums in the accounts. Over the last 77 years (ἐξ ἐτέων ἑβδομήκοντα καὶ ἑπτά), some amounts presented a discrepancy with the totals (or with the other pieces of information) and this impeded the resolution of some conflicts, probably those concerning financial arbitration and land disputes. By giving access to all the accounts rendered by the help of a new transcription (πάντες οἱ ἀπό<λ>ογοι ἀναγραφῶντι), Philocrates referred probably to the records in the form validated by *logistai* or other officials and thus authoritative. The inscription says nothing about the material used for the transcription: was it an *anagraphe* on stone or on another type of material? But the problem of the city of Camiros was that discrepancy between the information coming from several registers. The solution was to refer to the original records as a legal reference. This inscription points to a hierarchy between the accounts after their validation (οἱ ἀπό<λ>ογοι) and the other registers stored in the archives.

These relations between the different registers that constitute the financial documentation of the city ensured not only the good functioning of bookkeeping, but also more opportunities for capital movements.[27] The god's assets under supervision of city's administrators were integrated within a financial and administrative system. The Delian accounts shed light on the fact that the city of Delos went very far in experimenting the integration of the sacred chest and of the public chest in a unified system of accounting. As a matter of fact, it is clear from the accounts of the 2nd century that both assets were calculated together in the final balance of the account: it was probably the most convenient method of bookkeeping for the administrators, because of intensive movements of capital between the public and the sacred chest, due to loans, reimbursements of loans and several other payments in both directions.[28]

Some other inscriptions show that the Delian case was not an exception. For instance, in Athens at the end of the 4th century BC, a gift of 140 talents received from Antigonos

---

24 Lambrinoudakis & Wörrle 1983, 349, n. 336 : « Belege für πρόχειρα in dieser technischen Bedeutung sind mir freilich nicht bekannt" ; Faraguna 2000, 86–87.

25 Despite of the opinion of Migeotte 2014, p. 82, n. 192.

26 Délos, *ID* 399, A, l. 40 ; Apollonia under Salbakè, L. & J. Robert, *La Carie* II, 1954, n°167, 303–304, l. 19–20; Chankowski 2008, 86 (διαφωνεῖν).

27 For Athens, see also the argumentation of Faraguna 2008.

28 Chankowski 2013.

Monophthalmos for military purposes was placed in the sacred chest of Athena under the supervision of her treasurers (*IG* II^2, 1492B). Part of this money was probably used for loans or cash advances to the city. Another document from Lindos (*Lindos II*, 419 = *LSCG Suppl.* n° 90), dated from 22 AD, refers to the creation of a *parakatatheke* for Athena Lindia and Zeus Polieus. In order to facilitate some expenses for religious purposes, the Lindians decided to create a special fund coming from several financial surpluses and from a subscription. The so called "sacred administration" is in fact the area where public management of funds is implemented with an obligation of publicity and open access. The assets of the gods were the major financial reserve of capital for a city-state and became therefore the core of the elaboration of public bookkeeping, on which came the management of other complementary funds. We are thus very far away from an only symbolic function of the engraving.

All these bookkeeping and accounting experiences were made possible due to the expertise of citizens. It is a fact that has to be emphasized, since some recent publications tend to favor the role of public slaves as experts in technical and financial aspects of public administration, because they were not sharing in the democracy.[29] The testimonies coming from accounting documents are proof of the contrary. Even if some limited and subordinate work was done by *demosioi douloi*, it is clear from all these financial inscriptions that the participation in accounting and administration of public finances was the duty not only of officials, but also of the *ekklesia* and the *boule* and sometimes of specific commissions of citizens. The citizens were certainly gaining skills when participating in these various procedures, from the beginning of their political activity in the *ekklesia*. Some of them, probably because of their private business, were more involved than others in budgeting and accounting techniques, as Silenos on Delos, Philocrates in Camiros, or Pamphilos in his small city of Caria: in Apollonia under Salbake, during the 2nd century BC, this model citizen is honored for the help that he had provided to his city by reorganizing the administration of the state incomes.[30] Greek citizens shared, in various degrees, both technical and political expertise. They collectively contributed to the development of accounting methods that resulted in the gradual development of consolidated forms of books and accounts, despite of the rotation of charges.

29 For instance Ismard 2015, highlighting a model of ancient Greek democracy "against the experts".

30 Robert 1954, n°167, p. 303–304 (Pamphilos); Segrè, Pugliese Carratelli 1951 n°110 (Philocrates); Chankowski 2008 (Silenos).

Bibliography

Andreau, J., « Les archives des banquiers romains et leur conservation », *in* M.-Fr. Boussac, A. Invernizzi (éds.), *Archives et sceaux du monde hellénistique, BCH Supplément* XXIX, 1996, 423–437.

Bogaert, R., *Banques et banquiers dans les cités grecques*, Leyde, 1968.

Burford, A., *The Greek Temple Builders at Epidauros*, Liverpool, 1969.

Chankowski, V., « Un nouveau procès délien : les comptes des naopes de Délos et la procédure athénienne au IVe siècle », *Bulletin de Correspondance Hellénique* 125, 2001, 175–193.

Chankowski, V., *Athènes et Délos à l'époque classique. Recherches sur l'administration du sanctuaire d'Apollon délien, BEFAR 331*, Athènes, 2008.

Chankowski, V., « Banquiers, caissiers, comptables. A propos des méthodes financières dans les comptes de Délos », *in* K. Verboven, K. Vandorpe, V. Chankowski (eds), *Pistoi dia tèn technèn. Bankers, Loans and Archives in the Ancient World, Studia Hellenistica* 44, Leuven, 2008, 77–92.

Chankowski, V., « Nouvelles recherches sur les comptes des hiéropes de Délos : des archives de l'intendance sacrée au "grand livre" de comptabilité », *Comptes rendus de l'Académie des Inscriptions et Belles Lettres*, 2013, 917–953.

Chankowski, V., *Parasites du dieu. Comptables, financiers et commerçants dans la Délos hellénistique*, Athènes, *BEFAR*, to be published.

Chankowski, V., Rousset, D. (eds), *A propos des* Finances des cités grecques *de Léopold Migeotte*, *Topoi* 20, 2015, 339–494.

Davies, J., « Greek Archives : from Record to Monument », *in* M. Brosius (ed.), *Ancient Archives and Archival Traditions. Concepts of Record-keeping in the Ancient World*, Oxford, 2003, 325–328.

De Roover, R., « The Development of Accounting prior to Luca Pacioli according to the Account-books of Medieval Merchants » *in* A. C. Littleton, B. S. Yamey (eds), *Studies in the History of Accounting*, London, 1956, 118–123.

de Ste Croix, « Greek and Roman Accounting », *in* A. C. Littleton, B. S. Yamey (eds), *Studies in the History of Accounting*, Homewood, 1956, 14–74.

Dreher, M., « Die Rechte der Götter », *in* M. Gagarin, A. Lanni (eds), *Symposion 2013. Papers on Greek and Hellenistic Legal History*, 2014, 1–26.

Epstein, Sh., « Attic Building Accounts from *Euthynae* to *Stelae* », *in* M. Faraguna (ed.), *Legal Documents in Ancient Societies IV. Archives and Archival Documents in Ancient Societies*, Trieste, 2013, 127–142.

Faraguna, M., « A proposito degli archivi nel mondo Greco: terra e registrazione fondiarie », *Chiron* 30, 2000, 65–115.

Faraguna, M., «Calcolo economico, archivi finanziari e credito nel mondo greco tra VI e IV sec. A.C. », *in* K. Verboven, K. Vandorpe, V. Chankowski (eds), *Pistoi dia tèn technèn. Bankers, Loans and Archives in the Ancient World, Studia Hellenistica* 44, Leuven, 2008, 33–58.

Faraguna, M. « Archives in Classical Athens. Some Observations », *in* M. Faraguna (ed.), *Legal Documents in Ancient Societies IV. Archives and Archival Documents in Ancient Societies*, Trieste, 2013, 163–171.

Fröhlich, P., *Les cités grecques et le contrôle des magistrats*, Paris-Genève, 2004.

Glotz, G., « Le prix du papyrus dans l'Antiquité grecque », *Annales d'histoire économique et sociale* 1, 1929, 3–12.

Harris, E., « The Plaint in Athenian Law and Legal Procedure », *in* M. Faraguna (ed.), *Legal Documents in Ancient Societies IV. Archives and Archival Documents in Ancient Societies*, Trieste, 2013, 156–175.

Ismard, P., *La démocratie contre les experts. Les esclaves publics en Grèce ancienne*, Paris, 2015.

Kahrstedt, U., « Untersuchungen zur athenischen Behörden », *Klio* XXXVII, 1938, 25–32.

Kritzas, Ch., « Aspects de la vie politique et économique d'Argos au Ve siècle avant J.-C. », *in* M. Piérart (ed), *Polydipsion Argos. Argos de la fin des palais mycéniens à la constitution de l'Etat classique*, *BCH Supplément* XXII, Athènes-Fribourg-Paris, 1992, 231–240.
Kritzas, Ch., « Nouvelles inscriptions d'Argos : les archives des comptes du Trésor sacré (IVe s. av. J.-C.), *Comptes rendus de l'Académie des Inscriptions et Belles Lettres* 2006, 397–434.
Lambrinoudakis, V., Wörrle, M., « Ein hellenistischen Reformgesetz über das öffentliche Urkundenwesen von Paros », *Chiron* 13, 1983, 283–368.
Linders, T., « The purpose of inventories : a close reading of the Delian inventories of the Independence », *in* D. Knœpfler (ed.), *Comptes et inventaires dans la cité grecque*, Genève, 1988, 37–47.
Migeotte, L., « La comptabilité publique dans les cités grecques », *in* K. Verboven, K. Vandorpe, V. Chankowski (eds), *Pistoi dia tèn technèn. Bankers, Loans and Archives in the Ancient World*, *Studia Hellenistica* 44, Leuven, 2008, 59–76.
Migeotte, L., *Les finances des cités grecques*, Paris, 2014.
Minaud, G., *La comptabilité à Rome*, Lausanne, 2005.
Parker, R., Obbink, D., « Aus der Arbeit der "Inscriptiones Graecae" VI. Sales of Priesthoods on Cos I », *Chiron* 30, 2000, p. 415–449.
Robert, L., Robert, J., *La Carie. Histoire et géographie historique avec le recueil des inscriptions antiques. II. Le plateau de Tabai et ses environs*, Paris, 1954.
Rousset, D., « Sacred Property and Public Property in the Greek City », *JHS* 133, 2013, 113–133.
Rousset, D., « Les fonds sacrés dans la cité grecque », *Topoi* 20, 2015, 369–393.
Schärlig, A., « Les moyens de calcul du comptable antique », in V. Chankowski, G. Minaud (eds), *Comptables et comptabilités dans l'Antiquité, Comptabilité(s). Revue d'histoire des comptabilités* [On line] 6, 2014, URL : http://comptabilites.revues.org/1491.
Segrè, M., Pugliese Caratelli, G., « Tituli Camirenses », *Annuario della Scuola archeologica di Atene e delle missioni italiane in Oriente*, 27–29 (n.s. 11–13), 1949–1951, 141–318.
Vial, C., *Délos indépendante (314–167 avant J.-C.), BCH Supplément* X, Paris, 1984.

The Evolving Format of Building Accounts in Classical Athens

Cristina Carusi, Parma

The aim of this article is to show how the format of Athenian building accounts inscribed on stone evolved over the course of time as well as to discuss possible reasons for this development and for the concurrent appearance of building specifications in the epigraphic record.

Building accounts emanated from the work of ad-hoc appointed boards of officials known as *epistatai*, i.e. "overseers", which the Athenian council and assembly put in charge of supervising the financial and technical aspects of public projects.[1] The size and term of office of each board of *epistatai* varied on a case-by-case basis.[2] The epigraphic evidence reveals that boards of *epistatai* in charge of different building projects consisted of between two and five members, plus or including the secretary, who was either designated as such at the time of the appointment or elected by the board itself from among its members. A board of *epistatai* held office for the entire length of a project, which could amount to a substantial number of years, such as fifteen in the case of the Parthenon. In most cases, the members of a board were entirely replaced from year to year, but there are exceptions to this rule: for example, the same board was probably in charge for the last five years of the Parthenon's construction. Similarly, the board for the bronze statues of Athena and Hephaestus remained probably in charge for the five years or more of the project. Though, there is no explicit evidence as to the method of appointment. Since *epistatai* had to manage substantial amounts of public money, it is plausible to assume that they were elected by show of hands, as in the case of other offices with huge financial responsibilities. It is also possible that some sort of census requirement had to be fulfilled. Finally, a board might be assisted by some ancillary figures, such as the co-secretary mentioned in the Parthenon accounts or the under-secretary of the Erechtheum accounts, which were probably city employees.

As we said, *epistatai* oversaw large sums of public money and, consequently, were financially liable for it. At the end of their appointment, members had to undergo an audit in front of the council (the *euthynai*) and thus had to keep accurate accounts of receipts and

---

1 Unfortunately, in the Attic epigraphic evidence, there is no extant decree concerned with the appointment of *epistatai*. Our only indication of how such a text might look like is the rider that established the board of *epistatai* in charge of the financial administration of the Eleusinian sanctuary, dated to around 432/1 (*I.Eleusis* 30; *IG* I³ 32). However, such *epistatai*, even if explicitly modeled on the *epistatai* of the acropolis' works (l. 9-12), were not an ad-hoc appointed board in charge of a specific project, but ordinary officials in charge of the entire administration of the sanctuary from year to year. In general, on the appointment and functions of Athenian officials see Hansen 1991, 225-245.

2 The following outline of the appointment and composition of boards of *epistatai* is based on Marginesu 2010, 57-65. Before Marginesu's work on the Athenian *epistatai*, the reference study on building committees in the Greek classical world as a whole was that of Wittenburg 1978.

expenditures incurred during their term of office so as to demonstrate their sound financial management of the project.[3] Some of these accounts, or, rather, a selective and rearranged version of them, were inscribed on stone and survive, albeit in fragments, until today.[4] These inscriptions almost exclusively belong to the second half of the 5th c., with very few and peculiar exceptions dated to the 4th c.

It is interesting to observe how the format and content of building accounts evolved during this period. The most ancient example of this category of inscriptions comes from a stele containing at least eight annual accounts of an unknown work (*IG* I³ 433).[5] Each year's section, starting on a new line and usually five to ten lines long, lists the names of the secretary and *epistatai* in office annually, followed by the total receipts and expenditures of that accounting year and the remaining balance, if any, handed down to the following year's board.[6] Since several lines at the top of the stele are missing, it is possible that a lost prescript mentioned the identity of the work. Unfortunately, the total lack of details concerning the source of money and the nature of items and labor paid for makes it difficult to venture any guess.[7] The traditional date of the inscription to the mid-5th c. is based on letterform.[8] More importantly, the format and content of this text, if compared to other building accounts, as we will see below, points to an early stage in the epigraphic evolution of this category of documents.

The next text, traditionally identified with the accounts of the bronze statue of Athena Promachos that Phidias erected on the acropolis in the 450s, consists of eleven fragments (pertaining to one or possibly two marble stelae), most of them found on the acropolis, where the inscription was probably set up (*IG* I³ 435). The extant fragments preserve at least nine annual accounts arranged in double columns.[9] Each year's section is separated from the previous one by a blank space and is dated by means of the annual *epistatai*'s

3 On the *euthynai* in the Athenian democracy, see Hansen 1991, 222-224.

4 The complex relationship between building accounts presented at the *euthynai* (and possibly deposited in public archives) and building accounts inscribed on stone has been recently discussed by Epstein 2013.

5 The stele (h. 1.39 cm, w. 0.45 cm, t. 0.22 cm) was found in Monastiraki. The most recent edition is Pitt 2015.

6 See, for example, the year VI section, at l. 31-40: Θ[ρ]ασί[π]πο γ[ρα]μ[ματεύ]ο[ντος] | Γαργε[τ]τ[ί]ο, [ἐπιστάται *v*] | Ἀμ[ο]ίβιχος [Λ]αμ[πτρε]ύ[ς], Ο[. c. 4 .] | hεστιαιόθ̣[εν] ⁚ [. . . c. 12 . . .] | Μυρρινόσ[ι]ος ⁚ . .]θο[. .]ο[. c. 5 .] | Κέττιος, Φ[. . .]λο[. . .] ⁚ Θ̣[ορίκιος ?] | λε̂μμα Μ[Μ]Μ[.]ΧΗΗΗ[. .]ΔΗ– – | ἀνάλομα ⁚ Μ[. .]ΧΧ[.]Η[. .]Δ̣Ͱ– – | τ[ο]ῖς νέοι[ς ἐ]πι[σ]τ[ά]τ[ε]σ[ι παρέ]|δομεν [ἀ]πὸ τ[. . . .]ο– – – – – "When Thrasippos of Gargettos was secretary, we, the *epistatai* Amoibichos of Lamptrai, O[...] of Hestiaia, [...] of Myrrhinous, [...] of Kettos, Ph[...] of Thorikos (?), receipts 32,332+ (?) dr., expenditures 14,231+ (?) dr., handed over to the new *epistatai* from [...]".

7 Since the few monetary figures preserved on the stone point to expenditures ranging from 15,000 to 35,000 dr. for the central years of the accounts, the total cost of the work was probably around 30-50 talents. This amount and the length of the works (8-9 years) suggest a substantial project, possibly linked to the agora or the lower city, if one considers where the stele was found.

8 See Pitt 2015, 700.

9 In the most recent re-edition of the accounts (Foley and Stroud 2019), the editors conclude that the extant fragments were not necessarily arranged in three double columns of text for a total of nine annual accounts, as traditionally thought. In reality, the stele could have included up to four double columns of text and up to a total of eleven annual accounts. In addition, it is possible that a second stele, possibly bearing the continuation of the accounts, adjoined the first stele on the right side.

Fig. 1

secretary. It opens with a statement of how much money the *epistatai* received from the *kolakretai* and how much from the previous accounting year. Then, it lists the expenditures the *epistatai* made from those sums, ending with a statement of how much money was spent as a whole and how much was left over for the next accounting year. Each double column breaks into two separate sub-columns, with a prescript and list of entries on the right and the related monetary figures on the left; horizontal lines separate monetary figures from each other (See Fig. 1).[10] Although the arrangement of the fragments and the heavily restored text must recommend caution, some expenditure entries seem to recur in more or less the same order in almost all sections. The most important are: copper talents (χαλκô τάλαντα), tin talents (καττιτέρο τάλαντα), charcoal and firewood (ἄνθρακες καὶ χσύλα καύσιμα), wages by the day, by the prytany, and by the job (μισθοὶ κατ' ἑμέραν, μισθοὶ κατὰ πρυτανείαν, μισθοὶ ἀπόπαχς), earth and hairs (γε̂ καὶ τρίχες), and wages for the *epistatai*, secretary, and assistant (μισθοὶ ἐπιστάτεσι καὶ γραμματεῖ καὶ hυπερέτει).

Recently, the traditional hypothesis that these accounts concerned the colossal bronze statue of Athena Promachos has been called into question. Similarly, their traditional dating to the 450s on the basis of letterform is no longer upheld.[11] Regardless of the identity of the accounts' subject, in my opinion it is crucial to emphasize that the format and content of the inscription strongly suggest placing it at an intermediate stage in the epigraphic evolution of building accounts. Unlike the unknown work's accounts, here the expenditures are broken down in different entries and, similarly to the Parthenon accounts, which securely date to 447/6-433/2, the text is arranged in double columns, with monetary figures on the left and

10 The only two sections whose length is completely preserved range from 23 to 26 lines (l. 36-61 and l. 63-85). For the opening of a section see l. 36-41 (following here the text of Foley and Stroud 2019): : – – – [hoῖς .]Α̣Λ[name . . 3-4 . . ἐγραμμάτευε] | [demotic . . 6? . .]Α[ἐπιστάται | – – – ἔλαβο]ν̣ π[αρὰ κολακρετôν σύμπαν·| – – – λε̂μμα] πε[ριγενόμενον | ἐκ τô π]ρο[τέρο ἐνιαυτô κτλ. “The *epistatai* to whom [name and demotic] was secretary took from the *kolakretai* all together […]; receipts left over from the previous year […] etc.”. For an ending see l. 58-61: [– – – κεφάλαιον ἀναλόματ]ος| [σύνπαντος] *vacat* | [– – – περιεγένετο τô λέμμ]ατος | [ἐς τὸ hύστερον ἔτος] *vacat*. “Total of the whole expenditures […]; of the receipts it was left over for the following year […]”.

11 For the traditional interpretation and dating see Dinsmoor 1921a. For a recent reappraisal of all arguments in favor or against the traditional interpretation see Foley and Stroud 2019. They argue that no conclusive link can be found between the literary and archaeological evidence for the bronze statue of Athena Promachos and the extant fragments of the accounts. Rather, since the accounts register a series of repeated actions year after year, they likely recorded a process of manufacturing repeated on an annual basis, possibly the forging of a number of bronze objects for either a practical or a dedicatory goal.

entries on the right. However, unlike the Parthenon accounts, no distinction is made among the different jobs and professions of workers. In addition, the wages of workers paid on a daily rate system, a prytany rate system, and a piecework system are all gathered under the same heading. On this basis, it is plausible to place these accounts after the unknown work's accounts and before the Parthenon accounts, possibly in the early 440s.[12]

The fifteen annual accounts of the Parthenon were inscribed on the four sides of a large marble stele set up on the Acropolis, of which only 25 fragments survive (*IG* I³ 436-451). The text was arranged in eight double columns, three on each of the two large sides of the stele and one on each of the narrow edges.[13] Each annual account opens with a prescript that runs for the entire length of the double column and gives the number of the annual account in the series by mentioning the board of *epistatai* with their own secretary and the first secretary of the council in charge for that year. Accounts from the year XI onwards also add the eponymous archon. After the prescript, the receipt entries follow, with monetary figures on the left and items on the right.[14] Then, the heading ἀναλόματα precedes the expenditure entries, again with monetary figures on the left and items on the right, followed by the remaining balance (περιεγένετο τô ἐνιαυτô τούτο) (See Fig. 2).

Fig. 2

The receipt entries list a variable number of sources, the most important ones being the treasurers of Athena, which usually appear at the top of the list, and the *hellenotamiai*, i.e. the treasurers of the Delian League. Entries also occasionally mention other boards of treasurers and, starting from the year X onwards, the proceeds of the sale of surplus materials, such

12 This dating is compatible with Tracy's observation (2016, 93-101) that the letter cutter who inscribed this document was active at least from 440 to 432, and possibly some more years before and after this time range. Considering that we do not know when the Parthenon accounts started to be inscribed on stone (years I-VI being apparently carved by the same letter cutter), it is certainly possible that *IG* I³ 435 predated them of a few years.

13 According to Dinsmoor's reconstruction (1921b, 233-245) the stele was a parallelepiped of 1.60x1.80x0.20m. The first six annual accounts were inscribed on the obverse, the following seven on the reverse, the year XIV on the left side, and the year XV on the right side. Different letter cutters were at work on these accounts (see Tracy 2016, 43 n. 5).

14 For a typical prescript see e.g. *IG* I³ 447, l. 344-346 (year XII): [τοῖς ἐπιστάτεσι hoῖς Ἀντικλε̃ς ἐ]γραμμάτευε [ἐπὶ] τε̣̃ς [δο|δεκάτες βολε̃ς hε̃ι . . . . . .] πρôτος ἐγρ[αμμ]άτευ[ε | ἐπὶ Λυσιμάχο ἄρχοντος Ἀθεναίοι]ς λέμματα τô [ἐνι]αυτô τά[δε κτλ. "For the *epistatai* to whom Antikles was secretary, in the 12th council to which [...] was first secretary, when Lysimachos was archon of the Athenians, the following are the annual receipts etc.".

as gold, wood, and ivory, as well.[15] Here, the list of expenditures contains much more detail than in previous accounts and the *epistatai* make a distinction among payments for different operations, such as the transportation and hoisting of stone, and to different categories of workers, such as quarrymen, carpenters, road-makers, and sculptors. In addition, they list payments for the purchase of materials – sometimes under a general heading (ὀνεμάτον), sometimes mentioning a specific commodity (e.g. wood and ivory) - and for monthly wages (καταμενίον), presumably for the architect and other city employees involved in the project.

The accounts of the Propylaea closely resemble the Parthenon accounts in both format and content. The five annual accounts (*IG* I³ 462-466), dated to 437/6-433/2, were inscribed on both sides of a marble stele set up on the acropolis, of which only 23 fragments survive. The text was arranged in four double columns, two on the front and two on the back of the stele, with monetary figures on the left and items on the right.[16] As in the Parthenon accounts, the receipt entries list a number of sources, most prominently the treasurers of Athena and the *hellenotamiai*.[17] Similarly, the expenditure entries, though very fragmentarily preserved, seem to list payments for some general operation, such as the transport of stone, and to different categories of workers, such as quarrymen and carpenters, as well as monthly salaries (καταμενίον).[18]

Even though the erection of the chryselephantine statue of Athena Parthenos, conceived and built by Phidias between 447 and 438, was ideologically and physically intertwined with the construction of the Parthenon, the ensuing accounts (*IG* I³ 453, 455-458) have no elements in common with the Parthenon and Propylaea accounts. In fact, they exclusively register the money that the treasurers of Athena allocated each year to the purchase of gold and ivory for the statue, with no mention of other materials (e.g. wood for the statue's core and for scaffolding) nor payments for any workers.[19] As such, they look more like a statement or an "inventory" of how much of the goddess' wealth was "hoarded" in the statue rather than building accounts, in line with the purpose of the statue itself, which was

15 Other boards allocating money include *xenodikai*, *trieropoioi*, the treasurers of the Hephaistikon, and some unknown treasurers linked to *balaneia*.

16 For the reconstruction of the stele, which was probably 1.23m large and 0.111-0.186m thick, see Dinsmoor 1913. For the conception of the Parthenon and Propylaea accounts as an unitary monument see Marginesu 2010, 33.

17 In addition to these, one can mention the treasurers of the Hephaistikon, the rent of a sacred house, the sale of hides from sacrifices, and the sale of dismantled materials, such as roof tiles, wood, and revetment slabs, probably deriving from the old entrance gate of the acropolis.

18 On the basis of format and content, it is possible to date to the years 440s another small fragment of building accounts found in Eleusis and probably concerning the construction of the "Periclean" phase of the Telesterion (*I.Eleusis* 23; *IG* I³ 395). Receipt and expenditure items were most certainly listed in a double column, with entries on the right and monetary figures, now lost, on the left. Both receipt and expenditure items are broken down in a series of entries, reminiscent of the Parthenon accounts. See Shear 2016, 170-174, and Clinton 2008, 44-45.

19 The jump-to-the-eye feature of these inscriptions, together with monetary figures always placed in prominent positions, is that each annual disbursement is accompanied by a list of all the treasurers that made up the allocating board (while the board of *epistatai* receiving the money is identified only by the name of the secretary). The accounts were inscribed on separate stelae and probably set up inside the temple. *IG* I³ 459 is a rejected and incomplete attempt to inscribe the same text as *IG* I³ 458, while *IG* I³ 454, originally considered part of the series, has now been recognized as a fragment of the Samian War expenses inscribed on *IG* I³ 363 (see Marginesu and Themos 2014).

not a cultic image but the repository of a large portion of the goddess' treasure.[20] The only exception is the summary account of the entire project, which was inscribed on a monumental and carefully polished stone, of which only two fragments survive (*IG* I³ 460). As far as we can tell from the scanty, extant portions of the text, the *epistatai* stated first how much money and gold they had received (l. 1-9) and then broke down their expenses in different categories, of which only execution (ἀπεργασία), structure (κατάβλεμα), and gold survive (l. 10-19). Each entry is separated from the other by a *paragraphos* and monetary figures appear to start on a new line. The beauty and large size of the script, especially of numerals, add to the conspicuous grandeur of the monument (See Fig. 3).

Fig. 3

The next extant accounts belong to the following decade and present an interesting development as compared to previous documents. These accounts, concerning the bronze statues of Athena and Hephaestus, are dated to the years 421-416 and were inscribed on a stele set up in the sanctuary of Hephaestus in the agora, of which only three large fragments survive (*IG* I³ 472)[21]. The text opens with a prescript listing the names of the *epistatai* and their secretary, followed by the date in which the work for the statue began (l. 2-6).[22] After a blank space, it follows a list, year after year, of the sums of money allocated by the annual boards of the treasurers of the Other Gods, whose names are carefully recorded (l. 9-20). While the prescript and list of receipts run for the entire length of the stone, the expenditures (l. 138-160) are arranged in two double columns, with monetary figures, now lost, on the left and the related entries on the right. *Paragraphoi*

20 See Marginesu 2009, 469-474, and 2010, 34. On the peculiar features of these accounts see also Shear 2016, 70. In this respect, they are similar to the so-called accounts of the Golden Nikai (*IG* I³ 467-471), which contain, in reality, statements or inventories of the golden parts of each statue with their respective weight (on the golden Nikai see Thompson 1944).

21 According to Vallarino 2012, these accounts do not concern the erection of the statues but some restoration works and the construction of the *anthemon*, i.e. a bronze palm tree at the back of the statues. In addition, the large lacuna following l. 20 might have contained the receipt entries of at least two more years; as such, works might have lasted eight rather than six years, ending in 414/3.

22 See l. 2-6: ἐπιστάται ἀγαλμάτοιν ἐ[ς τὸ] ḥεφαίστιον Ἀπόλεχσις Σμικύθο *v* | [Ἰ]φιστιάδες, Χαιρέας Ἐπι[. . .]ο hαγνόσιος, Πείσανδρος Γλαυκέτο | Ἀχαρνεύς, γραμματεὺς Ο[ἰκο]ṭέλες Γεισίο Λαμπτρεύς *vvvvvvvv* | *v* ἔρχσαντο τôν ἔργον ἐπὶ Ἀριστί[ονος ἄρχ]οντος, ἐπὶ τε̂ς βολε̂ς hε̂ι Μενεκλε̂ς Ἀναφλύστιος *vvv* | *v* πρôτ[ο]ς ἐγραμμάτευε, ἐπὶ τε̂ς Λε[οντίδος] πέμπτες πρυτανευόσες *vac.* "The *epistatai* of the two statues in the sanctuary of Hephaestus, Apolexis son of Smikythos of Iphistidai, Xaireas son of Epi[...] of Hagnous, Peisandros son of Glauketes of Acharnai, secretary Oikoteles son of Geisios of Lamptrai, started the work when Aristion was archon, in the council to which Menekles of Anaphlystos was the first secretary, in the fifth prytany of the tribe Leontis".

separate the entries.[23] The content of some of these entries is similar to the Parthenon accounts, with a simple mention of the materials and the categories of workers paid for.[24] In general, however, they tend to be decidedly more detailed and some, as Marginesu puts it, seem to have a certain "narrative flavor".[25] For example, at l. 155-160, the purchase of wood is accompanied by a careful description of its use: "wood was bought to make the two ramps on which the two statues were brought inside and on which the stone blocks for the base were transported, and to secure the base of the statues and the doors, and to erect the scaffolding around the statues and the ladders against the scaffolding".[26]

This level of detail represents a sort of prelude to the Erechtheum accounts, which mark a new stage in the evolution of building accounts. The construction of this temple, where the Athenians kept the most ancient and venerable cultic image of Athena, probably began in 421 though work halted in 413 in the aftermath of the disastrous Sicilian expedition.[27] When work resumed in 409/8, a decree of the assembly ordered the three *epistatai* of the project and the architect, Philocles of Acharnai, to prepare a report on the current progress of the work. This report was inscribed on the front face of an opistographic stele set up on the acropolis (*IG* I³ 474).[28] After the prescript, which ran along the entire length of the stele (l. 1-7), the report was arranged in two double columns and made up of two parts: first, a long and detailed survey of the unfinished parts of the temple (l. 8-92); then, an inventory of the stone blocks laying on the ground of the building site (l. 93-237). The description of each entry on the right takes up the largest part of the double column while the figures on the narrow left column refer to the number of architectural items of that kind.[29] Each entry starts on a new line and, similarly to the bronze statues' accounts, a *paragraphos* sometimes separates it from the previous one.

The accounts proper, preserved in fragments, were inscribed on separate stelae and cover the works completed in 409/8 and 408/7 (*IG* I³ 475-476).[30] Unlike previous accounts,

---

23 Despite the total amount listed on the front face of the stone (l. 166), the expenditure entries continue on the left side (l. 173-191), probably in a single column. See Thompson 1969 for the reconstruction of the stele.

24 See e.g. l. 151: – – – χσύλα καὶ ἄνθρακες τôι μολύβδοι "[? dr.] wood and charcoal for the lead"; l. 152: – – – τράπεζαν ποιέσαντι "[? dr.] to the one who made a table".

25 See Marginesu 2009, 463-468.

26 See l. 155-160: – – – χσύλα ἐονέθε τὸ κλίμακε ποιε͂σαι, ἐν hοῖν τὸ | ἀγάλματε ἐσεγέσθεν [κ]αὶ ἐφ' ὃν hοι λίθοι ἐσ|εκομίζοντο hοι ἐς τὸ βάθρον, καὶ φάρχσαι | τὸ βάθρον τοῖν ἀγαλμ̣ά̣τοιν καὶ ṭὰς θ̣ύρας, | καὶ ἰκριο͂σαι περὶ τὸ ἀγάλματε καὶ κλίμακε | πρὸς τὰ ἴκρια.

27 See Hurwit 1999, 206, Holtzmann 2003, 166, Shear 2016, 376-381.

28 On this stele (h. 1.835?, w. 0.505, cr. 0.139) see Caskey 1927, 280-321. The reverse of the stele, of which only two small fragments survive, contains the building specifications for the remaining works (l. 238-258), on which see Carusi 2006, 13-14.

29 See e.g. l. 8-15: τô νεὸ τάδε κατελάβομεν hεμίεργα·| ἐπὶ τε͂ι γονίαι τε͂ι πρὸς τô Κεκροπίο·| IIII | πλίνθος ἀθέτος με͂κος τετρά|ποδας, πλάτος δίποδας, πάχος | τριhεμιποδίος. | I | μασχαλιαίαν με͂κος τετράποδα, | πλάτος τρίποδα, πάχος τριôν | hεμιποδίον κτλ. "The following parts of the temple we took over half finished: at the corner towards the Kekropion: 4 blocks unplaced, length 4 feet, width 2 feet, thickness 3 half feet; 1 angular (?) block, length 4 feet, width 3 feet, thickness 3 half feet etc.".

30 See Caskey 1927, 322-416. Construction works continued for at least three other years, but only small fragments of these accounts survive. Recently, Lambert 2016 put some order in the material and was able to establish that one of them (*SEG* 50.69; *IG* II² 1654 + *IG* I³ 478) belongs to the accounts of the

they are organized per prytany. Each new section opens with the mention of the tribe holding the prytany and of how much money the treasurers of Athena allocated to the *epistatai*.[31] The list of expenditure entries follows, first the purchases (hονέματα) and then the payments for different kinds of operations (e.g. λιθοργικô, ἀγαλματοποικô, etc.) and for different categories of workers (e.g. κεροπλάσταις, ἐνκαυταῖς, χάλχας ἐργασαμένοις, etc.). Each entry ends with the total amount spent for that particular operation and category of worker, and each prytany section ends with the total amount spent in that prytany.[32] The text is arranged in columns, but figures are not set apart in a different sub-column; on the contrary, they are incorporated into the body of the text and flagged by means of punctuation. New entries sometimes start in a new line or after a short blank space on the same line, but most often no break occurs between one and the other. Also, new prytany sections usually begin on a new line or after a short blank space on the same line, often flagged by a *paragraphos* or by punctuation marks (See Fig. 4).

Fig. 4

What makes these accounts really peculiar is the level of detail describing each expenditure item. In particular, the accounts register the name of each single worker, his civic status, the exact content of his job, and the payment he received for such a job. For example, the accounts itemize the expenditures for a section of the roof thusly (*IG* I^3 475, l. 240-250): "To

years 407/6-406/5, while the other belongs to the accounts of the year 405/4 (*IG* I^3 477; *IG* II^2 1655). The fragment edited as *IG* I^3 479 does not belong to the Erechtheum accounts.

31 For the opening of a prytany section see e.g. *IG* I^3 476, l. 183-188: hεπὶ τε̂ς Πανδι|[ονί]δος ὀγδόες πρυτανευούσ|[ες] *v.* λέμματα παρὰ ταμιο̂ν τε̂ς | [θε]ô, Ἀρεσαίχμο hαγρυλε̂θεν κ|[αὶ] συναρχόντον, ΧΗΗΔΔΔΓΙΗΗ|[Η hα]ναλόματα κτλ. "In the eight prytany of the tribe Pandionis, receipts from the treasurers of the goddess, Aresaichmos of Agryle and his colleagues: 1,239 dr. 1 ob.; expenses: etc.".

32 For the ending of a section see e.g. *IG* I^3 476, l. 280-281: ⁚ λε̂μμα ⁚ ΧΗΗΔΔΔΓΙΗΗΗ|Ι. ἀνάλομα τὸ hαυτό *v.* :: "Receipts: 1,239 dr. 1 ob. Expenses: the same.".

wood-workers for planning planks for the roof, 7 palms long, 10 dactyls wide, at 1,5 ob. each: 45 dr. to Komon living in Melite, for 180 pieces; 17 dr. to Timomachos of Acharnai, for 68 pieces; 11 dr. 4,5 ob. to Tlesias of Kettos, for 47 pieces; 21 dr. to Mikion living in Melite, for 84 pieces; 2 dr. 1,5 ob. to Euthydomos of Melite, for 9 pieces. Sum total for work on the planks for the roof: 97 dr."[33]

After the Erechtheum work, it becomes difficult to follow the evolution of building accounts for the simple reason that this category of inscriptions seems to virtually disappear from the Athenian epigraphic record. Among the few exceptions, there are some short inscriptions concerning the reconstruction of the Piraeus walls, covering the years 395/4 to 392/1 and inscribed on separate blocks or stelae, which were probably set up in different locations (*IG* II² 1656-1664).[34] Unlike other accounts, they do not provide a general picture of all receipts and expenditures. In fact, each inscription registers only the operations and relative expenses that different annual boards of tribal wall-builders (*teichopoioi*) managed in different years.[35] Despite the fragmentary state of most of these inscriptions, it is possible to observe that in most of them monetary figures were incorporated into the body of the text and that contractors were often mentioned by name, similarly to the Erechtheum accounts.[36] After the disappearance of building accounts proper, expenses for building works are occasionally found within some examples of general accounts, the most important ones being the accounts of the sanctuary of the Two Eleusinian Goddesses dated to the year 329/8 (*I.Eleusis* 177).[37] These accounts were inscribed on a large stele set up in the Eleusinian sanctuary, of which the upper and lower portions survive, with a substantial

---

33 See *IG* I³ 475, l. 240-250: χσυλοργοῖς ἐσ τὲ[ν | ἐποροφία]ν hιμάντας ἀποχσέσασιν | [με̑κ]ος hεπταπαλάστος, πλάτος δεκ|[αδα]κτύλος, τρ̣ιο̣̑ν hεμιοβελίον ⁝ hέκα|[στ]ον ⁝ΔΔΔΔ𐅃⁝ Κ[ό]μονι ἐμ Με ⁝ οἰ ⁝ Η𐅄ΔΔΔ, | Δ𐅃ͰͰ⁝ Τιμομάχοι ⁝ Ἀχαρν[ει ⁝] 𐅄Δ𐅃ΙΙΙ, ΔͰΙΙ|ΙC⁝ Τλεσίαι Κεττίοι ⁝ΔΔΔΔ𐅃ΙΙ ⁝ΔΔͰ⁝ Μικ|ίονι ⁝ ἐμ Με⁝ οἰκ ⁝ 𐅄ΔΔΔΙΙΙΙ⁝ ͰͰΙC⁝ Εὐθυδόμο|ι Μελιτ ⁝𐅃ΙΙΙΙ⁝ ἐς τὲν ἐποροφίαν hιμάντ|ον ἐργασίας ἀργυρίο κεφάλαιον ⁝𐅄ΔΔ|ΔΔ𐅃ͰͰ. Note that the phrase "living in X" distinguishes metics from citizens, who are instead registered with their demotics. Slaves are identified by the possessive genitive of their owner.

34 See also Maier 1959, nr. 1-9, 21-39, and Rhodes and Osborne 2003, nr. 9A-B, 46-49. To these, one must now add *SEG* 19.145 and *SEG* 32.165.

35 See e.g. Maier 1959, nr. 3 (*IG* II² 1658): Αἰγεῖδος τεχο[ποιοὶ – – – – – – – – οἱ] | ἐπ' Εὐβολίδο αἱρ[εθέντες ἐτέχισαν? μ]|εταπύργιον· ἀνα[καθάρσεως τô] | λιθολογήματος [*pretium* μισ(θωτὴς) Ἀν]|τικράτης⁚ κεφ⁚ πλ[ίνθων ἀριθμὸς] | ΜΜΧΧΧ𐅅Η· <ἀ>νεβάλ[λοντο αἱ χίλιαι] | ΔͰͰͰ. μισ(θωτὴς) Κόνων [*demoticum* τούτ]|ων ΗΗΗ𐅃ͰΙΙΙ *v.* ΕΤ̣– – – – – – – –| μισ(θωτὴς) Εὐγείτων Α̣– – – – – – – "The *teichopoioi* of the tribe Aigeis […] those appointed under the archonship of Eubolis built (?) the curtain wall. For clearing away the foundation: […] dr. Contractor: Antikrates of Kephisia. Number of bricks: 23,600. A thousand were laid down for 13 dr. Contractor: Konon of […] of these 306 dr. 3 ob. […] Contractor: Eugeiton of […]". Even if *teichopoioi* are not explicitly mentioned in *IG* II² 1656-1657, it is quite probable that also these inscriptions were set up by annual boards of wall-builders.

36 For the sake of thoroughness, I must add that some fragmentary accounts, stemming from the construction of an Ionic temple in the sanctuary of Apollo at Delos in the 350s, were found both in Delos and Athens (see Chankowski 2008, nr. 52-55).

37 Building expenses are recorded also in the Eleusinian accounts dated to 336/5 or 333/2 (*I.Eleusis* 159), of which only three fragments of the right portion of the stele survive. Their format is similar to *I.Eleusis* 177. The portion of a stele edited as *IG* II² 1669 and dated to the second half of the 4th c. contains some building expenses related to the sanctuary of Zeus Soter at Piraeus. However, the surface of the stone is extremely corroded and difficult to read, so that restorations are far from sure. As far as it is possible to tell, their format is similar to the Eleusinian accounts.

lacuna between the two. The text is arranged in two wide columns. The accounts list receipts and expenditures on a prytany-by-prytany basis, with how much money the administrators of the sanctuary received or had in their hands at the beginning of each prytany and how much was left at the end of it.[38] Each prytany section starts on a new line or is separated from the previous one by a couple of blank lines. Figures are incorporated into the body of the text and flagged by means of punctuation. The level of detail is similar to the Erechtheum accounts, even if not as accurate. For example, as Epstein notes, the Eleusinian accounts are often vague about the identity and civic status of individual workers.[39] However, the layout of the text looks even more crammed than the Erechtheum accounts, especially given the breadth of each column (78 to 81 spaces) and the remarkably small size of the letters (only 4 mm high as compared to 5th c. accounts where, on average, letters are 8 mm high) (See Fig. 5).

It is interesting to observe that while building accounts seem to gradually disappear from the epigraphic record, building specifications inscribed on stone become more and more frequent in the course of the 4th c. These documents, called συγγραφαί in the Attic usage, contain a technical description of the works to be performed and some of the terms and conditions according to which works were to be contracted out, such as, for example, rules concerning the supply of material, appointment of guarantors, methods of payment, and deadlines for delivery. Building specifications were usually drawn up by architects appointed by the Athenian council and assembly and were a necessary step for the realization of building projects. Indirect evidence in the Attic epigraphic record indicates that they were part of the Athenian administrative procedure since at least the mid-5th c. Nevertheless, all building specifications inscribed on stone, with the exception of the document inscribed on the reverse of the Erechtheum report (*IG* I³ 474), belong to the 4th c.[40]

38 See e.g. the opening statement of the 6th prytany (l. 176-178): [ἐπ]ὶ τῆς Κεκροπίδος πέμπτης πρυτανείσας τὸ περιὸν παρὰ ταμίαιν τοῖν θεοῖν ⁝ X𐅅𐅄Δ𐅃IITX ⁝ καὶ τὸ περιὸν | [π]αρὰ ταμ̣ίαι τοῖν θεοῖν Νικοφίλωι Ἀλωπεκῆθεν ⁝ΔΔΔ⊢⊢III⁝ καὶ τὸ περιὸν παρ' ἐπιστάταις Ἐλευσινόθε | [I]Ϲ̣Χ̣ κ̣α̣ὶ τὸ μερισθὲν παρ' ἀποδεκτῶν ἐπιστάταις ⁝𐅅HHH𐅄· ἀπὸ τούτου ἀνήλωται κτλ. "Under the fifth prytany held by the tribe Kekropis, the surplus from the treasurers of the Two Goddesses: 1565 dr. 2 ¼ ob. 1 ch.; the surplus from the treasurer of the Two Goddesses, Nikophilos of Alopeke: 42 dr. 3 ob.; the surplus from the Eleusinian *epistatai* 1,5 ob. 1 ch. and the money allocated from the *apodektai* to the *epistatai*: 850 dr. From this money the following expenses have been made: etc." See also the closing statement of the same prytany (l. 196-198): κεφάλαιον ἀναλώματος ⁝ 𐅅HHH{H}𐅄<Δ>IϹX ⁝ κεφάλαιον λήμματος παρ' ἀποδε||[κτῶν 𐅅]Ḥ̣Ḥ̣Ḥ̣𐅄̣ ⁝ περίεστι[ν παρὰ] ταμίαιν τοῖν θεοῖν ⁝ X𐅅𐅄Δ𐅃IITX ⁝ καὶ παρὰ ταμ̣ίαι τοῖν θεοῖν Νικοφίλωι Ἀλ||[ωπε ΔΔ]Δ̣⊢̣⊢̣III. *vac.* "Grand total of the expenditures: 860 dr. 1,5 ob. 1 ch.; grand total of the receipts from the *apodektai*: 850 dr.; from the treasurers of the Two Goddesses there are left 1565 dr. 2 ¼ ob. 1 ch.; from the treasurer Nikophilos of Alopeke 32 dr. 3 ob.".

39 See Epstein 2013, 129, 138-139.

40 For a catalogue of all known Athenian *syngraphai*, with a detailed study of their structure and function, see Carusi 2006. For 5th c. decrees making reference to the existence of *syngraphai* see *IG* I³ 35, 45, 84, and *I.Eleusis* 41.

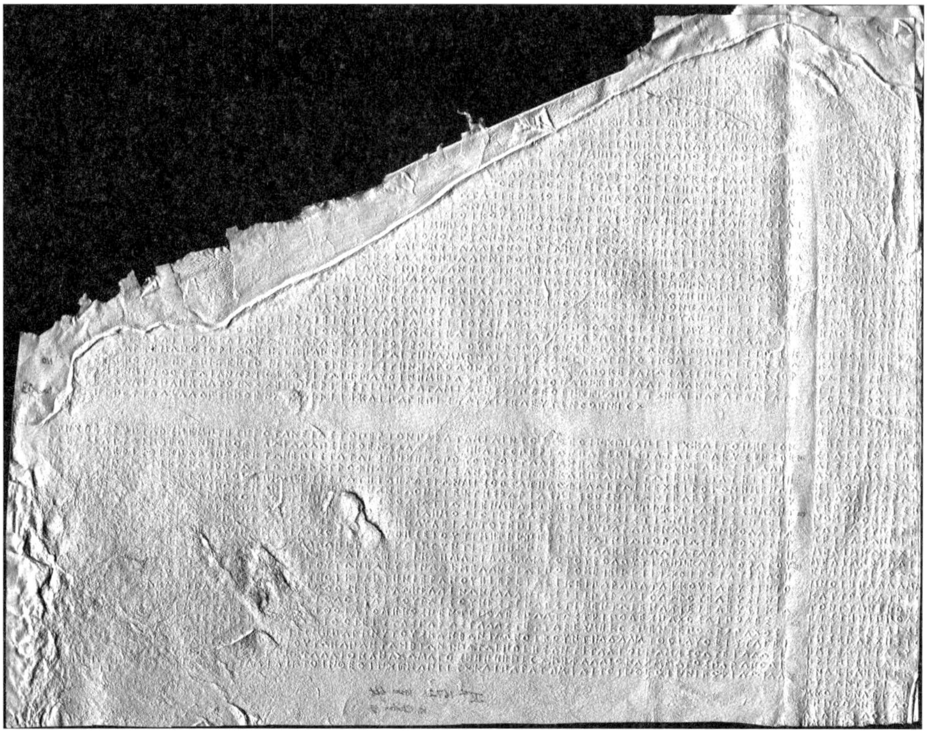

Fig. 5

The most famous example of this category of inscriptions is, without a doubt, the well-preserved stele with the *syngraphai* of Piraeus' arsenal (*IG* II² 1668), originally set up near the arsenal itself and probably dated to 347/6.[41] As the "title" of the inscription states, the *syngraphai* were drawn up by Euthydomus of Melite and Philon of Eleusis and concerned a stone arsenal for naval tackle and rigging to be built at Zea, between the ship-sheds along the harbor and the agora.[42] The rest of the text, which runs for 97 continuous lines,

41 For the arsenal and the relative inscription see Jeppesen 1958, 69-101. Construction works probably started in 347/6, when an *eisphora* for funding the project started to be levied (*IG* II² 505, l. 14-18), were interrupted in 339/8 because of the war against Philip II (Philoch. *FGrHist* 328 F 56a), and were completed under Lycurgus' administration (Plu. *Mor.* 841d, 852c), possibly by 330/29 (cf. *IG* II² 1627, l. 287-289) (See Fig. 6).

42 See l. 2-7: [σ]υνγραφαὶ τῆς σκευοθήκης τῆς λιθίνης τοῖς χρεμαστοῖς σκεύεσιν | Εὐθυδόμου Δημητρίου Μελιτέως, Φίλωνος Ἐξεκεστίδου Ἐλευσινίου. | σκευοθήκην οἰκοδομῆσαι τοῖς χρεμαστοῖς σκεύεσιν ἐν Ζείαι ἀρξά|μενον ἀπὸ τοῦ προπυλαίου τοῦ ἐξ ἀγορᾶς προσιόντι ἐκ τοῦ ὄπισθεν τῶν ν|εωσοίκων τῶν ὁμοτεγῶν, μῆκος τεττάρων πλέθρων, πλάτος πεντήκοντα π|οδῶν καὶ πέντε σὺν τοῖς τοίχοις "Specifications of the stone arsenal for naval tackle and rigging by Euthydomus son of Demetrios of Melite and Philon son of Exekestides of Eleusis. To build the arsenal for naval tackle and rigging in Zea, starting from the propylaion that leads from the agora as one approaches from behind the ship-sheds under the same roof, 4 plethra in length, 55 feet in width, including the walls". For Philon of Eleusis as the architect of the arsenal see Vitr. 7.*praef.*12, Cic. *de orat.* 1.62, Strabo 9.1.15, Plin. *NH* 7.125, Val. Max. 8.12.2, Plu. *Sull.* 14.7.

Fig. 6

describes how to construct the arsenal, including its foundations, walls, doorways, windows, roof, and the internal organization of the space with galleries and shelves. After an initial infinitive sentence, all instructions are given in the future indicative, with circumstantial participles in agreement with an implicit, singular subject. However, the last lines of the text (l. 94-97) state that "contractors" - in the plural - "will carry out the works according to the specifications and in reference to the measures and model that the architect indicates, and will deliver them within the deadline at which they will undertake each of the works".[43]Since such a massive building required the contribution of different kinds of craftsmen, such as stonemasons and carpenters, it is obvious that it was contracted out in multiple lots, probably different from each other in size and typology. This confirms that building specifications were inscribed on stone before construction works started and before the identity and number of the involved workers were known. Moreover, it reveals that *syngraphai* inscribed on stone usually gave a general description of the building but tended to leave out more detailed information, which would have been necessary for the contractors to complete their jobs (e.g. measures and deadlines).[44]

As I argued elsewhere, this text shows with particular force that the main purpose of inscribing building specifications on stone was not to provide prospective contractors, or whoever of the public might be interested, with practical information. On the contrary, inscribed *syngraphai* must be considered enduring monuments, erected to celebrate and perpetuate the memory of building enterprises that were felt as particularly significant to

43 See l. 94-97: ταῦτα ἅπαντα ἐξεργάσονται οἱ μισθωσάμ|ενοι κατὰ τὰς συγγραφὰς καὶ πρὸς τὰ μέτρα καὶ πρὸς τὸ παράδειγμα, ὃ | ἂν φράζηι ὁ ἀρχιτέκτων, καὶ ἐν τοῖς χρόνοις ἀποδώσουσιν, οἷς ἂν μισ|θώσωνται ἕκαστα τῶν ἔργων.

44 See Jeppesen 1956, 85-86. Some of the missing information could be transmitted to the contractors by means of the measures and model (*metra* and *paradeigma*) mentioned in the last clause. However, the inscription is certainly more focused on the monumental aspects of the building than on matters of detail and appears to address the general public rather than the actual contractors.

the city of Athens and its policies.[45] In this specific case, the construction of a massive stone arsenal was a meaningful political and military endeavor, meant to reassert the city's naval power while recovering from the Social War and facing Philip II's activism in northern Aegean.

This survey shows that during the years 440s and 430s building accounts moved progressively from a more cursory format (i.e. the unknown work's accounts) to a format in which a more detailed list of receipts and expenditures was laid out in an extremely "user-friendly" interface. Within this newer format, some "visual devices" immediately call to attention the main sources of money and items of expenditure with their relative monetary figures. For "visual devices", I mean here the blank spaces separating each year's section from the following one; each entry starting on a new line; and, above all, the listing of figures and items in separate and parallel sub-columns.[46] The Parthenon accounts represent the most mature form of this evolution and, with their large stele set up on the acropolis, its most monumental outcome. On the other hand, the Erechtheum accounts, a couple of decades later, reach an unsurpassed level of detail in accommodating much information that had been omitted in previous accounts, but, in doing so, they abandon most of the visual devices adopted before. As a result, for a passer-by it was probably not so easy to immediately identify, just looking at the stone, the sums of money spent for the different categories of purchases and payments. Finally, building accounts seem to go out of fashion in the 4th c. and are gradually replaced, in the epigraphic record, by building specifications.

There is a large scholarly consensus, I believe, that public documents inscribed on stone, as showed above in the case of building specifications, did not have a purely informative function. In fact, the temporary display of relevant texts on wooden tablets or whitewashed boards more conveniently fulfilled said function. In Athens, these temporary media were usually posted on special locations, such as, for instance, a wall in the Bouleuterion or the base of the monument of the Eponymous Heroes in the agora. It is to these temporarily displayed texts that whoever of the public was interested turned to get all sort of practical information.[47] In the case of building accounts it has been reasonably assumed, as said above, that this temporary display occurred when the *epistatai*, at the end of their term of office, were about to pass their *euthynai*.

It is clear, however, that the actual accounts submitted by the *epistatai*, previously posted on some prominent location and later stored in archives, were different from the texts inscribed on stone. The Parthenon accounts, as well as others mid-5th c. building accounts, omit too many relevant details and would be extremely inadequate to serve as a tool for accountability. As such, we have to assume that they represent only a selective and

45 See Carusi 2006, 28-29, and 2010, 214-223.

46 According to Meyer 2017, the columnar arrangement of building accounts, as well as of other category of inscriptions such as casualty lists and tribute lists, was adopted as a conscious visual reference to the inscribed stone posts that characterized the epigraphic landscape of the acropolis in the first half of the 5th c. and were used to dedicate to the gods achievements considered of particular importance to them. For the columnar arrangement as borrowed from the formatting of originals written on papyri see Del Corso 2002, 181-189. In either case, it cannot be denied that this arrangement was ideal for organizing and conveying lists of items in a functional way.

47 On the temporary display of public documents see the seminal article by Wilhelm 1909. More recently, see Davies 1994, 205-207, and Rhodes 2001, esp. 33-36.

rearranged version of the actual accounts presented by the *epistatai* at the time of the *euthynai*.[48] Their primary function was not to divulge practical information for whomever might be interested in checking the conduct of the *epistatai*, but to assert Athens' power by pointing to the grandeur of its achievements and the largesse of the sums of money involved.[49] Not surprisingly, monetary figures occupy a prominent position in these accounts. In addition, we must not forget that accounts set up in sacred spaces and concerning sacred buildings had an important religious dimension as dedications meant to both please and honor the gods.[50]

These elements - celebrating the city's achievements and honoring the gods - are certainly part of the goal of later accounts as well. However, the increasing level of detail and the concurrent abandonment of most visual devices seem to obscure the incisiveness and effectiveness of this goal in favor of what might appear - at first sight - a more "bureaucratic" concern. In order to explain this change of attitude and the unsurpassed level of detail of the Erechtheum accounts, scholars have looked at the difficult financial situation that Athens was facing in the war against Sparta and to the recent political crisis that had led to the abolition and then restoration of the democracy in 411-410. These political and financial factors would have sparked the need for an increased level of accountability and transparency from the part of public officials and led to the inscribing of documents that would have allowed the public to inspect with closer scrutiny the conduct of said officials.[51]

In my opinion, however, two arguments undermine this idea. First, the format of the Erechtheum accounts is not a complete watershed in the history of inscribed accounts, since some of its trends are anticipated by the accounts of the bronze statues of 421-416 (*IG* I^3 472). Such being the case, the new format cannot be considered a result of the specific financial and political situation in the aftermath of the Sicilian expedition and oligarchic coup. Second, the level of detail displayed in the Erechtheum accounts pays more attention

48 See Epstein 2013, 132. From the late-5th c. or early 4th c. onwards, public documents stemming from the activity of the council and the officials working in close relation with it were kept in a central record office located in the Metroon, the sanctuary of the Mother of the Gods in the agora. As such, it is likely that all documents related to building activities were kept in the same archive. Before such a central record office was created, the council as well as most Athenian officials probably maintained separate archives. For 5th c. record-keeping and the establishment of a central record office see Sickinger 1999, esp. 62-138. On the complex relationship between archival texts and documents inscribed on stone see Boffo 1995 and Davies 2003.

49 See, to quote only the most recent contributions, Marginesu 2010, 33-34, and Epstein 2013, 132-133. Even though inscribed accounts were not suitable to check the *epistatai*'s conduct, they can still be seen as symbols of the democratic principles on which the Athenian political and administrative system was based, i.e. transparency and accountability (see Davies 1994, esp. 211). As Rhodes argues, the celebration of Athens' power passed through the parading not only of the city's endeavors and financial prowess but also of the democratic principles that made such achievements possible (2001, 140-141).

50 On the religious dimension of public inscriptions see Meyer 2013.

51 The idea that the Erechtheum accounts aimed at attaining a tighter control on the expenses made by the *epistatai* is expressed by several scholars, even if with different nuances. See Davis 1948, 485-486 (to counteract possible political opposition to the project), Wittenburg 1978, 72-73 (to meet the principles of a more radical form of democracy), and Feyel 2006, 16-17 (to respond to the concerns created by the dire financial situation). Also Epstein 2013, 134-137, sees the Erechtheum accounts as a step further in attaining an increased level of accountability and transparency from the part of public officials.

to the identity of the workers who performed the different jobs and the description of each job than to the sums of money spent in the process. In these accounts monetary figures do not occupy a prominent place anymore and, despite the signs of punctuation meant to flag them, they are not particularly discernible, but rather obscured and "swallowed up" by the abundance of the surrounding details, some of them frankly superfluous, if one was primarily interested in the accountability of the *epistatai*.[52]

As Marginesu pointed out, the accounts of the bronze statues have a certain narrative flavor and seem to display a somewhat self-congratulating and proud tone for the complexity of the job achieved – in that particular case the transport of the statues inside the temple.[53] It seems to me that the same attitude is at play in the Erechtheum accounts and in other later accounts, such as the Eleusinian ones, where the density of the text makes even more difficult to find and check the monetary figures.

In other words, I argue that in the last quarter of the 5th c. building accounts became more and more focused on describing how a building achievement was completed rather than in showing how much money was spent to complete it. The purpose was still to celebrate that achievement and the effort the city made to realize it, but by pointing less to the financial aspect and more to the deployment of the human and technical resources necessary to realize it. One might even argue that this occurred, not accidentally, when the sums of money at stake became less important than had been before.[54] In alternative, one might assume that the evolving format of building accounts was influenced by other epigraphic documents in which the descriptive and detail-oriented flavor is predominant, for example the inventories of the treasurers of Athena, which, incidentally, were written in the continuous-line format.[55] In any case, I wish to emphasize that, in my opinion, this development concerned the epigraphic habit and the way in which the city chose to celebrate its achievements, not the administrative practice of the *euthynai* nor any increased preoccupation with the accountability of the *epistatai*.[56]

This trend might also explain why building specifications started to replace building accounts in the epigraphic record. These documents, where monetary figures were dispensable and frequently overlooked, while technical instructions took most of the space,

52 For the idea that this kind of building accounts were meant to commemorate the names of the individuals who made possible the realization of a building scheme, in the same way as votive inscriptions, see Burford 1971. However, as Epstein 2013, 137, rightly points out, this purpose would have been more effectively fulfilled by a list of names, as, for instance, in the case of casualty lists. In addition, there are workers who remain anonymous also in the Erechtheum accounts (see e.g. *IG* I³ 475, l. 272-285). As Meyer 2017, 244-248, points out, in the last years of the 5th c. the Athenian epigraphic record is marked by an increasing focus on individual names. This larger phenomenon reflects a change in the Athenian democratic culture, with a shift from a major emphasis on the role of the collectivity to a greater acknowledgment of the individual's role within the community.

53 See Marginesu 2009, 467-468.

54 The average cost of 1-year-works in the Erechtheum derived from the monetary figures preserved in the accounts, i.e. 24.500 dr., is 5 to 7 time smaller than the average cost of 1-year-works in the Parthenon, i.e. 136.000 to 188.000 dr., depending on what estimate of the Parthenon's cost one accepts (i.e. 340 to 470 t.).

55 On the "stamp-collector's pleasure" and the "stamp-catalogue compiler's professional satisfaction" that the inventories of Athena's treasurers convey see Davies 1994, 209.

56 In both these respects I dissent from Epstein 2013.

were certainly more focused than accounts on the level of accomplishment necessary to achieve a building project, and celebrated that achievement even when the building itself – the tangible proof of the city's accomplishment – was yet to come.

Illustrations

Fig. 1
IG I^3 435, fragments E and F - By courtesy of the Sara B. Aleshire Center for the Study of Greek Epigraphy, University of California, Berkeley (photo 21147)

Fig. 2
IG I^3 449, fragments D, E, and A - By courtesy of the Sara B. Aleshire Center for the Study of Greek Epigraphy, University of California, Berkeley (photo 21158)

Fig. 3
IG I^3 460 - By courtesy of the Sara B. Aleshire Center for the Study of Greek Epigraphy, University of California, Berkeley (photo 7327)

Fig. 4
IG I^3 476, fragment XIII - By courtesy of the Sara B. Aleshire Center for the Study of Greek Epigraphy, University of California, Berkeley (photo 21171)

Fig 5
I.Eleusis 177 (squeeze, detail of l. I.140-198, II.343-400) - By courtesy of Institute for Advanced Study (KP 1545)

Fig. 6
IG II^2 1668 (squeeze, detail of l. 1-26) - By courtesy of the Center for Epigraphical and Palaeographical Studies, Ohio State University

Bibliography

Boffo, L. 1995. "Ancora una volta sugli «archivi» nel mondo greco: conservazione e «pubblicazione» epigrafica", *Athenaeum* 83: 91-130.

Burford, A. 1971. "The Purpose of Inscribed Building Accounts", *Acta of the Fifth International Congress of Greek and Latin Epigraphy*, Oxford: 71-76.

Carusi, C. 2006. "Alcune considerazioni sulle *syngraphai* ateniesi del V e IV secolo a.C.", *ASAA* 84: 11-36.

Carusi, C. 2010. "La legge di Agirrio e le *syngraphai* ateniesi di IV secolo", in A. Magnetto, D.Erdas, and C. Carusi (eds.), *Nuovi studi sulla legge granaria ateniese del 474/3*, Pisa: 213-233.

Caskey, L.D. 1927. "The Inscriptions", in J.M. Paton (ed.), *The Erechtheum, measured, drawn, and restored*, Cambridge: 277-421.

Chankowski, V. 2008. *Athènes et Délos à l'époque classique. Recherches sur l'administration du sanctuaire d'Apollon délien*, Athènes.

Clinton, K. 2008. *Eleusis. The Inscriptions on Stone. Documents of the Sanctuary of the Two Goddesses and Public Documents of the Deme*. II: *Commentary*, Athens.

Davies, J.K. 1994. "Accounts and Accountability in Classical Athens", in R. Osborne and S. Hornblower (eds.), *Ritual, Finance, Politics: Athenian Democratic Accounts presented to D.M. Lewis*, Oxford: 201-212.

Davies, J.K. 2003. "Greek Archives: From Record to Monument", in M. Brosius (ed.), *Ancient Archives and Archival Traditions. Concepts of Record-Keeping in the Ancient World*, Oxford: 323-343.

Davis, P.H. 1948. "In the Workshop of the Erechtheion", *AJA* 52: 485-489.

Del Corso, L. 2002. "I documenti nella Grecia classica tra produzione e conservazione", *QS* 56: 155-189.

Dinsmoor, W.B. 1913. "Attic Building Accounts. III. The Propylaea", *AJA* 17: 371-398.

Dinsmoor, W.B. 1921a. "Attic Building Accounts. IV. The Statue of Athena Promachos", *AJA* 25: 118-129.

Dinsmoor, W.B. 1921b. "Attic Building Accounts. V. Supplementary Notes", *AJA* 25: 233-247.

Epstein, Sh. 2013. "Attic Building Accounts from *Euthynae* to *Stelae*", in M. Faraguna (ed.), *Archives and Archival Documents in Ancient Societies*, Trieste: 127-141.

Feyel, Chr. 2006. *Les artisans dans les sanctuaires grecs aux époques classique et hellénistique*, Athens.

Foley, E. and Stroud, R.S. 2019. "A Reappraisal of the Athena Promachos Accounts from the Acropolis (*IG* I³ 435)", *Hesperia* 88: 87-153.

Hansen, M.H. 1991. *The Athenian Democracy in the Age of Demosthenes*, Oxford, UK and Cambridge, MA.

Holtzmann, B. 2003. *L'Acropole d'Athènes. Monuments, cultes et histoire du sanctuaire d'Athèna Polias*, Paris.

Hurwit, J.M. 1999. *The Athenian Acropolis. History, Mythology, and Archaeology from the Neolithic Era to the Present*, Cambridge.

Jeppesen, K. 1958. *Paradeigmata. Three Mid-Fourth Century Main Works of Hellenic Architecture Reconsidered*, Aarhus.

Lambert, S.D. 2016. "The Last Erechtheion Building Accounts", *AIO Papers* 7: 1-10.

Maier, F.G. 1959. *Griechische Mauerbauinschriften*, I, Heidelberg.

Marginesu, G. 2009. "Note sui rendiconti ateniesi di statue del V secolo a.C.", *PP* 64: 460-474.

Marginesu, G. 2010. *Gli epistati dell'Acropoli: edilizia sacra nella città di Pericle, 447/6-433/2 a.C.*, Paestum.

Marginesu, G. and Themos, Ath.A. 2014. "Ἀνέλοσαν ἐς τὸν πρὸς Σαμίος πόλεμον. A New Fragment of the Samian War Expenses (*IG* I³ 363 + 454)", in A.P. Matthaiou and R. Pitt (eds.), *Athenaion Episkopos. Studies in Honour of Harold Mattingly*, Athens: 171-184.

Meyer, E.A. 2013. "Inscriptions as Honors and the Athenian Epigraphic Habit", *Historia* 62: 453-505.

Meyer, E.A. 2017. "Inscribing in Columns in Fifth century Athens", in I. Berti, K. Bolle, F. Opdenhoff, and F. Stroth (eds.), *Writing Matters. Presenting and Perceiving Monumental Inscriptions in Antiquity and the Middle Ages*, Berlin and Boston 2017.

Pitt, R. 2015. "Some Mid-Fifth century Athenian Building Accounts", in A.P. Matthaiou and N. Papazarkadas (eds.), *ΑΞΩΝ. Studies in honor of Ronald S. Stroud*, Athens: 693-707.

Rhodes, P.J. 2001. "Public Documents in the Greek States: Archives and Inscriptions", *G&R* 48: 33-44, 136-153.

Rhodes, P.J. and Osborne, R. 2003. *Greek Historical Inscriptions 404-232 BC*, Oxford.

Shear, T.L. jr. 2016. *Trophies of Victory. Public Building in Periklean Athens*, Princeton.

Sickinger, J.P. 1999. *Public Records and Archives in Classical Athens*, Chapel Hill and London.

Thompson, D.B. 1944. "The Golden Nikai reconsidered", *Hesperia* 13: 173-209.

Thompson, W.E. 1969. "The Inscriptions in the Hephaisteion", *Hesperia* 38: 114-118.

Tracy, S.V. 2016. *Athenian Lettering of the Fifth century B.C.. The Rise of the Professional Letter Cutter*, Berlin and Boston.

Vallarino, G. 2012. "Le epigrafi dello *Hephaisteion* e il culto di Efesto ad Atene", in G. Bevilacqua and S. Campanelli (eds.), *Ἀρετῆς ἕνεκεν καὶ σοφίας. Un omaggio a Paola Lombardi. Giornata di studio - Roma, 28 Ottobre 2010*, Roma: 61-74.

Wilhelm, A. 1909, "Über die öffentliche Aufzeichnung von Urkunden", in *Beiträge zur griechischen Inschriftenkunde*, Wien: 229-299.

Wittenburg, A. 1978. *Grieschische Baukommisionen des 5. und 4. Jahrhunderts*, München.

Misthos, *Apophora*, or Something Else? A Fresh Look at *SEG* XXXV 134*

David M. Lewis, Edinburgh

In 1985 Alan Johnston published a remarkable text incised onto the floor of a plate; the find itself was made in the Kerameikos before 1960.[1] The text predominantly comprises a series of abbreviated names followed by two sets of numerals. In Johnston's view, the most plausible interpretation is that the named individuals were slaves; the first set of numerals represents numbers of days, and the second set of numerals represents either payments of *misthos*, a rent paid to the slave's owner by a lessee for their hire; or *apophora*, a regular fixed payment made by slaves to their owners in circumstances where the slave operated independently.[2] Despite its many interesting features, not much discussion of this document has appeared in print since Johnston's initial publication.[3] This article represents an attempt to rekindle interest in this document; for if Johnston is correct then it is of prime interest to historians of Greek slavery. Appealing as that interpretation may be, however, both hypotheses are open to several objections; in my view, an alternative scenario can better account for the production of this text: the pooling of resources by an association of lower-class individuals, perhaps for a sacrifice.

* My Thanks to the audience at Schwetzingen (September 2016) and to the participants in the 'New discoveries in Greek epigraphy' seminar at Edinburgh (October 2018) for their comments and criticisms. I would also like to thank Stephen Lambert and Ilias Arnaoutoglou for discussing the text with me. Christian Amitzbøll Thomsen, Benedikt Eckhardt, Edward Harris, Jason Porter, and Mirko Canevaro read drafts of the article and provided invaluable criticisms and suggestions. The Deutsches Archäologisches Institüt Athen kindly permitted me to reproduce a photograph of the plate discussed herein; my thanks to its staff and to Dr J. Heiden for arranging this and supplying the image.

1 A. Johnston, 'A fourth century graffito from the Kerameikos' *MDAI(A)* 100 (1985): 293-307.

2 Johnston (n. 1): 303-7. I avoid the term 'living apart' (though many *apophora*-paying slaves likely did live elsewhere than their owner's house) in order that this group is not conflated with the *khoris oikountes* mentioned in Dem. 4.36. The latter were probably a category of freedmen: see M. Canevaro & D.M. Lewis, '*Khoris oikountes* and the obligations of freedmen in late Classical and early Hellenistic Athens' *Incidenza dell'antico* 12 (2014): 91-121. For *apophora*-paying slaves in classical Athens see now D. Kamen, 'Manumission and slave-allowances in Classical Athens' *Historia* 65.4 (2016): 413-26.

3 For instance, it is not discussed in C. Pébarthe's important book *Cité, démocratie et écriture* (Paris 2006). Brief discussion in R. Thomas, 'Writing, reading, public and private "literacies." Functional literacy and democratic literacy in Greece' in W.A. Johnson & H.N. Parker (eds.) *Ancient Literacies: The Culture of Reading in Greece and Rome* (Oxford 2009): 13-45, at pp. 28-9.

I. *SEG* XXXV 134: An Overview

We may begin by noting the chief features of the find. The plate is black-glazed, 14.8cm in diameter at its original undamaged extent, and was dated by Lucy Talcott to the mid-fourth century BC on ceramic grounds. Johnston dated the text to post-350 based on letter forms.[4] I present the following text based on Johnston's *editio princeps* and the edition at *SEG* XXXV 134:

SIDE A

1 [.c.6..]ς̣ ἄρ̣χων
[Ἑκ]α̣τ̣[ο]μβαιών

4 Date of plate: Johnston (n. 1): 293; date of text: ibid: 297.

Column I

[- - -]αν : ΔΔΙΙ
[ ] Ἑρμω : ΔΔΙΙΙ : ͰΙΙΙΙC
ἐν τῶι
ἱερ : ΙΙΙΙ :
Ẹ Ἀπολλω : ΔΔΔΙΙΙΙ : ͰΙΙΙ
[ ] Ἀταρβι : ΔΔ
[ ] Φιλιπ : ΔΔ𐅃Ι
[ ] ν? Ἱππω : ΔΔ𐅃ΙΙΙ : ͰͰΙ
[ ] ν Νιτα : Δ𐅃ΙΙΙ
Ε Ἀρτεμ : ΔΔ𐅃ΙΙΙ : ͰͰΙ
[ ]ν Τιμαρ : ΔΔ𐅃ΙΙΙ :
Ẹ Γαστρ : ΔΔΔ : ͰͰΙΙ
[- - -]αλλι : ΔΔ𐅃
[- - - -]νο : ΔΔ𐅃ΙΙΙ : ͰͰΙ

Column II

Θαλλω : ΔΔ𐅃ΙΙΙ : ͰͰΙ
Κολχ : ΔΔΙΙΙΙ
Ε Εὐβιω : ΔΔ𐅃ΙΙΙ : ͰͰΙ
Ἀμπελι : ΔΔ𐅃ΙΙΙ : ͰͰ
Ε Μικιω : ΔΔ𐅃ΙΙΙ : ͰͰΙ
Ε Ῥυνδα : ΔΔ𐅃ΙΙΙ : ͰͰΙ
Κ . τυ : ΔΔ𐅃ΙΙΙ
Ε Μελαν : ΔΔ𐅃ΙΙΙ : ͰͰΙ
Μακεδο : ΔΔ𐅃ΙΙΙ
Ε Δεξι : ΔΔ𐅃ΙΙΙ : ͰͰΙ
Ε Εὐμαθ : ΔΔ𐅃ΙΙΙ : ͰͰΙ
Ε Τιριβ : ΔΔ𐅃ΙΙΙ : ͰͰΙ
Φανια : ΔΔΙΙ
ποτήρια : Ηρακ : ΙΙ Ἀριṣτοδή-
ἡμικοαῖα : μεια : ΗΔΔΔ : καρχήσια ΙΙΙΙ
𐅃 Σιμια : ΔΔ𐅃ΙΙΙ : ͰͰΙ
Ιταμ : 𐅃ΙΙΙΙ . [- - -]

[- -]κτ : ΔΔ𐅃ΙΙΙ : ͰͰΙ Θραικ : ΔΔΙΙ Ε Παρμ [:] Δ̣ . . [- -]
[- -] . χ : ΔΔ𐅃 Ε Πετρω : ΔΔΙΙΙ : ͰΙΙΙΙC Ἀσθ . [- -]
ἐν τῶι ἱερ : 𐅃

SIDE B On the underside, inside the foot Ἡρακλ(—)

In order that the reader might more easily understand the text, I have translated the numbers and tabulated the information (table 1, *infra*).

Table 1

Individual no.	**Name**	**Numeral 1**	**Numeral 2 (payment)**	**Daily average**	**E?**	***EN ΤΩΙ ΙΕΡ***
1	]αν	22				
2	Ἑρμω	23	1dr 5.5 ob (= 11.5 ob)	0.5 ob		4
3	Ἀπολλω	34	1dr 3ob (= 9ob)	0.26 ob	E	
4	Ἀταρβι	20				
5	Φιλιπ	26				
6	Ἱππω	**28**	**2dr 2ob (= 14ob)**	**0.5 ob**		
7	Νιτα	18				
8	Ἀρτεμ	**28**	**2dr 2ob (= 14ob)**	**0.5 ob**	E	
9	Τιμαρ	28				
10	Γαστρ	30	2dr 3ob (= 15ob)	0.5 ob	E (?)	
11	]αλλι	25				
12	]νο	**28**	**2dr 2ob (= 14ob)**	**0.5 ob**		
13	Θαλλω	**28**	**2dr 2ob (= 14ob)**	**0.5 ob**		
14	Κολχ	24				
15	Εὐβιω	**28**	**2dr 2ob (= 14ob)**	**0.5 ob**	E	
16	Ἀμπελι	31	2dr (= 12ob)	0.39 ob		
17	Μικιω	**28**	**2dr 2ob (= 14ob)**	**0.5 ob**	E	
18	Ῥυνδα	**28**	**2dr 2ob (= 14ob)**	**0.5 ob**	E	
19	Κ . τυ	28				
20	Μελαν	**28**	**2dr 2ob (= 14ob)**	**0.5 ob**	E	
21	Μακεδο	28				
22	Δεξι	**28**	**2dr 2ob (= 14ob)**	**0.5 ob**	E	
23	Εὐμαθ	**28**	**2dr 2ob (= 14ob)**	**0.5 ob**	E	
24	Τιριβ	**28**	**2dr 2ob (= 14ob)**	**0.5 ob**	E	
25	Φανια	22				
26	Ηρακ	2	Payment in pots	?		
27	Σιμια	**28**	**2dr 2ob (= 14ob)**	**0.5 ob**		
28	Ιταμ	9	Text damaged			
29	]κτ	**28**	**2dr 2ob (= 14 ob)**	**0.5 ob**		
30	Θραικ	22				
31	Παρμ	Numeral incomplete	Text damaged		E	
32	]χ	25				
33	Πετρω	23	1dr 5.5 ob (11.5 ob)	0.5 ob	E	5
34	Ἀσθ	Text damaged	Text damaged			

Notable Features

Before turning to the question of interpretation, it is necessary to underscore certain key features of the text. This will involve running over some of the groundwork already well established by Johnston.[5]

Prescript

The first two lines comprise some manner of heading. In line 1 A[-]ΧΩΝ is tolerably clear; Johnston suggests that this could be θιασ]α[ρ]χῶν; but as 'that would leave a gap at the beginning of the line', he prefers the name of the eponymous archon followed by ἄρχων in the nominative; although this is unusual (as prescripts in official documents use the genitive form), this 'may be sufficiently explained by the fact that this is by no means an official text.'[6] As for line 2, Johnston notes that 'I can envisage no restoration other than Ἑκ]ατ[ο]μβαίων, which not only fits all existing traces but would start suitably close to the edge of the plate's interior.'[7] This latter restoration seems more secure than the former, and at least provides us with the month Hekatombaion during which (or concerning which) the text may have been composed.

Days and Payments

As Johnston points out, it is clear that the two main columns of names were composed first, and the other elements added later: note for example from the photograph how the numerals relating to Ἑρμω are squeezed in behind the pre-existing entry for Κολχ. The text was thus not composed in one go, but was updated over time: after an initial blocking-in of the main two columns of names (and perhaps the first set of numerals), the second set of numerals and some further names and numerals were later added, and finally the epsilons (on which see *infra*).[8] The most striking feature of the text is the consistency of thirteen of the entries (marked in bold in table 1), where the first numeral is 28, followed after the punctuation mark by 2 drachms 2 obols (ὁ δεῖνα : ΔΔΠΙΙΙ : ⊢⊢ΙΙ).[9] Johnston makes the compelling suggestion that the first column records days, the second daily payments. For these thirteen individuals, then, the daily payment was ½ obol. There are variations on this theme that use the same basic ratio. Note for instance Ἑρμω (23 : 11 ½ obols = ½ obol per diem), Γαστρ (30 : 15 obols = ½ obol per diem) and Πετρω (23 : 11 ½ obols = ½ obol per diem). This consistency is striking; but there are deviations from the rule. Ἀπολλω has 34 : 9 obols, which computes as 0.26 obols per diem. Ἀμπελι has 31 : 12 obols, which computes as 0.39 obols per diem. Most unusual is Ηρακ, whose first numeral (2) is vastly smaller than those of the other individuals, and whose payment or contribution is made in several kinds of pot.[10] This may point to a special role for Ηρακ; and he may indeed be the person who cut

5 I will avoid repeating in full Johnston's commentary, and stick only to those aspects that bear directly on the interpretations discussed in §II *infra*; readers are referred to Johnston's excellent commentary for further details.
6 Johnston (n. 1): 298.
7 Johnston (n. 1): 297.
8 On the order of composition, see Johnston (n. 1): 295.
9 Namely individuals 6, 8, 12, 13, 15, 17, 18, 20, 22, 23, 24, 27, 29 in table I.
10 For excellent notes on these pot types see Johnston (n. 1): 302-3.

the inscription, for the name Ἡρακλ appears on the other side (*viz.* the base) of the plate.[11] Finally, in eleven entries we have the name plus first numeral but no monetary payment.[12] (This is clear due to obvious vacats; due to damage it is impossible to assess properly the entries for Παρμ and Ἀσθ).

Epsilon

The inscriber has added the letter epsilon to the left of many of the 'payers.' As Johnston points out, no 'non-payer' is marked thus.[13] There are a number of possible explanations for this choice of letter; in particular, as the past indicative augment, epsilon could abbreviate various verbs denoting that payment had been made.[14]

EN ΤΩΙ ΙΕΡ

In two cases we find the phrase EN ΤΩΙ ΙΕΡ written to gloss entries with a reduced number of 'days' and a correspondingly smaller payment, but again on the ½ obol per diem system: Ἑρμω and Πετρω. Both paid 23 daily contributions, 11 ½ obols each. Beside the phrase EN ΤΩΙ ΙΕΡ in each instance there is marked a further numeral, 4 for Ἑρμω and 5 for Πετρω. This subsequent numeral probably represents the number of days that these individuals were ἐν τῶι ἱερ<ῶι>, *viz.* 'in the sanctuary.' If we add these numerals to the 23 completed payments, the figure comes to 27 'days' for Ἑρμω and 28 for Πετρω. It thus appears that presence 'in the sanctuary' (performing some task?) exempted these two individuals from several daily payments. Note too that the lower numeral for Ἑρμω may be explained by the punctuation mark (*viz.* :) following his entry, which could indicate that something more is owed.

Onomastics

It is clear from the text that the names are abbreviated and their endings missing; their grammatical case therefore cannot be determined. Johnston believes that this list is composed 'almost certainly all of slaves',[15] in part due to the presence of a number of clearly non-Greek onomastics: Ἀσθ, which may be Semitic[16]; Θραικ, obviously a Thracian ethnic name and common for slaves in Athens[17]; Κ.τυ, which suggests Thracian origins if we read the second letter as omicron, Celtic if we read it as alpha[18]; Κολχ, suggesting

11 For ownership marks on pottery see more generally M. Lang, *Graffiti and Dipinti* (Princeton 1976) = *The Athenian Agora* vol. XXI: 23-52.
12 Namely individuals 1, 4, 5, 7, 9, 11, 14, 19, 21, 25, 30, 32 in table I.
13 Johnston (n. 1): 299.
14 Johnston (n. 1): 304.
15 Johnston (n. 1): 307.
16 Johnston (n. 1): 300.
17 K. Vlassopoulos, 'Athenian slave names and Athenian social history' *ZPE* 175 (2010): 113-44 counts nine examples of Θρᾶιξ.
18 Johnston (n. 1): 301. Having only seen a photograph, I cannot profess complete certainty; but alpha appears to be far more likely: the letter seems to be formed in an angular manner, yet the cutter is perfectly capable of forming neat curves when needed (see e.g. the beta in Εὐβιω). Stephen Lambert (per. comm. December 2017) remarks to me that the cutter is skilled in forming letters, a judgement with which Thomas (n. 3, p. 30) concurs.

Colchian origins[19]; Ῥυνδα, Anatolian in flavour[20]; and Τιριβ, very likely reflecting the Persian name Tiribazos.[21] These names do indeed fit well with the hypothesis that the document concerns slaves; however, some caution ought to be exercised here. Most slaves in Athens did not bear ethnic or foreign names[22]; and even in Hellenistic documents where we possess sound evidence for slaves' foreign origins, the vast majority of these bore Greek names.[23] Such foreign and ethnic names usually provide a reasonable sense of the slave's ethnic origins when we know for other reasons that the individual is a slave. It is not safe, however, to use ethnic and foreign names as evidence for slave status where we do not have other reasons to suspect slave status; for such names can also be borne by freedmen and (occasionally) freeborn persons.[24] And it goes without saying that the standard Greek names (Ἑρμω-, Ἀπολλω-, Μελαν-, etc.) could be borne by individuals belonging to any of the known legal status groups. Regarding gender, although Johnston suspects mainly males, in several instances a female identity is also possible.[25] It is best, then, to reserve final judgement about the gender and status composition of the group. All that can be said with confidence is that the group is likely to be predominantly male, have a noticeable non-Greek element, and is probably lower-class.[26]

II. Interpretation

The individual who inscribed this text obviously knew its purpose, was writing an accounting record for his own needs, and did not feel the need to spell its context out in detail. In interpreting it, then, we are faced with a 'goodness of fit' exercise; that is, we must advance scenarios that can account for the production of this text, scenarios of a sort known from our contemporary Athenian sources (so as not to explain *ignotum per ignotius*), and test whether or not they comfortably accommodate the text's various features.[27]

---

19 On Colchian slaves see D. Braund & G.R. Tsetskhladze, 'The export of slaves from Colchis' *CQ* 39.1 (1989): 114-25.

20 Johnston (n. 1): 302. On Anatolian slaves see D.M. Lewis, 'Near Eastern slaves in classical Attica and the slave trade with Persian territories' *CQ* 61.1 (2011): 91-113; for the Hellenistic period, see idem 'Notes on slave names, ethnicity, and identity in Classical and Hellenistic Greece' *Studia Źródłoznawcze. U Schyłku Starożytności* 16 (2018): 169-99.

21 Johnston (n. 1): 302.

22 Vlassopoulos (n. 17) *passim.*

23 See Lewis (n. 20, 'Notes on slave names...'). I do not treat the Locrian manumissions in that article, but the same pattern holds for these: see T.V. Blavatskaja, 'Zur Geschichte der Sklavenhaltung in den nordwestlichen Gebieten Griechenlands' in T.V. Blavatskaja, E.S. Golubcova & A.I. Pavlovskaja, *Die Sklaverei in Hellenistischen Staaten im 3.-1. Jh. V. Chr.* (Wiesbaden 1972): 3-105, at pp. 60-62.

24 Lewis (n. 20, 'Notes on slave names...'): 174 n. 11 & n. 12.

25 O. Masson & L. Dubois, 'Bulletin Épigraphique' *Revue des Études Grecques* 100 (1987) pp. 342-3 no. 354 point to several such cases.

26 Johnston (n. 1) rightly points out (p. 302) that 'as long as we are unable to define the nature of the transactions involved we should not ignore the possibility of a mixed list, slave and free', but later asserts more confidently in his conclusion that the list is 'almost certainly all of slaves' due to his *misthos/apophora* theory. As I aim to show below, there are serious difficulties with both of these scenarios, and Johnston's earlier, more hesitant stance therefore ought to be retained.

27 My task is thus similar to the interpretation of another singular document, *SEG* L 276. On this document see E.M. Harris, 'Notes on a lead letter from the Athenian agora' *HSCP* 102 (2004): 157-70.

Misthosis

In testing the hypothesis that the text might record *misthos* payments to slaveowners for the hire of slaves, Johnston cites Xen. *Vect.* 4.14 and 4.23.[28] At 4.14 Xenophon writes that Nicias son of Niceratus owned a thousand slaves whom he rented out (ἐξεμίσθωσεν) in the mines to a man named Sosias the Thracian; in return Sosias paid a rent of an obol per capita per diem, and τὸν δ' ἀριθμὸν ἴσους ἀεὶ παρέχειν, a euphemistic way of saying that when any of these slaves died, Sosias was obligated to find a replacement. At 4.23 Xenophon engages in some calculations: if the Athenian state were to make slave mining at Laurion a public venture and buy 6,000 slaves, renting them out (like Nicias) for an obol per diem, then it could realise a profit of 60 talents per annum. His calculation can be broken down as follows:

60 talents = 360,000 drachms = 2,160,000 obols
2,160,000 obols ÷ 6,000 slaves = 360 obols per slave per annum

Xenophon is therefore reckoning that each state-owned slave would be working a 360-day year. This forcefully brings home a proverb noted by Aristotle (*Pol.* 1334a20), οὐ σχολὴ δούλοις. Here is an image of Athenian slavery at its most brutal and chrematistic, a grinding work-regime whose attendant attrition rate is nonchalantly figured into a calculation of projected annual profits.[29]

However, some reservations should be noted regarding the use of this calculation as our template for *misthosis*. Mine labour was not necessarily unskilled, and various aspects of the extraction and processing of silver required specialist knowledge[30]; but those slaves rented out by Nicias (whether or not he owned as many as a thousand of them[31]) clearly were being treated as a highly disposable, low-skilled workforce. The reason is obvious: no free person apart from the most desperate would work down Laurion's mineshafts, and thus there was no competition from free wage labour in this sector.[32] Profit margins could be adjusted (in line with very low slave prices) by entrepreneurs like Nicias working with economies of scale.[33] But our document comes from the city, where in most cases there was

28 Johnston (n. 1): 306.

29 On considerations of profit, loss, and risk see P. Christesen, 'Economic rationalism in fourth-century BC Athens', *G&R* 50 (2003): 31-56; M. Faraguna, 'Calcolo economico, archivi finanziari e credito nel mondo greco tra VI e IV sec. a.C.', in K. Verboven, K. Vandorpe & V. Chankowski (eds.), *Pistoi Dia Tèn Technèn. Bankers, Loans and Archives in the Ancient World: Studies in Honour of Raymond Bogaert* (Leuven, 2008): 33-57.

30 See T.E. Rihll, 'Skilled slaves and the economy: the silver mines of the Laurion', in H. Heinen (ed.) *Antike Sklaverei: Rückblick und Ausblick. Neue Beiträge zur Forschungsgeschichte und zur Erschließung der archäologischen Zeugnisse* (Stuttgart, 2010): 203-220.

31 The figure is so far above any parallels from the orators that several scholars have expressed doubts regarding its verity: see D.M. Lewis, *Greek Slave Systems in their Eastern Mediterranean Context, c. 800-146 BC* (Oxford, 2018): 171 for references and discussion. As E.M. Harris ('Homer, Hesiod, and the "Origins" of Greek slavery' *REA* 114.4 (2012): 345-66, at 359) points out, Lysias (19.47-8) remarks that many people believed Nicias' fortune to be far larger than it really was.

32 Cf. Lewis (n. 31): 271-4.

33 See P. Gauthier, *Un commentaire historique des Poroi de Xénophon* (Geneva & Paris, 1976): 155-6: Xenophon's plan to increase slaveholdings from 1,200 to 6,000 within 5 years implies a price of 158 drachms per slave; to do the same within 6 years implies a price of 195 drachms per slave. Cf. the slave prices assembled in K. Ruffing & H.-J. Drexhage, 'Antiken Sklavenpreise' in P. Mauritsch et al. (eds.)

some competition between free wage labour and slave labour. A better analogy is the Erechtheum accounts, where we can see free and slave labour working side by side; interestingly, wages here are paid at the same rate for the same work regardless of whether the worker is a citizen, metic, or slave (though legal title to slave wages lay with their owners).[34] The base rate of pay is around 5-6 obols per diem.[35] Even if we use the scenario sketched by Xenophon (with a mere 1 obol per diem trickling back to the owner) as our model, the economics hardly work, for a payment of half of that sum is an unbelievably tiny payment for a full work day. On the more reasonable assumption that slaves in the city who were rented out on a medium- or long-term basis earned around a drachma a day, the *misthos* hypothesis for our document is impossibly unprofitable, a mere twelfth of what a slave could plausibly earn per diem.

There is a further problem: the *misthos* hypothesis cannot easily account for our two instances of individuals 'EN TΩI IEP.' Johnston proposes an ingenious solution to this problem: a scholiast (*Anecdota Bekker* I 12) tells us that the Anakeion was a shrine of the Dioskouroi where slaves stood for hire; perhaps for these days Ἑρμω and Πετρω were at this shrine standing for hire as day labourers rather than working in medium- or longer-term employment.[36] Again, however, the economics do not work; for this explanation requires us to view sending a slave to the hire market as an *even less profitable* alternative than a medium- or longer-term lease bringing in a mere ½ obol per diem. In any of these scenarios, it is hard to see why a master would expend several hundreds of drachms on a slave for so paltry a daily return.[37]

Apophora

Johnston suggests an alternative to *misthosis*: the payments could represent instances of *apophora*, that is, a regular fixed payment that a slave operating independently paid to his or her master.[38] Here, Johnston cites Aeschin. 1.97: Timarchus' father bequeathed him a workshop of nine or ten slave shoemakers, each of whom paid him an *apophora* of 2 obols per diem, except the foreman, who paid 3 obols. Again, however, the same objection can be lodged as for the *misthosis* hypothesis: Timarchus' slaves were paying either four or six times as much *apophora* per diem as our individuals with their tiny ½ obol per diem payment.

We might rescue the hypothesis by conjecturing co-ownership and therefore a split *apophora* payment. The co-ownership of slaves is attested in e.g. Lysias 4, *On a Wounding by Intent* (§§ 10, 12, 16), and if we postulate such a scenario with an *apophora*-paying slave, we can whittle down the fee by assuming that what we are seeing does not represent

Antike Lebenswelten: Konstanz, Wandel, Wirkungsmacht: Festschrift für Ingomar Weiler zum 70. Geburtstag (Wiesbaden, 2008): 321-51, at pp. 321-3.

34 See Lewis (n. 31): 43-4.

35 See R.H. Randall, 'The Erechtheum workmen' *American Journal of Archaeology* 57.3 (1953): 199-210, esp. pp. 207ff. More broadly, see W.T. Loomis, *Wages, Welfare Costs and Inflation in Classical Athens* (Ann Arbor MI, 1998).

36 Johnston (n. 1): 306.

37 On slave prices in Athens see Lewis (n. 31): 170-1 for references and discussion. For hired labour see A. Fuks 'Κολωνὸς μίσθιος, labour exchange in classical Athens' *Eranos* 49 (1951): 171-3.

38 See Kamen (n. 2) *passim*.

the full fee, but the part-share that went to a co-owner. Yet this runs up against an obvious objection: why would a slaveholder co-own thirty-four slaves? Surely it would make sense to singly-own half as many slaves and avoid the attendant fuss. Yet the scenario is not impossible; we might consider the case of a workshop of slaves inherited by multiple heirs who decide to keep it as a unit and split the income. Yet this fails to explain the exemptions for being ΕΝ ΤΩΙ ΙΕΡ. Another way to work around the problem of the tiny size of the daily payment is to conjecture a scenario such as we find in Hypereides 1, *In Defence of Lycophron.* Here we find described a racket arranged between a sycophant named Ariston and a man named Theomnestus.[39] In order that Ariston could specialise in sycophancy full time, Theomnestus used the money that Ariston extorted from his victims to buy slaves, each of whom would pay Ariston an obol per diem (Hyp. 1.2). In such an arrangement our 34 individuals, paying ½ obol per diem each, could have furnished a joint daily contribution of 17 obols, *viz.* 2 drachms 5 obols, quite a handsome per diem wage. Yet to such a scenario one might object that (a) arrangements like this can hardly have been common, making the solution *a priori* an unlikely one; (2) such a solution cannot explain the recurrent numeral 28, the variant payments, the non-payers, Ηρακ's payment in pots, or why Ἑρμω and Πετρω were given exemptions for several days each for being ΕΝ ΤΩΙ ΙΕΡ. The *apophora* hypothesis on any of these permutations is thus possible, but nonetheless strains credulity.

A Private Association

Before venturing his *misthosis* and *apophora* hypotheses, Johnston proposed another possibility:

> A second possibility is that we have here a rare document from an eranos group, i.e. a record of contributions paid in by club members, in this case slaves, for some specific purpose, most likely manumission or cult expenses. Monthly contributions and expenditure are often mentioned in this context; preserved lists on stone are of a roughly similar character, mentioning those who contribute as well as those comparatively dormant. In detail, however, there are difficulties. If we think of a manumission fund, Herak's vases become problematic and there is no apparent reason for exemption being granted to those ›in the sanctuary‹. The sanctuary could indeed be the centre of the eranos-group, but on this, or any other interpretation the numerals are very worrying; there seems little that can intervene between the member of the group and his contribution. If the numerals are taken as days, the fact that they are noted at all is perplexing, not to mention the patchy ›attendance‹ of some members and the non-contributory ›attendance‹ of others; the daily contribution of half an obol also seems very high. If the numerals are not days, we again face the problem of the regular appearance of 28.[40]

Although Johnston abandoned this hypothesis, a fresh appraisal is warranted; for the context of private associations can account for many of this document's singular features, and the sticking points that led Johnston to discount this line of enquiry can be accounted

---

39 On sycophancy in Athens see F.D. Harvey, 'The sycophant and sycophancy: vexatious redefinition' in P. Cartledge, P. Millett & S. Todd (eds.) *Nomos: Essays in Athenian Law, Politics and Society* (Cambridge 1993): 103-21.

40 Johnston (n. 1): 305-6.

for. If we suppose that our text derives from a private association that was pooling money towards some common goal – a sacrifice or festival for example – then a good parallel can be found in a contemporary Attic document, *IG* II^2 1361, a decree of the *orgeones* of Bendis.[41] In this decree the association's *hieropoioi* (the club officials who organise the sacrifice) must collect two drachms per member during the month of Thargelion to go towards the association's annual festival and sacrifice. Lines 16-20 state:

> ἀγο[ρὰν δὲ κ]αὶ [ξ]ύ[λλ]ογον ποιεῖν τοὺς ἐπιμελητὰς καὶ τοὺς ἱεροποιοὺς ἐν τῶι ἱερ-
> [ῶι] πε[ρὶ τῶν κοιν]ῶν τῆι δευτέραι ἱσταμένου τοῦ μηνὸς ἑκάστου. vv διδόναι δὲ
> [τοῖς ἱ]εροποιοῖς εἰς τὴν θυσίαν : ⊢⊢ : δραχμὰς ἕκαστον τῶν ὀργεώνων οἷς μέτεστι
> [το]ῦ [ἱε]ροῦ τοῦ Θαργηλιῶνος πρὸ τῆς ἕκτης ἐπὶ δέκα, ὃς δ' ἂν ἐπιδημῶν Ἀθήνη-
> [σι] καὶ ὑγιαίνων μὴ συνβάλληται, ὀφειλέτω : ⊢⊢ : ἱερὰς τῆι θε[ῶι].

The supervisors and the *hieropoioi* shall arrange an assembly and convocation in the sanctuary to (discuss) the association's affairs on the second day of each month. *Vacat.* Each of the *orgeones* who have a claim in the sanctuary shall give to the *hieropoioi* 2 drachmae during Thargelion for the sacrifice, before the 16th day (of the month). Whoever is at home in Athens and in good health but does not contribute, owes 2 drachmae, sacred to the goddess. (tr. Kloppenborg & Ascough)

This 2-drachma fee for the month of Thargelion provides a close parallel for the apparent fee of just over 2 drachms per 'payer' in our text, (probably) in the month of Hekatombaion, and shows that Johnston's belief that the fee is too high for an association is unwarranted: it need not be seen as a daily fee paid year-round. It is also worth underscoring Jones' view that the *orgeones* of Bendis lay at the poorer end of the spectrum of attested associations.[42] That parallel would fit with our onomastics, which suggest low-status individuals. One might note as a further parallel *IG* II^2 2940, a fourth-century list of individuals (probably composed of slaves) who constituted an association of *eranistai* operating in and around Laurion, and perhaps dedicated to the worship of the Anatolian god Men (if the restoration is correct).[43]

Nevertheless, as Johnston points out, the figure 28 (and variants thereof) present problems. The Athenians did not have months of 28 days, but 'full' months of 30 days and 'hollow' months of 29 days; Hekatombaion should have 30 days.[44] A straightforward

41 On this group see N.F. Jones, *The Associations of Classical Athens: The Response to Democracy* (New York & Oxford, 1999): 256-62; I. Arnaoutoglu, 'Cult associations and politics: worshipping Bendis in Classical and Hellenistic Athens' in V. Gabrielsen & C.A. Thomsen (eds.) *Private Associations and the Public Sphere* (Copenhagen 2015): 25-56.

42 Jones (n. 41): 260-261: 'Taken together, these particulars suggest the absence of an endowment and, again, of wealthy benefactors by the earnings or generosity of whom the association might perpetuate itself. Rather, the impression is left of dependence upon a trickle of small dues and fines, with cash reserves so small that the association cannot finance its annual festival without collecting a small fee (or equivalent fine) from its entire membership.'

43 The restoration is far from certain: see the remarks of H. Pleket and R. Stroud in *SEG* XXIX 163. For *eranistai* as members of an association, see C. Thomsen, 'The eranistai of classical Athens' *GRBS* 55.1 (2015): 154-75. See also M. Faraguna, 'Diritto, economia, sociètà: riflessioni su *eranos* tra èta omerica e mondo ellenistico' in B. Legras (ed.) *Tranferts culturels et droits dans le monde grec et hellénistique* (Paris 2012): 129-53.

44 B.D. Meritt, *The Athenian Year* (Berkeley & Los Angeles, 1961): 12-13.

solution can be proposed, however, if we think of the payments being organised not around a 'month' of 28 days, but around the figure of 2 drachms 2obols per member. What if, like the *orgeones* of Bendis, this putative association decided to pool resources for a sacrifice or festival, and the group's treasurer came up with a sum of 2dr 2ob per person, a figure based on the projected total cost of the sacrifice (or festival) divided by the number of members of the group? For an association of poor individuals, this would have been a sum not to be sniffed at; and so the treasurer could have made subscription to the fee more manageable by breaking it down into daily contributions of ½ obol which, paid into the common pot, would eventually amount to the required fee of 2dr 2ob per person. The figure 28, then, can be seen as an incidental figure, the product of a calculation for breaking down the overall fee into affordable daily payments. Those who paid more (*viz.* Γαστρ) might then have been the more public-spirited members of the group (or perhaps they had outstanding debts to the association from an earlier event). But what about those who underpaid or whose payment was missing?

A common genre of inscription relating to associations is the honorary decree for officers of the association who had done a good job.[45] In some of these, one of the virtues for which that the honorand is praised concerns dealing admirably with the association's funds. For example, *IG* II[2] 1323 honours Theon for his scrupulousness and promptness in dealing with funds when he was treasurer of an association of *thiasotai*. In *IG* II[2] 1329 the *orgeones* of the Mother of the Gods honour Chaireas for his public-spiritedness towards the association, especially during his term as secretary, and praise his consistent contribution of funds (line 10) and his contribution of interest-free loans to the association when the treasurer was absent (line 17). In *SEG* XXIV 156 a priest is honoured by *thiasotai* for making sure that the *eranos* (common fund) was always full by promply paying over any donations that were deposited with him. So our text could fit into a context where an association's *tamias* or *hieropoios* was chasing up members to pay their fees for an annual sacrifice: the text then records what each member owes; some had paid up in full, others had not, and one had delivered a load of pots in kind, perhaps as a bond whilst he scraped the money together for his contribution. (If Ηρακ was indeed the author of the text and treasurer for this group, perhaps he exercised more effort in chasing up the payments of the other members than setting a good example himself).[46] One can cite as a parallel *Agora* 16: 161 (3rd c BC), an inscribed list of debtors to an association: the fact that the members went to the trouble of inscribing this list of debtors shows how seriously they took the problem of members lagging in paying what they owed. So on this interpretation, the presence of 'non-payers', or perhaps 'tardy payers' is not all that surprising. Theophrastus, indeed, lampoons various attitudes to *eranos* contributions – grudging payment, for

45 I. Arnaoutogou, *Thusias Heneka Kai Sunousias: Private Religious Associations in Hellenistic Athens* (Athens, 2003): 115-118.

46 Benedikt Eckhardt suggests to me another possibility: that Ηρακ's contribution comprised the crockery needed for the ceremony in the sanctuary. Alternatively, Johnston (n. 1): 302-3 argues that the total value of this crockery may have been equivalent to the 'full payment' of 2 drachms 2 obols.

example (*Char.* 15.7), or boasting about one's contribution (*Char.* 23.6). We ought not, then, to be surprised to see inconsistency in payment.[47]

What about discounted payments for Ἑρμω and Πετρω, whose entries on the text bear the phrase EN ΤΩΙ ΙΕΡ? This can be paralleled too: Migeotte has recently drawn attention to a document from Callatis on the Black Sea (*IScM* III 35, 3rd c BC), where several of an association's subscribers offer days of labour instead of monetary payments.[48] Perhaps our individuals 'in the sanctuary' also did not have to pay for the days in which they were employed in sacred duties, their labour representing a fungible alternative to daily payments. Note too the mention of a meeting ἐν τῶι ἱερ[ῶι] in the decree of the *orgeones* of Bendis (lines 16-17) and instructions in lines 8-9 for the upkeep of ἡ οἰκία καὶ τὸ ἱερόν. It is customary in decrees of praise passed by associations in Attica that the document be inscribed and set up in the association's shrine.[49] The list of members with outstanding fees in *Agora* 16:161 is likewise to be set up ἐν τῶι ἱερῶι (line 7). For some poorer associations it was necessary to rent a plot of land or use a public shrine, or a shrine belonging to a wealthier association.[50] As we can see in *IG* II^2 1324 and 2499, these sites might be a little dilapidated and require some work to set in order for the celebration; and this sort of work may explain the discounts to Ἑρμω and Πετρω in our document: they had to take time off work to prepare the shrine, and therefore were not charged contribution fees for the days when they were working ἐν τῶι ἱερ<ῶι>.

A variant explanation could lie in a subscription[51] by a private association for e.g. the repair of a shrine, which has some attractive parallels. This would explain the variant payments rather better than the aforementioned scenario; but it does not account as well for the consistent 2 drachma 2 obol payments. As noted above, there is a close parallel for discounts for those working ἐν τῶι ἱερ<ῶι> in *IScM* III 35. Another variation on the private association theme requires a dramatic rethink of the meaning of the first numeral; that is, to discount the notion that the collection is for a sacrifice or festival, and to view our document as an account for the month of Hekatombaion of a year-round collection aimed at reaching 28 drachms per member per annum.[52] The figure of 2 drachms 2 obols is exactly one twelfth of 28 drachms. The advantages of this interpretation are several: (i) it does not

47 In these instances in Theophrastus the *eranos* is a loan, not an association fund; but attitudes towards both kinds of contribution may have been similar. On collecting fees see also Arnaoutoglou (n. 45): 101.

48 L. Migeotte, 'Les souscriptions dans les associations privées' in P. Fröhlich & P. Hamon (eds.) *Groupes et associations dans les cites grecques (IIIe siècle av. J.-C. – IIe siècle apr. J.-C.)* (Geneva, 2013): 113-27, at 116.

49 e.g. *IG* II^2 1252+999.16-17; 1253.11; 1256.11-12; 1263.26; 1277.35-6; 1278.14 (restored); 1284.17-18; 33-4; 1292.27; 1297.5; 1298.11; 1314.23-4; 1315.27-8; 1316.21-2; 1324.27-31; 1325.31; 1326.50; 1327.27; 1328.20; 1329.29-30; 1335.6-7; 1343.39-40; 2499.41-2; *SEG* 2:9.9; *IRhamnous* II 59.29-30; *AM* 66:228 no. 4.20.

50 For associations renting out their shrines see Arnaotouglou (n. 45): 110. On association shrines in Athens, see J. Steinhauer, *Religious Associations in the Post-Classical Polis* (Stuttgart, 2014): 118-21; C.A. Thomsen, 'The place of honour: association sanctuaries and inscribed honours in late Classical and early Hellenistic Athens', forthcoming in A. Cazemier & S. Skaltsa (eds), *Private Associations in Context: Rethinking Associations and Religion in Context.*

51 This was suggested to me by Edward Harris, who further suggests that the epsilon could denote ἐπέδωκε.

52 This suggestion – and what follows in this paragraph – I owe wholly to Christian Amitzbøll Thomsen.

require our *tamias* to be keeping a constant tally of daily payments, but instead collect just one monthly payment (somewhat like the 2 drachms paid by members of the *orgeones* of Bendis in Thargelion, but in our case the payment would be monthly rather than once per annum); (ii) it rids us of the need to explain the figure 28 in terms of either an impossibly short month, or a calculation aimed at producing, through ½ obol per diem payments, the figure of 2 drachms 2 obols, which is open to criticism on the grounds of being overly elaborate and, again, requiring a busybody *tamias* collecting money on a daily basis. As in the previous scenario, the lower payments from ῾Ερμω and Πετρω can be accommodated by them providing labour ἐν τῶι ἱερ<ῶι> instead. The reason for irregular payments for Ἀπολλω, Ἀμπελι, and Ηρακ remains a problem; Christian Thomsen has suggested to me a discounted fee for members of more slender means. Another attractive aspect of this hypothesis is that Hekatombaion is the first month of the Athenian year, and thus the regular 2 drachms 2 obols as the most frequent second numeral would represent in our text the projected first instalment; perhaps in the accounts for the following month, Metageitnion, the next instalment would be added to the previous one, thus slowly climbing across the year towards the projected 28 drachma total until the second numeral tallied with the first.

At any rate, if all 34 of our individuals had contributed what they owed per annum (on the assumption that this is what the first numeral indicates), then our putative association was in better financial health than the previous scenario based on the model of the *orgeones* of Bendis allows; for its annual income would then be over 1,000 drachms. This would not place it in the top tier of private associations, such as the *orgeones* of Amynus and Asclepius, which on one occasion spent 1,000 drachms on golden crowns to honour philanthropic members (*IG* II^2 1252 + 999); but it would be rather better off than the poorest private associations. This scenario is still compatible with our foreign-looking (and possibly servile) names: 2 drachms 2 obols per month would be a serious financial commitment for lower-class individuals, but the sum is not implausibly onerous.

Conclusion

Once we realise that the several servile-seeming names in this document do not need to be accounted for in terms of a group wholly composed of slaves, we need not be locked into an explanation based on *misthosis* or *apophora*, which as I have argued are hardly credible based on the very small size of the 'daily payments.' The size of the group, the amount and consistency of the payment in thirteen of the entries, and especially the mention of a shrine and discounts to those individuals working (?) there, all fit better with a scenario involving a private association. That is not to say that this line of interpretation is without its problems. However, if this article manages to rekindle interest in and debate over this enigmatic and unique document, I will count that as success enough. If the hypothesis that this text was produced by a private association is indeed correct, then it provides us with a unique insight into the accounting practices of such groups, and perhaps a rare example of a mixed-status association at quite an early point in the history of private associations in the Greek world.

Graeco-Roman Egypt

Headers for lists and accounts in ancient documents and in modern editions

Willy Clarysse, Leuven

Accounts and lists form a large group among the papyri and ostraca. A quick search in TM resulted in 5607 Greek accounts and 3820 lists. There are, however, numerous overlaps. The German word "Verzeichnis", for instance, used in the HGV and in TM, can indicate both a list (e.g. Verzeichnis von Einwohnern, von Inhabern von Grundstücken) or an account (Abrechnung; Verzeichnis; Verzeichnis von Ausgaben; Verzeichnis von Personen mit nachfolgenden Summen).

1) The headers of modern editions

The papyrological terminology for the types of texts we are discussing in this conference is created by the editors, who usually group their texts according to types (contracts, letters, receipts, with "accounts and lists" often at the end of the documentary texts) and/or provide each text with a header. These headers are chosen by individual editors and there is no uniform terminology in TM nor in HGV because the online databases simply copy the terms used by the editors. A typical example of editorial practice is provided by the table of contents of P. Bingen (accounts and lists are underlined):

27. Ptolemaic tax <u>account</u>
31. <u>Elenco</u> di indigeni con connotati personali
36. Ptolemaic apomoira <u>account</u>
38. <u>Abrechnung</u>
42. <u>List</u> of names
43. <u>Conto</u>
71. Aufstellung über Personen und Land
72. Aufstellung über Personen und Beträge in Weizen
76. <u>Conto</u>
77. Registre de navires marchands
79. Ausgaben für Faustina
99-101. <u>Liste</u> de noms
109. Registro di ekphoria
116. Greek <u>account</u> on a clay tablet
117. <u>List</u> of household items
119. <u>Account</u> of expenditures in wheat
120. <u>Account</u> of expenditures in money
127. <u>Abrechnung</u> über Kornverteilung an die Bettler
135. <u>List</u> of payments

136. Abrechnung über Getreidelieferungen
137. Verzeichnis von Ausgaben
139. Verzeichnis über Getreideablieferung
140. Verzeichnis von Landbesitz
142-144. Namensliste
145. Zahlungsliste
146. Verzeichnis von Abgaben

Table 1. P. Bingen headers

The lack of interest in terminology is also visible in the recent *Handbook of Papyrology*, where B. Palme wrote a chapter on "the range of documentary texts", with a short paragraph called "accounts" (Palme 2009, 370-371). Here he speaks about "an extensive group of private documents (where are the administrative accounts in this typology?), described broadly as economic texts, includes accounts of all kinds, receipts, orders for payment, proofs of banking, lists of incoming and outgoing money or goods, transport lists and much more." Different types of documents (such as receipts and orders for payment) are here lumped together with the accounts and lists. One also wonders what are "lists of payments", "Verzeichnis von Ausgaben/Abgaben" (items 137 and 146 in the list above), "lists of incoming and outgoing money", "Zahlungsliste" (*P. Vindob. Salomons* 17-18) and "Abrechnungsliste" (*SB* VIII 9697) if not accounts.

My study starts from a database of all lists, accounts, registers and inventories, which do have a header in the Greek text [http://www.trismegistos.org/tmcorpusdata/7/]. I excluded from the present study headers consisting of a date, a place (*SB* X 10220), the name of a person or a group (*BGU* VI 1495: Πτολεμαίου παρουσίας; *SB* XXII 15602 : οἱ ἀπομίναντες; *P. Strasb.* VII 651 : κατοίκων; *SB* XVI 12379 : σκοπελάριοι; *CPR* XXII 24 : ἀτελῶν; *O. Mich.* I 356 : οἱ ἀπελθόντες), the name of an item (*P. Cairo Zen.* I 59004 : ἀλεύρων; *P.Cairo Zen.* IV 59771 : τὰ ἀγορασθέντα πρόβατα; *P. Cairo Zen.* V 59850 : σησάμου; *CPR* X 51 : ἰχθύες) or even a number, though I kept these in a separate (but incomplete) database. In many cases the word for "account" is omitted, as e.g. in *P. Cairo Zen.* IV 59542, which is introduced by παρὰ Ξένωνος εἰς τοὺς ἵππους, but here it is identified on the back as λόγος παρὰ Ξένωνος (and therefore included). The database underlying the present study is limited to list-like documents which identify in their header (or, rarely, on the back) the type of document, e.g. λόγος, γραφή, γνῶσις, βρέουιον, but also ἀναλώματα, δαπανήματα, λήμματα, or (ἀπ)έχω and ἀπέδωκα. This resulted in some 1200 texts, i.e. nearly 13 % of the accounts and lists (9400 items) bear a header indicating the type of text. Given that there are many overlaps between the two categories and that maybe a quarter of our texts have lost their first lines, this is number is higher than I expected.

Starting from this material, I have tried to bring some order into the different types of documents. The two main categories are accounts and lists. This distinction is for instance the basis of two chapters in *O. Bodl.* When I made this distinction explicit, I had to decide for every text and every text type to which category it belonged. I started of course from the typology of the editors, but it was soon clear that their decision to call a text "account" or "list" was sometimes subjective. This is illustrated by a few examples in table 2.

ed. princ.	type	other edition	type
P. Cairo Zen. I 59014	porterage account	*SB* XXVI 16505 and HGV	Liste von Transportgütern
SB XVI 12822	Abrechnung	*P. Gen.* IV 204	liste de sommes dues pour l'impôt
P. Strasb. V 320	liste de contribuables	*P. Sakaon* 8	account of meat
P. Tebt. I 96	list of arrears	Berkeley homepage	account of arrears
P. Tebt. IV 1126	list	*P. Tebt.* IV 1128	account

Table 2. Different headers in different editions of the same or similar texts

P. Bingen 150 is called a "Coptic account", but the header ⲧⲉⲅⲛⲱⲥⲓⲥ ⲛⲉⲥⲟⲩ is translated as "the list of wheat". The text looks indeed like a shipping list, but as there is a total of artabae at the end, I have classified it as an account.

By trial and error I gradually defined the difference between lists and accounts : for an account one needs at least figures. But not every enumeration with figures is automatically an account. An account also needs a common denominator, which allows the user to count the number of items. Thus one can have an account of oxen, of pigs, of fishes delivered, of requisitioned donkeys, of workmen on a building plot, of pastries, but not an account of cloths, ceramics and metal objects mixed together. There is, however, a way to count different objects as if they are not a single category : by giving them a common denominator, usually by adding a price in money or in grain. This allows to count different objects together, though the price alone is not enough to speak of an account : there must be the intention to count the total value of the things enumerated. Therefore dowry lists (with value added) or registers of land (no totalisation of the areas of the plots) are not considered by me as accounts.

Often a text can therefore be recognised as an account because it has a total at the end (or at the beginning), or when it contains the words "income and expense" (λήμματα, ἀναλώματα, δαπανήματα). In most cases it is not too difficult to make the distinction between simple lists and accounts. The following table shows 30 of about 100 instances where I have corrected the headers of the editors. Some problems remain, however, especially with fragmentary texts.

typology of the editor	reference	my typology	Greek header
Liste von Einnahmen und Ausgaben	*CPR* VIII 22	account, money	λόγος λημμάτων καὶ ἀναλωμάτων
Liste von Ausgaben	*P. Amst.* 76	account, money	ἔκθεσις
Ausgabenliste	*SB* X 10742	account, fragmentary	λόγος δαπανῶν
Ausgabenliste	*SB* XVI 12291	account, money	δόσις
Ausgabenliste	*P. Strasb.* II 119	account, money	διαστολὴ τῶν διδομένων
Liste von Zahlungen	*P. Amst.* 85	account, money, end total	γνῶσις (recto), λόγος (verso)

Liste von Zahlungen	*SB* XX 14216	account, money, end total	λόγος τῶν δοθέντων
Liste von Zahlungen	*SB* XX 14537	account, money	λόγος
Liste von Zahlungen	*SB* X 10551	account, money	λόγος δραχμῶν
Namenliste mit Abgaben	*P. Köln* XIII 533	account, grain, with end total	Βουσίρεως δημοσίων
Liste mit Namen und Zahlungen	*SB* XX 14077	account, money, with initial and end total	*no header*
List of expenses	*P. L. Bat.* XXV 79	account, grain	γνῶσις τῶν ἀναλωμάτων
List of expenses	*P. Kellis* I 53 and 54	account, money	λόγος ἀναλωμάτων
Liste von verschuldetem Wein	*P. Amst.* 78	account, wine (in dipla)	λόγος ὧν χρεωστοῦσιν οἱ ἀμπελουργοί
Steuerliste	*P. Münch.* III 139	account, money, end total	εἴσπραξις χρυσίνους
Liste von Steuerschulden	*P. Amst.* 84	account, money	*header lost*
Liste de sommes dues pour l'impôt	*P. Gen.* IV 204	account, money	ἔκθεσις
List of payments in kind	*P. Mich.* VI 376	account, grain	εἴσπραξις
Auflistung von Weizenmengen	*SB* XX 14700	account, grain	γνῶσις σίτου ἀρταβῶν
List of festal payments	*P. Oxy.* LXVII 4617	account, money	γνῶσις ἑορτικῶν
Liste von Festbeiträgen	*SB* XIV 12130	account, wine, with end total	λόγος ἑορτικῶν
Auflistung von Zahlungen	*SB* XVIII 13145	account, money	ἔκθεσις
Auflistung von Kosten	*SB* XXII 15332	account, money	λόγος ἔργων
Einnahmeliste	*BGU* XVII 2724a	account, grain, with end total	γνῶσις σίτου
Zahlungsliste	*Eirene* III 13	account	γνῶσις πραγμάτων
Aufstellung	*P. Louvre* I 48	account	λόγος ἀναλωμάτων
account of oxen	*P. Mil. Vogl.* III 148-149	list of oxen	ἀπεργασία βοικῶν
account of requisitioned animals	*O. Kellis* 103	list of requisitoned donkeys	λόγος ἀγγαρίας
account of arrears of oil	*O. Kellis* 98	list of arrears (no figures)	ἔκθεσις περισσοτέρου ἐλαίου
compte de patisseries	*P. Strasb.* V 339	list (no value)	λόγος
private account	*P. Wash.* I 58	inventory, with value of the items	λόγος σκευῶν τῶν εὑρεθέντων ἐν κληρώσει of NN

Table 3. Headers in the editio princeps different from my typology

The database now lists 825 accounts and 358 lists. Fourty-seven texts of similar type remained unclassified and there are some overlaps. Part of the unclassified texts were too fragmentary to be determined, others are registers of landed property. Though lists of owners of land [there are 28 of them] often contain figures of the area in possession of a person or even of the produce of the land, they are nowhere considered accounts by the editors (see e.g. the *P. Bingen* listing in table 1 above).

Among the lists a special mention is due to inventories [33 in the database]. These offer a complete enumeration of all possessions of an individual or an institution at a certain point in time (dowry lists at marriage, lists of inherited property, lists of books in a library). Sometimes the value of the items listed is added, but they clearly are not accounts.

Among the 837 accounts 478 are accounts of money, 185 accounts of grain and 197 accounts where neither money nor grain were involved. In 70 cases the account registers both income and expense, in 168 they deal with income alone and in 208 with expenses alone. Since income for one person, group or institution usually means expense for other parties, it is not always clear what category is meant. Datives of personal names or groups are counted as expenses; παρὰ NN is listed as income; but what to do when the name is in the nominative? In a document of the administration taxes are income, in a private document they are expenses; therefore the type of document is not always clear to the modern reader.

Both lists and accounts can be private or official (emanating from or directed to a governmental office). There are many more private lists, but only a minority has a header.

	private	**official**	**estate**
account	298	357	70
list	87	198	8

Table 4. Accounts and lists. Private, official and estate documents.

2) Headers in the Greek papyri

The most common header by far is the word λόγος, which is found in 552 out of 1156 instances, from the Ptolemaic up to the Arab period. Even in Coptic this is a common header[1]. The word is used for both lists and accounts, which means that the translation given by the editors ought to be checked : English or French have no word for the two, like German Verzeichnis.

1 *P. Köln ägypt.* II 62, Coptic text written on paper is an account of wine (λογος ⲛⲏⲣⲡ) dated to the 10th cent. AD.

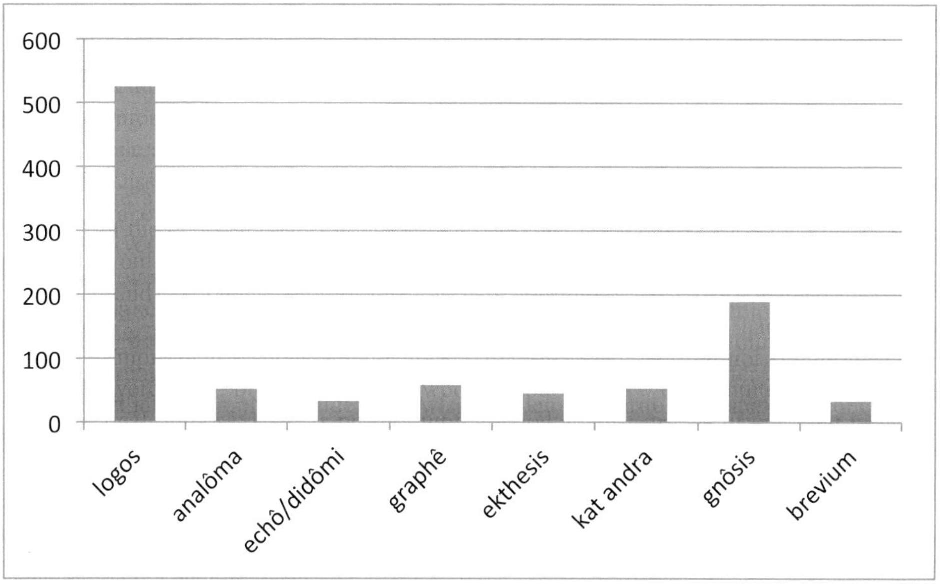

graph 1 : The main Greek words used as headers for lists and accounts

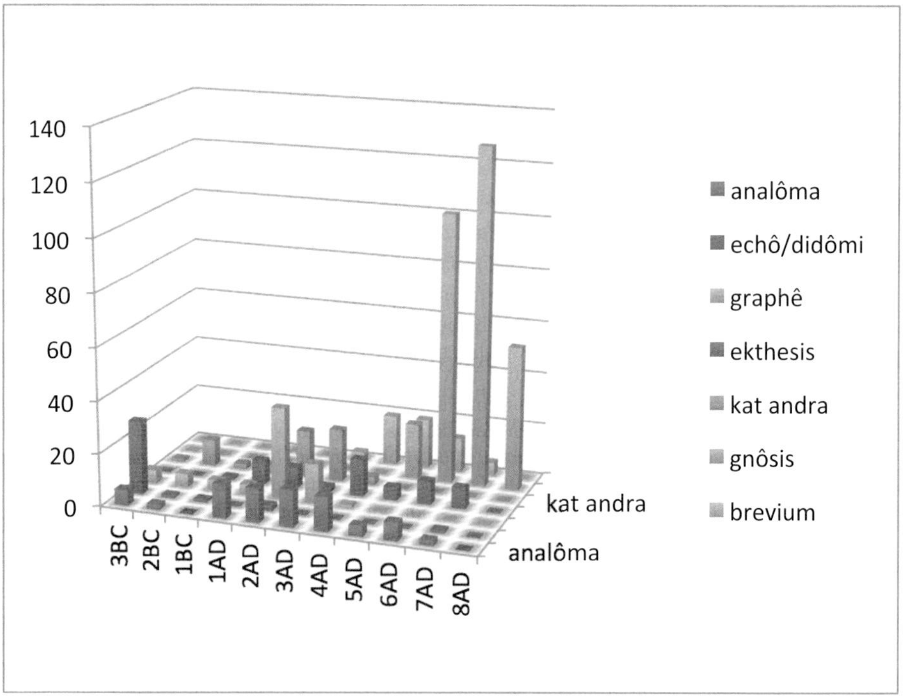

graph 2 : The main Greek words used as headers in lists and accounts (omitting λόγος)

The words ἀνάλωμα (rarely δαπάνη) and λῆμμα are often put in the genitive at the beginning of an account. There are 52 instances of ἀνάλωμα, of which 32 λόγος ἀναλώματος, 5 δαπάνη of which 2 λόγος δαπάνης, 58 λῆμμα of which 42 λόγος λήμματος. In many cases λόγος is no doubt to be understood, as also with expressions as σιτικός etc. These are certainly accounts, with indication of income and expense.

Logos is also to be understood with κατ' ἄνδρα [there are 56 κατ' ἄνδρα items in the database], though this expression is never explicitly combined with λόγος (once with σωματισμός)[2]. The expression κατ' ἄνδρα clearly belongs to the administrative language in the Ptolemaic and Roman period. The earliest examples are found in the second cent. BC, the term occurs repeatedly in the archive of Menches (late 2nd cent. BC), also as a header for land surveys. It disappears after the third century AD, with only three fourth cent. examples, one of which is uncertain[3].

In 12 cases ἀπαιτήσιμον (with a variant ἀπαίτησις) is used as a header, four times combined with κατ' ἄνδρα[4]. Though *LSJ* translates the word as "list of land subject to dues" it can indicate all kinds of stately dues. In all cases amounts in money or grain are mentioned and we have listed the *apaitesima* as accounts rather than simple lists.

In a few instances accounts are introduced by a verb (ἔχω and ἔχει 25, δίδωμι, ἐδόθη 10). This is not a real header, like λόγος or βρέουιον. Expressions with ἔχω are only found in Ptolemaic texts (mainly in the Zenon and Dryton archives), those with δίδωμι continue sporadically into the Arab period (e.g. *P. Oxy.* XVI 2045).

ἔκθεσις

With a single exception, which may belong to the very end of the first cent. BC (*P. Tebt.* II 573 descr.) all 45 examples of this word date from the Roman to the Arab period. Editors often translate it as "arrears", probably on the basis of Preisigke's *Fachwörterbuch*, p. 7, but as a header it simply means "list"[5]. Forty out of 45 instances are clearly accounts, but there are also some lists of cloths without valuation in money, which are therefore lists. The term comes from the administrative language (31 out of 45 texts are official and none is clearly private).

Γραφή occurs 63 times as a header. In the Ptolemaic period it is used for any kind of list or inventory (e.g. *P. Dryton* 38), in the Roman period it is the usual word for administrative lists of persons, especially lists of liturgists and lists/inventories of priests and possessions of the temple [γραφὴ ἱερέων καὶ χειρισμοῦ][6]. In the private sphere the word is used both for

2 *P. Eirene* IV 13 (λόγος κατ' ἄνδρα χωματικῶν ἔργων), *BGU* I 141 (σωματισμὸς κατ' ἄνδρα ἀργυρικῶν).

3 *P. Sakaon* 8 (AD 309); 4 (AD 336). *SB* XX 14468 is dated AD IV by Sijpesteijn, but the names and the money figures (drachmas and obols) rather point to a date before AD 275.

4 *BGU* II 659; *BGU* XIII 2282; *SB* XIV 11505; *Stud. Pal.* XXII 88.

5 Even in the Adrados, *Diccionario griego-espanol* 6 (2002), s.v. ἔκθεσις the word is translated as "lista de atrasos de pago pendientes o sumas adeudadas al fisco". In LSJ the meaning "list" is mentioned sub VIII, with one single example from the papyri.

6 Cf. F. Burkhalter, *Le mobilier des sanctuaires d'Egypte*, ZPE 59 (1985), p. 123-134.

lists and for accounts [*SB* VI 9245; *P. Lond.* VII 1994; *PSI* IV 427, with a total on the back], but in the public sphere it became a terminus technicus for listing groups of persons with a special status[7]. Ἀναγραφή is used 12 times from the Ptolemac to the Arab period. In at least five cases it clearly points to an inventory[8], but it can also be a list of fishermen (*P. Oxy.* LXIV 4440) or an account of expenses (*P. Lond.* IV 1447).

In the later Roman period two new words make their appearance : γνῶσις and the Latin loanword βρέουιον. Only the former also makes it into Coptic.

Γνῶσις (190 examples) is not attested before the fifth century[9], the earliest dated example is even sixth century (AD 514; *P. Cairo Masp.* I 67014). Since lists of the Byzantine period are normally undated and palaeographical datings are often vague (two centuries timespan or even more) the graph above probably mispresents the real situation and gnôsis becomes common only from the sixth century onwards (texts dated AD 400 - 599 are divided over the fifth and sixth centuries in the graph, but no doubt most of them belong to the sixth century). The word remains popular up to the eight century, and is also used in Coptic, both for accounts (e.g. *SB* I 5303) and lists (e.g. *P. Bingen* 150; *CPR* XII 6), though editors tend to prefer the translation "list" even in cases where gnôsis is certainly an account[10].

The Latin loanword βρέβιον / βρέουιον is less common (33 instances)[11]. The earliest examples date from the late third or early fourth century, the time of the tetrarchy, when many Latin loanwords entered the administrative language. Again the word indicates both lists and accounts; in the archive of Abinnaeus it is used as an official term, but some of the fourth century examples are private (estates). Most occurrences date to the fourth century and in the fifth century the word seems to fall out of use (only two uncertain examples of the 6th century, no examples in Coptic). With three exceptions (an inscription from Chalkis = *Sylloge* II 905.17, the *Vita Chrysostomi* of Palladius 3.90 and two passages in the codex of Iustinianus) all examples given in Adrados' lexicon are from the papyri.

---

7 Therefore in the report of a village scribe *PSI Communicazione* 6 12.3 the general [λόγος] μηχανῶν is a more likely supplement the the editor's [γραφὴ] μηχανῶν.

8 E.g. ἀναγραφὴ σκευῶν in *BGU* XVI 2669 (BC 21-AD 5), *Stud. Pal.* XX 67 (AD 100-299) and *P. Ryl.* IV 627 (AD 300-325); ἀναγραφὴ τῶν ἁγίων κειμηλίων in *Wilcken, Chrest.* 135 and *P. Prag.* II 178 (AD 400-599). For inventories, see W. Clarysse, *Inventories in Coptic churches and monasteries*, in : K. Vandorpe - W.Clarysse (edd.), *Archives and inventories in the Eastern Mediterranean*, Contactforum Koninklijke Vlaamse Academie, Brussels 2006, pp. 85-93.

9 Three instances are dated AD 300 - 699 in TM: *SB* I 4759 B, 4888, 5303 (all three dated by Wessely, to the "byzantine period" and certainly 5th century at the earliest).

10 The meaning "list" seems clear in an important inscription from Perge, dated about AD 500, quoting a speech by the emperor Anastasius. The text is now published in Gephyra 14 (2017), p. 133-212, see Bull. ép. 2018.451 : γνῶσις ἀνδρῶν καὶ ἀννωνῶν ὑποτεταγμένων τῷ θείῳ σέρμωνι.

11 For this word, see most recently A. Maravela-Solbakk, *ZPE* 149 (2004), p. 184, who refers to *Lex. Lat. Lehnwörter* II, 207-210.

The word ὑπομνηστικόν, usually meaning memorandum[12] sometimes also heads a list or account, though perhaps the term only gets this meaning from the context[13]. See for instance *P. Jena* II 37 (ὑπομνηστικὸν σκευῶν ἀγορασθέντων μοι ἐν Ἀλεξανδρείᾳ; AD 500-599); *P. Fouad* 74 (list of objects to buy in Alexandreia, introduced by a short memorandum, followed by the usual οὕτως), P. *Iand.* IV 67 (called a ratiuncula by the editor; the header † σὺν θ(εῷ) ὑπομνηστικό(ν) is followed by a paragraphos and a list of items; *P. Mich.* XIV 684 (a list or cloths, perhaps an inventory, introduced by ⳩ ὑπομνιστικὼν εἱματίων (l. ὑπομνηστικὸν ἱματίων); *P. Oxy.* X 1343, a list of cloths, styled [ὑ]πομ\ν/ηστικ(όν) on the verso.

3. The lay-out of accounts and lists

Papyrus texts are usually written in *scriptio continua* and features of lay-out are the exception rather than the rule. Contracts for instance go on without interruption from beginning to end, letters and petitions are often marked by a separate last line with the final greeting formula (ἔρρωσο, ἐρρῶσθαί σε εὔχομαι, εὐτύχει, sometimes followed by a date). In accounts and lists the lay-out of the text is much more elaborate than in most other papyrus texts :

- a new line is usually taken for each item in the list
- figures are usually put in a separate column towards the right margin
- headers are often marked by a separate first line.

12 E.g. in *P. Abinn.* 42 (AD 326-375); *P. Ant.* II 92 and *PUG* I 29 (AD IV-V); *SB* XII 11084 and XX 15191 (AD V); *P. Köln* XIII 545 (AD 400-599); *P. Flor.* III 359 (AD 500-599); *P. Oxy.* XVI 2059 (AD VII).

13 *P. Fouad 74* (AD IV) is a memorandum followed by a list; *P. Cairo Masp.* III 67319 is headed as ὑπ]ο[μν]ηστικ(ὸν) [τ]ῶ̣ν̣ βοσκημάτων μο(υ) [τ]ῶν β̣ρωθ̣[έν]τ(ων) παρὰ διαφόρων ἀν[θρ]ώπ(ων) in l.1, but called a γνῶσ(ις) on the back.

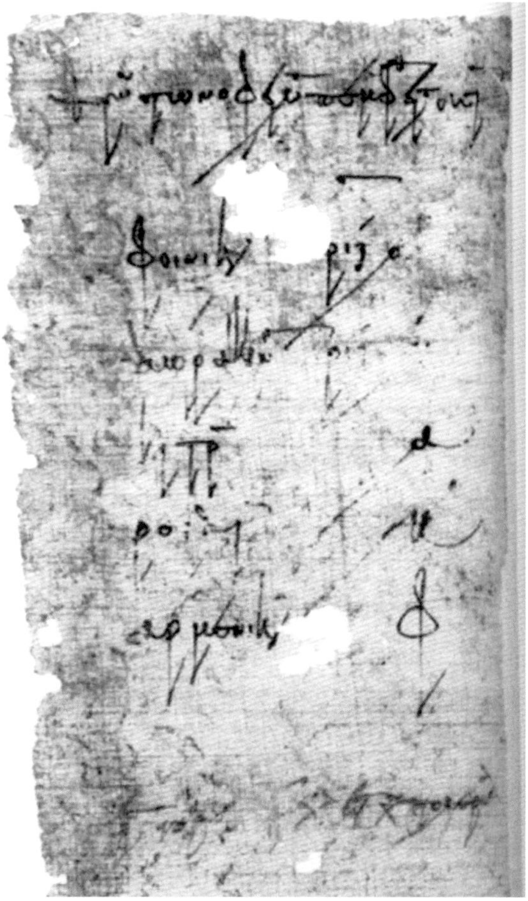

plate 1: *CPR* X 62 (AD VII; "Obstliste", with as header + γνῶ(σις) ὀφειλ(ημά)τ(ων) πεμφθ(έντων) εἰ(ς) τ(ὴν) οὐσί(αν), followed by a line with the symbol for οὕ(τως) introducing the actual list of fruits, with their numbers and prices. The last line, in a different hand, gives the date and the destination ("for the chorion Ptolemais") of the goods bought.

Official accounts and lists are often incorporated into memoranda or letters. Here too the lay-out clearly shows where the list itself begins : usually a new line is started, often there is an open space between the introductory formula and the list and this can be accentuated by the use of some expressions, such as ἔστι δέ and οὕτως.

The use of a paragraphos under the header lines is exceptional. I found it sporadically in the Menches archive (*P. Tebt.* I 67, 69, 70, 84) and then again in some papyri from the Arab period (*CPR* XII 8, though these are rather division lines; *P. Lond.* IV 1413; 1418), but fourteen instances on more than a thousand papyri shows that this device remained uncommon.

In official documents of the Roman period the list or account proper is often introduced by the expression ἔστι δέ, sometimes written in *scriptio continua* with what precedes ("unmarked") but more often positioned at the end of a line (often marked by a space before it) or in a separate short line, dividing the prescript from the list of objects or persons. This is found in 75 texts in the database, 60 of them clearly official (texts written by village scribes or sitologoi for instance) and in 10 belonging to large estates like that of Appianus, who copied administrative habits. Because the texts are nearly all official most of them carry a date. This allows us to date the expression rather precisely : the earliest examples date from AD 116 (*P. Giss.* I 58, a list of liturgists) and 134 (*BGU* IX 1891) respectively, the latest from AD 338 (*P. Lips.* I 97) and 361 (*P. Oxy.* LXVII 4599).

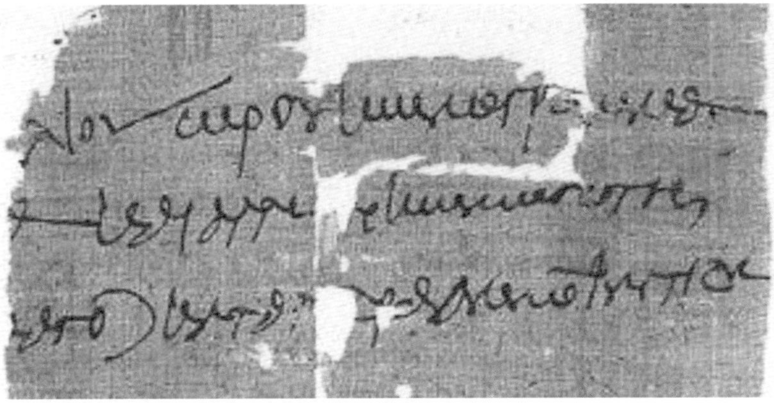

plate 2: SB XXVI 16824 : ἔστι δέ at the end of l.3 (unmarked)

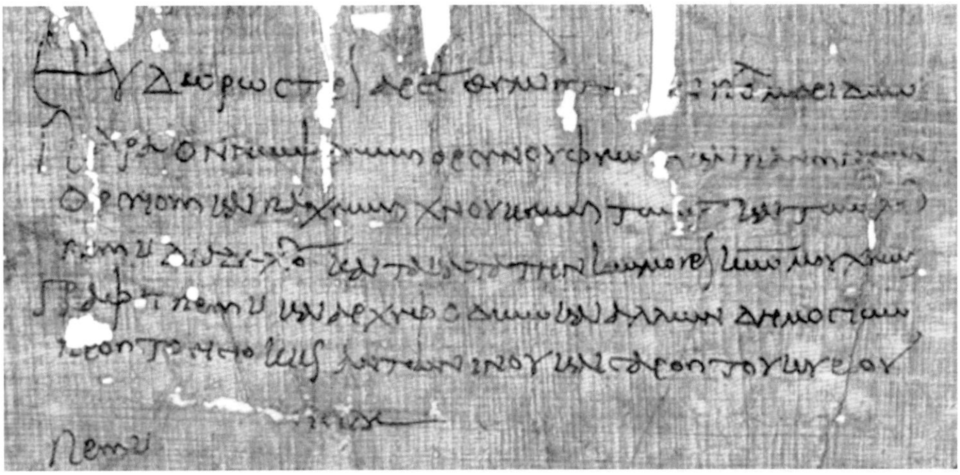

plate 3: BGU I 6 : ἔστι δέ in a separate line 7

Only once, in *P. Oxy.* LXVII 4599 (AD 361) the ἔστι δέ formula is found side by side with a new expression, introducing the list proper by means of the word οὕτως. This word is found from the fourth cent. AD up to the Arab period, both in private and official texts, often difficult to date (because of the indiction system). At first the word is written fully out at the end of the prescript or in a separate line, later on it is usually abbreviated into a horizontal line beginning with a short omikron. In a few cases older editors have even transcribed it as a paragraphos, but that is clearly not the case.

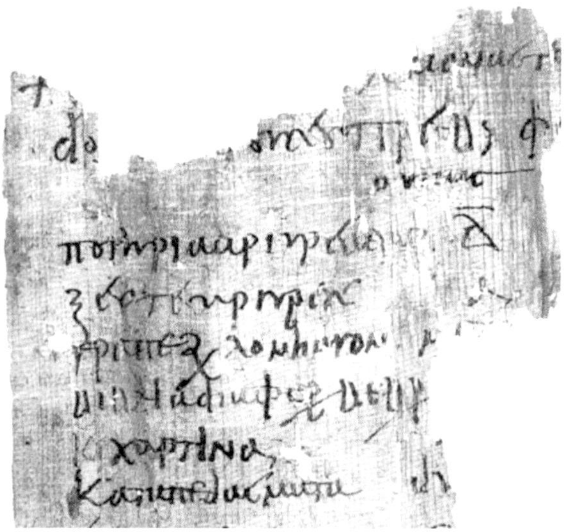

plate 4: P. Prag. II 178 (οὕτως written fully out in l.3)

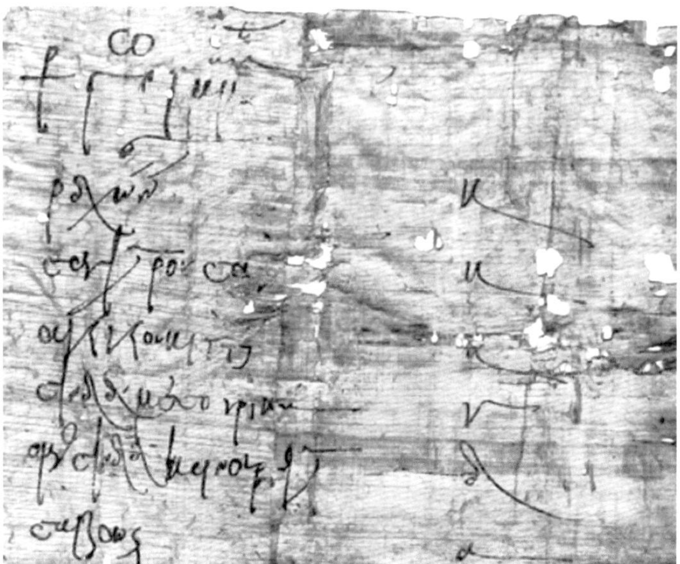

plate 5: P. Oxy. LXXVII 5126 (οὕτως abbreviated in l.2)

In the Byzantine period the headers are often preceded by a cross (see plate 1), a chrisma or a monogrammatic cross (plates 4 and 5). The earliest certain example of a cross is *CPR* VIII 37, which can be dated to about AD 350 because bishop Dios mentioned here in l. 10 must be identical with the bishop in *P. Landl.* II l. 147 (AD 346)[14]. The more elaborate christian symbolic figures XMΓ and ϘΘ are not attested before the fifth century[15].

4. The order inside accounts and lists

The headers of accounts and lists do not usually give explicit information about the order followed in the texts, except for the 52 κατ' ἄνδρα lists which list persons by name (this order is called κατ' ὄνομα in *CPR* VIII 44). Alphabetic order remains exceptional, I found only three instances (*BGU* IX 1897, AD 166; *P. Strasb.* I 27, AD I-II; *Stud. Pal.* XXII 88, AD 214)[16]. Other possibilites are listing by date (usually by day), by place and by item (normal with inventories). The following table shows how these different possibilities are spread

	lists	**accounts**	**total**
by person	160	330	511
by date	21	182	213
by place	30	60	91
by item	94 (24 inventories)	90	185

14 See K.A. Worp, *ZPE* 100 (1994), p. 300.

15 *P. Mich.* VI 378, which presents a cross, XMΓ and ϘΘ was dated by the editor to the early fourth century (date accepted in the *HGV* and *TM*), but see *BL* VIII, p. 213 (P.J. Sijpesteijn), *P. Sorb.* II, p. 46 (J. Gascou) and *BASP* 32 (1995), p. 52 (P. van Minnen), who all plead for a fifth century date.

16 For alphabetical order in Ptolemaic land lists as early as the late second century BC, see A. Verhoogt, *Menches, komogrammateus of Kerkeosiris*, Pap. Lugd.-Bat. 29, p. 215.

Surveying the land in Ptolemaic Egypt. The Information flow from village to nome level

Katelijn Vandorpe and Nick Vaneerdewegh, Leuven

Egypt may have been a gift of the Nile as suggested by Herodotus (2.5), but a complex administration was needed to deal with the agricultural realities of the yearly Nile inundations. This paper discusses the compilation of land surveys by the Ptolemaic administration. The Ptolemies continued the, undoubtedly costly, twofold Pharaonic survey operation: after the flood, land and its holders were listed, while after sowing but before the harvest, a crop report was drawn up, which formed the basis for estimating tax revenues. Both operations resulted in many forms of listings: by landholder, land category and crops, and these surveys were compiled at village, toparchy and nome level, and beyond.

The survey operations have been discussed by, among others, D.J. Crawford (1971),[1] H. Cuvigny (1985)[2] and A. Verhoogt (1998).[3] The data processing in late Ptolemaic surveys has been studied in detail by N. Reggiani (2016).[4] The evidence available for these studies were surveys at the village level, mainly from the Fayum oasis (third to first century BC).[5] Surveys at the toparchy level, originating from the Herakleopolite nome in Middle Egypt and probably dating from the (late) second century BC,[6] have not been included in the aforementioned studies and surveys at the nome level were not extant at the time. With

1 D.J. Crawford, *Kerkeosiris. An Egyptian village in the Ptolemaic period.* 1971. Cambridge: Cambridge University Press, pp. 5–38.

2 H. Cuvigny, *L'arpentage par espèces dans l'Égypte ptolémaïque d'après les papyrus grecs* (Papyrologica Bruxellensia 20). 1985. Brussels: Fondation égyptologique Reine Élisabeth.

3 A. Verhoogt, *Menches, Komogrammateus of Kerkeosiris. The Doings and Dealings of a Village Scribe in the Late Ptolemaic Period (120–110 BC)* (Papyrologica Lugduno-Batava 29). 1998. Leiden: Brill, esp. pp. 131–142. See now also D. Rathbone, D.J. Thompson and A. Verhoogt, 'A Reconstructed Land Survey from Kerkeosiris,' in R. Ast, H. Cuvigny, T. Hickey and J. Lougovaya (eds.), *Papyrological Texts in Honor of Roger S. Bagnall* (American Studies in Papyrology 53). 2013. Ann Arbor: University of Michigan Press, pp. 243–265.

4 N. Reggiani, 'Data processing and state management in Late Ptolemaic and Roman Egypt: The project 'Synopsis' and the archive of Menches,', in T. Derda, A. Łatjar and J. Urbanik (eds.) in cooperation with G. Ochała and A. Mirończuk, *Proceedings of the 27th International Congress of Papyrology, Warsaw 29 July – 3 August 2013* (Journal of Juristic Papyrology, Supplement 28). 2016. Warsaw: University of Warsaw, pp. 1415–1444. The project "Synopsis: Data Processing and State Management in Roman Egypt (30 BCE–300 CE)" is supervised by A. Jördens and U. Yiftach.

5 See e.g. the texts presented in Cuvigny 1985; for Demotic examples from the late third-century BC Fayum, see now e.g. P. Agri. Dem. 1, 2 (cols. v–vi) and 3.

6 BGU XIV 2441–2450. For the late second century date, rather than first century BC, see R. Scholl, in *C. Ptol. Sklav.*, p. 977; S. Scheuble-Reiter, *Die Katökenreiter im ptolemäischen Ägypten* (Vestigia. Beiträge zur alten Geschichte 64), Munich: C.H. Beck, p. 333; K. Maresch, in P. Herakl. Bank, pp. 10–12.

the publication in 2017 of the Edfu land survey of 118 BC (P. Haun. IV 70), a report at the nome level is available for the first time; moreover, this report originates from Upper Egypt, a region that has not yielded Greek land surveys in the past.[7] Therefore, it is now possible to discuss the information flow from village through toparchy[8] to the nome level, although it must be admitted that we are still by far best informed on the reports at the village level. In order to be able to make reliable comparisons, we will confine ourselves to the surveys of the late second century BC, which constitute the majority of the reports.[9]

1. Topographical surveys at the village level

In the villages, the survey reports were the responsibility of the village scribe or *komogrammateus*. The archive of the village scribes (also known as the archive of Menches)[10] from Kerkeosiris[11] in the Fayum oasis is revealing in this respect, as it contains numerous reports and informs us in detail about the role of the village scribe in the survey operations.

Two reports at the village level are at the basis of all other reports:
(a) a **cadastral survey** (in the Fayum called εὐθυμετρία κατὰ περίχωμα or εὐθυμετρία κατ' ἄνδρα κατὰ περίχωμα, "exact measurement (by man) by basin")[12] was drawn up after the inundations (in September–October),[13] a necessary operation, because after the flood the borders between the plots of land could have become blurred, or land near the river or a canal could have disappeared because it was flushed away. These cadastral surveys are preserved in different forms, a kind of working copies compiled immediately after the actual survey: they list the name of the holder or farmer (not mentioned when the plot was derelict land), the land category (i.e. the land's fiscal status, see below, 4) and the area of the plot, expressed in arouras[14]; more detailed surveys may also add information on the tax regime (e.g. land rented at x artabas[15] per aroura) or crops to be sown. A few surveys[16] include the dimensions of the plot in detail, that is the dimensions of the plots' three or four

7 Only a few Demotic land surveys at the village level were preserved for Upper Egypt, see U. Kaplony-Heckel, 'Demotische Verwaltungsakten aus Gebelein: Der grosse Berliner Papyrus 13608', *ZÄS* 121 (1994): pp. 75–91; eadem, 'Zur Landwirtschaft in Oberägypten. Demotische Akten und Urkunden aus Gebelein (II. Jht. v. Chr.) und der arabische Leitfaden des Maḫzūmī (†1189 n. Chr.)', in I. Shirun-Grumach (ed.), *Jerusalem Studies in Egyptology* (Ägypten und Altes Testament 40). 1998. Wiesbaden: Harrassowitz, pp. 57–66.

8 The Fayum or Arsinoite nome also has a *meris*-level in between the toparchies and nome (the *meris* of Herakleides, Themistos and Polemon).

9 Late second century reports: at the village level: surveys in P. Tebt. I and IV, Verhoogt 1998, Rathbone, Thompson, and Verhoogt, in P. Bagnall, and Reggiani 2016, App. pp. 1439–1444; at the toparchy level: BGU XIV 2441–2450; at the nome level: P. Haun. IV 70.

10 K. Vandorpe, W. Clarysse and H. Verreth, *Greco-Roman archives from the Fayum* (Collectanea Hellenistica 6). 2015. Brussels and Leuven: Peeters, pp. 440–446.

11 Crawford 1971.

12 E.g., P. Tebt. I 84b + IV 1117c, P. Tebt. I 84a, 84c, 85, IV 1117b, 1118, 1120, 1121; see also Rathbone, Thompson and Verhoogt, in P. Bagnall, p. 244.

13 See e.g. the date of the *euthymetria* in P. Tebt. I 84a: 30 Sept. 118 BC.

14 1 aroura is 100 cubits square or 2756 m^2.

15 An artaba is a measure of capacity of about 40 l.

16 E.g. P. Tebt. I 86 and 87.

sides, expressed in *schoinia*[17] and represented schematically, e.g. P. Tebt. IV 1123, ll. 6–7 (with translation):[18]

> Adjacent on the north, projecting ½ 1/3 1/8 1/16 *schoinion* west of the property previously surveyed:
>
> 4 ½ arouras taxed at 4 artabas per aroura, held by Phmouis son of Pathebis, measuring

●[19]

1 ½ ¼ 1/16 *schoinion* ●[20], total 4 ¼ 1/16 1/64 arouras ...

2 1/4 1/8 1/32 *schoinion*

This *schoinismos*-procedure, also found in Demotic topographical surveys,[21] has to be distinguished from the proper *euthymetria*-procedure.[22] As some have more details than other surveys, one may distinguish between "outline"[23] cadastral surveys (without the *schoinismos*-procedure) and cadastral surveys including the latter procedure. The *schoinismos*-procedure may also turn up in other types of surveys.[24]

(b) the cadastral survey was the basis for the **survey of agricultural production** (in the Fayum called ἡ κατὰ φύλλον γεωμετρία, "land measurement by crops"), drawn up in February–March after sowing and before the harvest.[25] On this occasion, officials surveyed the condition of the plots to see whether the inundated parts had been sown or not, and estimated the tax revenues per plot and holder, e.g. P. Tebt. IV 1119, l. 24 ff.:

> Adjacent on the south, while the irrigation channel is in between:
> Portis the elder son of Teos, Crown land, 6 arouras, of which
> 3 arouras rented at 3 artabas per aroura
> 3 arouras rented at 2 1/2 artabas per aroura,
> the crops are: 3 ar. with wheat, 1 ar. with *telis* (fenugreek), 2 ar. with *phaselos* (kind of bean, calavance).

The cadastral survey and survey of agricultural production were initially drawn up by officials who went from plot to plot. We are well informed for the Fayum oasis, where villages were divided into basins or *perichomata*, areas enclosed by canals and dykes; the Fayum village of Kerkeosiris for instance had ten such basins in 120/119 BC.[26] Within each basin, the officials surveyed the land clockwise; when the surveyors changed direction, this was recorded, e.g. P. Tebt. IV 1119, l. 22 ff.:

---

17 A *schoinion* is a unit of linear measurement of 100 cubits or 1 side of the aroura.
18 See also P. Tebt. I 87, with introduction; P. Tebt. IV 1122.
19 The dot-symbol means that the dimensions are the same as these of the opposite side (2 1/4 1/8 1/32).
20 1 ½ ¼ 1/16, see previous note.
21 See the late third-century BC surveys P. Agri. Dem. 2, cols. v–vi, and P. Agri. Dem. 3 (with introduction).
22 Reggiani 2016, pp. 1425–1426, with reference to P. Tebt. I 12, ll. 6–7.
23 E.g. Rathbone, Thompson and Verhoogt, in P. Bagnall, p. 244.
24 E.g. P. Tebt. III 1003 (of 176 or 165 BC), see Cuvigny 1985, pp. 47–50.
25 E.g. P. Tebt. IV 1117a, 1119.
26 P. Tebt. IV, p. 141.

> Adjacent on the west - and the survey now proceeds from north (to south), while the canal is in between:
> *kleros*-plot of the 100-aroura holder Protarchos son of Dionysios: 10 arouras, of which 5 arouras with *arakos* (wild chickling), 5 arouras with *phaselos* (kind of bean, calavance), the farmer is Cheuris.

The extant Greek topographical reports are rather fair copies, undoubtedly compiled at the office of the village scribe, while hardly any working files composed during the survey proper are extant, such as a Demotic "diary" from Upper-Egyptian Pathyris: one of the inspectors, Sesostris son of Harsiesis, inspected the farm land of the local temple in January of 90 BC; the diary records his day-to-day activities, mainly measuring the plots and cultivated parts; on the birthday of his son, he takes a day off and that is recorded too, as were the names of the men who presented him a gift in kind for the anniversary.[27]

One may wonder whether the cadastral surveys (a) were performed on a yearly basis because we know of special cadastral surveys on key dates, such as the start of a new reign or after a troublesome period. Ptolemy II, for instance, ordered a cadastral survey shortly after his new revenue laws,[28] and the Edfu land survey refers to such key dates for year 1 of Ptolemy VI (180 BC) and year 12 (170/169 BC), the start of the joint reign of Ptolemy VI, VIII and Cleopatra II.[29] Such references to key dates are also found in pre-Ptolemaic times, for instance, the Edfu donation text refers to land surveyed "up to year 18 of Nectanebo (II)", the last year of the king's reign after which a new survey followed with the start of a new reign.[30] What was the difference between these special surveys and the regular surveys, assuming the latter were conducted on a yearly basis? Perhaps the *euthymetria* was a yearly procedure, while the *schoinismos* was not. Or perhaps the data of the regular cadastral surveys were kept at the village level, while only the data of the special cadastral surveys on key dates flowed to the higher levels. Changes in between two cadastral surveys (enlargement or reduction of the plot, new owner, etc.) may have been declared by the owners to the proper authorities,[31] or may have been found either during the second survey of February-March, or during re-surveys (*episkepseis*) performed upon instructions of higher authorities.[32]

Since the taxes individual owners or farmers had to pay depended on the geometria-surveys of agricultural production (b), these were certainly performed each year,[33] except in

27 The papyrus is not yet fully published, see Kaplony-Heckel 1994, esp. p. 79.

28 W. Clarysse and D.J. Thompson, *Counting the People in Hellenistic Egypt*. Vol. 2. 2006. Cambridge: Cambridge University Press, p. 16 on E. Bresciani, 'Registrazione catastale e ideologia politica nell' Egitto tolemaico. A completamento di la "Spedizione di Tolomeo II in Siria', *Egitto e vicino oriente* 6 (1983): 15–31.

29 P. Haun. IV 70, pp. 37–38.

30 D. Meeks, *Le grand texte des donations au temple d'Edfou* (Bibliothèque d'étude 59). 1972. Cairo: Institut français d'archéologie orientale du Caire, p. 20*, 1.

31 For a discussion of such declarations, see Crawford 1971, pp. 19–20.

32 On the *episkepsis* procedure, see Cuvigny 1985, pp. 122–125.

33 See e.g. a papyrus from Lycopolis, 190 BC, ll. 46–48: "of the cultivated (σπόριμος) area nothing has been overlooked, because the land measurement of what is sown has taken place each year (καθ' ἔτος),

times of trouble. During this second survey, owners or farmers were individually informed, in writing, about the results of the survey and the tax amount to be paid after the harvest. Several such individual measurement-receipts addressed to the holders are preserved from second-century BC Upper Egypt and show that the holders were informed on a yearly basis, except in periods of unrest.[34]

These initially topographical surveys at the village level, with details on the holders or farmers of the plots, on the crops grown, and on the land category (e.g. *kleros*, or cleruchic land), served as a basis for other types of surveys, of which we discuss the best known in the following sections.[35] Typical of these secondary reports is the addition of subtotals and grand totals, often introduced by the symbol for γίνονται, an oblique line well visible in the lengthy reports.[36]

2. Alphabetical (tax) lists by person and summary reports (village level)

The personal details of the topographical land survey were copied in a more or less alphabetical list (by first letter) of the holders (of e.g. cleruchic land) or of the farmers (of e.g. crown land): all the plots owned or farmed by one person were gathered and the charges to be paid on the cultivated parts were recorded;[37] in some cases extra taxes to be paid were also added (e.g. the granary-guard tax, see below);[38] P. Tebt. IV 1103 may be such an alphabetical list, e.g. l. 34 ff. (with translation):

> "Harchypsis son of Peteesis. Year 1: out of 6 ½ 1/8 ar. renting at 31 art., 1 ¼ 1/8 ar. for 4 ½ art.; and apportioned from the land formerly held by Totoes son of Phagates, ½ 1/4 ar. for 3 art. Total, 2 1/8 ar. for 7 ½ art. Of these 1 1/8 ar. rented at 4 art. per ar., 4 ½ art. due; and 1 rented at 3 art. per ar., all in wheat."
> "Marres son of Petosiris (...)"
> "Mestasytmis son of Petesouchos, and associates, ..."

Subsequently, this alphabetical list was turned into a tax list in which not only the charges on the cultivated parts were registered, but also the extra taxes to be paid, such as a scribal fee and the granary-guard tax. A blank space was left between the persons in order to add the actual payments in one or more installments. Information on the payments was provided by the granary director, whose administration kept a logbook on a daily basis of those who had made a payment.[39] P. Tebt. IV 1105 (+ I 93) was such an alphabetical tax list of crown

and the payments on the produce are being exacted', see B. McGing, 'Revolt Egyptian style. Internal opposition to Ptolemaic rule', *AfP* 43 (1997): pp. 273–314.

34 K. Vandorpe, 'The Ptolemaic Epigraphe or Harvest tax (shemu)', *AfP* 46 (2000): pp. 165–228; Eadem, 'Paying Taxes to the Thesauroi of the Pathyrites in a Century of Rebellions (186–88 BC)', in L. Mooren (ed.), *Politics, Administration and Society in the Hellenistic and Roman World. Proceedings of the International Colloquium, Bertinoro, 19–24 July 1997* (Studia Hellenistica 36). 2000. Leuven: Peeters, pp. 405–436.

35 See also the overview in Reggiani 2016, esp. p. 1423.

36 See also Reggiani 2016, p. 1429.

37 E.g. P. Tebt. IV 1103, called κατ' ἄνδρα καὶ φύλλον.

38 E.g. P. Tebt. IV 1106.

39 Lists of payments per day are e.g. P. Tebt. I 90 and 91.

tenants,[40] where all payments are calculated in terms of wheat, although people were, for instance, allowed to pay in lentils. We present a short extract (P. Tebt. IV 1105, l. 1 ff., with translation):

> "Petesouchos son of Petosiris. 9 ½ 1/4 ar. renting for 47 ½ 1/4 art., and out of the property formerly held by Orses, 2 ar. for 10 1/12 art.; total 11 ½ 1/4 ar., 57 ½ 1/3 art., (the extra taxes:) ½ 1/12 for the 24th tax, ½ art. for deposit charges, 1 art. for *trichoinikon*-tax, 1/3 1/12 art. for granary-guard tax, 1/3 1/12 art. for fodder tax, 1/6 art. for *lochi( )*-tax, 3 art. for scribal fees. Total for taxes: 6 1/12 art.; total rent and taxes: 63 ½ 1/3 1/12 art. Plus ½ art. survey fee and 5 ½ ¼ art. for crown tax, total 6 ¼ art. Grand total 70 1/6 art.
>
> Of these were paid:
>
> on Pharmouthi 10: 36 1/3 art. wheat by 6-choinix measure, on (Pharmouthi) 29: 21 art. wheat by 6-choinix measure, total 57 1/3 art., on (Pharmouthi) 30: 5 ½ 1/3 art. wheat, on Payni 10, from his private deposit: 1 1/3 art. wheat, on (Payni) 19: 4 art. lentils,
>
> Total reckoned in terms of wheat: 68 ½ art., plus 2 art. scribal fee, total 70 ½ art."
>
> "Paapis son of Petosiris (...)"
>
> "Pnepheros son of Petesouchos ..."

This information on payments by individuals at the village level was (probably) not taken over in lists on toparchy- and nome-level.

Preliminary (*prodialogismoi*) summary (*epikephalaiou*) reports at the village level are extant,[41] summarizing the grand total of the above-mentioned charges to be paid followed by the totals actually paid per 10 days (e.g.: "Pharmouthi, from day 11 to 20"[42]); subtotals are recorded for rents and land taxes, and for the extra taxes (e.g. scribal fee[43]), but no details on the people who paid their rents or taxes are provided in these summary reports. The rents and taxes in this type of reports are always expressed in wheat, so that payments in e.g. olyra are converted to their wheat equivalent ("olyra, calculated in terms of wheat: 94 art."[44]).

3. Crop summary reports (village level)

The crop details of the topographical survey of agricultural production were taken over in a summary (*epikephalaiou*) report of the crops, a κατὰ φύλλον ἐπικεφαλαίου, where details of the holders or farmers and their plots are no longer listed. Such reports are extant at the village level for crown land, e.g. P. Tebt. I 67, l. 2 ff. (with translation),[45] but were undoubtedly also available on higher levels; totals of crops were often calculated in terms of wheat:

40 Another example is: P. Tebt. I 94 + IV 1107.
41 E.g. P. Tebt. I 89; Reggiani 2016, App. pp. 1439–1444.
42 P. Tebt. I 89, l. 15.
43 P. Tebt. I 89, l. 56.
44 Reggiani 2016, App. pp. 1439–1444, l. 9.
45 See also P. Tebt. I 66, 68 and 69.

Summary list of crops for the said year. In the 52nd year there were sown including pastures 1139 ¼ arouras of land, at a rent of 4642 1/12 art., the supposed calculation of which was:

- wheat, 1644 2/3 art.,
- barley calculated in terms of wheat: 2877 ¼ art.,
- olyra calculated in terms of wheat: 91 ½ 1/4 art.,
- copper calculated in terms of wheat: 39 1/3 1/12 art.,
- total, calculated in terms of wheat: 4642 1/12 art.

For the 53rd year there have been sown:

- with wheat: 576 ½ ¼ 1/8 arouras at a rent of 2567 1/3 art. (...)
- with barley are sown 178 ¼ 1/8 arouras at a rent of 787 1/3 art. (...)
- with lentils are sown ... "

4. Land category reports (village-, toparchy- and nome-level)

The topographical surveys of agricultural production at the village level detailed above were reorganized per land category (such as sacred, cleruchic, crown land, etc.). As the tax regime was different for each land type, the land categories may also be considered fiscal categories. In the Fayum villages, separate land category reports were sometimes compiled for sacred and cleruchic land on the one hand, and for crown land on the other hand. By contrast, in the nome land survey from Edfu, these and similar land categories were presented in one list.

In the reports, the land categories are divided into subcategories, e.g. sacred land in the Fayum consists of land of the temples of first rank, of second rank, etc.; in the Edfu nome land survey, the dedicated land had "land dedicated to god Soter up to year 12" as one of the subcategories (see below, 4.1). Information on these subcategories, not found in the basic topographical surveys, must derive from other types of reports.

Historical details on the plots or land categories, which were not recorded in the topographical surveys either, were also added from other sources. Especially historical details on cleruchic plots were reported on all levels, such as the date on which a cleruch was granted his *kleros*, or who was responsible for the grant. For the total areas of privately-owned land subject to charges as recorded in the Edfu nome survey (P. Haun. IV 70) of 118 BC, the compiler went back to the situation before 207/206 BC, almost a century earlier (l. 283).

Village level:

- A first, detailed land category report was compiled at the village level,[46] called a κατὰ φύλλον,[47] whereby each category (e.g. sacred land) had a clear set of subcategories (e.g. land of temples of first rank). Per subcategory, details on the holders or farmers, productive parts and crops (wheat, barley, lentils, ...) were recorded, followed by a subtotal of the land and its productive parts. A grand total for the land category was added at the start and/or at the end of the overview.
- a summary land category report (τὸ ἀναγραφόμενον πᾶν ἔδαφος) brought together the subtotals per subcategory and the grand totals per land category, leaving out details on

46 E.g. P. Tebt. I 61, 62, 63 and 64.

47 P. Tebt. I 63, l. 2.

holders or famers.[48] P. Tebt. I 60 is, in our view, such a report, presenting the subtotals and totals for sacred, cleruchic and crown land, followed by a more detailed overview of special (usually temporary) categories of land and derelict land.

Toparchy level:
A group of villages formed a toparchy, where the reports were compiled under the supervision of the toparchy scribe or *topogrammateus*:

- all the detailed land category reports of the villages were brought together in a long survey, copying per village all the details on holders, productive parts and crops, as well as the (sub)totals.[49] The information in the detailed land category reports at the village level seem to have been copied more or less word for word at the toparchy level.
- summary reports must have existed, but are not preserved.

Nome level:
Two or more toparchies formed a nome; the Edfu nome (the Apollonopolites), for instance, consisted of 4 toparchies at the end of the second century BC:

- the city of Apollonopolis Megale (the metropolis of the nome, west bank; modern Edfu),
- the lower toparchy (northern part of the nome, west bank),
- the upper toparchy (southern part of the nome, west bank),
- Arabia (the part of the nome located on the east bank of the Nile).

The overall structure of the Edfu nome report is reminiscent of the summary report at the village level: first the subtotals and totals for dedicated, cleruchic and the Upper-Egyptian counterpart of crown land are recorded, while derelict land and special land categories are listed last.[50]

The land category report at the nome level gathers the subtotals per subcategory and per toparchy, e.g. P. Haun. IV 70, l. 18 ff. (with translation):

> "land dedicated to god Soter up to year 12 (...):
> in the Apollonopolis(-toparchy): 196 1/16 arouras (...), 1372 1/3 1/12 artabas, (...) of which have been sown: 60 arouras, 420 artabas."

Thus, contrary to the reports on the lower levels, the details on individual plots and their holders or farmers have totally disappeared (except for the larger cleruchic plots, see 4.2). Subtotals and grand totals are added per subcategory and/or per land category, often broken down first per toparchy, e.g. P. Haun. IV 70, l. 25 ff. (with translation):

> "Of the land in release,
> in the Apollonopolis(-toparchy): 247 $^{1}/_{16}$ arouras (...), of which sown 65 arouras,
> in the lower toparchy: fertile land 64 arouras, uninundated,
> in the upper toparchy: fertile land 2 arouras, of which sown 2 arouras,
> in Arabia: 10 arouras, of which dry land 8 arouras.

48 E.g. P. Tebt. I 60.
49 E.g. BGU XIV 2441–2450.
50 P. Haun. IV 70, pp. 12–13.

Total, 323 $^{1}/_{16}$ arouras, (...) of which sown 67 arouras."

In the case of the land category "land subject to taxes", the subtotals per toparchy and totals for the nome are presented in columnar format: column one records the name of the toparchy, the second the surface involved in arouras, the third column the yield in artabas of wheat. These numbers are then added up to reach the nome total, e.g. P. Haun. IV 70, l. 293 ff. (with translation):

"And up to year 1 (180).
These consist of:
Private island land,

in Apollonopolis,	484 ½ 1/8 1/32 arouras,	3,144 ½ artabas;
in the lower toparchy,	2,291 ½ 1/8 arouras,	15,152 1/3 artabas;
in the upper toparchy,	1,341 1/8 1/16 1/32 arouras,	9,291 2/3 artabas;
in Arabia,	372 ½ ¼ 1/32 arouras,	2,531 artabas;
Total,	4,490 ¼ 1/32 arouras,	30,119 ½ artabas."

The nome report further copies the historical details on certain land categories from the village and toparchy level (see below, 4.2). P. Haun. IV 70 of 118 BC thus gives a longue durée overview of land usage in the Edfu nome going back to the end of the third century BC.

The nome report was checked by both the village and toparchy scribes, who were probably present at the spring meeting in the nome capital. This review operation explains why details or corrections have been added in smaller characters between the lines or in the margins of P. Haun. IV 70, both by the agency of the village scribes as explicitly stated ("the village scribes (report) as follows", ll. 120–121, 190, 229) or of the toparchy scribes (ll. 339–343). Likewise, the subtotals per toparchy were all checked, undoubtedly by the *topogrammateis* themselves, as shown by the checking marks (small dots) in the left margins. Conspicuously, several checking marks for the lower toparchy subtotals are missing.[51]

While the crops are specified (wheat, barley, lentils, *arakos*, ...) in the detailed overview per holder on village and toparchy level, details on the crops are no longer recorded in the subtotals and grand totals on village and toparchy level, and are never specified at the nome level: crop estimates, if mentioned, are in (sub)totals, and always calculated in terms of wheat.

4.1. Information flow for sacred and/or dedicated land

The sacred or dedicated land was divided into subcategories, e.g. for the Fayum into land of temples of first rank, of second rank, land of the chapels for the sacred ibis, etc.; for the Herakleopolite toparchy into land of the great gods Stotoetis and (perhaps) Herakles, etc.; for the Edfu nome into land dedicated by Horus to minor gods, land dedicated to the god Soter, etc. (see table 1). These subcategories are found on all levels, but while on village and toparchy level the details on the farmers, surface and crops per plot were added, at the

51 See P. Haun. IV 70, p. 11 and 55.

nome level such details were left out and were replaced by the grand totals of the surface and productive parts per toparchy, at the end added up for the entire nome (see examples above). The summary report at the village level (e.g. P. Tebt. I 60, l. 8 ff., see above) also contains the same subcategories.

Table 1. Information flow for sacred and/or dedicated land

Village level	**Toparchy level**	**Nome level**
Sacred and/or dedicated land	*Sacred and/or dedicated land* **Overview per village**	*Sacred and/or dedicated land*
Subcategories:[52] → → → → • land of temples of first rank, second rank, ... • land of the *ibiones* (chapels for the sacred ibis), • …	Subcategories:[53] → → → → → • land of the great gods Stotoetis and ?Herakles • …	Subcategories:[54] • … [lost] • land dedicated by Horus to minor gods • land dedicated to the god Soter
+ per subcategory: details on farmers, priests, productive parts, crops → →	+ per subcategory: details on farmers, priests, productive parts, crops	+ per subcategory: /
& subtotal of land and its productive parts → → →	[& subtotal of land and productive parts?]	/
+ grand total for sacred land & its productive parts for village → → → → → → →	[+ grand total for sacred land & its productive parts for each village in toparchy?]	
↓ ↓ ↓ ↓ ↓	[+ grand total for toparchy?] →	grand total of land & its productive parts per toparchy + grand total for dedicated land & its productive parts for entire nome
Summary report (e.g. P. Tebt. I 60, l. 8 ff.)	[Summary report?]	[Summary report?]
Info from the Fayum oasis	Info from Herakleopolite nome, Middle Egypt	Info from Edfu nome, Upper Egypt

52 See P. Tebt. I 62, l. 4 ff.

53 See BGU XIV 2441, l. 108 ff. The part of the survey on sacred land is not well preserved.

54 See P. Haun. IV 70, l. 1 ff.

4.2. Information flow for cleruchic land

For cleruchic land, the same categories are found on all three levels: (1) larger plots of cleruchic land belonging to cavalrymen (*katoikoi hippeis*), and (2) smaller plots belonging to infantrymen (*machimoi*, called *andres* in the Edfu land survey). Within these main categories, similar subcategories are present on village, toparchy and nome level in a mainly chronological order, referring to the date on which the respective cleruchs were granted their plot (see examples below).

Under Ptolemy VIII the chronological overview of the *kleroi* of cavalrymen starts with the older cleruchs, who received their grants under the grandfather, father and brother of the ruling king, followed by the cleruchs who were assigned a *kleros* under the ruling king.[55] Under his successor Ptolemy IX Soter II, an extra generation was added to the overview, which started now with the cleruchs who received their grants under the great-grandfather (or simply "under Philopator"[56]), grandfather, uncle ("brother of the father", or simply "Philometor"[57]), and father and/or brother of the ruling king.[58] Some Herakleopolite surveys at the toparchy level simply bring together the cleruchs added to the cleruchy under the previous kings under the heading "old (*archaioi*) cleruchs".[59]

The names of the cavalrymen who were granted the largest plots, and details on these plots are found on all levels, even the nome level (*in casu*: plots of 120 and 280 arouras), while details on the land of cavalrymen and infantrymen with smaller plots are only recorded on village and toparchy level, not at the nome level: e.g. the nome Edfu land survey does not list the individual plots and names of the "*katoikoi hippeis* formerly from the troop of Ptolemaios, son of Apollodoros", only the total area, that is 40 1/8 arouras (P. Haun. IV 70, ll. 63–68).

When individual plots and their holders are recorded, the order within this category is not alphabetical, but probably the order of the names as found in the topographical lists.

Table 2. Information flow for cleruchic land

Village level	Toparchy level	Nome level
Cleruchic land	*Cleruchic land* **Overview per village**	*Cleruchic land*

• cavalrymen: → → → → →
  ○ several subcategories
• infantrymen: → → → → →
  ○ several subcategories
	cavalrymen: → → → → →
	  ○ several subcategories
	[-] → → → → → →
		cavalrymen:
		  ○ several subcategories
		
		infantrymen:
		  ○ several subcategories

55 Village level: P. Tebt. I 62, IV 1108, 1109; toparchy level: see note 59; nome level: P. Haun IV 70.

56 E.g. P. Tebt. IV 1114, l. 9.

57 P. Tebt. I 1113, l. 10, 1115, l. 12.

58 E.g. P. Tebt. I 63, l. 32, 39, 51, 95; see also P. Tebt. IV 1110, 1113, 1114, 1115.

59 E.g. BGU XIV 2441, l. 135, 147.

+ per subcategory: → → → → mainly chronological order often with exact dates + details on persons → → → → + details on their plots: crops, productive, non-productive parts & subtotal of land and its productive parts → → → + grand total for cleruchic land & its productive parts for village → → → → → ↓ ↓ ↓ ↓	+ per subcategory: mainly chronological order (without exact dates) + details on persons + details on their plots: crops, productive, non-productive parts + subtotals per subcategory per village + grand total for cleruchic land per village [+ grand total per subcategory for entire toparchy?] → → → → → + grand total for cleruchic land for entire toparchy?] →	+ per subcategory: mainly chronological order often with exact dates + details on land of cavalrymen owning large plots only; + details on their plots: productive, non-productive parts / for smaller plots of cavalrymen and for infantrymen: no details on persons and plots, only subtotals + subtotals per subcategory per toparchy + grand total per subcategory for entire nome + grand total for cleruchic land for entire nome
Summary report (e.g. P. Tebt. I 60, l. 18 ff.)	[Summary report?]	[Summary report?]
Info from the Fayum oasis	Info from Herakleopolite nome, Middle Egypt	Info from Edfu nome, Upper Egypt

Survey of cleruchic land at the ***village level*** *(Kerkeosiris, Fayum oasis). Extract from P. Tebt. I 62, l. 27 ff. (with translation).*

Cavalrymen (*katoikoi hippeis*)
(old catoicic cavalrymen:)

- "cleruchic land under the grandfather of the king" (l. 29 ff.):
  + non-alphabetical list of individuals and their plots
  + subtotal of land, broken down in productive, non-productive parts and crops
- "cleruchic land under the father of the king" (l. 38 ff.), with four further subcategories:
  + non-alphabetical list of individuals and their plots
  + subtotal of land, broken down in productive, non-productive parts and crops

- "cleruchic land under the brother of the king" (l. 57 ff.), with several subcategories:
    1. "those who belong to the noble catoicic cavalrymen":
        + non-alphabetical list of individuals and their plots
        + subtotal of land, broken down in productive, non-productive parts and crops
    2. "those who became catoicic cavalrymen through Dionysios in year 31" (l. 66 ff.):
        + non-alphabetical list of individuals and their plots
        + subtotal of land, broken down in productive, non-productive parts and crops
    3. "those who became catoicic cavalrymen in year 34" (l. 84 ff.):
        + one individual and his plot
    4. "those who were promoted to the rank of catoicic cavalrymen from the rank of road inspectors" (l. 87 ff.):
        + non-alphabetical list of individuals and their plots
        + subtotal of land
    5. "those who were promoted to the rank of catoicic cavalrymen from the rank of desert guards in year 32" (ll. 99–100 ff.):
        + non-alphabetical list of individuals and their plots
        + subtotal of land
    6. "those who were promoted to the rank of catoicic cavalrymen from the rank of policemen in year 33" (l. 107 ff.):
        + non-alphabetical list of individuals and their plots
        + subtotal of land, broken down in productive, non-productive parts
- "cleruchic land under the king" (l. 116 ff.), with several subcategories:
    1. "those who became catoicic cavalrymen through Kriton in year 37" (l. 116 ff.):
        + non-alphabetical list of individuals and their plots
        + subtotal of land
    2. "those who were promoted to the rank of catoicic cavalrymen from the rank of road inspectors in year 34" (l. 139 ff.):
        + non-alphabetical list of individuals and their plots
        + subtotal of land
    3. "those who were promoted to the rank of catoicic cavalrymen from the rank of road inspectors in year 34" (l. 151 ff.):
        + non-alphabetical list of individuals and their plots
        + subtotal of land
    4. "those who were promoted to the rank of catoicic cavalrymen through Chomenis in year 41" (l. 159 ff.):
        + non-alphabetical list of individuals and their plots

Infantrymen (*machimoi*):

- "promoted in year 41" (l. 178 ff.):
    + non-alphabetical list of individuals and their plots
    + subtotal of land
- "promoted in year 42" (l. 241 ff.):
    + non-alphabetical list of individuals and their plots
    + subtotal of land
- ...

Subtotals per subcategory (l. 315 ff.):

- cleruchic land under the grandfather of the king: 104 1/16 1/32 arouras land
- ...

Grand total of cleruchic land, and grand total of productive cleruchic land (l. 337 f.).

Survey of cleruchic land at the ***toparchy level*** *(Herakleopolite nome, Middle Egypt). Extract from BGU XIV 2441.*

Cavalrymen (*katoikoi hippeis*)

- "old (archaioi, that is assigned under previous kings) catoicic cavalrymen" (l. 135 ff.):
  + non-alphabetical list of individuals and their plots
  + subtotal of land, broken down in productive and non-productive parts
- "(those who became catoicic cavalrymen) through Exakon" (l. 149 ff.):
  + non-alphabetical list of individuals and their plots
  + subtotal of land, broken down in productive and non-productive parts
- [-] (l. 172 ff.)
- "(those who were promoted to the rank of catoicic cavalrymen) from the rank of road inspectors" (l. 186 ff.):
  + non-alphabetical list of individuals and their plots
  + subtotal of land, broken down in productive and non-productive parts
- "(those who were promoted to the rank of catoicic cavalrymen) from the rank of policemen" (l. 218 ff.):
  + non-alphabetical list of individuals and their plots
  + subtotal of productive land
- "(those who were promoted to the rank of catoicic cavalrymen) from the rank of river guards" (L 225 ff.):
  + non-alphabetical list of individuals and their plots
  + subtotal of productive land
- "(those who were promoted to the rank of catoicic cavalrymen) from the rank of desert guards" (l. 229 ff.):
  + non-alphabetical list of individuals and their plots
  + subtotal of land, broken down in productive and non-productive parts
- "(those who became catoicic cavalrymen) through Totheios (?)" (l. 245 ff.):
  + non-alphabetical list of individuals and their plots
  + subtotal of land, broken down in productive and non-productive parts

Grand total of land of the catoicic cavalrymen (l. 260 ff.), broken down in productive and non-productive parts

(no infantrymen or *machimoi* recorded in the extant parts of this survey)

Survey of cleruchic land at the ***nome level*** *(Edfu nome, Upper Egypt). Extract from P. Haun. IV 70 (with translation).*

Cavalrymen (*katoikoi hippeis*):

- "Cleruchic land up to year 16 under the grandfather of the king (207/206 BC)" (l. 33 ff.):
    - 120 arouras for a cavalryman from the polis
      + detailed report on holder (Sommounis, plot transferred to Ptolemaios son of Pasas) and plots and their location (toparchies and villages)
    - plots (40 arouras in total) of the cavalrymen of the troops of Ptolemaios son of Apollodoros
      + no details for these smaller plots, only totals of productive and non-productive parts per toparchy (all located in the toparchy of Arabia)

  Subtotal of cleruchic land up to year 16, broken down in productive and non-productive parts
- "(Cleruchic land) since year 12 under brother of the king (170 BC)" (l. 73 ff.):
    - 280 arouras assigned in year 15 (167/166 BC)
      + detailed report on holder (Pasas, plot later transferred to his son Ptolemaios) and plots and their location (toparchies)

  Subtotal of cleruchic land since year 12 under brother of the king, broken down in productive and non-productive parts

Infantrymen (*andres*):

- "(Cleruchic land) that in year 36 of the (ruling) king (Ptolemy VIII) was assigned, ... " (135/134 BC) (l. 93 ff.):
    - no details for these smaller plots, only totals of productive and non-productive parts per toparchy

Grand totals of cleruchic land per toparchy, broken down in productive and non-productive parts
Grand total of cleruchic land for the nome, broken down in productive and non-productive parts.

4.3. Information flow for crown land and land subject to tax

The information flow for crown land is more difficult to retrieve for several reasons. First, crown land, rented by farmers, is well-attested in the Fayum, where we have surveys at the village level, but in the extant surveys at the toparchy level this land type is not preserved, while the only survey available at the nome level originates from Upper Egypt, where crown land is hardly found. Instead of crown land, Upper Egypt has a large area of privately-owned land, for which the owners paid a tax at a similar rate to the rent paid by the farmers of crown land. Therefore, privately-owned land may, for tax purposes, be considered the equivalent of crown land.

A second problem lies in the differences in irrigation regime: the Fayum area is not inundated directly by the Nile, but by a branch of the river, and the influx of water in this semi-oasis is controlled by a system of canals and sluices; the agricultural area in the Nile valley, on the contrary, is divided in island-land (land in or near the Nile, irrigated directly by the river) and high-land (irrigated during the Nile flood through a system of canals and dykes). Hence the land surveys from the Fayum do not have the subcategories of island-land and high-land, found in the land survey of the Edfu nome.

Conclusion

The rich papyrological evidence of Ptolemaic Egypt provides a wealth of data on the information flow of land surveys from village through toparchy to nome level (see figure). For the Fayum, an additional administrative level is attested – the so-called *meris* between toparchy and nome (see note 8), but there are no indications that the level of tax districts between village and toparchy played any role in land surveys, as it did for tax lists of the third century BC.[60] Data collection started at the village level with two topographical surveys: a cadastral survey (*euthymetria*) in Sept.–Oct. after the inundation, on the basis of which a crop survey (*geometria*) was performed in Febr.–March after the sowing, but before the harvest. Based on these two surveys, a number of secondary reports were created for the village level and/or for transmission to the higher levels. Firstly, an alphabetical list of land holders was drawn up and then turned into a tax list, meticulously recording the dues each individual had to pay. This was further summarised in a more general report recording dues and actual payments (often in wheat equivalent). Secondly, based on the *geometria*, a summary was made of agricultural production (also regularly using wheat equivalents). Thirdly, a land survey report per land category (e.g. sacred, cleruchic or crown land) was created. Each category was further divided into subcategories, and details were added on the crops grown, while historical information was taken from other sources, e.g. for *kleroi* it is mentioned when a cleruch received his grant, who previously held it, etc. In contrast to the previous two types of report, this report did transmit information on individual plot holders to the toparchy level. At the toparchy level, the information of the survey reports per land category was copied almost verbatim, and the resulting list was then passed on to the nome level. Here, the toparchy lists were compiled into a single nome report. This summary no longer contained information on individual plot holders and farmers, except for larger cleruchic plots and (probably) derelict land, betraying a keen interest in the longue durée history (going back to the 3rd century BC) of these types of land. The nome report further gave the grand totals per land category and its subcategories, broken down into subtotals per toparchy only, checked in a systematic way by the toparchy scribes. Village scribes added corrections to the detailed data on some cleruchic plots and probably also to details on derelict land, assuming derelict land was included in the nome report. (Sub)totals were always expressed in wheat, no longer in the actual crops cultivated. We may assume that, as was the case for tax lists, only the summary nome reports were sent to Alexandria.

60 Clarysse and Thompson, in P. Count II, pp. 63–65.

Figure. Information flow from village to higher levels

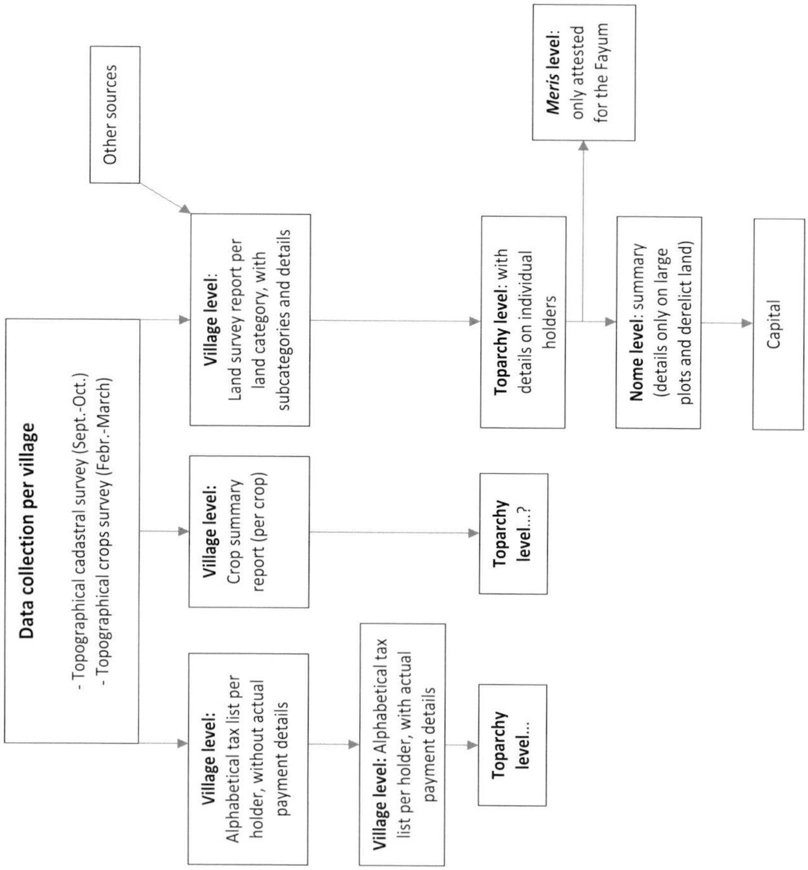

Bibliography

Brashear, W.M. (ed.), *Ptolemäische Urkunden aus Mumienkartonage* (Ägyptische Urkunden aus den Staatlichen Museen Berlin: Griechische Urkunden 14). 1980. Göttingen: Staatliche Museen Preussischer Kulturbesitz. (= BGU XIV)

Bresciani, E., 'Registrazione catastale e ideologia politica nell' Egitto tolemaico. A completamento di la 'Spedizione di Tolomeo II in Siria', *Egitto e vicino oriente* 6 (1983): pp. 15–31.

Christensen, Th., D.J. Thompson and K. Vandorpe (eds.), *Land and Taxes in Ptolemaic Egypt: An Edition, Translation and Commentary for the Edfu Land Survey (P. Haun. IV 70)*. 2017. Cambridge: Cambridge University Press. (= P. Haun. IV 70)

Clarysse, W. and D.J. Thompson, *Counting the People in Hellenistic Egypt*. 2 vols. 2006. Cambridge: Cambridge University Press.

Crawford, D.J., *Kerkeosiris. An Egyptian village in the Ptolemaic period*. 1971. Cambridge: Cambridge University Press.

Cuvigny, H., *L'arpentage par espèces dans l'Égypte ptolémaïque d'après les papyrus grecs* (Papyrologica Bruxellensia 20). 1985. Brussels: Fondation égyptologique Reine Élisabeth.

Grenfell, B.P., A.S. Hunt and J.G. Smyly (eds.), *The Tebtunis Papyri. Part I*. 1902. London: Oxford University Press. (= P. Tebt. I)

Hunt, A.S., J.G. Smyly and C.C. Edgar (eds.), *The Tebtunis papyri. Volume 3, Part 2*. 1938. London: Cambridge University Press. (= P. Tebt. III)

Kaplony-Heckel, U., 'Demotische Verwaltungsakten aus Gebelein: Der grosse Berliner Papyrus 13608', *ZÄS* 121 (1994): pp. 75–91.

Kaplony-Heckel, U., 'Zur Landwirtschaft in Oberägypten. Demotische Akten und Urkunden aus Gebelein (II. Jht. v. Chr.) und der arabische Leitfaden des Maḫzūmī (†1189 n. Chr.)', in I. Shirun-Grumach (ed.), *Jerusalem Studies in Egyptology* (Ägypten und Altes Testament 40). 1998. Wiesbaden: Harrassowitz, pp. 57–66.

Keenan, J.G. and J.C. Shelton (eds.), *The Tebtunis Papyri. Volume IV*. 1976. London: Egypt Exploration Society. (= P. Tebt. IV)

Maresch, K., *Ptolemäische Bankpapyri aus dem Herakleopolites (P. Herakl. Bank). Papyri der Sammlungen in Heidelberg, Köln und Wien* (Papyrologica Coloniensia 35). 2012. Paderborn: Ferdinand Schöningh.

McGing, B., 'Revolt Egyptian style. Internal opposition to Ptolemaic rule', *AfP* 43 (1997): pp. 273–314.

Meeks, D., *Le grand texte des donations au temple d'Edfou* (Bibliothèque d'étude 59). 1972. Cairo: Institut français d'archéologie orientale du Caire.

Monson, A., *Agriculture and Taxation in early Ptolemaic Egypt. Demotic land surveys and accounts (P. Agri. Dem.)* (Papyrologische Texte und Abhandlungen 46). 2012. Bonn: Habelt. (= P. Agri. Dem.)

Rathbone, D., D.J. Thompson and A. Verhoogt, 'A Reconstructed Land Survey from Kerkeosiris,' in R. Ast, H. Cuvigny, T. Hickey and J. Lougovaya (eds.), *Papyrological Texts in Honor of Roger S. Bagnall* (American Studies in Papyrology 53). 2013. Ann Arbor: University of Michigan Press, pp. 243–265.

Reggiani, N., 'Data processing and state management in Late Ptolemaic and Roman Egypt: The project 'Synopsis' and the archive of Menches,', in T. Derda, A. Łatjar and J. Urbanik (eds.), in cooperation with G. Ochała and A. Mirończuk, *Proceedings of the 27th International Congress of Papyrology, Warsaw 29 July – 3 August 2013* (Journal of Juristic Papyrology, Supplement 28). 2016. Warsaw: University of Warsaw, pp. 1415–1444.

Scheuble-Reiter, S., *Die Katökenreiter im ptolemäischen Ägypten* (Vestigia. Beiträge zur alten Geschichte 64), Munich: C.H. Beck.

Scholl, R., *Corpus der ptolemäischen Sklaventexte*. 1990. Stuttgart: Steiner.

Vandorpe, K., 'The Ptolemaic Epigraphe or Harvest tax (shemu)', *AfP* 46 (2000): pp. 165–228.
Vandorpe, K., 'Paying Taxes to the Thesauroi of the Pathyrites in a Century of Rebellions (186–88 BC)', in L. Mooren (ed.), *Politics, Administration and Society in the Hellenistic and Roman World. Proceedings of the International Colloquium, Bertinoro, 19–24 July 1997* (Studia Hellenistica 36). 2000. Leuven: Peeters, pp. 405–436.
Vandorpe, K., W. Clarysse and H. Verreth, *Greco-Roman archives from the Fayum* (Collectanea Hellenistica 6). 2015. Brussels and Leuven: Peeters.
Verhoogt, A., *Menches, Komogrammateus of Kerkeosiris. The Doings and Dealings of a Village Scribe in the Late Ptolemaic Period (120–110 BC)* (Papyrologica Lugduno-Batava 29). 1998. Leiden: Brill.

Agreements and accounts. On-going research on economic activities of the temple of Soknopaiou Nesos according to the Demotic texts[1]

Sandra L. Lippert, Paris and Maren Schentuleit, Oxford

Introduction

At the 1st International Fayum Congress in Sommerhausen in 2003 we presented a paper on the economy of the temple of Soknopaios with results of the then still on-going five-year research project initiated by Karl-Theodor Zauzich in 2000 which aimed at the edition of the late Demotic documentary texts from Dime/Soknopaiou Nesos (30 BCE to 2nd century CE).[2] At the time, our study was based mainly on ostraca and receipts pertaining to the temple's financial administration, whereas two text types which are essential to this subject were still largely unexplored: accounts and agreements, both of which are very well represented in the Demotic material from Soknopaiou Nesos. We gave a preliminary report on the agreements at the 2nd International Fayum Congress in Lecce in 2005[3], and by the end of the project, the edition volumes on ostraca and receipts were under press[4]. But although Karl-Theodor Zauzich and ourselves had done preliminary work by making transliterations and translations of those accounts and agreements of which we already had photographs, the two volumes on theses texts were far from publication-ready, especially since the known source material had exponentially increased through our research in collections.

In 2008 Martin Stadler reignited the Soknopaiou Nesos flame at Würzburg with a new DFG-financed project "Dime im Fayum – ein Tempel im Spannungsfeld von Tradition und Multikulturalität im hellenistisch-römischen Ägypten" in which Carolin Arlt (Würzburg) is

1 This contribution was not presented at the 8th LDAS meeting, but is based on the paper "Research on economic activities of the Soknopaios temple according to the Demotic Texts – 16 years on" which we gave at the Round Table of the *Texts in Context* project, "The Island of the Divine Crocodile – Recent Research on Textual and Other Archaeological Remains from Soknopaiou Nesos", organised by Francisca Hoogendijk at the University of Leiden, October 10–12, 2019. The acts of this event are not going to be published, we are therefore grateful to Andrea Jördens, who also attended, to give us the opportunity to include our manuscript into the present volume.

2 S. L. Lippert/M. Schentuleit, "Die Tempelökonomie nach den demotischen Texten aus Soknopaiu Nesos", in: S. L. Lippert/M. Schentuleit (eds.), *Tebtynis und Soknopaiu Nesos. Leben im römerzeitlichen Fajum. Akten des internationalen Symposions vom 11.–13. Dezember 2003 in Sommerhausen*, Wiesbaden, 2005, 71–78.

3 S. L. Lippert, "Die Abmachungen der Priester – Einblicke in das Leben und Arbeiten in Soknopaiou Nesos", in: P. Davoli/M. Capasso (eds.), *New Archeological and Papyrological Researches on the Fayyum. Proceedings of the International Meeting of Egyptology and Papyrology. Lecce, June 8th–10th 2005* (= *Papyrologica Lupiensia* 14), Lecce, 2005, 145–155.

4 S. L. Lippert/M. Schentuleit, *Demotische Dokumente aus Dime I. Ostraka*, Wiesbaden 2006; eadd., *Demotische Dokumente aus Dime II. Quittungen*, Wiesbaden, 2006.

employed as scientific collaborator.[5] While this project concentrated on religious texts, on the Ptolemaic period documentary texts housed at Oxford and the mainly Roman period material that the on-going excavation of the university of Lecce at Soknopaiou Nesos brought to light, it also gave the opportunity to Marie-Pierre Chaufray to spend one year as a post-doc at Würzburg in 2012/13, where she worked on around 100 accounts and set up a database that lists all hitherto known book keeping papyri from Dime with metadata.[6] This led to a joint research project "DimeData", launched by Würzburg and Bordeaux Universities in 2018, funded by the French *Agence Nationale de la Recherche* (ANR) and the *Deutsche Forschungsgemeinschaft* (DFG) and directed by Marie-Pierre Chaufray (Bordeaux) and Martin Andreas Stadler (Würzburg), that is concentrating on temple accounts from Soknopaiou Nesos.[7] The scientific collaborators are Déborah Vignot-Kott (since September 2018), Maren Schentuleit (November 2018–August 2019), and now Robert Kade who replaced Maren Schentuleit in October 2019. The planned editing platform will provide transliterations and translations as well as annotations of about 40 texts and will, together with the agreements, furnish the basis for further analyses of the administrative and economic system of Dime in the Roman period.

Additionally, we have recently resumed our work on the agreements in view of a future edition project in collaboration with Karl-Theodor Zauzich. The edition of these texts will be published as *Demotische Dokumente aus Dime* IV.

Agreements

The temple agreements or *hnw.w*, as they are called in Egyptian, are agreements between the priesthood as a whole and priestly functionaries, dependent craftsmen or persons in charge of certain temple-owned enterprises; they regulate the rights and duties of these individuals or groups in the exercise of professional activities in the context of the temple.

The vast majority of these agreements are still unpublished, although one of them, pBerlin P. 7059[8], is known to Egyptologists since it appeared as a phototype image in Wilhelm Spiegelberg's *Demotische Papyrus aus den Königlichen Museen zu Berlin* (Leipzig/Berlin), in 1902; it was there identified as a letter, but is in fact an agreement for the

5 < www.aegyptologie.uni-wuerzburg.de/forschung/dime-im-fayum/ >.

6 M.-P. Chaufray was at that time research associate for the project *Dime im Fayum – ein Tempel im Spannungsfeld von Tradition und Multikulturalität im hellenistisch-römischen Ägypten* funded by the DFG (project no. 107273930) directed by M. A. Stadler and based at the University of Würzburg.

7 M. Schentuleit, "Keeping Track of Accounts: The Editing Platform DimeData", in: C. E. Römer (ed.), *News from Texts and Archaeology. Acts of the 7th International Fayoum Symposium 29 October – 3 November 2018 in Cairo and the Fayoum*, Wiesbaden, 2020, 27–32; M.-P. Chaufray, "Comptes du temple de Soknopaios à Dimé à l'époque romaine", in: T. Derda/A. Łajtar/J. Urbanik (eds.), *Proceedings of the 27th International Congress of Papyrology in Warsaw, 29 July – 3 August*. Journal of Juristic Papyrology Supplement 28, Warsaw, 2016, 1737–1749; ead., "Registres comptables et pratique scribale à Dimé à l'époque romaine", in: R. Ast/J. Cromwell/M. Choat/J. Lougovaya-Ast/R. Yuen-Collingridge (eds.), *Observing the Scribe at Work: Scribal Practice in the Ancient World*. OLA (in press).

8 TM 45755. W. Spiegelberg, *Demotische Papyrus in den Königlichen Museen zu Berlin*, Berlin 1902, 22, pl. 45. The *Lexikon der Ägyptologie* took this identification over: E. Lüddeckens, s.v. *Papyri, Demotische*, in: *Lexikon der Ägyptologie* IV, Wiesbaden 1982, col. 777. For the date cf. K.-Th. Zauzich, "Spätdemotische Papyrusurkunden IV", *Enchoria* 7 (1977), 152 [151–180].

lesonis (*mr-šn*, "chief controller")[9] of a sanctuary of Isis Nepherses at Dionysias. The hitherto only fully published agreement from Soknopaiou Nesos is pVienna D 4852[10]; it concerns the regulations for the scribe's office at the Soknopaios temple[11].

Other priestly functionaries and dependent craftsmen who have already been identified as parties of such agreements are the priests on active duty (*pꜣ sꜣ nty ꜥq* 'the phyle who enters (scil. the sanctuary)'), lesoneis as representatives of the whole priesthood in Dime, as well as the lesoneis of subsidiary sanctuaries[12], i.e. temples and chapels outside Dime which were administratively dependent on the Soknopaios sanctuary, the priests deputized as public tax collectors (*nꜣ sḥn.w pr-ꜥꜣ nꜣ wꜥb.w* 'the royal tax collectors of the priests'[13]), for those sent out to collect grain from dependant farmers, for the responsible of the temple granary, and for those collecting the professional fees of the weavers. Besides, we find regulations for the running of temple-dependent businesses like the brewery/bakery of Dime, the dressmaker's shop, the dying workshop, the ferry service and for the temple's cattle farmers.

Given the sheer amount of papyrus fragments with agreements from Soknopaiou Nesos stored mainly in Berlin and Vienna, but also in Paris, London and Aberdeen – over 80! –, and the fact that we have not photographs of all of them nor, of course, finished joining the fragments for which we already have images, it is still impossible to assess the total number of manuscripts, and even more so, of individual texts: each manuscript may (and usually did) contain several agreements, and the length of these varies from a few lines to several large columns.

Accounts

Only a few individual fragments[14] of the 850 inventory numbers already identified as accounts from the temple of Soknopaiou Nesos have so far been published. The bulk of the

9 See M.-P. Chaufray, *La fonction du lésônis dans les temples égyptiens de l'époque saïte à la fin de l'époque ptolémaïque*. Studia Hellenistica, Leuven (forthcoming).

10 = pRainer Cent. 5 = TM 45643 (year 15 of Domitian, i.e. 95/96 CE).

11 E. Bresciani, "Un documento dell' anno 15 di Domiziano dall'archivio templare di Dime (P. Vindob. D 4852): Le condizioni previste per lo scriba e l'addetto alla spese dei sacerdoti", in: *Festschrift zum 100-jährigen Bestehen der Papyrussammlung der österreichischen Nationalbibliothek Papyrus Erzherzog Rainer (P. Rainer Cent.)*, Wien, 1983, 181–184. Corrections are published by K.-Th. Zauzich, "Die Bedingungen für das Schreiberamt von Soknopaiu Nesos", *Enchoria* 12 (1984), 87–90.

12 Lippert/Schentuleit, *Demotische Dokumente aus Dime II. Quittungen*, 15–18; M.-P. Chaufray, "Des lésônes en action dans le temple de Soknopaios à Soknopaiou Nesos à l'époque ptolémaïque", in: P. Piacentini/C. Orsenigo (eds.), *Egyptian Archives*, Milan, 2009, 153–164. M. Schentuleit, "Organization of the the Priesthood in Soknopaiou Nesos. Transition between the Ptolemaic and Roman Periods", in: M. Capasso/P. Davoli (eds.), *Soknopaios, the Temple and Worship. Proceedings of the First Round Table of the Centro di Studi Papirologici of Università del Salento Lecce – October 9th–10th 2013*. Edaphos 1, Lecce/Rovato, 2015, 167–185.

13 Cf. Lippert/Schentuleit, in: *Tebtynis und Soknopaiou Nesos*, 75 and Lippert/Schentuleit, *Demotische Dokumente aus Dime II. Quittungen*, 21–22.

14 pBerlin P. 23545 = TM 45592 (K.-Th. Zauzich, "Spätdemotische Papyrusurkunden IV", *Enchoria* 7 (1977), 167, no. 10), pVienna D 6151 = TM 47526 (A. Migahid, "Eine spätdemotische Abrechnungsliste über Naturallieferungen (P. Vindob. D 6151)", *ZÄS* 130 (2003), 99–102), pVienna D 6141 = TM 47527 (A. Migahid, "Ein Auszug aus einem spätdemotischen Kassenbuch", *ZÄS* 127 (2000), 54–59); pVienna D 6454 = TM 47523 (A. Migahid, "Eine neue spätdemotische Abrechnungsliste aus

documents are stored in the collections of Berlin, London, Paris and Vienna, but there are also fragments in collections in North America. During her time at Würzburg, Marie-Pierre Chaufray was able to identify more than 120 rolls that are more than 1 metre long each.

The layout of the accounts written as lists is easily recognisable, as they consist of generally narrow columns of up to 40 short lines that are often split into two separate vertical rows of entries: a) the text entries and b) the number entries. The number entry is either an amount of money or a quantity of a good or a product. Occasionally, headlines of lists are preserved which consist of a date with a regnal year and an indication like *ỉp* 'account', as well as a more detailed description of the purpose of the entries. However, not in all cases is it clear whether the account concerns income or expenses of the temple. It is to be presumed that in many cases the columns without headings simply present fragments of lists for which the headings at their beginning are not preserved.

Chaufray has set up a preliminary typology[15] which now, after one year of studying the documents, has been somewhat refined. The following typology combines formal and content-related criteria: Type 1 shows under the heading *pꜣ ỉp (n) nꜣ hwe(.w) (n) ḥw.t-nṯr (n) Sbk-nb-Pay pꜣ nṯr ʿꜣ* "the list/the account of the expenses of the temple of Soknopaios the great god" enumerations of goods, personal names – occasionally specified with a title –, titles alone, occupational designations and entries mentioning the names of fees or taxes or other specifications of the purpose of the payment (e.g. "the salary") to which sums of money are assigned. Type 2 consists of lists of names in one column and amounts of money in the other. The headings show that these accounts most likely served the redistribution of the syntaxis, that is the priestly income the state paid to temples that had accepted to have their agricultural domains turned into public land. They enumerate the priests receiving the syntaxis by order of their phylai. In one instance, the amount of money every priest is entitled to is given as 1 silver deben. Type 3 shows calculations of grain quantities on the occasion of processions (*ḫʿ*). Type 4 seems to be a sort of cash ledger, detailing income and expenses in money. Type 5, which mainly concerns shorter accounts, list outstanding payments from taxes, fees and loans. However, there are still texts which are unclear to us.

The agreements and the accounts are part of the extensive Demotic documentation of the temple administration, which also includes the aforementioned receipts and ostraca. Viewed together, they not only give us an idea of the administrative processes of the temple, but also provide a context for the very concisely phrased entries in the accounts, without which these would not have been comprehensible to us.

Soknopaiu Nesos oder Umgebung", *BIFAO* 103 (2003), 342–344); pVienna G 19818 vso = TM 112348 und pVienna G 19877 vso = TM 171852 (F. Hoffmann, "Doppelte Buchführung in Ägypten. Zwei Wiener Abrechnungen (P. Wien G 19818 Verso und 19877 Verso)", in: M. Depauw/Y. Broux (eds.), *Acts of the Tenth International Congress of Demotic Studies, Leuven, 26–30 August 2008*. OLA 231, Leuven [et al.], 2014, 86–96), pVienna D 6500 = TM 47537 und pVienna D 6502 = TM 47538 (A. Migahid, "Zwei spätdemotische Listen", *MDAIK* 55 (1999), 326–328, no. 1; 331–332, no. 2), pVienna D 6788 = TM 128993 (A. Migahid, "Ein Auszug aus einem spätdemotischen Steuerbuch", in: K. Daoud/S. Abd el-Fatah (eds.), *The World of Ancient Egypt. Essays in Honor of Ahmed Abd el-Qader el-Sawi*. ASAE Suppl. 35, Cairo, 2006, 167–199).

15 Chaufray's preparatory work is the basis for the typology of accounts used in the article by Schentuleit, in: *News from Texts and Archaeology*, 27–32.

Temple book keeping

The system of temple book keeping and the accounting process can, according to our current knowledge[16], be described as follows:

Ostraca were used to record expenditure and income in money, wheat, bread etc. on a daily or rather a short-term basis as well as the presence of priests in the temple on specific days.[17] We have not yet found such ostraca for all types of entries we find on papyrus, which could mean that ostraca were used where the scribes had to take down complicated information on place, that is, not in their office, but in the granary, bakery, during festival processions etc., where the temple scribe could not carry around his long account scrolls, nor wanted to waste smaller papyrus sheets for data that had to be recopied only a short time later anyway. Such smaller sheets of papyrus were, however, used for receipts that were handed to those who delivered goods and or paid money to temple officials.[18] The ostraca with short accounts of goods or money, attendance and allocation lists[19] were taken back to the accounting office and kept there until, after a certain period of time (rather hours or days than months), a scribe transferred the information to papyrus as part of his account lists on long papyrus scrolls. These in turn were periodically audited and, if the numbers turned out to be correct, the priesthood issued discharge receipts on papyrus for the scribe of the priests who acted as book keeper of the temple.[20] The lists also served as basis of recapitulating accounts in Greek which the temple drew up to fulfil their obligations toward the state administration.[21]

Contexts

The following examples can show how entries in accounts are sometimes only understandable on the basis of other text types from Soknopaiou Nesos. The first example concerns an entry that occurs repeatedly:

sw-x nḥḥ nꜣ sbꜥ.w (n) Pꜣ-ḥꜣ-n-Ỉs.t "Day x: oil for the doors of Pa-ha-en-Iset[22]

All by itself, this would be quite cryptic, but the agreement pBerlin P. 7059, which concerns sanctuaries in Dionysias, contains the following instruction (ll. 17–20):

16 The following update slightly modifies our view of the accounting procedures already presented in S. L. Lippert, "Seeing the Whole Picture: Why Reading Greek Texts from Soknopaiou Nesos is not Enough", in: T. Gagos (ed.), *Proceedings of the Twenty-Fifth International Congress of Papyrology, Ann Arbor July 29 – August 4, 2007*. American Studies in Papyrology, Special Edition, Ann Arbor, 2010, 427–434 (esp. 432).

17 O.Dime I 1–85, 176–204.

18 P.Dime II 1–55.

19 Cf. S. L. Lippert/M. Schentuleit, "Demotic Ostraca and their Use in Egyptian Temple Context from the Graeco-Roman Period – Soknopaiou Nesos and Hut-Repit", in: C. Caputo/J. Lougovaya (eds.), *Using Ostraca in the Ancient World: New Discoveries and Methodologies. Heidelberg, 12–14 October 2017.* Materiale Textkulturen 23 (forthcoming).

20 P.Dime II 56–69. Lippert/Schentuleit, *Demotische Dokumente aus Dime II. Quittungen*, 236–237.

21 P.Louvre I 4; SPP XXII 183; SB VI 9199; W. Chr. 93 = BGU I 149. See now L. Capron, "Déclarations fiscales du temple de Soknopaiou Nêsos: éléments nouvaux", *ZPE* 165 (2008), 133–160.

22 Cf. pVienna D 8a recto col. 4, l. 30, col. 7, l. 33 and col. 10, l. 10; pVienna D 8b recto col. 6, l. 30 (the toponym is lost).

"[The lesonis] of Per-hy-Iset (*Pr-ḥy-(n-)Ỉs.t*[23]) shall give a ½ (measure) (and) [a] chous of oil for the door of the western gate and the door of the northern gate and the .[.] of the 'room of the lionesses'[24] at the day of procession. He shall cause the lemeisa of the priests to stand/be present and have them oint [them]. If he does not act accordingly, he shall give the priests one deben of silver money."

This passage shows that the oil listed in the accounts is used in the context of a ritual treatment of the doors in connection with a procession, i.e. the days for which these entries are made would have been festival days. The agreement specifies the quantity as 'half a (measure) (and) [a] chous' – unfortunately, it is not quite clear what unnamed measure is meant here[25] – the keramion or metretes? –, and which capacity it had[26], but from the mention of more than a chous we already see that this treatment did not simply mean that the hinges were oiled, but that the large wooden door leaves were anointed. This probably had a practical purpose, such as preserving the wood against insects or cracking in the hot sun, even though it was done in a ritual context, i.e. on a festival day and by the priests themselves instead of hired workmen. In the account pVienna D 8, for which no year date is preserved, no quantity is given, but simply the value of the oil, in one case 16 obols[27]. But since oil prices fluctuated vastly, between 2,5 and 10 obols per lok[28], this does not help us determine the quantity used.

The second example does not simply concern a detail, but the fundamental understanding of the account keeping at Soknopaiou Nesos. As mentioned above, most accounts consist of long lists of entries such as food stuff or objects in one row and the amounts of money in the other. The obvious explanation would be that these amounts correspond to revenues or expenditure of money for these products.

---

23 The writing is an alternative rendering of *Pꜣ-ḥꜣ-n-Ỉs.t*.

24 pBerlin P. 6848B Col. 3 l. 6: Th. Dousa/F. Gaudard/J. Johnson, "P. Berlin 6848, a Roman Period Temple Inventory", in: F. Hoffmann/H. J. Thissen (eds.), *Res Severa Verum Gaudium: Festschrift für Karl-Theodor Zauzich zum 65. Geburtstag am 8. Juni 2004*. Studia Demotica 6. Leuven/Paris/Dudley, MA, 2004, 148 [139–222], cf. fn. 81 for the feminine form *mꜣy.wt*.

25 In the accounts from Roman Soknopaiou Nesos, an unnamed measure for wine occurs which constitutes a daily ration for one person and thus can hardly be more than 1,5 to 2 litres – on the basis of the prices, it might have been half a *chous* (cf. S. L. Lippert, "Of Pots, Sherds and Drachmas. Demotic Ostraca from *Ḥw.t-Rpy.t* (with a detour to Soknopaiou Nesos)", in: F. Naether (ed.), *New Approaches in Demotic Studies. Acts of the 13th International Conference of Demotic Studies*. ZÄS Beihefte 10, Berlin/Boston, 2019, 153–154 [151–174]). However, this unnamed wine measure cannot be the same as the one used here for oil, because it would then have been mentioned after the chous, and not before.

26 For the discussion of the varying capacities of the keramion/metretes see N. Kruit/K. Worp, "Metrological Notes on Measures and Containers of Liquids in Graeco-Roman and Byzantine Egypt", *APF* 45 (1999), 120–127 [96–127].

27 pVienna 8a recto col. 7 l. 33.

28 2,5 obols per lok: pBM gr. 262 (the Demotic accounts are written upside-down in the interstices of a Greek account), col. 6, l. 6, 15; 10 obols per lok: pBerlin P. 9563 A, col. x+2, l. 5–6, 11 (1,5 lok oil = 15 obols), 18, 23; x+3, l. 3, 9, 11 (6 lok oil = 2 kite (à 27 obols) and 4 obols).

pVienna D 8b recto col. 3, ll. 23–25:

23	*snsn (n pꜣ) sẖ-tmy*	*ḏbꜥ.t 7 ½*	bread (for the) village scribe	7 ½ obols
24	*ꜣwš*	*ḏbꜥ.t 4*	resin	4 obols
25	*ỉrp*	*[ḥḏ sp-2] qd.t 4 (ḏbꜥ.t) 3*	wine	4 kite [of silver money] 3 (obols)

Even though it is not stated explicitly, these are certainly expenses of the temple, and the scribe received bread, resin and wine. But what about the money? Did the temple pay for the bread etc. and gave it then to the scribe? Since we know that the temple had a bakery and most likely also a wine cellar, since there are receipts for wine deliveries, this scenario is not very likely. But if in reality these goods simply came out of the temple stocks, why do they appear in an account of money? The solution can, in our opinion, be found in a passage of the already mentioned agreement for the function of the scribe of the priests of Soknopaiou Nesos, pVienna D 4852 (ll. 7–17):

"He shall draw up the running (account of) expenses until it (the account) is settled with him (…) He shall enter large bread(s) (and) small bread(s) into the (account of) expenses according to the estimated street price. (...) He shall enter olive oil, radish oil (and) safflower(?) oil into the (account of) expenses of the priests according to the estimated street price. (...) Each pigeon that one will roast, he shall count it at 1 ½ obols. Any resin that one will burn, [he] shall [count it] at 2 obols (...) Any green fodder[29] which he will give, he shall count it according to [the estimated street price.] (…)"

Our working hypothesis is that this means that certain expenses made in kind, that is, from products that came directly from temple factories, storage or farms, were converted into monetary values, mainly according to the current market price, sometimes also according to a pre-set fixed price, in order to be entered into the accounts of temple expenses.

A possible explanation for this practice is that in this way, the total volume of temple expenses could be numbered as monetary value, which might have played a role for the declaration of expenses which the temple had to make for the state authorities in the form of financial statements in Greek. At least one example of this type of text shows not only the total expenses, but also the surplus, which in this specific case had to be paid in total to the tax authorities "for the poll tax of the supernumerary priests" (P.Louvre I 4, l. 41). Thus, it looks like the above-mentioned accounting method served to minimize the surplus which had to be paid in money.

Viewed in this context, the practice to enter into the accounts the expenses connected to various officials of the state administration can also be better understood. Especially interesting are those entries that contain several lines for goods and food stuff, like this elaborate example from pVienna D 8b recto col. 3, ll. 1–21:

29 For *swb* meaning "green fodder" and not "weeds" (cf. *Chicago Demotic Dictionary* < https://oi.uchicago.edu/research/publications/demotic-dictionary-oriental-institute-university-chicago >, letter *s*, 72–73), see S. L. Lippert/M. Schentuleit, "Papyrus Berlin P. 7056: division of a *kleros* between members of a priestly family from Roman Soknopaiou Nesos", in: B. Bryan/Ch. Di Cerbo/M. Escolano Poveda/M. Smith (eds.), *One Who Loves Knowledge. Studies in Honor of Richard Jasnow* (forthcoming).

1	*... [...]. šmw sw-1*		... [...]. shemu-season, day 1	
2	*ḫnṯ št pꜣ fy-sfy*	*ḏbʿ.t 1 ½*	acacia wood (and) cushion(s) (for) the swordsman	1 ½ obols
3	*snsn*	*ḏbʿ.t 5*	bread	5 obols
4	*mw ḏyt*	*ḏbʿ.t 2*	water (and?) olives	2 obols
5	*nḥḥ*	*ḏbʿ.t 2*	oil	2 obols
6	*sw-2 snsn tꜣwy*	*ḏbʿ.t 5*	Day 2: breakfast bread	5 obols
7	*ḏyt*	*ḏbʿ.t [.]*	olives	[.] obols
8	*snsn rhe*	*ḏbʿ.t 5*	dinner bread	5 obols
9	*ꜣwš*	*ḏbʿ.t 3*	resin	3 obols
10	*nḥḥ*	*ḏbʿ.t 2*	oil	2 obols
11	*wstʿ*	*ḥḏ sp-2 qd.t 4.t*	travelling allowance(?) 4 kite silver money	
12	*ḫbs*	*[ḏbʿ.t] ½*	lamp	½ [obol]
13	*(...)*		(...)	
14	*ḫnṯ trns pꜣ mḫr*	*ḏbʿ.t 2 ½*	acacia wood for (the) telones of the magazine	2 ½ obols
15	*s.t sḏr 2*	*ḏbʿ.t 5*	2 sleeping places	5 obols
16	*nḥḥ lq 1*	*ḏbʿ.t 8*	oil, 1 lok	8 obols
17	*snsn*	*ḏbʿ.t 15(?)*	bread	15(?) obols
18	*ꜣwš*	*ḏbʿ.t 4*	resin	4 obols
19	*mw*	*[ḥḏ sp-2] qd.t 8.t*	water	8 kite silver money
20	*ỉrp(?) snsn*	*ḏbʿ.t 10*	wine(?) (and?) bread	10 obols
21	*ḏyt*	*[ḏbʿ.t] 1.t ½*	olives	1 ½ obols

These examples show that different officials visited Dime, or at least spent time there on their journey elsewhere, and had to be accommodated by the temple: up to now, we have discovered temple expenses for the village scribes of Tama(u)is[30], Dionysias and Neilupolis, for a strategos (*stryqs*), a *sḥn* (tax collector or governor?), an inspector (*rmṯ-šn*, epistates), a scribe of "the one of the private person" (*pa-pꜣ-rmṯ-nmḥ*), that is, of the βιβλιοθήκη ἐγκτήσεων[31], a register or private property kept in the nome capital Arsinoe, telones of the magazine, a nomarch (*sḥn-dnỉ.t*) and a state scribe or perhaps even a basilikos grammateus (*sḫ pr-ʿꜣ*)[32]. The nomarch travelled with his retinue: in his entry, three sleeping

30 For the identification of *Tꜣ-mꜣy.t* as Tama(u)is (modern Tamiya) instead of an abbreviation of *Tꜣ-mꜣy.t-Sbk-nb-Pay* (Soknopaiou Nesos), see below.

31 Cf. the term *pa-rmṯ.w-nmḥ.w* in pBerlin P. 8092, ll. 7, 8, 12 and perhaps 18 (S. L. Lippert/M. Schentuleit, "Stoetis in geheimer Mission – Der Brief pBerlin P 8092", in: H. Knuf/C.Leitz/D. von Recklinghausen (eds.), *Honi soit qui mal y pense. Studien zum pharaonischen, griechisch-römischen und spätantiken Ägypten zu Ehren von Heinz-Josef Thissen*. OLA 194, Louvain, 2010, 365, 372–373 [357–381]).

32 For the basilikos grammateus, see Ch. Armoni, *Studien zur Verwaltung des ptolemäischen Ägypten: das Amt des Basilikos Grammateus*. Pap.Col. 36, Paderborn, 2012, and T. Kruse, *Der Königliche Schreiber und die Gauverwaltung. Untersuchungen zur Verwaltungsgeschichte Ägyptens in der Zeit von Augustus bis Philippus Arabs (30 v. Chr.–245 n. Chr.)*. APF Beihefte 11, München/Leipzig, 2002. For *sḫ pr-ʿꜣ*

places are mentioned.[33] But other officials also were accompanied by a body guard, armed with a sword, that is, a *fy-sfy* or machairophoros.[34]

When staying overnight, these people received a sleeping place or at least bedding, fire wood, lamps and oil, resin to be burnt to chase off mosquitoes, and of course food and drinks. Occasionally, not just bread and olives were provided, but real cooking seems to have taken place, because at least once, a metal kettle is entered into the account.[35] The corresponding monetary values for the consumed goods or even just provided objects were again calculated and then entered into the running account of temple expenses. As with the bedding and lamps, putting a price on the mere use of cooking utensils was probably justified by the fact that even though they were given back to the temple afterwards, they had to be cleaned. Some people even received travel provisions (*snsn ỉw=f mš*ʿ) for the next part of their journey and/or *wst*ʿ, which, according to the agreement pVienna D 4852, could be a travelling allowance in money.

When it is possible to analyse accounts running over a longer time period, this will hopefully provide us with information about the frequency of such official visits in Dime, and also which parts of the state administration thus came into direct contact with the priests. As for the reasons for such visits and the tasks accomplished there, these might rather be gleaned from the agreements and Greek documents.

Regional Networks

The agreements show that the economic network of the Soknopaios temple was largely linked to cultic activity. Already in the Ptolemaic period, the priests of Soknopaiou Nesos leased out two branch sanctuaries, one of Isis Nepherses in Dionysias and one of Isis Nephremmis in a place called *Tꜣ-ꜣte.t*, outside of Dime[36]. In the Roman period, these were administered by lesoneis subordinate to the priesthood of the Soknopaios temple for which agreements were drawn up, but we no longer find lease offers – perhaps the system had changed to one of appointment on fixed terms rather than lease offers from the applicants. These branch sanctuaries were used as a kind of administrative "outposts" of the Soknopaios temple in the sense that their lesoneis had to take on tasks pertaining to the enterprises and dependent workers of the temple in their vicinity, in addition to their duties within the sanctuary itself.

The sanctuary called Pa-ha-en-Isis, "the chapel of Isis", containing an altar (*ẖwy.t*) of Isis Nepherses, was situated within the temple precinct of the Sobek temple of Dionysias alias *Pꜣ-tmy-mꜣy* "The New Town", at the western end of the Themistou meris. The lesonis of this sanctuary also administered the "room of the lionesses", equally located within the temple precinct. The relation of the "room of the lionesses" to the "Bubasteion" mentioned in a Greek text from Dionysias[37] is unclear, since the latter gave its name to a quarter of the

simply meaning "scribe of the state administration", see P.W. Pestman, "Bail à ferme de la terre « La Pointe »", in: E. Boswinkel/P.W. Pestman (eds.), *Textes grecs, démotiques et bilingues*, P.L.Bat. 19, Leiden, 1978, 10 n. i) [3–12].

33 pVienna D 8b recto col. 5 l. 16.

34 pVienna D 8a recto col. 7 l. 8 mentions a swordsman of the *sẖ pr-ʿꜣ*.

35 pVienna D 8a recto col. 9 l. 7.

36 Cf. P.Ox.Griff. 42–44, 48–51.

37 BGU I 53, l. 13 (133 CE).

village. Either, this Bubasteion is a different sanctuary outside the temenos, or, if it is to be identified with the "room of the lionesses", it was situated inside the temenos, but was directly accessible via a secondary gate in the temenos wall and thus could still have served as eponymous sanctuary of the town area just outside this gate.

In one of the agreements pertaining to this lesonis, there is a clause allowing him to sublease the altar of Isis Nepherses and the room of the lionesses[38], but in an addendum to the same text, this permission – presumably copied from an earlier agreement – is retracted and the licence to lease out these sanctuaries is granted to the lemeisa (*mr-mšʿ.w*) and elders of the temple of Soknopaiou Nesos instead[39]. Nevertheless, the lesonis of Pa-ha-en-Iset retains the permission to lease out the altar of Isis Nepherses at Neilupolis and the "house of the nomographos" (*nwmqlps* = νομογράφος 'notary'), probably also at Neilupolis, but the rent he is allowed to demand is capped at 25 deben.

One of his obligations is to do an inventory on the first day of the year, at the first hour of the day, that is, immediately after he takes over[40]. By chance, one such inventory list[41] has actually survived and tells us that in the chapel of Isis Nepherses, the deified Satabus had a cult, while in the room of the lionesses, the deified Harpagathes and Peteamonipe were venerated (and perhaps their mummies kept). This is interesting because "Panomieus", i.e. "The one of the lionesses", "Satabus" and "Harpagathes" are three of the most common personal names of Soknopaiou Nesos. Indeed, these close connections between Dionysias and Soknopaiou Nesos date back to the Ptolemaic period: documents from the 2nd century BCE show that the agricultural domain of the temple of Soknopaiou Nesos was situated at Dionysias, meaning the grain supply for the temple came from there, via boat[42]. For the Roman period, we have no information about a temple domain – it is likely that the ἱερὰ γῆ of Soknopaiou Nesos was, as elsewhere, turned partly into public land.[43] But a grain receipt following the pattern of receipts for offering wheat[44], but made by the phyle in service not for the "responsible of the offering" (*pꜣ rd n pꜣ fy*), that is, the manager of the temple granary, but to the lesonis of Pa-ha-en-Isis, could point to the fact that the grain supply for the Soknopaios temple, at least in part, still came from Dionysias, and that, perhaps due to delivery problems, the phyle in this particular case had to get the grain for baking the offering breads directly from there instead of simply collecting it at the temple granary of Soknopaiou Nesos.

38 pBerlin P. 7059, l. 6.

39 Cf. pBerlin P. 7059, l. 24–25.

40 Cf. pBerlin P. 7059, l. 20–21.

41 pBerlin P. 6848 = P.Zauzich 12 (TM 46246) (see fn. 24 above).

42 Cf. S. L. Lippert, "Chapels, Chambers and Gateways: the religious architecture of Soknopaiou Nesos according to the demotic documentary papyri", in: M. Capasso/P. Davoli (eds.), *Soknopaios. The Temple and Worship. Proceedings of the First Round Table of the Centro di Studi Papirologici of Università del Salento, Lecce, October 9th 2013*. Edaphos 1, Lecce 2015, 161–162.

43 Cf. A. Monson, *From the Ptolemies to the Romans. Political and Economic Change in Egypt*, Cambridge, 2012, 136–138.

44 For this category of receipts, see Lippert/Schentuleit, *Demotische Dokumente aus Dime* II. *Quittungen*, 145–183 (esp. 181–183) and S. L. Lippert, "Au clair de la lune – The organisation of cultic service by moon calendar in Soknopaiou Nesos", in: Gh. Widmer/D. Devauchelle (eds.), *Actes du IXe congrès international des études démotiques. Paris, 31 août–3 septembre 2005*. BdE 147, Le Caire, 2010, 183–194.

We have already heard that the lesonis of Pa-ha-en-Isis had to organise the impregnation of the doors of the Isis chapel and of the "room of the lionesses" with oil. Another task of this lesonis was the supervision of the fishermen, for whom he has to establish (*smn*) something "for the god" – presumably the fees which they had to pay to the temple for exercising their trade[45]. On the other hand, the agreements mention that he should not spend too much time on the lake shore either (more precisely, no more than five days per month, not even when it was his time to do his five days of compulsory dike work), probably because some lesoneis had made this their main activity instead of taking care of the Isis chapel. On the other hand, he had the right to take off a day to go fishing during the summer months (more precisely, between May 15 and the end of August)[46].

While two Ptolemaic lease offers for the chapel of Pa-ha-en-Iset in Dionysias contain the promise to build "the room of Harpsenesis"[47],we do not know where this room was and which status it had in relation to the Soknopaios temple in the Roman period, because we have not yet been able to find it in the Roman period sources. It cannot be the Harpsenesis temple at Soknopaiou Nesos, which existed well before 118 BCE[48], and it is unlikely to be the sanctuary of Harpsenesis near *Tꜣ-ꜣte.t* which will be discussed below. The likeliest solution is that this "room of Harpsenesis" was also in Dionysias, and in that case, it might well be the sanctuary that gave its name to the ἀ[μ]φόδ( ) Ἁρποχρατ( ) in Dionysias[49], as "Harpokrates" is the common Greek translation of Harpsenesis[50].

The chapel (*ʿby.t*) of Isis Nephremmis at Ta-atet (*Tꜣ-ꜣte.t*) was another branch sanctuary which, in the Roman period, was administrated by lesoneis subject to agreements made with the priesthood of Soknopaiou Nesos. Like for Pa-ha-en-Iset, there are also Ptolemaic lease offers for this chapel. Greek documents show that a cult of Isis Nephremmis existed in Neiloupolis (Νείλου πόλις)[51], Pelusion (Πηλούσιον)[52] and Gynaikon Nesos (Γυναικῶν Νῆσος, also Νῆσος Γυναικῶν λεγομένη)[53]. Of these, the Demotic name of Neiloupolis – *Pr-Ḥʿpy* – is known, so the remaining two have to correspond to the two other Demotic toponyms, namely *Pr-ḥḏ* and *Tꜣ-ꜣte.t*. But which is which? While we cannot be absolutely sure, a number of indications point to *Pr-ḥḏ* being Pelusion and *Tꜣ-ꜣte.t* being Gynaikon Nesos:

45 pVienna D 6869 + 6877 + 6880 + 6888 B, ll. 9–10.
46 pVienna D 6869 + 6877 + 6880 + 6888 B, col. 3, l. 8–9.
47 P.Ox.Griff. 43 (118 BCE) and 44 (end of the 2nd C. BCE).
48 Cf. CPR XXIX 2 (122 BCE); CPR XXIX 3 (119 BCE). See also M. Schentuleit/G. Vittmann, *"Du hast mein Herz zufriedengestellt ..." Ptolemäerzeitliche demotische Urkunden aus Soknopaiu Nesos*. CPR 29, Berlin/New York, 2009, 119–121.
49 BGU I 53, l. 12 (133 CE). The editors have dissolved the abbreviation to ἐπ[ὶ τοῦ] ἀ[μ]φόδ(ου) Ἁρποχρατ(ίωνος) "in [the] quarter of Harpokration", but regarding the existence of a quarter named after the Bubastis-temple (ἐπ' ἀμφόδ(ου) Βουβαστ(είου)) in the very same text (see above) and the new evidence from the Demotic texts, it seems possible that in fact the quarter of the Harpokrateion was mentioned (ἐπ[ὶ τοῦ] ἀ[μ]φόδ(ου) Ἁρποχρατ(είου)).
50 See also below (Isis Nephremmis and Harpsenesis-Harpokrates in Gynaikon Nesos).
51 P.Louvre I 4, ll. 4–7; SPP XXII 183, ll. 31–33.
52 SB XVI 12685 = SPP XXII 184, ll. 37–38; SPP XXII 15, ll. 1–2.
53 BGU III 916, ll. 9–10; BGU XIII 2217, col. 2 ll. 8–9; P.David 1 = SB X 10281, col. 2 ll. 3–4; SPP XXII 183, ll. 93–94.

1) The Demotic accounts, agreements and receipts never mention a lesonis of *Pr-ḥḏ*, but simply payments for the altar of Isis Nephremmis made directly to the main temple at Soknopaiou Nesos. Indeed, a Greek complaint by a group of priests of Soknopaiou Nesos who accuse someone to have deprived them of their rightful income from the altar of Pelusion[54] states that this sanctuary was family-owned, which means that the altar would not have had yearly changing lesoneis selected by the main temple.

On the other hand, the lesoneis of the *ʿby.t*-chapel of Isis Nephremmis at *Tꜣ-ꜣte.t* are well attested through a receipt[55] and several agreements[56], and these find their counterparts in the lesoneis of Isis Nephremmis at Gynaikon Nesos who, in the second half of the 1st century CE, lease out the altar of Isis Nephremmis at Neilupolis[57].

2) The name *Tꜣ-ꜣte.t* means "the (mountain) back", "the ridge", which fits a Greek toponym containing the element νῆσος "island" such as Gynaikon Nesos. However, this "island of the women" does not need to be an island today, or even still have been one during the Roman period, when the water level of the lake had already sunk to its modern height of about 45 m below sea level[58]: in order to receive this Greek name, it would have sufficed that it was one in the early Ptolemaic period, when due to the hydraulic endeavours of the first Ptolemies, the Fayum lake only just started to drop from its former, much higher level of about 20 m above sea level[59], or perhaps simply that people at that time still remembered that it had once been an island (as was the case with Soknopaiou Nesos). We will come back to a possible location for this ridge later.

For *Pr-ḥḏ*, which means "treasury, storage room" and Pelusion, called after the eastern Delta town of the same name, no such similarity in meaning between the two names can be detected. However, it is possible that *Pr-ḥḏ* "storage room" is an Egyptian pseudo-etymology of "Pelusion" based on a phonetic similarity (remember the tendency of the Fayumic dialect to pronounce /r/ as /l/), and perhaps also an allusion to one of the Egyptian names of Pelusion, *Swnw*, which translates as "emporium".

The cultic activities of the lesonis of the chapel of Isis Nephremmis at *Tꜣ-ꜣte.t* also include care for "the house of Stothoetis the god", another deified person who, like the afore-mentioned Satabus and Harpagathes at Dionysias, also had a heavy influence on naming practices at Soknopaiou Nesos. And of course, Panephremmis "The one of (Isis) Nephremmis" is another of the typical Soknopaiou Nesos names.

---

54 SPP XXII 184 = SB XVI 12685 (139 CE).

55 P.Dime II 54 (pBerlin P. 15505). The toponym (ll. 6 and 9) had been read *Tꜣ-mꜣyn* by K.-Th. Zauzich, "Spätdemotische Papyrusurkunden II", *Enchoria* 2 (1972), 65, and we proposed *Tꜣ-ỉwe.t(?)* in our re-edition in *Demotische Dokumente aus Dime* II. *Quittungen*, 185. However, comparison with other attestations shows that *Tꜣ-ỉwṯ(.t)* or *Tꜣ-ꜣṯ(.t)* should be read.

56 pBerlin P. 15654 (late 1st–2nd c. CE); pVienna D 4854 + 4855 + 4856 + 4857 + 4861 + 4864 + 4866 + 4867 + 6011 + 6110 (late 1st–2nd c. CE); pVienna D 6054 + 6055 + 6874 + 6078 (1st half 1st c. CE);

57 BGU III 916 (69–79 CE).

58 C. Römer, "The Nile in the Fayum. Strategies of Dominating and Using the Water Resources of the River in the Oasis in the Middle Kingdom and the Graeco-Roman Period", in: H. Willems/J.-M. Dahms (eds.), *The Nile: Natural and Cultural Landscape in Egypt*, Bielefeld, 2017, 180 [177–191].

59 Römer, in: *The Nile*, 180, 185 n. 44; see also M. Rebentisch, "Notes on the Maps "Fayyum Blue Moeris", in: C. E. Römer (ed.), *News from Texts and Archaeology. Acts of the 7th International Fayoum Symposium 29 October – 3 November 2018 in Cairo and the Fayoum*, Wiesbaden, 2020, 192 [189–195].

The accessory tasks of the lesonis of *Tȝ-ȝte.t* are even more varied than those of the lesonis of Pa-ha-en-Iset. He leases out the altar of Isis Nephremmis at Neilupolis and also the "house of the nomographos", probably also at Neilupolis, since *Tȝ-ȝte.t*/Gynaikon Nesos seems not to have had much village infrastructure, and again the rent is capped at 25 deben. That probably means that this "house of the nomographos" was sometimes leased out by the lesonis of Pa-ha-en-Iset and sometimes by the lesonis of *Tȝ-ȝte.t*. Both of these had, as we have seen, the task to lease out the altars of "their" respective goddesses at Neilupolis, so the responsibility for the "house of the nomographos" might have switched at some point – or perhaps annually? – from one to the other.

The lesonis of *Tȝ-ȝte.t* also collected the professional tax of the "shipmasters of *Tȝ-ȝte.t*" (*nȝ ʿ-n-mr.w Tȝ-ȝte.t*). These were, like the "shipmasters of Soknopaiou Nesos", responsible for running a ferry service and transporting goods between Soknopaiou Nesos and temple properties on the other side of the Fayum lake. The lesonis of *Tȝ-ȝte.t* had to have boats built and steering oars produced for them, and he is also involved in the wood trade: the agreements explicitly mention olive, acacia and tamarisk wood, and he has to deliver specified quantities to the temple of Soknopaios – it is therefore likely that there were groves in the vicinity of *Tȝ-ȝte.t* which could be used for this purpose. Finally, he is the only one allowed to sell wine at *Tȝ-ȝte.t,* so perhaps there were vineyards on the hill of *Tȝ-ȝte.t*.

A third branch sanctuary with its own lesoneis was a temple of Harpsenesis: it is never labelled through a toponym, but always simply by the theonym. It seems most likely that it was also at *Tȝ-ȝte.t*/Gynaikon Nesos or in its close vicinity: there is an early Roman agreement for the lesonis of Isis Nephremmis, Harpsenesis and Stothoetis, which at that period seems to have been a single post, and in the later Roman agreements for the lesonis of Ta-atet, Harpsenesis is still occasionally mentioned.[60] Two Greek inventory rolls kept at the Soknopaios temple even mention that in the branch sanctuary of Gynaikon Nesos, there was, besides the naos for Isis Nephremmis, also a wooden naos for Harpokrates[61], and a Greek account lists grain for the purificatory meals of the priests of Soknopaios who participated in the festival processions of Isis Nephremmis and Harpsenesis at Gynaikon Nesos (κω[μασίαις] ἐν Νήσῳ Γυναικῶν (94) λε[γομέν]ῃ [῞Ισιδος Ν]εφρέμιδο(ς) καὶ Ἁρποκράτο(υ) (95) θεῶν μ[ε]γίστων)[62]. A clue to the location of Gynaikon Nesos and the temple of Harpsenesis lies in the fact that the main extra-cultic activity of the lesonis of Harpsenesis is the supervision of oil production and oil trade to which we will come back more in detail later: Greek texts mention a toponym Psenharpsenesis or Psinharpsenesis[63] in the Herakleidou meris which is quite often connected with olive groves. This Psenharpsenesis was not a village[64], but rather a region[65] – the toponym is generally used in

60 E.g. in pVienna D 6054 + 6055 + 6874 + 6078, l. x+6, x+10.

61 P.David 1 = SB X 10281, col. 2, l. 7 (138–161 CE); BGU XIII 2217, col. 2, ll. 11–12 (after 161 CE).

62 SPP XXII 183, l. 93–96 (138 CE?); P.Louvre I 4, col. 3 l. 74–76 (before 166 CE) is restored after this passage.

63 The latter form only in P.Petrie III 104 (244/3 BCE).

64 E. A. Selim, "Where was Psenharpsenêsis", *ICDS* XXVII.3, 1980, thus corrects the two instances where editors had once wrongly restored *kômê* in a lacuna before Psenharpsenesis and once wrongly restored Psenharpsenesis instead of Karanis after *kômê*.

the phrase "the plain (πεδίον) of Psenharpsenesis"[66], and this plain was cultivated with wheat, date palms and especially olive trees[67]. Several τόποι are mentioned within this region, but documents concerning Psenharpsenesis are generally written in Karanis[68], with which it also shared the police force[69]. Moreover, the "priest of Harpokrates" called Phanomgeus, son of Phanomgeus (i.e. *Pa-nȝ-mȝy.wt*, as mentioned above, a name typical for Soknopaiou Nesos) who appears in several tax accounts from Karanis as paying the ἐπιστατικὸν ἱερέων[70] might well be the lesonis of the Harpsenesis temple mentioned in the documentation from Soknopaiou Nesos. As said before, the territory of Psenharpsenesis must have bordered the territory of Karanis, presumably on the north[71], but we do not know how far this plain stretched east, south and west[72]. While it has been proposed that the element Pse-/Psi- of Psenharpsenesis means "the sand" (*pȝ šʿ*)[73], and that the Harpsenesis in question was an individual who had land there, it is phonetically more convincing that this

65 Selim, *ICDS* XXVII.3, 1973.

66 Selim, *ICDS* XXVII.3, passim. Cf. BGU I 282 (175–181 CE), BGU II 558 (201–225 CE), BGU XIII 2341 (2nd c. CE), W. Chr. 364 (169–171 CE), P.Alex.Giss. 6 (2nd half 2nd c. CE), P.Gen. III 145 (206 CE), P.Mich. Mchl 11 (180–210 CE); SB XXII 15779 (98–100 CE) mentions special "watchmen of the plain".

67 Cf. Selim, *ICDS* XXVII.3, 1974–1975. Texts mentioning olive groves on the territory of Psenharpsenesis: P.Mich. IX 539 (53 CE), P.Mich. IX 540 (53 CE), BGU II 379 (67 CE), SB XXII 15346 (88–89 CE), P.Mich. IX 554 (93 CE), BGU II 444 (98–117 CE), SB XIV 12022 (100 CE), P.Lond. II 151 (p. 215) = BASP 55 224 (2nd c. CE), P.Prag. II 171 (106–117 CE), P.Corn. 7 (126 CE), BGU II 657 (151–200 CE), P.Lond. II 168 (p. 190) (162 CE), SB XXIV 16252 (163 CE), W. Chr. 364 (ca. 169–171 CE), SB IV 7379 (177 CE), P.Mich.Mchl. 11 (180–210 CE), BGU I 282 (175–180 CE), BGU II 558 (201–225 CE), P.Gen. III 145 (206 CE). The tax receipts for Petheus, son of Phaesis on P.Mich. VI 383 (107–109 CE), l. 26–27 and 34–35 mention his "garden land of Psenharpsenesis" and immediately afterwards the tax for transporting olives.

68 E.g. P.Corn. 7 (126 CE) or W. Chr. 364 (ca. 169–171 CE).

69 Selim, *ICDS* XXVII.3, 1975.

70 W. J. R. Rübsam, *Götter und Kulte in Faijum während der griechisch-römisch-byzantinischen Zeit,* Bonn, 1974, 98–99 and n. 4: P.Mich. IV 223, l. 1467 (171/2 CE), P.Mich. IV 224 l. 802 (172/3 CE) and P.Mich. IV 225 l. 1135 (173/4 CE).

71 Selim, ICDS XXVII.3, 1976. Joint mention of Karanis and Psenharpsenesis e.g. in P.Lond. II 151 (p. 215) = BASP 55 224 (2nd c. CE) περ<ι> Καρανίδα καὶ̣ (5) Ψεναρψενῆσιν „in the vicinity of Karanis and Psenharpsenesis"; P.Mich.Mchl. 11 (ditto, phrased as π̣ε̣ρ̣ὶ πε̣[δ]ίο̣ν Ψ̣ε̣(5)ναρ̣[ψ]ε̣ν̣ῆσιν κώμης Κα̣ρ̣α-(6)νίδος „in the plain of Psenharpsenesis of the village Karanis"), P.Alex.Giss. 6 (2nd half 2nd c. CE): περὶ κώ(μην)(6) [Καρα]νίδα πεδί[ο]υ̣ Ψεναρψε-(7)[νήσε]ω̣ς̣. "near the village Karanis, of the plain of Psenharpsenesis". Proximity is also implied in P.Mich. IX 554 (93 CE) in which an inheritance consisting of property in Karanis and Psenharpsenesis is divided.

72 Selim suggests on the basis of the *penthemeros* certificate P.Grenf. II 53g for work ἐν χώμ(ατι) (4) Ψε̣( ) Φιλαδελ( ), which he understands as 'on the dike of Pse(nharpsenesis) and Philadel(phia)', that the two places should have been connected by a dike and canal, which he supposes to be the Bahr Wardan, i.e. the early Ptolemaic canal following the desert edge around the eastern and northern border of the Herakleidou meris. However, as G. Claytor, "Penthemeros Certificates of the Granary C123, Karanis", *BASP* 50 (2013), 55 [49–75], note to l. 2, points out, the extension of the abbreviation Ψε( ) as "Psenharpsenesis" is by no means obligatory, as there are the dikes of Psenalitis and Psenonnophris attested in this region (cf. also *op.cit.*, 59–60).

73 Selim, *ICDS* XXVII.3, 1974, n. 7. Given the unsatisfactory phonetics (Demotic *šʿ* "sand" > Coptic ϣⲱ, ϣⲟⲩ, cf. W. E. Crum, *A Coptic Dictionary*, Oxford, 1939, 549b; W. Westendorf, *Koptisches Handwörterbuch*, Heidelberg, 1965/1977, 302) it is hard to believe that this etymology was really suggested to him by Willy Clarysse, as he claims.

initial element Pse-/Psi- is in fact *Pꜣ-šy-* "the lake"[74]. Now, a body of water called Μικρὰ Λίμνη, or "small lake" existed once in the Herakleidou meris: when the water level of the Fayum lake started to fall in the early Ptolemaic period[75], it must have split off from the main lake. It is only attested in Greek texts of the 3rd century BCE[76] and had disappeared by the Roman period, when the water level had fallen another 40 meters[77]. Geomorphological modelling suggests that in its latest stage, the Mikra Limne had retracted to the south of the prominent elongated ridge to the west of Tama(u)is/Tamiya[78]. But since this toponym[79] can certainly be identified with Demotic *Tꜣ-mꜣy.t*, "The Island", a toponym frequently occurring in the agreements for the lesonis of *Tꜣ-ꜣte.t*[80], it is obvious that earlier on, this lake must have extended north, around this ridge and Tama(u)is/Tamiya; the ridge itself is thus a very obvious candidate for *Tꜣ-ꜣte.t* "the mountain back" alias Gynaikon Nesos "the island of the women", where the above-mentioned chapel of Isis Nephremmis was situated, and quite likely the sanctuary of Harpsenesis as well. Thus, it seems plausible to propose that the plain of Psenharpsensis – "the lake of Harpsenesis" (*Pꜣ-šy-Ḥr-pꜣ-šr-n-Ỉs.t*) – took its name from this former lake, in the middle of which was an island with a sanctuary of Harpsenesis, and which by slowly shrinking towards the south, had left behind a fertile agricultural plain in the north.

As mentioned earlier, the main non-cultic activity of the lesonis of Harpsenesis was the supervision of oil production and oil trade in this region. He kept the official oil measure and collected the professional fees – in oil for the oil producers and in money, at 4 obols per log oil, from the oil sellers[81]. He was allowed or even encouraged to exercise these activities himself, as some of the agreements show, but obviously should not neglect his priestly service in the temple of Harpsenesis: he still has to burn incense there each day. Part of the oil he produced and what he levied from the other oil mills[82] was sent to the

74 *Šy* "lake" > Coptic ϢΗΙ, ϢΕΙ "pit, cistern" (Crum, *Coptic Dictionary*, 547b; Westendorf, *Koptisches Handwörterbuch*, 306). So already proposed by *Trismegistos Places* <https://www.trismegistos.org/geo/>, GEO_Id 1955.

75 Römer, in: *The Nile*, 180, 185 n. 44.

76 *Trismegistos Places*, Geo_Id 1256. Cf. also E. Van 't Dack/T. Reekmans, *Ptolemaica*. Studia Hellenistica 7, Louvain/Leiden, 1951, 46; P.W. Pestman, *Greek and Demotic Texts from the Zenon Arch*ive. P. L. Bat. 20A, Leiden, 1980, 268.

77 D. Bonneau, *Le Régime administratif de l'eau du Nil dans l'Égypte grecque, romaine et byzantine*. PdÄ 8, Leiden, 1993, 53. Cf. also H. Geremek, *Karanis, une communauté rurale de l'Égypte romaine au IIe–IIIe siècle de notre ère*. Archiwum Filologiczne 17. Wrocław, 1969, 50.

78 Rebentisch, in: *News from* Texts *and Archaeology*, map 3.

79 *Trismegistos Places*, Geo_Id 2238.

80 At first, we had taken the toponym *Tꜣ-mꜣy.t* as an abbreviation of *Tꜣ-mꜣy.t-Sbk-nb-Pay*, Soknopaiou Nesos (cf. S. L. Lippert/M. Schentuleit, *Demotische Dokument aus Dime III. Urkunden*, Wiesbaden, 2010, 405, commentary to pVienna D 10085 = P.Dime III 36, DT l. 1), but it would indeed be strange that in the agreements, this abbreviation was only used in texts also mentioning *Tꜣ-ꜣte.t*.

81 An unpublished account, pBerlin P. 15579 rto, is labelled "Year 5. The account of oil from *Tꜣ-ꜣte.t*" and then listed at least 21 persons who each gave half a *ššw*-jar of oil.

82 Cf. the agreement pVienna D 4854 + 4855 + 4856 + 4857 + 4861 + 4864 + 4866 + 4867 + 6011 + 6110, col. 2, l. 34–35: each oil producing priest had to give him 15 log oil for the illumination before Soknopaios.

Soknopaios temple for the illumination there – if the lesonis of Harpsenesis failed to do so, he had to pay one silver kite per day[83].

As mentioned above, the "small lake" no longer existed in the Roman period, but there was still a canal, which might be the "canal of Tared" (*tꜣ ḥny.t Ta-rd*) that appears once in a very fragmentary agreement[84] which does not help us locating it. However, it is also mentioned in a Greek lease offer[85] for an oil radish field[86] in the plain of Psenharpsenesis as διῶρυξ Ταραιτις λεγομένη "the canal called Taraitis". Therefore it might have been on this canal that the "shipmasters of *Tꜣ-ꜣte.t*", which had to pay their dues to the lesonis of *Tꜣ-ꜣte.t*, were active, although they might also have crossed the Fayum lake in order to reach Soknopaiou Nesos.

Conclusion:

Taking together the various Demotic sources from the temple book keeping has allowed us to retrace the different steps of accounting, such as the inclusion of virtual expenses, perhaps as a means to reduce the surplus of income that had to be paid to the tax authorities, although much is still to be learned from the many meters of papyrus rolls that are currently being studied. The comparisons between Demotic and Greek sources has helped us locate the two main branch sanctuaries, Pa-ha-en-Iset at Dionysias and the sanctuary of Isis Nephremmis at *Tꜣ-ꜣte.t* alias Gynaikon Nesos: their convenient situation at the western and eastern end of the Fayum lake probably prompted the priesthood to saddle their lesoneis with administrative tasks and thus make these places anchor points for the economic network of the Soknopaios temple.

The agreements also show that over time, such arrangements could change. We have seen that at some point, the lesonis of Pa-ha-en-Isis-Nepherses at Dionysias was allowed to lease out the altar of Isis Nepherses and the "room of the lionesses", but later he was expressly forbidden to do so, as this now fell to the lemeisa and elders of the priests, i.e. was organised directly by the Soknopaios temple. Another example is the creation of a separate office of lesonis of Harpsenesis, who took over the administration of everything oil-related, at some point in the 1st or early 2nd century CE, while in an agreement from the beginning of the Roman period, the offices of lesonis of the chapel of Isis Nephremmis at *Tꜣ-ꜣte.t*/Gynaikon Nesos and of lesonis of Harpsenesis were joint into a single function[87].

This is of course still a very preliminary assessment. It will take more time, and intensive study of the hundreds of fragments of agreements and accounts, to get to the point where we can draw a complete picture of the temple administration of Soknopaiou Nesos not only at a given moment in time, but also in its chronological development.

83 pVienna D 4854 + 4855 + 4856 + 4857 + 4861 + 4864 + 4866 + 4867 + 6011 + 6110, col. 2, l. 9–10.

84 pBerlin P. 15661+15666 (col. 2, l. 4): agreement for the transport of wheat from temple domain land to Soknopaiou Nesos by boat.

85 BGU XI 2123, l. 11.

86 For the interpretation of λαχανόσπερμον as oil radish seed, instead of sesame, see Lippert/Schentuleit, in: *One Who Loves Knowledge* (forthcoming).

87 pVienna D 6054 + 6055 + 6874 + 6078 text A, 1st half of the 1st century CE (year 22 of Tiberius? = 35/6 CE).

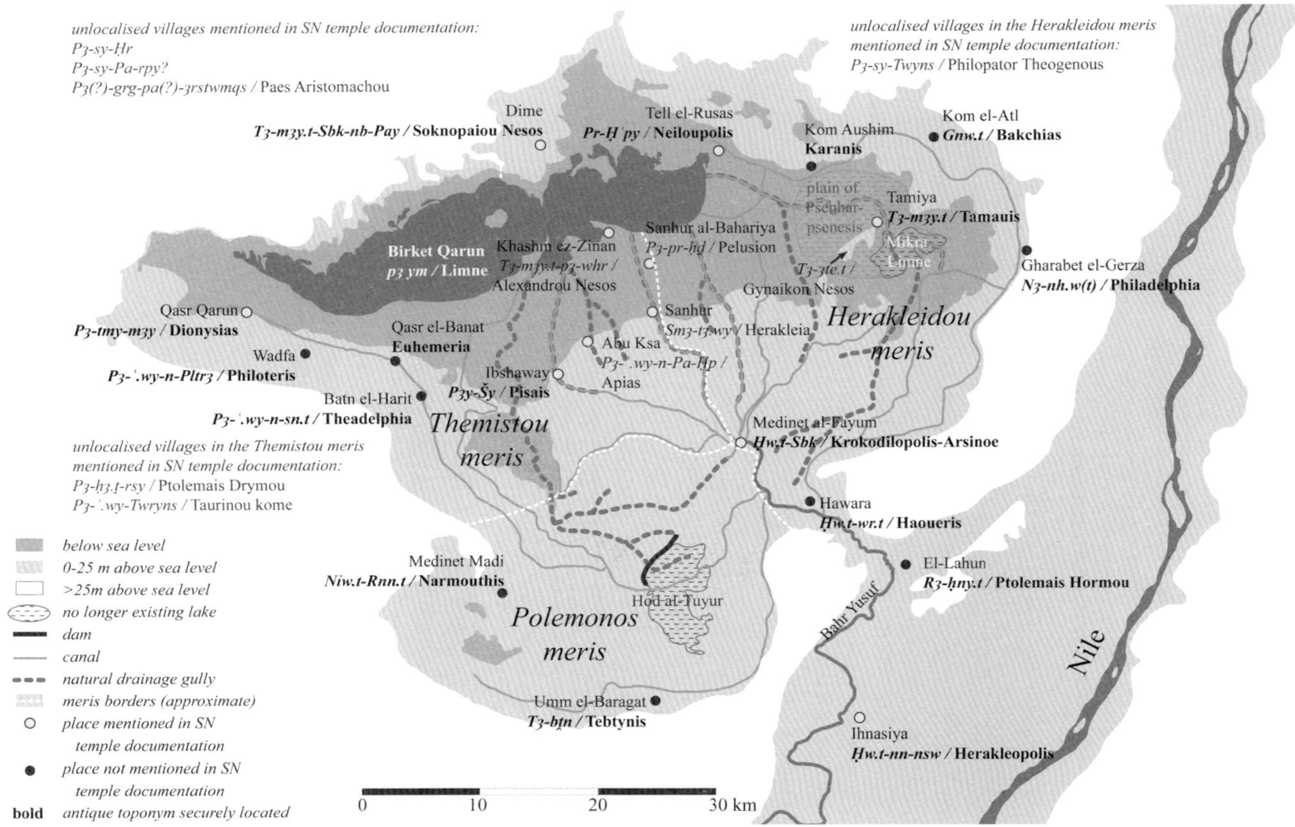

Fig. 1:
Map of the Fayum including the new identifications and locations of toponyms (drawing by the authors, combining information from the map in J. Ball, *Contribution to the Geography of Egypt, Cairo*, 1939, 126; U.S. Army map "Al Fayyūm", NH 36-9, series P502, edition 1-AMS (1953); Rebentisch in: *News from Texts and Archaeology*, map 3); Lippert/Schentuleit, in: *One who loves knowledge* (forthcoming), fig. 4).

Buchführung und Rechnungswesen in der Gutsverwaltung

Andrea Jördens, Heidelberg

Ausgangspunkt des mehrjährigen Gemeinschaftsprojektes „Synopsis: Data Processing and State Management in Roman Egypt (150 BCE-300 CE)“[1] war die staatliche Organisation der Datenverwaltung, wie sie in den verschiedenen Stufen von der Sammlung aller mutmaßlich relevanten Informationen vor Ort bis zur Übermittlung einer kondensierten Fassung an die Spitze der Verwaltungspyramide verlief. Beim endgültigen Empfänger – in der Kaiserzeit also den verschiedenen Stäben der römischen Zentrale, wenn nicht gar beim Kaiser höchstpersönlich – gingen die zuvor erhobenen Daten dabei nurmehr in Auswahl ein, in der gleichwohl zumindest der Idealvorstellung nach alle als wesentlich erachteten Elemente in gebündelter Form enthalten waren.

Man wird kaum fehlgehen in der Annahme, daß entsprechende Prinzipien und vergleichbare Verfahren auch im privaten Bereich gebräuchlich waren, wo immer ein Wirtschaftsbetrieb einen gewissen Umfang überstieg, so daß direkte mündliche Kommunikationswege sich nicht mehr als ausreichend erwiesen. Dies galt gleichermaßen, ob der fragliche Betrieb aus einer einzigen, aber übermäßig gewachsenen und womöglich weitverzweigten Einheit bestand oder sich aus vielen kleineren Einheiten zusammensetzte, die wiederum der Koordination bedurften. Letzteres war namentlich bei der Gutsverwaltung der Fall, und zwar nicht erst zu einer Zeit, als der seit jeher übliche Streubesitz sich bei manchen Angehörigen der führenden Schichten des Imperium Romanum mitunter bis weit in ferne Provinzen erstreckte.

In der Forschung waren Fragen nach Buchführung und Rechnungswesen in diesem Bereich freilich nochmals weniger im Blick als in der staatlichen Administration. Einige Überlegungen hierzu finden sich immerhin schon, wiewohl aus ganz anderer Perspektive, in der grundlegenden Studie von Eckhard Christmann zu den Aussagen der literarischen Quellen; neue Impulse dürften zudem von dem soeben erschienenen Überblicksartikel von Kai Ruffing zu „Schriftlichkeit und Wirtschaft im Römischen Reich“ ausgehen.[2] Relativ allge-

---

1 GIF Grant No: G-38-111.4/2011, Laufzeit 01/2013-12/2016; Principal Investigators: Prof. Dr. Andrea Jördens (Universität Heidelberg), Prof. Uri Yiftach-Firanko (Hebrew University, Jerusalem, ab 10/2014 Tel Aviv University); Mitarbeiter: Dr. Shimon Epstein (Jerusalem), Nikolaos Theodorakopoulos und besonders Dr. Nicola Reggiani (beide Heidelberg). Vgl. auch bereits das Vorwort dieses Bandes.

2 E. Christmann, 'Zum Verhältnis von Autor und Leser in der römischen Agrarliteratur. Bücher und Schriften für Herren und Sklaven', *Antike Fachschriftsteller: Literarischer Diskurs und sozialer Kontext*, hrsg. v. M. Horster – C. Reitz (Palingenesia 80), Stuttgart 2003, 121-152; K. Ruffing, 'Schriftlichkeit und Wirtschaft im Römischen Reich', *Literacy in Ancient Everyday Life*, hrsg. v. A. Kolb, Berlin – Boston 2018, 221-236. Eckhard Christmann habe ich sehr herzlich für die freundliche Übersendung seines Manuskriptes zu danken, das ich bereits für meine noch unpublizierte Marburger Antrittsvorlesung zum Thema „Schreibkundige Gutsverwalter – Wunsch oder Wirklichkeit?“ im WS 2002 nutzen konnte,

mein bleiben die entsprechenden Überlegungen in dem wichtigen Buch von Jean-Jacques Aubert zu der rechtlichen und gesellschaftlichen Stellung der „Business Managers in Ancient Rome“, der zwar auf die Bedeutung der dabei geforderten Rechnungslegung hinweist, dies jedoch eher beiläufig behandelt und auch kaum einmal konkreter zu fassen sucht.[3] Eine eigene Linie verfolgt wiederum Gérard Minaud, der als Wirtschaftswissenschaftler den Prinzipien ökonomischen Denkens und Handelns von der mittleren Republik bis in die Spätantike nachgeht.[4] Diese Prinzipien sucht er insbesondere über die Analyse der einschlägigen Begriffe und also des Instrumentariums zu erschließen, das sich aus den von ihm daraufhin befragten Texten von Plautus' *Asinaria* bis zu Cassiodor, aber eben auch dokumentarischen Quellen wie den pompejanischen Wachstäfelchen, den *Vindolanda tablets* und den Papyri des Heroneinos-Archivs ergibt. Zu seinen wichtigsten Schlußfolgerungen zählen hierbei die tiefgreifenden Differenzen, die diesbezüglich zwischen der grundsätzlich großen Eigenständigkeit römischer *vilici* und der zentralisierten Wirtschaftsform etwa der appianischen Besitzungen im Heroneinos-Archiv festzustellen seien,[5] was uns am Ende nochmals beschäftigen wird.

Schon aus allgemeinen Erwägungen wird man es jedenfalls auch in der Gutsverwaltung für geläufige Praxis halten, daß insoweit bedeutsame Informationen zunächst vor Ort gesammelt und dann in gestraffter Form an die Spitze der Verwaltungspyramide – hier also den Gutsherrn – weitergeleitet wurden. Einschlägige Nachrichten hierüber sind am ehesten, wie schon Ruffing notierte, in den aus Ägypten überlieferten Papyri zu finden.[6] Dabei wird man zunächst an die aus Hunderten von Papyri bestehenden und entsprechend berühmten sog. Archive des Zenon und eben des Heroneinos denken wollen, die zu unseren größten geschlossenen Funden überhaupt gehören und jeweils für ihre Zeit – das erste im III. Jhdt. v. Chr., das zweite im III. Jhdt. n. Chr. – wünschenswerte Einblicke in die Details der antiken Gutsverwaltung bieten. Trotz manch durchaus vergleichbarer Grundzüge weisen sie jedoch auch signifikante Unterschiede auf, so bereits durch die Zusammensetzung des Materials.

Zenon, Sohn des Agreophon aus dem südwestkleinasiatischen Kaunos, hatte im Jahr 256 v. Chr. die Leitung der 10.000 Aruren umfassenden δωρεά beim arsinoitischen Philadelpheia übernommen, die der hohe Hofbeamte und zeitweilige Finanzminister Apollonios als Geschenk von Ptolemaios II. erhalten hatte.[7] Berühmt sind seine Papiere vor allem für die intensive Korrespondenz, die uns über die Kultivierung bislang unbewirtschafteter

desgleichen Kai Ruffing für seine damalige und noch heute anhaltende Unterstützung (nicht nur) in allen Wirtschaftsfragen.

3 J.-J. Aubert, *Business Managers in Ancient Rome. A Social and Economic Study of* institores, *200 B.C. - A.D. 250*, Leiden – New York – Köln 1994.

4 Vgl. nur G. Minaud, *La comptabilité à Rome. Essai d'histoire économique sur la pensée comptable commerciale et privée dans le monde antique romain*, Lausanne 2005.

5 So bes. G. Minaud, 'Rationalité modulable des comptabilités', *Topoi* 12-13, 2005, 271-281; vgl. auch bereits ders., *La comptabilité* (wie Anm. 4), 91 f. und passim.

6 Vgl. nur Ruffing, 'Schriftlichkeit und Wirtschaft' (wie Anm. 2), 228 f.

7 Vgl. nur zuletzt K. Vandorpe, '[Professional archive of] Zenon son of Agreophon (Philadelpheia)', *Graeco-Roman Archives from the Fayum* (Coll. Hell. 6), hrsg. v. K. Vandorpe – W. Clarysse – H. Verreth, Leuven – Paris – Bristol, CT 2015, 447-455 = <https://www.trismegistos.org/arch/archives/pdf/256.pdf> (Zugang am 04. 01. 2019).

Flächen in ehemaligem Sumpfland aufklärt, und dies in Gegenden, die überhaupt erst zwei Generationen zuvor in griechische Hand gelangt waren. So nehmen die Abrechnungen denn auch nur ungefähr 10% des Erhaltenen ein und betreffen vornehmlich die sog. Sitometrie, also Aufstellungen über die Mengen an Getreide und anderen Nahrungsmitteln – besonders Öl und Wein –, die an Gutsarbeiter, Sklaven oder auch Gäste gingen.[8] In oft langen Listen sind hier einzelne Namen mitsamt den ihnen ausgefolgten Mengen verzeichnet, wobei die Ordnungsprinzipien der Auflistung oft im dunkeln bleiben und auch über die Hintergründe der gelegentlich höheren Zuteilungen nichts zu erfahren ist. Als Beispiel mag hier die – mit lediglich 14 Namen recht kurze – Sitometrieliste P. Cair. Zen. IV 59676 dienen:[9]

Ἔστιν ὁ ἀνηλισκόμενος σ[ῖτος] καθʼ ἡμέραν τοῖς κατὰ τ[ὴν] οἰκίαν σώμασιν ἀκολουθικο[ῖς·]		Es beträgt das aufgewendete Getreide pro Tag für das im Hause tätige Dienstpersonal:	
Πεισικλεῖ	χ(οῖν.) α ∠	dem Peisikles	Choin. 1½
Βανναίωι	χ(οῖν.) α ∠	dem Bannaios	Choin. 1½
Ὀλυμπίχωι	χ(οῖν.) α ∠	dem Olympichos	Choin. 1½
Ἄγρωνι	χ(οίν.) β	dem Agron	Choin. 2
Μενίππωι	χ(οῖν.) α ∠	dem Menippos	Choin. 1½
Νικάνορι	χ(οῖν.) α ∠	dem Nikanor	Choin. 1½
Μικίωνι	χ(οῖν.) α ∠	dem Mikion	Choin. 1½
Γλαυκίαι	χ(οῖν.) α ∠	dem Glaukias	Choin. 1½
Ἀκάμαντι	χ(οῖν.) α ∠	dem Akamas	Choin. 1½
Νικασίαι	χ(οῖν.) α ∠	dem Nikasias	Choin. 1½
Χάρμωι	χ(οῖν.) α ∠	dem Charmos	Choin. 1½
Ξένωνι	χ(οίν.) β	dem Xenon	Choin. 2
Ἀδράστωι	χ(οῖν.) α ∠	dem Adrastos	Choin. 1½
Λεπτίνει	χ(οῖν.) α ∠	dem Leptines	Choin. 1½

Selbst diese relativ einfach konzipierte Liste weist bereits einige der für diese Aufstellungen charakteristischen Elemente auf, so die durch Ausrückung und ein deutliches Spatium vom folgenden abgesetzte Überschrift, unter der jeweils in gerader Linie links die Namen, rechts die Beträge stehen; keine Unterschiede sind hingegen bei Buchstabengröße oder Zeilenabstand zu vermerken.[10] Deutlich komplexer ist die am Rand als παρὰ Μάρωνος·

8 Vgl. Vandorpe, 'Zenon son of Agreophon' (wie Anm. 7), bes. 453; hierzu grundlegend weiterhin T. Reekmans, *La sitométrie dans les Archives de Zénon* (Pap. Brux. 3), Bruxelles 1966; vgl. auch C. Orrieux, 'Les comptes privés de Zénon à Philadelphie', *CE* 56, 1981, 314-340 sowie die Übersicht bei P. W. Pestman u.a., *A Guide to the Zenon Archive* (Pap. Lugd. Bat. 21), Leiden 1980, 194; kommentierte Neueditionen zuletzt bei R. Scholl, C. Ptol. Sklav. I 98-114, mit der Zusammenfassung S. 512 ff.

9 P. Cair. Zen. IV 59676 = C. Ptol. Sklav. I 98 (258-256 v. Chr.), beim Wiederabdruck allerdings durchweg ohne die Sigle ∠ (für ἥμισυ '½'). Die Frühdatierung ergibt sich nach Scholl, Komm. zu C. Ptol. Sklav. I 98 aus den später veränderten Rationen, der aus diesem Grund wie auch der möglichen Identifikation einiger Personen die Liste in Alexandria zu verorten bzw. dem dortigen Haushalt zuzuordnen erwägt.

10 Vgl. nur die Abb. unter <http://ipap.csad.ox.ac.uk/PCZ-colour/300dpi/P.Cair.Zen.IV.59676.jpg> (Zugriff am 03. 01. 2019). Danach scheint der rechte Rand zudem original zu sein, so daß wohl keine weiteren, erst später abgebrochenen Kolumnen folgten. Zu dem für solche Aufstellungen typischen Layout

σιτικός (Z. 1 f.) gekennzeichnete, auf zahlreiche Fragmente verteilte und daher sehr viel umfangreichere Getreideabrechnung des Maron P. Cair. Zenon II 59292 ausgefallen, die sich über mehr als 660 Zeilen erstreckt und teilweise auch tagesgenaue Einträge bietet. Beispielshalber seien nur zwei der auffällig niedrigen, da lediglich aus 10 bis 15 Zeilen bestehenden Kolumnen angeführt:[11]

Frg. A col. VIII	
ι̅ϛ̅ Πεμενᾶι εἰς δέ[λ-]	am 16. dem Pemenas für Fer-
φακας τῆς ἐπιγον[ῆς] κρ(ιθῆς) ι	kel des neuen Wurfs Gerste 10
ι̅ζ̅ σπέρμα εἰς ἰδιόσ[πορα]	am 17. Saatgut für die Selbstaussaat
Παλοῦτι [- - -]	dem Palus [- - -]
Ὥρωι Πάιτος κρ(ιθῆς) [- - -]	dem Horos, Sohn des Pais Gerste [- - -]
Λαβόιτι ἐρεβίν[θου - - -]	dem Labois Kichererbse [- - -]
μεικτοῦ [- - -]	gemischt [- - -]
(γίν.) δοχ(ικῶι) κρ(ιθῆς) β∠,	macht im Empfängermaß Gerste 2½,
ἐρεβ[ίνθου - - -]	Kichererbse [- - -]
κ̅ Πεμενᾶι εἰς δέ[λ-]	am 20. dem Pemenas für Fer-
φακας τῆς ἐπιγ[ονῆς - - -]	kel des neuen Wurfs [- - -]

Frg. A col. IX	
κ̅ε̅ Ἀνδρεία̣[ι εἰς] τὴν σιτο-	am 25. dem Andreias für die Sito-
μετρί[αν] πυ(ροῦ) α	metrie Weizen 1
ὄνοις τοῖς [τὰ] ἐκκαύμα-	den Eseln, die das Heizmate-
τα προσ[άγ]ουσι εἰς τὸ	rial herbeischaffen für das
βαλανε̣[ῖον] κρ(ιθῆς) ε	Bad Gerste 5
κ̅ϛ̅ σπέρμα	am 26. Saatgut
διὰ Διογέ̣[νο]υς	durch Diogenes
Ἁρμάι Π̣[α]θ̣ῶυτος κρ(ιθῆς) ηγ´	dem Harmais, Sohn des Patoys
	Gerste 8⅓

Bei dieser langen Liste wurde die Arbeit mit Ek- und Eistheseis – Aus- bzw. Einrückungen – nochmals systematischer durchgeführt als im vorigen Fall, wobei sich das sehr bewußt eingesetzte Layout vor allem durch die gestaffelten Eistheseis auszeichnet.[12] Dadurch lassen sich die oft mehrzeiligen Einträge unmittelbar voneinander unterscheiden, was wesentlich zur leichteren Erfassung der Struktur beiträgt und eine Suche, sollte sie denn nötig werden, zweifellos vereinfachen mußte. Dabei steht das schon durch die Überstreichung hervorgehobene Tagesdatum regelmäßig in deutlicher Ekthesis, während der unterschiedliche Grad der Einrückung nicht nur Weiterführung oder Beginn eines – dann neuen – Eintrags, sondern auch eine Art Rangfolge anzeigt, so namentlich bei mehreren Einträgen unter ein und demselben Tagesdatum. Erneut sind die jeweils ausgeteilten Getreidemengen je-

mit ‘Pseudokolumnen’ auch Clarysse, in diesem Band; Lippert – Schentuleit, ebenfalls in diesem Band, bes. 144.

11 P. Cair. Zenon II 59292 = C. Ptol. Sklav. I 101 (250 v. Chr.), Z. 84-101 auf Frg. A col. VIII und IX; Übers. R. Scholl, mit Modifikationen.

12 Vgl. nur die Abb. unter http://ipap.csad.ox.ac.uk/PCZ-colour/300dpi/P.Cair.Zen.II.59292r(iv).jpg (Zugriff am 23. 12. 2018).

weils leicht abgesetzt und nach rechts gerückt, im Einzelfall auch einmal Zwischensummen gezogen, bevor nach leicht vergrößertem Zeilenabstand der Eintrag des nächsten Tages begann.

Eine übergeordnete Rechnungslegung, die Einblick in die gesamten wirtschaftlichen Aktivitäten des Gutsbetriebes mit all ihren Einnahmen und Ausgaben gewährte, sucht man unter Zenons Papieren freilich vergebens. Dies stellt sich im Fall der Heroneinos gänzlich anders dar, der Mitte des III. Jhdts. n. Chr. auf den Besitzungen des alexandrinischen Ratsherrn und ehemaligen Exegeten Aurelius Appianos als Verwalter tätig war. Neben der erneut reichhaltigen Korrespondenz trat in seinem 'Archiv' auch eine Fülle von Aufstellungen zutage, die diesbezüglich ein ungleich vollständigeres Bild vermitteln.[13] Sie sind bei genauerer Betrachtung insgesamt drei verschiedenen Kategorien zuzuweisen, nämlich „drafts of the monthly accounts submitted by *phrontistai* to the owners of the Appianus estate", die in der griechisch-römischen Antike nicht ihresgleichen kennen und daher unter Wirtschaftshistorikern einige Berühmtheit genießen; „a variety of accounts or records which were drawn up by the *phrontistai* for their own use. Some of these, such as the day-by-day lists of disbursements of wine or of payments made, may be termed 'primary' records", wobei es ebenso mancherlei hierauf aufbauende Zwischenstufen gab, die sich nach dem damit verfolgten Zweck nochmals in weitere Untergruppen einteilen ließen, wie umgekehrt auch anderes, das kaum mehr ernsthaft als Auflistung zu bezeichnen, sondern allenfalls ein bloßer Notizzettel war; schließlich einige wohl aus der Zentraladministration stammende Fragmente.[14]

Von all diesen verschiedenartigen Aufstellungen hatte die Forschung bislang fast ausschließlich die mit großer Sorgfalt gefertigten Abrechnungen im Blick, die in monatlichem Abstand an eine übergeordnete Stelle zu übersenden waren. Sie sollten Heroneinos weit über den engeren Kreis der Papyrologen hinaus Bekanntheit verschaffen, stellt das von ihm praktizierte Abrechnungssystem, das bereits die doppelte Buchführung kannte, doch ohne jede Frage einen Höhepunkt antiker Rechnungsführung dar; nicht ohne Grund wurde es von Dominic Rathbone, der die Feinheiten in seiner eingehenden Untersuchung erstmals in vollem Umfang herauszuarbeiten vermochte, als das „most sophisticated presently known from the Graeco-Roman world" beschrieben.[15]

Genau genommen haben wir es bei den Monatsberichten nur mit wohl erst gegen Jahresende erstellten Entwürfen zu tun, da sie bis zu ihrer Auffindung um das Jahr 1900 am

13 Vgl. H. Verreth – K. Vandorpe, '[Professional archive of] Heroninos, estate manager (Theadelpheia)', *Graeco-Roman Archives* (wie Anm. 7), 170-175 = <https://www.trismegistos.org/arch/archives/pdf/103.pdf> (Zugang am 04. 01. 2019); grundlegend hierzu nach wie vor D. W. Rathbone, *Economic Rationalism and Rural Society in Third-Century A.D. Egypt. The Heroninos Archive and the Appianus Estate*, Cambridge 1991.

14 So zusammenfassend Rathbone, *Economic Rationalism* (wie Anm. 13), 334; ihm folgend auch C. Ferro, 'I rendiconti dell'archivio di Heroneinos', *AnPap* 6, 1994, 37-51, hier erneut mit Schwerpunkt auf der ersten der drei dort aufgeführten Kategorien „1) conti mensili dei φροντισταί ...; 2) registrazioni primarie e appunti; 3) conti dell'amministrazione centrale" (so 37 f.). Neue Texte jetzt vor allem in P. Prag. III 236-242, vgl. auch allgem. <http://www.accademiafiorentina.it/?pg=cr_hero> unter *types: Account* (Zugriff am 19. 12. 2018).

15 So Rathbone, *Economic Rationalism* (wie Anm. 13), 331.

Ort ihrer Aufzeichnung in Theadelpheia verblieben.[16] Darin wurde nicht nur nach Einnahmen und Ausgaben unterschieden, vielmehr waren die Abrechnungen auch systematisch aufgebaut; so wurden zunächst die ausgegebenen Gelder – für Löhne, Büromaterialien, Steuern usw. – und sodann die Aufwendungen für die einzelnen Anbauprodukte gelistet, während am Ende die Ausgaben für Fässer, Gerätschaften und sonstige Infrastrukturmaßnahmen standen. In anderem wich Heroneinos wiederum von der Praxis seines Vorgängers Eirenaios ab, der unterdessen zu der Gutseinheit im benachbarten Euhemereia gewechselt war, da er sich, statt die Ausgaben für die Arbeitskräfte je nach Einsatzort geographisch anzuordnen, für eine Bündelung nach Tätigkeiten entschied und beispielsweise die Kosten für Zimmermannsarbeiten in verschiedenen Weingärten oder für Erntearbeiter im Gemüsebau zu nur einem Eintrag zusammenfaßte.

Weitaus weniger Aufmerksamkeit wurde demgegenüber den allfälligen Vorstufen dieser Monatsberichte zuteil, die von einfachen Notizblättern bis zu manch spezifischen Zwecken dienenden Aufstellungen reichten und in den unterschiedlichsten Bearbeitungsstufen erhalten blieben. Dies betraf etwa auch die „day-by-day lists of disbursements“, von denen einige wenige schon bisher bekannt geworden waren, da sie sich gelegentlich auch auf anderweitig genutzten Rollen fanden; vermutlich wurden sie hier zunächst nur vorläufig notiert, um sie später in die regulären Bücher zu überführen.[17] Dem erst kürzlich publizierten P. Prag. III 240 ist nunmehr jedoch zu entnehmen, daß es daneben auch speziell hierfür angelegte Aktenstücke gab, die die Abrechnungen gleich einer Reihe von Personen enthielten, von denen jeder einzelnen eine eigene Kolumne gewidmet war.[18] Über Monate, wenn nicht gar Jahre hinweg geführt, stellten offenkundig auch sie nicht mehr denn bloße Vorarbeiten zu den heutzutage ungleich geläufigeren Monatsberichten dar, in die die hier noch separat festgehaltenen Daten nachmals einfließen sollten. Als Beispiel hierfür sei nur der

16 Hierzu wie zum folgenden Rathbone, *Economic Rationalism* (wie Anm. 13), 331 ff., bes. 338 „Although the 'monthly' accounts each cover one Egyptian month, they were not drawn up each month but drafted in groups, probably all together at the end of each Egyptian year“; zur Fundsituation knapp auch Verreth – Vandorpe, 'Heroninos, estate manager' (wie Anm. 13), 171.

17 So die beiden undatierten, in diesem Fall auf Heroneinos' Vorgänger und nachmaligen Kollegen Eirenaios zurückgehenden Belege P. Laur. III 99 col. III, 8-20 (auf dem Verso von P. Flor. I 97b) bzw. SB XVI 12526, 1-8 (als sekundärer Eintrag auf dem Rekto, vgl. schon P. J. Sijpesteijn – K. A. Worp, 'Zwei Wiener Papyri', *Scritti in onore di Orsolina Montevecchi*, hrsg. v. E. Bresciani u.a., Bologna 1981, 363-369, bes. 365 in der Ed. pr. sowie <https://www.trismegistos.org/tm/detail.php?tm=30282> [Zugriff am 02. 01. 2019]); hierzu jetzt allgem. Rathbone, Einl. zu P. Prag. III 240 (9.-12. 250 n. Chr.), bes. S. 110, vgl. auch *Subtype 13 Pay records of employees* auf der einschlägigen Datenbank <http://www.accademiafiorentina.it/?pg=cr_hero> (Zugriff am 19. 12. 2018).

18 So jetzt der auf dem Verso des Entwurfs für den [λόγος χό]ρτου τοῦ Θὼθ μηνὸς τοῦ ἐνεστῶ(τος) β (ἔτους) 'Monatsbericht für Grünfutter im Monat Thoth des laufenden 2. Jahres' (Z. 1) P. Prag. III 239 (9. 250 n. Chr.) festgehaltene P. Prag. III 240 (9.-12. 250 n. Chr.). Als Paradebeispiel dieses Typs wurde schon von J. Bingen, 'Les comptes dans les archives d'Héroninos', *CE* 26, 1951, 378-385, bes. 380 f. der offenbar weiterhin unpublizierte P. Brux. descr. beschrieben, der auf dem Verso und teilweise auch in freigebliebenen Zwischenräumen des Rekto der Vorarbeit zur Episkepsis SB XVI 12493 + P. Prag. I 24 = SB I 4325 (= z.T. W. Chr. 236) + P. Flor. III 372 (Ende II./Anf. III. Jhdt.; TM 30277) niedergelegt wurde (= TM 11174). Im Vergleich dazu enthalte P. Prag. III 240 nicht mehr als nur „rough working accounts … However, the basic format and function of all these records are the same“ (so Rathbone in der Einl., S. 110 bzw. 111).

Beginn der ersten vollständig erhaltenen Kolumne dieses im Spätjahr 250 entstandenen Rechnungsbuches gegeben:[19]

Λόγος Πωλίωνος γεωργ(οῦ)	Aufstellung des Bauern Polion
ἕως Μεσορὴ β κατ' ἀρχαίους	bis zum 2. Mesore nach dem Wandeljahr[20]
12 λοιπ(ὸν) ἐπ' ἐμοὶ (δρ.) π (ὀβ.) [̣η] η	Rest bei mir: 80 Dr., ~~8~~ 8 Ob.
(δρ.) κ (τετρώβ.), διὰ τῆς	20 Dr. 4 Ob., durch die Tochter
θυγ(ατρὸς) (δρ.) η̅	8 Dr.
(ὧν) Θὼθ ε̅ μο(ν.) [α̅] (δρ.) η̅ (ὀβ.) η̅	davon am 5. Thoth 1 Monoch.: 8 Dr. 8 Ob.
ἐλαίου κοτ(ύλαι) β (δρ.) δ (τετρώβ.)	2 Kot. Olivenöl: 4 Dr. 4 Ob.
16 δ τοῖς παι̣δίοις μο(ν.) β (δρ.) ις (ὀβ.) ις̅	am 4. für die Sklaven 2 Monoch.: 16 Dr. 16 Ob.
ιγ διὰ τῆς γυν(αικὸς) αὐτοῦ (δρ.) η̅	am 13. durch seine Frau: 8 Dr.
κβ τῇ πό̣λ̣(ει) ὧν λόγ(ον) [φ]ύ̣λακι (δρ.) η̅	am 22. für die Stadt, davon auf Rechnung für den Wächter: 8 Dr.
δαπ(άνη̣) κώμ̣ης (δρ.) δ	für Aufwendungen des Dorfes: 4 Dr.
20 ὑπὲρ κωμάρχων (δρ.) η	für die Komarchen: 8 Dr.
καὶ ὑπὲρ Θὼθ η ἕως λ̅ σὺν τῇ̣	und für Thoth, vom 8. bis zum 30., mit den
δαπάν̣η̣ τῆς κ(ώμης) (δρ.) [ξ̅] νβ	Aufwendungen des Dorfes: ~~60~~ 52 Dr.
(ὧν) τῇ̣ αὐτῇ̣ ἡμέρα̣ (δρ.) [ιζ] \`κα´,	davon am selben Tag: ~~17~~ 21 Dr., Rest:
(λοιπὸν) (δρ.) [λα̅] \`λς̅´	~~31~~ 36 Dr.

19 Vgl. P. Prag. III 240 (9.-12. 250 n. Chr.), hier mit Z. 10-23; hierzu auch der entsprechende Eintrag im HGV <http://aquila.zaw.uni-heidelberg.de/hgv/130565> unter *Erwähnte Daten*: „Zahlreiche Tagesdaten von 26. Juli 250 bis 26. Dez. 250" (Zugriff am 26. 11. 2018).

20 Wie Rathbone im Komm. zu P. Prag. III 240, 11, 35, 51, 70 zu recht bemerkt, muß der üblicherweise in dem formelhaften κατ' ἀρχαίους enthaltene Verweis auf das ägyptische Wandeljahr angesichts des nunmehr schon seit Jahrhunderten gebräuchlichen alexandrinischen Kalenders befremden, weswegen er hier wie in Z. 51 für ein Verständnis „'in the old accounts' (sc. λόγους)", in Z. 35 und 70 dagegen für eine proleptische Verwendung plädiert. Die Parallelität der Einträge – Z. 35 ἕως Χοιὰκ ι̣α κατ' ἀρχαίους, Z. 51 ἕως Θὼθ λ κα[τ'] ἀ̣ρχαίους, Z. 70 [ἕ]ως Χοιὰκ λ κατ' ἀρχαίους – spricht freilich eher gegen unterschiedliche Deutungen, zumal ein solcher Zusatz zum Datum nach D. Hagedorn – K. A. Worp, 'Das Wandeljahr im römischen Ägypten', *ZPE* 104, 1994, 243-255, bes. 253 gerade auch in „Listen" häufiger begegnet, nämlich „P. Mil. Vogl. II 52 (138; Zahlungen); P. Mil. Vogl. VII 304 (166; Ausgaben für Arbeiten); BGU VII 1717 (II/III; Abrechnung); O. Narm. Gr. 172 (II/III; Agenda)". Abgesehen davon, daß alle vier Belege ebenfalls arsinoitischer Herkunft sind, scheint der Künstlervertrag P. Med. I 47 = SB X 10439 (nach 212) sogar aus demselben Ort Thraso (TM GeoID 2417) wie das Heroneinos-Archiv und damit auch P. Prag. III 240 zu stammen. Selbst wenn das ägyptische Jahr nach Hagedorn – Worp, a.a.O. 245 zu dieser Zeit dem alexandrinischen um volle 68 Tage voranging, wird man die Geltung des alten ägyptischen Kalenders trotz aller Bedenken daher nicht für völlig abwegig halten dürfen. Demnach wäre mit der hiernach im Mesore und also zum Jahresabschluß zusammengestellten Übersicht bereits mehr als zwei Monate vor dem üblichen Jahresende und also schon vor der Ernte Bilanz gezogen worden, was freilich noch mehr als das Phänomen als solches nach einer überzeugenden Erklärung verlangt. Hatte man womöglich mit zwei verschiedenen Kalendersystemen gearbeitet und für die „'primary' records" noch das – im Alltag vielleicht gar gebräuchlichere – Wandeljahr verwendet, während man erst in einem fortgeschrittenen Stadium der Bearbeitung zum alexandrinischen Jahr wechselte?

Auch hier treffen wir wieder das nun schon vertraute, letztlich unverwechselbare Layout mit dem durch Überstreichung hervorgehobenen und in Ekthesis gestellten Tagesdatum sowie den bei längeren Einträgen gestaffelten Eistheseis an, ebenso die Angewohnheit, die jeweils ausgeteilten Beträge – bei Zenon die Getreidemengen, bei den „pay records" des Heroneinos die gezahlten Gelder – um der besseren Übersichtlichkeit willen separat zu stellen und an den rechten Kolumnenrand zu rücken. Wenn letzteres hier nochmals augenfälliger wird als bei der oben gegebenen Getreideabrechnung P. Cair. Zenon II 59292, so deswegen, weil die Einträge anders dort zumeist nur einzeilig, die Rollen und damit auch die Kolumnen hingegen sehr viel höher sind. Auch wenn die Blatthöhe von P. Prag. III 240 mit knapp 22 cm immer noch deutlich unter dem seinerzeit etwa 30 cm hohen Standardformat bleibt, tritt daher doch derselbe Effekt wie bei der zuvor angeführten Sitometrieliste P. Cair. Zen. IV 59676 ein, nämlich daß die rechtsbündig untereinandergesetzten Beträge gleichsam als eigene Kolumne innerhalb der Kolumne – 'Pseudokolumne' – erscheinen.

Von Format, Anlage und Art der Aufstellungen her lassen sich diese „'primary' records" des Heroneinos jedenfalls ohne weiteres denjenigen des Zenon zur Seite stellen, auch wenn sie ihnen, da rund ein halbes Jahrtausend später, in manchen Details überlegen sein mögen. Anders sieht dies hingegen im Fall der weitaus komplexeren Monatsberichte aus, wie sie für Heroneinos so typisch waren. Zwar sind hinsichtlich des Layouts keine nennenswerten Differenzen zu vermerken, läßt man einmal die deutlich längeren, da oft mit zusätzlichen Detailinformationen gespickten Zeilen außer Betracht. Doch ist von vergleichbaren Aufstellungen über sämtliche Arten von Einnahmen und Ausgaben, die dazu in regelmäßigen Abständen an den Gutsherrn zu übersenden waren, in Zenons Papieren bekanntlich nichts zu finden, was zweifellos einer Erklärung bedarf.

Sie könnte möglicherweise in dem besonderen Vertrauensverhältnis liegen, das zwischen Zenon und seinem Dienstherren Apollonios, dem mächtigen Finanzminister Ptolemaios' II., bestand. Mit ihm durch die gemeinsame Herkunft aus Kaunos verbunden, hatte Zenon schon bei Apollonios' syrischen Unternehmungen, später auch als sein Sekretär eine bedeutende Rolle gespielt, bevor er die Verwaltung der δωρεά bei Philadelpheia übernahm und sich auch bei dieser neuen Aufgabe bestens bewährte. Diese besonderen Umstände mochten Apollonios bewogen haben, im Fall seines Landsmannes von den sonst üblichen Formen der Berichterstattung abzusehen. Ebenso wäre denkbar, daß Zenon zwar entsprechende Aufstellungen fertigte und nach Alexandria sandte, sich aber im Unterschied zu Heroneinos niemals Entwürfe davon zurückbehielt. Allerdings besitzt beides nicht unbedingt große Plausibilität. So wird man dies am ehesten auf die Organisation des Aktenbestandes zurückführen wollen – daß aus uns unbekannten Gründen eben nur der 'Korb' mit der Korrespondenz, nicht aber der mit den Monatsberichten erhalten blieb.[21] Genaueres hierüber werden wir wohl nie mehr in Erfahrung bringen, weil die Papyri nicht aus systematischen Grabungen stammen, was insofern noch einmal mehr zu bedauern ist.

21 Vgl. zur Fundsituation knapp auch Vandorpe, 'Zenon son of Agreophon' (wie Anm. 7), bes. 448; zu einer entsprechenden Organisation nach Inhalt bzw. Adressaten, wenn auch in völlig anderem Kontext, A. Archi, 'Archival Record-Keeping at Ebla 2400-2350 BC', *Ancient Archives and Archival Traditions. Concepts of Record-Keeping in the Ancient World*, hrsg. v. M. Brosius, Oxford 2003, 17-36, bes. 33 Fig. 2.7.

Die Position des Heroneinos war demgegenüber eine gänzlich andere. Denn während es bei Zenon wohl auch aufgrund des Nahverhältnisses zu Apollonios keine wie auch immer geartete Zwischeninstanz gab, nahm Heroneinos, so selbständig er als φροντιστής auf der von ihm geleiteten Gutseinheit beim arsinoitischen Theadelpheia agierte, in der Verwaltungshierarchie der appianischen Besitzungen nur eine untergeordnete Stellung ein. Zwar pflegte er die Monatsabrechnungen dem Präskript zufolge stets direkt an den Eigentümer Aurelius Appianos zu richten.[22] Gleichwohl spricht einiges dafür, daß auch sie zuvor über den Schreibtisch des in der Gauhauptstadt angesiedelten „general manager“ Alypios gingen, der – möglicherweise gestützt auf seine Erfahrungen als kaiserlicher Prokurator, falls er den Titel nicht wie viele andere nur ehrenhalber führte – im Auftrag des Appianos von dort aus die Arbeiten auf den verschiedenen φροντίδες im Arsinoites koordinierte und später vielleicht sogar Schwiegervater von Appianos' Tochter und Erbin Diodora wurde.

In den „'primary' records“ fanden derlei Differenzen freilich keinerlei Niederschlag, was andererseits auch kaum überraschen kann. Denn wer auf welcher Ebene auch immer zur Berichterstattung verpflichtet war, benötigte entsprechende Nachweise, sein Handeln gegenüber der übergeordneten Instanz zu belegen. Dazu galt es zunächst die Daten auf der alleruntersten Ebene zu sammeln und zu sortieren. Dies betraf letztlich jeden, der am Beginn der Produktionskette stand, freie und unfreie Verwalter ebenso wie den Eigentümer, der seine kleine Gutswirtschaft noch selbst betrieb. Auch für ihn mochte sich schließlich eine wenigstens rudimentäre Buchführung empfehlen, wollte er den Überblick über die in seinem Bereich getätigten Geschäfte wahren. Hierüber klären uns die Dokumente denn auch hinlänglich auf – über die Anbauprodukte, die Mengen, allerlei Arten von Sonderausgaben usw. Über den jeweiligen Kontext als solchen ist ihnen dagegen nichts zu entnehmen.

Dies ist, wie gesehen, auch bei den beiden hier in Rede stehenden Archiven der Fall. Zwar erscheinen die Unterschiede auf den ersten Blick weitaus größer als die Gemeinsamkeiten, die sich zumal von Zuschnitt und Zusammensetzung her in erstaunlich engen Grenzen halten. Vieles davon wird man jedoch bereits der Überlieferungslage, anderes aber auch dem Interesse der Forschung anzulasten haben. So ist die Fülle der Studien zur frühptolemäischen Zeit und namentlich zum Zenon-Archiv kaum mehr zu überschauen, während das Heroneinos-Archiv zwar zu großen Teilen, aber immer noch nicht vollständig publiziert und letztlich bis heute nur unzureichend erschlossen ist. Von seinen zahllosen Aufstellungen waren zudem vor allem die singulären Monatsberichte im Blick, wohingegen die vorausgehenden Bearbeitungsstufen kaum je eingehendere Würdigung erfuhren. Dies hängt zweifellos damit zusammen, daß gerade Listen aller Art sich ohnehin eher selten besonderer Wertschätzung erfreuen, da sie meist nur begrenzten Informationswert besitzen und bestenfalls als serielle Texte Bedeutung erlangen. So gilt dies gemeinhin als relativ undank-

22 Vgl. nur stellvertretend für andere SB XX 14197, 1-5 Αὐρηλίῳ Ἀπιανῷ ἐξη(γητεύσαντι) βουλ(ευτῇ) τῆς λαμπ(ροτάτης) πόλεως τῶν Ἀλεξανδρέων καὶ ὡς χρημ(ατίζει) παρὰ Αὐρηλίου Ἡρωνείνου φρ(οντιστοῦ) Θεαδελφείας· λόγος λήμματος καὶ ἀναλ(ώματος) τοῦ Παῦνι μη(νὸς) τοῦ ἐνεστῶ(τος) γ (ἔτους)· ἐστὶ δέ· κτλ. 'An Aurelius Appianos, ehemaligen Exegeten und Ratsherrn der glänzendsten Stadt der Alexandriner und wie er sonst noch heißt, von Aurelius Heroneinos, Verwalter von Theadelpheia. Verzeichnis der Einnahmen und Ausgaben im Monat Payni des laufenden 3. Jahres, und zwar: usw.' (nach dem 24. 6. 253 n. Chr.).

bares Geschäft, was sich oftmals – so vielleicht auch hier – schon vorneweg auf die Bereitschaft zur Edition auswirkt.

Damit wuchs den Differenzen eine nachgerade alles überlagernde Bedeutung zu, so daß die gleichermaßen vorhandenen Parallelen völlig in den Hintergrund gerieten. Sieht man jedoch vom Inhaltlichen ab, läßt eine nähere Betrachtung rasch erkennen, daß beide Archive uns nur mit unterschiedlichen Arten der Datenerfassung konfrontieren. Denn im Falle Zenons blieb ausschließlich eine eng begrenzte Gruppe von „'primary' records" erhalten, während wir bei Heroneinos sämtliche Stufen des Rechnungswesens vorfinden, nur das Hauptaugenmerk stets den so singulären Monatsberichten gilt. Durch die – mehr oder weniger zufällige – Zusammensetzung des Materials wird damit zugleich die Perspektive bestimmt, ohne dennoch eine Basis für weiterreichende Schlüsse zu bieten.

Danach ist jedenfalls so viel klar, daß sich hieraus nichts zu der Form der Bewirtschaftung ergibt. Einblick in die tatsächlichen Verhältnisse und damit den Entstehungskontext ist vielmehr allein durch die Überprüfung sämtlicher zugehörigen Dokumente, eine sorgfältige Analyse der spezifischen Rolle und Funktion aller darin auftretenden Personen sowie die hierauf aufbauende Rekonstruktion der jeweiligen Strukturen zu erlangen. Hieraus wiederum ließen sich im Idealfall sogar Rückschlüsse auf etwaige Prinzipien bei der Betriebsführung ziehen, sofern angesichts der Lückenhaftigkeit unserer Evidenz überhaupt ein – womöglich gar sicheres – Urteil in der Sache zu gewinnen ist.

Folglich wird man stets eine Einzelfallprüfung vorzunehmen haben, deren Addition erst ein hinreichend profiliertes Gesamtbild entstehen läßt, welches wiederum den Blick auf gemeinsame Grundsätze eröffnen mag. Als erster Schritt in diese Richtung bietet sich der Vergleich einer Art Kontrollgruppe an, näherhin zweier weiterer 'Archive', die vor noch nicht langem publiziert wurden und durchaus verwandte Aufstellungen aus der Gutsverwaltung enthalten. Dabei handelt es sich zum einen um das sog. 'Archiv des Pakysis', das sich zu großen Teilen heute im Pariser Louvre befindet,[23] und zum anderen um das sog. Kellis Agricultural Account Book, kurz KAB, einen aus acht Holztafeln bestehenden Kodex, dessen mustergültige Edition Roger Bagnall vorlegte.[24] Beide stammen aus relativ später Zeit. Pakysis, ein Priester aus dem kleinen Ort Soknopaiu Nesos im Norden des Faijum, war unter Caracalla auf nicht näher zu fassenden Besitzungen in diesem Gebiet tätig, während das anonym überlieferte KAB aus den 360er oder 370er Jahren datiert und Aufzeichnungen aus einem Gutsbetrieb in der Großen Oase enthält. In beiden Fällen liegen recht umfangreiche Textmengen vor, die bei weitem nicht mit der Dokumentation des Zenon oder gar Heroneinos mitzuhalten vermögen, aber dennoch geeignet erscheinen, dem bisher gewonnenen Bild gewisse Tiefenschärfe zu verleihen.

Von Pakysis besitzen wir inzwischen mehr als 20 Aufstellungen über die verschiedensten Einnahmen und Ausgaben in Geld wie Naturalien, die sich größtenteils auf dem Verso bereits anderweitig verwendeter Papyri finden und von seinen Aktivitäten im landwirtschaftlichen Bereich zeugen. Auch hier fallen immer wieder die tagesgenau vorgenommenen Einträge ins Auge, wie sie nach den obigen Ausführungen für die „'primary'

23 Vgl. P. Louvre I 48-65 sowie K. Geens, '[Private archive of] Pakysis, son of Tesenouphis, priest (Soknopaiou Nesos)', *Graeco-Roman Archives* (wie Anm. 7), 267-268 = <https://www.trismegistos.org/arch/archives/pdf/165.pdf> (Zugang am 04. 01. 2019); hierzu jetzt auch Ruffing, 'Schriftlichkeit und Wirtschaft' (wie Anm. 2), 228.

24 P. Kell. IV 96 (361-364 oder 376-379 n. Chr.).

records“ charakteristisch waren. Demnach gab diese Art Aufstellung offenbar auch das Modell für Pakysis ab, das er freilich oft nur mit Mühe sauber durchzuhalten vermochte, so daß die Grenzen zu eilig hingeworfenen Notizzetteln vielfach fließend sind. Zu den wenigen besser gelungenen Exemplaren zählt P. Louvre I 48, den er offenbar sogar über einen längerfristigen Zeitraum zu führen gedachte und daher geradezu vorschriftsmäßig begann:[25]

Ἀγαθῇ Τύχῃ. Γέρτων Ἑρμῇ Ἀφροδίτη.	Mit gutem Glück! Kerdon, Hermes, Aphrodite.
Λῆμα γενηματωυ κ̅ (ἔτους) ἕως	(An?) Einnahmen an Naturalien im 20. Jahr bis zum
Ἐπὶφ α̅. κριθὴ ἁλονίας ἀρτ(άβ.) ι̅θ̅	1. Epeiph: Gerste von der Tenne 19 Art.
μέτ(ρ.) ζ· ναύ(λου) μέτ(ρ.) ζ χύν(ικ.) β	7 Metra; an Naulon: 7 Metra, 2 Choin.
ϛ ἀπὸ τῆς ἁλονίας (πυρ. ἀρτ.) μ̅ζ̅∠	am 6. von der Tenne: 47½ Art. Weizen
ζ ὁμ(οίως) ἄλ(λας) (πυρ. ἀρτ.) κη∠	am 7. ebenso weitere 28½ Art. Weizen
ναύλ(ου) κριθῆς μέτ(ρ.) ι̅ζ̅	an Naulon: 17 Metra Gerste
Κ̣αμβελις κριθῆ(ς) μέτ(ρ.) κ̅η̅	Kambelis: 28 Metra Gerste
η̅ Σενι ἄλ(λας) (πυρ. ἀρτ.) γ̅ μέτ(ρ.) ϛ̅	am 8. Seni: weitere 3 Art. 6 Metra Weizen
θ Σελ̣ιτι (πυρ. ἀρτ.) ϛ∠d	am 9. Seliti: 6¾ Art. Weizen
ι̅ζ̅ ναύλ(ου) κριθῆ(ς) μέτ(ρ.) γ∠	am 17. an Naulon: 3½ Metra Gerste
καὶ ἀπὸ ἄλ(λης) ἁλο{λο}νίας (πυρ. ἀρτ.) κγ μέτ(ρ.) β·	und von der anderen Tenne: 23 Art. 2 Metra Weizen

1 l. Κέρδων Ἑρμῆς 2 l. λῆμμα [vel fortasse λημμά(των)] γενημάτων 3 l. Ἐπείφ 3, 5, 12 l. ἁλωνίας 4 l. χοίν(ικας)

Schon die zu Beginn gestellte Segensformel läßt dabei eine gewisse Schulung in solcherlei Aufstellungen erkennen.[26] Dennoch zeigt sich Pakysis den hiermit verbundenen Anforderungen kaum gewachsen. Dies beginnt bereits damit, daß die – ursprünglich vielleicht durchaus längere – Rolle nicht etwa einen einzigen Sachverhalt betraf, da nur in den ersten beiden Kolumnen Einnahmen, in der dritten und wohl auch vierten dagegen Ausgaben in Naturalien aufgelistet waren, während die fünfte Notizen zur Kontoführung im Nachbarort Dionysias enthielt. Es zeichnet sich jedoch auch im Erscheinungsbild ab. So sind zwar Ansätze zu einer Strukturierung mit Hilfe von Ek- und Eistheseis vorhanden, doch ist nicht einmal das Tagesdatum durchgehend ausgerückt, wie auch Beträge bzw. Mengenangaben meist ohne größeres Spatium direkt an die Zahlungsdetails – den Leistungszweck oder wie hier die Herkunft des eingegangenen Getreides – anschließen.

Deutlich besser ist Pakysis dies bei den Aufstellungen über Geldbeträge gelungen, bei der die jeweils gezahlten Summen wie gewohnt eine eigene Kolumne innerhalb der Kolumne bilden.[27] Auch dort läßt das Layout jedoch jede Konsequenz vermissen, wobei der insge-

25 P. Louvre I 48, 1-11 (6. 11. 212 n. Chr.); hierzu auch der entsprechende Eintrag im HGV <http://aquila.zaw.uni-heidelberg.de/hgv/11860> unter *Erwähnte Daten*: „Viele Einzeldaten vom 25. Juni – 6. Nov. 212" (Zugriff am 25. 11. 2018).

26 Hierzu jetzt B. Sippel, ‘Agathe Tyche, Kerdon, Hermes, Aphrodite: Ein Ausbildungsnetzwerk unter Landgutverwaltern des kaiserzeitlichen Fayum?’, *ZPE* 213, 2020, 213-220.

27 So bes. bei dem bemerkenswerterweise als λό̣γος Απις βουκ(όλ-) ‘Aufstellung zum Rinderhirten (?) Apis’ überschriebenen P. Louvre I 51 (vor 216 n. Chr.?), aber etwa auch P. Louvre I 53 verso; 54; 61 (sämtlich o.D.) sowie 57, 28-35 (217/18, 218/19 oder 222/23 n. Chr.).

samt recht unbeholfene Eindruck durch die beharrliche Verwendung ausgeschriebener Kalamoi noch befördert wird. Zu dem ungelenken Schriftbild und einer mehr als bedenklichen Orthographie kommen die offenkundigen sprachlichen Defizite, so nicht zuletzt der weitgehende Verzicht auf die Kasusendungen bei ägyptischen Namen, was um so mißlicher ist, als wir oft nicht wissen, ob sich darunter Orte oder Personen verbergen.

Nach alldem vermochte Pakysis den üblichen Vorgaben nur sehr bedingt gerecht zu werden, was sich vermutlich auch durch seinen persönlichen Hintergrund erklärt. Von Haus aus nicht nur muttersprachlicher Ägypter, sondern sogar Angehöriger der einheimischen Priesterschaft, bekleidete er als Stolistes nachweislich eine der ranghöchsten Positionen im Soknopaios-Heiligtum.[28] In welcher Funktion Pakysis seine hier in Rede stehenden Aufzeichnungen fertigte, ist indessen unbekannt. So könnte er sie ebenso als Eigentümer wie im Auftrag des Heiligtums angelegt haben; manches spricht allerdings dafür, daß er für den bekannten alexandrinischen Großgrundbesitzer Ti. Claudius Syrion tätig war.[29] Den Texten selbst ist hierzu nichts zu entnehmen, erst recht nicht zu irgendwelchen Fragen der Organisationsstruktur.

Bei Pakysis haben wir demnach offenbar mit dem Typus des bestenfalls semi-professionellen Quereinsteigers in der Gutsverwaltung zu tun, dem Buchführung und Rechnungswesen nicht gerade 'in die Wiege gelegt' waren. Aus der Art der Dokumentation ist zugleich zu folgern, daß er auf der untersten Ebene der Verwaltungshierarchie stand, vermutlich auch direkter in die Bewirtschaftung eingebunden war als Zenon oder auch Heroneinos.

Einem fortgeschritteneren Stadium der Datenerfassung gehört demgegenüber das KAB an, das 1988 bei Ismant el-Kharab, dem antiken Kellis in der Großen Oase, *in situ* entdeckt wurde, dies sogar noch mitsamt der Kordel, die es einst zusammengehalten hatte. Auf insgesamt acht jeweils beidseitig in mehreren Kolumnen beschriebenen Holztafeln waren darin in insgesamt fast 1800 Zeilen über drei Jahre hinweg die Abrechnungen eines Guts-

28 So nach einer in vier nahezu wortgleichen Exemplaren vorliegenden Eingabe vom 7. April 216 n. Chr., da die Hand des eigenhändig unterzeichnenden Petenten auf dem Rekto mit derjenigen der Aufstellungen auf dem Verso identisch ist, vgl. nur BGU I 321 = M. Chr. 114, 26 und P. Berol. 7081 recto, 25 an den Strategen (http://berlpap.smb.museum/01724/ bzw. W. Schubart, *Papyri Graecae Berolinenses*, Bonn 1911, Taf. 34b) bzw. BGU I 322 = M. Chr. 124, 29 und P. Louvre I 3, 30 f. an den Centurio (http://berlpap.smb.museum/01755/ bzw. P. Louvre I, Taf. 3); die von F. Mitthof, Bespr. von P. Louvre I, *ZRG R.A.* 118, 2001, 408-413, bes. 412 f. geäußerten Vorbehalte gegenüber einer Identifikation erscheinen angesichts des so eigenwilligen Schriftbildes unbegründet. Hierzu zuletzt A. Jördens, 'Unerwartete Kohärenzen. Vom Erkenntniswert artefaktbedingter Vergesellschaftung bei (nicht nur) dokumentarischen Papyri der Kaiserzeit', *Vergesellschaftete Schriften. Beiträge zum internationalen Workshop der Arbeitsgruppe 11 am SFB 933*, hrsg. v. U. Ehmig (Philippika 128), Wiesbaden 2019, 41-61, bes. 57 ff.

29 In diese Richtung deutet jedenfalls der singuläre Posten von 4 Drachmen für die Kleidung eines Sklaven in P. Louvre I 54, 20 ff. τούτο(υ) δέτοκα δούλου (l. δέδωκα δούλῳ) Συρίων(-) ἐπὶ τον (l. τῶν) ἱματίων αὐτοῦ (δραχμὰς) δ 'davon habe ich gegeben dem Sklaven Syrion für seine Kleider 4 Dr.', falls statt des zunächst ergänzten Dativs Συρίων(ι) 'dem Sklaven Syrion' der Genetiv Συρίων(ος) herzustellen und also 'dem Sklaven des Syrion' zu übersetzen ist; so auch schon erwogen im Korrekturzusatz zum Komm. zu P. Louvre I 54, 21 ff. Hierin ließe sich gut der bekannte αἰωνογυμνασίαρχος dieses Namens erblicken, der in den fraglichen Jahrzehnten über weitgestreuten Grundbesitz in der Chora verfügte, vgl. nur zuletzt Jördens, Einl. zu P. Louvre I 41, wonach bislang Ländereien bei Memphis, im Oxyrhynchites und im Arsinoites bezeugt sind.

verwalters niedergelegt. Selbst hier sind teilweise noch tagesgenaue Eintragungen zu finden:[30]

	Taf. 4 verso col. III, kopfstehend	
	λόγ(ος) δοθέντ(ων) εἰς τὴν	Aufstellung des Ausgegebenen für die
	δαπάν(ην) ἀπὸ μην(ὸς) Μεσορή,	Versorgung ab dem Monat Mesore,
856	τοῦ μην(ὸς) μ(άτια) ο	pro Monat 70 Matia
	…	…
864	Θὼθ κγ μ(άτια) ιε	am 23. Thoth: 15 Matia
	Φαῶφι γ μ(άτια) κε	am 3. Phaophi: 25 Matia
	ς ὁμοί(ως) μ(άτια) οε	am 6. ebenso: 75 Matia
	κ μ(άτια) ι·	am 20.: 10 Matia
868	Ἀθὺρ κδ μ(άτια) λ	am 24. Hathyr: 30 Matia
	Χοιὰκ ς μ(άτια) μ	am 6. Choiak: 40 Matia
	κ ὁμοί(ως) μ(άτια) ν	am 20. ebenso: 50 Matia
	κζ μ(άτια) μ	am 27.: 40 Matia

Freilich handelte es sich hierbei nur um einen Nachtrag, wie schon die Drehung gegenüber den früheren Eintragungen um 180° anzeigt. Tatsächlich wurde die Liste im freien Raum unterhalb der dritten Kolumne positioniert, die nur gut die Hälfte der Tafel einnahm; so war dies wohl kaum mehr als eine Art Notlösung, bei der auch keinerlei Platz für Layoutelemente wie etwa Ek- oder Eistheseis blieb. Doch auch sonst erweist sich das Rechnungsbuch bei genauerer Betrachtung als keineswegs so systematisch geführt, wie es auf den ersten Blick erscheint und zumal die auffälligen Kontrollstriche vor den jeweiligen Einträgen suggerieren. Denn es sind zwar mancherlei Ansätze zu einer gewissen Ordnung vorhanden, da die verschiedenen Rechnungsposten – Einnahmen, Ausgaben, Lagerbestände, eigene Konten – separat voneinander geführt und innerhalb dessen zumeist nach Indiktionen gegliedert sind. Daneben gibt es jedoch auch eine Reihe von Inkonsequenzen, vielerlei Sprünge und dazu unverbundene Einschübe, so daß kein wirklich durchdachtes und vor allem streng befolgtes Konzept ersichtlich wird.

Nicht viel anders als bei Pakysis ist also auch hier darauf zu schließen, daß diese Aufzeichnungen vornehmlich dem Eigengebrauch dienten. Hierzu paßt etwa auch die Kargheit der Einträge, die erneut unbefriedigende sprachliche Gestaltung, der recht eigenwillige Umgang mit den Maßeinheiten und nicht zuletzt die Fülle der Korrekturen. Was seine Position betrifft, hatte unser Verwalter außer dem Gutsbetrieb in Kellis offenbar noch einige kleinere Einheiten unter sich, die wie das nahegelegene Mesobe teilweise sogar über eigene Lagerkapazitäten verfügten. Eigentümer scheint der wohl in der 150 km entfernten Metropole Hibis ansässige γ(εοῦ)χ(ος) Faustianus, Sohn des Aquila gewesen zu sein; dort wohnte jedenfalls seine mutmaßliche Ehefrau – oder Mutter? –, die nicht namentlich genannte οἰκοδέσποινα.[31] Daneben begegnet ein weiteres Dutzend Gutsangestellter, einschließlich

30 So etwa die zur Illustration hier angeführten P. Kellis IV 96, 854-856 bzw. 864-871 (361-364 oder 376-379 n. Chr.).

31 Vgl. nur P. Kellis IV 96, 341 f. ὁ γ(εοῦ)χ(ος) Φαυστιανὸς Ἀκύλου; 1136 ὁ γ(εοῦ)χ(ος) Φαυστιανός; 1336 τῷ γ(εού)χ(ῳ) Φαυστιανῷ; 1399 ὁ γ(εοῦ)χ(ος) Φαυστιανός bzw. 334 f. ṭ[ῇ] ọ[ἰ]κοδεσπο(ίνῃ) [ἐν Ἴ]βι; 1145 f. τῇ οἰκοδεσποίνῃ ἐν Ἴβει. Die unterschiedliche Benennung ist allerdings bemerkenswert, weswegen zu erwägen wäre, ob es sich bei der οἰκοδέσποινα nicht um die – inzwischen verwitwete? –

einiger als ἀδελφοί titulierter 'Kollegen', unter denen sich vielleicht nicht nur dann, wenn sie explizit als προνοηταί bezeichnet sind, Verwalter in ähnlicher Stellung verbergen mochten.[32] Insgesamt würde man unseren Mann am ehesten auf mittlerer Ebene verorten, ohne daß sich freilich aus den Aufstellungen als solchen etwas zur Organisationsstruktur des Gutsbetriebes ergibt, wie mangels sonstiger Evidenz auch nichts zur mutmaßlichen Berichtspflicht gegenüber dem Gutsherrn zu sagen ist. In mancherlei Hinsicht könnte man ihn insofern durchaus mit Zenon vergleichen, wenngleich die Maßstäbe dort fraglos ganz andere waren.

Nach alldem sehen wir uns in den vier hier vorgestellten Beispielen mit den verschiedensten Arten von Buchführung und Rechnungswesen in der Gutsverwaltung konfrontiert, die einem Zeitraum von mehr als 600 Jahren entstammen. Darunter gab es ebenso private Notizen, die von vornherein niemals für fremde Augen gedacht waren, wie es sicherlich bei Pakysis, aber wohl auch bei unserem zuletzt erwähnten Gutsverwalter in der Großen Oase der Fall war und gewiß ebenso für manche Dokumente des Heroneinos galt. Bei Zenon könnte zwar das sorgfältige Layout auf eine Rezeption durch Dritte deuten, doch lassen bloße Ausschnitte des ehemaligen Aktenbestandes, wie sie hier nun einmal vorliegen, schwerlich belastbare Aussagen zu. Die Position des jeweiligen Gutsverwalters hing wiederum von einer ganzen Reihe von Faktoren ab, die von einer persönlichen Nahbeziehung mit flachen Hierarchien wie bei Zenon über ein den öffentlichen Strukturen verwandtes, da über mehrere Stufen verlaufendes System wie bei Heroneinos bis zu anscheinend relativ großer Selbständigkeit wie bei unserem letzten Beispiel in der Großen Oase reichen. Wenn hieraus überhaupt eine Schlußfolgerung zu ziehen ist, so diejenige, daß es eine erhebliche Breite unterschiedlicher Konzeptionen gab, von denen im Grunde keine der anderen glich. So sind denn auch nicht gut Erkenntnisse von hier nach dort zu übertragen, wie und wo immer sie gewonnen sein mögen.

Gemeinsam scheint indessen allen hier in den Blick genommenen Dokumentengruppen zu sein, daß die Texte als solche schlechterdings nichts über die Bewirtschaftungsform aussagen. Zwar enthalten sie eine Fülle von Details, die uns über die verschiedensten mehr oder weniger interessanten Aspekte antiker Gutsverwaltung im griechisch-römischen Ägypten aufklären. Über die Organisationsstruktur des Betriebs als solchen verraten sie dagegen nichts, wie ohnehin höchstens in Ausnahmefällen überhaupt etwas darüber in Erfahrung zu bringen ist. Erinnert sei zudem daran, daß wir auf vergleichbare „day-by-day lists" schließlich auch in ganz anderem Kontext stoßen; als Beispiel hierfür sei nur die auf einem Ostrakon vom Mons Claudianus festgehaltene „List of All Personnel for Several Days" benannt, die das Erfordernis entsprechender Aufstellungen auch in der Verwaltung der Steinbrüche belegt.[33]

Ehefrau des Aquila und Mutter des Faustianus handelt. Für diesen Gedanken wie auch die Durchsicht des Manuskripts habe ich einmal mehr Rudolf Haensch herzlich zu danken.

32 Vgl. bes. P. Kellis IV 96, 1150 ff. τοῖς ἀδελ(φοῖς) Ἀπολιναρίῳ καὶ Βελλῆτι προνοητ(αῖς); allgem. auch Bagnall, Einl. zu P. Kellis IV 96, bes. S. 70 ff., wonach – anders als etwa bei Heroneinos – zumindest keine klaren Indizien für eine Hierarchie innerhalb des Verwaltungspersonals vorliegen: „What is particularly unclear is whether any of those mentioned was the superior of the writer" (71).

33 Vgl. nur O. Claud. IV 723 (um 136/37 n. Chr.) mit der Abb. S. 310, wo die erneut in Ekthesis gesetzten Tagesdaten besonders augenfällig sind.

Um so mehr Interesse kommt einer literarischen Parallele zu, die sich in dem großenteils verlorenen, meist als *Satyricon* bezeichneten Roman des Petronius Arbiter findet. Zu den teilweise bizarren Programmpunkten, die die Festgesellschaft beim sog. 'Gastmahl des Trimalchio' über sich ergehen lassen muß, zählt auch der Auftritt eines *actuarius*, der den neuesten Rechenschaftsbericht von Trimalchios Gütern verliest. Ist schon vom Genus her mit einer Persiflage zu rechnen, erscheint die Absurdität der Szene nochmals gesteigert durch den scharfen Kontrast zwischen Inhalt und Form der Präsentation, da der Verwalter mit zweifellos todernster Miene ein Sammelsurium von durchweg maßlos übertriebenen Zahlen und buntgemischten Kalamitäten aller Art zum besten gab. Der eintönige Vortrag besaß auf den Ich-Erzähler geradezu einschläfernde Wirkung, so daß er nur den Beginn noch einigermaßen exakt wiederzugeben vermochte:[34]

2	*VII. Kalendas sextiles. In praedio Cumano ...* *nati sunt pueri XXX, puellae XL* *sublata in horreum ex area tritici millia modium quingenta* *boves domiti quingenti*	26. Juli: auf dem Landgut bei Cumae ... geboren 30 Jungen, 40 Mädchen von der Tenne in den Speicher überführt: 500.000 Scheffel Weizen zum Gebrauch abgerichtet: 500 Stück Ochsen
3	*eodem die: Mithridates servus in crucem actus est, quia Gai nostri genio male dixerat*	am selben Tag: der Sklave Mithridates ans Kreuz geschlagen, weil er den Genius unseres Gaius gelästert hatte
4	*eodem die: in arcam relatum est quod collocari non potuit, sestertium centies*	am selben Tag: in den Tresor verbracht, wofür es keine Investitionsmöglichkeit gab, 10 Millionen Sesterzen
5	*eodem die: incendium factum est in hortis Pompeianis, ortum ex aedibus Nastae vilici*	am selben Tag: es gab einen Brand in den pompejanischen Gärten, ausgebrochen im Haus des Verwalters Nasta

Namentlich was die tagesgenaue Aufzählung betrifft, sind hierbei indes erstaunliche Analogien zu den oben betrachteten Aufstellungen aus Ägypten zu vermerken. Dies dürfte dafür sprechen, daß es nicht nur dort, sondern auch in der römischen Gutsverwaltung eine mehr oder weniger regelmäßige Übermittlung entsprechender Nachrichten von einzelnen Gütern gab, die offenbar jeweils mit Tagesdatum festgehalten wurden und die Grundlage für die Ausführungen des *actuarius* bildeten. Tatsächlich wissen wir schon aus den Agrarschriftstellern, daß die Erstellung von *rationes* zu den grundlegenden Pflichten eines jeden Verwalters zählte.[35] Erhalten blieb hiervon jedoch nichts, so daß wir über deren Gestalt auf bloße Mutmaßungen verwiesen sind. Dies ist wohl auch der Grund, warum die Fragen der Rechnungslegung bei Jean-Jacques Aubert eine solch nachgeordnete Rolle spielen.[36]

Von Gérard Minaud wird Petron dagegen sogar als Kronzeuge dafür angeführt, daß wir hier mit ganz unterschiedlichen Prinzipien des antiken Wirtschaftens zu tun haben. Ihm zufolge handele es sich bei der von dem *actuarius* präsentierten Liste nämlich nur um eine Art

34 Petr., Sat. 53, 2-5; Übers. C. Hoffmann, mit Modifikationen.

35 Eingehend dazu bes. Christmann, 'Zum Verhältnis' (wie Anm. 2).

36 Vgl. etwa die „Social and economic aspects of the vilicus system" bei Aubert, *Business Managers* (wie Anm. 3), 146 ff., wo sich nichts dazu findet; knapp allenfalls 189 f. mit Anm. 254 ff.

breviarium in Form eines bloßen Inventars, das dem Grundherrn zwar einen Überblick über den aktuellen Besitzstand erlaube, ihm jedoch in keiner Weise als Grundlage ökonomischer Entscheidungen dienen könne.[37] Hierzu stünden die ungleich komplexeren Monatsabrechnungen des Heroneinos in schroffem Gegensatz, zielten sie anders als die aus Petron ersichtliche, typisch römische Form der Aufstellung doch genau darauf ab, den Grundherrn mit allen für unternehmerische Aktivitäten erforderlichen Daten zu versorgen.

Zu fragen bleibt indes, ob derlei Differenzen sich tatsächlich unterschiedlichen Wirtschaftsstrukturen oder nicht vielmehr den unterschiedlichen Genera unserer Quellen verdanken. Schließlich haben wir in den Monatsabrechnungen der appianischen Besitzungen reale, der Verwaltungspraxis entstammende Dokumente vor uns, während die Figur von Petrons *actuarius* wie auch seine Auflistung trotz des wahren Kerns, der dem zweifellos innewohnt, doch nur literarische Fiktionen sind. Auch die Situierung der Nachrichtenübermittlung könnte kaum unterschiedlicher sein, war ein detaillierter und reich mit Zahlen ausgestatteter Monatsbericht doch niemals für einen mündlichen Vortrag gedacht. Es spricht daher alles dafür, daß Petron sich bewußt für ein 'abgespecktes' Format entschied, das die eingegangenen Informationen auf das Wesentliche reduzierte, was wohlgemerkt allein schon ausreichte, Geduld und Aufnahmefähigkeit der Zuhörerschaft aufs äußerste zu strapazieren. Daraus ergibt sich jedoch noch lange nicht, daß einem römischen Grundherrn wie Trimalchio ausschließlich solche, aber keinerlei den Monatsabrechnungen vergleichbare Dokumente zugingen, wie umgekehrt auch Appianos bei anderer Gelegenheit durchaus ähnliche Kurzberichte erhalten haben mag.

Auch wenn Minauds Rekonstruktion der antiken Buchführung nicht zuletzt durch die so reiche Ausbeute an einschlägigen Texten viele ansprechende Züge besitzt, erheben sich aus quellenkritischer Sicht doch mancherlei Bedenken. Zum einen scheint die Lückenhaftigkeit unserer Evidenz nicht immer hinreichend in Rechnung gestellt, was gerade in Bezug auf die vermutete Repräsentativität und etwa darauf aufbauende Vergleiche kein ganz unwesentlicher Faktor ist. Zum anderen bewegt sich die Diskussion oft sehr im Abstrakten. Allzu wenig wird berücksichtigt, daß letztlich jede Aussage unserer Quellen ebenso zeit- wie situationsgebunden ist, während sich eine stärkere Einbettung in den jeweils gegebenen Kontext noch einmal seltener findet; gelegentliche Versuche einer Konkretisierung können mitunter sogar eher in die Irre führen.[38] Im Fall Petrons kommt noch hinzu, daß der Realitäts-

37 Vgl. nur Minaud, *La comptabilité* (wie Anm. 4), 93.

38 So etwa die Diskussion des Layouts der nach Minaud, *La comptabilité* (wie Anm. 4), 79 § 120 bis zu neun Kolumnen umfassenden *tabulae*, wofür er sich auf den Wortlaut von P. Mich. III 166 = CPL 151 = C. Sánchez-Moreno Ellart, Professio Liberorum. *Las declaraciones y los registros de nacimientos en derecho romano, con especial atención a las fuentes papirológias*, Madrid 2001, 128 ff. F (13. 4. 128) beruft, freilich ohne sich intensiver mit der umfänglichen einschlägigen Literatur auseinanderzusetzen; eingehend hierzu bes. R. Haensch, 'Das Statthalterarchiv', *ZRG R.A.* 109, 1992, 209-317, bes. 289 Anm. 241; vgl. auch Sánchez-Moreno Ellart, a.a.O. 104 ff. und bes. 107 f. Wenn Minaud im Anschluß daran bemerkt, daß „[d]'autres documents papyrologiques offrent la même interprétation“ und dafür in Anm. 137 „[p]ar exemple le papyrus BU (richtig: BGU) VII 1694 en date de 163 ap. J.-C.“ anführt, ist es ihm offenbar lediglich um die Wendung *tabul(a) IIII pag(ina) V* in Z. 13 getan. Denn als Beleg für die vorausgehende Behauptung „Il existait des *tabulae* de grandes dimensions susceptibles de comporter neuf colonnes“ kann dieses Wachstafeldiptychon schon deswegen nicht dienen, weil es wie die anderen in BGU VII 1690-1694 publizierten Geburtsanzeigen lediglich 12-14 cm hoch und 17-18 cm breit ist, vgl. nur die Einl. zu BGU VII 1690. So stellt der fragliche Satz offenbar die Schlußfolgerung aus dem

gehalt seiner Darstellung schon vom Genus her als höchst fragwürdig einzuschätzen ist. Dies hat selbstredend auch für den Auftritt von Trimalchios *actuarius* und seine Berichterstattung zu gelten. Was immer von den dort angeblich registrierten Details zu halten sein mag, ist hieraus allein jedenfalls weder ein zuverlässiges noch ein hinreichendes Bild über Gestalt und Konzeption der römischen *rationes* zu gewinnen.

Ähnliches gilt freilich auch für das kaum minder singuläre Heroneinos-Archiv. Denn was die berühmten, von Minaud so hoch veranschlagten Monatsberichte anbelangt, ist schließlich nicht nur für Rom, sondern auch für das gesamte griechische Millennium Ägyptens nichts auch nur annähernd Vergleichbares zu konstatieren. Doch ist abgesehen davon ohnedies kaum zu sagen, wie typisch die hier faßbare Verwaltungsstruktur für das Nilland als ganzes war; letztlich ist eine solche Aussage nicht einmal nur für den hier in Rede stehenden Arsinoites der hohen Kaiserzeit zu treffen. Andererseits ist die vermeintliche Einzigartigkeit von Heroneinos' Papieren, wie schon von Dominic Rathbone festgestellt, vor allem auf die überaus günstige Fundsituation zurückzuführen. So wird man zuversichtlich annehmen dürfen, daß andernorts sehr wohl Parallelen zu diesem einen und noch dazu ungewöhnlich gut erhaltenen Archiv existierten.[39] Nur wurde davon bislang nichts entdeckt, so daß wir auch nicht wissen, wie sich dies im Einzelfall gestaltet haben mag.

Sicher dürfte nach alldem aber immerhin so viel sein, daß der Standard in der privaten Buchführung weitaus höher als gemeinhin angenommen war. Wenn man diesbezüglich also die aus dem Heroneinos-Archiv gezogenen Erkenntnisse ohne weiteres verallgemeinern darf, hat dies erst recht im Fall der „'primary' records" zu gelten, von denen wir nun tatsächlich Belege aus den verschiedensten Zeiten und Orten besitzen. Dies läßt zum einen darauf schließen, daß zumindest bei größeren Besitzungen eine entsprechende, vorzugsweise tagesgenaue Datenerfassung zu Einnahmen und Ausgaben, Anbauprodukten, Personal usw. allgemein verbreitet und üblich war. Zum anderen gab es darin zwar allerlei durch die Umstände bedingte Differenzen. Dennoch wiesen sie in ihrer Anlage eine erstaunliche Verwandtschaft auf, freilich ohne daß sich daraus bestimmte oder gar verbindliche Prinzipien des Wirtschaftens ableiten ließen.

---

zuvor zitierten Passus in P. Mich. III 166 pag. III, 1 ff. *tab(ula) VIII pag(ina) II ... et post alia pag(ina) IX* dar, ohne die vermutete Gleichsetzung von *pagina* und Kolumnen weiter zu erhärten oder gar archäologische Zeugnisse dafür beizubringen. Ähnliches gilt für die Darstellung, daß die Seiten römischer Rechnungsbücher durch die – als Abkürzung für *D(ebitum)* bzw. *Cr(editum)* gedeuteten – Buchstaben D bzw. C (oder CR in Ligatur) gekennzeichnet seien, wofür Minaud, a.a.O. 79 § 121 auf ein Relief des Rheinischen Landesmuseums Trier verweist, vgl. auch 353 im „Annexe" die stark vergrößerte Abbildung des geöffneten Codex aus der Zahlungsszene auf dem sog. Elternpaarpfeiler aus Neumagen Inv. 970 (II./III. Jhdt. n. Chr.). Tatsächlich sind darin jedoch keine Buchstaben, sondern die für aufwendigere Wachstafelensembles typischen und bezeichnenderweise in der Mitte des Schriftspiegels befindlichen kleinen Schutzzapfen zu erblicken, die die in die umgebende Wachsschicht eingeritzte Schrift vor Beschädigung bzw. Abrieb bewahren sollten; dazu jetzt A. Jördens, 'Codices des Typs C und die Anfänge des Blätterns', *Material Aspects of Reading in Ancient and Medieval Cultures. Materiality, Presence and Performance*, hrsg. v. A. Krauß – J. Leipziger – F. Schücking-Jungblut (MTK 26), Berlin – Boston 2020, 115-148, bes. Anm. 67.

39 So auch schon die Schlußfolgerung von Rathbone, *Economic Rationalism* (wie Anm. 13), 359: „The accounts of the Appianus estate show some signs of development, but they were not unique either in concept or in format".

unabhängig von dem Maß an Autonomie, das *vilici* oder φροντισταί auf unterer Ebene zugestanden wurde. Insofern scheint eher Vorsicht geraten, was die von Minaud verfochtene Gegenüberstellung römischer und ägyptischer Wirtschaftsformen betrifft – hier separate Einheiten unter der Leitung eigenverantwortlicher *vilici*, dort φροντίδες, deren Vorsteher gleichsam als bloße 'Rädchen' in einer zentralisierten Verwaltung agierten.[40] Bis zum Beweis des Gegenteils wird man vielmehr in Rom, ja im gesamten Reich wie auch schon innerhalb der ägyptischen Evidenz je nach Ort, Zeit und Konstellation der beteiligten Personen mit ganz unterschiedlichen Konzeptionen zu rechnen haben.

40 Vgl. bereits oben Anm. 4 f.

Registrierung und Beurkundung von νόμοι im Grapheion von Tebtynis

Patrick Sänger, Münster

Unter den Urkunden, die im römerzeitlichen Grapheion von Tebtynis hergestellt wurden, findet sich mehrfach auch die Bezugnahme auf die Textgattung νόμος, die sich hier auf Satzungen – „rules“ – von Vereinigungen bezieht. Die Bezeichnung νόμος kann in diesem Kontext freilich irreführend sein, denn für gewöhnlich versteht man darunter – dem Rechtsdenken der griechischen Klassik entsprechend – ein Gesetz, dessen Quelle die Legislative einer Polis war und bei dem es sich um einen schriftlich fixierten oder – wie in Sparta – mündlich überlieferten Rechtssatz handelte.[1] Im ptolemäischen Ägypten kam es hinsichtlich der Semantik des Begriffes νόμος zu einer nicht unwesentlichen Inhaltsverschiebung, weil dieser – gemäß einer überzeugenden Interpretation von Joseph Mélèze Modrzejewski – von seinem Zusammenhang mit Äußerungen des öffentlichen oder staatlichen Ordnungswillens getrennt wurde. Es war nunmehr der königliche Wille, der die Gesetze bestimmte. Die daraus hervorgehenden Rechtssätze wurden in der Form eines διάγραμμα oder πρόσταγμα erlassen, aber nicht mehr als νόμοι bezeichnet. Vielmehr wurde der Begriff νόμος auf jene Rechtsbereiche beschränkt, die neben der „staatlichen“ bzw. königlichen, von den διαγράμματα und προστάγματα abgedeckten Gesetzgebung existierten. Er wurde dadurch – freilich auch mit Bezug auf die νόμοι der auf ägyptischem Boden gegründeten griechischen Städte – auf die gewohnheitsrechtliche Sphäre bezogen und seiner klassischen Bedeutung entfremdet.[2] Beachtenswert ist dabei, dass das, was unter den Ptolemäern als Gewohnheitsrecht aufgefasst wurde, tatsächlich nur mit dem Begriff νόμος, nicht aber mit semantisch naheliegenden Bezeichnungen wie ἔθος, ἐθισμός oder συνήθεια in Verbindung gebracht wurde.[3] Das ändert sich in römischer Zeit, in der νόμος und ἔθος zu austauschbaren Begrifflichkeiten werden, und das gilt sowohl mit Bezugnahme auf das römische Recht als auch auf gewohnheitsrechtliche Regelungen.[4]

Damit sind wir im römischen Ägypten angelangt, das den Hintergrund für diese Untersuchung bildet. Der einleitende Hinweis auf die Bedeutungsverschiebung des Begriffes νόμος war notwendig, um auf die semantische Verwendung vorzubereiten, mit der wir im

---

1 Wolff 1962a; Mélèze Modrzejewski 2014, 7–18.

2 Mélèze Modrzejewski 2014, 23–24, 115–169. Ders. ebenda, 50–51, 224 betrachtete das ägyptische und griechische Gewohnheitsrecht unter dem Modell des Rechtspluralismus und argumentierte ausschließlich für eine Legalisierung des Gewohnheitsrechtes durch die Gerichtspraxis, so dass er sich in diesem Punkt von Wolffs Hypothese entfernt, das ptolemäische Rechtssystem sei als ein einziges Gebilde, als ein allumfassendes Königsrecht zu verstehen; Wolff 1953, 28; 1960, 213–217; 1962b, 27, Anm. 22a, 194–201; 1979, 60.

3 Mélèze Modrzejewski 2014, 22.

4 Mélèze Modrzejewski 2014, 24–26.

Zusammenhang mit Satzungen von Vereinigungen konfrontiert werden. Denn diese νόμοι entstammen der gewohnheitsrechtlichen Sphäre. Im bürokratischen Sprachgebrauch kann der Begriff νόμος nachweislich auf die Satzung einer Vereinigung bezogen werden: Das beweist P.Enteux. 20 (Ars.) aus dem Jahr 221 v. Chr., wo in Z. 5 und 9 von einem θιασιτικὸς νόμος die Rede ist, wobei die zweite Erwähnung in der Subskription des Strategen erfolgt. Weitaus zahlreicher ist der angezeigte Wortgebrauch in zwei ἀναγραφαί bzw. Registern bezeugt, die aus dem Kontext der lokalen, als Grapheion bezeichneten Urkundsbehörde des im Gau Arsinoites gelegenen Dorfes Tebtynis stammen und zu dem Archiv des Kronion, Sohn des Apion, dem Vorsteher des Grapheion, gehören;[5] es handelt sich um P.Mich. II 123 (45/6) und 124 (46–49), die kurz vor die Mitte des 1. Jahrhunderts n. Chr. datieren, also in die Regierungszeit des Claudius gehören, und in denen in insgesamt sieben Einträgen die νόμοι von Vereinigungen Erwähnung finden:

— P.Mich. II 123 Rekto, Kol. VI, 18: νόμος συνόδο(υ) Ψοσνε(ῦτος) ἐλεουργο(ῦ) (*l.* ἐλαιουργο(ῦ)) ἐλέου (*l.* ἐλαίου) κο(τύλαι) δ
— P.Mich. II 123 Rekto, Kol. IX, 45: [-] νόμος συνόδο(υ) Κρονι. . [-]
— P.Mich. II 123 Rekto, Kol. X, 6: δ (l. θ) νόμο(ς) συνόδο(υ) Κρονίωνο(ς) Καμήους (ὀβολοὶ) ια
— P.Mich. II 123 Rekto, Kol. XI, 36: νόμος [σ]υνόδου Ἡρακλήου Πίχιο(ς) ἐπαύλεω(ς) (ὀβολοὶ) κ
— P.Mich. II 123 Rekto, Kol. XVI, 12: νόμος πυμένων (l. ποιμένων) (ὀβολοὶ) η
— P.Mich. II 123 Rekto, Kol. XVII, 38 νόμο(ς) οἰκοδόμων (ὀβολοὶ) ι
— P.Mich. II 124, Kol. II, 23: νόμος συνώδο(υ) (l. συνόδο(υ)) θεοῦ . [.]. . . .

Bevor näher auf diese Belege eingegangen wird, sei darauf hingewiesen, dass die Dokumentation von Vereinigungen in Tebtynis nicht auf besagte ἀναγραφαί beschränkt ist, sondern durch insgesamt sechs Zeugnisse aus dem Archiv des Kronion, Sohn des Apion, erweitert wird, die ebenfalls aus der Mitte des 1. Jahrhunderts n. Chr. stammen und damit ungefähr zeitgleich zu den ἀναγραφαί stehen. Es handelt sich einerseits um drei Papyri, auf denen jeweils die Satzung einer Vereinigung verzeichnet wurde,[6] sowie andererseits um drei weitere Dokumente, die sich lediglich als Auflistungen von Mitgliedern jeweils einer Vereinigung präsentieren.[7] Welche Gruppen sich hinter diesen Vereinigungen verbergen, kann zweifelsfrei nur zwei Satzungen und einer Mitgliederliste entnommen werden: P.Mich. V 244 betrifft ἀπολύσιμοι – also Personen, die von irgendwelchen Pflichten oder auch Steuerzahlungen befreit waren[8] –, die der Großgrundbesitzung (οὐσία) des Claudius zugewiesen waren, Nr. 245 ἁλοπῶλαι bzw. Salzhändler; Nr. 246 ist der Vereinigung des hellenisierten Horus-Kindgottes Harpokrates zuzuweisen. Diese Evidenz wirft zusammen mit den ἀναγραφαί ein Schlaglicht auf die zahlreichen Vereinigungen, die es im frühkaiser-

5 Zu dem Archiv siehe zusammenfassend Van Beek 2013 sowie die auf dieser Dokumentation aufbauenden Studien von Micaela Langellotti (2015; 2016a; 2016b).
6 P.Mich. V 243 (14–37); 244 (43); 245 (47); siehe bereits Boak1937, 212.
7 P.Mich. V 246 (Mitte 1. Jh.); 247; 248 (beide: frühes 1. Jh.).
8 Zu der Wortbedeutung von ἀπολύσιμος siehe Preisigke, WB I 188 *s. v.*; LSJ[9] 208 *s. v.*; A. E. R. Boak, P.Mich. V 244, Einleitung, S. 100–101.

zeitlichen Tebtynis gegeben hat.[9] Die betreffenden Zeugnisse gewähren aber auch einen Einblick in die bürokratische Praxis, die den Satzungen zugrunde lag – ein Aspekt, der bislang bei der Beschäftigung mit diesen Dokumenten erstaunlicherweise ausschließlich ohne genauere vergleichende Berücksichtigung der ἀναγραφαί behandelt wurde. Das trifft auch auf Karl Heinrich Schnöckel zu, der der Textgruppe P.Mich. V 243–248 seine im Jahr 1956 vorgelegte Dissertation widmete, die im Jahr 2006 schließlich veröffentlicht wurde.[10]

Zwei Fragen, die sich ursächlich aus den ἀναγραφαί ableiten, sind hier von zentraler Bedeutung: Wurden Satzungen von Vereinigungen üblicherweise in einem Grapheion aufgesetzt, und welcher Urkundstyp lag ihnen zugrunde?

Zunächst sei auf die bekannte Tatsache verwiesen, dass die Institution des Grapheion, die von der Mitte des 2. Jahrhunderts v. Chr. bis in das 4. Jahrhundert n. Chr. nachweisbar ist, ab der frühen Kaiserzeit weite Verbreitung fand und über die Dörfer der Chora verteilt war. Die örtlichen Grapheia bildeten gewissermaßen Nebenstellen der Agoranomieämter, die als zentrale Urkundsbehörden der Gaue in den jeweiligen Gauhauptstädten konzentriert waren. Hinsichtlich ihrer Funktion bestanden zwischen den zentralen Agoranomieämtern und den Grapheia keine Unterschiede; auch in letzteren wurden Urkunden jeglicher Art aufgesetzt.[11] Einen lebhaften Einblick in die Schreibarbeit, die in den Grapheia geleistet wurde, gewähren die ἀναγραφαί.[12] Sie waren auf Griechisch verfasste Listen, in denen die Urkunden, die in dem jeweiligen Grapheion aufgesetzt wurden, mit kurzen Angaben zu ihrem Typ, den Urkundsparteien, dem Gegenstand oder Wert des Rechtsgeschäftes und für gewöhnlich die Höhe der veranschlagten Schreibgebühr (γραμματικόν) in chronologischer Reihung verzeichnet wurden. Einen anschaulichen Eindruck von derartigen Registern vermitteln unsere ἀναγραφαί P.Mich. II 123 und 124, wobei erstere tatsächlich eine praktisch durchgängige Dokumentation der während des sechsten Regierungsjahres des Claudius im Grapheion von Tebtynis aufgesetzten Urkunden bietet. Die einzelnen Posten werden verschiedenartig kategorisiert: man findet zahlreiche Verträge, die als ὁμολογίαι ausgewiesen und danach näher präzisiert werden; sie können etwa ein Pacht- und Kaufgeschäft oder eine ἔκστασις, einen Verzicht auf Vermögensteile, zum Inhalt haben. Andere Einträge nennen allein den Inhalt der Urkunde: hierbei kann es sich um eine μίσθωσις (Pacht), ein δάνειον (Darlehen), eine πρᾶσις (Verkauf), eine συγγραφὴ τροφῖτις (Unterhaltsvertrag), eine διδασκαλία (Lehrlingsvertrag), eine δόσις (Geschenk) und eine ἐκχώρησις (Verzichtsurkunde) handeln.[13] Der alleinige Verweis auf eine συγγραφή – die allgemeine technische Bezeichnung für (staatsnotarielle) „Urkunde"[14] – scheint sich aufgrund der weiteren Inhaltsbeschreibung überwiegend auf einen Mitgiftsvertrag zu beziehen,[15] und für Eingaben bzw. Petitionen werden zwei Begriffe verwendet: ὑπόμνημα und – ein einziges Mal in unseren

9 Damit setzt sich die relativ gute Quellenlage zu den Vereinigungen in Tebtynis fort, die sich in ptolemäischer Zeit in neun demotischen Satzungen der Suchos-Vereinigung niederschlägt, die allesamt aus dem 2. Jahrhundert v. Chr. stammen; siehe dazu Muhs 2001.

10 Schnöckel 2006.

11 Zu den örtlichen Grapheia siehe einschlägig Wolff 1978, 18–23.

12 Zu der Anagraphe siehe grundlegend Wolff 1978, 35–45.

13 Zu dieser Aufzählung vgl. A. E. R. Boak, P.Mich. II 123, Einleitung, S. 88.

14 Wolff 1978, 84; Lippert 2012, 141.

15 P.Mich. II 123 Rekto, Kol. II, 18; Kol. V, 22; Kol. VI, 10; Kol. VII, 13, 15, 31; Kol. XI, 10; Kol. XII, 17, 28, 29; Kol. XIV, 20, 21, 30; Kol. XV, 23; Kol. XVIII, 38; Kol. XXI, 24.

beiden ἀναγραφαί – ἀξίωμα. Bei ersterer Urkunde wird oftmals betont, dass sie gegen (κατά) eine andere Partei gerichtet ist,[16] wohingegen bei letzterer – eingeleitet durch εἰς – der Fokus auf den Empfänger gelegt wird.[17] Schwieriger gestaltet sich demgegenüber die Einschätzung, welche Urkunden sich hinter den Bezeichnungen ἀναφόριον, γραφή, ὑπομνημάτιον und χειρογραφία verbergen. Betrachtet man die Einträge, dann könnten die ἀναφόρια als Zahlungen oder Abrechnungen, die γραφαί als Listen zu identifizieren sein. Wie genau das in den dokumentarischen Quellen nur in den Grapheionregistern aus Tebtynis bezeugte ὑπομνημάτιον zu verstehen ist, muß fraglich bleiben; in der Edition wird „report" wiedergegeben.[18] Eine nähere Definition von χειρογραφία wird sich aus einer Gegenüberstellung mit unseren Satzungen ergeben, zu denen nun zurückzukommen ist.

Auch wenn die Satzungen von Vereinigungen, wie bereits erwähnt wurde, in P.Mich. II 123 und 124 an sieben Stellen begegnen – und wir werden gleich sehen werden, dass auf derartige Dokumente durchaus häufiger Bezug genommen wird, als es auf den ersten Blick erscheinen mag –, so gibt es abgesehen von diesen Belegen keinen Hinweis auf einen bürokratischen Zusammenhang zwischen ihnen und einer Urkundsbehörde. Das verwundert umso mehr, als P.Mich. II 123 und 124 den Anschein erwecken, als wäre es allgemeiner Usus gewesen, die Satzungen von Vereinigungen in einem Grapheion aufsetzen zu lassen. In der Tat scheinen es sieben unterschiedliche Vereinigungen zu sein, die diesbezüglich die Dienste des Grapheion in Anspruch nehmen; es sind dies die Vereinigungen der Hirten (ποιμένες) und der Maurer (οἰκοδόμοι), eine weitere, die einem unbekannten Gott gewidmet ist, und vier andere, die sich über einen Eigennamen definieren; zwei von diesen geben einen Zusammenhang mit Ölbauern (ἐλαιουργοί) und mit einem bäuerlichen Betrieb (ἔπαυλις) zu erkennen.

Was genau ließen sich die Vereinigungen von dem Grapheion ausstellen bzw. welcher Urkundstyp stand hinter einem νόμος? Diese Frage mag zunächst banal erscheinen, geht doch aus der Bezeichnung νόμος mit wünschenswerter Deutlichkeit der Inhalt der Urkunde hervor. Betrachtet man die äußere Form der erhaltenen Satzungen P.Mich. V 243–245, dann fallen überdies Charakteristika ins Auge, die gut zu einem Grapheion zu passen scheinen – man beachte nur das Anfangsdatum, die objektive Stilisierung und die Unterschriften am Ende. Dementsprechend hat die Forschung bislang den Vertragscharakter der Satzungen hervorgehoben.[19] Auch Schnöckel beschritt diesen Weg, indem er zu der Beo-

16 κατά: P.Mich. II 123 Rekto, Kol. III, 44; Kol. IV, 15, 35; Kol. V, 31; Kol. X, 11; Kol. XII, 18; Kol. XIV, 28; P.Mich. II 124 Verso, Kol. I, 7. In P.Mich. II 124 Rekto, Kol. I, 18 könnte κατά durch πρός ersetzt worden sein: ὑπόμνη(μα) Αὔνγο(υς) Σεκον[ώπιος] π̣ρ̣ὸ̣(ς) . . . .[. .] . .το( ) α . . .[.

17 P.Mich. II 123 Rekto, Kol. II, 24; vgl. P.Mich. II 123 Rekto, Kol. XIV, 9, wo die Konstruktion im Bezug auf ὑπομνήματα auftritt.

18 Wie Anm. 13. Hinsichtlich der Interpretation der in besagten Registern verzeichneten αναφόρια hat sich jüngst Langellotti 2016a, 129–134 für die Bedeutung „written bids for state concessions" (S. 132) ausgesprochen.

19 Boak 1937, 220; ders., P.Mich. V 243, Einleitung, S. 95; Préaux 1947, 191–193; Taubenschlag 1955, 644–646. Das entspricht der generellen Auffassung von dem Charakter der Satzungen antiker Vereinigungen: Als um die Mitte des 19. Jahrhunderts das rechtshistorische Interesse an den Satzungen antiker Vereinigungen einsetzte, ging es ausgehend von der Identifizierung der *lex collegii aquae* (CIL VI 10298 = FIRA III 32 [Rom, augusteische Zeit]) durch Adolf A. F. Rudorff (1850) und der darauf bezogenen Reaktion von Theodor Mommsen (1850, 345–353) im Wesentlichen um die Frage, ob diese Satzung einer *lex publica* oder *lex privata* nahestehe; und ferner, ob die in ihr festgehaltenen Bestimmun-

bachtung gelangte, dass Gestaltung und Formular der Satzungen an jene der staatsnotariellen Urkunde, eines δημόσιος χρηματισμός, erinnerten, und daraus folgerte bzw. bestätigte, dass „der Nomos seinerzeit offenbar als eine Art Vertrag angesehen" wurde.[20]

Es wäre nun aber zu einfach, mit Schnöckel zu dem verallgemeinernden Schluss zu gelangen, die Satzungen P.Mich. V 243–245 hätten allesamt einen „speziellen Vertragstyp" namens νόμος verkörpert, der „beurkundungstechnische Varianten" aufgewiesen habe.[21] Die Wirkung der Satzungen war zweifelsfrei eine rechtlich bzw. vertraglich bindende, und deren formale Gestaltung mag den Vergleich mit einer staatsnotariellen Urkunde nahelegen. Ein genauerer Blick auf die Art der Beurkundung der Satzungen lässt aber dennoch erste Zweifel an Schnöckels Einschätzung aufkommen, P.Mich. V 243–245 mit einem einzigen Urkundstyp in Verbindung zu bringen. Hier spielt hinein, was auch Schnöckel durchaus bewusst war, und zwar der Umstand, dass die Texte, die die Satzungen überliefern, gleichzeitig auch deren Beschlussfassung durch die Mitglieder der Vereinigungen dokumentieren.[22] Dieser Charakter tritt bei P.Mich. V 244 und 245 besonders deutlich, ja gerade plakativ hervor, denn denkt man sich bei diesen beiden Satzungen die Datierung am Beginn und die Unterschriften am Ende weg, dann verbleibt als Kern des Dokumentes der äußeren Form nach ein einfacher gemeinschaftlicher Beschluss; hätte man ihn auf einer Steininschrift gefunden, würde man diese ohne Zögern der Kategorie „Dekret" zuordnen. Eine derartige Gestaltung scheint von den beschlussfassenden Mitgliedern auch intendiert gewesen zu sein: jeweils in Z. 3 werden die Satzungen mit ἔδοξαν eingeleitet, ein Wortgebrauch, der in den epigraphisch überlieferten Beschlüssen bzw. Dekreten massenhaft überliefert ist. Wie man die Wiedergabe des gemeinschaftlichen Beschlusses auf formaler Ebene auffasste, dürfte sich auch darin manifestieren, dass der Vorsteher und ein weiteres Mitglied ihren Originalunterschriften am Ende von P.Mich. V 244 (Z. 45 und 46) die Bemerkung ἐψήφισμαι beifügen[23] – ein Textelement, das in P.Mich. V 245 nicht mehr erhal-

gen bezüglich interner Gerichtsbarkeit dieser Form der Rechtspflege einen öffentlichen Charakter verliehen habe und als übertragene Staatsgewalt oder aber lediglich als Ausdruck der Autonomie der Vereinigung aufzufassen sei. Diese Fragestellung wurde von Mariano San Nicolò (1927) anlässlich einer Untersuchung der internen Gerichtsbarkeit jener Vereinigungen des hellenistischen Ägypten aufgegriffen, deren Satzungen seinerzeit bekannt waren. Er unterstrich den Vertragscharakter der Satzungen und – ähnlich wie Mommsen – den Aspekt der „Privatautonomie", so dass die interne Gerichtsbarkeit von Vereinigungen des hellenistischen Ägypten den Charakter einer Schiedsgerichtsbarkeit angenommen habe. Und in der Tat ist es heute auch im Bezug auf die römischen Satzungen (*leges collegiorum*) allgemeiner Tenor, diese – vergleichbar etwa mit *leges templorum* – als „rechtsgeschäftliche Vereinbarungen im privaten […] Bereich" anzusehen, womit sie zu den *leges dictae* zu reihen sind (Bleicken 1975, 61–62). Dazu passt, dass Jinyu Liu (2009, 98–99) betonte, der in den Digesten (47,22,4) überlieferte, von Gaius auf Solon zurückgeführte Grundsatz der Zwölftafelgesetze – wonach *collegia* intern Vereinbarungen (*pactiones*) treffen konnten, sofern diese die *lex publica* nicht verletzten – habe prinzipiell für die gesamte Kaiserzeit gegolten.

20 Schnöckel 2006, 19–35; Zitat: 31.

21 Schnöckel 2006, 29–31; 31–32.

22 Schnöckel 2006, 19, 23, 52, 55; zu der Form eines Beschlusses, den die Satzungen antiker Vereinigungen annahmen, siehe generell auch San Nicolò 1972 (zweiter Teil), 21.

23 Dieser Wortgebrauch tritt auch in den Mitgliederlisten P.Mich. V 246, 20–24 (Ars., Mitte 1. Jh.); 247, 17/18 (Ars., frühes 1. Jh.); 248, 8–10 (Ars., frühes 1. Jh.) entgegen, die uns zu drei weiteren Vereinigungen vorliegen.

ten ist.[24] Demnach scheint der reine Satzungstext zumindest im Fall von P.Mich. V 244 und 245 als ψήφισμα formuliert und verstanden worden zu sein.[25] Wenn es darum ging, den Beschluss, das ψήφισμα, von einem professionellen Urkundsschreiber abfassen zu lassen, wird sich dieser bei der Stilisierung an den üblichen Typen öffentlicher Urkunden orientiert haben.

Liefert das aber genügend Indizien, um die in Frage stehenden Satzungen einem einzigen Urkundstyp zuzuordnen? Einen Hinweis darauf, als welcher Urkundstyp die Satzung P.Mich. V 244 aus der Sicht des Grapheion definiert wurde, dürfte das Verso des Papyrus bieten. Dort hat der Urkundsschreiber die Kürzung χ<ε>ιρογρ( ) und darauf folgend den Personennamen Κρονίωνο(ς) τοῦ Ἡρωδίωνος vermerkt, womit der auf dem Rekto in Z. 21 und 45 als Kronion, Sohn des Herodes, bezeichnete Vorsteher der Vereinigung angesprochen sein dürfte.[26] Hinsichtlich der Interpretation von χ<ε>ιρογρ( ) gehen die Meinungen auseinander. Sowohl Hans Julius Wolff als auch Schnöckel haben χ<ε>ιρόγρ(αφον) aufgelöst, diesen Begriff aber auf unterschiedliche Weise interpretiert: Wolff erachtete ihn als Indiz, dass die Satzung einen privaten Handschein dargestellt habe, also als Privaturkunde aufzufassen sei;[27] Schnöckel meinte, χ<ε>ιρόγρ(αφον) beziehe sich auf die originale „unterschriftliche Erklärung" des Vorstehers auf dem Rekto (Z. 45) und sei in dieser Bedeutung namengebend für die gesamte Urkunde gewesen.[28] Folgende Einträge in unseren ἀναγραφαί P.Mich. II 123 und 124 führen aber zu einer anderen Überlegung:

— P.Mich. II 123 Rekto, Kol. III, 41: χιρογρ(αφία) (l. χειρογρ(αφία)) πλήθους γερδίων εἰς τοὺς {εἰς} ἐπιστάτας (δραχμαὶ) η
— P.Mich. II 123 Rekto, Kol. VI, 25: χιρογραφία (*l.* χειρογραφία) πλήθο(υς) ἐριοπολῶν (*l.* ἐριοπωλῶν) (δραχμαὶ) η
— P.Mich. II 123 Rekto, Kol. XXII, 44 (mit Sänger 2016): [χιρ]ογρ(αφία) (*l.* χειρογραφία; ed. pr.: [συ]νγρ(αφὴ) (l. συγγρ(αφή)) πλῆθος (l. πλήθους) ἀπολυσ[ίμων -]
— P.Mich. II 124 Rekto, Kol. II, 15: χιρογρ(αφία) (l. χειρογρ(αφία)) πλῆθος (l. πλήθους) ἐριοπολῶ(ν) (l. ἐριοπωλῶ(ν)) (δραχμαὶ) η

Löst man χειρογρ( ) in P.Mich. II 124 Rekto, Kol. II, 15 gemäß dem Beispiel von P.Mich. II 123 Rekto, Kol. VI, 25 auf, erhält man zwei Belege für den Eintrag „*cheirographia* der Versammlung der Wollhändler, 8 Drachmen". Folgt man diesem Beispiel weiter, so begegnet die Formulierung zudem jeweils einmal im Zusammenhang mit der Versammlung der Weber (betreffs der Vorsteher)[29] und mit der Versammlung der ἀπολύσιμοι, zu deren Ver-

24 Siehe dazu weiter unten bei Anm. 33.
25 Vgl. Schnöckel 2006, 60.
26 So auch die Einschätzung von A. E. R. Boak, P.Mich. V 244, Komm. zum Verso (S. 107), die von Schnöckel aufgegriffen wurde; siehe dazu weiter unten Anm. 28.
27 Wolff 1978, 128.
28 Schnöckel 2006, 21–22.
29 Mit P.Mich. II 123 Rekto, Kol. XXI, 31 liegt ein weiterer Eintrag vor, bei dem eine χειρογραφία in Verbindung mit einer Vereinigung, und zwar eben jener der Weber, genannt wird; Bezugspunkt der handschriftlichen Erklärung ist in diesem Fall ein namentlich nicht genannter, das bevorstehende 7. Jahr des Claudius betreffender Vorsteher der Weber: χιρογρ(αφία) (*l.* χειρογραφία) ἡγουμένου γερδίων τοῦ ἰσιόντος (*l.* εἰσιόντος) ζ (ἔτους). Aufgrund dieser Formulierung und dem anschließenden Auftreten der Präposition ἐπί, auf die wiederum ein Lücke folgt, kann der angezeigte Beleg nicht als Parallele zu

einigung die Satzung P.Mich. V 244 vorliegt. Da hier ein als χειρογραφία bezeichneter Urkundstyp im Kontext von Vereinigungen in Erscheinung tritt, liegt im Kontext eines Archives die Vermutung doch recht nahe, dass sich hinter der in Frage stehenden Kürzung χ<ε>ιρογρ( ) auf dem Verso von P.Mich. V 244 das Wort χειρογραφία verbirgt.[30] Für einen derartigen Analogieschluss könnte auch sprechen, dass auf ein χειρόγραφον, also einen privaten Handschein, an keiner Stelle der ἀναγραφαί P.Mich. II 123 und 124 explizit Bezug genommen wird.[31] Überdies ließe sich die Bedeutung von χειρογραφία als „handschriftliche Erklärung“[32] gut mit dem Inhalt von P.Mich. V 244 in Einklang bringen, handelte es sich doch um ein urkundlich verbrieftes ψήφισμα der Vereinigung der ἀπολύσιμοι. Wenn P.Mich. V 244 auf dem Verso tatsächlich als χειρογραφία bezeichnet worden wäre, dann würde das außerdem gut dazu passen, dass man nachfolgend auf den Vorsteher der ἀπολύσιμοι Bezug nahm, denn dieser hatte den Beschluss der von ihm vertretenen Vereinigung auf dem Rekto mit seiner Originalunterschrift bestätigt.

Verfolgt man diese Überlegungen konsequent weiter, dann könnten die in den ἀναγραφαί verzeichneten χειρογραφίαι, die in Zusammenhang mit dem πλῆθος einer Vereinigung genannt werden, Satzungen nach dem Muster von P.Mich. V 244 enthalten haben. Schließlich wird das ψήφισμα bzw. der Beschluss, der P.Mich. V 244 zugrunde liegt, anlässlich einer Versammlung (πλῆθος) der Vereinigung gefasst worden sein. Im übrigen wird in dieser Satzung – wie auch in P.Mich. V 243 und 245 – an erster Stelle die Wahl eines neuen Vorstehers festgehalten, und dieses wesentliche Textelement könnte in der ἀναγραφή mit εἰς τοὺς ἐπιστάτας umschrieben worden sein. Damit müsste man in Erwägung ziehen, dass in den ἀναγραφαί zwei Bezeichnungen auf die Satzung einer Vereinigung Bezug nehmen konnten: νόμος und χειρογραφία.

Angesichts dessen erhebt sich unweigerlich die Frage, ob der angezeigte Wortgebrauch mit der bürokratischen Praxis des Grapheion zusammenhängt, in deren Rahmen unter einem νόμος und einer χειρογραφία unterschiedliche Arten von Urkunden verstanden wurden, die man für die Widergabe von Satzungen verwendete, oder ob wir hier einfach mit der Verwendung von austauschbaren Begriffen konfrontiert werden. Wie bereits angedeutet wurde, wissen wir zwar nichts Genaueres darüber, welche allgemeine Urkundspraxis den Satzungen von Vereinigungen zugrunde lag. Allerdings lohnt in diesem Zusammenhang abermals eine formale Betrachtung unserer drei Exemplare P.Mich. V 243, 244 und 245, denn aus ihnen dürften sich entgegen bisherigen Deutungen – die die in den ἀναγραφαί erwähnten χειρογραφίαι nicht in die Überlegungen miteinbezogen haben – zwei unterschiedliche Urkundstypen ableiten lassen, auf die für schriftliche Niederlegung von Satzungen zurückgegriffen wurde. Diese Beobachtung nimmt ihren Ausgang darin, dass P.Mich. V 243 die Originalunterschriften der unterzeichneten Mitglieder – an erster Stelle die des neuen Vorstehers (Z. 17) – enthält. Dagegen werden in 244 die Mitglieder der Vereinigung unter dem Text des Beschlusses vom Schreiber lediglich aufgelistet, und es sind

jenen oben angeführten Formulierungen gereiht werden, die sich auf ein πλῆθος einer Vereinigung und, wie im Folgenden argumentiert wird, die schriftliche Fixierung einer Satzung beziehen.

30 So bereits Sänger 2016, 284, Anm. 32.

31 Damit ist nach Wolff 1978, 39 auch zu rechnen, der konstatierte, „dass zumindest in römischer Zeit private Handscheine (Cheirographa) niemals anagraphiert wurden.“

32 Preisigke, WB 781; LSJ^9 1985; Langellotti 2016a, 125 mit Anm. 59.

am Ende der Urkunde unterschreiben; 245 bricht mit dem Einsetzen der Auflistung der einzelnen Mitglieder ab und dürfte daher ebenfalls die von 244 repräsentierte Form der Beurkundung widerspiegeln.[33]

Im Fall von P.Mich. V 243 wurde die Satzung also durch die Unterschriften der Mitglieder bestätigt, so wie es von der am Ende der Satzung formulierten Klausel in Z. 12–13 κυρία (*l.* κύριος) <ἔ>στωι ὁ νόμος ὑπογραφεὶς ὑπὸ τῶν πλείστων („der von den meisten unterschriebene νόμος soll rechtskräftig sein") gefordert wird. Als rechtsgültige Urkunde sei der unterschriebene νόμος dem Vorsteher zu übergeben: κύριος τῶι προστάτῃ ἀποδοθήτωι (*l.* ἀποδοθήτω) (Z. 13). Eine andere Variante, den νόμος urkundlich zu verbriefen, begegnet in P.Mich. V 244 und 245: In ihnen wird der Beschluss der ὑπογεγραμμένοι (Z. 2), der unterzeichneten bzw. aufgelisteten Mitglieder, festgehalten; über die Satzung und die Wahl des Vorstehers ist bereits positiv entschieden worden. Anders als im Fall von P.Mich. V 243 scheint in P.Mich. V 244 und 245 der Fokus also nicht darauf zu liegen, den νόμος mittels der Urkunde mehrheitlich zu bestätigen bzw. zu beschließen, sondern das betreffende und im Prinzip bereits geltende ψήφισμα über die Satzung bzw. den νόμος im Rahmen eines Sitzungsprotokolls urkundlich zu dokumentieren. Passend dazu fehlen in diesen Satzungen die in P.Mich. V 243 enthaltenen κύριος-Formulierungen. Dennoch mussten auch die Urkunden, in denen die bereits erfolgte Beschlussfassung der Vereinigungen festgehalten wurden, ordnungsgemäß bestätigt werden; dies taten der Vorsteher und ein weiteres Mitglied, indem sie ihre eigenen kopierten Unterschriften noch einmal eigenhändig bekräftigten.

Vor diesem Hintergrund wäre es denkbar, dass Satzungen, wie sie in P.Mich. V 244 und 245 vorliegen, in den ἀναγραφαί mit dem Begriff χειρογραφία umschrieben worden sind; präzisiert wurde diese Angabe dann – unter Bezugnahme auf ein πλῆθος – durch die jeweilige Bezeichnung der betreffenden Vereinigung. Demgegenüber könnten Urkunden, die in der Form von P.Mich. V 243 gestaltet waren, gemäß dem Wortlaut der darin anzutreffenden κύριος-Formulierungen, einfach als νόμος bezeichnet worden sein; das war ihr Inhalt, unabhängig davon, ob dieser schon bestätigt war oder nicht. Ob die Personennamen, nach denen einige Vereinigungen benannt waren, die im Zusammenhang mit den in den ἀναγραφαί genannten νόμοι auftreten, auf den Gründer, den noch amtierenden oder aber den zukünftigen Vorsteher Bezug nehmen, muss offen bleiben.

Auch wenn es momentan nicht möglich ist, bei der formalen Unterscheidung von Satzungen, die als νόμος und χειρογραφία bezeichnet wurden, über Vermutungen hinauszugelangen, so gibt es zumindest ein Indiz, das den hier entwickelten Ansatz zu unterstützen vermag: für die νόμοι wird eine Gebühr verlangt, die zwischen 8 und 20 Obolen lag und im Fall der Ölbauern durch eine Naturalabgabe in Form von Öl (4 Kotylen) ersetzt wurde. Demgegenüber hatten die χειρογραφίαι einen weitaus höheren Preis: für sie waren durchgehend 8 Drachmen zu entrichten. Es wird also klar, dass es zwischen den νόμοι und χειρογραφίαι irgendeinen Unterschied geben muss, der sich schließlich in der Höhe des erhobenen γραμματικόν niederschlägt. Wie ist der auffällige Preisunterschied aber tatsächlich zu erklären? Kann er daran liegen, dass in die χειρογραφίαι – sollten die hier angestellten

33 Zu der unterschiedlichen Gestaltung der die Satzungen abschließenden Mitgliederlisten vgl. auch Schnöckel 2006, 29–31.

Überlegungen zutreffen – die Mitgliederliste der jeweiligen Vereinigung inkorporiert wurde?[34] Man wird auch hier nichts weiter als spekulieren können.

Abschließend steht die Frage, ob es sich bei den νόμοι bzw. χειρογραφίαι von Vereinigungen nun um öffentliche oder private Urkunden handelte. Aufgrund der disparaten Quellenlage zu den Satzungen und deren hybrider Gestalt wird man diesbezüglich zu keiner klaren Lösung gelangen können. Gewiss spricht die Stilisierung der hier untersuchten Urkunden eher für einen öffentlichen Charakter. Der bloße Umstand, dass die Satzungen zum Archiv des Kronion gehören und daher zu den im Grapheion verbliebenen Dokumenten zu zählen sind,[35] mag diese Einschätzung zwar nicht von vornherein stützen. Wir wissen nämlich, dass im Grapheion neben Vertragsurkunden nicht nur andere Dokumente wie etwa Petitionen, Abrechnungen und Listen, sondern auch private Handscheine, also χειρόγραφα, abgefasst wurden.[36] Dennoch ist zu bedenken, dass das Verzeichnen privater Handscheine in ἀναγραφαί nicht zu erwarten ist.[37] Somit könnte das Faktum, dass νόμοι bzw. χειρογραφίαι zu jenen Urkunden gehören, die in P.Mich. II 123 und 124 aufscheinen, den öffentlichen Charakter der Satzungen nahelegen: Die Originale der νόμοι und χειρογραφίαι könnten also dazu bestimmt gewesen sein, mit anderen öffentlichen Urkunden zum Zweck der weiteren Archivierung zu einem τόμος συγκολλήσιμος verarbeitet zu werden.[38]

Sollte diese Überlegung zutreffen, dann gäbe es gleichwohl keinen Grund, den öffentlichen Charakter der Satzungen als einen Reflex auf eine Kontrolle der Vereinigungen durch die römische Verwaltung zu sehen, wie sie ausgehend von der hypothetischen *lex Iulia de collegiis* immer wieder postuliert wurde.[39] Es genügt, in diesem Kontext auf Ilias N. Arnaoutoglou zu verweisen, der überzeugend zeigen konnte, dass generelle Züge einer derartigen Politik im römischen Ägypten des 1. Jahrhunderts nicht nachzuweisen sind.[40] Wenn es also intendiert war, die Satzung in einer öffentlichen Urkunde festzuhalten, dann wird man dies nicht auf irgendwelche Vorschriften zur Überwachung von Vereinigungen zurückführen müssen.[41] Vielmehr wird man erwägen dürfen, dass es seit dem Bestehen griechischer Urkundsbehörden in ptolemäischer Zeit gebräuchlich wurde, die urkundliche Verbriefung von griechischen Satzungen in die Hände von professionellen Urkundsschreibern zu legen: einerseits um auf deren sachliche Kompetenz zurückzugreifen, andererseits um die zugrundeliegende Satzung bei dieser Gelegenheit im Rahmen einer öffentlichen Urkunde festzuhalten und ihr damit eine stärkere Publizität und Autorität zu verleihen. Die

34 Reine Exemplare solcher Mitgliederlisten liegen vielleicht mit P.Mich. V 247 und 248 (beide: Ars., frühes 1. Jh.) vor.

35 Schnöckel 2006, 21.

36 Van Beek 2013, 4.

37 Siehe weiter oben Anm. 31.

38 Zu dieser Archivierungspraxis siehe Wolff 1978, 41–42.

39 Vertreten wurde diese Auffassung bereits von Mommsen 1843 und fand danach weite Verbreitung. Ihr zufolge seien Vereinigungen von römischen Behörden ab der Promulgation der Augustus zugeschriebenen *lex Iulia de collegiis*, auf deren Existenz eine Passage in Suet. Aug. 32, 1 schließen lasse, streng kontrolliert worden.

40 Arnaoutoglou 2005; zu der in der römischen Kaiserzeit gegenüber Vereinigungen verfolgten Politik vgl. etwa auch San Nicolò 1972 (zweiter Teil), 11–14, Harland 2013, 142–151, Tran 2012, 76–77 und Langellotti 2016a, 120–128.

41 In diese Richtung interpretierte andeutungsweise aber Schnöckel 2006, 35, 46–51 den Befund.

hier untersuchten Quellen könnten diesen Trend schlaglichtartig zumindest für das frühkaiserzeitliche Grapheion von Tebtynis beleuchten.

Kurz zusammengefasst, hat der vorliegende Beitrag gezeigt, dass die Textgattung νόμος im Zusammenhang mit den Satzungen von Vereinigungen und der hinter diesen Rechtstexten stehenden bürokratischen Praxis verschiedene Gesichter haben kann. Die ἀναγραφαί, die aus dem Kontext des Grapheion von Tebtynis bzw. dem Archiv des Kronion stammen, haben Anlass zu der Vermutung gegeben, dass in diesen Registern nicht nur die verzeichneten νόμοι, sondern auch die auf die Versammlung einer Vereinigung Bezug nehmenden χειρογραφίαι mit Satzungen in Verbindung zu bringen sind. Eine Betrachtung von P.Mich. V 243–245 hat nahegelegt, dass der formale Unterschied in der Art und Weise, wie ein νόμος im Rahmen einer Urkunde festgehalten wurde, gelegen haben könnte: mit νόμος wurde eine Satzung bezeichnet, die im Rahmen der Urkunde zu bestätigen war; eine χειρογραφία war dagegen eine Urkunde, in der ein bereits gefasstes ψήφισμα über die Satzung bzw. den νόμος einer Vereinigung verbrieft wurde. Die Unterscheidung dieser Urkundstypen ist unabhängig von deren Einstufung als private oder öffentliche bzw. staatsnotarielle Urkunde. Letztere Variante dürfte aber doch die wahrscheinlichere sein, ohne daraus eine Reaktion auf eine behördliche Überwachung der Vereinigungen durch die römische Verwaltung ableiten zu müssen.

Für die hinter den Satzungen stehende bürokratische Praxis sind die hier untersuchten Quellen von ungemeiner Bedeutung; vor jeglicher Verallgemeinerung warnt aber der Umstand, dass sie in örtlicher wie zeitlicher Hinsicht äußerst begrenzt sind.

Literaturverzeichnis

Arnaoutoglou, I. N. (2005) Collegia in the Province of Egypt in the First Century AD, AncSoc 35, 197–216.

Van Beek, B. (2013) Kronion son of Apion, head of the grapheion of Tebtynis, in: Trismegistos Archives, Stand: ArchID 93. Version 2, http://www.trismegistos.org/arch/archives/pdf/93.pdf (abgerufen am 4. April 2018).

Bleicken, J. (1975) Lex Publica. Gesetz und Recht in der römischen Republik, Berlin.

Boak, A. E. R. (1937) The Organization of Gilds in Greco-Roman Egypt, TAPhA 68, 212–220.

Harland, P. A. (2013) Associations, Synagogues, and Congregations. Claiming a Place in Ancient Mediterranean Society, 2. Aufl., Minneapolis.

Langellotti, M. (2015) Sales in Early Roman Tebtunis: the Case of the *Grapheion* Archive of Kronion, in: Jakab, E. (Hrsg.), Legal Documents in Ancient Societies V. Sale and Community Documents from the Ancient World, Trieste, 117–132.

Langellotti, M. (2016a) Professional Associations and the State in Roman Egypt: the Case of First-Century Tebtunis, CE 91, 111–134.

Langellotti, M. (2016b) Contracts and People in Early Roman Tebtunis: a Complex Affair, in: Derda, T. – Łajtar, A. – Urbanik, J. (Hrsg.), Proceedings of the 27th International Congress of Papyrology, Warsaw, 29 July – 3 August 2013 (JJP Suppl. 28), Warszawa, 1725–1736.

Lippert, S. (2012) Einführung in die altägyptische Rechtsgeschichte (Einführungen und Quellentexte zur Ägyptologie 5), 2. Aufl., Berlin.

Liu, Jinyu (2009) *Collegia Centonariorum*. The Guilds of Textile Dealers in the Roman West (Columbia Studies in the Classical Tradition 34), Leiden, Boston.

Mélèze Modrzejewski, J. (2014) Loi et coutume dans l'Égypte grecque et romaine (JJP Supplements 21), Warszawa.

Mommsen, Th. (1843) De collegiis et sodaliciis romanorum. Accedit inscriptio Lanuvina, Kiliae.

Mommsen, Th. (1850) Römische Urkunden, ZRG 15, 287–371.

Muhs, B. (2001) Membership in Private Associations in Ptolemaic Tebtunis, JESHO 44, 1–21.

Préaux, C. (1947) À propos des associations dans l'Égypte gréco-romaine, RIDA 1, 189–198.

Rudorff, A. A. F. (1850) Die sogenannte Lex de Magistris Aquarum, eine altrömische Brunnenordnung, ZRG 15, 203–272.

Sänger, P. (2016) Korr. Tyche 831: P.Mich. II 123 Rekto, Kol. XXII, 44: χειρογραφία statt συγγραφή, in: Tyche 31, 283–284.

San Nicolò, M. (1927) Zur Vereinsgerichtsbarkeit im hellenistischen Ägypten, in: ΕΠΙΤΥΜΒΙΟΝ. Heinrich Swoboda dargebracht, Reichenberg, 255–300.

San Nicolò, M. (1972) Ägyptisches Vereinswesen zur Zeit der Ptolemäer und Römer, Erster Teil: Die Vereinsarten (Münch.Beitr. 2,1); Zweiter Teil: Vereinswesen und Vereinsrecht (Münch.Beitr. 2,2), zweite, durchgesehene Auflage mit Nachträgen von Johannes Herrmann, München.

Schnöckel, K. H. (2006) Ägyptische Vereine in der frühen Prinzipatszeit. Eine Studie über sechs Vereinssatzungen (Papyri Michigan 243–248) (Xenia. Konstanzer Althistorische Vorträge und Forschungen 48), Konstanz.

Taubenschlag, R. (1955) The Law of Greco-Roman Egypt in the Light of the Papyri: 332 B.C.–640 A.D., 2nd ed., Warszawa.

Tran, N. (2012) Associations privées et espaces public. Les emplois de *publicus* dans l'épigraphie des collèges de l'Occident romain, in: Dondin-Payre, M. – Tran, N. (Hrsg.), *Collegia*. Le phénomène associatif dans l'Occident romain (Scripta Antiqua 41), Paris, 63–80.

Wolff, H. J. (1953) Faktoren der Rechtsbildung im hellenistisch-römischen Ägypten, ZRG RA 70, 20–57.

Wolff, H. J. (1960) Plurality of Laws in Ptolemaic Egypt, RIDA 7, 191–223.

Wolff, H. J. (1962a) Gewohnheitsrecht und Gesetzesrecht in der griechischen Rechtsauffassung, Deutsche Landesreferate zum VI. Internationalen Kongress für Rechtsvergleichung in Hamburg 6, 3–18 (= E. Berneker [Hrsg.], Zur griechischen Rechtsgeschichte, Darmstadt 1968, 99–120).
Wolff, H. J. (1962b) Das Justizwesen der Ptolemäer (= Münch.Beitr. 44), München.
Wolff, H. J. (1978) Das Recht der griechischen Papyri Ägyptens in der Zeit der Ptolemaeer und des Prinzipats, Zweiter Band: Organisation und Kontrolle des privaten Rechtsverkehrs (HdAW X 5, 2), München.
Wolff, H. J. (1979) Das Problem der Konkurrenz von Rechtsordnungen in der Antike (= Sitzungsberichte der Heidelberger Akademie der Wissenschaften, Philosophisch-Historische Klasse 1979, 5), Heidelberg.

Identifying People in Official Reports: The Administrative Practice in Roman Egypt*

Nicola Reggiani, Parma

"La réalité transcrite par les documents se révèle riche et complexe
et il est évident que la terminologie s'est adaptée
aux besoins pratiques d'une fiscalité nuancée et diversifiée"[1].

Introduction

Identifying people for official purposes is a key concern of every public administration. At a time when no ID card existed, such as Graeco-Roman antiquity, it became crucial to provide unique identification for each person involved in public business, documents and registrations, like contracts or tax receipts. The most usual and common way to distinguish individuals was to provide personal details such as genealogy (most commonly the father's, grandfather's, and mother's names[2]), age, geographical provenance, current residence, and physical appearance. A second group of identifiers aimed at describing the individual's place within the society as well as his/her administrative position: social status, tax liability, occupation. These have already been well studied from several viewpoints. The fundamental monograph published more than fifty years ago by Gerbert Hübsch provides a general and detailed overview of personal descriptions in Greek and Demotic public and private documents from the Ptolemaic to the Byzantine age, with a final discussion on their juridical purpose[3]. The ways of indicating the belonging to particular privileged social classes have been widely analysed too[4]. Very recently, the third volume of the series "Legal Documents in Ancient Societies" has been devoted to the theme "Identifiers and identification methods in the ancient world"[5], and Mark Depauw's contribution in it carefully

* This paper stems from the project "Synopsis: Data Processing and State Management in Roman Egypt (30 BCE-300 CE)", conducted by Prof. Dr. Andrea Jördens (Universität Heidelberg) and Prof. Uri Yiftach (Tel Aviv University) under a grant of the German-Israeli Foundation for Scientific Research and Development (G-38-111.4/2011). I wish to mention and thank Nikolaos Theodorakopoulos and Giuditta Mirizio, who at different stages worked on some data that I re-used for the present research, and above all Uri Yiftach for helpful discussions on many topics I dealt with and Andrea Jördens for precious suggestions given to a preliminary version of the work.

1 Aubert 2007: 395.

2 On the emergence of metronymics in early Roman Egypt see Depauw 2010. Recent discussion of the term *apatōr* by Yiftach 2015b.

3 Hübsch 1968. Detailed discussions of the juridical use of the record of physical details had already been provided by Hasebroek 1921 and Caldara 1924.

4 Especially Nelson 1979; cf. also Whitehorne 1982, Delia 1991, and, more recently, Jördens 2012.

5 Depauw-Coussement 2014.

surveys all the possible identifiers used in Egypt since Pharaonic times[6]. In the same volume, Uri Yiftach deals with the particular issue of identifying people in contracts from Greco-Roman Egypt[7], and another research conducted by him has highlighted the trend of distinguishing the use of identifying markers according to the different branches of public administration[8]. It is apparent that while marking personal identities in legal documents is a preferential means of guaranteeing the juridical validity of the act, in our present focus, i.e. the official reports, more concrete aims are on the ground – namely, population control and/for tax collection management. I will therefore concentrate on the terms related to the tax/administrative status, more closely connected to the purposes of the reports themselves, in order to verify the existence of a bureaucratic vocabulary specifically devoted to this public branch and to shed light on its mechanics. For this sake, I will consider the official reports within the framework traced by the project "Synopsis"[9], that is regarding each report as a synoptic assembly of earlier, basic, "lower-level" documents, and as the basis, in turn, for more comprehensive, "upper-level" accounts.

Though the known issues deriving from the scattered preservation of the papyri themselves prevent from any statistically (chronologically, geographically) conclusive – nor even relevant – usage of the data at our disposal[10], it is still possible to trace some general trends. It is worth recalling and stressing that the overall framework sketched below – as regards not only declarations, but also administrative reports and tax accounts, in the following parts of the contribution – was not a monolythic structure, working in the same way everywhere and at any time. The system exhibited differences even from office to office – in the formularies that have come down to us, which reflect the respective administrative methodologies employed – and underwent improvements and changes through time (see below, passim). Yet, this apparent "bemerkenswerte Flexibilität der Römer", which was certainly inherited by the previous arrangements of the Ptolemaic administrative system and adapted to the Romans' interests, always conceals "sehr klare Vorstellungen"[11] about the final outcome of their administrative strategies. Whatever the diverse or non-standard administrative choices, all the documents filed and issued in the local offices were

---

6 Depauw 2014.

7 Yiftach 2014: 113-4 traces the main trends of personal identification in legal documents, from the two main systems used in the Arsinoites (physical marks, patronymic, age) and in the Oxyrhynchites (extended genealogy) to the integration of the two during the mid II century, with the addition of legal residence as a further identifier.

8 Yiftach forthc.1, where a preliminary discussion of identification methods in census declarations and derived documents is sketched.

9 See first footnote, and Yiftach 2012; Yiftach 2015a; Reggiani 2016: 1415-7; Yiftach-Reggiani forthc.; as well as Uri Yiftach's contribution in these same proceedings.

10 Warnings about that issue can be found in Bagnall 1995: 62-4; see also the remarks by Hombert-Préaux 1952: 40-1, in relation with census declarations, and by Scheidel 1999: 64-5, for census declarations and death notifications. Noteworthy are the words of Messeri Savorelli 1989: 7-8 on the population registers: "Questo tipo di fonte è scarso in assoluto, qualora si pensi che registri di tal fatta venivano prodotti ogni anno in ciascuna unità territoriale amministrativa". Data on the distribution of the material findings can be found in Bagnall-Frier 1994: 6-9.

11 This meaningful dichotomy is employed by Jördens 2009: 92 with reference to the provincial differences in the census mechanics, but seems well exportable to every aspect of Roman administration in Egypt. Of the Romans' administrative flexibility in Egypt speaks also Yiftach 2019.

intended to reach the higher vertices of the central State management, which reconduced everything to a unity. Accordingly, we will be speaking of main trends and general schemes, well recognizable in the extant documents from the I to the early III century AD[12].

1. Official terminology in the personal declarations

Roman Egypt knew several types of documents aimed at providing personal information about the individuals to the official administration. We call most of them under the label "declaration"[13]. The main example is of course the group of the **house-by-house census declarations** (*kat'oikian apographai*), which can be defined as written personal reports concerning the inhabitants of a dwelling[14]: they are the documents attesting the widest variety of identifiers, thanks to their deep degree of detail[15] (see below). I consider also other documents pertaining to the categories of personal declarations, because in all of them the set of data is homogeneous, and their purpose uniform: to allow the State to manage population control and tax collection, with particular reference to the capitation tax or poll tax, the *laographia*[16]. **Death notifications** are closely related to poll tax: "The notice requested that the deceased be enrolled among the dead and that his name be stricken from the tax-lists, if he was liable to payment of taxes"[17]. Their focus is of course on a piece of information not to be found in census declarations, namely the death of the individuals, but of the deceased do they exhibit almost all the identifying categories considered in the *apographai*: family relations, place of residence, occupation, tax status[18]. **Birth declarations** (*hupomnēmata epigennēseos*) and ***epikrisis*** **applications** are both related to tax-exempted categories[19]. Any claim to belong to a privileged social category rested on the status of the applicant's family, especially the father's lineage: genealogical and personal

12 Afterwards, things changed substantially: cf. e.g. Jördens 2009: 65-6.

13 On the documentary type of the "declaration" (*apographē*) see the observations by Bickermann 1930: 25-8. See also Avogadro 1935, passim; Jördens 2009: 95-6.

14 Wallace 1938: 98. For discussion of a possible, slightly different meaning of the parallel phrase *kat'oikian epikrisis* (cf. Hombert-Préeaux 1952: 48-9 & 101; Falletti 1964: 113) see Biscottini 1966: 74-6. On Roman census and personal declarations see Jördens 2009: 62 ff., and Claytor-Bagnall 2015, with references to previous literature.

15 See in general Wilcken 1893: 240 ff.; Wilcken 1912: 192-5 & 202 ff.; Wallace 1938: 98 ff.; Taubenschlag 1955: 611-2; Braunert 1968; Kruse 2002, I: 64-6 ff.; and especially Hombert-Préaux 1952, which "ist immer noch das Standardwerk zu allen Aspekten der Zensusdeklarationen" (Duttenhöfer 2002: 157); more recently, Bagnall-Frier 1994: 1-30.

16 For a general overview on the *laographia* see Johnson 1936: 531-7; Wallace 1938: 116 ff.; Tcherikover 1950; Lewis 1983: 169; Rathbone 1993: 86-99. See also my notes on the *praktores laographias* in Yiftach-Reggiani forthc. for a short summary and further bibliography.

17 Wallace 1938: 106. Cf. on this category also Wilcken 1912; 196; Grassi 1922: 208-11; Montevecchi 1946; Mertens 1958: 65-77; Casarico 1985; Scheidel 1999; Kruse 2002, I: 139-68; Reggiani 2016b. It is worth noting, after Scheidel 1999: 63, that "about a quarter of all known texts report the death of individuals who were not liable to pay poll tax": this might be explained, as already Mertens 1958, 131 thought, with the fact that sometimes the heirs had to pay for residual dues, and therefore it was important to declare the privileged status of the deceased himself. For the importance of the date of death for the liability of the heirs see Wilcken 1912: 196; P.Col. II: p. 82; P.Petaus 9: note *ad* l. 17; Kruse 2002, I: 139-41.

18 Cf. Casarico 1985: 11-13 (the declarant's data) and 13-17 (the deceased's data); see also Reggiani 2016b.

19 Wallace 1938: 105; Sánchez-Moreno Ellart 2010: passim, part. 114-9.

details prevail here[20]. **Notices of *anachōresis*** ("flight" from the place of dwelling) are "similar in form to the notices of birth and death, and similarly designed to supplement the official registers of taxable population"[21]. It is quite a rare type of declaration, occurring only at Oxyrhynchus in the first century AD: "no doubt they reflect the growing economic distress of the period. When *anachōresis* next became a major problem, in the second century, the government had ceased to waste energy on the pursuit of individuals, and confined itself to redistributing the defaulters' taxes"[22]. Apart from a generic personal identification of the missing person, profession included, they provided important information on the location of the taxpayers. **Property declarations** (mostly of uninundated land and of livestock)[23] may contain, sometimes, identification records, though not as a primary purpose of the submission. As Taubenschlag stated, "The Romans did not employ ἀπογραφαί of land for taxation purposes; they used only land-ἀπογραφαί which refer to the inundation of the Nile with regard to its unfavourable effect on the productiveness of land (ἄβροχος; ἔμβροχος γῆ). The aim of these declarations is to obtain κουφοτέλεια or ἀτέλεια"[24], i.e. partial or total exemption from taxes. Thus they do provide relevant information for tax categorization, but no direct details on the declarers. In Avogadro's words, "le dichiarazioni di proprietà sono, fra tutte le ἀπογραφαί, le meno adatte a fornire una completa presentazione degli individui che le hanno redatte; si comprende facilmente perché manchino in questi documenti le indicazioni intese a caratterizzare un individuo, come l'età e i segni somatici salienti, se si pensa che la notazione era un elemento atto a garantire l'identificazione personale e perciò poteva benissimo mancare qui, dove non era il caso di temere sostituzione di persona"[25]. The rare mentions of *aphēlikes* (underage

20 On the declarations of birth see Wilcken 1912: 195-6; Grassi 1922: 206-8; Montevecchi 1947 (with noteworthy observations about the connections with the census declarations); Taubenschlag 1955: 625-6; Mertens 1958: 48-65; Sánchez-Moreno Ellart 2001: passim; Kruse 2002, I: 171-6; Sánchez-Moreno Ellart 2010 (who analyses their connection with applications to register a privileged status). It is worth referring to Schulz 1942: 83, for a summary of the differences between these birth declarations and those submitted by Roman citizens. On the *epikrisis* procedure and the related documentation see Wilcken 1912: 196-7; Bickermann 1930: 30-1 ff.; Nelson 1979; cf. also Wallace 1938: 109-12 & 403-5; Hombert-Préaux 1952: 145-7 & 104-5; Taubenschlag 1955: 612-3 ("supplementary to the κατ' οἰκίαν ἀπογραφαί"); Braunert 1956: 53-6; Mertens 1958: 99 ff.; Kruse 2002, I: 252 ff.; Bussi 2008: 14-16. *Epikrisis* applications were submitted also with reference to slaves: see Bieżuńska-Małowist 1977: 64 ff. Recently, Yiftach 2010 discussed an *epikrisis* report with a particular focus on the data recorded in it.

21 P.Oxy. XXXIII 2669: Introduction, p. 97; cf. Lewis 1937: 68-9; Braunert 1955-6: 264-5 ff.; Hanson 1988: 271-7, esp. 274; Hanson 2007a: 267 ; Jördens 2009: 309-11.

22 P.Oxy. XXXIII 2669: Introduction, p. 97. A group of similar documents, dated to the same chronological range, comes from the *meris* of Herakleides in the Arsinoites; they are quite different as to the formulary, but can be ascribed to the same typology: cf. Hanson 2007a.

23 Cf. Wilcken 1912: 203-5; Avogadro 1935; Wallace 1938: 82 ff.; Habermann 1997; Kruse 2002, I: 180 ff.; Jördens 2009: 106-34 (on property *apographai* in general, *abrochia* and livestock declarations in particular, and other categories of such documents).

24 Taubenschlag 1955: 613; cf. Wilcken 1912: 204; Avogadro 1935: 137-9; Kruse 2002, I: 235 ff..

25 Avogadro 1935: 161: "I connotati appaiono eccezionalmente in una dichiarazione [POxy. 72; cfr. inoltre POsl. 1126 a 1 dove la presenza dei connotati non è motivata da nessuna ragione particolare], inviata alla βιβλιοθήκη ἐγκτήσεων, nella quale il denunziante e quegli che ha scritto per lui ἀγράμματος, hanno aggiunto alla firma l'indicazione della loro età e delle οὐλαί: Zoilus, figlio di Apollonius, ha steso l'ἀπογραφή in sostituzione del proprietario assente e certamente, per legittimare e garantire il suo

children) are not intended to provide relevant information to the tax officials, but to account for the role of their representatives, since property declarations may have been submitted by minors[26]; the same can be said of the indication of residence[27]. Professions are, instead, widely mentioned[28]. **Lists of priests** (*graphai hiereōn*) are somehow different, in that they are not submitted by individuals but by temple priesthoods, yet they are yearly declarations issued to the administrative authorities and share more or less the same technical vocabulary with the census-related documents[29]. Finally, a particular document that I will include in this group, though not being a proper personal declaration as well, is the **extract from the census registers** (*ex eikonismou*, or also *ex apographēs* or *ek kat'oikian apographēs*): although the *eikonismos* itself is in fact an official register[30], it was made up of the raw, unprocessed data coming from the census declarations[31], and can therefore be equalled to them in terms of information level. The word *eikonismos* itself alludes to the detailed personal descriptions provided by the *apographai* (cf. ⟨ε⟩ἰκονισμοῦ ἀπογραφῆς in P.Ryl. II 161, 16, and see below)[32].

Despite the strong local idiosyncrasies[33], it is still possible to trace some general trends applying to census declarations. The personal markers are almost always recorded in full, for both the issuer of the declaration (usually the owner/tenant of the housing unit, with some exceptions) and any other inhabitant, according to the indications of the prefectural edict that launched the census: typically are mentioned not only the interpersonal relations

intervento, egli, che non pare sia stato ordinariamente l'intermediario dell'assente Marcus Porcius, ha aggiunto i connotati personali".

26 Cf. Avogadro 1935: 162-3.

27 Cf. Avogadro 1935: 165, who indeed states that such pieces of information are not as numerous as in the *kat'oikian apographai*.

28 Cf. Avogadro 1935: 163-5.

29 The lists were usually issued in the form of the *graphē hiereōn kai cheirismou*, the *cheirismos* being an inventory of the temple properties (cf. on this Burkhalter 1985), attached to the declaration but by no means connected to the mechanism of population survey. These *graphai* provided some basic personal (names, patronymics, papponymics, metronymics, age) and administrative (see below) pieces of information to at least five different officials: *stratēgos, basilikos grammateus, bibliophulax, eklogistēs, exetastēs* i.e. the inspector appointed by the *idios logos* (cf. Montevecchi 1932; Gilliam 1947: 191-8; Evans 1961: 159-60; Battaglia 1984). Bibliography can be found in Gilliam 1947: 191 n. 60, and CPR XV 22: Introduction, pp. 52-3.

30 An extensive treatment of this type of document is provided by Braunert 1956: 56-62; cf. also Sijpesteijn 1995: 274 nn. 2-3, and more recently Kruse 2002, II: 807 n. 122 ("Mit εἰκονισμὸς κατ' οἰκίαν ἀπογραφῆς ist offenbar ein Register von Haushalten und ihrer Bewohner auf der Grundlage der den Behörden eingereichten Zensusdeklarationen gemeint. Dieses Register verzeichnete (unter anderem?) hauptsächlich die Personalbeschreibungen der mittels der besagten κατ' οἰκίαν ἀπογραφαί gemeldeten Personen, daher wohl auch seine Bezeichnung als εἰκονισμός"); see also below.

31 "Typically, in such extracts, a part of a house (and other appurtenances) is listed followed by the name of the owner [...]. These entries are followed by the names of the persons who lived in and rented this part of the house. Besides their own names those of father, grandfather, and mother of the tenants are given" (Sijpesteijn 1986: 158).

32 Cf. Depauw 2011: 190 ff. for the meaning of *eikonismos* and related words since Ptolemaic age.

33 For an extensive description of the local formularies, see Hombert-Préaux 1952: 106 ff.; local variants are discussed also by Kruse 2002, I: 66 ff., and Jördens 2009: 75-87. The high variety of formularies even within the same nome is stressed by Falletti 1964: 111.

between the registered people, but also their genealogy[34], age[35], occupation (see below), provenance or residence[36], and the most striking physical features[37]. The social position of each person is always considered: for example, we find *douloi* (further qualified – as to their provenance – as *oikogeneis*, *agorastoi* etc.) and *apeleutheroi*[38], and the women's guardians are sometimes mentioned, with the usual formula μετὰ κυρίου. The dichotomy *Rhomaios* / *Aiguptios* does not apply, because Roman citizens had a different way of declaring themselves[39] and they were not subject to the capitation tax. Alexandrians appear very seldom, only with reference to women[40]. In several census declarations from Oxyrhynchus the declarant concludes by swearing that in the house there live no-one else but the people declared, "no *epixenos*, no *Rhomaios*, no *Alexandreus*, no *Aiguptios*", but this is a mere formulaic occurrence[41]. The *Hellēnes*, which in the Roman age had disappeared as a true ethno-social category[42], are mentioned only with reference to the Arsinoitic "6475" *katoikoi*[43].

From this viewpoint, there are no big differences with the legal documents mentioned above[44]. Nevertheless, the said types of documents also provide an almost complete overview of the terms identifying tax and/or administrative status, i.e. referred to taxation liability and/or official registrations of any kind. It is declared whether people are subject to poll tax (***telōn tēn laographian*** or the like[45]), which was indeed the main purpose of such

34 Cf. Wallace 1938: 102; Hombert-Préaux 1952: 102-3; Bagnall-Frier 1994: 22.

35 Cf. Wallace 1938: 102; Hombert-Préaux 1952: 118 ff.

36 Hombert-Préaux 1952: 107-8; Bagnall-Frier 1994: 22. "The local residence is designated more exactly when the owner of the house lived in a city than when his home was in a village" (Wallace 1938: 100).

37 Cf. Wallace 1938: 102; Hombert-Préaux 1952: 118 ff.; see above. That the physical marks were recorded following a strict technical vocabulary has been proved by Daris 1993.

38 In general, on slaves cf. Bieżuńska-Małowist 1977; Clarysse 1989; Straus 2004. On slaves in the census declarations see the observations by Scheidel 1997: 160-2. On the *oikogeneis* (house-born slaves) cf. Bieżuńska-Małowist 1975. On manumission of slaves in Graeco-Roman Egypt cf. Straus 2009.

39 Cf. Braunert 1968.

40 *Astē*: P.Wisc. I 36 [Theadelphia, Ad 147]; SB XXVI 16671 [Oxyrhynchus, AD 216/7]. On the terminology of *astos* cf. Arangio-Ruiz 1950 and Delia 1983: 82; also Delia 1991. On the tax privileges of the Alexandrians (and, as of AD 130, of the inhabitants of Antinoupolis) cf. Jördens 2009: 331-8.

41 Cf. Bickermann 1930: 40; Delia 1983: 56-7; Yiftach forthc.1: [2]. For the three ethno-social categories in the Greek papyri from Roman Egypt, moving from their occurrence in the *Gnōmōn* of the *idios logos*, see the very recent discussion by Yiftach forthc.1.

42 Cf. Montevecchi 1985.

43 SB XXIV 16013 [Tebtunis, AD 132/3]; BGU XIII 2220 [Soknopaiou Nesos, AD 133]; SB XII 10842 [Tebtunis, AD 133]; SB XX 14163 [Samareia, AD 133]; SB XX 14303 [Ptolemais Euergetis, AD 147]. Cf. Canducci 1990; for *katoikoi* see below.

44 Cf. Yiftach 2019.

45 Actually, this term does not appear in the census declarations themselves, since it was the implicit "default" condition of anyone not subject to exemptions; it is however stated in some notices of death (C.Pap.Gr. II 47, 10-11; 54, 1 [restored]; 61, 5-6; 63, 11; 72, 5 [Ptolemais Euergetis, AD 160]; P.Prag. I 19, 9 [Soknopaiou Nesos, AD 177-180]), usually followed by the indication of the place introduced by *epi* (cf. Casarico 1985, 14-15). Compare the same usage in P.Petaus 9 = C.Pap.Gr. II App.2, 9 [Kerkesoucha Orous, AD 185], a request to abolish the *laographia* for two sentenced to death, redacted "nella forma consueta della denuncia di morte" (Casarico 1985, 223), and the opposite term ***en tē ateleia*** in P.Oxy. XXXVIII 2837 = C.Pap.Gr. II 7, 9 [Oxyrhynchus, AD 50]. A derivative from *laographia* is used only in PSI X 1146, an extract from the census lists of Tebtunis [*p*. AD 138], where some slaves are said to be λ̣α̣ογραφοῦνται ὡς οἱ δεσπόται (l. 12). A unique case is represented by

declarations[46], or whether they belong to any group entitled to full exemption or to reduced rates (see below), and particular conditions of registration – ***(pro)anagraphomenos***, ***(sun)apogegrammenos***, ***anagegrammenos*** – followed by the mention of the place of registration[47].

The information about place were also important for fiscal purposes, since the poll tax had to be paid in the place of residence[48], as we know – beside the Gospels! – e.g. from SB IV 7461 = P.Graux I 1 [Arsinoites, AD 45], an official letter related to the exaction of the poll-tax from people legally resident at Philadelphia but living in a different nome. Villagers were legally allowed to leave their dwelling place temporarily, though remaining registered in the lists of their legal residence[49]: in some cases, the change of dwelling was stated in the personal declarations with the formula ***metabasin poioumenos epi...*** or ***epi***

P.Cair.Isid. 8, a census declaration from AD 309 Karanis, where the declarant provides a brief summary of the relevant persons in the household (himself and his own son) categorizing them between **ὑποτελής** ("taxable", himself, l. 9) and **ἀτελής** ("non-taxable", his son, being underage, l. 10). The information is repeated by a different hand (most likely a registering officer) below, providing a quick account of the relevant data (γείνεται ὑπ[οτελ]ὴς εἷ[ς], | ἀτελὴς [εἷς], "in total: taxable, one; non-taxable, one", ll. 15-16), just before the Latin subscription of the *censitor*. The dichotomy recalls a couple of Ptolemaic *prostagmata* that ordered a census of livestock and enslaved natives in Syria and Phoenicia (SB V 8008 = C.Ord.Ptol. 21-22 [260 BC]), e.g. τήν τ[ε ὑ]π[ο]τελῆ καὶ τὴν [ἀ]τελῆ | [λείαν] (ll. 3-4).

46 Not the only one: interesting enough is P.Lips. II 132 [Leukos Pyrgos, Hermopolites, AD 132], stating that all the *laographoumenoi* (l. 6) should perform the dyke works (cf. commentary *ad loc.*); see also BGU II 618 [Mendes, Arsinoites, AD 213/4], a κατ' ἄνδρα τῶν ὀ[φ]⟨ε⟩ιλόντων ἐργάσασθαι | τὰ χωματικὰ ἔρ[γ]α (ll. 6-7) where men ἀ[π?]ὸ μὲν ὁμολ(όγου) λαογρ(αφίας) (l. 13 + BL I 57 = Rostowzew 1910: 221) are listed. Cf. Bonneau 1993: 138 with n. 138, according to whom *laographoumenoi* means here "indigènes inscrits". Somehow related to this interconnection between tax status and public work dues seems also the term ***apoiētos*** "not useable" referred, as a marginal addition, to an underage in the population report P.Petaus 93, 125 [Ptolemais Hormou, AD 182-187].

47 Hombert-Préaux 1952: 67 interpreted *anagraphomenos* in relation with the term *ephestion* "le lieu d'une résidence stable où l'on est astreint à des prestations fiscales"; Bagnall-Frier 1994: 16 refer it to the filing of the record in a different place than that of residence (i.e., where the person was already registered in previous lists); Kruse 2002, I: 64 speaks of "fiskalischen Domizil". The term is normally used also in contracts and in similar documents. For *anagraphē* see Braunert 1956: 62-5. *Apogegrammenos* (used only at Arsinoe) means that the person was declaring a house of his own property but he had already declared himself for the house where he lived (Hombert-Préaux 1952: 106; CPR XV 24, note to l. 13). *Anagegrammenos*, according to Casarico 1985: 106 n. 11, is an equivalent of *apographomenos*, but we may wonder whether it was (at least sometimes) a shortened form of *anagegrammenos en epigegenēmenois* (see below), since it sometimes appears in relation with *aphēlikes* (as in the very same C.Pap.Gr. II 32 [Philadelphia, AD 48/9 or 62/3] republished by Casarico) and in a negative form (*mē anagegrammenos*, see P.Stras. VIII 768, 7, 8, 13 [Tebtunis, AD 174/5]), which would make very scarce sense if it meant a previous registration in a different place (the editor of the Strasbourg papyrus points indeed to the formula related to the registration of newborns). *Proanagraphomenos* appears only twice in the entire papyrus corpus: in PSI X 1112, 24-5 [Oxyrhynchus, AD 231] it refers to a previous owner of the house, now deceased, while in SPP II 1 [Herakleopolis, AD 216] the context is unfortunately fragmentary (the word occurs also in P.Oxy. III 504, 17 [Oxyrhynchus, early II AD], but it seems to bear a different meaning). Slaves are sometimes recorded with the unique term ***logizomenos*** "counted" (P.Brux. I 19, 8 & 12 [Arsinoe, AD 117/8]; SB XXII 15704, 73, 79, 81, 83 [Karanis, *p.* AD 138]), which is used in some camel declarations with reference to animals (BGU III 762, 8; P.Lond. II 328, 8 [both from Soknopaiou Nesos, AD 163]).

48 Cf. Braunert 1955-6: 226 ff.; Jördens 2009: 69-75.

49 Cf. Mirković 2007: 747-9.

xenēs (gegonōs)[50]; if one returned, he was defined ***apo xenēs***. In the deprecated event that people fled away from their usual residence without communicating their new location, the most infamous phenomenon of *anachōrēsis* occurred[51]. As we said, at the beginning of the Roman age special declarations had to be submitted to the authorities in order to communicate this situation, because fled people escaped tax payments[52]: "the fact that he [i.e. the declared person] is a fugitive will result in his being entered in the list of tax delinquents"[53] (see below). In these documents it was also stated that the ***anakechōrēkotes*** left no *poros*, i.e. no property[54], and were not ***estrateumenoi***, i.e. did not join the army, which was a possibility reserved to the metropolitans and eventually entitling to gain Roman citizenship[55]. Coming back to the main point, the place of residence was important also in order to distinguish the privileged persons living in the *mētropoleis* (see below): P.Gen. I^2 4 [Arsinoites, c. AD 87], a petition by a metropolitan challenging his deceitful official registration in a different village, is a clear example of that.

The same data, when applicable, are mentioned also for the underage children, i.e. younger than 14 years[56]. These were categorized with the term ***aphēlix***, and it was further remarked whether they were already entered or not in the lists of the newborns (***anagegrammenos en epigegenēmenois*** or ***mē anagegrammenos en epigegenēmenoi***[57]) through birth declarations[58]. Minors were fully exempted from the poll-tax[59], and it seems that the indication of registration into the population lists was a matter of the privileged classes[60] (see also below). The opposite situation, i.e. boys adjudged to be 14 years old, seems to be represented by the term ***anakekrimenos***, which occurs only once, in P.Coll.Youtie I 20 (c. AD 56), a text that I will be discussing below.

A common reference to partial exemptions from the poll tax is made by means of the terms ***epikekrimenos***[61], meaning that the person belonged to any of the privileged groups

50 Sánchez-Moreno Ellart 2010: 111; cf. Braunert 1964: 25-7. On ***epixenoi*** as tax payers see also Hanson 1988: 265-6.

51 Cf. Lewis 1937; Braunert 1955-6: 260 ff.; Mirković 2007: 748-50; Bussi 2008: 51-8; Jördens 2009: 304-30.

52 Link 1993 argues that the main reason for *anachōrēsis* was not the impossibility to pay for taxes due to poverty, but rather the actual will to escape payment.

53 Lewis 1982: 75.

54 "In emphasizing that the fugitive has left behind no taxable or seizable property the declarants are obviously concerned lest anything of theirs be seized by the authorities in compensation of his tax default" (Lewis 1982: 75; cf. Hanson 2007a: 267).

55 Cf. Lewis 1982: 75-6. On the relationship between *anachōrēsis* and the Roman army see also de Blois 2007: passim. For the military enrolment as a way to gain social advancement, see Bussi 2008: 83-4 ff.

56 Cf. Wilcken 1912: 197; Taubenschlag 1932; Wallace 1938: 105; Taubenschlag 1955: 167.

57 Cf. Kruse 2002, I: 171. In SB XXII 15704, 49 [Karanis, *p.* AD 138] a child is recorded as μὴ ἀπογεγρ(αμμένος), but it is probably a mistake for μὴ ἀναγεγρ-. The indication of the inscription among the newborns seems to be an Arsinoite idiosyncrasy: cf. Sánchez-Moreno Ellart 2010: 102. Probably this annotation was added only the first time that the person was entered to the tax lists.

58 Cf. Wilcken 1893: 245.

59 Few cases in which they seem to be liable (namely P.Mich. X 577 [AD 47/8 or 61/2] and P.Col. II 1 r2, passim [Theadelphia, AD 129]) are to be interpreted as conventional forms of indicating former *aphēlikes*, now adults: see discussion in the introduction to the latter papyrus.

60 Wallace 1938: 105; Hombert-Préaux 1952: 116-7.

61 Wilcken 1912: 201-2; Bickermann 1930: 35; Taubenschlag 1955: 613.

identified through the procedure of *epikrisis*: ***apo gumnasiou*** and ***apo mētropoleōs / mētropolitēs***[62] above all, with some local distinctions (***oktadrachmoi, dōdekadrachmoi***, according to the reduced rate[63]), and the case of the ***katoikoi*** (the descendants of the privileged class of settlers called with the same name), a special category of gymnasial status attested in Arsinoe only[64]. The word ***epikrinomenos*** refers to a candidate for this selection[65], and it is attested also the negative form ***anepikritos***[66]: Chr.W. 220 [Arsinoites, *p*. AD 117] contains a wonderful testimony of a person scrutinized ἀπὸ ἀνεπικρίτ(ων) εἰς λαογρ(αφουμένους) (l. 16)[67]. Other special exempted categories can be mentioned, like the ***hieronikai*** "victors at the sacred games" (BGU I 119, 9 [Arsinoites, AD 175]); they may be further identified with the term ***atelēs*** "non-taxable"[68].

One of the most common terms used in personal declarations, ***laographoumenos***[69], seems to be related to the *epikrisis* as well: against Wallace, who had stated that *laographoumenos* meant a person fully liable to the poll tax[70], Hombert and Préaux considered it a shortened variant of *laographoumenos epikekrimenos*[71]. It must be said that Wallace himself was aware of the fact that this was a relative term[72]. According to Bagnall and Frier, it refers to metropolitans paying the tax "at a reduced rate"[73]; it sometimes occurs in combination with *idiōtēs* and with some professions (see below). We should consider also the hypothesis that it might simply mean "recorded (or: to be recorded) in the census list"[74].

The mention of the **profession,** apparently not systematically recorded, arises more specific questions. We know that some occupations of particular rank were partially

62 Cf. Bickermann 1930: 35-40; Whitehorne 1982. Recently, Van Minnen 2002 and Broux 2013 argued that the two categories were two distinct groups that developed side by side, and that the former was not an elite part of the latter, as previously thought.

63 Broux 2013: 144: in the Hermopolites, Herakleopolites and in the Mendesian nome the metropolitans paid 8 drachmas instead of 16, while in Oxyrhynchus they paid 12. According to Sánchez-Moreno Ellart 2010: 102, the *apo gumnasiou* of Oxyrhynchus were a sub-category of metropolitans.

64 For full discussion on the privileged categories subject to *epikrisis* see Nelson 1979: passim; see also Bickermann 1930: 35-43; Mertens 1958: 99-128, focused on the city of Oxyrhynchus; Bussi 2008: 16-20; Jördens 2009: 331-54. For such categories in the census declarations see Hombert-Préaux 1952: 104-5 ff. (esp. 115), and Bagnall-Frier 1994: 22; for *katoikoi* also P.Mich. XI 603, 8 n.; Canducci 1990; Rathbone 1993: 96; Sánchez-Moreno Ellart 2010: 102; Broux 2013: 144.

65 Bickermann 1930: 30.

66 Wilcken 1912: 198; Taubenschlag 1955: 613.

67 Cf. Bickermann 1930: 34.

68 This term occurs e.g. in the said BGU I 119 with reference to the *hieronikēs* (cf. BGU I 328, ii, 1), and in a fragmentary context in SB XX 14303, 7; see also above, the peculiar case of P.Cair.Isid. 8. On *ateleia* cf. Wallace 1938: 120.

69 Hombert-Préaux 1952: 104-5.

70 Wallace 1938: 110, keeping on Wilcken's interpretation (Wilcken 1893: 249, and introductions to Chr.W. 63 & 64) and followed e.g. by Taubenschlag 1955: 613.

71 Hombert-Préaux 1952: 115.

72 Wallace 1938: 405 n. 85.

73 Bagnall-Frier 1994: 22.

74 Sánchez-Moreno Ellart 2010: 103 n. 44; see below for *laographia* meaning "list of persons".

exempted from the poll tax (i.e., some **priests**[75] and **officials**[76]), and this should account for their mention. The occurrences of everyday jobs are more problematic, since their relation with tax liability is still not completely clear: some are recorded along with the term *laographoumenos*, and some are not. A recent Italian study[77] has revised the general matter, and keeping Wallace's interpretation of *laographoumenos* as "subject to the full capitation tax" (see above) the author states that the professions recorded without any further specification point to exempted guilds (e.g. the *chrusochooi*, "goldsmiths"), while those flanked by the term *laographoumenos* point to guild members individually liable for some legal reasons. The matter might be more complex, if we consider the possible interpretation of *laographoumenos* as a metropolitan "liable in part" (see above), and that even professional categories which do not appear as *laographoumenoi* are elsewhere subject to a poll tax (the *laographia chrusochoōn* in BGU II 434, 4 [Memphis, AD 169]). Anyway, the statement that some artisans were exempted from the *laographia* because they had to pay for other capitation taxes connected to their professions (especially the *cheirōnaxion*)[78] is striking: it is probably not a chance that one of the most attested profession in the census declarations, the weavers (*gerdioi*), was subject to a specific *cheirōnaxion* due, called *gerdiakon*[79]. In

75 Hombert-Préaux 1952: 103. For tax exemption of priests see also Hobson 1984: 848-52; Bussi 2008: 23 ff.; Jördens 2009: 338-45.

76 Hombert-Préaux 1937: 260; Wallace 1938: 106 and 120; Jördens 2009: 346-7. We know for sure that the *stratēgos*, the *basilikos grammateus*, the *topogrammateis*, the *kōmogrammateis*, the *exēgētēs*, the *epistatēs phulakitōn*, as well as their *hupēretai* "assistants", were exempted: cf. P.Oxy. IX 1210, 9 ff. [Oxyrhynchites, I BC – I AD], a list of exempted officials, and P.Hamb. IV 272 [Arsinoites, AD 41-68], discussed by Kruse 2002, II: 920, where the officials requesting to be released from the *laographia* apparently call themselves **ἀλαογράφητοι** (l. 4), which is a *hapax*.

77 Rolandi 2007, to which the reader is referred for earlier bibliography and for the complete list of the professions attested in census documents. Some notes on the professions also in Calderini 1923: 24 ff. For a general overview of Roman professions as attested in the documentation from Egypt refer to Ruffing 2008.

78 Rolandi 2007: 194; see below. On *cheirōnaxion* and its exemption cf. Wallace 1938, 191-2; Jördens 2009: 347-9.

79 Cf. Hombert-Préaux 1952: 117, "Toutes le branches de l'industrie texile sont soumises à une fiscalité spéciale et c'est peut-être pour cette raison qu'on indique avec un soin particulier les professions relevant de cette industrie"; cf. also Bagnall-Frier 1994: 24; see below. For the weavers' tax and its collection in Roman times see Reiter 2004, 111-44. Other peculiar documents related to the weavers' profession and their particular tax status are the apprentice registrations, with which new weavers were declared and therefore added to the pertinent lists (*tōn mathetōn taxeis*): see discussion of this in the introduction to P.Mich. III 170 [Oxyrhynchus, AD 49], with particular stress on the formula διὸ ἀξιῶ ἀνα|γράψεσθ[α]ι τὸν υἱὸν ἐν τοῖς τοῦ αὐ|τοῦ ἔτους μαθηταῖς ὡς καθήκει (ll. 12-4: "I therefore ask you to register my son in the list of apprentices of the said year, as appropriate"). The topic is further discussed by Forselv 1998; Kruse 2002, I: 176-80 & 271; Reiter 2002; cf. Bergamasco 2004: 33 with footnote 14. See also P.Mich. III 171 & 172 [AD 58 & 62]; PSI VIII 871 [AD 66]; SB XXIV 16186 [AD 70, all of them from Oxyrhynchus]; Lewis 1983: 171. Bergamasco 2004: 34-5 proposes that the tax involved was not the *gerdiakon* but a sort of tax on the apprenticeship itself; this does not affect the fiscal purpose of the documents. After P.Oxy. II 288, 36 & 314, 2 = SB X 10220, 2 [Oxyrhynchus, AD 25], where an ἀπογ(ραφὴ) γερ(δίων) is read by Vandoni 1974: 5, one could infer that special declarations had to be submitted by the weavers. The term, however, appears to be a *hapax* in the entire papyrological *corpus*, and is resolved from an abbreviation: considering the context, a census extract (see Biscottini 1966, 74-6) containing a viritim list where the term follows the first name of the list, i.e. the declarant's, we may

this case, the specification of the job would be aimed at avoiding double tax payments. Further evidence is provided by the notifications of death: if the deceased "was a member or a guild subject to taxes on trades a notice was sent to the collector of the tax"[80]. Still, we do find *laographoumenoi gerdioi* in some declarations[81]. Sometimes the profession comes along with the specification ***apolusimos (tēs laographias)*** "released" [82]: this is the case, more often, with the priests, since not all of them were relieved of the dues[83] and it was necessary to further specify that circumstance. Other categories which could be *apolusimoi* were, apparently, some artisans (*ergatai* and an *elaiourgos* in P.Oxy. VI 984 = P.Oxy.Census, passim [Lykopolis, AD 91/2?])[84]. The term, by itself, "indicates a person who is either discharged or exempted from a service or an obligation"[85]; the same concept works in the phrase τῆς λαογραφίας ἀπολυθῆναι used in a request for release of *laographia* submitted by some officials in P.Hamb. IV 272 [Arsinoites, AD 41-68]. Generally speaking, it is hard to trace any general interpretation of the data pertaining to the professional status: while occupations like the *iatroi* are surely a privileged one (see below), others like the *dēmosioi geōrgoi* are not – the reasons for their inclusion must therefore be different, as we will guess better below[86]. On the other hand, the frequent mention of the profession in the declarations of property (see above), as well as in secondary population lists, seems not to apply to tax purposes but rather to general personal identifications[87]; this makes sense indeed, since "designation of occupation seems unique to the branch of administrative activity concerned with, or resulting from census declarations.

wonder whether it could be interpreted as something else, namely ἀπογ(ραφόμενος) γέρ(διος). Further on the relationships between the State and the textile industry see Wipszycka 1966.

80 Wallace 1938: 106 (ref. to P.Oxy. II 262 [Oxyrhynchus, AD 55], a notice of death addressed to an *eklemptōr gerdiōn*).

81 BGU I 115 = Chr.W. 203 [Karanis, AD 60/1]; SB XII 11232 [Tebtunis, AD 76]; P.Narm.2006 7 [Narmouthis, AD 135].

82 Hombert-Préaux 1952: 118.

83 Montevecchi 1932: 323; Hombert-Préaux 1937: 260; Evans 1961: 249-50; Nelson 1979: 62; see also below.

84 There is a soldier (*hippeus*) qualified as *apolusimos tēs laographias* in SB XXII 15704, 28 [Karanis, p. AD 138], but his exemption seems to depend on his being overage (*huperetēs*, see below): see also the comment *ad l.* by Sijpesteijn 1993: 289. As for soldiers, this term must not be confused with the same word meaning "discharged" from the army (in this sense it appears in at least two census declarations, SB XII 10788, 29 & 50 [Oxyrhynchus, AD 62-64], and SB X 10219, 8 [Arsinoe, p. AD 161]; therefore, the two meanings are often distinguished by adding *tēs laographias* (as in SB 15704) or *apo strateias*.

85 Parássoglou 1978: 62. Martin 1950: 147 speaks of "l'extinction d'une obligation légale d'une durée determinée". Both are dealing with *apolusimoi tēs ousias* and *apolusimoi tēs strateias*. It is quite evident that apolusim*os tēs laographias* points to a full exemption, therefore the recording of *apolusimoi* in tax accounts (cf. Hanson 1984: 1113-7) must refer to the cultivators *apolusimoi tēs ousias*, who were granted with special privileges but not full tax exemption (cf. Parássoglou 1978: 61-4). A different interpretation could be that the *apolusimoi* recorded in tax accounts were people previously liable and therefore listed in earlier register, then released but entered anyway to officialize their new tax status.

86 Cf. below, footnote 91. According to Casarico 1985: 16-17, "l'assenza [...] dell'indicazione di un'attività si può forse attribuire alla mancanza di un mestiere specifico o di una professione ben definita; in questo caso doveva per lo più trattarsi di agricoltori o comunque di individui che vivevano dei prodotti di un appezzamento di terreno".

87 See the discussion of this in Yiftach forthc.1: [7-8].

Consequently, the term is also found in extracts or lists of persons, directly deriving from census declarations"[88].

It has been proposed that even the terms ***argos / atechnos*** ("unemployed", perhaps "temporary unable to work"?, the former found in Memphis only[89]) referred to a privileged category "de gens qui ne s'adonnent pas aux métiers manuels"[90], but in few cases it refers to slaves or to overage people[91]. The same might be supposed also for ***idiōtēs***, "indicating a private person, i.e., an adult, male citizen without a trade"[92], but see the payment λα(ογραφίας) ἰδι(ωτῶν) recorded in SB XVI 12645 [Memphis, AD 141] ("tax incumbent on unskilled workers", as tentatively interpreted by Youtie[93]) and the ἰδιῶται ἐργατευόμενοι interpreted as "unskilled, manual labourers"[94] listed in SB XX 15024, iii 9 [Tebtunis, II AD] in a *laographia* context (see below). The situation looks very complex and unfortunately we lack solid ground to draw final conclusions; for instance, the term ***amisthos*** "unwaged" is supplied once in the census declaration SB VIII 9870, 8 [Hermopolites, II AD] (ἄμ]ισθ[ο]ς) without a clear context.

Priests are characterized by further identifiers, connected to their special social position[95]. Apart from *apolusimos*, which we discussed above, a category of youth between the proper underage *aphēlikes*[96] and their official registration in the priestly lists is recorded

88 Yiftach forthc.1: [9]. Some exceptions are occasionally recorded. The most outstanding overlap is represented by the *dēmosioi geōrgoi*, "public cultivators", systematically recorded in the personal declarations and in the population registers. This was not a privileged category at all, but was in fact one of the two main groups in which the rural population was categorized within land registers and related tax reports: *(dēmosioi) geōrgoi* ("cultivators") and *klērouchoi* ("owners"), as showed by the outstanding P.Tebt. II 288 [AD 226], a memorandum addressed by the joint *stratēgos* of the Themistos and Polemon *merides* in the Arsinoites to the tax collectors in which τῶν [γε]ωργ(ῶν) | καὶ κληρούχων (ll. 2-3, then again at ll. 7-8) are distinguished. It is remarkable that the term *klērouchos* never seems to occur in census-related documents, but we should also note that it was a local variant (limited, apparently, to the said *merides* in the II-III century) of the more widespread category of the *katoikoi*, who are opposed to the *dēmosioi geōrgoi* everywhere else (this dichotomy is best known through its administrative outcome, the distinction of revenues, and consequently of tax collectors, *dia dēmosiōn* and *dia katoikōn*). Since it has been stressed that *katoikoi* as privileged census group are limited to Arsinoe (see above), we may wonder whether the *katoikos* recorded in the census declaration P.Oslo III 98 [Herakleopolis, AD 132/3] refers, instead, to the rural category. The issue of the dichotomy in land-related documents is discussed by Yiftach forthc.1: [9-11], with further references. For the distinction between *praktores dia dēmosiōn* and *praktores dia katoikōn / klērouchōn* see my contribution to Yiftach-Reggiani forthc. with bibliography.

89 Cf. already Calderini 1923: 25.

90 *Argos*: Hombert-Préaux 1952: 105 (and also p. 122); cf. Bagnall-Frier 1994: 22. *Atechnos*: Hombert-Préaux 1952: 120-1.

91 Casarico 1985: 16.

92 Bagnall-Frier 1994: 24. For earlier discussion of this problematic term see Youtie 1982: 597-8; cf. also Calderini 1923: 29.

93 Cf. Youtie 1982, with discussion of the matter.

94 Bülow-Jacobsen 1989: 127.

95 Messeri Savorelli 1989: 14 argues that "l'amministrazione fiscale teneva registri separati per i sacerdoti e per i civili".

96 For *aphēlikes* in the *graphai hiereōn* see Montevecchi 1932: 320; Gilliam 1947: 189-90; Battaglia 1984: 85; Battaglia 1986: 87-8.

as ***aneikonistos*** "not yet registered"[97]. Those who passed the selection (*eiskrisis*) to become priests are called *epikekrimenoi*[98] just as those who passed the *epikrisis* (see above), while another special term to be found only in *graphai hiereōn* is ***paradochimos***, which should identify a particular tax reduction or privilege[99]. The lists of *aphēlikes* and *aneikonistoi* could be issued separately[100]; dead priests (*teteleutēkotes*) were recorded somehow, too[101]. In the *graphai hiereōn* the individuals are arranged by ***phulē*** ("tribe") and/or by order, according to the priestly tradition[102]. Both categories were used to provide separate accounts. A nice example, among the others, is P.Tebt. II 298 [Tebtunis, AD 108], where the viritim list starts with τῶν μ̣ὲν παραδοχίμω[ν] | [κα]ὶ ἐπικεκριμ[έ]νων ἀπολυσίμων (ll. 10-11) and goes on with different priestly groups.

A further reference to tax exemption is ***apolelumenos (tēs laographias)***, "der befreit worden ist von der Kopfsteuer"[103], which might occur alone (BGU I 95, 13) or in combination with some other explanations for the exemption itself, like ***huperetēs*** "overage"[104], ***episinēs / ensinēs*** "disabled"[105], ***asthenēs*** "sick"[106], perhaps in the sense of "(permanently) disabled"? (SB V 8025, 1 [Arsinoites, AD 91/2] – a nice certificate of tax exemption), which makes us think (but the evidence is very scarce) that it could have been related to physical deficiencies[107]. An even rarer term indicating exemption is ***apoluomenos***, which appears with this meaning e.g. in an extract from a census declaration from Tebtunis (PSI X

97 This term appears in the *graphai hiereōn* only: cf. Montevecchi 1932: 320 with n. 2; Battaglia 1984: 85 n. 30. The meaning is connected to that of *eikonismos* etc., for which see above.

98 Parássoglou 1973: 8.

99 Hobson 1984: 849 & 851-2; Bussi 2008: 34-6; see also below. According to P.Tebt. II 298, note to l. 10, and Montevecchi 1932: 323, it was probably related to the heredity of the charge. Hanson 2007b: 180 offers a different explanation: it could mean "receipt" or "reception", with reference to "taxpayers whose payments of the *laographia* are gathered not by collectors from the local tax office, but through other processes". Both interpretations do not exclude each other. See also below.

100 Battaglia 1984: 85. They are by no means equivalent to the lists of special categories redacted by the officials for administrative purposes, of which we will discuss below.

101 Montevecchi 1932: 327.

102 Tribes: Montevecchi 1932: 318 ff.; Evans 1961: 180-3. Orders: Montevecchi 1932: 320 & 323 ff.

103 Wilcken 1893: 249.

104 C.Pap.Gr. II 25, 7 [Karanis, AD 111]; BGU I 95, 13 [Karanis, AD 147]. Cf. Wilcken 1893: 249; Casarico 1985: 14. On the age limit for tax payment see Hombert-Préaux 1937: 261; Wallace 1938: 106-9; Hombert-Préaux 1952: 140 & 144. Some new thoughts on the issue have been recently presented by Dominic Rathbone at the 28th International Congress of Papyrology (Barcelona, August 2016: "Age and Fiscality in Roman Egypt", abstract at http://papyrologia.upf.edu/programme); he demonstrated that exemption was due in the civil year after a man became 60 years old (i.e. the time when they were put in the list of the *hupereteis*), and sometimes not until he was 62 (cf. e.g. P.Mich. IV 223, 2415-6 [Karanis, AD 172]). For old age as a reason for tax exemption see also Jördens 2009: 350-1.

105 P.Oxy. VI 984 = P.Oxy.Census, 220 [Lykopolis, AD 91/2?]; SB VI 9105, 17-8 [Arsinoites, AD 198?]; SB VIII 9870, 9-10 [Hermopolites, II AD]; cf. also Bagnall-Frier 1994: 226, on the unpublished P.Berl.Leihg. III 52a. "It is evident that disability provided release from capitation taxes, but we do not know what was required as proof of disability" (P.Oxy.Census, p. 39, note to l. 220); cf. Hombert-Préaux 1937: 262. On physical affections as reasons for tax exemption see also Jördens 2009: 349-50.

106 Hombert-Préaux 1937: 261-4.

107 As for *apolusimos*, also *apolelumenos* can bear the meaning of "discharged" veteran.

1146, 8-9 [*p.* AD 138]). People not liable to the poll tax might be referred to as ***ektos sunopseōs***, "excluded from the estimate of taxes to be collected" following the translation by the editors of P.Mich. XI 603 (see below).

To conclude this lexical overview of tax exemptions, it may be worth quoting P.Phil. 1, a dossier of documents related to tax payments by weavers [Arsinoites, *p.* AD 119], which at ll. 26-34 records a list of categories exempted (*apoluomenoi*) from some public dues, perhaps liturgies, unfortunately lost in the right-hand lacuna, but still interesting for the terminology used and the professions mentioned:

εἰσὶ δὲ οἱ ἀπ[ολ]υόμενοι δημο[σίων
ἱερεῖς λογίμων ἱερῶν οι τ̣ ̣ ̣ ̣[ ] ̣αδ̣[
μ̣οι κτηνοτρόφοι οι τ̣η̣[
ὑπερετεῖς ἐπισινεῖς ἐπικριθέντε[ς
ἰατροὶ α[̣ ̣ ̣] ̣εις αυ̣[̣ ̣ ̣]αι φυλα[
πῶλα[ι]αμεῖς [ἐλ]αιουργοὶ [
γν[α]φεῖ[ς] τέκτονες [
χρυσο[χόοι] καὶ εἴ τινες ὀνομασ[
] ̣ετο χει[ρω]νάξιον [

"The following are exempted from public (duties?): priests of the high-ranking temples … maintainers of animals for transportation … old men, men officially recognized as disabled … physicians … guards (?) … merchants of … potters, manufacturers of oil … fullers … carpenters … goldsmiths and whoever pay the tax on trades…"[108]

We can in conclusion sketch the following theoretical categorization of administrative identifiers in personal applications, and then turn to the re-use of them in the official reports:

A. references to previous or different census registrations
- 1. *anagraphomenos* "registered"
  - *a.* *proanagraphomenos* "formerly registered"
- 2. *(mē) apogegrammenos* "(not) registered"
- 3. *anagegrammenos* "inscribed"
- 4. *metabasin poioumenos* "transferred, moved away"
- 5. *epi xenēs* "away"
- 6. *logizomenos* "counted"

B. references to the registration of children
- 1. *aphēlix* "underage"
  - *a.* *(mē) anagegrammenos en epigegenēmenois* "(not) inscribed among the newborns"
- 2. *anakekrimenos* "adjudged"

C. references to the *epikrisis*
- 1. *epikekrimenos* "adjudged to the *epikrisis*"
  - *a.* *apo mētropoleōs / mētropolitēs* "metropolitan"
    - *i.* *oktadrachmos* "eight-drachmas metropolitan"
    - *ii.* *dōdekadrachmos* "twelve-drachmas metropolitan"
  - *b.* *apo gumnasiou* "gymnasial"

108 The translation follows *Ancient Roman Statutes* #207, with slight adjustments.

c. *katoikos* (Arsinoites only)
2. *epikrinomenos* "candidate to the *epikrisis*"
3. *anepikritos* "not adjudged to the *epikrisis*"

D. other forms of tax liability
1. *telōn tēs laographias* "paying the poll tax" = *hupotelēs* "taxable", or the like
2. *laographoumenos* (unclear meaning)
3. special professional categories (priests, officials…)
4. exempted professional categories
   a. *apolusimos* "released"
   b. *argos* / *atechnos* "(temporary) unable to work" (?) / "unemployed" (?)
   c. *idiōtēs* "private"
5. other forms of exemption
   a. generic
      i. *atelēs* "non-taxable"
      ii. *ektos sunopseōs* "excluded from the tax estimate"
      iii. *apolelumenos* "released"
      iv. *apoluomenos* "exempted"
   b. specific
      i. *huperetēs* "overage"
      ii. *asthenēs* "permanently disabled" (?)
      iii. *episinēs* / *ensinēs* "(temporary?) disabled"
      iv. *teteleutēkōs* "dead"
      v. *anakechōrēkōs* "fled away"

Fiscal identification	**Full liability**	**Partial liability**	**Exemption**
LIFE STATUS	*anakekrimenos* (14 y.o.) 14-60 y.o.	(dead's legal heirs)	*aphēlix (< 14)* *huperetēs (> 60)* *teteleutēkōs*
RESIDENCE	*anagraphomenos* *apogegrammenos* *anagegrammenos* *epixenos et sim.*	*metropolitēs*	*anakechōrēkōs*
SOCIAL STATUS	*anepikritos* *epikrinomenos*	*epikekrimenos* *laographoumenos?*	*aporos*
PROFESSIONAL STATUS	non-exempted jobs? *aneikonistos*	*epikekrimenos* *paradochimos* officials	exempted guilds? *apolusimos* *argos, atechnos, idiōtēs?* *apolelumenos (episinēs, asthenēs)* *apoluomenos*

2. Official terminology in the administrative reports

The census declarations, collected and assembled in *tomoi sunkollēsimoi*[109], allowed the public administration to draw lists, accounts, and estimates, with the main purpose of managing the operations of tax collection: in Wallace's words, "[t]he primary purpose of the census in Roman Egypt was the numbering of the population for the efficient collection of taxes"[110]. General registers of census declarations (***eikonismoi***) were kept at various archives: we know that copies of the same document were addressed by the declarants to different officials, at the level both of the village (*kōmogrammateus* and *laographoi*; in the nome capitals, they were replaced by the *mētropoleōs grammateus* and the *amphodarchēs* / *amphodogrammateus*[111]) and of the *nomos* (*stratēgos* and *basilikos grammateus*)[112]. "The duplication of records caused by the filing of the census returns in four or five different bureaux must have been a heavy expense to the administration of Egypt, but it shows how carefully the officials watched the census to collect information for all types of taxation and for other purposes, and to prevent fraud and connivance with the populace on the part of the lower officials"[113]. The general registers "were a basic source of authoritative information concerning the identity, parentage, status, and age of individuals, and they were thus sometimes copied for private purposes, whether in short extracts or in full copies. This information might be required to help establish eligibility for *epikrisis* as a member of a privileged class, or to show entitlement to inherit"[114].

Such registers represented also the starting point for later processing of the collected data: we know that both general population lists and special rosters of certain categories were redacted, within the different offices, with administrative and tax purposes. P.Mich. XI 603 provides us with an outstanding example of that workflow. It is a contract issued by nine scribes to the secretaries of Arsinoe in AD 134, where they state the different types of documents they had been hired to write (ll. 5-18):

ἐπεὶ συνεθέμεθα ὑμ{ε}ῖν | χω̣ρὶς τῆς κατ' οἰκίαν ἀπογραφῆς συν|θε̣ῖναι μόνα ἀντίγραφα λαογραφιῶν | [κ]α̣τ̣' ἄνδρα καὶ λόγους κατοίκων καὶ | ἀ̣πολογισμοὺς ἀφηλίκων καὶ ἐκτὸς | συνόψεως καὶ νῦν δὲ συνεθέμεθα | συνθεῖναι καὶ μόνα ἀντίγραφα λαογρ[α]φ(ιῶν) | ἐν κεφαλαίωι τοῦ αὐτοῦ ιη (ἔτους) Ἁδριανοῦ | Καίσαρος τοῦ κυρίου, παρεχομένων | ὑμῶν ὅσων ἐὰν χρή\α̣ν̣/ (*l.* χρείαν) σ̣χῶμεν λό|γων τοῦ ιζ (ἔτους) πρὸς τὴν σύνθεσιν, | ἐπὶ τῶι

109 Hombert-Préaux 1952: 131 ff.; Bagnall-Frier 1994: 19 & 28; Kruse 2002, I: 86, 108, 129 ff. (see SPP II pp. 27-8 = Chr.W. 209 = P.Vet.Aelii 5, 8: ἐξ συγ̣κολλησίμων (= ἐκ συγκ-) κατ' οἰκ(ίαν) ἀπογρ(αφῶν) [Ankyron, Herakleopolites, AD 217/8], with commentary in Wilcken's and Sänger's editions). In general, on such an archival practice, that became standard in Roman times, see Clarysse 2003, who states that the *apographai* are by far the most frequent type of document filed into *tomoi sunkollēsimoi* (p. 355).

110 Wallace 1938: 96; cf. Rathbone 1993: 89.

111 Mertens 1958: 1-30.

112 Wallace 1938: 99-100; Kruse 2002, I: 65. "Good luck has preserved one splendid illustration, the declaration of a household which survives in six copies, all in the same hand and identical except for the address, addressed to the *strategos* (in duplicate), to the *basilikos grammateus,* to the *komogrammateus* of Soknopaiou Nesos (in duplicate), and the *laographoi* of that village" (Bagnall-Frier 1994: 19, with reference to BGU I 90 = I 224 = I 225 = II 410 = II 537 = P.Grenf. II 55: cf. Calderini 1922).

113 Wallace 1938: 104.

114 Bagnall-Frier 1994: 28.

λαβόντας ὑμᾶς τῶν πρ̣[οκε]ι̣|[μ]έ̣νων βιβλίων μόνα τὰ ἀ̣ντίγρ̣α̣φ̣α̣ | [πρ]ὸς μηδὲν ἁπλῶς κατασχεῖ̣ν̣ σ̣ε̣ ἔ̣τι.

"Whereas we agreed with you, apart from the house-by-house registration, to draw up single copies of the population lists arranged person-by-person, lists of *katoikoi*, and lists of minors and of those excluded from the tax estimate; now also we have agreed to draw up single copies of population lists in summary for the same 18th year of Hadrian Caesar the lord, with you supplying whatever records of the 17th year we require for the compilation, on condition that once you receive the copies of the above-stated documents we shall not be detained(?) further for any purpose whatsoever".[115]

The documents mentioned here are:

(1) ***kat'oikian apographē*** "declaration by houses", which must refer, as already noted by the editors of the papyrus, to the "τόμος συγκολλήσιμος composed of individual κατ' οἰκίαν ἀπογραφαί" – not the original one, of course, because the latter was composed by gluing the actual declarations issued by the individuals, and not redacted by the scribes at the central office. It must be a copy of what is elsewhere called *eikonismos* (see above – note that the extracts from such registers are called either *ex eikonismou* or *ek kat'oikian apographēs*, or even *ex apographēs*, which makes it clear that the terms were interchangeable). P.Oxy. VI 984, now extensively re-edited as P.Oxy.Census [Lykopolis, AD 91/2?], can be a fair instance of this case. It is a wide census register listing the full details of each declarant and of the other members of each household[116]; the noteworthy recurring annotation ἐξ ἀπογρα(φῆς) α(ὐτοῦ) (or occasionally of someone else) makes the provenance of the data clear[117].

(2) ***laographiai kat'andra / laographiai en kephalaiō*** "population lists by persons" / "summary population lists". What is called *laographia*, here, is not the tax, but a mere population list, "a list of the λαοί"[118]. It appears under the two main formats of *kat'andra*, i.e. detailed *viritim* register, and *en kephalaiō*, its summarized version[119]. Both are

115 Translation from *Papyri.info*; the *ed.pr.* has the last sentence as follows: "on condition that when you receive single copies of the above-stated documents you hold us responsible for nothing more whatever". Cf. Bagnall-Frier 1994: 27.

116 A detailed description is provided in P.Oxy.Census: pp. 19-20.

117 Cf. P.Oxy.Census: p. 19; Kruse 2002, I: 271. See also Mertens 1958: 83.

118 *Ed.pr.*, note *ad loc.* The fact that in the Arsinoites the capitation tax was usually collected, together with other dues, under the name of *suntaximon* (cf. Keyes 1931; Wallace 1938: 116 ff.; Tcherikover 1950; Forselv 1996: 157; Rathbone 1993: 88: "Another practice attested only in the Arsinoite nome is the use of *laikē suntaxis* [contribution of the *laos*/people] in place of the term *laographia* in some private contracts and declarations of decease") might have made it easier to use the term *laographia* with the meaning discussed here, which seems to stem from the Ptolemaic usage (cf. Chr.W. 288, Introduction). For *laos* meaning "population of the country" see Montevecchi 1979: 56-61.

119 I spend few words on the different purposes of *kat'andra* and *epi kephalaiou* (the same as *en kephalaiō*) arrangements in Reggiani 2016: 1432-3: the structure by persons is "the key to the fiscal usage of data, in that each person is registered as a tax-paying unit", while the summary reports were intended to provide very resumed information about relevant data "and were used as a basis for the more general 'regional' reports issued by the higher instances of the *nomos*". For this categorization applied to the laographic lists see Henne 1925: 333-4. In spite of the commentary of P.Heid. IV 310 *ad* 20-1, I would suggest that the phrase κατ' ἄνδρα λαογρα( ) in P.Ross.Georg. V 20r, 5 [Korphotoi,

mentioned also in P.Heid. IV 310 (ll. 20-1), a list of official documents (*graphē bibliōn*) redacted likely by the *kōmogrammateus*[120] of Euhemeria between AD 117 and 138 among several registers and accounts.

We can glean the structure of a ***laographia kat'andra*** from the very well known cases of P.Lond. II 257-259 [AD 94/5], three huge detailed registers of persons from some group of villages of the Herakleides *meris* in the Arsinoites[121]. The first two papyri and the beginning of the third one are arranged by house[122]: the caption οἰκί(α), or οἰκία(ς) with further specifications, followed by the owner's name, introduces each section. Of each individual are given genealogical details (family relationship with the preceding person, or father's, grandfather's, mother's, maternal grandfather's names), profession (not always, as usual), age. Almost all the words, even the proper names, are abbreviated, which shows a high degree of bureaucratic standardization. In the extant examples no indication of tax status appears, which makes us suspect that we are dealing with a list of fully liable people only: the impression is confirmed by the lack of female names and the age range, going from 14 to 60[123]. Attached to this, accounts of other administrative categories are given in the third papyrus: the *aphēlikes* of the *epikrinomenoi* (ll. 54-60), the *hupereteis* (l. 64), the dead (ll. 65 ff.), with detailed chronological references[124]. The relevant data could be

---

Herakleopolites, AD 222/3] refers to a *kat'andra* report of payments for the poll tax rather than a mere population list (see Thomas 1975, 114: "the papyrus contains a report of poll-tax collected") and is therefore to be expanded as κατ' ἄνδρα λαογρα(φίας): cf. P.Oxy. XLVI 3272, 2 [Oxyrhynchus, c. AD 61/2]: [κατ' ἄνδρα λαογ]ραφίας correctly translated as "individual list of the poll-tax". Kruse 2002, I: 276-7 proposes κατ' ἄνδρα λαογρα(φουμένων), which bears the same meaning but seems unparalleled.

120 Such *graphai bibliōn* were submitted by the village secretary to the *eklogistēs*: see below, the case of P.Sijp. 20.

121 Cf. P.Lond. II: p. 20, and CPR XV 25 (fragments belonging to the same roll [Arsinoe, AD 94/5]; similar registers are preserved in BGU II 493-510 [Arsinoites, II AD] and CPR XV 28 [Soknopaiou Nesos, second half II AD]). The issuing office might have been a joint *kōmogrammateia*, like those discussed by Derda 2006: 152 ff., or some other bureau in charge of a toparchy or a similar wide geographical area (such cases are not unknown to tax collection: see the *praktores* in charge of some places καὶ ἄλλων τόπων / κωμῶν, or even of toparchies, of which I discuss in Yiftach-Reggiani forthc.). P.Tebt. II 391 [AD 99] provides a unique testimony of the division of duties among a group of *praktores laographias*, who agree that two of them will collect the dues in the village of Tebtunis, while the other two colleagues will be in charge of the people from Tebtunis living in other places or in the *mētropolis* itself. Indeed, in P.Lond. II 259, 35 [Philadelphia, AD 94/5] we find a reference to καὶ τῶν ἐν ἑτέραις κ[ώμαις] καταγι(νομένων) Ἡρακλ[ε]ίδου μ[ερί]δ(ος) Φιλωτερίδο(ς) which might refer to some kind of deplaced residence.

122 This legacy feature, obviously inherited from the *eikonismoi*, influenced also some types of *kat'andra* tax ledgers that appear later in the administrative process: not those recording the daily payments, which are of course arranged chronologically, but those structured alphabetically, where some particular combinations of names betray the original *kat'oikian* fabric, as pointed out by Hanson 1991: 188 with n. 109.

123 Cf. P.Lond. II: p. 19.

124 The terminology exactly parallels the one in the census declarations and related documents. We only find the new category of the ***homologoi*** (P.Lond. II 259, 63 [Philadelphia, AD 94/5]), which according to Wilcken, introductions to Chr.W. 63 & 64, means "die Kopfsteuerpflichtigen" (= *laographoumenoi* according to him, but see above for the controversial meaning of this term); cf. Rostowzew 1910: 219-23 ("den Kopfsteuerpflichtigen innerhalb seiner ἰδία", p. 222); Kruse 2002, I, 278. This seems to find a parallel use in the categorization of land: in some texts from the Fayum

managed differently, on occasion[125], but the general frame is clear. It is the case described by Bagnall and Frier in the following passage: "Listmaking began with lists as comprehensive as the declarations themselves, omitting the repetitious formulaic elements and extracting only the list of persons with data about them. These included both sexes and all ages and statuses. Such lists were in general kept up to date with information from declarations of birth and death, as can be seen for example in P.Oxy. VI 984 [see above]. It is certain that they were composed anew with each census, but checked against existing lists and recent declarations of additions and subtractions. Those on previous lists who had failed to register this time and who were not known to have died were added. These lists will at least have saved the authorities the trouble of referring frequently to the *tomoi* which were cumbersome to use, and will thus have served as a handy reference tool. [...] Tax lists for everyday use, like P.Lond. II 257-259, needed only to record males subject to taxation, i.e., between the ages of 14 and 62. The giving of ages allowed the authorities to remove the small minority who passed the end of tax liability by surviving to old age"[126].

The other typology, the ***laographia en kephalaiō*** , must have been a sort of summary of the *kat'andra* report. One more mention of it appears among the items of the *graphē bibliōn* preserved on P.Sijp. 20 (l. 21), issued in AD 169/70 by Horion, *kōmogrammateus* of Dinnis in the Arsinoites, to the office of the *eklogistēs*[127].

(3) ***logoi katoikōn*** "lists of *katoikoi*". The contract is redacted in Arsinoe and *katoikoi* are the special exempted local category (see above); no doubt that elsewhere similar lists of privileged classes were filled out: the *ekthesis mētropolitōn* P.Col. V 1v 1b [Theadelphia, c. AD 160], recording amounts of taxes paid, must have been based on a raw list of metropolitans taken from census declarations and *epikrisis* applications. P.Stras. VII 651 verso

---

homologos refers to a type of land "in normal condition", "liable to its normal taxation" (P.Fay.: pp. 286-7). The latest discussion of this term is provided by Mirković 2007: 744-8: "*homologoi* were inhabitants of the villages and registered there in the tax lists" (p. 746).

125 In such derived documents as SB I 5118, an ἀντίγραφον διαστρώματος ("copy of the abstract") λαογραφίας κατ' ἄ[νδρα from Philopator alias Theogenous [AD 129/30], and showing the very same structure (the age is probably lost in the right-hand lacuna), at least one tax status (*laographoumenos*) is recorded; in another example of extract, P.Phil. 5 [Philadelphia, AD 48/9 or 62/3], containing data for one person, the maternal grandfather is omitted: ἐκ λαογραφίας κα[τ]' ἄνδρα θ (ἔτους) | Φιλαδελφείας. | μέρο(ς) οἰκ(ίας) ἴδ(ιον)· Ἡρακ( ) Μένωνος | μητρὸ(ς) Φιλοῦτος (ἐτῶν) νθ.

126 Bagnall-Frier 1994: 27. A particular discussion is deserved by the *kat'andra apographē* mentioned in P.Princ. III 127 [Theadelphia, AD 161], the beginning of a letter addressed by the Theadelphian *laographoi* to the officials charged of carrying the reports to the *eklogistēs* at Alexandria. They say (ll. 8-11 updated after BL VIII 284): κατεχωρίσαμεν ὑμ{ε}ῖν κατ' ἄνδρα | ἀπογρ(αφὴν) τῶν ἀπογραψαμένω(ν) ἡμ{ε}ῖν | πρὸς τὴν τοῦ κγ (ἔτους) θεοῦ Αἰλίου | Ἀντωνίνου κατ' οἰκί(αν) ἀπογρ(αφήν), i.e. "we have filed with you the viritim *apographē* of those registered by us in the house-by-house census of the 23rd year of divine Aelius Antoninus". The editors leave the term (which appears to be a *hapax* in the entire papyrological corpus) undiscussed, translating it as "census return". This "supplement" (συν|τεθεῖσα, ll. 11-2) is clearly a list taken from the data collected with the *kat'oikian apographai*, and it might well be just an erroneous or non-standard way of referring to a *kat'andra laographia*.

127 See Hoogendijk 2007 for discussion of this papyrus, and above for a similar case. The report is addressed, as usual, to the *paralēmptai bibliōn* of the *eklogistēs*, the board of officers in charge of receiving the documents (cf. Reggiani 2017: 62).

[Bakchias, mid II cent.] might have been a (draft?) example of such lists: under the caption κ[α]τ(οίκων) (l. 1) several persons are registered with detailed family information (patronymic, papponymic, metronymic); that we are in a fiscal context is probably shown by the fact that the list is followed by another one of *aporoi* (ἀπόρων, l. 12; see below)[128].

(4) ***apologismoi aphēlikōn kai ektos sunopseōs*** "registers of minors and of those excluded from the estimates". It is not clear if the reference is to one inclusive list or to two different lists (one for the minors and one for the others). In fact we have several examples of separate lists of underage children, clearly compiled on the basis of both census and birth declarations[129], but titled *graphē*[130]or sometimes *logos*[131] *aphēlikōn*. "It was also essential [...] to maintain lists of those under 14 who would become liable when they reached that age, so that each year the year's cohort of 14-year-olds could be added to the main list of taxpayers. These lists accounted carefully for every taxpayer, to the point sometimes of giving *tomos* and sheet number references for their declarations in previous censuses. From these lists could be computed the numbers liable in each tax category and thus the amount to be collected"[132]. However, here the term *apologismos* must refer to something more detailed than a simple "list" or "roster" of names[133]; it usually occurs in declarations or reports advising "reductions", or more generally speaking corrections to be applied to previous accounts[134]. We find reference to a couple of *apologismoi aphēlikōn* in P.Sijp. 20,

128 For other hints see the Introduction to the papyrus, p. 74.

129 Hombert-Préaux 1952: 75.

130 P.Mil.Congr.XIV pag. 22 [Ptolemais Euergetis, AD 96/7 or 98]; P.Lond. III 915 [Memphis, AD 160]; P.Oxy. LXV 4489 [Oxyrhynchus, AD 197]; CPR XV 32 [II/III AD]; O.Bodl. II 1961 [Thebes, II/III AD]; SB XVIII 13129 [Oxyrhynchites, AD 207/8]; SPP II 1 [Herakleopolis, AD 216]; P.Oxy. XLIII 3096 [Oxyrhynchus, AD 223/4]; P.Ryl. II 110 (?) [Hermopolis, AD 259]; P.Oxy. XL 2927 [Oxyrhynchus, AD 268-271]; P.Ups.Frid 6 [Oxyrhynchus, AD 273]; P.Oxy. X 1256 [Kynopolites, AD 282]; P.Oxy. XLVI 3295 [Oxyrhynchus, AD 285]; P.Oxy. XLIV 3183 [Oxyrhynchus, AD 292]; P.Oxy. XLIII 3137 [Oxyrhynchus, AD 295].

131 P.Coll.Youtie I 25 [Tebtunis, AD 147]; SB VI 9619 (?) [Ptolemais Euergetis, AD 184]; SB VI 9219 [Hermopolis, AD 319].

132 Bagnall-Frier 1994: 28.

133 Cf. Bickermann 1930: 25 (*apologismos* as a sub-category of declaration, i.e. report); Avogadro 1935: 169 ("rendiconto": cf. *ibid.*, n. 1, on the difference between *apographē* and *apologismos*); Reggiani 2016: 1429 (Ptolemaic *apologismos* as a very detailed land register). On the difference between *graphai* "lists, rosters" and other types of official documents see, e.g., Lewis 1970: 162-3. The typical *graphē* included only a header and a simple *kat'andra* list (cf. Montevecchi 1932: 318), without accounting features. See below, Conclusions, and the contribution by Willy Clarysse in this same volume, for a tentative reassessment of the relevant vocabulary.

134 In II-century Soknopaiou Nesos the term is used to define applications to remove sold camels from the appropriate lists (hence, Kruse 2002, I: 186-7 "rechnerische(r) Abzug" or "Abmeldung"): P.Lond. II 304, 18 [AD 144]; BGU I 89, 1 [AD 163]; cf. SPP XXII 90, 17 [AD 144]; SB XVI 12689, 11 [*p.* AD 162]. Consider also P.Mich. I 43, 2-3 [Philadelphia, 253 BC]: an *apologismos* of corn and sesame is requested in order to evaluate wrong measurements; P.Tebt. III/2 856, 25 [Arsinoites, c. 171 BC]: *apologismos* of seeds to be added (τὰ παρακείμενα); P.Tebt. I 79c, 4-5 [Arsinoites, c. 148 BC]: lands to be taken into account διὰ τοῦ | [ἀπολο]γισμοῦ; P.Oxy. II 297, 5-6 [Oxyrhynchus, AD 54]: an ἀπολογισμὸν | τῶν [π]ρ[ο]βάτων is requested in order to estimate how many sheep have been added by the lambing beyond those included in a previous account; P.Sarap. 52, 65 [Hermopolites, AD 118/9]: a further account of lambs within a more general λόγος προβάτ(ων); P.Berl.Möller 5, 4-9 [Psei,

23-4, i.e. the aforementioned *graphē biblīōn* of the *kōmogrammateus* of Dinnis: here, among several *apaitēsima* of various taxes and three seed registers, and beside the aforesaid *laographia en kephalaiō*, are listed an *apologismos* of the minors and another one of the underage sons of the priests (*aphēlikōn huiōn hiereōn*)[135]. SB XXVI 16384 = O.Narm. I 102, 14 [Narmouthis, II-III AD] is a draft of a similar list and again cites *apologismoi aphēlikōn*.

We can gain a better idea of the paperwork concerning the registration of children from SPP IV pagg. 58-78 (= P.Lond. II 261 + P.Lond. II 260 + previously unpublished parts of a Rainer papyrus), which is another outstanding document for the understanding of administrative mechanisms, and thus deserves a closer attention[136]. In this large *tomos*

Arsinoites, AD 145]: a customs ἀπολογισμόν is sent περὶ τοῦ μηδὲν | περιγεγονέναι "concerning what have been left over"; P.Amh. II 69 = Chr.W. 190, 11-2 & 15-6 [Arsinoites, AD 154]: report of *sitologoi* mentioning an ἀπολογισμὸν περὶ τοῦ μηδὲν | ἡμ{ε}ῖν μεμετρῆσθ(αι) "report concerning (the rents) not measured by us". In Ptolemaic times we find many attestations of the *apologismos hupologou*, a register of unproductive land which was clearly to be subtracted from the due rents (P.Tebt. III/2 826, 4-6 [Berenikis Thesmophorou, 172 BC]; P.Tebt. I 74, 2 & 32 [Kerkeosiris, 113 BC]; P.Tebt. I 75, 16 [Kerkeosiris, *p.* 112 BC]: cf. Reggiani 2016a: 1433 – see BGU VI 1216, 12-3 [Memphis or Aphroditopolis, 110 BC?]: ὑπολόγου τοῦ ἀναφερομένου | διὰ τοῦ ἀπολογισμοῦ, "of the unproductive land to be reported according to the *a.*"). However, the Ptolemaic and early Roman *apologismos tou edaphous* was a more inclusive, detailed register (P.Tebt. I 61, viii, 216 [Kerkeorisirs, 117 BC]; P.Tebt. I 30, 26 [Kerkeosiris, 115 BC]; P.Tebt. I 72b, 2 [Kerkeosiris, 113 BC]; P.Berl. Möller 9, 11-2 [AD 45]), just as the *a.* τῶν σωμάτων τοὺς μὲν πρὸς τοῖς | ἀμπελικοῖς εἶναι of P.Col. IV 87, 24-5 [Philadelphia, 244 BC?] or the *a.* κρίσεων of P.Ryl. II 78, 35 [AD 157]. Also *apologismoi epistolōn* "registers of letters" are attested (P.Phil. 4, 1 [Philadelphia, *p.* AD 141]; P.Laur. I 2, 17-8 [Arsinoites, AD 148]; P.Flor. I 67, 54 [Arsinoe, AD 162?]; P.Panop.Beatty 1, 64 [Panopolis, AD 298]; SB XXVI 16384, 15-6 [Narmouthis, II-III AD].

135 Hoogendijk 2007: 139 nn. 23-24.

136 For general discussion see the P.Lond. and SPP commentaries, as well as Kruse 2002, I: 272 ff. For the sake of clarity, I provide here the general outlines of the roll:

(1) ll. 1-27 (P.Lond. II 261, coll. i-ii = ancient *kollēmata* 21-22): the end of a sort of general tax register of the *amphodon* (cf. l. 9 ἐπὶ τοῦ ἀμφόδ(ου) τελο(ῦντες)).

(2) ll. 28-244 (P.Lond. II 261, coll. iii-xvi = ancient *koll.* 1-14): **ἀπολογισμὸς ἀφηλίκων υἱῶν [λ]α[ογ]ραφουμένων** "register of the underage sons of the *laographoumenoi*",

(3) ll. 245-78 (P.Lond. II 261, coll. xvii-xviii = ancient *koll.* 15-16): supplementary *graphē* of those whose births had been reported during the current year.

(4) ll. 279-330 (SPP IV pp. 67-8, coll. I-III): final part of a list of slaves and freedmen taken from the census declarations (cf. l. 327: δ[οῦλοι ἀ]ν̣[α]γεγραμμέ(νοι) [διὰ] τ̣ῆ̣ς κ[ατ'] οἰκίαν ἀ[πογραφῆς).

(6) ll. 378-431 (SPP IV pp. 70-1, coll. VII-X): **λόγος χειρωναξίου** "account of the *cheirōnaxion* tax" income for the current year

(7) ll. 432-88 (SPP IV pp. 71-2, coll. XI-XIII = Chr.W. 61 = CPJ II 421): **ἀπαιτήσιμ[ον] Ἰ̣[ουδαικοῦ τελέσ]ματος** "register of the tax on Jews" of the same year.

(8) ll. 489-506 (SPP IV p. 72, col. XIV): **γραφῇ{ι} ὑπερετῶν καὶ ἀσθενῶν** "list of the overage and of the weak" registered in the *amphodon*.

(9) ll. 507-82 (P.Lond. II 260, coll. i-v): final part of a list of men said to have passed the *epikrisis* (see P.Lond. II, pp. 42-3 and 46).

sunkollēsimos composed of several documents redacted by Herakleides, *amphodarchēs* of the quarter *Apolloniou Parembolē* in Arsinoe around AD 73, we find a complete "register of the underage sons of the *laographoumenoi*" (ἀπολογισμὸς ἀφηλίκων υἱῶν [λ]α[ογ]ρα̣φουμένων, ll. 28-244) and large part of a "register of the underage sons of the *katoikoi*" (ἀπολογισμὸς ἀφηλίκων υ̣ἱ̣ῶν κατοίκων, ll. 583-703), as well as a γραφὴ{ι} ὑπερετῶν καὶ ἀσθενῶν, "list of the overage and of the weak" (ll. 489-506)[137] which must fall into the case of the *apologismoi ektos sunopseōs* mentioned by the scribes of P.Sijp. 20.

The accounts of the minors where drawn basically from both census declarations and birth notifications. The amphodarch himself states that the data for the underage sons of the *laographoumenoi*, recorded for the current fifth regnal year of Vespasian (AD 72/3), regard τῶν [δ]ι̣ὰ̣ τ̣ῆς κα̣τ' οἰκίαν ἀπογραφ[ῆ]ς | τοῦ η (ἔτους) Νέρωνος ἀναγε[γ]ραμμένων (διετῶν) | μέχρι (ἑνὸς ἔτους) ἐπανακειμέν[ων (ll. 31-3) as well as τ]ῶ̣ν ἀπὸ θ (ἔτους) | μέχρι δ (ἔτους) Οὐεσπασιανοῦ δι' ὑπομνημάτων | σημανθέντων ἐπιγεγεννῆσθαι (ll. 33-5), that is those registered through the declarations of the latest census, dating back to Nero's eighth year (AD 61/2), and those registered through the birth notifications (*hupomnēmata*) from Nero's ninth year (AD 62/3) to Vespasian's fourth year (AD 71/2). The same applies for the sons of the *katoikoi*. The children are divided by age (those who are 13 years old in the current year, those who are 12 years old in the current year, and so on) and within each category calculations are made to sum those enlisted during the latest census (οἱ διὰ [συ]νκεφαλαιώσεως [η (ἔτους)] ἀ̣ν̣αγεγρ(αμμένοι): ll. 38, 90, 593, 617) with those registered through the birth declarations in the following years (ὁ τῶ̣ι δ (ἔτει) σημανθ(εὶς) ἐπιγεγε(ννῆσθαι), passim). Of the former, only the figures are given, while the latter are further divided by house and filed in *kat'andra* lists, as a sort of update to the *laographia* register[138]. Dead children are taken into consideration too. "The minuteness with which the age, birth, date of registration, &c., of each individual is noted, among both the adults and the ἀφήλικες, shows the extreme care with which each person was followed and accounted for from census to census"[139].

The SPP roll is complementary to P.Sijp. 20 (which by the way, as noted above, reports an *apologismos aphēlikōn huiōn hiereōn*) in providing us with evidence of the administrative paperwork concerning population registers and reports. It uses passim, for example, data from the accounts of the deceased (***taxeis teteleutēkotōn***)[140] redacted with the

---

(5) ll. 331-77 (SPP IV pp. 68-9, coll. IV-VI): **γραφῆ{ι} Ῥωμαίων κ[αὶ Ἀλεξανδρέων** "list of Romans and Alexandrians", which of course was not based on any census-like declaration since Romans and Alexandrians were not subject to that procedure (see above).

(10) ll. 583-703 (P.Lond. II 260, coll. vi-xiii): **ἀπολογισμὸς ἀφηλίκων υ̣ἱ̣ῶν κατοίκων** "register of the underage sons of the *katoikoi*".

137 Cf. Hombert-Préaux 1937: 262.

138 On updating population lists see Wallace 1938: 105-6, and Kruse 2002, I: 279-80.

139 P.Lond. II: pp. 45-6.

140 The current official term for this register seems to have been *taxis*, which occurs in the standard formulary of the declarations of death (see those collected in C.Pap.Gr. II, to which add SB XX 15037 [Arsinoites, AD 49]; P.Gen. III 137 [Philadelphia, AD 50]; P.Monts.Roca IV 68 [I/II AD]; SB XX 15038 [Tebtunis, AD 117]; SB XX 15011 [Tebtunis, AD 117-138]; P.Prag. I 19 [Soknopaiou Nesos, AD 177-180]; P.Gen. III 139 [Soknopaiou Nesos, AD 178]; P.Oxy. LXXIV 4992 [Oxyrhynchus, AD

purpose of both crossing out dead people from the tax lists and assessing the tax liability of their heirs[141]. The latter purpose explains why a particularly careful attention was paid to the month of death (a notice directly taken from death notifications), as is clear from the text of P.Coll.Youtie I 20 presented below, because the tax liability of the heirs depended on that[142]. The former use is attested also in P.Sijp. 26, 121 (an administrative document from Philadelphia [AD 51], which we will discuss below) and SB XVI 12816, 48, 53, 69, a population register from Soknopaiou Nesos (AD 179) recording variations, by reduction (*elassōmata*: cf. l. 20; the same vocabulary occurs in the aforesaid P.Lond. II 259) of the dead and addition of new adults, affecting the tax liability of the local priesthood[143].

The people *ektos sunopseōs* were those excluded from the tax estimates (see below), because exempted or released for some reason from the payment. The need for separated lists of them is clearly shown by the first provision of P.Oxy. XXXVI 2754, 1-2 [Oxyrhynchus, AD 111], a messy collection of prefectural edicts: here it is stated that "the village secretaries are to present under oath the names of those who are infirm or who wish to be released on other grounds, with the strategus supervising" (τῶν ἐπισινῶν ἢ ἄλλαις αἰτίαις ἀπολυθῆναι βουλομένων οἱ κωμογραμματεῖς | ἔνορκοι τὰ ὀνόματα διδότωσαν τοῦ στρατηγοῦ παρακολουθοῦντος). Terminology is rather generic, but we find the *ektos sunopseōs* mentioned together with the tax-exempted categories of Romans and Alexandrians in the obscure CPR VIII 20, the final part of a letter of unknown provenance and dated to the third century, in which the writer speaks of two differents "accounts" (εἰς λόγον, ll. 5 & 8), one Ῥωμαίων καὶ Ἀλεξανδρέων | καὶ τῶν ἐκτὸς συνόψεως (ll. 6-7) and one τῶν κατοί|κων (ll. 8-9). As the editors stated, the context is completely unclear, not to say surprising, but it is at least evident the relationship of the *ektos sunopseōs* with groups that did not pay taxes in full (the *katoikoi* being, as we noted above, exempted in part). The mention of this category in P.Mur. 117 = SB X 10307, 3 [Palestine, end II AD], though the context is too fragmentary to understand it, proves the use of the term also outside Egypt; at any rate, the fiscal meaning is clear also by comparison with SB I 5230, iv, 50 [after AD 10/11], where εἰδῶν τῶν ἐκτὸς συγόψεως (= συν-) τεθέ⟨ντ⟩ων refers to taxes in kind not considered in the regular estimate[144]. Most interesting is PSI XII 1230, a declaration of a slave for *epikrisis*

223/4]; cf. Casarico 1985, 17-19). It may have had the proper meaning of "established roster" as opposed to the *graphē* (used in the *epikrisis* application P.Mil.Congr.XIV p.22, 22 [see above]; the occurrence in C.Pap.Gr. II 2 [Theadelphia, AD 12], a notice of death, is probably a mistake for the more usual formula, since the whole phrase looks quite unique) that might conceal the actual registration act, resulting in a more or less raw list. Outside these two terminological cases falls SB XVI 12816, 48, 53, 59, 69 [Soknopaiou Nesos, AD 179] in referring to a *gnōmōn teteleutēkotōn* "register of the dead": here, the cited document relates to specific chronological ranges, and this might explain the special term *gnōmōn*, on which see below, Conclusions.

141 Cf. Kruse 2002, I: 141-3 ff.; see above, and Reggiani 2016b.

142 Cf. Casarico 1985: 17.

143 For discussion of this text see Hobson 1984: part. 848-52; cf. CPR XV 26 [Soknopaiou Nesos, AD 179], which belongs to a similar document (see below). Here, in the note to l. 5, the editor G. Messeri Savorelli holds as "probabile che l'amministrazione fiscale registrasse in registri separati la popolazione civile e i sacerdoti" (cf. Messeri Savorelli 1989: 10-12).

144 Cf. Wessely 1882: 189 and commentary to P.Mur. 117.

from AD 203 Oxyrhynchus. The applicant follows the usual procedure[145], in declaring his 13-years-old slave and his own belonging to the metropolitan group of the *dōdekadrachmoi* (see above); but he states to be currently ἐκτὸς | συνόψεως διὰ τὸ ἐπὶ ξ̣ή|νη⟨ς⟩ (= ξέ-) (ll. 9-11)[146]. This stresses once more the difference between the *ektos sunopseōs*, not paying taxes at all, and the privileged categories entitled to reduced payments, such as, in this last case, the metropolitans.

A particular attention was paid to those who changed tax status, due to either death or age shift: "the town and village clerks would know from their census records when each boy within their territory became liable for the tax and when to remove the deceased and the superannuated from the rolls"[147]. The data extracted from the lists of deads and minors were further processed into more comprehensive accounts like SB XVI 12816 [Soknopaiou Nesos, AD 179], widely discussed by Hobson 1984[148], which must have been based on drafts like P.Coll.Youtie 20 and, in turn, must have been the base for the general tax *sunopseis* like P.Sijp. 26[149]. P.Coll.Youtie 20, written on the verso of P.Corn. 24, belongs to the papers of Nemesion, tax collector of Philadelphia, and provides a general summary account of the population in the year AD 56[150]. Its main purpose is clearly to state how many men were liable to the poll tax, by subtracting exempted groups. It is worth transcribing the relevant text (the whole papyrus except ll. 1-2, which relate to a different account[151]) followed by the interpretation of the editor, which sketches the relevant administrative data flow:

ἄνδ(ρες) ψπβ
(ὧ̣ν) παρ(αγενόμενοι) καὶ παραι(τησάμενοι) ἄνδ(ρες) σι
ὑπερ(ετεῖς) θ ⟦μὴ ἔχω(ντες, *l.* ἔχο-) ἀγχ(ιστεῖς)⟧
(γίνονται) ἄνδ(ρες) σιθ
κατα̣λ(είπονται) ἄνδ(ρες) φξγ
ὑπερ(ετεῖς) (ἐτῶν) ξα ϛ
ἀνακ(εκριμένοι) ιδ (ἐτῶν) θ
β (ἔτους) ἄνδ(ρες) δ
παρα(γεγραμμένος) α
κατη(γμένος) α
(γίνονται) ἄνδ(ρες) φπδ
προ(σγίνονται) ἀφή(λικες) λϛ

145 Cf. Bieżuńska-Małowist1977: 65 ff.: slaves were declared when they reached their thirteenth year, and followed the social-fiscal group of their master.

146 The editor, followed by Bieżuńska-Małowist1977: 66, interprets *sunopsis* as census list, but see below for its meaning as tax estimate.

147 Lewis 1983: 169-70.

148 A more fragmentary, yet noteworthy example is provided by CPR XV 26 [Soknopaiou Nesos, AD 179]. It contains parts of a list of dead priests to be subtracted (ἀ]πογείνε̣[ται, l. 1) from the *laographia* entries and only the handwriting prevented the editor to consider it part of the same register as SB 12816.

149 Hanson 2007b: 173 actually considers the documents like SB 12816 as tax *sunopseis* like P.Sijp. 26.

150 Cf. Hanson 2007b: 173.

151 The text has been improved very much by new readings made by Ann Hanson in two past occasions: Hanson 1988: 270 nn. 43 & 47 (the latter recorded as BL IX 57) and 2007: 173 n. 10. Here I set up the most updated transcription.

(γίνονται) ἄνδ(ρες) χκ (τάλαντα) δ Γτνζ (τριώβολον)
γνόμονα (*l.* γνώ-) τετελευτη(κότων)
ἐντὸς μην(ὸς) Χοι(ὰκ) δ (δραχμαὶ) ϙη (τετρώβολον)
Χοι(ὰκ) α (δραχμαὶ) κδ
Τῦβ(ι) δ (δραχμαὶ) ρδ
Μεχ(εὶρ) γ (δραχμαὶ) [φ] (δραχμαὶ) πδ
μετὰ τὸ(ν) καταχ(ωρισμὸν) τῶν λόγω(ν) ϛ (δραχμαὶ) ρμϛ
(γίνονται) τετ(ελευτηκότων) (δραχμαὶ) υμϛ (τετρώβολον)
(γίνεται) (τάλαντα) δ Γωδ (ὀβολὸς)

"We have in lines 3 to 6 a total number of men and two categories of men who are subtracted from this total. 210 are called present and excused; whether they are ἄποροι or of a privileged class we do not know. Nine men are overage[152]. Lines 7-15 reckon the total number of persons liable for payment of laographia. Each item in this list appears to come from a separate document listing persons in different categories. First there is the standard list of those regularly liable for the poll tax, a κατ' ἄνδρα. This is followed by those 61 years old who have probably been segregated into a separate list since they would be transferred the following year to exempt status. A third item in line 9 lists nine who have been adjudged to be 14 years old. The next three categories are unclear[153]. In line 13 the total of lines 7-12 is given. Then 36 ἀφήλικες are added and the total number of 620 men liable for poll tax given. These ἀφήλικες must be those who reached the age of 14 in this year. There may have been a separate list of this age cohort, or Nemesion may simply mean that they are being transferred from a comprehensive list of minors to the κατ' ἄνδρα list of those liable to taxation. Lines 16 through 22 reckon the tax liability of those who died in the first six months of this year"[154].

The amphodarch roll included also an account for *cheirōnaxion*, the tax on handicrafts (λόγος χειρωναξίου, l. 379). As we already noted, there was a strong connection between the payment for or the exemption from the *laographia* and the special dues related to some professions. In particular, it is ascertained that "the population registers which were prepared for the *laographia* were also used to collect other charges such as the *cheirōnaxia* (craft-dues) and, for (non-metropolite) villagers only, the *huikē* (pig-tax) and *halikē* (salt-tax), and these taxes were often collected together with the *laographia*"[155]: it will produce

152 The phrase *mē echontes anchisteis* "not having heirs-at-law", recovered by Hanson 2007b: 173 n.10, was deleted by Nemesion because it usually applied to dead, not to overage: cf. Hanson 2007b: 179 n. 1 (and see below).

153 The first one, with reference to a "second year", must refer to the *anakekrimenoi* moved to tax liability during the second year of Nero (AD 55/6, fitting the dating of the recto), i.e. the same category as in the line before, which according to a revised reading by Hanson 1988: 270 n. 43 was registered in the first year (AD 54/5). The second one is now to be read ***paragegrammenos*** "added to the list" after Hanson 1988, 270 n. 47, meaning another supplementary addition (Oates, *ed.pr.*, transcribed παρα(γενόμενος), cf. l. 4). The third one is now to be read ***katēgmenos*** "led down" (cf. P.Sijp. 26, 50 & 84) after Hanson 2007b: 173 n. 10 (I just propose to start the abbreviation after the *ēta* instead of after the *gamma*, according to what I see in the picture published in the *editio princeps*, plate IX).

154 Oates 1976: 190-1.

155 Rathbone 1993: 87; cf. also Hobson 1984: 852-3 on the *halikē* (and another tax) along with *laographia* in the register of priests mentioned above (SB 12816).

no surprise to state that some declarations of death were directly submitted to tax exactors like those of the weavers' dues[156]. The attention to the profession is made clear by documents like SB XX 15024 [Tebtunis, II AD], which can be placed – within the administrative workflow – somewhere between the *laographiai kat'andra* and the summary *en kephalaiō*, approximately at the same level of the *logos katoikōn* of P.Sijp. 20. The papyrus contains a *kat'andra* list of people arranged by category, with a high detail of personal data (patronymic, papponymic, metronymic, age). The first fragment preserves several sections of occupational categories: weavers (γέρδιοι, l. ii 3) among other wool merchants (ἐ̣ριοπῶλαι, l. ii 9), then priests (ἱερεῖς θεῶν κώμης, l. ii 12), herdsmen (ποιμένες, l. ii 17), builders/carpenters (τέκτονες, l. iii 1), the sons of the public cultivators working (?) for their fathers (υἱοὶ δημοσίων γεωργῶν ὑ̣π̣ο̣[- - -]ῦ̣ν̣τες τοῖς πατράσι, l. 4), the ἰδιῶται ἐργατευόμενοι (l. iii 9, see above for this category). The second fragment from the same document starts with a section (unfortunately, very fragmentary) dealing with ὑπερετεῖς ἄνδ̣ρ̣[ες (l. 2) and τῶν ἐκτὸς σ̣υ̣ν̣[όψεως (l. 3), and followed by the beginning of a list of ὑπερετεῖς (l. 8), making it clear that the whole document relates to the *laographia* or a similar context[157]. Such secondary registers served as a basis for tax accounts like that for *cheirōnaxion* filed in the SPP *tomos*, where indeed, after a general introductory section, a *kat'andra* list arranged by profession is drawn up, and the only difference from the SB list is that the record of the amount paid takes the place of the age indication[158] (which was, at this step, irrelevant).

To sum up, "eine wichtige Funktion der κατ' οἰκίαν ἀπογραφαί sowie der Geburts- und Todesanzeigen, aber auch des Verfahrens der ἐπίκρισις bestand zweifellos darin, die relevanten Daten zu liefern, die die Behörden zur Zusammenstellung von Listen benötigten, in denen die Bevölkerung entweder nach Haushalten oder getrennt nach den diversen Statusgruppen erfaßt wurde"[159]. The wide variety of such derived lists has been well shown by Hombert and Préaux[160]; we can now outline a general scheme of how the relevant personal data (the "identifiers") were processed within this administrative workflow. The basic individual identification was provided by the genealogical details and the physical marks; they tend to decrease in the very first steps of the process, but we may find quite a detailed genealogy even in tax registers. This is fairly understandable, since tax collection (even on land) was almost always conducted on an individual basis. Details on the social status allowed for extracting data on privileged categories, while the determination of age was fundamental to frame the liable men between the two opposite poles of the lowest legal age (under which the *aphēlikes* were grouped) and the highest one (above which the *hupereteis* were placed). Geographical provenance was a way to both determine particular privileges and define the local boards responsible for tax control and collection. The specification of the profession, which arises the most puzzling questions, could serve as a futher tax categorization, if not as a mere individual identifier, at least in some occasions.

---

156 Casarico 1985: 11; see above.
157 Cf. Bülow-Jacobsen 1989: 127-8.
158 Cf. Bülow-Jacobsen 1989: 128.
159 Kruse 2002, I: 271.
160 Hombert-Preaux 1952: 135 ff.

3. Official terminology in the tax accounts

A further passage in the registering chain was the use of population / administrative lists to draw up tax accounts. The most complex and inclusive among the latter is without doubts the so-called ***sunopsis***, i.e. the estimate of the taxes to be exacted during a certain year in a certain place. We have already encountered this term when we noted that the categories exempted from the poll tax were sometimes grouped under the general title of ***ektos sunopseōs***, meaning indeed their exclusion from such "estimates". The best example of such general registers is P.Sijp. 26 [Philadelphia, AD 51], the structure of which is clear: the entries are arranged by categories, providing totals and lists of names[161]. Formally, it can be considered a parallel of the *laographiai kat'andra*. The pieces of personal information are reduced to the essential elements (patronymics, sometimes metronymics), and the categories show a terminology which we do find in the personal declarations only in part. Apart from the *hupereteis* "overage", the *teteleutēkotes* "dead" (with further annotations, certainly taken from death notifications), the *aphēlikes* "underage" (the number of which is taken, it is said, ἐξ εἰκονισμ(οῦ), l. 96) and some exempted professional categories (*phulakes, hiereis*), we find ***hoi mē echontes anchisteis*** "those not having heirs-at-law"[162], ***estrateumenoi*** "enlisted in the army" (see above and below), ***kakourgoi*** "criminals"[163], ***hoi opheilontes en paradochē anechthēnai*** "those who need to be carried over in *paradochē*", which corresponds to οἱ ἐν παραδοχῇ ἀναφερόμενοι of SB XVI 12816, 45 [Soknopaiou Nesos, AD 179][164]; ***hoi pros gnōmōna aneilēmmenoi*** "those who had been included according to the schedule"[165], the ***anapographoi tessareskaidekaeteis*** "14-years-old boys uncensused".

This is a noteworthy trend of the population registers: it seems that a technical, bureaucratic terminology existed at the level of the offices, and it was used to further specify categories and sub-categories of the population, pointing out special cases and crossing data coming from other public branches. The military sector, for instance, could be one of these: "separate lists of **ἐστρατευμένοι** are not infrequent in the Philadelphia tax documents, as

---

161 Cf. Hanson 2007b. "Two other fragments of *synopseis* can be identified among the papers of Nemesion, but these are from other tax years and written in different hand [P.Mich. inv. 849v and inv. 843v]. Portions of *synopseis* from other villages are also known: the first century *synopsis* from Aueris (SB XVIII 13244) and the *synopsis* of 178/79 from Soknopaeu Nesus (SB XVI 12816 and CPR XV 26). The rubrics that punctuate the lists in the *synopseis* show many similarities" (*ibid.*: 173; see above).

162 Cf. Hanson 2007b: 179 & 173 n. 5. "In the absence of ἀγχιστεῖς the fisc received the inheritance" (Taubenschlag 1955: 188). See also above for the issues related to the death of taxpayers. The phrase is known to the administrative vocabulary, see above and below apropos of SB IV 7462.

163 For criminals not paying for *laographia* see e.g. P.Petaus 9 = C.Pap.Gr. App.2, 9, the abovementioned request to abolish the poll tax for two sentenced to death. About tax exemptions for criminals, prisoners, and the like, see Jördens 2009: 351-2.

164 See above for discussion of this term. *Paradochimos* is often used is connection with priests, but here those who have to be carried over in the *paradochē* are, beside three priests, a huge number of people belonging to tax-free estates and therefore *apolusimoi* (Hanson 2007b: 180) and a couple of guards.

165 The reference must be to the γνώμων τῆς λαογρ(αφίας) cited in CPR XV 26, 5, which is almost certainly the same as mentioned in SB 12816, iii 5 as γνώμων only (and cf. γνωμο( ) in P.Stras. 651, 23 – see above). Following the interpretations offered by the editors of the involved papyri, it should refer to a schedule or assessment of rates for the poll-tax. Whether it was the same as the *laographia kat'andra*, or some different register, is not clear.

e.g. P.Ryl. IV 595, 114-22 (+ BL VI 123), where the enlisted are booked for full payment of the *laographia* in arrears. Repeated isolation of the enlisted in discrete lists suggests that the tax bureau considers the category one that requires special attention. The I-cent. declarations of *anachoresis* from the Oxyrhynchite nome occasionally note that the missing taxpayer as not enlisted (P.Oxy. XXXIII 2669, P.Gen. II 94): the concern of tax authorities may reside in both a change of domicile and a change of status"[166]. Another impressive example is provided by the lists of those lacking means (***graphai aporōn***). As far as our documentation goes, no-one declares himself as ***aporos***[167] in any known *apographē*, but since dedicated registers existed, the definition of such a category was probably duty of the officials themselves, or perhaps followed some special application similar to those submitted in order to avoid liturgical appointments for the same reason[168], or to declare the status of *anakechōrēkōs* (see above). P.Lond. III 911 [AD 149] is a fragment from such a list, interestingly exhibiting the title ἀντίγραφον γραφῆς ἀπόρων (l. 1; the entries are then introduced by the heading ἔστι δὲ ἐν ἀπọροις, l. 6[169]). The already mentioned P.Stras. 651 took its list of ἀπόρων (l. 12) from such *graphai*, filed with data not gathered from the personal declarations we discussed above. It could be the same case also for the ***anakechō-rēkotes***, the people "fled away"[170], also known as ***aneuretoi aporoi***, the "untraceable delinquent taxpayers"[171]: apart from the declarations of *anachōrēsis*, limited in the space and time (see above), these terms never appear in personal applications, as is again understandable, but are used in official lists of runaway (the ***anakechōrēkotōn taxeis*** referred to in the closing formulas of the declarations of *anachōrēsis*[172]) and tax reports such as statements of arrears issued by the collectors of the *laographia*. Outstanding examples of that are P.Corn. 24 [Philadelphia, AD 56]; SB XVIII 13862 [Tebtunis, AD 57], where the category is further qualified as οἱ καὶ ὄντες | ἀνευρέτων καὶ ἐν ἀναχωρήσ⟨ε⟩ι εἰς ἀγνοου|μένους τόπους [ll. 6-8], "those who have disappeared and have left for unknown places"; P.Ryl. IV 595 [Philadelphia, AD 57], a report by the *praktōr laographias* stating the total amount of the poll dues and then providing a *kat'andra* list ἀνακεχωρηκότων ἀπόρων (ll. 11 ff.) and ἄλλων ἀνακεχωρηκότων (ll. 57 ff.)[173]. Particularly relevant, and

166 Hanson 2007b: 179-80; see above for the declarations of *anachōrēsis*.

167 Rémondon 1951: 226 ff.

168 E.g. Chr.W. 325 [Soknopaiou Nesos, AD 140]; P.Leit. 5 [Tebtunis, AD 180]; P.Lips. II 146 [Arsinoites, AD 189]; SB XXII 15494 [Nilopolis, Ars., II-III AD]; PSI XII 1243 [Dionysias, Ars., AD 208]; SB XX 14335 [early III AD]; cf. P.Lips. II 145, 52-6 [Arsinoe, AD 189] (mention of a petition); P.Oslo III 81, 8-9 [Arsinoites, AD 197] (trial proceedings); SB XXIV 15904, 9 [Theadelphia, II-III AD] (designation of substitutes); P.Oxy. LXXVII 5107, 23-4 [Oxyrhynchus, AD 210/1] (mention of *aporoi* in a contract of substitution). For *aporoi* in the liturgy system cf. Lewis 1963: 13; Drecoll 1997: 333-4; Lewis 1997, 159-60.

169 The editors interpreted the papyrus as "a copy of an official certificate of lack of means", but the title itself points to a "copy of a list of *aporoi*", and *esti de* is the typical formulaic heading of lists of any type. Indeed already Johnson 1936, 251 identified it as a "copy of a register of paupers".

170 Rémondon 1951: 229 ff.; see above. A similar term, also to be found in reports only, is ***aparastatos*** (e.g. SPP IV pagg. 58-83; cf. Wilcken 1912: 198).

171 Hombert-Préaux 1937: 261; cf. the instructions given by the prefect to the *stratēgos* in SB XIV 11374 (Arsinoites?, AD 168) with the comment by Świderek 1974. On the coincidence of the *anakechōrē-kotes* with the *aneuretoi aporoi* see Lewis 1980: 64.

172 Cf. Hanson 2007a: 267.

173 Cf. Lewis 1980 : 64.

often quoted, is SB IV 7462 = P.Graux I 2, a draft petition to the prefect by the *praktores laographias* of some Arsinoitic villages who, in AD 57, worried because tax collection was endangered διὰ τὸ τοὺς μὲν | ἀνακεχωρηκέναι ἀπόρους, τοὺς δὲ τετε|λευτηκέ[ναι] μὴ ἔχοντας ἀγχιστεῖς (ll. 9-11), "due to those lacking means who fled away and those who died without heirs-at-law". The importance of drawing such lists is apparent: they had to be subtracted from the general tax *sunopseis*, and, later on, they would be the base for calculating the *merismoi aporōn* and *anakechōrēkotōn*, the assessments imposed to compensate the deficits[174].

P.Sijp. 26, the *sunopsis*, was found among the papers of Nemesion, the *praktōr laographias* of Philadelphia, and was most likely written by himself[175]. It served as a comparison to check the payments collected against the tax ledgers ("daybooks")[176], and it was certainly drawn up on the basis of information provided by the *kōmogrammateus* (or the amphodarch) in the form of the *apaitēsima kat'andra*, i.e. viritim tax checklists[177], likely along with copies of the different types of lists that we already discussed. This allowed the tax officials to avoid stuffing their documents with lots of personal information, which could be easily retrieved backwards elsewhere. The lack of detailed personal descriptions at the upper levels of the reporting paperwork flow is, therefore, quite rational: what mattered were just the data about tax collection (payments and exemptions), and there was no need to further identify the tax-payers. Moreover, the higher offices themselves were in possession of copies of the census declarations and of equally detailed population registers, so that they were able to cross the information.

This interplay of reports at different detail levels can explain, for example, a weird occurrence among the official medical reports. It is a particular group of official documents issued by physicians, and from the 160s by the *dēmosioi iatroi* (doctors practicing a public service), to the civil authorities in order to attest the actual conditions of a sick or a dead; at least in the latter case they may be considered connected in some way to the notifications of death[178]. The public medical reports (*prosphōnēseis iatrou*) follow a regular formulaic scheme drawing from both scientific and administrative technical phraseology, and their authors are always identified through the shortest, and most common, personal attributes:

---

174 Lewis 1937; Rémondon 1951; Forselv 1996: 159.

175 Hanson 2007b: 173.

176 The checking procedure is described by Hanson 2007b: 173 n. 4.

177 Cf. P.Fay. 40: Introduction, p. 157; Hoogendijk 2007: 135-6. The procedure is clarified by BGU II 457 = Chr.W. 252 [Karanis, *p.* AD 132/3], the copy of an "additional notice" (ἀντί[γ]ρ(αφον) προσγράφου, l. 1) sent by the *kōmogrammateus* to the *praktōr sitikōn* in order to correct the data from a previous viritim *apaitēsimon* of grain dues (ἐπ⟨ε⟩ὶ [δ]ι̣' οὗ ἐπιδέδωκά σοι ἀπαιτησίμου | κατ' ἄνδρ[α] σιτικῶν καθη[κ]όντων, ll. 4-5): cf. Larson 1954: 22; Youtie 1973: 1001-2. On the composition of the *apaitēsima* see Rostowzew 1906: 212: "Daneben werden von den Dorfschreibern noch Listen κατ' ἄνδρα alphabetisch angelegt, wohl auf Grund und als Material für die ἀπαιτήσιμα geführt".

178 There was no direct connection between death notifications and official medical reports, since the latter were requested by the *stratēgos* after receiving special petitions, and were by no means a routine practice. Yet the purpose of both was the same (to state someone's death in an official way), and the administrative results may have been the same as well (cancellation from the census lists, etc.). I dealt with the topic of official medical reports elsewhere: I refer to Reggiani 2016c & 2018a/b for general information and further bibliography, and to Reggiani 2015 for the special context of the papyrus mentioned here below.

name + patronymic, and provenance. It is therefore surprising the fact that in one report, P.Oxy. III 476, redacted at Oxyrhynchus in AD 159-161 by two mummifiers (*entaphiastai*), the senders are identified with a very detailed personal recording: patronymic, metronymic, age, physical marks, provenance (ll. 2-9: παρὰ Θώνιος Φλώρου | μητρὸς Πτολέμας | ὡς (ἐτῶν) λε οὐ(λὴ) καρπ(ῷ) ἀρ(ιστερῷ) καὶ Θώ|νιος Πεταῦτος μητρὸς | Ταουῆτος ὡς (ἐτῶν) ξβ ἀσήμ(ου) | ἀμφοτέρων ἀπ' Ὀξυρύγ|χων πόλεως ἐνταφι|αστῶν[179]). As has been recently shown[180], the identification of a doctor was a complex matter involving social, cultural and legal issues. We know that the public physicians, in particular, were subject to a *dokimasia*, i.e. an official evaluation of their privileged status[181], and we must guess that the authorities were in possession of official lists of them (just as they kept lists of priests, metropolitans, and other privileged categories). We may infer that thanks to this pre-existing official registration the (public) doctors did not need any particular description, while other specialists involved in the same matters did. The same, likely, happened with all the population lists and registers we have dealt with so far[182].

Conclusions

A main trend can be outlined in the administrative steps from personal declarations to local registers and further reports and lists. Most of the personal details (including the place of residence expressed by the *anagraphomenos*-clause) tend to disappear, since the identity of the indivuals is no longer concerned and they are not specific to the relevant administrative branch, and are replaced with new identifying technical terms, related to the procedure of registration and of categorization of the population, for the eventual purpose of tax management. The following table visualizes the processing workflow.

Phase 1: submission of personal declarations	→ Phase 2: collection of personal declarations	→ Phase 3: extraction of data from personal declarations	→ Phase 4: processing of data for fiscal purposes	→ Phase 5: tax registers
Census declarations Death notifications Birth notifications *epikrisis* applications *abrochia* declarations Livestock declarations Priest registrations *anachōrēsis* declarations	*Eikonismos*	*laographia kat'andra* *laographia en kephalaiō* Lists of privileged categories Lists of *aphēlikes* Lists of *ektos sunopseōs* Lists of dead Lists of *aporoi* Lists of *anakechōrēkotes*	*apaitēsimon* ↓ *sunopsis*	(several types)

179 The papyrus is cited by Hübsch 1968: 55 just because the physical description is located in a different place than the usual.

180 Israelowich 2014.

181 In the medical reports from the Hermopolites we find even a standard formula highlighting the belonging of the local *dēmosioi iatroi* to the group τῶν ἐν τῷ ὡρισμένῳ ἀριθμῷ τῶν δοκίμων τῆς αὐτῆς πόλεως, "of those included in the fixed number of the selected of the same city": cf. Reggiani 2016c, with further bibliography in footnote C-19.

182 One final question would concern the use of personal identifiers in non-*laographia* tax and land reports, but a full overview of the different types of documentation stemming from the various tax offices would require a separate discourse, and space is a tyrant. I attempt a sort of preliminary categorization, limited to the offices of the *sitologoi* (collectors of taxes in kind) and *praktores* (collectors of taxes in cash), in Yiftach-Reggiani forthc., to which I refer for further bibliography. On tax accounting mechanics cf. Yiftach 2015a.

A further acquisition of the proposed survey is the outline of a very strict sectorial vocabulary in defining the population lists, which are the keystone of the entire processing workflow and can be summarized as follows[183]. ***Kat'andra*** is not a typology of list by itself, but rather a type of arrangement. For examples, *graphai* can be organized *kat'andra* (see e.g. P.Tebt. II 298 [Tebtunis, AD 108]) as well as *apaitēsima* (see e.g. P.Poethke 20 [Arsinoites, II/III AD]) or many other reports and registers. There were special scribes, called *katandrographoi*, "whose speciality was to draft itemized tax records"[184]: the ones hired in P.Mich. 603 (see above) belonged certainly to this category. Frequently juxtaposed to the *kat'andra*, ***epi kephalaiou / en kephalaiō*** is the summarized version ("by headers", literally[185]) of any type of report / register. Specific types of listing documents are instead: ***apologismos***, a detailed account containing, or used for, calculations; ***logos***, an accounting list (usually less detailed than the *apologismos*) containing, or used for, calculations; ***taxis***, an officially established roster; ***graphē***, a list consequent to, or aimed at, a registration act; ***gnōmōn***, a register or index ("assessment") containing updated data to check other reports.

---

183 For a wider overview of the terminology related to "lists" see the contribution by Willy Clarysse in this same volume.

184 Hanson 1991: 188. This profession is attested in one of the famous tax rolls from Karanis, P.Mich. IV.1 224, 2333 (AD 173). It apparently required some special skills to extract the relevant information from scattered records and to transfer them into viritim lists.

185 Assuming *kephalaion* = "header" in the sense of Italian idiom "per [sommi] capi": the metaphor is the very same.

Bibliography

V. Arangio-Ruiz, Intorno agli ΑΣΤΟΙ dell'Egitto greco-romano, RIDA 4 (1950), 7-20.

J.-J. Aubert, Le vocabulaire de la fiscalité en Egypte gréco-romaine, in Vocabulaire et expression de l'économie dans le monde antique, eds. J. Andreau, V. Chankowski, Bordeaux 2007, 385-97.

S. Avogadro, Le ΑΠΟΓΡΑΦΑΙ di proprietà nell'Egitto greco-romano, "Aegyptus" 15 (1935), 131-206.

R.S. Bagnall, Reading Papyri, Writing Ancient History, London-New York 1995.

R.S. Bagnall, B.W. Frier, The Demography of Roman Egypt, Cambridge 1994.

E. Battaglia, Dichiarazioni templari. A proposito di P.Oxy. XLIX, 3473, "Aegyptus" 64 (1984), 79-99.

E. Battaglia, Due liste di sacerdoti, "Aegyptus" 66 (1986), 85-99.

M. Bergamasco, Tre note a tre ΔΙΔΑΣΚΑΛΙΚΑΙ, SEP 1 (2004), 31-41.

E. Bickermann, Beiträge zur antiken Urkundengeschichte, APF 9 (1930), 24-46.

I. Bieżuńska-Małowist, Gli schiavi nati in casa ("oikogeneis") e il carattere del lavoro servile nell'Egitto greco-romano, in Storia sociale ed economica dell'età classica negli studi polacchi contemporanei, ed. I. Bieżuńska-Małowist, Milano 1975, 111-29.

I. Bieżuńska-Małowist, L'esclavage dans l'Égypte gréco-romaine. Seconde Partie: Période romaine, Wroclaw - Warszawa - Kraków - Gdansk 1977.

M.V. Biscottini, L'archivio di Tryphon, tessitore di Oxyrhynchos, "Aegyptus" 46 (1966), 60-90 & 186-292.

H. Braunert, ΙΔΙΑ. Studien zur Bevölkerungsgeschichte des ptolemäischen und römischen Ägypten, JJP 9-10 (1955-6), 211-328.

H. Braunert, Zur Terminologie der Volkszählung im frühen römischen Ägypten, "Eos" 48 (1956), 53-66.

H. Braunert, Die Binnenwanderung. Studien zur Sozialgeschicthe Ägyptens in der Ptolemäer- und Kaiserzeit, Bonn 1964.

H. Braunert, Cives Romani und ΚΑΤ' ΟΙΚΙΑΝ ΑΠΟΓΡΑΦΑΙ, in Antidorum Martino David obltatum. Miscellanea papyrologica, edd. E. Boswinkel, B.A. van Groningen, P.W. Pestman [P.Lugd.Bat. 18], Lugdunum Batavorum 1968, 11-21.

Y. Broux, Creating a New Local Elite: The Establishment of the Metropolitan Orders of Roman Egypt, APF 59 (2013), 143-53.

A. Bülow-Jacobsen, Two Greek Papyri Carlsberg from Tebtunis. P.Carlsberg 53 and 57, ZPE 78 (1989), 125-31.

F. Burkhalter, Le mobilier des sanctuaires d'Egypte et les "listes des pretres et du cheirismos", ZPE 59 (1985), 123-34.

S. Bussi, Le élites locali nella provincia d'Egitto di prima età imperiale, Milano 2008.

A. Caldara, L'indicazione dei connotati nei documenti papiracei dell'Egitto greco-romano, Milano 1924.

A. Calderini, Sei esemplari di un'unica scheda di censimento romano, "Aegyptus" 3 (1922), 341-5.

A. Calderini, La composizione della famiglia secondo le schede di censimento dell'Egitto romano, Milano 1923.

D. Canducci, I 6475 cateci greci dell'Arsinoite, "Aegyptus" 70 (1990), 211-55.

L. Casarico, Il controllo della popolazione nell'Egitto romano, 1. Le denunce di morte, Azzate 1985 [C.Pap.Gr. II].

W. Clarysse, Slaven en papyri, "Kleio" 19 (1989), 1-22.

W. Clarysse, *Tomoi Synkollesimoi*, in Ancient Archives and Archival Traditions. Concepts of Record-Keeping in the Ancient World, ed. M. Brosius, Oxford 2003, 344-59.

W.G. Claytor, R.S. Bagnall, The Beginnings of the Roman Provincial Census: A New Declaration from 3 BCE, GRBS 55 (2015), 637-53.

S. Daris, Il lessico fisionomico nei papiri greci, in Lingue tecniche del greco e del latino. Atti del I Seminario internazionale sulla letteratura scientifica e tecnica greca e latina, eds. S. Sconocchia, L. Toneatto, Trieste 1993, 99-104.

L. de Blois, The Military Factor in the Onset of Crises in the Roman Empire in the Third Century AD, in Impact of the Roman Army (200 BC - AD 476). Economic, Social, Political, Religious and Cultural Aspects. Proceedings of the Sixth Workshop of the International Network Impact of Empire: Roman Empire, 200 B.C. - A.D. 476 (Capri 2005), eds. L. de Blois and E. Lo Cascio, Leiden-Boston 2007, 497-507.

D. Delia, Roman Alexandrian: Studies in Its Social History, Diss. New York 1983.

D. Delia, Alexandrian Citizenship During the Roman Principate, Atlanta 1991.

M. Depauw, Do Mothers Matter? The Emergence of Metronymics in Early Roman Egypt, in The Language of the Papyri, eds. T.V. Evans, D.D. Obbink, Oxford 2010, 121-39.

M. Depauw, Physical Descriptions, Registration and εἰκονίζειν with New Interpretations for P.Par. 65 and P.Oxy. I 34, ZPE 176 (2011), 189-99.

M. Depauw, Elements of Identification in Egypt, 800 BC – AD 300, in Depauw-Coussement 2014, 75-102.

M. Depauw, S. Coussement (eds.), Legal Documents in Ancient Societies III: Identifiers and Identification Methods in the Ancient World, Leuven-Paris-Walpole (MA) 2014.

T. Derda, Ἀρσινοΐτης νομός. Administration of the Fayum under Roman Rule, Warsaw 2006 (JJP Suppl. VII).

C. Drecoll, Die Liturgien im römischen Kaiserreich des 3. und 4. Jh. n. Chr., Stuttgart 1997

R. Duttenhöfer (Hg.), Griechische Urkunden der Papyrussammlung zu Leipzig (P.Lips. II), München-Leipzig 2002.

J.A.S. Evans, A Social and Economic History of an Egyptian Temple in the Greco-Roman Period, YCS 17 (1961), 143-283.

M. Falletti, Textes concernant le recensement dans l'Hermoupolite, CE 39 (1964), 111-9.

I.L. Forselv, Receipt for Payments of *Syntaximon* and *Merismoi*, SO 71 (1996), 156-71.

I.L. Forselv, Registration of an Apprentice: P.Osl. Inv. no. 1470, SO 73 (1998), 116-24.

E.H. Gilliam, The Archives of the Temple of Soknobraisis at Bacchias, YCS 10 (1947), 179-281.

T. Grassi, Formulari, "Aegyptus" 3 (1922), 206-11.

W. Habermann, Aspekte des Bewässerungswesens im kaiserzeitlichen Ägypten I: Die „Erklärungen für nicht überflutetes Land" (Abrochia-Deklarationen), in Miscellanea oeconomica. Studien zur antiken Wirtschaftgeschichte, hrsgg. K. Ruffing, B. Tenger, St. Katharinen 1997, 214-83.

A.E. Hanson, Caligulan Month-Names at Philadelphia and Related Matters, in Atti del XVII Congresso Internazionale di Papirologia (Napoli 1983), Napoli 1984, III, 1107-18.

A.E. Hanson, The Keeping of Records at Philadelphia in the Julio-Claudian Period and the "Economic Crisis under Nero", in Proceedings of the XVIII International Congress of Papyrology (Athens 1986), ed. B.D. Mandilaras, Athens 1988, II, 261-77.

A.E. Hanson, Ancient Illiteracy, in Literacy in the Roman World, Ann Arbor (MI) 1991, 159-98.

A.E. Hanson (2007a), Sworn Declarations of Removal from Herakleides Division, Arsinoite Nome, in Akten des 23. Internationalen Papyrologenkongresses. Wien, 22.-28. Juli 2001, ed. B. Palme, Wien 2007, 267-71.

A.E. Hanson (2007b), Estimate for Capitation Tax of Philadelphia for Year 11 of Claudius: A Synopsis of the Village, in Papyri in Memory of P.J. Sijpesteijn (P.Sijp.), eds. A.J.B. Sirks, K.A. Worp, with the assistance of R.S. Bagnall and R.P.Salomons, Oakville (CT) 2007, 172-84 [P.Sijp. 26].

J. Hasebroek, Das Signalement in den Papyrusurkunden, Berlin-Leipzig 1921.

H. Henne, Deux papyrus grecs du Musée du Caire, "Aegyptus" 6 (1925), 330-4.

D.W. Hobson, P.Vindob. Gr. 24951 + 24556: New Evidence for Tax-Exempt Status in Roman Egypt, in Atti del XVII Congresso Internazionale di Papirologia (Napoli 1983), Napoli 1984, III, 847-64.

M. Hombert, C. Préaux, Les papyrus de la Fondation Égyptologique reine Élisabeth II, Certificat d'exemption de laographia, CE 12 (1937), 259-64.

M. Hombert, C. Préaux, Recherches sur le recensement dans l'Egypte Romaine [P.Lugd.Bat. V], Bruxelles 1952.

F.A.J. Hoogendijk, Amtliche Korrespondenz zwischen Dorfschreiber und Eklogistes, in Papyri in Memory of P.J. Sijpesteijn (P.Sijp.), eds. A.J.B. Sirks, K.A. Worp, with the assistance of R.S. Bagnall and R.P. Salomons, Oakville (CT) 2007, 128-39 [P.Sijp. 20].
G. Hübsch, Die Personalangaben als Identifizierungsvermerke im Recht der gräko-ägyptischen Papyri, Berlin 1968.
I. Israelowich, Identifications of Physicians during the High Empire, in Depauw-Coussement 2014, 233-52.
A. Jördens, Statthalterliche Verwaltung in der römischen Kaiserzeit. Studien zum *praefectus Aegypti*, Stuttgart 2009.
A. Jördens, Status and Citizenship, in The Oxford Handbook of Roman Egypt, ed. C. Riggs, Oxford 2012, 247-59.
A.C. Johnson, An Economic Survey of Ancient Rome, II. Roman Egypt to the Reign of Diocletian, Baltimore (MY) 1936 [repr. New York 1959].
C.W. Keyes, *Syntaximon* and *Laographia* in the Arsinoite Nome, AJP 52 (1931), 263-9.
Th. Kruse, Der königliche Schreiber und die Gauverwaltung, Untersuchungen zur Verwaltungsgeschichte Ägyptens in der Zeit von Augustus bis Phillipus Arabs (30 v. Chr. – 245 n. Chr.), I-II, München 2002.
M.E. Larson, The Officials of Karanis, 27 BC-227 AD. A Contribution to the Study of Local Government in Egypt under Roman Rule, PhD Diss., Ann Arbor 1954.
N. Lewis, ΜΕΡΙΣΜΟΣ ΑΝΑΚΕΧΩΡΗΚΟΤΩΝ: An Aspect of the Roman Oppression in Egypt, JEA 23 (1937), 63-75.
N. Lewis, Leitourgia Papyri. Documents on Compulsory Public Service in Egypt under Roman Rule, Philadelphia 1963.
N. Lewis, The γραφὴ δημοσίων of Roman Egypt, CE 45 (1970), 161-5.
N. Lewis, *Notationes Legentis*, BASP 17 (1980), 61-5.
N. Lewis, *Notationes Legentis*, BASP 19 (1982), 71-82.
N. Lewis, Life in Egypt under Roman Rule, Oxford 1983.
N. Lewis, The Compulsory Public Services of Roman Egypt, 2nd ed., Firenze 1997.
S. Link, *Anachoresis*. Steuerflucht im Ägypten der frühen Kaiserzeit, „Klio“ 75 (1993), 306-20.
V. Martin, Une ΓΡΑΦΗ ΑΝΔΡΩΝ du premier siècle, JJP 4 (1950), 143-9.
P. Mertens, Les Services de l'État Civil et le contrôle de la population à Oxyrhynchus au IIIe siècle de notre ère, Brussel 1958.
G. Messeri Savorelli, La popolazione di Soknopaiu Nesos nel 178/9 d.C., AnPap 1 (1989), 7-14.
M. Mirković, Foreshadowing Later Development or Existing Practice: Diocletian's Fiscal Reforms and Changes in the First Three Centuries, in Proceedings of the 24th International Congress of Papyrology (Helsinki 2004), eds. J. Frösén, T. Purola, E. Salmenkivi, Helsinki 2007, II, 743-55.
O. Montevecchi, ΓΡΑΦΑΙ ΙΕΡΕΩΝ, "Aegyptus" 12 (1932), 317-28.
O. Montevecchi, Ricerche di sociologia nei documenti dell'Egitto greco-romano, V. Le denunce di morte, "Aegyptus" 26 (1946), 111-29.
O. Montevecchi, Ricerche di sociologia nei documenti dell'Egitto greco-romano, VI. Denunce di nascita di greco-egizi, "Aegyptus" 27 (1947), 3-24.
O. Montevecchi, *Laos*. Linee di una ricerca storico-linguistica, in Actes du XVe Congrès International de Papyrologie (Bruxelles-Louvain 1977), eds. J. Bingen, G. Nachtergael, IV, Bruxelles 1979, 51-67.
O. Montevecchi, *Aigyptios – Hellen* in età romana, in Studi in onore di Edda Bresciani, eds. S.F. Bondì, S. Pernigotti, F. Serra, A. Vivian, Pisa 1985, 339-53.
C. Nelson, Status Declarations in Roman Egypt, Amsterdam 1979.
J. Oates, Census Totals: Nemesion's Notes, in Collectanea Papyrologica. Texts Published in Honor of H.C. Youtie, ed. A.E. Hanson, Bonn 1976, I, 189-96 [P.Coll.Youtie I 20].
G. Parássoglou, On Priests and Their Affairs in Roman Egypt, "Studia Papyrologica" 12 (1973), 7-21.

G. Parássoglou, Imperial Estates in Roman Egypt, Amsterdam 1978 [ASP 18].
D. Rathbone, Egypt, Augustus and Roman Taxation, CCG 4 (1993), 81-112.
N. Reggiani, Ispezionare cadaveri: mummificatori, medici e anatomisti nell'Egitto greco-romano (a proposito di P.Oxy. III 476), MBAH 33 (2015), 75-86.
N. Reggiani (2016a), Data Processing and State Management in late Ptolemaic and Roman Egypt: The Project 'Synopsis' and the Archive of Menches, in Proceedings of the 27th International Congress of Papyrology (Warsaw, 28 July – 3 August 2013), eds. T. Derda, A. Lajtar, J. Urbanik, Warsaw 2016, III, 1415-44.
N. Reggiani (2016b), Declaration of Death, in Medicalia Online, ed. I. Andorlini, Parma 2016, URL: http://www.papirologia.unipr.it/CPGM/medicalia/vocab/index.php?tema=177.
N. Reggiani (2016c), Medical Report, in Medicalia Online, ed. I. Andorlini, Parma 2016, URL: http://www.papirologia.unipr.it/CPGM/medicalia/vocab/index.php?tema=171.
N. Reggiani, Tax Collection and Grain Measures in Roman Egpyt: An Account Involving *paralēmptai* and a Receipt Issued by the *sitologoi* of Berenikis Aigialou, With Some Notes on Measure Standards (*paralēmptikon*, *epaiton*), APF 63 (2017), 59-88.
N. Reggiani (2018a), Ispezioni e perizie ufficiali nell'Egitto greco-romano: il *corpus* dei rapporti professionali (*prosphoneseis*), in Lavoro, lavoratori e dinamiche sociali a Roma antica: persistenze e trasformazioni. Atti delle giornate di studio (Roma Tre, 25-26 maggio 2017), ed. A. Marcone, Roma 2018, 203-19.
N. Reggiani (2018b), I papiri greci di medicina come fonti storiche: il caso dei rapporti dei medici pubblici nell'Egitto romano e bizantino, "Aegyptus" 98 (2018), 107-30.
F. Reiter, P.Osl. inv. 1470 und die Webersteuer für Minderjährige in Oxyrhynchos, APF 48 (2002), 116-24.
F. Reiter, Die Nomarchen des Arsinoites. Ein Beitrag zum Steuerwesen im römischen Ägypten, Paderborn-München-Wien-Zürich 2004.
R. Rémondon, Ἀπορικόν et Μερισμὸς ἀπόρων, ASAE 51 (1951), 221-45.
M. Rolandi, I mestieri artigiani nelle κατ' οἰκίαν ἀπογραφαί e nelle liste di popolazione dell'Egitto romano: aspetti e problemi, "Aegyptus" 87 (2007), 181-97.
M. Rostowzew, Kornerhebung und -transport im griechisch-römischen Ägypten, APF 3 (1906), 201-24.
M. Rostowzew, Studien zur Geschichte des Römischen Kolonates, Leipzig-Berlin 1910 [APF Beih. 1].
K. Ruffing, Die berufliche Spezialisierung in Handel und Handwerk. Untersuchungen zu ihrer Entwicklung und zu ihren Bedingungen in der römischen Kaiserzeit im östlichen Mittelmeerraum auf der Grundlage griechischer Inschriften und Papyri, St. Katharinen 2008.
C. Sánchez-Moreno Ellart, *Professio Liberorum*. Las declaraciones y los registros de nacimientos en derecho romano, con especial atencion a las fuentes papirologicas, Madrid 2001.
C. Sánchez-Moreno Ellart, ὑπομνήματα ἐπιγεννήσεως: the Greco-Egyptian Birth Returns in Roman Egypt and the Case of P.Petaus 1–2, APF 56 (2010), 91-129.
W. Scheidel, Quantifying the Sources of Slaves in the Early Roman Empire, JRS 87 (1997), 156-69.
W. Scheidel, The Death Declarations of Roman Egypt: A Re-appraisal, BASP 36 (1999), 53-70.
F. Schulz, Roman Registers of Births and Births Certificates, JRS 32 (1942), 78-91.
P.J. Sijpesteijn, Another Extract from a Census Register, ZPE 62 (1986), 158.
P.J. Sijpesteijn, Settlement of a Debt and Extracts from Census Registers, ZPE 98 (1993), 283-91.
P.J. Sijpesteijn, Three Papyri Concerning Census, ZPE 107 (1995), 271-6.
J.A. Straus, L'achat et la vente des esclaves dans l'Égypte romaine. Contribution papyrologique à l'étude de l'esclavage dans une province orientale de l'Empire romain, München-Leipzig 2004.
J.A. Straus, L'affranchissement dans l'Égypte gréco-romaine. À propos d'un ouvrage récent sur l'affranchissement et le statut des affranchis dans le monde grec antique, « L'Antiquité classique » 78 (2009), 233-9.
A. Swiderek, ΟΙ ΤΩ ΟΝΤΙ ΑΝΑΚΕΧΩΡΗΚΟΤΕΣ (P Berlin 16036 verso col. II 1-20), in Festschrift zum 150jährigen Bestehen des Berliner Ägyptischen Museums, Berlin 1974, 425-9.

R. Taubenschlag, ΕΝΝΟΜΟΣ ΗΛΙΚΙΑ nel diritto dei papiri, "Aegyptus" 12 (1932), 141-4.
R. Taubenschlag, The Law of Greco-Roman Egypt in the Light of the Papyri (332 BC-640 AD), Warszawa 1955[2].
J.D. Thomas, The Introduction of *Dekaprotoi* and Comarchs into Egypt in the Third Century A.D., ZPE 19 (1975), 111-9.
V. Tcherikover, *Syntaxis* and *Laographia*, JJP 4 (1950), 179-207.
P. Van Minnen, Αἱ ἀπὸ γυμνασίου. 'Greek' Women and the Greek 'Elite' in the Metropoleis of Roman Egypt, in Le rôle et le statut de la femme en Egypte hellénistique, romaine et byzantine. Actes du colloque international Bruxelles-Leuven 27–29 novembre 1997, eds. H. Melaerts, L. Mooren, Leuven 2002, 337-53.
M. Vandoni, Testi per il corso di papirologia. I documenti di Trifone (dai papiri di Ossirinco), Milano 1974.
S.L. Wallace, Taxation in Egypt from Augustus to Diocletian, Princeton (NJ)-London 1938.
C. Wessely, Der Wiener Papyrus Nr. 31, "Wiener Studien" 4 (1882), 175-96.
J. Whitehorne, The Ephebate and the Gymnasial Class in Roman Egypt, BASP 19 (1982), 171-84.
U. Wilcken, ΑΠΟΓΡΑΦΑΙ, "Hermes" 28 (1893), 230-51.
U. Wilcken, Grundzüge und Chrestomathie der Papyruskunde, I Bd. Historischer Teil, II Hälfte Chrestomathie, Leipzig-Berlin 1912.
E. Wipszycka, Das Textilhandwerk und der Staat im Römischen Ägypten, APF 18 (1966), 1-22.
U. Yiftach, A Gymnasial Registration Report from Oxyrhynchus, BASP 47 (2010), 45-65.
U. Yiftach, P.Col. inv. 33r and the Processing of Data in Early Roman Egypt, in Papyrological Texts in Honor of R.S. Bagnall, eds. R. Ast., H. Cuvigny, T.M. Hickey, J. Lougovaya, Durham (NC) 2012, 349-54 [= P.Bagnall 70].
U. Yiftach, Did BGU XIV 2367 Work?, in Depauw-Coussement 2014, 103-18.
U. Yiftach, From Arsinoe to Alexandria and Beyond: Taxation and Information in Early Roman Egypt, JJP 45 (2015), 291-312.
U. Yiftach, *Apator Metros*: The Rise of a Formula in Bureaucratic Perspective. Response to Maria Nowak, in Symposion 2015. Conferências sobre a História do Direito grego e helenístico (Coimbra, 1-4 Setembro 2015), eds. D.F. Leão, G. Thür, Wien 2016, 115-20.
U. Yiftach, The Rise of the Flexible Template: Patterns of Change in Identification Methods between the Ptolemaic and the Roman Period, in L'identification des personnes dans les mondes grecs, eds. R. Guicharrousse, P. Ismard, M. Vallet, A.-E. Veïsse, Paris, forthcoming.
U. Yiftach (forthc.1), The *Gnomon* in Context: Status Designations and Bureaucratic Compartmentalization in Roman Egypt, in Dienst nach Vorschrift? Vergleichende Studien zum *Gnomon* des *Idios Logos*, 3. Wiener Kolloquium zur antiken Rechtsgeschichte (19.-20.6.2014), ed. T. Kruse, forthcoming.
U. Yiftach (forthc.2), The Notion of a Flexible Template, in Proclamation et preuve d'identité dans le monde grec (18 -20 juin 2015), Paris, forthcoming.
U. Yiftach, N. Reggiani, *Synopsis*: Data Processing in Ptolemaic and Roman Egypt, forthcoming.
H.C. Youtie, Notes on Papyri, in Scriptiunculae, II, Amsterdam 1973, 1001-17 [= BICS 11 (1964), 15-30].
H.C. Youtie, P.Mich.inv. 3244: Receipt for Poll Tax, in Scriptiunculae Posteriores, II, Bonn 1982, 597-8 [= ZPE 38 (1980), 287-8].

Fiskalische Buchführung in Theadelpheia

Thomas Kruse, Wien

Im Oktober/November des Jahres 1912 unternahm Wilhelm Schubart seine dritte Reise nach Ägypten, unter anderem mit der erklärten Absicht, dort Papyri anzukaufen. Schubart wurde, wie auch schon früher, begleitet von seiner Frau Frida, die über die gemeinsam mit ihrem Mann unternommenen Reisen ein kleines Büchlein mit dem Titel „Von Wüste, Nil und Sonne" geschrieben hat, in welchem sie in sehr lebendiger und anschaulicher Weise ihre Reiseeindrücke verarbeitet hat. Es wurde im Jahr 1922 in Berlin herausgebracht,[1] und in diesem kleinen Buch berichtet Frida Schubart auch von einem Papyrusankauf in einem Dorf in der Nähe von Kairo und gibt eine sehr humorvolle Schilderung von den Verhandlungen mit dem geschäftstüchtigen Ägypter, dem sie das Pseudonym Abul Much – „Vater der List" – gegeben hat. Dieser Mann machte die Schubarts zunächst mit einigen kleineren Papyri neugierig und präsentierte ihnen dann eine Schachtel mit acht gut erhaltenen Papyrusrollen, deren Preis er bei den Verhandlungen in geschickter Weise in die Höhe zu treiben versuchte.[2]

Diese schließlich für die Berliner Sammlung erworbenen Rollen gehören zusammen mit anderen ähnlichen Texten offensichtlich zu einem Archiv administrativer bzw. fiskaladministrativer Provenienz, in dessen Mittelpunkt das Dorf Theadelpheia im Gau Arsinoites (dem heutigen Fayum) und sein Umland stehen. Bei Trismegistos.org firmiert das Archiv unter dem Namen „Administrative Archive of Theadelpheia".[3] Die frühen Editoren des Archivs, wie William L. Westermann und Clinton W. Keyes sowie Heinz Kortenbeutel, vermuteten das Büro des Toparchen als seinen Entstehungsort, und ihrer Auffassung haben sich weitere Autoren angeschlossen. Auf die Problematik dieser Zuweisung wird noch zurückzukommen sein. Der exakte Umfang des Archivs und seine zeitliche Erstreckung ist aufgrund der vielen Texte, die ihm nicht sicher zugewiesen können, und weil außerdem einige Rollen unpubliziert sind, noch unklar. Seinen Kernbestand bilden aber sicherlich die erwähnten Rollen in Berlin sowie weitere in der Sammlung der Columbia University in New York. Sie enthalten Abrechnungen über Geld- und Naturalsteuereinnahmen sowie Bankquittungen. Die Rollen datieren aus dem 2. Jh., wobei die Rektoseiten in der Regierungszeit der Kaiser Hadrian und Antoninus Pius beschriftet und die Versoseiten in der Zeit des Antoninus Pius und des Marc Aurel wiederverwendet wurden. Nach einem kurzen Vorbericht über den Inhalt der Berliner Rollen, den Schubart kurz nach ihrem Ankauf in den Beiheften der Berliner Museen gegeben hat, publizierte Wilhelm Schubart selbst im Jahr 1919 ihre berühmteste Versoseite, nämlich die Epitome des Gnomon des Idios Logos, einer Sammlung von Vorschriften und Präzedenzfällen zu Rechts- und Verwaltungsma-

1 Frida Schubart, Von Wüste, Nil und Sonne. Mit Zeichnungen von Alfred Bollacher, Berlin 1922.
2 Schubart, Von Wüste, Nil und Sonne (siehe o. Anm. 1) 71–77.
3 Siehe https://www.trismegistos.org/arch/archives/pdf/247.pdf.

terien, welche in die Kompetenz des *procurator* des Idios Logos fallen, einer Finanzverwaltungsbehörde bei der Provinzverwaltung in Alexandria.[4] 1924 folgte die Publikation weiterer Stücke durch Karl Thunell (P.Berl. Thun.), die 1932 von Thure Kalén neu herausgegeben wurden (P.Berl. Leihg. I). In demselben Jahr erschien auch die Edition der Rektoseiten der in der Sammlung der Columbia University befindlichen Rollen durch William L. Westermann und Clinton W. Keyes (P. Col. II), und bereits ein Jahr zuvor hatte Hjalmar Frisk eine weitere Berliner Rolle mit Bankquittungen publiziert (P.Berl. Frisk 1). 1937 erschien dann die Publikation weiterer Berliner Steuerlisten aus der Feder von Heinz Kortenbeutel (BGU IX), und 1956 wurden schließlich die Versoseiten der Rollen in der Columbia University durch John Day und Clinton W. Keyes publiziert (P.Col. V). Weitere Listen in Berlin sind noch unpubliziert, eine davon wird von Günther Poethke (P.Berol. inv. 11654), die andere von mir selbst (P. Berol. inv. 11670) publiziert werden. Außerdem gehört zu dem Bestand des Theadelpheia-Archivs eine Papyrusrolle in der Biblioteca Medicea Laurenziana (P.Laur. inv. 19655), über die ihre Editoren Paul Heilporn, Diletta Minutoli und Rosario Pintaudi anläßlich des 28. Internationalen Papyrologenkongresses in Barcelona 2016 einen kurzen Vorbericht gegeben haben.[5] Ebenfalls zu dem Bestand des Archivs gehören weitere Texte in Berlin (BGU XIII 2270–2271) und Paris (P.Graux 30) sowie einer in Groningen (SB XVI 13060). Weitere zu dem Archiv gehörende Texte wurden schließlich Ende 2018 als BGU XXII 2905–2913 publiziert.

Wie bereits gesagt, handelt es sich bei den meisten der Rollen des Archivs von Theadelpheia um Listen über die Einnahme von Geld- und Naturalsteuern. Erstere wurden von den πράκτορες ἀργυρικῶν, den Geldsteuereinnehmern, die letztgenannten von den σιτολόγοι, den Verwaltern der öffentlichen Getreidespeicher, in welche das zumeist in Form von Weizen gezahlte Steuergetreide floß, erstellt.[6] Ich möchte nun im Folgenden insbesondere anhand der Akten der Geldsteuereinnehmer einige Details der fiskalischen Buchführung in Theadelpheia etwas näher beleuchten.

Eine Methode der fiskalischen Buchführung ist die Verbuchung von Einnahmen unter dem Namen der einzelnen Einzahler. Dieser Vorgang wird in der entsprechenden Dokumentation mit dem *terminus technicus* κατ' ἄνδρα bezeichnet und meint mithin eine Aufzeichnung "Mann für Mann". Beispielhaft hierfür ist etwa BGU IX 1891, ein κατ' ἄνδρα-Register über die täglichen Eingänge der Kopfsteuer aus dem 18. Jahr Hadrians (= 133/34 n.Chr.), welches vom 3. Dezember 133 n.Chr. datiert. Der erhaltene Teil dieses Textes umfaßt 20 Kolumnen mit mehr als 600 Zeilen und enthält die Namen von 432 verschiedenen Personen. Das Register wurde von den πράκτορες ἀργυρικῶν von Theadelpheia erstellt und enthält in Kol. I–XV die Abrechnung über Einzahlungen an Kopfsteuer (λαογραφία) und anderen kleineren Steuern (μερισμοί) für den Monat Phaophi des 18. Jahres des Kaisers Hadrian, also den Zeitraum von Ende September bis Ende Oktober 133 n.Chr. Diese Steuern fließen auf Provinzebene in das Finanzressort der διοίκησις, in welches für ge-

4 BGU V 1210.

5 *P.Laur. inv. 19655: un nouveau rouleau fiscal de Théadelphie*, in: 28th International Congress of Papyrology, Barcelona From 1 to 6 August 2016, Programme & Abstracts S. 81.

6 Zur agrargeschichtlichen Interpretation dieser Texte sowie zu ihrer Bedeutung für die Landbesitzverhältnisse siehe insbes. M. SHARP, *The Village of Theadelphia in the Fayyum: Land and Population in the Second Century*, in: A.K. Bowman – E. Rogan (Hg.), Agriculture in Egypt from Pharaonic to Modern Times (Proceedings of the British Academy 96), Oxford 1999, 159–192.

wöhnlich die regulären Steuereinnahmen flossen. Ich zitiere zur Veranschaulichung beispielhaft das Präskript und die ersten drei Einträge:

Παρὰ Ἥρωνος τοῦ Νείλου καὶ Ἥρωνος τοῦ Ἀκείους
2 τῶν β πρακ(τόρων) ἀργυ(ρικῶν) κώμης Θ̣εαδελφείας.
Κατ᾽ ἄνδ[ρ]α τῶν διαγεγραμμένων ἡμεῖν (l. ἡμῖν) ε[ἰ]ς ἀρίθμη(σιν)
4 μη[ν]ὸς Φαῶφι τοῦ ἐνεστῶ(τος) ιη (ἔτους) Ἁδριανοῦ Καίσα[ρ]ος τοῦ κυρίου.
Ἔστι δέ· λαογρα(φίας) καὶ ἄλλων μερισ(μῶν) λα Ἁ[θ]ὺρ δ
6 νθ / / / Ψεναμοῦνις Πρωτᾶ τοῦ Ἁρμιύσ̣ι(ος) μη(τρὸς) Ἐσον̣έ̣ω(ς) η χ(ωματικοῦ) στατ(ίωνος)
μζ / / / Πνεφερῶς ἀδελφὸς μη(τρὸς) τῆς αὐ(τῆς) η χ(ωματικοῦ) στατ(ίωνος)
8 μη / / / Πρωτᾶς Ἁρμιύσεως το(ῦ) Ἀφροδ(εισίου) μη(τρὸς) Τετα ̣( ) η χ(ωματικοῦ) στατ(ίωνος)

κ.τ.λ. (Z. 1–8).

„Von Heron, Sohn des Neilos, und Heron, Sohn des Akes, den beiden Einnehmern der Geldsteuern des Dorfes Theadelpheia. Liste nach Individuen über die an uns getätigten Einzahlungen auf Rechnung des Monats Phaophi des gegenwärtigen 18. Jahres des Hadrianus Caesar, des Herrn. Im Folgenden die Aufstellung über die Kopfsteuer und die anderen Merismoi. Hathyr 4.

59 (*3 Kontrollzeichen*) Psenamunis, Sohn des Protas, des Sohnes des Harmiysis, die Mutter ist Esoneus: 8, Chomatikon, *statio*-Abgabe

47 (*3 Kontrollzeichen*) Pnepheros, (sein) Bruder von derselben Mutter: 8, Chomatikon, *statio*-Abgabe

48 (*3 Kontrollzeichen*) Protas, Sohn des Harmiysis, des Sohnes des Aphrodisios, die Mutter ist Tetạ ( ): 8, Chomatikon, *statio*-Abgabe" etc. (Übersetzung Verf.).

In Kol. XVI beginnt dann ein weiteres solches Register für den Folgemonat Hathyr, also Ende Oktober bis Ende November 134 n.Chr.:

Παρὰ Ἥρωνος καὶ μετόχ(ων) πρακ(τόρων) ἀργ(υρικῶν) κώμης Θεαδελφείας,
468 [κ]ατ᾽ ἄνδρα τῶν διαγεγρα(μμένων) ἡμεῖν (l. ἡμῖν) εἰς ἀρίθμη(σιν) μη(νὸς) Ἁθὺρ τοῦ
ἐνεστῶτος ιη (ἔτους) Ἁδριαν(οῦ) Καίσαρος τοῦ κυρίου. Ἔστι δέ·
470 δ̣ι̣ο̣ι̣κ̣(ήσεως) λημμάτων ι̣η̣ (ἔτους (?)) λαογρα(φίας) καὶ ἄλλων μερισμ(ῶν)
μηνὸς Ἁδριανοῦ δ.
472 λ / / Μύστης Ἁρμιέως το(ῦ) Ἰμούθ(ου) μη(τρὸς) Ἡρῶτος η
λα / / Νικίας Ἥρωνος το(ῦ) Τεσεν̣ο̣(ύφεως) μη(τρὸς) Τεσενο( ) μη(τρὸς) Ταπετε-σου( ) η χ(ωματικοῦ) μαγ(δωλοφυλάκων) δεσ(μοφυλάκων) πο(ταμοφυλακίδος)

474 νβ / / Σαταβοῦς Σισόιτ(ος) τοῦ Μύσθου μη(τρὸς) Εὐδαι(μονίδος) η χ(ωματικοῦ) μαγ-
(δωλοφυλάκων) δεσ(μοφυλάκων) πο(ταμοφυλακίδος)

κ.τ.λ. (Z. 467–474).

„Von Heron und Kollegen, Einnehmern der Geldsteuern des Dorfes Theadelpheia. Liste nach Individuen über die an uns getätigten Einzahlungen auf Rechnung des Monats Hathyr des gegenwärtigen 18. Jahres des Hadrianus Caesar, des Herrn. Im Folgenden die Aufstellung über die Einnahmen für (das Ressort) Dioikesis des 18. Jahres (?) für die Kopfsteuer und die anderen Merismoi. Monat Hadrianos[7] 4.

30 (*2 Kontrollzeichen*) Mystes, Sohn des Harmieus, des Sohnes des Imuthes, die Mutter ist Heros: 8

31 (*2 Kontrollzeichen*) Nikias, Sohn des Heron, des Sohnes des Tesenuphis, die Mutter ist Teseno( ), die Mutter ist Tapetesu( )[8]: 8, Chomatikon, Abgabe für Wachturmbesatzung, die Gefangenenwächter und die Flußwachtschiffe.

52 (*2 Kontrollzeichen*) Satabus, Sohn des Sisois, des Sohnes des Mysthes, die Mutter ist Eudaimonis: 8, Chomatikon, Abgabe für Wachturmbesatzung, die Gefangenenwächter und die Flußwachtschiffe“ etc. (Übersetzung Verf.).

Bei den in den beiden Präskripten genannten Abrechnungsmonaten handelt es sich jeweils um denjenigen Monat, in welchem die Steuer fällig wird – dieser Fälligkeitsmonat wird in anderen Texten des Archivs auch als προθεσμία bezeichnet.[9] Gezahlt werden die Steuern jedoch nicht im Phaophi, sondern erst mit dem Beginn des Folgemonats Hathyr, denn die Liste nennt als erstes Zahlungsdatum den 4. Hathyr, also den 31. Okt. 133 (oben BGU IX 1891, 5). Ebenso beginnen in dem folgenden Register die Zahlungen nicht im Fälligkeitsmonat Hathyr, sondern zu Beginn des darauffolgenden Monats, nämlich am 4. Choiak, also am 30. November 133 (oben BGU IX 1891, 470).

Jeder Eintrag beginnt zunächst mit einer Ziffer (auf deren Bedeutung wir sogleich noch zu sprechen kommen werden), sodann folgt der Personenname des jeweiligen Steuerzahlers, gefolgt vom Namen des Vaters und des Großvaters sowie der Mutter. Danach wird eine Summe von 8 Drachmen angegeben, bei der es sich um die von der betreffenden Person bezahlte Rate für die Kopfsteuer (λαογραφία) handelt; darauf folgen die abgekürzten Bezeichnungen für die kleineren Steuern, die im Präskript unter dem Sammelbegriff ἄλλοι μερισμοί zusammengefaßt werden, der soviel bedeutet wie: „Sonstige Abgaben“. Hierbei handelt es sich um das χωματικόν (einer Steuer für den Unterhalt der Dämme) und die Abgaben δεσμοφυλάκων, μαγδωλοφυλάκων und ποταμοφυλακίδος (oder

7 Der ägyptische Monat Choiak trug unter der Regierung des Kaisers Hadrian auch den Namen Ἁδριανός. Entgegen der ed. pr. steht μηνός nach der Abb. unter http://berlpap.smb.museum/Original/P_11656-Pl-F_R_4_001.jpg bereits am Beginn von Z. 471.

8 Anscheinend hat der Schreiber hier zweimal unterschiedliche Namen der Mutter des Steuerzahlers eingetragen. Der Herausgeber kommentiert dies nicht. Denkbar wäre, daß der erste Name Τεσενο( ) eine Dittographie des Großvatersnamens ist, deren Tilgung vergessen wurde, oder daß der zweite Muttername Ταπετεσου( ) die Korrektur des ersten Τεσενο( ) ist und auch in diesem Fall der Schreiber vergessen hat, den ersten Namen zu tilgen.

9 Siehe etwa BGU IX 1894, 11. 14. 18. 25.

ποταμοφυλακίδων)[10] für den Unterhalt von Gefängniswächtern, Wachturmbesatzungen sowie der Flußwachtschiffe; schließlich zählt dazu noch eine weitere als στατίωνος bezeichnete Steuer, deren Natur noch nicht abschließend geklärt ist.[11] Bei der Nennung aller dieser μερισμοί wird im Gegensatz zur Kopfsteuer kein Betrag angeführt, woraus zu schließen ist, daß diese Steuern in festen Beträgen gezahlt wurden, während die Raten für die Laographia schwanken konnten.

Der Eintrag eines jeden Personennamens wird von zwei bis drei verschiedenen Zeichen begleitet. Regelmäßig erscheint zunächst ein Schrägstrich vor dem Namen, ein weiterer Strich unter dem Namen und mitunter noch ein Punkt hinter dem Schrägstrich. In den obigen Zitaten werden alle diese drei Kontrollzeichen jeweils mit / wiedergegeben.

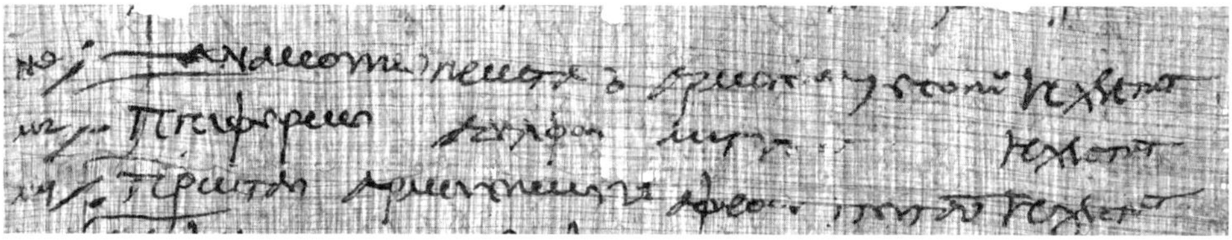

BGU IX 1891 (P.Berol. inv. 11656), Z. 6–8 (Bildnachweis: Berliner Papyrusdatenbank)

Diese Zeichen, die sich auch in anderen ähnlichen Akten mitunter finden, werden als Kontrollzeichen gedeutet, die zum Zeichen eines erfolgten Abgleichs mit einer oder mehreren anderen Akten gemacht wurden. Gedacht wurde hierbei etwa an das originale Erhebungstagebuch der Praktoren, denn ein solches ist BGU IX 1891 angesichts der regelmäßigen Schrift wohl nicht, sondern eher ein Auszug oder eine Kopie desselben.[12] Die Herausgeber von P.Col. II 1 Rekto, wo sich dieselbe Form der Kontrollstriche findet, meinten, diese zeigten an, daß die individuellen Steuerzahlungen in das Hauptbuch der Bank übertragen worden seien, welches in alphabetischer Reihenfolge eine vollständige Liste der kopfsteuerpflichtigen Einwohner Theadelpheias enthalten habe.[13] Warum ein solches „Hauptbuch" nur bei der Staatsbank, welcher die Steuereinnahmen zuflossen, geführt worden sein soll, wird nicht näher begründet. Mir scheint indes, daß auch die Praktoren selbst, von deren Hand BGU IX 1891 ja stammt, ein solches Register mit den Namen sämtlicher steuerpflichtiger Einwohner des Dorfes benötigt haben dürften. Die zwei bis drei unterschied-

10 Zu dieser Steuer, deren vollständige Bezeichnung ὑπὲρ μερισμοῦ (oder μερισμῶν) ποταμοφυλακίδος (oder ποταμοφυλακίδων) lautete, siehe F. Reiter, Einleitung zu P.Köln IX 377.

11 Die Bezeichnung weist auf das lateinische Wort *statio* und mithin ebenfalls auf eine Abgabe, die in irgendeiner Form für Bewachung bzw. Kontrolle erhoben wird. In O.Bankes 34, 3–4 (Elephantine, 138 n.Chr.) findet sich die Zusammenstellung: ὑπ(ὲρ) μερισ[μοῦ] | σκοπέλ(ων) καὶ κ̣ο̣στω̣δ̣(ίας) στα̣(τίωνος) (δραχμὴν) α (τριώβολον(?)) (zur Lesung von Z. 4 s. R. Duttenhöfer, ZPE 202, 2017, 242). Eine *statio* ist aber auch für die Flußwachtschiffe bezeugt, s. O.Wilck. 278, 6–7 (Elephantine, 190 n.Chr.): στατίωνος | ποταμοφυλακ(ίδων), siehe auch S.L. Wallace, *Taxation in Egypt from Augustus to Diocletian*, Princeton 1938, 148 u. 432 Anm. 52. Dies weist auf eine Anlegestelle bzw. einen Posten der Flußwachtschiffe (s. auch Duttenhöfer, *loc.cit.*). Es ist aber nicht sicher, ob sich alle Belege für στατίων in den Steuerlisten darauf beziehen lassen; denkbar wäre wohl auch eine Abgabe für den Unterhalt von Kontrollposten römischer Soldaten, wie beispielsweise der *beneficiarii*.

12 Siehe auch F. Kortenbeutel, BGU IX p. 2.

13 W.L. Westermann – C.W. Keyes, P.Col. II p. 3.

lichen Kontrollzeichen sind wohl in der Tat am ehesten so zu deuten, daß jedem Kontrollzeichen eine jeweils eigene Akte, mit der die in BGU IX 1891 erfaßten Daten abgeglichen worden sind, entspricht – das wären dann also bis zu drei andere Register. Es ist jedoch einstweilen keine Klarheit darüber zu gewinnen, welche genau diese anderen Akten waren. Es wäre indes wohl auch möglich, daß den Kontrollzeichen jeweils ein eigener Kontrolleur zuzuordnen ist, daß also zwei bis drei Personen die Angaben jeweils mit derselben Akte abgeglichen haben, um die Gefahr von Irrtümern zu minimieren, die größer wäre, wenn nur eine einzige Person den Abgleich vorgenommen hätte.

Ganz zu Beginn eines jeden Eintrags und noch vor dem ersten Kontrollstrich steht eine Ziffer (siehe auch die obige Abbildung). Diese Ziffern stehen nicht in einer numerischen Ordnung, sondern ihre Abfolge erscheint auf den ersten Blick beliebig. Manche Ziffern erscheinen außerdem mehrfach. So beginnen etwa die Einträge mit der Nennung der Steuerzahler in BGU IX 1891, 6–17 in der folgenden Weise:

6	νθ (= 59) / / / Ψεναμοῦνις Πρωτᾶ …
	μζ (= 47) / / / Πνεφερῶς ἀδελφός …
8	μη (= 46) / / / Πρωτᾶς Ἁρμιύσεως …
	ϛ (= 6) / / / Ἁρφαῆσις Πεθέως …
10	ιη (= 18) / / / Ἥρων Ὥρου …
	νη (= 58) / / / Χαρητᾶς Ἥρωνος …
12	θ (= 9) / / / Ἀφροδείσιος Ἀφροδ(εισίου) …
	κζ (= 27) / / / Κρονίων ἀπάτω(ρ) …
14	νϛ (= 56) / / / Τιθοῆς Ἀμψάϊτος …
	ιβ (= 12) / / / Δίδυμος Ἀλεξίων̣(ος) …
16	νϛ (= 56) / / / Τιθοῆς ἀπάτωρ …
	ε (= 5) / / / Ἁρφαῆσις ἀπάτωρ …

Betrachtet man nun aber die Namen der Steuerzahler in den Einträgen, die mit den betreffenden Ziffern bezeichnet sind, so erweist sich die Reihenfolge der letzteren mitnichten als beliebig. Vielmehr müssen diese Ziffern offensichtlich eine Referenz auf Kolumnen einer anderen (nicht mehr erhaltenen) Akte bzw. Rolle sein, wo diese einzelnen Steuerzahler der alphabetischen Ordnung ihrer Personennamen folgend verzeichnet waren – was in BGU IX 1891 ja ganz offensichtlich nicht der Fall ist. Demgemäß war der in der oben zitierten Passage in Z. 6 zuallererst genannte Psenamunis in der Kolumne 59 (= νθ) dieser Akte eingetragen, weil sein Name mit Ψ (Psi), dem vorletzten Buchstaben des griechischen Alphabets, beginnt. Die in den Z. 9 u. 17 genannten beiden Steuerzahler mit Namen Harphaesis (Ἁρφαῆσις) sowie der in Z. 12 genannte Aphrodisios (Ἀφροδείσιος) fanden sich dagegen in den Kolumnen 5 (= ε), 6 (= ς) und 9 (= θ) dieses Registers, ganz am Anfang also, bei den mit Alpha, dem ersten Buchstaben des griechischen Alphabets, beginnenden Personennamen. Die beiden Träger des mit dem Buchstaben Tau beginnenden Namen Tithoes in den Z. 14 und 16 waren dagegen beide in der Kolumne 56 (= νς) des Registers eingetragen usw.

Wie bereits erwähnt, wurde die Kopfsteuer (Laographia) in Raten bezahlt, deshalb erscheinen manche Personen in dem Register BGU IX 1891 zweimal, nämlich immer dann, wenn die betreffende Person nicht nur im Hathyr auf Rechnung des Vormonats Phaophi, sondern auch im Monat Choiak auf Rechnung des Monats Hathyr eine Rate für die Kopfsteuer bezahlt hat, die sich zu dieser Zeit im Fayum auf 44 Dr./Jahr belief. So erscheint beispielsweise der gleich zu Beginn des ersten Monatsberichts für den Phaophi in Kol. I Z. 6 genannte Psenamunis, Sohn des Protas und der Esoneus, Enkel des Harmiysis, für den dort am 4. Hathyr die Zahlung einer Rate von 8 Dr. für Laographia und *statio*-Abgabe verbucht wird,[14] ein weiteres Mal in Kol. XX Z. 565, wo für ihn am 7. Hadrianeios (Choiak) die Zahlung einer weiteren Rate für die Laographia in Höhe von 4 Dr. verbucht wird.[15]

Am Schluß einer Monatsabrechnung wird die Gesamtsumme der Einnahmen aus der λαογραφία und den ἄλλοι μερισμοί gezogen, darauf folgen weiterhin Vereinnahmungen aus etwaigen Rückständen und Einnahmen aus Geldsteuern, die außerhalb der Hauptgruppe der Laographia und der ἄλλοι μερισμοί stehen, die aber ebenfalls von den πράκτορες ἀργυρικῶν von Theadelpheia eingezogen werden. Die Gesamtsumme für die auf Rechnung des Monats Phaophi verbuchten Einnahmen beläuft sich laut der Endabrechnung in Kol. XV Z. 466 auf 4264 Dr.

Es stellt sich nunmehr die Frage, zu welchem Zweck solche Listen wie das soeben behandelte Register BGU IX 1891 angelegt worden sind. Allem Augenschein nach handelt es sich hierbei nicht um das originale Einnahmetagebuch der Praktoren, in welches die täglichen Einnahmen eingetragen worden sind, sondern entweder – falls die Praktoren ein gemeinsames Tagebuch für alle Steuersorten geführt haben sollten – um einen Auszug daraus, oder – falls solche Tagebücher nach Steuersorten getrennt geführt worden sein sollten – eine Kopie aus solch einem Tagebuch. Sehr wahrscheinlich waren solche monatsweise von den Praktoren zu erstellenden Register zu Einreichung an eine vorgesetzte Behörde bestimmt. Bei dieser könnte es sich etwa um den Gaustrategen handeln, von dem wir wissen, daß er etwa auch die regelmäßig (oft monatlich erstellten) Abrechnungen der Sitologen über die Naturalsteuereinnahmen erhalten hat.[16] Für Theadelpheia ist bisher keine Einreichung einer so großen Geldsteuerliste wie BGU IX 1891 an den Gaustrategen bezeugt. In dem ganzen reichhaltigen bisher publizierten Material aus Registern zu den Geld- und Naturalsteuereinnahmen aus Theadelpheia findet sich ohnehin keine einzige, die mit einer Adresse versehen worden wäre, wohingegen die verantwortlichen Ersteller solcher Listen regelmäßig namentlich genannt werden, wie es ja auch bei BGU IX 1891 der Fall ist.

Eine Ausnahme bildet P.Berol. inv. 11670, denn diese bisher unedierte Papyrusrolle enthält ein Register derselben Praktoren, welche auch für die Erstellung von BGU IX 1891 verantwortlich waren. Der Inhalt dieses sehr schwer lesbaren Registers, welches mir zur Edition anvertraut worden ist, betrifft unter anderem die Aufstellung von Rückständen aus der Kopfsteuer und anderer Merismoi von Land- bzw. Steuerflüchtigen, die in dem Text als ἄποροι ἀφανεῖς („mittellose Unauffindbare") bezeichnet werden, also solche Personen, die

14 νθ / / / Ψεναμοῦνις Πρωτᾶ τοῦ Ἁρμιύσι̣(ος) μη(τρὸς) Ἐσον̣έ̣ω(ς) **η** χ(ωματικοῦ) στατ(ίωνος).

15 ν̣θ̣ / / Ψ[ε]ναμοῦνις Πρῶτα τοῦ Ἁρμιύσ(ιος) μη(τρὸς) Ἐσονέως **δ**.

16 Siehe etwa P.Berl. Leihg. I 11 (Theadelpheia, 7. Aug. 168 n.Chr.); P.Mert. II 77 (Karanis, 4. Nov. 182 n.Chr.); P.Amst. I 36 (Sethroites, 2. Jh. n.Chr.).

nicht über die nötigen Mittel zur Erfüllung ihrer fiskalischen Verpflichtungen verfügten und deshalb ihre Dörfer verlassen hatten bzw. sich verborgen hielten, also ἀφανεῖς („unsichtbar") geworden waren. Das Register wird für die Abrechnung des Monats Pharmuthi des 17. Jahres des Hadrian erstellt (Ende März bis Ende April 133). Eine der Besonderheiten dieses Registers liegt nun darin, daß es an den βασιλικὸς γραμματεύς adressiert ist, also den zweithöchsten Beamten nach dem Gaustrategen in der Hierarchie der Gauverwaltung.[17] Meines Wissens ist dieser Text damit der einzige Text dieser Art, der an den Königlichen Schreiber adressiert ist, und er bestätigt mithin die Kompetenzen dieses Beamten über insbesondere fiskalische Angelegenheiten.[18] Generell läßt sich aber wohl sagen, daß eine ausdrückliche Adressierung solcher Register an vorgesetzte Beamten nicht unbedingt nötig war. Es reichte wohl, wenn klar war, wer sie verfaßt hatte, und sie mußten außerdem auch noch weiteren Behörden als nur der Gauverwaltung eingereicht werden, so vor allem dem Eklogistes, welcher als der der zentralen Provinzverwaltung Alexandria zugeordneter Rechnungsprüfer des Gaus ebenfalls die monatlichen Einnahmeberichte der Praktoren und der Sitologen erhielt.[19] Es läßt sich also vermuten, daß von solchen Registern mehrere Exemplare für verschiedene höhere Beamten anzufertigen waren, so daß die Praktoren aus Bequemlichkeit im Regelfall auf ihre ausdrückliche Adressierung verzichtet haben mochten.

Neben solchen Registern wie dem soeben behandelten BGU IX 1891, in welchen die monatlichen Eingänge von Steuerzahlungen verzeichnet wurden, wurden von den Praktoren von Theadelpheia auch Gesamtabrechnungen über die Geldsteuereingänge eines ganzen Jahres erstellt. Eine solche Gesamtsteuerliste liegt in BGU IX 1894 vor, die ebenfalls interessante Details der fiskalischen Buchführung aufweist.[20] Der Text ist vollständig und umfaßt 16 Kolumnen, in denen die Einnahmen aus 126 verschiedenen Geldsteuern der Toparchie (des „Bezirks") von Theadelpheia zusammengeführt werden. Dabei gliedert sich das Register in zwei Teile. Der erste Teil (Kol. I–XI) enthält die Geldsteuereingänge für das 20. Regierungsjahr der Kaiser Antoninus Pius und Lucius Verus (= 156/57); im zweiten Teil (Kol. XII–XVII) werden die Eingänge der Geldsteuern auf Wein- und Gartenland aus dem 19. Jahr (= 155/56) verzeichnet. Die Liste ist allerdings insofern unvollständig, als in manchen Zeilen nur der Name der Steuer ohne irgendwelche Einnahmen verzeichnet ist. Ein größerer Zwischenraum unter diesen Einträgen läßt indes vermuten, daß daran gedacht war, die fehlenden Angaben über die Eingänge aus den betreffenden Steuern zu ergänzen. Ich zitiere im Folgenden zur Illustration den Beginn dieses Registers:

17 Z. 1–3 lauten nach meiner (vorläufigen) Transkription: [Ἀ]ρ̣χ̣ιβίωι βασιλ(ικῷ) γρ̣(αμματεῖ) Ἀρσι(νοίτου) Θεμίστου μ̣ε̣ρ̣ίδος | [π]αρὰ Ἥρωνος τοῦ Νείλου καὶ Ἥρωνος τ̣ο̣ῦ̣ Ἀκείους | τ̣ῶν β⁻ πρακ(τόρων) ἀργυ(ρικῶν) κώμης Θεα̣[δε]λ̣φ̣ε̣ί̣α̣ς.

18 Siehe hierzu insbes. TH. KRUSE, *Der Königliche Schreiber der Königliche Schreiber und die Gauverwaltung. Untersuchungen zur Verwaltungsgeschichte Ägyptens in der Zeit von August bis Phlippus Arabs (30 v.Chr. – 245 n.Chr.)*, 2 Bde. (APF-Beih. 11), München – Leipzig 2002, insbes. II 610–655.

19 Siehe etwa für die Sitologen P.Amh. II 69 (Arsinoites, 28. Aug. 154 n.Chr.) sowie für die Praktoren P.Oxy. LXXVII 5107, 28–30 (Oxyrhynchites, 27. Dez. – 25. Jan. 211 n.Chr.).

20 Zu den Details der Berechnungen in diesem Text, ihrer Fehlerquote und den (natürlich zugunsten des Fiskus!) jeweils erfolgenden Aufrundungen siehe auch E. BAYER, *Zu BGU 1894*, Aegyptus 19, 1939, 89–99.

1 Τοπαρχικὸς λημμάτων κ (ἔτους) Ἀντωνίνου
2 Καίσαρος τοῦ κυρίου Θεαδελ(φείας). Ἔστι δε·

3 **ναυ̣[β]ίου κ[α]τοίκ(ων)** α τό(μου) κολ(λήματος) δ
4 (γίνονται) [(δραχμαὶ)] χμη (ὀβολοὶ) γ ∠ (χαλκοῦς 1) προ(σδιαγραφομένων) (δραχ-
μαὶ) ξε (ἡμιωβέλιον) (γίνονται) (δραχμαὶ) ψιγ (τετρώβολον)
(χαλκοῦς 1) ε τό(μου) κόλ(λημα) ζ κ̣ [(τετρώβολον)]
5 ψλ̣δ (διώβολον) (χαλκοῦς 1)

6 **ναυβί̣ο̣(υ) ἐναφεσί(ων)** α τό(μου) κολ(λήματος) δ
7 (δραχμαὶ) ρνϛ (χαλκοῦς 1) προ(σδιαγραφόμενα) (δραχμαὶ) λα (ὀβολὸς) α ∠
(χαλκοῦς 1) (γίνονται) (δραχμαὶ) ρπζ (ὀβολὸς) α ∠ (χαλκοῦς 1)
ε τό(μου) κόλ(λημα) ζ (ὀβολὸς) α ∠

κ.τ.λ. (Z. 1–7).

„Toparchieliste über die Einnahmen des 20. Jahres des Antoninus Caesar, des Herrn, für Theadelpheia, wie folgt:
Für das Naubion der Katöken, Rolle 1 Kolumne 4:
Macht 648 Drachmen 3½ Obolen 1 Chalkûs, Aufschlagszahlungen 65 Drachmen eine halbe Obole, macht 814 Drachmen 4 Obolen 1 Chalkûs. Rolle 5 Kolumne 7: 20 Drachmen [4 Obolen]. 834 (*sc.* Drachmen) 2 Obolen 1 Chalkûs.
Für das Naubion für die *ge enapheimene*, Rolle 1 Kolumne 4:
156 Drachmen 1 Chalkûs, Aufschlagszahlungen 31 Drachmen 1½ Obolen 1 Chalkûs, macht 187 Drachmen 1½ Obolen 1 Chalkûs. Rolle 5 Kolumne 7: 1½ Obolen" etc. (Übers. Verf.).

Jeder Eintrag nennt zunächst drei wesentliche Elemente (im obigen Zitat durch Fettdruck und unterschiedliche Unterstreichungen kenntlich gemacht), nämlich (1) den Namen der betreffenden Steuer, sodann wird auf eine Liste verwiesen, die (2) mit der Nummer einer Rolle (τόμος) und (3) mit einer Kolumne derselben (κόλλημα) angegeben wird. Aus dieser (nicht erhaltenen) aus mehreren Rollen bestehenden Hauptliste, in der die Eingänge für die einzelnen Steuern entweder nach einzelnen Dörfern oder nach den Steuerzahlern (also κατ' ἄνδρα) verzeichnet gewesen sein dürften, wird sodann die Gesamtsumme für die betreffende Steuer erhoben. BGU IX 1894 ist also technisch gesehen ein Auszug aus sehr viel umfangreicheren, uns heute verlorenen Akten.

Der erste Eintrag im obigen Beispiel verzeichnet das Aufkommen aus dem Naubion der Katöken. Hierbei handelte es sich um eine Steuer, mit der die privilegierte landbesitzende Schicht der Katöken im Fayum (der Nachfahren der ptolemäerzeitlichen Militärsiedler) ihre Verpflichtung zur Arbeit an Dämmen und Kanälen ablöste. Interessanterweise wird in diesem Eintrag auf zwei verschiedene Tomoi verwiesen. Zunächst wird mit Verweis auf τόμος 1 κόλλημα 4 ein Gesamtaufkommen für das Naubion der Katöken in Höhe von 648

Drachmen 3½ Obolen 1 Chalkûs verzeichnet; hierzu treten die üblichen Zuschläge (προσδιαγραφόμενα) in Höhe von fast 1/10, was eine Gesamtsumme von 713 Drachmen 4 Obolen 1 Chalkûs ergibt. Unmittelbar anschließend wird nun aber mit Verweis auf τόμος 5 κόλλημα 7 eine weitere kleine Summe in Höhe von 20 Drachmen 4 Obolen genannt, die zu dem aus τόμος 1 κόλλημα 4 gewonnenen Steueraufkommen hinzugezählt wird, woraus sich eine neue Gesamtsumme von 734 Drachmen 2 Obolen 1 Chalkûs ergibt. Offenbar fand sich also, als man im Büro der Praktoren die Gesamtsteuerliste auf der Grundlage der Einzelsteuerlisten erstellte, im 5. τόμος auf dem 7. κόλλημα noch eine weitere kleinere Einnahme für das ναύβιον κατοίκων, die zu der vorher dem 1. τόμος 4. κόλλημα entnommenen Summe hinzuzuzählen war, woraus sich eine höhere Gesamtsumme ergab (Z. 5).

Dasselbe Phänomen findet sich auch im zweiten Eintrag der Liste (Z. 6–7), der die Naubionsteuer betrifft, die auf die γῆ ἐναφειμένη, eine spezielle Kategorie des Staatslandes,[21] erhoben wurde. Auch hier wird zunächst mit Verweis auf τόμος 1 κόλλημα 4 ein Gesamtsteueraufkommen verzeichnet, das sich in diesem Fall auf 187 Drachmen 1½ Obolen 1 Chalkûs beläuft, und sodann wie im ersten Eintrag mit Verweis auf τόμος 5 κόλλημα 7 ein weiterer, diesmal ganz winziger Eingang für dieselbe Steuer in Höhe von 1½ Obolen genannt. Im Gegensatz zum ersten Beispiel folgt auf den aus demselben (!) 7. κόλλημα des 5. τόμος gewonnenen Nachtrag keine erneute Gesamtsumme (die sich nunmehr auf 194 Drachmen 3 Obolen 1 Chalkûs belief) – sie wurde wohl vom Schreiber vergessen. Die beiden Beispiele zeigen aber anschaulich, daß offenbar auf dem 7. κόλλημα des 5. τόμος in irgendeiner Form nachträgliche Einnahmen bzw. Ergänzungen zu der Haupterhebung im 1. τόμος verzeichnet waren.

Die Verweise in BGU IX 1894 auf die τόμοι und κολλήματα der Hauptsteuerlisten gehen in ihrer Bezifferung durcheinander, daher kann, wie schon der Herausgeber Heinz Kortenbeutel bemerkt hat,[22] die Liste nicht so entstanden sein, daß ihr Kompilator die τόμοι einfach beginnend mit der Nr. 1 von vorn bis hinten durchgesehen und sich jeweils die betreffenden Steuern herausgesucht hat, denn in diesem Fall müßte die Zahl der τόμοι und κολλήματα ansteigen. Im ersten Teil des Textes (der Abrechnung für das 20. Jahr in BGU IX 1894 Kol. I–XI) reichen die Ziffern der τόμοι, auf die verwiesen wird, von 1 bis 6; im zweiten Teil (der Abrechnung für das 19. Jahr in Kol. XII–XVII) sogar von 1 bis 10. Die τόμοι müssen z.T. sehr umfangreich gewesen sein; so enthielt der im ersten Teil des Auszugs BGU IX 1894 am häufigsten genannte τόμος 1 mindestens 204 Kolumnen. Es läßt sich allerdings nicht sagen, nach welchen Prinzipien diese τόμοι angelegt worden sein könnten. Manchmal finden sich gleiche oder verwandte Steuern auf ein und demselben κόλλημα eines τόμος – so etwa die beiden Naubion-Steuern in den ersten beiden Einträgen der Liste, die wir soeben besprochen haben, jeweils auf τόμος 1 κόλλημα 4; manchmal erscheint hingegen ein und dieselbe Steuer auf verschiedenen κολλήματα; so wird etwa bei der Abrechnung über einen Pachtzins auf bestimmtes Acker- und Weideland (φόρος ἐδαφῶν καὶ χερσονομῶν) für das 20. Jahr auf die κολλήματα 68, 69, 85, 86 sowie 202, 203 und 204 verwiesen. Denkbar wäre daher vielleicht, daß die großen τόμοι, auf die in BGU IX 1894 jeweils verwiesen wird, jeweils verschiedene Zeitpunkte der Erhebung einer Steuer im Jahresverlauf und/oder verschiedene Orte der Erhebung, also in den diversen

21 Siehe hierzu auch KRUSE, *Der Königliche Schreiber* (siehe Anm. 18) I 584–597.
22 BGU IX p. 86.

Dörfern der Toparchie von Theadelpheia widerspiegeln. Aber diese Frage harrt nach wie vor der Klärung.

Der Auszug über das Gesamtaufkommen an Geldsteuern für das 20. Jahr, der im ersten Teil von BGU IX 1894 vorliegt, ist offenbar nach den einzelnen Finanzressorts der Fiskalverwaltung gegliedert, in die die jeweiligen Steuern flossen. Zuerst werden die Steuereingänge für das Ressort διοίκησις (das allgemeine Finanzressort der Provinz) aufgeführt (Z. 1–58), dann diejenigen für das Ressort ἱερατικά (das aus der Verwaltung des Tempellandes hervorgegangen ist) (Z. 59–77), dann diejenigen für das Ressort des Idios Logos (in das vor allem Einkünfte aus Konfiskationen und diverse spezielle Abgaben flossen) (Z. 78–92) und schließlich diejenigen für das Ressort οὐσιακά (welchem die Steuererträge der mittlerweile verstaatlichten großen Landgüter der iulisch-claudischen Kaiserfamilie und ihrer Freigelassenen zuflossen) (Z. 93–126).

Nicht immer flossen die Einkünfte aus einer bestimmten Steuer einem einzigen dieser Finanzressorts zu, wie etwa die aus der Kopfsteuer dem Ressort διοίκησις. Vielmehr konnten Einkünfte ein und derselben Steuer durchaus auch verschiedenen Ressorts zufließen. Diesem Umstand wird in dem Auszug über das Gesamtsteueraufkommen der Toparchie von Theadelpheia durchaus Rechnung getragen, wie etwa der im folgenden zitierte Eintrag über die Gebühr, die für die Dienerschaft in einem Heiligtum von Heroen zu entrichten war, zeigt, welche – wenn die Abkürzung vom Herausgeber richtig gedeutet worden sein sollte – vielleicht dem besonderen Schutz der Straßen dienten (BGU IX 1894, 78–81):

78 ἰδίου λόγου ὁμοίως

79 ὑπηρεσίας ἱεροῦ Ἡρώων ἀγυ(ιέων) (?)[23] α τό(μου) κολ(λήματος) β·

80 (δραχμαὶ) πθ (διώβολον) (ἡμιωβέλιον) (χαλκοῖ 2), (ἑκατοστῶν)[24] δ (δραχμαὶ) γ
(τετρώβολον), (γίνονται) (δραχμαὶ) ϙγ (ἡμιωβέλιον) (χαλκοῖ 2)·
(ἑκατοστῶν) (δραχμαὶ) β (τέταρτον)

81 ἐν διοικ(ήσει) λ̣ογιζό(μεναι) (δραχμαὶ) β (ἡμιωβέλιον) (χαλκοῖ 3), σ(υμβολικοῦ)[25]
(δραχμὴν) α, (γίνονται) (δραχμαὶ) γ (ἡμιωβέλιον) (χαλκοῖ 3)

23 Siehe zur möglichen Auflösung der Abkürzung H. KORTENBEUTEL im Komm. zu BGU 1894,79.

24 Zur Schreibweise der Sigle für ἑκατοστή, mit welcher die Zuschläge in Höhe von 1 %, 2¼ % und 4 % in BGU IX 1894 bezeichnet werden und die sich mit derselben Schreibweise etwa auch in P.Col. II 1 recto 4 Kol. X Z. 18 (155 n.Chr.); SB XXVI 16420, 7. 9. 22 (173 n.Chr.) und P.Flor. II 131 recto *passim* findet, siehe insbes. D. HAGEDORN, *Bemerkungen zu Urkunden*, AnPap 27, 2015, 129–138, bes. 131–136 (vgl. auch Westermann und Keyes im Komm. zu P.Col. II 1 recto 4 Kol. X Z. 18). Das Zeichen ist von Kortenbeutel an den entsprechenden Stellen in BGU IX 1894, 9. 13. 17. 24. 27. 60. 65. 80. 83. 89. 90 als Kombination von Rho (= ἑκατοστή) und Drachmenzeichen gedeutet worden, was jedoch unzutreffend ist, weshalb, wie schon HAGEDORN, op.cit. 135 richtig festgestellt hat, die auf dieser Grundlage jeweils in der Form (ἑκατοστῆς) (δραχμῆς) α oder gar (ἑκατοστῆς) ρ´ (δραχμαὶ) [alternativ (δραχμῶν)] δ bzw. β δ´ hergestellten Transkriptionen in der Duke Databank of Documentary Papyri (siehe http://papyri.info/ddbdp/bgu;9;1894, Zugriff am 29.01.2019) „keinesfalls adäquat" sind.

25 Zu dieser Lesung statt des ἐ(πὶ) (δραχμὴν) α der *editio princeps* siehe HAGEDORN, *Bemerkungen zu Urkunden* (siehe o. Anm. 24) 134–135.

„(Einnahmen für den) Idios Logos in gleicher Weise:

Für den Dienst im Heiligtum der Heroen der Straßen (?), Rolle 1 Kolumne 2:
89 Drachmen 2½ Obolen 2 Chalkoi; 4 % Aufschlag: 3 Drachmen 4 Obolen, macht 93 Drachmen ½ Obole 2 Chalkoi; 2¼ % Aufschlag,
für die Dioikesis angerechnet: 2 Drachmen ½ Obole 3 Chalkoi, Quittungsgebühr: 1 Drachme, macht 3 Drachmen ½ Obole 3 Chalkoi" (Übers. Verf.).

Der Eintrag ist der erste in der Aufstellung über die in das Ressort des Idios Logos fließenden Steuern. Zunächst wird mit Verweis auf τόμος 1 κόλλημα 2 eine Summe von 89 Drachmen 2½ Obolen 2 Chalkoi für diese Steuer genannt, gefolgt von einem vierprozentigen Zuschlag in Höhe von 3 Drachmen 4 Obolen, woraus sich eine Gesamtsumme von 93 Drachmen 4 Obolen 2 Chalkoi ergibt. Von dieser Summe wird sodann auf der Grundlage der Erhebung eines 2¼-prozentigen Aufschlags auf die vorher für das Ressort des Idios Logos abgerechneten Steuersumme eine kleine Summe in Höhe von 3 Drachmen ½ Obole 3 Chalkoi für das Ressort der Dioikesis verbucht, was mit ἐν διοικ(ήσει) λ̣ογιζό(μεναι) zum Ausdruck gebracht wird.[26] Der Aufschlag in Höhe von 4 % fließt also dem Ressort des Idios Logos zu, wohingegen der Aufschlag in Höhe von 2¼ % gemeinsam mit der Quittungsgebühr für das Ressort der Dioikesis verbucht wird.[27]

Abschließen möchte ich die obige Behandlung der Methoden der Buchführungspraxis der Geldsteuereinnehmer von Theadelpheia mit einigen Bemerkungen zu der Beziehung des Archivs, aus dem die oben behandelten Dokumente stammen, zur Toparchie von Theadelpheia. W.L. Westermann und C.W. Keyes, die Editoren eines Teils der in der Sammlung der Columbia University befindlichen Rollen des Archivs, waren zunächst der Auffassung, daß die von ihnen 1932 in P.Col. II edierten Texte „were all filed together in the branch office of the βιβλιοθήκη δημοσίων λόγων which was in Theadelphia."[28] Das Gauarchiv ist indes, wie bereits Ulrich Wilcken in der Besprechung von P.Col. II im Rahmen seines „Urkundenreferates" anführte, nur in den Gaumetropolen nachzuweisen.[29] Diesen Befund hat die seitdem verbesserte Quellenlage bestätigt. Heinz Kortenbeutel, der 1937 die in BGU IX versammelten Dokumente des Archivs ediert hatte, glaubte hingegen gute Indizien dafür zu haben, daß das Archiv im Büro des Toparches, also des Vorstehers der Toparchie von Theadelpheia, entstanden sei.[30] J. Day und C.W. Keyes haben in ihrer 1956 erschienen Edition weiterer Texte des Archivs in P.Col. V die These Kortenbeutels zwar erwähnt, sie jedoch lediglich für eine „equally plausible explanation" für die Herkunft der Dokumente erklärt.[31] Als Argument für eine Entstehung des Archivs in der Behörde des Toparchen wurde zunächst die Tatsache angeführt, daß sich in dem Archiv sowohl Register der πράκτορες ἀργυρικῶν über Geldsteuereinnahmen als auch solche seitens der σιτολόγοι über Naturalsteuereinnahmen befänden. Das Büro, in welchem diese Berichte zusammengeführt

26 Siehe zu diesen Berechnungen auch BAYER, *Zu BGU 1894* (siehe o. Anm. 20) 93–94.
27 Siehe hierzu auch HAGEDORN, *Bemerkungen zu Urkunden* (siehe o. Anm. 24) 135–136.
28 P.Col. II p. xi.
29 APF 10, 1931, 273.
30 BGU IX p. VI.
31 P.Col. V p. xv–xvi.

wurden, müsse in der administrativen Hierarchie deshalb über den Praktoren und den Sitologen gestanden haben.[32]

Das Argument, dieses Büro mit dem des Toparchen zu identifizieren, gewann man sodann aus dem Umstand, daß BGU IX 1894 als τοπαρχικὸς λημμάτων bezeichnet wird, also als auf die Toparchie bezüglicher Bericht über Einnahmen. Sein Herausgeber Heinz Kortenbeutel war der Meinung, daß zu dem Adjektiv τοπαρχικός, das im Übrigen nur an dieser einen Stelle sowie in einem noch unpublizierten Text bezeugt ist, das Bezugssubstantiv λόγος hinzuzufügen sei, was er in seiner Transkription des Textes dann auch tat.[33] Diese Hinzufügung ist wohl unnötig, da in einer weiteren noch unedierten Rolle des Archivs aus Berliner Beständen eine ähnliche Zusammenstellung wie die in BGU IX 1894 mit ἐκ τοπαρχ(ικοῦ) ια (ἔτους) überschrieben ist.[34] Τοπαρχικός scheint also in der Bürokratensprache der Fiskalbeamten ein ähnlich verkürzter Ausdruck zu sein, wie κατ' ἄνδρα o.dgl. Es kann sich als Adjektiv sowohl auf τοπάρχης als auch auf τοπαρχία beziehen. Fritz Kortenbeutel statuierte indes in der Einleitung zu BGU IX 1894: „Hier kommt wohl nur die Beziehung auf τοπάρχης in Frage …",[35] und führt als Beleg für eine verantwortliche Rolle des Toparchen für die Steuererhebung P.Tebt. II 289 aus dem Jahr 23 n.Chr. an, einen Brief des Gaustrategen an den Toparchen von Tebtynis im Arsinoites, in welchem er letzteren unter Androhung von Konsequenzen ermahnt, ihm Steuerunterlagen zu schicken.[36] Auch eine ebenfalls von Kortenbeutel angeführte Liste über Naturalsteuerabgaben der Staatsbauern, wo in unklarem Kontext τοπαρχη( ) erscheint, datiert in die tiberische Zeit.[37] Aus der Zeit, in der die Texte des Theadelpheia-Archivs entstanden sind, findet sich dagegen kein einziger vergleichbarer Text. Lediglich drei Belege sind bisher für das Amt des Toparchen im 2. Jh. n.Chr. bekannt geworden, nämlich die Erwähnung eines Toparchen in unklarem Zusammenhang in einem Privatbrief unbekannter Herkunft, der vom Herausgeber in das 2. Jh. datiert wird,[38] sowie zwei Überstellungsbefehle an einen Archephodos, der zugleich das Amt des Toparchen versieht, aus dem 2.–3. Jh. aus Soknopaiu Nesos.[39] Das letzte Zeugnis für das Toparchenamt ist seine Erwähnung in einem Dokument über die

32 Siehe H. KORTENBEUTEL, BGU IX p. VI.

33 BGU IX 1894,1: Τοπαρχικὸς <λόγος> λημμάτων κ (ἔτους) Ἀντωνίνου κ.τ.λ.

34 P.Berol. inv. 16036 Verso Kol. III Z. 1, s. A. ŚWIDEREK, *The Date of the Prefecture of Baienus Blastianus*, in: D.H. Samuel (Hg.), Proceedings of the Twelfth International Congress of Papyrology AnnArbor 13–17 August 1968 (ASP VII), Toronto 1970, 461–463, bes. 461 Anm. 1.

35 BGU IX 1894 Einl. p. 83.

36 Ἀ]πολλώνιος στρατηγὸς Ἀκοῦτι | τοπάρχῃ Τεβτύνεως χαίρειν. | ἐξαυτῆς πέμπε μοι πρόσγραφον | τῶν μέχρι τῆς σήμερον διαγεγρ(αμμένων) |[5] κατ' εἶδος, οὕτως γὰρ γνώσομαι | πότερον ἐπὶ τόπων σε ἐάσω | πράττοντά τι ἢ μεταπεμψάμε(νος) | πέμψωι̣ (*l.* πέμψω) τ̣ῶι ἡγεμ[όνι] ὡ̣ς ἀ̣[με-]|λοῦντα τῆς εἰσπρά[ξεως]. |[10] ἔρρωσο. vac. ? | (ἔτους) ἐνάτου Τιβερίου Καίσαρος | Σεβαστοῦ | Μεχ(εὶρ) κα. Verso: [Ἀκοῦτι] τ̣[ο]π̣[ά]ρ[χ(η̣)] Τεβτύν(εως). – „Apollonius, Stratege, an Akûs, Toparchen von Tebtynis, Gruß. Schicke mir sofort die Zusatzliste über die bis zum heutigen Tag erfolgten Zahlungen für die einzelnen Steuerarten, denn auf diese Weise werde ich wissen, ob ich dich in deiner derzeitigen Stellung, in welcher du tätig bist, belassen oder dich vorladen und vor den Präfekten schicken werde wegen der Vernachlässigung der Steuereintreibung. Leb wohl! Neuntes Jahr des Tiberius Caesar Augustus, Mecheir 21." Verso: „An Akûs, Toparchen von Tebtynis" (Übers. Verf.).

37 P.Osl. III 112, 6.

38 P.Mich. III 208, 4–5.

39 BGU XI 2083 (= BGU I 148); SPP XXII 1.

Nominierung von Liturgen für ein Dorf im Hermopolites aus dem Jahr 265 n.Chr.[40] Eine Verantwortlichkeit des Toparchen für die Steuererhebung ist im 2.–3. Jh. n.Chr. nirgendwo ersichtlich, und dasselbe gilt im Übrigen auch für das Amt des Topogrammateus.

Ansonsten betreffen die übrigen 409 Ergebnisse, die man erhält, wenn man in papyri.info nach der Buchstabenfolge τοπαρχ– im Zeitraum zwischen 100 und 300 n.Chr. sucht,[41] ausschließlich die Toparchie als einen administrativen Distrikt bzw. – und hier wird es dann wiederum für unseren Zusammenhang interessant – als Amtssprengel der Praktoren und der Sitologen. Das Amt des Toparchen scheint dagegen, wenn es nicht ohnehin ganz verschwunden war, so doch zumindest erheblich an Bedeutung eingebüßt zu haben. Diejenigen Kompetenzen für die Steuererhebung (oder zumindest für deren Buchführung), die er im 1. Jh. n.Chr. ausweislich des obengenannten P.Tebt. II 289 noch besessen hat, könnte er vielleicht im Zuge der Ausweitung des Liturgiesystems und der damit einhergehenden Reorganisation der Geld- und Naturalsteuererhebung in der Regierungszeit des Kaisers Traian – als etwa auch die Funktion des πράκτωρ ἀργυρικῶν zu einer Liturgie wurde[42] – verloren haben. Nichts deutet also darauf hin, daß der Toparch oder der Topogrammateus zur Zeit der Entstehung des „administrativen Archivs von Theadelpheia" eine irgendwie bedeutende, den Erhebungsbeamten übergeordnete Rolle in der Steuererhebung gespielt hätte, die dazu hätte führen können, daß Akten der Geld- und Naturalsteuerhebung in seinem Büro archiviert worden wären. Nach wie vor sehr prominent in der Dokumentation bleibt aber die Toparchie als administrative bzw. fiskaladministrative Verwaltungseinheit, auf deren Bedeutung insbesondere als Steuerbezirk bereits Ulrich Wilcken in seinen monumentalen Studie zu den griechischen Ostraka aus Oberägypten hingewiesen hatte.[43]

Zurückkommend auf die Frage nach der administrativen Verortung des Archivs von Theadelpheia könnte man als Ort seiner Zusammenstellung und Archivierung – wenn nicht das Büro des Komogrammateus (des Dorfschreibers) – vielleicht auch eine Art von gemeinsamen Zentralbüro der Praktoren und Sitologen in Theadelpheia vermuten, gewissermaßen eine zentrale Instanz für die Erhebung der Geld- und Naturalsteuern für die Toparchie von Theadelpheia, in welchem die Steuerregister des „administrativen Archivs von Theadelpheia" erstellt worden sein könnten. In jüngster Zeit konnte etwa Amin Benaissa überzeugend zeigen, daß die Aktenführung der Sitologen im Oxyrhynchites viel zentralisierter

40 P.Flor. I 1 Kol. I, Z. 7 u. 21.

41 Zuletzt durchgeführt am 19.12.2018.

42 Siehe hierzu etwa N. Lewis, *The Compulsory Public Services of Roman Egypt* (Second Edition) (Papyrologica Florentina XXVIII), Firenze 1997, 42; M. Sharp, *Shearing Sheep: Rome and the Collection of Taxes in Egypt*, 30 BC – AD 200, in: W. Eck (Hg.), Lokale Autonomie und römische Ordnungsmacht in den kaiserzeitlichen Provinzen vom 1. bis 3. Jahrhundert (Schriften des Historischen Kollegs 42), München 213–241, bes. 227–228.

43 U. Wilcken, *Griechische Ostraka aus Aegypten und Nubien. Ein Beitrag zur Antiken Wirtschaftsgeschichte*, Leipzig – Berlin 1899, Erstes Buch, 428–429. Es ist übrigens nicht ganz richtig, wenn H. Kortenbeutel, BGU IX p. VI auf diese Stelle für „die Beteiligung des Toparchen bei der Steuererhebung" verweist, denn Wilcken handelt hier ausschließlich über „die wichtige Rolle der Toparchie als Steuerbezirk". – Zur Bedeutung der Toparchie als administrativen bzw. fiskaladministrativen Bezirks siehe auch T. Derda, *Toparchies in the Arsinoite Nome: A Study in Administration of the Fayum in the Roman Period*, JJP 33, 2003, 27–54; ders., Ἀρσινοΐτης νομός. *Administration of the Fayum under Roman Rule* (JJP Suppl. VII), Warsaw 2006, 117–146.

organisiert war, als man bisher gedacht hatte.[44] Bezüglich des Archivs von Theadelpheia muß es hier indes einstweilen bei Vermutungen bleiben, zumal große Teile des Archivs noch ihrer Edition harren, die auch für das Problem seiner administrativen Verortung vielleicht noch Aufschlüsse bereithalten könnten.

44 A. BENAISSA, *Giro Transfer in the Oxyrhynchite Nome: A New Document in the Beinecke Library*, ZPE 179, 2011, 221–230.

Reconstructing Karanis: Tax Collection and Administrative Innovation in an Arsinoite Town of the Second Century CE

Uri Yiftach, Tel-Aviv[1]

The term *kollêma* is translated in *LSJ* Greek lexicon as "sheets of papyrus gummed together to form a roll" (s.v. p. 972).[2] In the Roman period, the term acquired new meaning, denoting a column of text within a roll, regardless of whether it originally made an independent sheet. In documentary texts, the term is used whenever a scribe wishes to refer the exact location, in another document, of a piece of information he now uses for his own purposes.[3] A reference to the *kollêma* would naturally be required only when the related document is exceedingly long. One such area is the collection of revenues. Tax collectors, *sitologoi*, *praktores*, bankers, and others would compose daybooks, filling out the pages (*kollêmata*) with an account of their revenues. At the top of each page, they would then add the page number. Synoptic accounts, drawn from the data collected from daybooks, would sometimes record the exact page in which the data were originally registered. Reports giving evidence of this practice are quite abundant.[4] Tax collectors, in turn, required, for the collection of the taxes, lists reporting the identity of the tax subjects and how much each of these individuals should pay. This list, prepared by the central village administration, was called *apaitêsimon*.[5]

---

1 This paper stems from the project "Synopsis: Data Processing and State Management in Roman Egypt (30 BCE-300 CE)", conducted by the author in collaboration with Prof. Dr. Andrea Jördens (Universität Heidelberg) under the auspices of the German-Israeli Foundation for Scientific Research and Development (G-38-111.4/2011).

2 Preisigke, *WB* 1, s.v. (p. 818): *Das in die Aktenrolle eingeklebte Blatt.* See also W. Clarysse, 'Tomoi synkollesimoi', in: M. Brosius (ed.), *Ancient Archives and Archival Traditions: Concepts of Record-Keeping in the Ancient World* (Oxford 2003) 344-359 at 345-346.

3 Clarysse (supra n. 2) 349; W.A. Johnson, *Bookrolls and Scribes in Oxyrhynchus* (Toronto 2004) 88.

4 References to daybooks: *BGU* VII 1618 (II CE, Philadelphia); *P.Aberd.* 25 (II CE, unknown provenance); *P.Amh.* II 122 (211/2 CE, Hermopolis); *P.Berl.Leihg.* I 2^{v} = *P.Berl.Thun.* 2^{v} = *SB* III 7194^{v} (168 CE, Theadelphia?) (?); *P.Bour.* 42 (166/7 CE, Hiera Nêsos); *P.Col.* V 1^{v} 2 (not directly from a daybook) (ca. 160 CE, Theadelphia); V 1^{v} 3 (155 CE, Theadelphia); *P.Erl.* 42 (II CE, unknown provenance); *P.Flor.* III 386 (83/4 CE, Hermopolis) (?); *P.Fouad* I 14 = *P.Bacch.* 24 = *SB* V 8070 [second copy: *P.Lund* IV 7] (mid II CE, Bacchias); *P.Fuad I Univ.* 33 (II/III CE, unknown provenance) (?); *P.Gron.* 4 (IV CE, Theadelphia); *P.Lond.* III 1212 (p. 90) (253/4 or 254/5 CE, unknown provenance); *P.Mil.Congr.* XVII page 47 = *SB* XVI 12730 (end II/III CE, unkown provenance); *P.Oxy.* XXII 2346 (late III CE, Oxyrhynchitês) (?) [cf. L.C. Youtie, ZPE 30 (1978) 177-186 at 178-179, 185-186]; XLIV 3168 (after 7.4.155 or 177, Hermopolitês (?)); 3169 (ca. 200-212 CE, Oxyrhynchitês); *P.Petaus* 44 (before 11.1.185 CE, Arsinoitês) (?); *P.Ryl.* II 185 (II CE, Hermopolitês?); 203 (II CE, Hermopolitês); *P.Stras.* I 23 (I/II CE, Hermopolis); *SPP* IV pp. 119-121 (58-64 CE, Arsinoitês).

5 Cf. Preisigke, FWB p. 24 s.v.: "Forderungsliste"; Th. Kruse, *Der königliche Schreiber und die Gauverwaltung. Untersuchungen zur Verwaltungsgeschichte Ägyptens in der Zeit von Augustus bis Philippus* Arabs (30 v.Chr. - 245 n.Chr.) (Munich 2002) 610-612; S.L. Wallace, *Taxation in Egypt from Augustus*

Twenty-two texts recording *apaitêsima* have come down to us. Yet, of these, in eight only is the text sufficiently well preserved to reveal the structure of the document. Among these, five stem from the Arsinoitês, all drawn up in Soknopaiou Nêsos over the course of a relatively short time in the second and third decades of the third century CE.[6] We do not possess, in other words, direct and unequivocal evidence of the structure of the *apaitêsimon* in other parts of the nome, and from earlier or later periods. But indirect evidence abounds: once composed, the *apaitêsimon* was handed over to tax collectors who used it to find out the tax liability of each tax subject. In most cases, we can perhaps infer the verification process from checkmarks, one or more, added before the name of some of the tax payers.[7] Upon this hypothesis, the tax collector inspected both the *apaitêsimon* and his daybook, and, once the name of the tax subject was found in the former, he checkmarked both. This is, of course, not the only possible explanation for these checkmarks, nor does it yield any information about the structure of the *apaitêsimon*. Fortunately, in several cases, tax collectors went beyond that.

---

to Diocletian (Princeton 1938) 32-33, 295; *P.Sijp.* 20 (170 CE, Dinnis Onneiton) with introduction and commentary.

6 The *apaitêsimon* records the names of the tax subjects and their liabilities. It is clearly identifiable only whenever the beginning of the report, where the *apaitêsimon* has been presented as such, has been preserved. Among the preserved, certain *apaitêsima*, the structure is evident in *BGU* I 145 (213 CE, Soknopaiou Nêsos) (τῶν ἐλάσσω φανέντων πραξίμου) [not alphabetical]; II 457 = *WChr* 252 (132/3 CE, Karanis) (an update to an earlier list) [not alphabetical]; 659 (229 CE, Soknopaiou Nêsos) [alphabetical]; *CPR* I 33 (215 CE, Soknopaiou Nêsos) [alphabetical]; *O.Wilck.* II 1308 (298/9 CE, Thebes) (very short); *P.Lond.* II 322 (pp. 159-160) = *WChr* 358 (214/5 CE?, Soknopaiou Nêsos) [not alphabetical] (πρὸς ἀπαίτησιν); III 1170 R (p. 92) (ca. 144 CE, Theadelphia ? [*ZPE* 13 (1974) 153]) [alphabetical]; *P.Oxy.* LXIII 4372 (341-399 CE?, Oxyrhynchos) [not alphabetical]; *SB* I 4522 *descriptum* (242/3 CE, Alabanthis) [partly alphabetical]; XX 14512 (II/III CE, Soknopaiou Nêsos) (very short); *SPP* IV pp. 58-78 ll. 378-488 = *WChr* 61 = *CPJ* II 421 (ll. 432-488) (ca. 70 CE, Ptolemais Euergetis) [not alphabetical] (ἤχθησαν εἰς ἀπαίτησιν); XXII 88 + *Stud.Pal.* XX 26 [BL VII, p. 266] (214/5 CE, Soknopaiou Nêsos) [alphabetical]; 174 + *Stud.Pal.* XXII 169 (?) [BL VII, 267] (218 CE, Soknopaiou Nêsos) [not alphabetical]. In others, while the document is identifiable as *apaitêsimon*, the structure can no longer be gauged: *BGU* I 175 (II/III CE, Soknopaiou Nêsos); 299 (ca. 143/4 CE, Arsinoitês); II 598 (173/4 CE, Soknopaiou Nêsos); XIII 2282 (229/30 CE, Ptolemais Arabôn); *P.Fay.* 40 (162/3 CE, Theadelphia); *P.Laur.* IV 171 (III CE, unknown provenance); *P.Matr.* 1 (119/20 CE, Oxyrhynchitês); *P.Stras.* IV 220^{v} (229/30 CE, Oxyrhynchos) (πρὸς ἀπαίτησιν). Certain, not yet edited: *P.Fay.* 208 *descriptum* (222-235 CE, Bacchias). The corpus of lists which could perhaps be identified as *apaitêsima*, viz. a list of names with a record of the tax liability/payment, is vast: see, e.g., *P.Phil.* 18 (II CE, Tebtynis) [alphabetical]; *SB* XIV 11481 (38-48 CE, Philadelphia) [not alphabetical]; *SPP* XXII 165 (early III CE, Soknopaiou Nêsos) [not alphabetical] (cf. further *BL* V, p. 144). I thank Marius Gerhardt, curator of the papyrus collection of the Staatliche Museen zu Berlin, Stiftung Preußischer Kulturbesitz, for allowing me to inspect *SB* I 4522 *descriptum.*

7 Checkmarks in daybooks: *BGU* IX 1891 (133 CE, Theadelphia); *P.Col.* II 1^{r}.1a (133/4 CE, Philadelphia); 1^{r}.1.b (134/5 CE, Theadelphia); *P.Fouad.* 68 (180 CE, Arsinoitês); *P.Giss.Univ.* VI 49^{v} (after 28.8.221 CE, Tebtynis); *P.Hamb.* IV 274 (198 CE, Theadelphia?); *P.Hib.* II 218^{v} (198 CE, Theadelphia); *P.Mich.* IV.1 223 + *SB* XIV 11710 (171/2 CE, Karanis); 224 (172/3 CE, Karanis); 225 (174/5 CE, Karanis); IV.2 359a (175 CE, Karanis) (partial); *PSI* X 1154 (II CE, Tebtynis); *SB* XII 11011 (130-175 CE, Karanis?); XVI 12737 col. 2 (30 CE, Philadelphia). See also Th. Kruse, 'Fiskalische Buchführung in Theadelpheia', above, p. 228.

BGU IX 1891 contains two reports, ll. 1-466 (cols. 1-15) and 467-615 (cols. 16-20), recording the daily revenues in cash collected by the *praktores argyrikôn* of the village of Theadelphia for the months of Phaôphi and Hathyr in the 18th year of Hadrian, respectively (28.9-26.11.133 CE).[8] The addressee is not reported, but can be assumed to be the nome's *stratêgos*.[9] In the title, the *praktores* name the types of taxes collected; these are the *laographia* and "the remaining *merismoi*."[10] As a rule, one line is dedicated to each tax payer who is identified by his father, paternal grandfather, and mother, as is commonly the case in administrative documentation from the Roman period.[11] In the present case, the author also details, in a systematic manner, the types of taxes exacted from each individual person.[12] The list is not alphabetical, but arranged presumably by the exact moment in each day in which the tax subjects came to pay their due. This pattern accounts well for the consecutive registration of members of the same family.[13] The *praktores*, engaged in collecting the taxes, relied on the *apaitêsimon*. Yet, in the present case, instead of simply checkmarking the two documents, they also recorded in their daybook before each entry a *kollêma* number. This is the *kollêma* in which the registered tax subject's liabilities were recorded in the *apaitêsimon*. What can these numbers tell us about the structure of the *apaitêsimon*?

Let us start with stating what seems to me to be the obvious: *BGU* IX 1891 contains two reports, but the *apaitêsimon* is identical: a list of tax payers recording their individual liabilities that was handed over to the *praktores* at the beginning of the tax collection year and was kept by them through its end.[14] The original roll contained as many as 63 columns,

8 K. Geens, 'Administrative Archive from Theadelphia', in *Leuven Homepage of Papyrus Collections*, ArchID 247. Version 1 (2011) https://www.trismegistos.org/archive/247#archdetail-table and Th. Kruse (supra n. 7) passim.

9 U. Yiftach, 'From Arsinoe and Alexandria and Beyond: Taxation and Information in Early Roman Egypt: A Discussion of P. Bagnall 70', *Journal of Juristic Papyrology* 45 (2015) 291-312 at 292 and Kruse (supra n. 7), 231.

10 *BGU* IX 1891.1-5: παρὰ Ἥρωνος τοῦ Νείλου καὶ Ἥρωνος τοῦ Ἀκείους | [2] τῶν β πρακ(τόρων) ἀργυ(ρικῶν) κώμης Θεαδελφείας | [3] κατ' ἄνδ[ρ]α τῶν διαγεγραμμένων ἡμεῖν ε[ἰ]ς ἀρίθμη(σιν) | [4] μη[ν]ὸς Φαῶφι τοῦ ἐνεστῶ(τος) ιη (ἔτους) Ἁδριανοῦ Καίσα[ρ]ος τοῦ κυρίου | [5] ἔστι δὲ λαογρα(φίας) καὶ ἄλλων μερισ(μῶν).

11 I have treated this question in U. Yiftach, 'Apator metros: The Rise of a Formula in Bureaucratic Perspective,' in, D.F. Leão, G. Thür, *Symposion 2015: Vorträge zur griechischen und hellenistischen Rechtsgeschichte (Coimbra, 1.-4. September 2015)* (Vienna 2016) 215-219, and *idem*, 'The Rise of the Flexible Template: Patterns of Change in Identification Methods between the Ptolemaic and the Roman Period', in P. Ismard, M. Vallet, A.-E. Veïsse (eds.), *l'identification des personnes dans les mondes grecs* (Paris 2019) 77-89.

12 E.g., l. 91: ιϛ / / / Ἥρων Ὀρσενο(ύφεως) τοῦ Ὥσεως μη(τρὸς) Ἐσονέως η χ(ωματικοῦ) μαγ(δωλοφυλάκων) δεσ(μοφυλάκων) πο(ταμοφυλακίδος) σ(τατίωνος). Such a detailed account in *viritim* reports is quite exceptional and may well derive from the personal inclinations of the scribe or the administrative tradition in early second-century CE Theadelphia. A study of the scribal idiosyncracies at the offices of Theadelphian tax collectors is still missing. Elsewhere, scribes would usually do with the name, patronym, and the amount of payment. See, e.g., *P.Hib.* II 218.2.5 (late I/early II CE, Hêrakleopolitês): Σαρῦθις Πανινούτιος α ∠.

13 Cf., e.g., ll. 183-185, with three siblings registered together.

14 As shown by the congruity of *kollêma* numbers of persons recorded in both reports. Cf., e.g., Nikandros son of Isidôros, grandson of Nikandros, mother Hêrôs (*kollêma* 31 in both reports); or Tithoês son of Hêraklês, grandson of Hêraklês, mother Hêrôs (*kollêma* 56). There are some discrepancies, as in the

which seems to be normal, even if not standard, for this period and sphere of activity.[15] Following the numbers, we can easily gauge the system by which the original list was created. It was alphabetical: the first ten columns incorporate names beginning with an *alpha* and the 10th column consists of names beginning with *beta*, *gamma*, and *delta*. Names beginning with *delta* also occupy columns 10 through 13, names with *epsilon* appear in the 13th and 14th columns, *zeta* in the 14th, *êta* from the 15th through the 23rd, *theta* in the 24th, *iota* in the 24th through the 26th, *kappa* in the 26th and 27th, *lambda* in the 28th, *mu* in the 28th through the 31st, *nu* in the 31st and 32nd, *omikron* through the 36th, *pi* through the 49th, *sigma* through the 54th, *tau* through the 56th, *phi* through the 57th, *khi* in the 58th, *psi* through the 60th, and *omega* in the final three columns. Some names are especially well attested and occupy multiple columns, thus giving us some notion of their popularity: this is the case with *Harphaêsis*, which occupies three columns, and *Hêrôn*, which takes up as many as five columns. The number of names per column varies, typically somewhere between 10 and 15 names; at the same time, the list is hardly exhaustive, but represents those who paid the taxes in the months of Phaophi and Hathyr. In the case of *BGU* IX 1891 itself, the number of names per column is between 30 and 35. If we assume that this was also the case with the *apaitêsimon*, the current evidence represents between one third and one half of the names originally recorded in that document.[16]

BGU IX 1891 is not the only document representing this type of reference. *P.Col.* II 1^r 1 fragments a and b, with eight and six columns of text respectively, represents the same method of recording the liability of tax subjects: a collection, over the course of at least eight days (four in each fragment) based on an *apaitêsimon* in an alphabetical order.[17] There are also at least three cases of preserved *apaitêsima* that are constructed according to the same structure: *BGU* II 659 (229 CE), *CPR* I 33 (215 CE), and *Stud.Pal.* XXII 88 (214/5 CE), all stemming, as indicated earlier, from Soknopaiou Nêsos.[18] The alphabetical order would seem to be the obvious categorization method. But in Roman Egypt it was not:[19] three *apaitêsima* from Soknopaiou Nêsos (*BGU* I 145, 213 CE; *P.Lond.* II 322

---

case of Areios the elder, son of Tesenouphis (?), grandson of Papos, mother Hêraklous, recorded in the *apaitêsimon* referred to in the papyrus from Columbia in *kollêma* 6, while in that relied upon in the text from Berlin in *kollêma* 7. If the reading is correct, such discrepancies are probably due to scribal slip.

15 Cf., e.g., Clarysse (supra n. 2) 351-352.

16 However, the total number of persons subject to the payment of the *laographia* would thus amount to 1,800. Using a ratio of 1:3,1 tax payers: inhabitants (see briefly D.Rathbone, "Village, land and population in Greco-Roman Egypt", *PCPS* 216 (1990) 103-142 at 130), on the assumption that the list is exhaustive, the population of Theadelphia would be 5,580 persons large.This is a very high estimate, compared with between 2,100 and 2,300 inhabitants assumed by Rathbone (op.cit., p. 133), and M. Sharp, "The Village of Theadelphia in the Fayyum: Land and Population in the Second Century", in A.K. Bowman, E. Rogan (eds.), *Agriculture in Egypt from Pharaonic to Modern Times, Proceedings of the British Academy* 96 (Oxford 1989) 159-192 at 164.

17 Fragment a columns 4-7 records the collection of taxes on Hathyr 10th-12th of the 19th year of Hadrian (6-8.11.135). The exact dates of columns 1-3 of the same fragment, as well as the days recorded in fragment b, are not certain. See *P.Col.* II, p. 7.

18 See above n. 6.

19 According to Clarysse (supra n. 2), 344 the alphabetical order was only introduced into Egypt in the second century BCE.

(pp. 159-160) = *WChr* 358, 214/5 CE?; *Stud.Pal.* XXII 174, 218 CE), and another from Oxyrhynchos (*P.Oxy.* LXIII 4372, 341-399 CE?), are not arranged alphabetically.[20] With this in mind, I turn my attention to the evidence provided by the daybooks of the *praktores argyrikôn* from Karanis, as represented in particular in two documents, *P.Mich.* IV.2 359a + *P.Cair.Mich.* 359, which recorded a collection in January and February 175 CE, and *P.Mich.* IV.1 225 whose main section (ll. 1-3,022) covers the period between February and August 174 CE, both from the same archival context—that of the tax collector Sokratês, or rather, in this specific chronological context, his son Sarapiôn.[21]

P.Mich. IV.2 359a + *P.Cair.Mich.* 359 is an extensive document: 2,207 lines of text, recording the collection of revenues in cash over the course of two months, Tybi through Pachon in the 15th year of Marcus Aurelius (31.12.174-28.2.175 CE). The structure of the individual entries is quite similar to that of *BGU* IX 1891, with the name of each tax subject occupying one line and incorporating the personal name, the name of the father, the name of the paternal grandfather, the name of the mother, and the amount of tax collected. It also records, in the following line, the *kollêma* from which the details of the person were collected, that is the *apaitêsimon*.[22] The papyrus from Karanis shows then that the practice of 'detailed cross-referencing' was common in different parts of the Arsinoite nome. This is, however, where the similarities end: first, while the Theadelphian *apaitêsimon* consisted of approximately 60 *kollêmata*, its counterpart from Karanis reaches just about 120.[23] Second, the number of persons recorded in each column of origin is somewhat smaller, no more than seven. Taking into account that *P.Cair.Mich.* 359 records a collection of just two months—even this period is not fully documented—we would assume a *kollêma* recording of about 10 persons, compared to the 30 names assumed in the Theadelphian counterpart.[24] This fact is a first indication that the *kollêma* of the Karanis *apaitêsimon* is of a different nature from its Theadelphian counterpart. Finally, and most importantly, when we list the names of tax payers per *kollêma*, we find no alphabetical order. This fact was already noticed by the editors of the text who correctly assumed a topographical ordering.[25] Karanis was divided into 120 collection areas, each with roughly 10 tax payers.

20 This is also the case in *P.Lond.* III 1170 R (p. 92) (ca. 144 CE, Arsinoitês), if indeed an *apaitêsimon*. Cf. L.C. Youtie, 'P.Lond. III 1170 and the Strategos Julius Isidorus', *ZPE* 13 (1974) 151-160.

21 K. Geens, 'Sokrates, tax collector and family', in Leuven Hompage of Papyrus Collections, ArchID 109. Version 2 (2013) http://www.trismegistos.org/arch/archives/pdf/109.pdf.; P. van Minnen, 'House to House Enquiries: An Interdisciplinary Approach to Roman Karanis', *ZPE* 100 (1994) 227-251; S. Strassi Zaccaria, 'Prosopografia e incarichi amministrativi a Karanis nel II sec. d.C. Proposte interpretative', *ZPE* 85 (1991) 245-262 at 254; *P.Cair.Mich.* II, pp. 9-18.

22 Cf., e.g., ll. 20-21: Πετσ̣[ῖ]ρις Πασοκνοπαίου τοῦ Πετσίρεως μη(τρὸς) Ἡρῶτος (δραχμὰς) η | ξ.

23 The currently highest *kollêma* number recorded in our contexts is 113. See n. 43 below.

24 *P.Mich.* IV.1 225, covering comprehensively 8 Feb. through 14 Aug. 174 CE, records seven persons as registered in the *apaitêsimon*'s 54th *kollêma*. In one case, that of Ptolemaios, son of Pasoxis, grandson of Satabous, mother Hêras, the name is recorded in as many as five different entries; most others are recorded in three. Four of these persons are also recorded in *P.Cair.Mich.* 359, covering just two months at the beginning of 175 CE. As the odds are low that the remaining three became nontaxable or died, we could assume payment on their part later that year. Drawing on this assumption, we may imagine additional tax subjects in the *apaitêsimon* of 174 CE, in addition to those recorded in *P.Mich.* IV.1 225. But they would not be more than two or three.

25 H. Riad, J.C.Shelton, *A Tax List from Karanis (P.Cair.Mich.* 359): 2 (Bonn 1977) 2-4.

The topographical theory is supported by the order in which the numbers are registered in the daybook. In *P.Mich.* IV.1 225, the tax collector records for Mecheir 14th (8.2.174) collection from payers registered in *kollêmata* 3, 4, 5, 5, 5, 9, 9, 9, 10, 12, 12, 15, 16, 18, 21, 21, 21, 23, 25, 31, 33, 34, 36, 36, 36, 36, and 44, roughly in that order; the next day (Mecheir 15th), 41, 41, 42, 42, 45, and 46; and on the third (Mecheir 16th) are registered tax payers whose names have been for the most part recorded in *kollêmata* numbers 47 through 67, and in the following day (Mecheir 17th) primarily in *kollêmata* 69 through 95. In the fifth day (Mecheir 18th) , the tax collector starts all over again: he deals with tax subjects recorded in *kollêmata* 3 to 45; following day six, with little collection, he resume work in the seventh, with tax payers recorded in *kollêmata* 41 to 65, and in day eight in *kollêmata* 64 to 103. He then holds to the same routine over the next two months.[26]

The best explanation for this pattern is naturally topographical. In Karanis, the tax collector, rather than waiting for the tax subjects in his office, paid each a personal visit. For this purpose, an *apaitêsimon* arranged alphabetically would be of little use. The purpose would be well served, on the other hand, by a 'map' listing the tax payers' places of residence. Unfortunately, the tax list does not indicate where each unit was located, but considering the pattern relayed above, we can identify some larger areas: roughly 1-45, 45-75, and 75-120. In the course of his circuit, the tax collector likely devoted an entire day to one neighborhood: he would move from one unit to the next and collect taxes from whomever he could. Within a cycle of three to four days, the circuit would be complete.

This system simplified the collection of the taxes and made it more effective: usually the *praktôr* did not work alone. We assume a group of between two and four *praktores*, probably with additional staff (perhaps other local functionaries), going from one collection area to the next.[27] Some residents were more compliant and would pay immediately, while others would try to avoid payment. The *praktores* did not have to make a fuss. They could simply go on to the next unit and return a couple of days later, thus building up psychological pressure even on the most reluctant of tax subjects. Within a couple of weeks, we guess, most paid. To be sure, not all tax collectors would show tolerance, and some were more willing to resort to coercion to exact their dues. This would lead to

26 P.*Mich.* IV.1 225: Day 1: 26 collections, range: 3-36. Day 2: 6 collections, range: 41-46. Day 3: 19 collections, 47-67. Day 4: 8 collections, 69-95. Day 5: 15 collections, 1-32. Day 6: 4 collections (day of rest?). Day 7: 8 collections, 41-65. Day 8: 17 collections, 76-96. Day 9: 8 collections, 3-49 (day of rest?). Day 10: 8 collections, eight between 47 and 75. Day 11: 9 collections, (3) 14-16, (5) 67-103. Day 12: 23 collections, 1-39.Day 13: 13 collections, 46-75. Day 14: 14 collections, 76-104. Day 15: 23 collections, 1-41. Day 16: 15 collections, 45-75. Day 17: 12 collections, 70-101. Day 18: 28 collections, 2-42. Day 19: 19 collections, 46-72. Day 20: 12 collections, 76-104. Day 21: 15 collections, 4-41. Day 23: 10 collections, 80-105. Day 24: 14 collections, 1-42. Day 25: 9 collections, 46-65. Day 26: 1 collection (day of rest). Day 27: 18 collections, 67-99. Day 28: 23 collections, 7-47. Day 29: 16 collection, 45-69. Day 30: 25 collections, 58-103.

27 Th. Kruse, 'Zu den Kompetenzen des administrativen Hilfspersonals der enchorischen Beamten in der römischen Kaiserzeit', in: T. Derda et al. (eds.), *Proceedings of the 27th International Congress of Papyrology Warsaw, 29 July – 3 August 2013* (Warsaw 2016) III, 1761–1771 at 1763; F. Oertel, *Die Liturgie. Studien zur ptolemäischen und kaiserlichen Verwaltung Ägyptens* (Leipzig 1917) 203, 410-423.

complaints, amply recorded in petitions, and endeavors by the provincial administration to curbe malpractice.[28]

P.Mich. IV.1 225 and *P.Mich.* IV.2 359a + *P.Cair.Mich.* 359 were composed during two consecutive years, 174 CE and 175 CE, respectively. Many of the tax payers that appear in the former are also recorded in the latter. But the *apaitêsimon* they refer to is different, that of *P.Mich.* IV.1 225 being subject to updates and additions by the authors of the *apaitêsimon* that anticipated the collection of taxes reported in *P.Mich.* IV.2 359a + *P.Cair.Mich.* 359. With the update, new *kollêmata* were added and tax subjects were moved over to higher numbers.[29] In the case of some persons, the change of *kollêma* may also mirror internal migration: persons now registered in a completely different tax unit.[30] Even so, not all data were up to date by the time the *praktôr* came to collect the tax. Accordingly, the 36th day of the collection in *P.Mich.* IV.1 225 records the *praktôr*'s visit to units 1-45. Yet the eighth, ninth, and tenth entries record persons registered in *kollêma* 83. They were apparently still located, by the time the *apaitêsimon* was drafted, in *kollêma* 83 and had moved to a 'smaller number' before the taxes were actually collected.[31]

The update of *apaitêsima* over the course of two consecutive years is not particular to Karanis.[32] As already indicated above, the authors of the Theadelphian daybooks *BGU* IX

28 Twenty four petitions directed against tax collectors and related officials in the period from the early Principate to the end of the fourth century. *BGU* I 340 (after 148/9 CE, Ptolemais Euergetis); II 515 = *WChr.* 268 (193 CE, Arsinoitês); IV 1188 (15 BCE-14 CE, Koma, Hêrakleopolitês); *P.Amh.* II 83 = *WChr* 230 (301-307 CE, Arsinoitês); *P.Col.* VIII 209 with *P.Med.* I 43 = *SB* VI 9010 + *P.Mert.* I 8 (3 CE, Theadelphia); *P.Kell.* I 15 (357 CE, Kellis); *P.Lund* IV 1 = *SB* VI 9340 (198 CE, Bacchias); *P.Oxy.* II 285 = *P.Lond.* III 796 descr. (ca. 50 CE, Oxyrhynchos); XII 1460 (219/20 or 223/4 CE, Oxyrhynchitês); XIX 2235 (ca. 346 CE, Oxyrhynchitês); L 3584 (before 460 CE, Tampemou, Oxyrhynchitês); *P.Sakaon* 37 = *P.Thead.* 18 (284 CE, Thrasô, Arsinoitês); 46 = *P.Thead.* 22 (342 CE, Theadelphia); *P.Tebt.* II 302 (71/2 CE, Tebtynis); *P.Vind.Tand.* 5 (IV CE, unknown provenance); *PSI* VIII 927 (after 186 CE, Soknopaiou Nêsos ?); *SB* VI 9105 (198 CE?, Arsinoitês); 9458 (2nd half II CE, Tebtynis); XIV 11902 = *P.Oxy.* II 393 descr. (49/50 CE, Oxyrhynchos); XIV 12087 (162 CE, Theadelphia); XVI 12678 (late IV CE, Oxyrhynchitês); XVIII 13260 (328 CE, Hêrakleopolitês); 13733 (195 CE, Narmouthis); XXIV 16252 = *SB* XII 11114 (partial) = *P.Mich.Mchl.* 12 (163 CE, Karanis); *SPP* XXII 49 (200/1 CE, Soknopaiou Nêsos). Most recent discussions by B. Kelly, *Petitions, Litigation, and Social Control in Roman Egypt* (Oxford 2011) 198, 249, 273-274, and A.Z. Bryen, *Violence in Roman Egypt* (Philadelphia 2013) with English translations of some of the above-listed texts.

29 Four tax subjects, for instance, who have been recorded, in the case of *P.Mich.* IV.1 225, in the *apaitêsimon*'s 54th *kollêma*, appear in the next year, in the *apaitêsimon* used by the authors of *P.Cair.Mich.* 359, in *kollêma* 59. Three persons, originally recorded in column 55, moved in the next year to columns 59 and 60; all three persons recorded in column 63 move in the next *apaitêsimon* to column 69. Cf. also *P.Cair.Mich.* 359, pp. 3-4.

30 Onnôphris, son of Pnepherôs, grandson of Phanomgeus, registered in the older *apaitêsimon* in *kollêma* (= collection area) 58, was moved to the fourth *kollêma* in the younger counterpart, and Petaus, son of Petheus, grandson of Petesouchos, also originally located in *kollêma* 58, appears in the new list in *kollêma* 14.

31 In the same vein, in the collection record relating to days 1-30 in P.*Mich.* IV.1 225, already sampled above (n. 26), day 3, generally covering people in *kollêmata* 47-67, also records two persons registered in *kollêmata* 13 and 18, and the record of the 19th day, generally recording persons in *kollêmata* 46 through 72, reports one person registered in *kollêma* 11.

32 Cf., in particular, *BGU* II 457 = *WChr* 252 (132/3 CE, Karanis) a *kômogrammateus*' letter to a *praktôr sitikôn* informing him of corrections to an *apaitêsimon*. The corrective nature of any *apaitêsimon* is stressed in *P.Oxy.* XIX 2241.2-9 (283/4 CE, Oxyrhynchitês): [2] [ἀπαιτή]σιμον ἐκφορίων καὶ φόρων

1891 of 9-11.133 and *P.Col.* II 1r 1, fragments a and b, approximately dated by the editor to 134/5 CE, followed in the tax collection process an alphabetical *apaitêsimon*. Quite unsurprisingly, many of the tax payers recorded in the former were also registered in the latter. But the two texts clearly relied on different *apaitêsima*. Tax payers who were registered in a certain *kollêma* in *P.Col.* II 1r 1a and b tended to move down in *BGU* IX 1891.[33] In the case of Theadelphia, the task was quite simple: one simply needed to insert the new names in the right alphabetical order. In Karanis, updating the *apaitêsimon* required more intensive effort. The author needed to traverse the town and register new inhabitants, removing those who were no longer present or taxable and changing the taxation unit of those who had changed residence.

How were the topographical *apaitêsima* created? One may be tempted to connect the information gathered over the course of the census: the tax subjects would declare their residence, whereupon these data would be used to create the topographic collection units.[34] The main problem with this explanation is that, unlike their counterparts in the nome's metropolis, census returns from Karanis record only irregularly the place of residence of the declarant within the village.[35] This is the case in 11 census returns, while 10 clearly omit these data.[36] There is another possibility. There are sixteen documents from Roman Egypt that record tax payers by domicile. The order of registration is not alphabetical and, at least in five, it is clearly topographical.[37] In some cases, the data seem not to have been

σιτ̣ικ(ῶν) ἐδαφῶ(ν) | [3] [τοῦ ἐνε]σ̣τ(ῶτος) β (ἔτους) τῶν κυρίων ἡμῶν Καρείνου | [4] [καὶ Νουμε]ρ̣ιανοῦ Σεβαστῶν. τὸ συντεθὲν | [5] [ἐκ τῶν προ]τ̣(έρων) ἀπαιτησίμων κ̣α̣ὶ τῆς γενομένης | [6] [ὑπὸ Α̣ὐ̣ρ̣η̣λ̣ί̣ο̣υ̣] Σεουήρου τοῦ τῆς ο̣ὐσίας γεωμέτ(ρου) | [7] [ἐπισκ(έψεως) ἔστ]α̣ι ἢ καὶ ἐν μέρει ἄπεσται ὅ τι δ' ἐν | [8] [τόμοις ἐγ]ν̣ώσθη ἠγνοημένον ὀφεῖλ(ον) ὁ̣ποτέ|[9][ρως οἰκον]ομηθῆναι.

33 See, for example, Aunês, son of Marrheios, grandson of Pnepherôs, mother Thermouthis, who is registered in the *apaitêsimon* referred to in *P.Col.* II 1r 1 in column 8, and in that of *BGU* IX 1891 in column 9; Hêrôn, son of Hôros, grandson of Onnôphris, mother Tausiris, recorded in *P.Col.* II 1r 1 in *kollêma* 17 and in *BGU* IX 1891 in *kollêma* 19; and Tithoês, son of Hêraklês, grandson of Hêraklês, mother Hêrôs, recorded in the Columbia papyrus in col. 63 and then moved down to col. 66 in the papyrus from Berlin.

34 V.B. Schuman, 'P.Mich. IV: A Commentary', *APF* 29 (1983) 41-57 at 43.

35 See N. Reggiani, 'Identifying People in Official Reports: The Administrative Practice in Roman Egypt', above, p. 193 n. 36 with literature.

36 Eleven census declarations from Karanis indicate the *amphodon* in which the reported house is located. *BGU* I 59.25-26 (175 CE, Karanis); 95.11 (145/6 CE); 97.2 = *WChr* 204 = *Jur.Pap.* 2b (201/2 CE); 154.19-20 (145/6 CE); II 577.7-8 (201/2 CE); *P.Mich.* IX 542.14 (before 212 CE); *P.Oslo* II 25.15-19 (217 CE); *SB* VI 9554 (2c) (146/7 CE) (place of residence of the declaring party); 9555a.3-5 (153-160 CE); 9555b.3-5 (174 CE); XXII 15810.2,3 (203 CE). At the same time, indicating the location of the house within the village was never indispensable. It is clearly avoided in another ten texts: *BGU* I 54 (161 CE); II 447 (173/4 CE); 524 (159/60 CE); XI 2018 (187/8 CE); *P.Mich.* VI 370 (187/8 CE); IX 540 (ca. 53 CE); *SB* VI 9554 (3) (147 CE); 9554 (4) (147 CE); XIV 11577 (104 CE); XX 14326 (160/1 CE).

37 In topographical sequence: *P.Oslo* III 110 (after 131/2 CE, unknown provenance) (?); 111 (235 CE, Oxyrhynchos); *P.Oxy.* XLVI 3300 (late III Oxyrhynchos); *SB* VIII 9870 (II CE, Hermopolitês); XXIV 15930 (III CE, Arsinoitês); 16000 = *P.Berl. Bork.* = *SB* VIII 9902 (early IV CE, Panopolis). Uncertain: *BGU* III 734 (after 235 CE, Arsinoitês); 735 (235 CE, Arsinoitês); *P.Lond.* II 257 + *CPR* XV 25 (p. 19) (94/5 CE, Ptolemais Euergetis); 258 (p. 28) (ca. 94/5 CE, Ptolemais Euergetis); 259 (p. 36) = *WChr* 63 (94/5 CE, Philadelphia?); *P.Oxy.Census* (91/2 CE ?, Oxyrhynchos); *P.Ross.Georg.* II 12 (after 48 CE, Arsinoitês); *PSI* III 231 (after 174/5 CE, Thmouis); *SB* VI 9555a (162-174 CE, Karanis); XIV 11266

independently collected, but to derive from the census declarations. At the same time, in at least some of the texts, the report is structured as a house-by-house survey: the surveyor records the location and residents of each house vis-à-vis that surveyed immediately beforehand.[38] Such a survey could then be conveniently used by the composer of the Karanis topographic tax collection *kollêmata.* The *kollêmata* would be assembled into a roll that would then be given to the *praktores* who used it for collecting the taxes. There is no text that could unequivocally be identified as a topographic tax collection *kollêma*, but at least two papyri merit our attention, both now in the Papyrus Collection of the University of Michigan. In the first, *P.Mich.* XV 710 (II CE, Karanis), the letter π is followed by a list of ten persons with patronyms and some also with papponyms, metronyms, and their occupations.[39] Is this the tax unit referred to in our daybooks?[40] We are on somewhat firmer ground in the case of *P.Cair.Mich.* II 22 (II CE, Karanis). Five columns of a text written on the verso against the fibers are introduced by consecutive *kollêmata* numbers: 29 through

(I/II CE, Arsinoitês?); 11267 (II CE, unknown provenance); XXIV 15930 (III CE, Arsinoitês); *Stud.Pap.* IV pp. 58-78 = *P.Lond.* II 261 (p. 53) + *WChr* 61 + *P.Lond.* II 260 (p. 42) (partial) (ca. 73 CE, Ptolemais Euergetis). Cf., e.g., Z. Borkowski, *Une description topographique des immeubles à Panopolis* (= P.Berl.Bork.) (Warsaw 1975) 33-41; P. Mertens, *Les services de l'État civil et le contrôle de la population à Oxyrhynchus au IIIe siècle de notre ère* (Brussels 1958) 83-98.

38 See, e.g., *P.Oxy.* XLVI 3300 (late III, Oxyrhynchos): ἀρχο(μένων) ἀπὸ οἰκ(ίας) Διογένους | 2 Διογένης | 3 Διονύσιος ἀδελ(φός) | 4 λιβ(ὸς) ἐχο(μένη) Ἡρακλεί[δ]ου οἰκ(ία) | 5 αὐτὸς Ἡρακλείδης | 6 καμψ(άντων) ἐπὶ νότ(ον) (πρότερον) Αν .[. . .] | 7 Ἀρανάις καψ[άριος] | 8 Ἀκυλειανός | 9 βορ(ρᾶ) ἐχο(μένη) Θωνίου οἰκ(ία) | 10 Θῶνις ἁλιεύς | 11 νότ(ου) ἐχο(μένη) Πασόις ἁλιεύς | 12 νότ(ου) ἐχο(μένη) Πτολεμαίου Ἀμόϊτ(ος) | 13 Φιλέας καὶ Ἰσίδωρος | 14 Ἀπολλω( ) καὶ Ὦρ[ο]ς | 15 νότ(ου) ἐχο(μένη) Ἁρποκ( ) [ο]ἰκοδόμ(ος) | 16 νότ(ου) ἐχο(μένη) Ἀφυγχίου ποικιλ(τοῦ) | 17 αὐτὸς Ἀφῦγχις | 18 Θῶνις ἀδελφ(ός) | 19 νότ(ου) ἐχο(μένη) Ἀνεικήτου βαφ(έως) | 20 αὐτὸς Ἀνείκητος | 21 νότ(ου) ἐχο(μένη) Φιλάμμω(νος) λαχ(ανοπώλου) ἀοίκ(ητος) | 22 νότ(ου) ἐχο(μένη) Σαραπιάδος | 23 Ἡρακλῆς | 24 νότ(ου) ἐχο(μένη) Διογ( ) λινούφ(ου) | 25 Ἄρειος | 26 νότ(ου) ἐχο(μένη) Ἡρακλ( ) α(ὐτὸς) Ἡρακλ (..) | 27 ν[ό]τ(ου) ἐχο(μένη) Μυ . . . .[.] | 28 Παυ̣σ̣ᾶς Ἀχιλ( ) υἱός | 29 Ἡραίσκος ἕτερος | 30 καμ(ψάντων) ἐπ' ἀπηλ(ιώτην) Διονυσίου | . . λας τέκτω(ν) | 32 ἀπηλ(ιώτου) ἐχο(μένη) Ἀπολ( ) Κιχόϊς | 33 καμ(ψάντων) ἐπὶ βορ(ρᾶν) Σαραπιάδος | 34 Παγᾶς | 35 [βορ(ρᾶ)] ἐχό(μενον) κλειβαν⟨ε⟩ῖο(ν) | 36 [. . . . . . .] .ο̣ς̣[-ca.?-]. On the context see I.F. Fikhman, 'Die Bevölkerungszahl von Oxyrhynchos in byzantinischer Zeit', *ArchPF* 21 (1971) 110-120 = A. Jördens (ed.), *Wirtschaft und Gesellschaft im spätantiken Ägypten. Kleine Schriften Itzhak F. Fikhman* (Stuttgart 2006) 184-189.

39 *P.Mich.* XV 710 (II CE, Karanis): π Πρόκλος Τιτο̣ή̣ους σακκοφόρο(ς) | 2 Γάιο(ς) Σατορνείν[ου] (l. Σατορνίλ[ου]) τοῦ Κιαπέ | 3 Πετεσοῦχο(ς) Πεθέως τοῦ Χαριδή(μου) Ἡρᾶτος | 4 Πεθεῦ̣ς Ὀννώ(φρεως) τοῦ Ἥρωνος μ̣η(τρὸς) Τασουχαρίο(υ) | 5 Πτολε̣μ̣αῖο[ς] Πετ̣ε̣αρμώ̣θ(εως) τοῦ Ἀγχώφεως | 6 Χαρίδη(μος) Πε̣θ̣έως [τοῦ] μη(τρὸς) Ἡρᾶτος σακκο( ) | 7 Πτολεμαῖο(ς) Σοκ̣μ̣ήνε̣(ως) τοῦ Παούσεως (l. Παύσεως) | 8 Πιτιρω[. . .]ς̣ Σοκ[.]ι̣ο̣(ς) τοῦ Ἁρμά̣χεως | 9 Π̣ά̣σω[ν . .] .[. . . . .]ν̣ος τοῦ Πε̣ .υ̣[.] .[.]θο(υ) | 10 [-ca.?-] .υ̣ . .[.] . .ῶτος | (verso) ιϛ δ κο(λλήματος). The *kollêma* was probably never integrated into a *tomos synkollesimos.* Compare Clarysse (supra n. 2) 349.

40 Pace *P.Mich.* XV, p. 51: 'undoubtedly the number of the klerouchie to which the person listed belonged', and H. Geremek, *Karanis, communauté rurale de l'Égypte romaine au IIe-IIIe siècle de notre ère* (Warsaw 1969) 77. I could not find an adequate explanation, in terms of the interpretation proposed here, for the text on the verso.

32.[41] The pattern of record is identical to that reconstructed using the daybooks: no alphabetical order, frequent next-of-kin in each column. Moreover, according to the editors, the handwriting is similar to *P.Cair.Mich.* 359A, col. xliv.[42]

According to our description so far, information on place of residence was gathered through house-to-house topographical surveys. The geographical data extracted from the surveys was used for the creation of topographical tax units, each registered in a different *kollêma*. The *kollêmata*, naturally assembled into rolls, were handed over to the tax collector; in the case of *P.Cair.Mich.* 359 and *P.Mich.* IV.1 225, the tax collector took pains to register, in his daybooks, the *kollêma* number next to each tax payer. The *apaitêsima* were also annually updated, yet it seems unreasonable to assume that the exacting work involved in a house-by-house survey would be undertaken every year.

A Berlin papyrus, published by W. Brashear in 1976, *BGU* XIII 2362, may shed some light.[43] The text consists of two columns, only one of which was published in the *editio princeps*. In the published column, there is a list of names, in what seems to be a random, or at least non-alphabetical, order. There are, of course, many lists on papyri exhibiting such a pattern, but, in the present case, a second hand has added, interlinearly, the word κολ(λήματος), followed by numbers—an addition that is pivotal to the understanding of the nature of the text. The text, as drafted by the first hand, is a scrap of an *apaitêsimon*, a *kollêma* recording members of one topographic collection unit, of the type assumed here in the case of *P.Mich.* XI 710 and *P.Cair.Mich.* II 22. Should we assume in its first, unpublished column the same context as in subsequent text, *BGU* XIII 2362 would resemble, in particular, *P.Cair.Mich.* II 22:[44] a fragment of an extensive document, from the village of Karanis recording the tax subjects by their topographical collection units. In the present

---

41 *P.Cair.Mich.* II 22 (II CE, Karanis): (column i) κθ | 2 Πτολε(μαῖος) Ἀθᾶτ̣ος | 3 Ἁτρῆς Π . . . .[.] .[.]αιο̣υ | 4 Ἰσᾶς Πακύσεως | 5 Καμῆς Ἱερανούφεως | 6 Κάστωρ ἀδελ(φός) | 7 Δίδυμος Σαραπίων(ος) | 8 Λεοντᾶς υἱός | 9 Ἀ̣φροδίσις Βα<κ>χίω̣ν̣ος | 10 [Ἀ]μ̣μωνᾶς Καμπᾶ | 11 [Π]ετεσοῦχος Ἑριέως | 12 [Φ]ιλάδελφο̣ς Πτολε[μαίου] | 13 [. .] . .[. .]α̣υ̣ς Πετεσού[χου] | 14 [-ca.?-]α̣μ̣ος .υ .[.] .ατ̣[-ca.?-] (column ii) λ̣ | 2 Σερῆ̣νος [Ἀ]χιλλᾶ | 3 Κ̣ . .το̣[ς] ἀ̣δελ(φός) | 4 Ἀμ̣μ̣ώνιος μη(τρὸς) Σαραπιάδος | 5 Λογ[γῖ]νος Ἀπονείτου | 6 Ἁτρ̣ῆ̣ς Ἀπίωνος | 7 Σα̣βῖνος Πτολε(μαίου) σαρ̣υς | 8 Πεταῦς Ἑρ̣ιέως | 9 Ἑριεῶς υἱός | 10 Σα̣βῖνος βουκόλος | 11 Π̣εθεῶς ἀδελ(φός) | 12 [Ὀ]ννῶφρις Τα̣ύρωνο̣ς | 13 Ἑ̣ρᾶς Ω[. . .]φ[. .] .ι̣ρ̣[.] | 14 [-ca.?-] . .[-ca.?-] (column iii) (two missing lines) | 3 [- -] Π̣[-ca.?-] .[-ca.?-]ο̣υ | 4 . [-ca.?-] . . . .[.]. .ως | 5 [-ca.?-] . .ιος | 6 . [-ca.?-] . . . | 7 [-ca.?-] . . .ας | 8 [- -] … [- -] | 9 [- -] … [- -] | 10 Λ̣[-ca -] | 11 Σ̣[-ca [?.] (two missing lines) | (column iv) λβ | 2 Ου̣μερ .ς Η .[-ca.?-] | 3 Ὧρος Πτολεμ̣α̣ί(ου) | 4 Π̣τολε(μαῖος) Σεμ[. . . .]περου | 5 Σωτᾶς Ἀχιλλᾶ .ηρα | 6 Δημᾶς . .ουα̣ο̣[.] . . .στου | 7 Σαταβοῦς .α . .ς | 8 Κάστωρ [-ca.?-] .ριου | 9 Σαραπί[ων] Ἑρμοῦς | 10 [-ca.?-] .[-ca.?-] | [-ca.?-] . (two missing lines) | (column v) [λ]γ | 2 Μ̣έ̣ν̣[τ]ωρ Λεον̣[-ca.?-] | 3 Εὐήμερο̣ς̣ [-ca-] | 4 [-ca.?-] .π̣ .[-ca.?-] (two missing lines).

42 *P.Cair.Mich.* II, pp. 120-121.

43 *BGU* XIII 2362 (= P. 21469r) (II CE, Karanis): . . .[-ca.?-] | 2 (hand 2) κο̣λ̣(λήματος) ρ̣ [-ca.?-] | 3 (hand 1) Κάστωρ Κ[-ca.?-] | 4 (hand 2) κολ(λήματος) ια̣ .[-ca.?-] | 5 (hand 1) Λεωνίδης [.]ανω̣( ) υ( )[-ca.?-] | 6 (hand 2) κολ(λήματος) . | 7 (hand 1) Νααρ(αῦς) Ναα[ρ(αῦτος)] Να .[-ca.?-] | 8 (hand 2) κολ(λήματος) ριγ[-ca.?-] | 9 (hand 1) Ζηνᾶς Φαήσεως υ( ) δ̣[-ca.?-] 10 (hand 2) κολ(λήματος) ριβ | 11 (hand 1) Λε̣ . .σσ . Τεσεν[ο]ύφ[εως -ca.?-] | 12 (hand 2) [κο]λ(λήματος) ιε | 13 (hand 1) Πα̣[-ca.?-] Ὀρσενού[φεως -ca.?-] | 14 (hand 2) [κολ(λήματος) -ca.?-] | 15 (hand 1) Φανομ[-ca.?-] νεώτ(ερος) υ( ) Φ̣α̣ν̣[-ca.?-] | 16 (hand 2) κολ(λήματος) ρια | 17 (hand 1) Πτολεμαῖς Ὀννώφρ[εως -ca.?-] | 18 (hand 2) κολ(λήματος) α . .| 19 (hand 1) Φανομγεὺς Πασο( ) . . .[-ca.?-] | 20 (hand 2) κολ(λήματος) ι̣ς̣ | 21 (hand 1) Μελανᾶς [-ca.?-] | 22 (hand 2) κολ(λήματος) π̣η.

44 See picture.

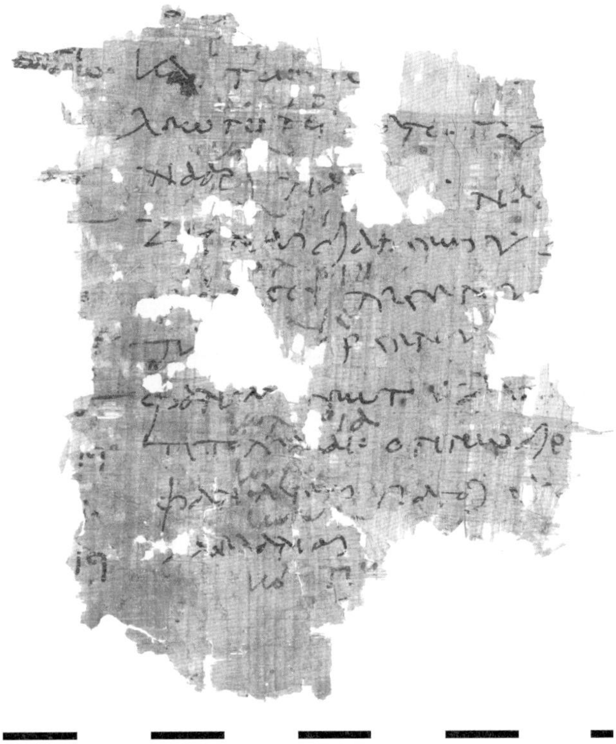

© Staatliche Museen zu Berlin - Ägyptisches Museum und Papyrussammlung, Scan: Berliner Papyrusdatenbank, P 21469

case, after the collection was over, the scribe used the document for yet another purpose. Instead of collecting the information from scratch, he simply verified the current whereabouts of payers recorded in each column and assigned them new tax units accordingly. In addition, differently from its two counterparts, *BGU* XIII 2362 can be prosopographically linked to the topographical tax collection units, as discussed in this paper: lines 10-11 of the Berlin text record a certain Zênas son of Phaêsis, now to be assinged to the 112th *kollêma*.[45] A Zênas son of Phaêsis, grandson of Zênas, whose mother being Tapasiôn, is registered four times in *P.Mich.* IV.1 225 of 174 CE; in three cases we are also informed of his tax-collection unit: 103.[46] In the following year, the same Zênas son of Phaêsis is recorded twice in *P.Cair.Mich.* 359; his *kollêma* here is 109.[47] Upon this evidence, it is now possible not only to connect the *kollêmata* of *BGU* XIII 2362 with the topographical taxation unit evidenced in two extensive daybooks, but also to propose a date. Zênas, who was registered in 174 in *kollêma* 103, was moved over in the next year to *kollêma* 109. Assuming the same pattern in the long run, *BGU* XIII 2362, where Zênas is recorded in *kollêma* 112, could be plausibly dated to any of the immediately following years, probably to 176 CE.

Our direct, secure evidence of the topographic taxation units derives from an extremely short period. The two extensive daybooks, which bear testimony to the topographic taxation units, date to 174 CE and 175 CE; the remaining documents mentioned above cannot be dated with any accuracy. A seemingly negative proof is provided by other daybooks. The

45 Supra n. 43.
46 ll. 275, 1845, 2244, 2589 and <http://oxrep.classics.ox.ac.uk/databases/people/391_zenas_s_phaesis_gs_zenas_m_tapasion/>.
47 ll. 225, 1682.

extensive *P.Mich.* IV.1 223, covering the period extending from September 171 CE to August 172 CE, does not record the *apaitêsimon*'s *kollêmata* numbers, nor does *P.Mich.* IV.1 224, which covers December 172 CE and almost entirely 173 CE. Does this mean that the topographic collection units were ephemeral, a one-time attempt to introduce a different categorization method that was soon abandoned? I don't believe so. *P.Cair.Mich.* II 22, and *P.Mich.* XI 710 give entirely different names from those recorded under the same *kollêma* numbers in *P.Cair.Mich.* 359 and *P.Mich.* IV.1 225. If the two shorter documents do, in fact, record topographic taxation units, they would relate to *apaitêsima* pre- or post-dating that recorded in the said tax lists. In addition, the fact that *P.Mich.* IV.1 223 and *P.Mich.* IV.1 224 do not explicitly record the *apaitêsimon*'s *kollêma* number does not prove its absence. Even for the two years for which the existence of the unit is secure not all tax reports contain such reference: the author of *P.Mich.* IV.1 225 added the *kollêma* numbers only as far as Epeiph 1st (25.5.174) , but have henceforth abandoned this practice: no *kollêma* number is recorded for payments made down to the end of the same year.[48]

The absence of an explicit reference does not imply, then, that the topographic collection units did not exist before and after 174 CE and 175 CE. Exhaustive coverage of the entire population by domicile is documented in Roman Egypt in the case of the capitals of the nomes, including Ptolemais Euergetis, where tax subjects were registered (ἀναγεγραμμένοι) in *amphoda.* Accordingly, Arsinoite tax reports that record the payer's place of residence stem from the nome's capital.[49] It is likely that the existence of this system would have inspired the creators of the topographic collection units in Karanis. *Amphoda* are also attested in the case of Karanis, but as they are not systematically applied as a means of identification in general, it is not plausible that they were used for the creation of the topographic collection units discussed in this paper.[50] There is thus hardly any ground to connect the tax-collection units with the *amphoda* system of Karanis. Our most direct prototype may be sought in the institution of the *klêrouchia*: as early as 141 CE, potential lessees of public land are divided into *klêrouchiai*, by which they are engaged in the forced cultivation of state land, their holdings and liabilities are recorded, and the assignment of seed loans is organized. In administrative terms, the *klêrouchiai* exhibit a close resemblance to the topographic taxation unit: the creation of an exceedingly small group of persons, each recorded in, and numbered by, their distinct *kollêma.*[51] It is thus not unreasonable to assume that the two systems were simultaneously introduced or that the taxation unit was introduced following the success of the *klêrouchia* system. Should the latter be the case, we could conjecture its introduction in the generation before its earliest secure attestation in 174 CE. Be that as it may, the bureaucratic experiment discussed here

48 *P.Mich.* IV.1 225.2414-3022 (27.5-14.8.174); *P.Mich.* IV.2 358b (14-22.8.174 CE); *P.Mich.* IV.1 225.3157-3334 (14-26.11.174); *P.Mich.* IV.2 358c (24-27.8.174 CE), 358d-e (28.8.–6.9.174); *P.Mich.* IV.1 225.3023-3053 (18-19.10.174); 358f (19-24.11.174); 358h (31.12.74-6.1.175).

49 *BGU* XIII 2280 + *BGU* IV 1087 + *BGU* I 9 = *WChr* 293 (cols. 1-2) (ca. 276 CE, Ptolemais Euergetis).

50 In *SB* VI 9555a (162-174), an abstract of data submitted in census declarations, the data from each *amphodon* are organized in different rolls, and independent numbering: γ τόμ[ο(υ) ἀ]μφόδο(υ) 'Ισίου [κ]ο(λλήματος) ιη [-ca.?-].

51 Geremek (supra n. 40), 74; O.M. Pearl, "The 94 Klerouchies at Karanis", in : E. Kießling, H.-A. Rupprecht (eds.), *Akten des XIII. Internationalen Papyrologenkongresses, Marburg/Lahn 2.-6. August 1971* (Munich 1974) 325-330.

seems to have been limited to Karanis. Even here, we have no idea whether it was still pursued after 175 CE. That the tax units were not founded on any preexisting topographic division may imply that it did not, but this is all, of course, just a hypothesis.

Rome and the Empire

Format and Features of Military Account-Books: the Case of PSI II 119 *recto* + ChLA IV 264*

Ornella Salati, Neapel

A well-known section of Vegetius' treatise is often quoted as testifying to the volume of the paperwork drawn up by the clerks of the Roman imperial army.[1] In comparison to the literary sources, however, the papyrological material has contributed more decisively to our knowledge of the ways in which military documents were written out, updated, and stored.[2] Furthermore, surviving records from different contexts – Egypt, Syria, Britain and elsewhere – make evident that much of this documentation was quite standard wherever the army was stationed. No great difference can be seen between (for example) accounts of an auxiliary unit in the West and those of an Egyptian legion. Neither did the writing support, in the form of papyrus, wooden tablet or ostracon, influence their general format.[3]

If one focusses on the Latin papyri from Egypt of the first three centuries AD, one discovers that a non-negligible number of documents appears to be related to financial aspects of the Roman army. Pay records, receipts, and different kinds of accounts were drawn up every day, even in times of peace.[4] In detail, the official evidence consists of 13 pay records,[5] 19 receipts,[6] 3 lists of materials,[7] and 5 accounts.[8] Only one bilingual account-

---

* The research leading to these results has received funding from the European Research Council (ERC) under the European Union's Horizon 2020 research and innovation programme (Grant agreement nº 636983); ERC-PLATINUM project 'Papyri and LAtin Texts: INsights and Updated Methodologies. Towards a philological, literary, and historical approach to Latin papyri' University of Naples 'Federico II' – PI Maria Chiara Scappaticcio.

1 Veg. *mil.* 2.19.2-4: *Totius enim legionis ratio, sive obsequiorum sive militarium munerum sive pecuniae, cottidie adscribitur actis maiore prope diligentia quam res annonaria vel civilis polyptychis adnotatur. Cottidianas etiam in pace vigilias, item excubitum sive agrarias de omnibus centuriis et contuberniis vicissim milites faciunt: ut ne quis contra iustitiam praegravetur aut alicui praestetur immunitas, nomina eorum, qui vices suas fecerunt, brevibus inseruntur. Quando quis commeatum acceperit vel quot dierum, adnotatur in brevibus.* On this passage see the remarks of Bowman 1998: 35-6, with further bibliography.

2 On the topic see Watson 1974; Phang 2007; Speidel 2007; Le Bohec 2010.

3 In literature, the level of standardization of military records has been discussed controversially. In addition to the studies cited in the previous footnote, see also Gilliam 1967: 233 (= Id. 1986: 317); Stauner 2004.

4 The following list updates that provided by R.O. Fink in his valuable work, *Roman Military Records on Papyrus* (hereafter RMR), in which papyri in Greek script and from Dura are also included. To give an example, in RMR the number of pay records, all in Latin script and from Egypt, amounts to 6 items (see RMR 68-73).

5 In chronological order they are: RMR 68; P.Harr. inv. 183e *recto*; RMR 69; RMR 73, although it is not a real pay record, but a list of sums held in deposit; ChLA X 410 + IV 228 + XVIII 663; ChLA IX 404; P.Ryl. II 273 a; RMR 71; ChLA XI 495; ChLA XI 473; perhaps RMR 130; ChLA X 446; ChLA III 212.

book survives.[9] Now a new account-book in Latin script can be added to the list of the extant documents: PSI II 119 *recto* + ChLA IV 264.

Discovered in Oxyrhynchus,[10] this roll has in fact been neglected so far and partially misinterpreted by scholars. One portion of the roll, provided by P.Laur. IV 134 *recto*, still remains unpublished, but for a specific reason which will explained in the next paragraph; ChLA IV 264 was published several years ago by R. Marichal in the fourth volume of *Chartae Latinae Antiquiores*.[11] As regards this portion, Marichal believed that the roll was an account-book, kept in an office of the central administration, probably that of the *idios logos*. Only very recently has a further portion of the roll, PSI II 119 *recto*,[12] come to light, showing the exact nature of this account-book: it started by recording properties and debts of soldiers, even dead and suicide victims; next it contained other accounts, such as those preserved by ChLA IV 264, in which payments and summaries of revenues to the fort are listed. Considering the content, the roll was likely stored in the same military context in which it was conceived and written out, instead of a civic office.[13]

This paper provides a more in-depth analysis of the evidence, in order to highlight its formatting and textual features. For this purpose, size of the roll and layout of the accounts will be discussed; then attention will be drawn to content and vocabulary. In both sections parallels provided by military papyri, even from different geographical contexts, will be cited. The use of comparative evidence, thus, will lead to a better understanding not only of the roll as such, but also of the bookkeeping system employed in the Roman army.

1. Date, Use and Re-use

A brief description of the evidence needs to be made at the outset. On the basis of internal elements, the roll can be closely dated: in ChLA IV 264 six auxiliary units (ll. 10-5) are mentioned, among them the *cohors I Lusitanorum* occurs (l. 10). This cohort made its first appearance in Egypt in AD 105,[14] and this date can thus be assumed as a certain *terminus post quem*. Furthermore, in PSI II 119 *recto* fr. *a* l. 17, the abbreviation for the *legio III Cyrenaica* can be read. The movements of this legion have been quite broadly discussed,

---

6 Together with O.Berenike III 275; 284; 290; 291; 312; 333; 361; 365; 392; 412; 414; 416; 433; 439, which feature receipts for water, see RMR 80; P.Mich. VII 435 + 440; ChLA XVIII 662; P.Oxy. IV 735 (which is in Latin and in Greek); ChLA XLI 1198.

7 P.Ryl. II 223; RMR 84; P.Grenf. II 110.

8 RMR 129; RMR 131; RMR 132; perhaps PSI inv. 2450 *recto*; perhaps ChLA XLV 1351 *descr*. There are two unpublished accounts from the fort of Maximianon, O.Max. inv. 288 and O.Max. inv. 1345, whose military connection is to be ascertained.

9 RMR 75.

10 On ChLA IV 264 (= TM 69879), found by B.P. Grenfell and A.S. Hunt in 1897, see P.Oxy. III (1903): Preface. PSI II 119 *recto* (= TM 70149) was found by E. Pistelli in an unknown year, between 1910 and 1913; see PSI II (1913): Introduzione, III n. 1. Details on P.Laur. IV 134, bought from the antiquarian market by E. Pistelli, are provided by Pintaudi 2014: 245-7.

11 ChLA IV (1967): 78-80; XLVIII 38. See also Marichal 1964: 110-1.

12 Just a brief reference can be found in ChLA XLVII 1461 *descr*.

13 Edition and commentary in Salati 2017b. Further remarks in Salati 2019.

14 See RMD 9, 40-1 (AD 105, 24th September); CIL III 13582 (AD 110). A list of the related documentation can be found in Alston 1995: 175. More recently, on the history of this cohort during I-II AD see Țentea, Matei-Popescu 2016.

but, according to the common view, it is from AD 127 that it was permanently transferred to Arabia.[15] It is also possible that its passage should be slightly backdated to AD 125.[16] The date of the roll, thus, falls within a narrow chronological frame; the script, a good form of ancient Roman cursive, is also consistent with early II AD.[17]

Through ancient use, the roll was subjected to considerable tearing, and, in some parts, it was covered by sheets from several Greek documents. For this reason, the *recto* of P.Laur. IV 134 has been completely lost;[18] PSI II 119 *recto* fr. *d* has also been partially covered by a small piece of a Greek document. Afterwards, when the Latin document was out of date, the roll was reused on the *verso* to write Plato's *Gorgia.*[19] Consequently, much scholarly attention has been devoted to this side of the roll, neglecting the other side. However, it is worth underlining that the present roll is among a very few instances of rolls bearing a Latin documentary text written before a Greek literary one. A relevant example, from Oxyrhynchus as well, is P.Oxy. L 3533 (II AD), containing 9 faint lines of a hitherto unpublished Latin register on the *recto*, and sections from Menander's *Epitrepontes* on the *verso.*[20] Regarding military evidence, four papyri deserve to be mentioned. The most famous is BGU II 696, the *pridianum* of the *cohors I Lusitanorum*. The document is dated to AD 156, 31st August, while an anonymous musical treatise was written on the *verso* between II and III AD.[21] A similar case is provided by P.Harr. inv. 183e *recto*, a pay record of I AD, which contains an anonymous lyrical work on the back, probably written during the same century.[22] ChLA XLII 1225 preserves a report of transfers of auxiliaries, as generally framed, dated to AD 144-63;[23] after a few decades, the *verso* was used to write a grammatical treatise. Lastly, P.Oxy. LXXXIII 5363 contains a sort of strength report dated to AD 244-9 or 247-9; a Greek recipe for a preparation for dental care was written on the other side, in the last few decades of the same century.

In general, such re-uses would suggest that (some) official military rolls needed to have specific morphological characteristics, not unlike those rolls in use in the civilian administration: the writing support was of high quality and could reach notable dimensions. That explains why, when they were out of date, military rolls were reused for literary works too. This assumption appears to have been true especially in the case of PSI II 119 *recto* + ChLA IV 264, as the next paragraph will show. Lastly, since the hand of the *recto* is the

15 Kennedy 1980: 283-308. See also Speidel 1977: 691-7.

16 Gatier 2000: esp. 357.

17 Among military papyri, comparisons can be made with P.Oxy. VII 1022, dated to AD 103, 24th February, and ChLA XLII 1212, of AD 113-7. A further parallel is provided by P.Oxy. LII 3692, of II AD, a copy of the will of Iulius Diogenes.

18 Pintaudi 1977: 112; Id. in P.Laur. IV (1983): 112; Puglia 1997: 45, 52, fn. 98. In general, on factors which could cause the deterioration of the papyrus see Leach-Tait 2000: 239-43.

19 In order, P.Laur. IV 134 + P.Oxy. III 454 + PSI II 119 (= TM 62613, LDAB 3798, MP3 1414.1). See also Crisci 1998: 107-8, nr. 26; Carlini, Violante 1999: 70-8. Only on P.Oxy. III 454 see Turner 1987: 106, nr. 62.

20 E.G. Turner, in P.Oxy. L (1983): 43.

21 Bibliography on the *recto* is listed in ChLA X (1979), 19 and in RMR 64, 228. On the *verso* see Pöhlmann, West 2001: 56-60, nr. 17-8 and 166-73 nr. 50-2, with previous bibliographical references.

22 On the *recto* see Salati 2017a; the *verso* has been published as P.Harr. I 35 (= TM 65564, LDAB 6815, MP³ 1960).

23 A different interpretation of the Latin document is suggested by Fink 1964: 297-9.

same, we should imagine a continuous roll, in which the individual accounts were written in succession, rather than a *tomos synkollesimos*.

2. Size and Layout

The literary content of the *verso*, arranged in columns of standard width of 5.7 cm and with standard intercolumnium of 1 cm, allows us to reconstruct the size of the roll and to work out the position of all the fragments within it. Here it is sufficient to say that, according to my reconstruction, the Platonic dialogue was presumably written in ca. [141] columns: which means that PSI II 119 *recto* was likely found at a distance of cols. [3] = ca. [20] cm from the beginning of the roll; in this space only one Latin column could be written. Then, a space of ± cols. [23] = ca. [154.1] cm separated this papyrus and ChLA IV 264, which was distant ± cols. [61] = ca. [408.7] cm from P.Laur. IV 134. Lastly, P.Laur. IV 134 was followed by a space occupied by ± cols. [42] = ca. [281.4] cm. On these accounts, it can be assumed that the length was about [944.7] cm. Adding the measures of the *protokollon* and *eschatokollon*, the total length was likely ca. [10] m, which was a standard measure. Since each Platonic column contained 48 lines on average and the margin was 2 cm, one may estimate that the height of the roll measured at least [31] cm.[24]

Such a roll height finds several parallels within military papyri: for instance, RMR 63, *pridianum-detulit* of the *cohors I Hispanorum Veterana equitata*, had a height of 32.4 cm,[25] and the abovementioned BGU II 696 of 35.5 cm.[26] Of greater interest is the comparison with similar financial documents: ChLA X 410 + IV 228 + XVIII 663, the pay record of an auxiliary unit, was 36 cm in height and RMR 68, preserving a legionary pay record, reached a maximum of 37 cm. In this light, the measure of PSI II 119 + ChLA IV 264 + P.Laur. IV 134 appears to be completely average.

As far as the layout is concerned, the two extant papyri show different features. To start with, PSI II 119 *recto* consists of four fragments,[27] in which parts of three columns survive altogether. In fact, fr. *d* is a small piece and does not need to be taken into account in the present discussion, as well as fr. *c*, being blank. In fr. *b* portions of 12 lines survive, whereas in fr. *a*, being the best preserved, the surviving column is complete on the left, right and bottom margins and shows 19 lines. By looking at the Platonic *verso*, it is possible to calculate the lost portion of both columns and to infer that the Latin document was arguably organized in columns of [33/4] lines, at least in this portion of the roll. This figure does not appear to be surprising: among the aforementioned examples, in RMR 63 the two surviving columns, being complete, consist of 38 and 44 lines, respectively; in BGU II 696

24 Fuller discussion in Salati 2017b. This reconstruction can be compared with that suggested by Puglia 1996: 56, who speaks about the same roll length, although suggests that the *Gorgia* was in [135] columns. By contrast, Johnson 2004: 141, 192, 221 indicates ca. [27.9] cm in height and [8] m in length, for a total of [119] Platonic columns.

25 See Marichal in ChLA III (1963): 127. On this document see also RMR: 217-27, and Stauner 2004: 102-4.

26 Marichal in ChLA X (1979): 19.

27 The fragments are, unfortunately, numbered with respect to the text on the *verso* and therefore come in reverse order with regard to the Latin document. Here the traditional numeration is followed in order to facilitate comparisons.

col. I contains a total of 40 lines, while col. II 43 lines. Lastly, in the pay record of ChLA X 410 + IV 228 + XVIII, col. II of frame *A*, preserved in its entirety, is made up of 42 lines.

Focusing solely on PSI II 119 *recto* fr. *a*, where sufficient text survives to afford generalizations about the layout, one can note that the column of writing is rather wide (12,7/13 cm) and is arranged into single blocks of information: the opening of each entry is signalled by the first line projected to the left. Moreover, the scribe left blank spaces at the end of entries, setting out on the right important elements, such as the abbreviations of *ad k(astra)* (l. 12, 15, 19) and *dr*(*achmae*) (l. 16). In this latter case, he also increased the modulo of the two letters. In the main, this layout is quite common in Roman military evidence and, more importantly, seems to be specific neither of a kind of document nor a period. It is continuously used in morning reports, even from different geographical contexts, such as PSI XIII 1307 *recto*, of mid. I AD, and P.Dura 82, of AD 223-33, stress. Such reports are characterized by columns containing numerous lines of writing and being very wide; a further common trait with PSI II 119 *recto* is the arrangement in single entries with the first line running out of the external right margin.[28] Sometimes this same layout can be found in lists: for instance, a close parallel is provided by P.Dura 97, a list of men and their horses (AD 251); here the lines of the only one surviving column are grouped into a single block, separated by blank spaces. In a similar way to the present papyrus, the monetary symbols are isolated in the right-hand margin.

It is tempting to think that this formatting uniformity was due to the needs of service and of managing vast amount of data: morning reports and lists, like the present document, comprised detailed material and needed thus to be readable and easy to consult. Interestingly, one may find some parallels also within the non-military evidence. A somewhat similar layout, with single sections of information and blank spaces at the end of the lines, occurs also in contemporary tax lists in Greek script: a comparison can be made with, for example, the well-known P.Col. II 1 *recto* 2, annual statement of receipts of poll tax (AD 128-9) and P.Col. V 1 *verso* 4, a register with tax payments in kind (AD 161-80). In both the texts the wide columns are made up of single entries, with isolated elements at the right-hand margin. This comparison may indicate the high level of specialization achieved by military clerks, who made their own document at any time, adapting the formatting conventions to their specific needs.

The second registration of the present roll, indeed, shows a different and convenient layout: in ChLA IV 264 only one column is preserved. On account of the Platonic column on the *verso*, one may conclude that the fragment preserves the greater part of the column and only the first 2 lines with the top margin are likely missing. The broad bottom margin, of 11 cm, clearly shows that we have here the last section of the record.

The arrangement of the narrow column marks the various steps taken by the scribe: l. 5, 9, and 16 are projected to the left. This last line is emphasized also through the increased size of the first letter. A blank space between ll. 18-9 underlines the end of the account. Furthermore, ll. 10-5, containing the list of the units involved, are centered in the middle of the column. This layout looks like that of numerous military lists. Among financial

28 A specific study of layout and graphical conventions of morning reports on papyrus is lacking. On the script of PSI XIII 1307 see Fioretti, Cavallo 2015. In general, on content and formulas of such records see Fink in RMR 179-80; Phang 2007: 292; and mostly Stauner 2004: 74-83.

evidence, comparisons can be made especially with RMR 73, bank deposits of the riders of an *ala* (AD 120-50), and with RMR 80, a receipt for hay from a *turma* (AD 130). During III AD a further parallel is provided by P.Oxy. IV 735, a receipt for wheat for cavalrymen and infantry (AD 205, 4th September). In all these examples, the most relevant elements of the document are isolated in separate lines written in the middle of the column.

3. Content and Language

Like the layout, the content of the two accounts will be examined separately.[29] As far as PSI II 119 *recto* is concerned, it is a record of goods belonging to the deceased and suicides among the soldiers, which appear partially to be under the supervision of a prefect of the camp. Both fr. *b* and fr. *a*, covering a period from February to April, show that the sequence of entries runs from the beginning of the year. Since fr. *a*, of these two pieces, is the better preserved, the analysis will focus mostly on this item.

Here parts of four entries remain: the first two are very poorly preserved, and it is sufficient to underline that entry 2 (l. 10) would contain, as it seems, a reference to dead soldiers. Fortunately, the following two items are preserved well enough to provide much more information. In addition, they follow a similar pattern. The text of this section runs as follows:

13 XIII K(alendas) M[ai]i[a]s i . ṭi . ṃ[.]u . r . . ex epistul[a Pe]troni praef[(ecti)]
14 castror(um) ex b[oni]s . ẹrv . [. .]m XỊỊỊỊ qui mortem
15 sibi conscit exit auri ob debit[u]m ad k(astra)
16 ṾIIIỊ K(alendas) Mai(as) Valerio Capitoni (centuria) Papiri heredi Valeri ca[. .] dr(achm-)
17 . . . . . m[. .] leg(io-) III Cyr(enaica-) ex epistul[a P]etroni praef(ecti) castr(orum)
18 [ex bonis] . ẹrvilụm XX̣Ṿ qui mortem sibi conscit
19 [exit auri] ob dẹbịṭ[um] ad k(astra)

Salient elements are the following: date (1), mention of written instruction (*ex epistula*) by the prefect of the camp (2), reference to some goods – whose interpretation remains problematic – followed by figures (3), and at the end, the information that the suicide victim owed an amount of gold, expressed with the partitive *auri*, to the camp to cover his debt (4). In addition to these elements, entry 4 makes mention of an unknown Valerius Capito, who belonged to the *centuria* of Papirius and who was appointed as heir of a homonymous Valerius. At the end of l. 16 the abbreviation of drachmae occurs, but no figures survive at all. At the beginning of l. 17 the mention for the *legio III Cyrenaica* is found.

The content of this latter entry might recall that of another military record, P.Mich. VII 435 + 440, which lists inheritances and payments of the *vicesima hereditatum* and concerns the *III Cyrenaica* as well. Nonetheless, one should also note that the Michigan papyrus consists only of autograph receipts, written by different hands, in which the language appears quite different and suicide is never mentioned as cause of death. In fact, the current evidence does not provide any parallel or model for such a record. PSI II 119 *recto* is, therefore, unique in its genre and a very important document: firstly, through the sentence

29 Texts and further details in Salati 2017b; Ead. 2019.

qui sibi mortem conscit, which is one of the traditional ways to refer to self-killers,[30] it is the only papyrological source attesting to cases of self-killings within the Roman army. Secondly and maybe more remarkably, this papyrus throws light on the financial outcome of the soldiers' suicide.

As is well known, military suicide was regarded as a form of desertion or oath breaking and, consequently, there was a general tendency by the state to discourage it.[31] Financial penalties, among other things, were also employed for this purpose.[32] In view of the dating of the roll, it is significant that an important change occurred at the beginning of II AD, when the emperor Hadrian narrowed down the valid and invalid motives for self-killing and established the cases in which a soldier could keep his testamentary rights. This was possible if the suicide was committed because of the burden of age or of grief. In addition to this, the emperor established that, without a legal will and heirs, the soldier's goods went to the camp as a whole.[33] As far as can be seen from what survives, the document seems to differ from the imperial disposition, as it makes mention neither of the reasons for the suicide nor heirs. For these features, it would seem to predate Hadrian's regulation (AD 119). Unfortunately, the evidence is not sufficiently explicit to support this assumption. Furthermore, this omission might be easily explained by the fact that the soldier was in debt with legionary cash, as the language would suggest. It is also significant that this debt is indicated by the word *aureus*, which is particularly rare among Latin papyri.[34] Regardless of its connection with the imperial rule, the document considers only economic aspects; it thereby gives us a glimpse of the Roman idea of army properties.

Focusing on ChLA IV 264, this portion contains a balance of cash payments, organized in 6 entries. Unfortunately, the text does not provide any detail about the source of these payments. The first editor spoke of a collection of taxes.[35] Alternatively, one might speculate that these sums were related to some financial activity of the units. A positive element could be the mention of Irinaeus *Augusti libertus* both in entry 1 and 2 (l. 2, 7). The role of imperial slaves or freedmen and their involvement both in the supply system and in

30 The sentence *qui sibi mortem conscit* is the traditional way to refer to self-killers. Latin, in fact, has no distinctive word to signify 'suicide' or 'self-murder'. For several phrases meaning 'to killing oneself' see van Hooff 1990: 139 fn. 11, 272, 246-50 (Appendix C). Among these, the most common was just *adsciscere/consciscere sibi mortem*.

31 For the ancient judgement on soldiers' suicides see the remarks of Andrieux 1927: 42; Carcani 1981: 92. The bibliography on the topic is particularly rich; see, lastly, Mentxaka 2010, and Manni 2013: 339-50.

32 A list of penalties can be read in in *D.* 49.16.3.1 (Mod. 4 *de poenis*): *Poenae militum huiuscemodi sunt: castigatio, pecuniaria multa, munerum indictio, militiae mutatio, gradus deiectio, ignominosia missio. Nam in metallum aut in opus metalli non dabantur nec torquentur*. See also *D.* 48.19.38.12 (Paul. 5 *sent.*): *miles, qui sibi manus intulit nec factum peregit, nisi impatientia doloris aut morbi luctusve alicuius vel alia causa fecerit, capite puniendus est: alias cum ignominia mittendus est.*

33 For the text see *D.* 28.3.6.7 (Ulp. 10 *ad Sab.*): *quam distinctionem in militis quoque testamento divus Hadrianus dedit epistulam ad Pomponium Falconem, ut, si quidem ob conscientiam delicti militaris mori maluit, irritum sit eius testamentum: quod si taedio vitae vel dolore, valere testamentum aut, si intestato decessit, cognatis aut, si non sint, legionis ista sint vindicanda*. See the analysis of Mentxaka 2010: 121-33, with further legal sources.

34 See P.Mich. VIII 470 l. 12 and 471 l. 16; ChLA V 299, fr. *i* l. 1, all from Tiberianus' archive, and PSI VI 730 l. 5.

35 Marichal in ChLA IV (1967): 79-80.

commercial transactions with the Roman army is a well-known phenomenon, as the papyrological evidence shows.[36]

Leaving aside these uncertain points, the language is meaningful and underlines important details of the account. Firstly, a variety of military ranks involved in the different stages of collecting the sums can be found. Entry 3 with the sentence *missae ab* (l. 9) shows the prominent role of the centurion named Valerius Perpetuus, who took care of the carriage of the cash. After the list of the auxiliary units, both *cohortes* and *alae*, involved in the collection, in l. 17 a *primus pilus* is recorded, who likely played an active role; at this point, however, the bad condition of the item does not allow us to reconstruct the details of his task. Lastly, entries 4 and 5, using similar sentences with the verb *fero* and the preposition *per* plus accusative of a personal name, refer to the carriage of drachmae. The two entries read as follows:

16 Item [a]llatae [±8] per Livium . [
17 ⟦(centurionis)⟧ p(rimi)pili sc . [±9]soṇ . . ḷụm[
18 ⟦ . . . . . ⟧
vac.
19 summa ac[cep]ta d[racm(arum)] CLXXXṾ[
20 et quae p[er B]rutu[m] l]atae eran[t

Unfortunately, we cannot know who Livius and Brutus were. Their names are very common and neither the rank nor the unit to which they belonged are stated. Probably they were ordinary soldiers. But, at the same time, these sentences invite comparisons with evidence from Vindolanda fort, and in particular with T.Vindol. II 190, a long daily account of foodstuffs, in which besides some entries one can find the similar notation *per Privatum*. The editors suggest that this Privatus was a slave. Perhaps our evidence might also refer to persons of servile (or libertine) status.[37]

The last entry gives the total expressed first in drachmae, the normal currency of Egypt, and then in other coinage, and makes use of stereotyped wording. It is useful to have the text before us:

21 fiunt dr[acm(ae) Aug(ustae) . .] CXXXVIII[
22 et calcul[atae sunt dr]acm(arum) Aug(ustarum) [±5 argenti]
23 Tyri XVI · aeris Italic[i

Once again Vindolanda evidence provides the main source of comparison for this entry: among the wooden tablets several financial documents survive, which similarly record sums received on a daily basis and, at the end, the total amount.[38] The occurrence of large sums in cash and of different coins also cannot be regarded as a striking feature of

36 P.Dura 64, a letter from the *praepositus* to the *tribunus cohortis Palmyrenorum* (AD 221), witnesses that the a *libertus* took care of the barley distribution to the soldiers. On commercial transactions, together with Vindolanda tablets (see Bowman 1998: 34; Groslambert 2012), see lastly O.Claud. III 417, in which one Gaion καιcαριανόc is involved in a lease contract, with the remarks of Cuvigny 2000: 60-2.

37 Bowman-Thomas in T.Vindol. II 153, 156. See also Bowman 1998: 35.

38 See mostly T.Vindol. II 178; 185 ll. 28-9; 191 ll. 14-5; 192 ll. 9-10; 201 l. 11.

ChLA IV 264, as Marichal believed;[39] Vindolanda tablets prove that the military clerks were accustomed to counting large sums in cash and converting money.[40] In comparison to the former text, it is evident that the pattern of the present one appears to be more standard. However, despite the many elements of similarity with military documentation from other forts, one should keep in mind that it is part of a larger body of evidence, which provides new insights into the bookkeeping system of the Roman army.

4. Conclusions

The financial documentation on papyrus mentioned at the start of this paper preserves only one bilingual account-book: RMR 75, of AD 139, consisting of three auxiliaries' receipts for money, of which one is in Latin, while the other two are in Greek. Moreover, each receipt was drawn up by a different scribe. If one pays attention to the evidence exclusively in Greek script, then one finds out that the surviving examples are particularly rare: in chronological order, PSI IX 1063, of AD 117, is a book of receipts for money deposited by recruits and written by different hands; P.Hamb. I 39, of AD 179, 9th January-10th April, is a complete book of receipts written by the soldiers of the *ala Veterana Gallica* for their yearly hay allowance. All the receipts are in Greek script and show the involvement of more scribes. Despite the rarity of the evidence, it is easy to see that these three papyri share important features: the pattern and the languages are the same, and the vocabulary too is rather standard. By contrast, they differ completely from the present roll. In other words, our papyrus has its own format. At this point, some relevant points of the evidence emerge:

1. Form and layout: PSI II 119 *recto* + ChLA IV 264 displays how the military registers were physically made and organized. They could also have the typical measurements of literary rolls and their medium was chosen according to its high quality. The layout was essential for reading and understanding of the document. The military clerks, therefore, drew up documents making use of formatting conventions. Obviously, this does not mean that there was no room for a few degrees of flexibility. This roll, indeed, offers proof of good documentary pragmatism, by alternating different layouts according to the specific needs of different sections.

2. Content: the greater portion of the roll has been lost and, unfortunately, we cannot know what other kinds of accounts were included. The surviving evidence, however, testifies to the fact that these ledgers were not only monothematic, but could combine different records. We might recall RMR 68, which contains on the *recto* a pay-record together with a record of men on special duty (= RMR 10), and a partial draft from a matricula (= RMR 37), while on the *verso* a summary of a century of *legio III Cyrenaica* (= RMR 58) and a daily duty roster (= RMR 9). Nonetheless, this papyrus is a single sheet from a roll, where the documents follow each other in an awkward manner. By contrast, our evidence is a whole roll, in which the accounts are written only on the *recto* and are well laid-out.

39 *Contra* the opinion of Marichal in ChLA IV (1967), 79-80 see Christiansen 1984: 279.

40 Bowman 1998: 34-5. In general, see also Alston 1995: 102, who points out that the Roman army was an 'important market and source of coinage'.

Furthermore, in both the sections, a high level of organization and scaling of the details can be appreciated.

3. Language: as far as we can see, the roll is entirely written in Latin. In the Roman army, Greek was acceptable and regularly used for official purposes too, as for instance the aforementioned account-books show. However, in some specific cases, Latin was chosen as a super-high language or as 'the language of power' by soldiers.[41] This choice clearly depended on the purpose of the document. In our evidence, thus, the use of Latin, instead of Greek, would suggest that we are dealing with one of the more formal documents from the Roman army.

4. Lifetime: How long did an official military roll live? The re-use of the item allows us to answer this question. As has been said, the Latin document was written between AD 105 and 125/7, whereas the uncial hand of Platonic *Gorgia* is dated to the middle or later part of II AD.[42] Therefore, we may conclude that this roll was in use for only a few decades. Through its use, it was probably kept in an archive of the camp in Nicopolis, or more likely in the governor's headquarters, since soldiers from several units are mentioned.

41 Adams 2003: 545-6 and 599-623.

42 Turner 1987: 106, nr. 62.

P.Dura 82

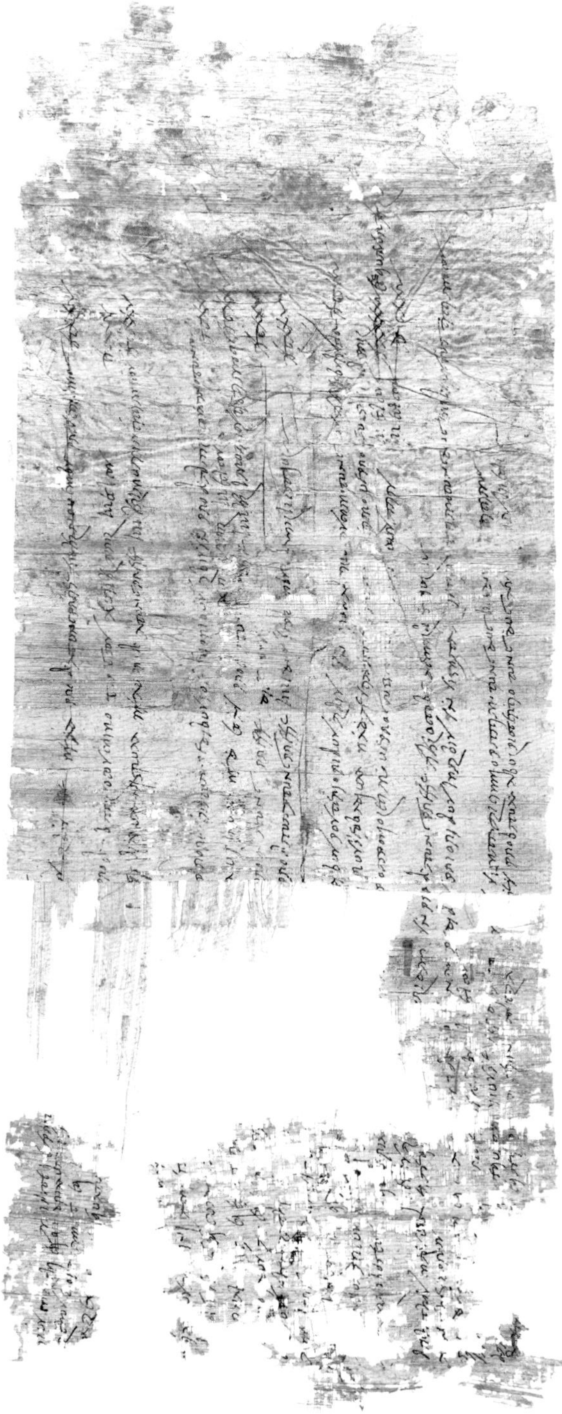

P.Dura 97

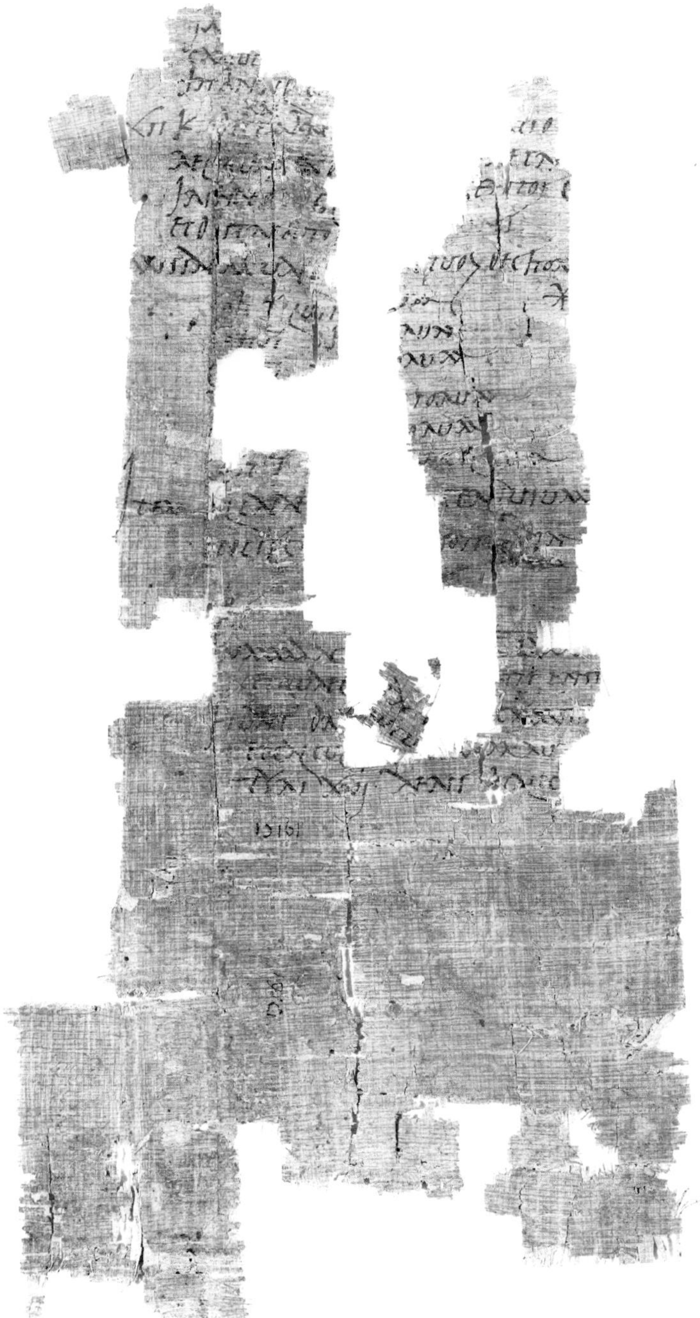

ChLA IV 264

PSI II 119 recto

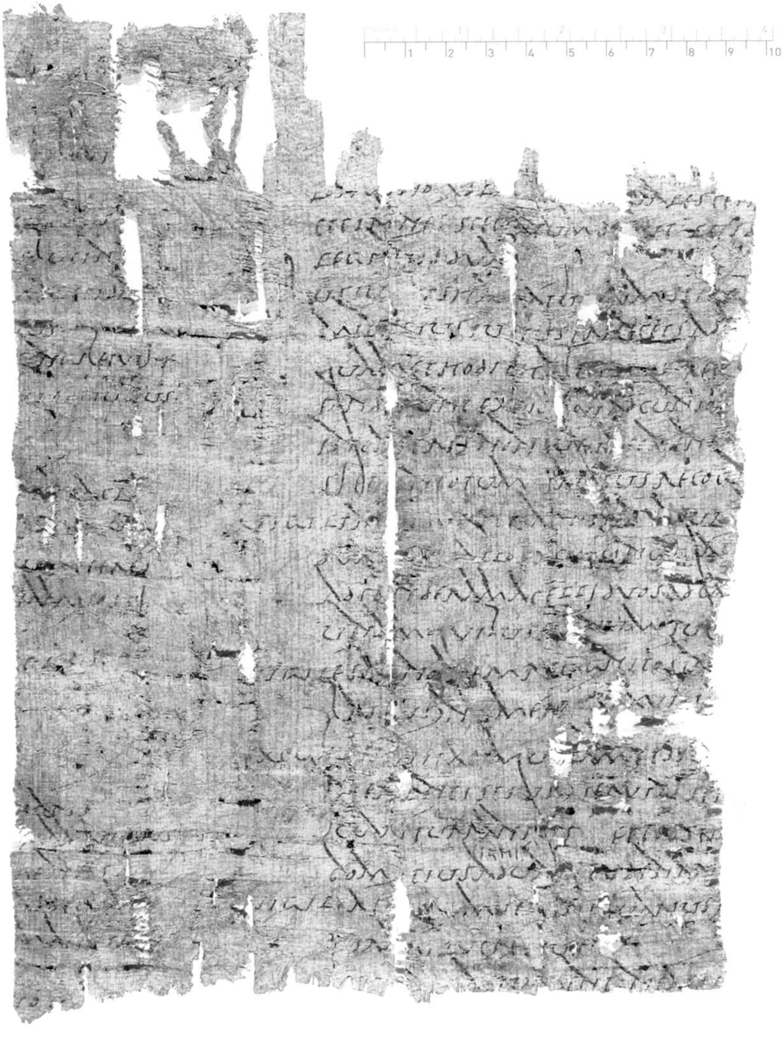

PSI XII 1307 recto

Appendix

List of military documents mentioned (in chronological order)

Publication	Papyrus	Other Publications	TM Number
PSI XIII 1307 recto	1307 recto	RMR 51 = ChLA XXV 786 = CPL 108	25148
RMR 68	P.Gen.Lat. 1 recto	ChLA I 7 a (= XLVIII 7 a) = CPL 106	69867
RMR 69	P.Gen.Lat. 4	ChLA I 9 (= XLVIII 9) = CPL 107	69868
RMR 129	MS Lat. Class. g. 3 recto (P)	ChLA IV 272 (= XLVIII 272)	69884
RMR 10	P.Gen.Lat. 1 recto	ChLA I 7 a (= XLVIII 7 a) = CPL 106	69867
RMR 37	P.Gen.Lat. 1 recto	ChLA I 7 a (= XLVIII 7 a) = CPL 106	69867
RMR 58	P.Gen.Lat. 1 verso	ChLA I 7 b (= XLVIII 7 b) = CPL 106	69867
RMR 9	P.Gen.Lat. 1 verso	ChLA I 7 b (= XLVIII 7 b) = CPL 106	69867
P.Harr. inv. 183e recto	183e recto		110834
T.Vindol. II 185	88.950		114444
T.Vindol. II 201	85.570		114457
P.Ryl. II 223	Gr. 223	ChLA IV 242 (= XLVIII 242) = CPL 312	27901
T.Vindol. II 153	20 i	T.Vindol. I 66 = CEL I 132	114863
T.Vindol. II 156	85.248	AE 1994, 1131	114420
T.Vindol. II 178	85.043		114437
T.Vindol. II 190	33, 47, 62	T.Vindol. I 4	114836
T.Vindol. II 191	11	T.Vindol. I 5	114837

Date	Provenance	Content
AD 65 ca.	Nicopolis	Morning report
AD 81		Pay record
AD 83-4		Pay record
AD 87		Pay record
AD 88		List of detached soldiers
AD 90 ca.		Draft of a matricula
AD 90 ca.		List
AD 90 ca.		Duty roster
I AD (before AD 83)		Pay record
AD 92-7 ca.	Vindolanda	Accounts
AD 92-7 ca.	Vindolanda	Accounts
I AD		Accounts
AD 97-103 ca.	Vindolanda	Renuntium
AD 97-103 ca.	Vindolanda	Daily report
AD 97-103 ca.	Vindolanda	Accounts
AD 97-103 ca.	Vindolanda	Accounts
AD 97-103 ca.	Vindolanda	Accounts

Publication	Papyrus	Other Publications	TM Number
T.Vindol. II 192	85.010.b		114449
RMR 131	P.Haw. 19	ChLA IV 239 (= XLVIII 239) = CPL 319 descr.	63268
P.Oxy. VII 1022	P.Lond. inv. 2049	RMR 87 = ChLA III 215 (=XLVIII 211) = CEL I 140 = CPL 111	78569
RMR 63	P.Lond. inv. 2851	ChLA III 219 (= XLVIII 219) = CPL 112	69875
ChLA XLII 1212	P.Cair. inv. SR 3049/31	CEL I 149	70013
PSI IX 1063	1063	RMR 74	17472
RMR 80	P.Lond. inv. 482	ChLA III 203 (= XLVIII 203) = CPL 114 = CEL I 150	78865
RMR 75	P.CtYBR inv. 249 (A)	ChLA IX 397 (= XLVIII 397) = CEL I 152	69907
ChLA XLII 1225	P.Lond. inv. 2723 + P.Mich. VII 477 recto	ChLA III 218 (= XLVIII 218) = CPL 121	70017
BGU II 696	P.Berol. inv. 14097 + 6870	RMR 64 = ChLA X 411 = CPL 118	69913
RMR 73	P.Lond. inv. 1196	P.Fay. 105 = ChLA III 208 (= XLVIII 208) = CPL 124	10770
P.Hamb. I 39	Gr. 184	RMR 76	44371
ChLA X 410 + IV 228 + XVIII 663	P.Berol. inv. 6866 A-B + P.Aberd. 133 + P.Reinach 2222	RMR 70 = CPL 122 + 123	63048
ChLA XI 495	P.Hamb. Gr. 310		69982
P.Mich. VII 435 + 440	inv. 510 + 511 + 511 bis	RMR 77 = ChLA V 277 (= XLVIII 277) = CPL 219 + 190 = CEL I 153	69887

Date	Provenance	Content
AD 97-103 ca.	Vindolanda	Accounts
I-II AD	Haueris	Accounts
AD 103, 24th February	Oxyrhynchus	Letter from C. Minucius Italus about the enrolment of six recruits
AD 105, 16th September		Strength report of Cohors I Hispanorum veterana equitata
AD 113-7	Theadelpheia	Request of probatio
AD 117, 3rd September		Receipts for deposita
AD 130 May	Alexandria	Receipts for hay for cavalrymen
AD 139 May-June		Receipts for the deposit of horses
AD 144-63	Karanis	Proposal of transfer of auxiliaries or civilian report mentioning centurions
AD 156, 31st August	Arsinoites	Pridianum cohortis I Augustae praetoriae Lusitanorum equitatae
AD 175 ca. or 184-5 ca.	Karanis	Bank deposit of the riders of an ala
AD 179 January-April	Nicopolis	Receipts for hay money
AD 192 or 193-6	Arsinoites	Pay record of auxiliaries
AD 193-211		Pay record
early II AD		Receipts for legacy

Publication	Papyrus	Other Publications	TM Number
ChLA XVIII 662	P.Clermont-Ganneau 4 a	ChLA XLVIII 662 = SB VI 9248 = CPL 136 = CEL I 165	27293
RMR 71	P.Vindob. L 72 + 82 verso	ChLA XLIV 1298	70085
P.Ryl. II 273 a	Gr. 273 a	RMR 72 = ChLA IV 243 (= XLVIII 243) = CPL 126	27910
RMR 84	P.Vindob. L 111	ChLA XLV 1322 = CPL 313	70108
RMR 130	MS. Lat. class. g. 4 (P)	ChLA IV 273 (= XLVIII 273)	69885
RMR 132	P.Aberd. inv. 2h recto	ChLA IV 230 (= XLVIII 230)	69876
ChLA XI 473	P.Berol. inv. 25046		69965
P.Oxy. IV 735	P. 735	RMR 81 = ChLA IV 275 (= XLVIII 275) = CPL 134	20435
ChLA XLI 1198	P.Cair. inv. s.n.	SB III 7181a = CPL 137 = CEL I 205	18859
P.Dura 64	P.CtYBR inv. D.P. 15	RMR 91 = ChLA VI 319 (= XLVIII 319) = CEL I 199	44792
P.Dura 82	P.CtYBR inv. D.P. 3 recto	RMR 47 = ChLA VII 337 = CPL 326	44813
P.Oxy. LXXXIII 5363	100/39(d) recto		786137
P.Dura 97	P.CtYBR inv. D.P. 3 verso	RMR 83 = ChLA VII 352 = CPL 327	44829
ChLA IX 404	P.Princ. inv. 7743 c	SB XX 14386	32180
P.Grenf. II 110	P.Lond. inv. 731	RMR 86 = ChLA III 205 (= XLVIII 205) = CPL 142	69873
PSI inv. 2450 recto	2450 recto		128489
ChLA III 212	P.Lond. inv. 1774		69874

Date	Provenance	Content
II AD	Syene	Receipt for wheat for a cavalryman
II AD		Pay record
II AD		Pay record of auxiliaries
II-III AD		Accounts
II-III AD		Pay record
II-III AD	Soknopaiou Nesos (?)	Accounts
II-III AD	Arsinoites	Pay record
AD 205, 4th September	Oxyrhynchus	Receipt for grain for a turma
AD 220, 4th March	Oxyrhynchus	Receipts for meat and wine supplies
AD 221	Dura Europos	Letter from Aurelius Rufinus praepositus to Iustillus tribunus
AD 223-33	Dura Europos	Morning report
AD 244-9 or 247-9	Oxyrhynchus	Strength report, perhaps of legio III Gallica
AD 251, 31st August (after)	Dura Europos	List of cavalryment and horses
AD 277-82		Pay record
AD 293		Receipt for money for cavalrymen
III AD	Oxyrhynchus	Accounts
III AD		Pay record

Publication	Papyrus	Other Publications	TM Number
ChLA X 446	P.Berol. inv. 14100 recto		69944
ChLA XLV 1351 descr.	P.Vindob. L 149		70126

Date	Provenance	Content
III AD		Pay record
III AD		Accounts

Bibliography

Adams, J.N. 2003, *Bilingualism and the Latin Language*, Cambridge.

Alston, R. 1995, *Soldier and Society in Roman Egypt. A Social History*, London & New York.

Andrieux, Ch. 1927, *La répression des fautes militaires dans les armées romaines*, Lyon.

Bowman, A.K. 1998, *Life and Letters on the Roman Frontiers. Vindolanda and its People*, London.

Carcani, M. 1981, *Dei reati e delle pene e dei giudizi militari presso i Romani*, Napoli.

Carlini, A., Violante, M. 1999, "Grg. 471d4-472b8; 507b8-508d6; 522b5-526a 6, PLaur IV 134 + POxy 454 + PSI 119", in *Corpus dei Papiri filosofici greci e latini. Testi e lessico nei papiri di cultura greca e latina. Parte I: Autori noti*, vol. 1, Nicolaus Damascenus-Platonis Fragmenta, Firenze, 70-8.

Christiansen, E. 1984, "On Denarii and other Coin-Terms in the Papyri", *ZPE* 54, 271-99.

Crisci, E. 1998, "P.Laur. IV 134 + PSI II 119", in Cavallo, G., Crisci, E., Messeri, G., Pintaudi R. (eds.), *Scrivere libri e documenti nel mondo antico. Mostra di Papiri della Biblioteca Medicea Laurenziana*, 25 agosto-25 settembre 1998 (Pap.Flor. XXX), Firenze, 107-8 (nr. 26).

Cuvigny, H. 2000, "Destinataires des chirographes et créanciers", in Ead., *Mons Claudianus. Ostraca graeca et latina*, III, *Le reçus pour avances à la familia, O.Claud. 417-631*, Le Caire, 55-78.

Fioretti, P., Cavallo, G. 2015, "Note sulle scritture di PSI XIII 1307", in Capasso, M., De Nonno, M. (eds.), *Studi paleografici e papirologici in ricordo di Paolo Radiciotti*, Lecce, 105-24.

Gatier, P.-L. 2000, "La Legio III Cyrenaica et l'Arabie", in Le Bohec, Y. (ed.), *Les légions de Rome sous le Haut-Empire*, Lyon, 341-9.

Gilliam, J.F. 1967, "The *deposita* of an Auxiliary Soldier (P. Columbia inv. 325)", *BJ* 167, 233-43 (= Id., *Roman Army Papers* (Mavors Roman Army Researches II), Amsterdam 1986, 317-27).

Groslambert, A. 2012, "Les soldat et l'argent sur le tablettes de Vindolanda", in Wolff, Ch. (ed.), *Le métier de soldat dans le monde romain.* Actes du cinquième congrès de Lyon organisé les 23-25 septembre 2010 par l'Université Jean Moulin Lyon 3, Lyon, 247-74.

van Hooff, A.J.L. 1990, *From Autothanasia to Suicide. Self-killing in Classical Antiquity*, London-New York.

Kennedy, D.L. 1980, "*Legio VI Ferrata*: The Annexation and Early Garrison of Arabia", *HSCP* 84, 283-308.

Johnson, W.A. 2004, *Bookrolls and Scribes in Oxyrhynchus*, Toronto-Buffalo-London.

Le Bohec, Y. 2010, "L'écrit au sein de l'armée romaine, du Ier au IIIe siècle de notre ère", in Perrin, Y. (ed.), *Neronia VIII. Bibliothèques, livres et culture écrite dans l'empire romain de César à Hadrien.* Actes du VIIIe Colloque international de la SIEN, Paris, 2-4 octobre 2008, Bruxelles, 192-207.

Leach, B., Tait, J. 2000, "papyrus", in Nicholson, P.T., Swan, I. (eds.), *Ancient Egyptian Materials and Technology*, Cambridge, 227-53.

Manni, A. 2013, Omnia mors solvit. *La morte del* reus *nel processo criminale romano*, Napoli.

Marichal, R. 1964, "Deux papyrus latins relatifs à l'administration financière de l'Égypte", *BAntFr* 1, 109-11.

Mentxaka, R.M. 2010, "El suicidio de los militares en época de Adriano", *Index* 38, 113-54.

Phang, S.E. 2007, Military Documents. Languages, and Literacy, in Erdkamp, P. (ed.), *A Companion to the Roman Army*, Main Street, 286-338.

Pintaudi, R. 1977, "Frammenti letterari laurenziani", *ZPE* 27, 107-17.

Pintaudi, R. 2014, "Mixtura Papyrologica", *APapyrol* 26, 241-60.

Pöhlmann, E., West, M.L. 2001, *Document of Ancient Greek Music*, Oxford.

Puglia, E. 1996, "Il catalogo di un fondo librario di Ossirinco", *ZPE* 113, 51-65.

Puglia, E. 1997, *La cura del libro nel mondo antico. Guasti e restauri del rotolo di papiro*, Napoli.

Salati, O. 2017a, "New Evidence on Latin Military Pay-Records: *P.Harr.* inv. 183e *recto*", *ZPE* 203, 263-71.

Salati, O. 2017b, "Un 'dimenticato' registro latino: PSI II 119 recto + ChLA IV 264", *Aegyptus* 97, 71-111.

Salati, O. 2019, "Accounting in the Roman Army. Some Remarks on PSI II 119r + ChLA IV 264", in Nodar, A., Torallas Tovar, S. (eds), Proceedings of 28th International Congress of Papyrology, Barcelona, 619-28.

Speidel, M.P. 1977, "The Roman Army in Arabia", *ANRW* II.8, 687-730 (= Id., *Roman Army Studies*, I, Amsterdam 1984, 229-72).

Speidel, M.P. 2007, "Einheit und Vielfalt in der römischen Heeresverwaltung", in Haensch, R., Heinrichs, J. (hrsg.), *Herrschen und Verwalten: der Alltag der römischen Admnistration in der hohen Kaiserzeit*, Köln-Wien, 173-94.

Stauner, K. 2004, *Das offizielle Schriftwesen des römischen Heeres von Augustus bis Gallienus, 27 v.Chr.-268 n.Chr. Eine Untersuchung zu Struktur, Funktion und Bedeutung der offiziellen militärischen Verwaltungsdokumentation und zu deren Schreibern*, Bonn.

Ţentea, O., Matei-Popescu, F. 2016, "The *cohors I milliaria Ituraeorum*. New Approach to Its Deployment", in *Studia Classica Serdicensia V. Monuments and Texts in Antiquity and Beyond. Essays for the Centenary of Georgi Mihailov (1915-1991)*, Sofia, 371-81.

Turner, E.G. 1987, *Greek Manuscripts of the Ancient World* (BASP Suppl. 46), London.

Öffentliche Abrechnungen: Cicero in Kilikien

Éva Jakab, Budapest

Marcus Tullius Cicero schrieb am 4. Januar des Jahres 49 v.Chr. in der Nähe von Rom einen Brief an einen gewissen Rufus, der interessante Details bezüglich der Aufgaben und Pflichten der römischen Magistrate, insbesondere ihrer Rechenschaftspflicht über den Verbrauch öffentlicher Gelder vermittelt. Es lohnt sich, den Sachverhalt näher anzuschauen – abgedruckt wird hier jedoch bloß der Absatz, der die Terminologie und Technik am besten demonstriert (Cic. ad fam. 5,20,8-9 – Cicero an Rufus):

> *Reliquum est de sestertiis centum milibus, de quibus memini mihi a te Myrina litteras esse adlatas, non mei errati, sed tui; in quo peccatum videbatur esse, si modo erat, fratris tui et Tulli. sed cum id corrigi non posset, quod iam depositis rationibus ex provincia decessimus, credo me quidem tibi pro animi mei voluntate proque ea spe facultatum, quam tum habebamus, quam humanissime potuerim, rescripsisse; sed neque tum me humanitate litterarum mearum obligatum puto neque me tuam hodie epistulam de HS* $\overline{C}$ *sic accepisse, ut ii accipiunt, quibus epistulae per haec tempora molestae sunt. (9) simul illud cogitare debes, me omnem pecuniam, quae ad me salvis legibus pervenisset, Ephesi apud publicanos deposuisse; id fuisse HS* $|\overline{XXII}|$*; eam omnem pecuniam Pompeium abstulisse. quod ego sive aequo animo sive iniquo fero, tu de HS* $\overline{C}$ *aequo animo ferre debes et existimare eo minus ad te vel de tuis cibariis vel de mea liberalitate pervenisse. quod si mihi expensa ista HS* $\overline{C}$ *tulisses, tamen, quae tua est suavitas quique in me amor, nolles a me hoc tempore aestimationem accipere; nam, numeratum si cuperem, non erat. sed haec iocatum me putato, ut ego te existimo. ego tamen, cum Tullius rure redierit, mittam eum ad te, si quid ad rem putabis pertinere. hanc epistulam cur conscindi velim causa nulla est.*[1]

1 „Nun noch ein Wort über die 100.000 Sestertien. Wie ich mich entsinne, hast Du mir aus Myrina geschrieben, nicht ich hätte mich geirrt, sondern Du. Der Fehler scheint hier, wenn überhaupt einer vorliegt, bei Deinem Vetter und Tullius zu liegen. Daran ist freilich nichts mehr zu ändern, weil ich die Provinz verlassen habe, nachdem die Abrechnungen bereits deponiert waren. Aber ich glaube doch, Dir entsprechend meinem eigenen Wunsche und meiner damaligen Aussicht auf die nötigen Mittel so entgegenkommend wie möglich geantwortet zu haben. Dass ich mit dem entgegenkommenden Ton meines damaligen Briefes eine Verpflichtung eingegangen sei, ist freilich nicht meine Meinung, und auch heute beim Empfang Deines Briefes wegen der 100.000 Sesterzen glaube ich nicht das Gefühl gehabt zu haben, das diejenigen überkommt, denen heutzutage jeder Brief ein Greuel ist. Im übrigen musst Du bedenken, dass ich das ganze Geld, das mir rechtmäßig zugefallen wäre, in Ephesus bei den Steuerpächtern deponiert habe – es waren 2.200.000 Sesterzen –, und dass Pompeius diese ganze Summe beschlagnahmt hat. Ob ich mich darüber ärgere oder nicht – Du musst über die 100.000 Sesterzen hinwegkommen und Dich damit abfinden, dass soviel weniger von Deinen Deputaten bzw. den Dir von mir zugedachten Remunerationen in Deine Tasche gelangt ist. Und wenn Du diese 100.000 Sesterzen als bereits von mir erhalten gebucht hättest, würdest Du doch, lieb und nett wie Du zu mir bist, im Augen-

Wie oben bereits erwähnt, ist das Schreiben mit dem 4. Januar des Jahres 49 v.Chr. datiert. Cicero war zu dieser Zeit Statthalter der Provinz Kilikien. Der Adressat ist ein gewisser L. Mescinius Rufus, der mit ihm eines der höchsten Ämter in der Provinzverwaltung bekleidete: Er war Quästor an seiner Seite.

Die Provinz Kilikien (*Cilicia*) lag im Südosten Kleinasiens und grenzte an Pamphylien und das Taurusgebirge. Zur Bedeutung der Provinz gehört die Tatsache, dass wichtige Handelsrouten durch das Gebiet nach Kappadokien und weiter in den Fernen Osten führten. Nach einer wechselvollen Geschichte wurde das Gebiet in der ersten Hälfte des 1. Jahrhunderts v.Chr. durch Pompeius von den „kilikischen Piraten" gesäubert, um dort eine neue römische Provinz einzurichten. In diese Provinz wurde Cicero im Jahre 51 v.Chr. (unter den Konsuln Ser. Sulpicius Rufus und M. Claudius Marcellus) als Statthalter entsandt; er trat die lange Reise am 1. Mai 51 an.[2]

I. Zur Provinzialverwaltung

Cicero blieb als *proconsul* in den Jahren 51/50 v.Chr. an der Spitze der Provinz, wobei der zweite Mann neben ihm, sein Quästor, L. Mescinius Rufus war. Der Quästor gehörte zu den so genannten „Hilfsorganen" des Statthalters: Kunkel betont, dass die Statthalter ursprünglich vor allem als militärische Befehlshaber dienten. Ihre Rechte und Aufgaben blieben in der römischen „Verfassung" der Republik gemäß dieser Prämisse festgelegt.[3] Nach diesem Konzept wurde auch der „Stab" der Statthalter zusammengesetzt, in dem zur Verwaltung der Staatsgelder regelmäßig auch ein Quästor ernannt wurde. Kunkel hebt hervor, dass der Quästor meistens ein junger Mann war, dessen Verhältnis zum Befehlshaber von den antiken Autoren nicht selten als Vater-Sohn Beziehung charakterisiert wird.[4] Verfassungsgemäß waren die Quästoren jedoch dem Statthalter keineswegs untergeordnet; ganz im Gegenteil, ihre Aufgaben bestanden hauptsächlich darin, gegen unerlaubte „Zahlungsaufforderungen" des Statthalters aufzutreten oder sogar Widerstand zu leisten.[5] Der Quästor prüfte also von Amts wegen die Einnahmen und Ausgaben der Provinzverwaltung und haftete für die Korrektheit der Buchführung und Abrechnung in eigener Person.[6] Bei uner-

blick keine Bezahlung durch abgeschätzte Güter von mir annehmen wollen; denn wollte ich in bar zahlen – unmöglich! Aber nimm das als einen Scherz, wie ich annehme, dass auch Du es nicht ernst meinst. Immerhin, sobald Tulllius vom Lande zurück ist, werde ich ihn Dir schicken, wenn Du glaubst, dass der Sache damit gedient ist. Warum ich wünschen sollte, dass dieser Brief zerrissen wird, sehe ich nicht ein." Übersetzung H. Kasten, Marcus Tullius Cicero: An seine Freunde, Lateinisch-deutsch, Düsseldorf-Zürich 1997, 291-292.

2 Vgl. E. Meyer, Caesars Monarchie und das Prinzipat des Pompeius. Innere Geschichte Roms von 66-44 v.Chr. 2. Aufl., Stuttgart-Berlin 1922.

3 W. Kunkel, Staatsordnung und Staatspraxis der römischen Republik, Zweiter Abschnitt: Die Magistratur (R. Wittmann Hg.), München 1995, 367.

4 Kunkel 1995: 368.

5 Kunkel 1995: 369.

6 Das heißt, dass bei Übergriffen des Statthalters auch er aufgrund der *lex Iulia de repetundis* verklagt und verurteilt werden konnte.

laubten Forderungen bezüglich öffentlicher Gelder war er sogar zum Einspruch verpflichtet.[7]

Um diesen verantwortungsvollen Aufgaben besser nachzukommen, wurde der Quästor nicht vom Statthalter ernannt, sondern durch Volkswahl bestellt. Etwaige personelle Wünsche des Statthalters wurden dabei nicht berücksichtigt. Das wäre auch gar nicht möglich gewesen, weil die Verteilung der gewählten Quästoren an die einzelnen Provinzen durch Los stattfand.[8] Insgesamt war jedoch die Lage der Quästoren nicht leicht, weil sie als Hilfspersonal dem Statthalter unterstanden, aber zugleich auch die Verantwortung für die Kontrolle seiner finanziellen Handlungen trugen. Sogar Kunkel unterstreicht, dass das rechtliche „Verhältnis zwischen Statthalter und Quästor somit kompliziert und in sich widersprüchlich" gewesen sei.[9] Quästor und Statthalter konnten bei mangelndem Vertrauen die Verwaltungshandlungen gegenseitig blockieren. In diesem Kontext ist der Inhalt des oben zitierten Briefes zu verstehen. Vor der weiteren Analyse müssen wir jedoch noch einen Blick auf die Protagonisten werfen, die in die aktuelle Affäre involviert waren.

Von L. Mescinius Rufus liest man in einigen Quellen der ausgehenden Republik: Cicero erwähnt ihn etwa in einem Brief an Atticus, der sogar die hier zu besprechende Angelegenheit betrifft.[10] Dazu noch später ...

Im Jahre 46 v.Chr., also einige Jahre nach dem oben zitierten Brief, schreibt Cicero wieder an Rufus, und zwar in einer hoch politischen Angelegenheit: Er will ihn überzeugen, sich im angehenden Bürgerkrieg für Pompeius zu entscheiden. In diesem Schreiben spricht Cicero von Rufus und dessen Leistungen in den höchsten Tönen.[11] Noch im selben Jahr tröstet Cicero den Rufus in einem anderen Brief, weil jener wegen seiner damaligen Positionierung in römischen politischen Kreisen höchst unglücklich war.[12] Anderswo tritt Cicero als Promotor für Rufus auf: Er empfiehlt ihn dem Statthalter der Provinz Achaia, Servius Sulpicius. Dieser soll Rufus, der in geschäftlichen Angelegenheiten nach Achaia reist, behilflich sein.[13] Im Bürgerkrieg gesellte sich auch Rufus zu den Republikanern. Er trat unter Cassius Longinus den Militärdienst an, dieser entsandte ihn gegen Tarsus.[14] Es gibt aber auch spätere Quellen, die von den politischen und militärischen Missionen des Rufus berichten: Mehrere Münzen, die aus dem Jahr 17/16 v.Chr. stammen, tragen die Prägung mit seinem Namen. Von besonderem Interesse ist eine mit der Aufschrift: IMP. CAES. AVGV. COMM. CONS. — *Imperator Caesar Augustus communi consensu.* Am Rand der Münze läuft die Schrift: L. MESCINIVS RVFVS III VIR. Gemäß dieser Münze ist L. Mescinius Rufus unter den Triumvirn dieses Jahres zu finden. Auf der Rückseite liest man: I. O. M. S. P. Q. R. V. S. PR. S. IMP. CAES. QVOD PER EV. R. P. IN AMP. ATQ. TRAN. S. E. Die Abkürzungen der Inschrift (die dem gewöhnlichen Formular folgen) kön-

7 Cic. Div. in. Caec. 32: *eras enim tu quaestor, pecuniam publicam tu tractabas, ex qua, etiamsi cuperet praetor, tamen ne qua deductio fieret, magna ex parte tua potestas erat.* S. auch Cato maior 3,5f.; Kunkel 1995: 369 Anm. 236.

8 Vgl. Liv. 30,33,2; Cic. Att. 6,6,4; s. dazu immer noch Kunkel 1995: 369.

9 Kunkel 1995: 369.

10 Cic. Att. 7(6),3,4.

11 Cic. ad Fam. 5,19.

12 Cic. ad Fam. 5,21.

13 Cic. ad Fam. 13,26 und 28.

14 W. Smith, A Dictionary of Greek and Roman Biography and Mythology, London 1873.

nen wie folgt aufgelöst werden: *Iovi Optimo Maximo S. P. Q. R. votum susceptum pro salute Imperatoris Caesaris, quod per eum res publica in ampliore atque tranquilliore statu est.* Die Historiker sind sich einig, dass die Widmung damit zu erklären ist, dass Augustus einige Jahre nach seinem Sieg über Varus glänzende Spiele zu Ehren des Jupiter Optimus Maximus veranstaltete,[15] die dann auch auf Münzen (als Teil der imperialen Image-Bildung) verewigt wurden.[16]

Kehren wir jedoch in das Jahr 49 v.Chr. zurück: Während Cicero seit dem 1. Mai 51 seinen Aufgaben als *proconsul* in der fernen Provinz Kilikien nachging, wurde er wegen der Zuspitzung des politischen Konflikts in Rom gegen Ende des Jahres 50 immer unruhiger.[17] Schließlich beschloss er, noch im Winter nach Rom zurückzukehren.[18] Seine Abreise scheint abrupt, fast überstürzt gewesen zu sein.

Der hastige Aufbruch – und vielleicht auch der Versuch, die undankbare Aufgabe der genauen Abrechnung zu vermeiden – führte aber dazu, dass Cicero den Abschluss seiner statthalterlichen Tätigkeit nicht präzise vornahm: Er hat seine *tabulae,* die Abrechnungen über die öffentlichen Finanzen, die ihm während seiner Verwaltung oblagen, mit dem Quästor L. Mescinius Rufus nicht ausreichend abgeklärt.

Aus den Berichten kann man darauf schließen, dass Cicero seine Abrechnungen sehr wohl mit seinem persönlichen Sekretär überprüft und abgeschlossen hatte. Er versäumte jedoch, diese mit denen des Quästors zu vergleichen, die Bilanz mit ihm gemeinsam zu erstellen und zu bestätigen. Damit scheint er einerseits dem damaligen Usus, andererseits der *lex Iulia* aus dem Jahre 59 v.Chr. zuwider gehandelt zu haben. Auf die Details des Sachverhalts ist unten noch zurückzukommen; davor müssen wir jedoch einen Blick auf den normativen Hintergrund werfen.

II. Zur Rechenschaftspflicht

Alle Magistrate des römischen Staates waren verpflichtet, während ihres Amtsjahres über die öffentlichen Gelder, die ihnen zur Verfügung standen, eine genaue Abrechnung zu führen und nach Ablauf ihres Amtsjahres diese Rechnungen zur Einsicht der öffentlichen Aufsicht vorzulegen. Diese Verpflichtung ging auf eine lange Tradition zurück: *leges publicae* gegen Korruption wurden bereits in der frühen Republik erlassen. Lintott konnte die einschlägige Gesetzgebung (mit präzisen Inhaltsangaben) ab dem Jahr 149 v.Chr. nachweisen.[19] Eine lange Reihe von Gesetzen versuchte, den (nicht selten vorkommenden)

15 Suet. Aug. 23.

16 Die Münzprägung oder die Schöpfungen der bildenden Kunst dienten oft als Mittel der imperialen Propaganda, die gerade unter Augustus auf hohem Niveau entwickelt wurde, vgl. dazu etwa H. Mouritsen, Plebs and Politics in the Late Roman Republic, Cambridge 2001, 18-37; P. Zanker, Augustus und die Macht der Bilder, München 1987.

17 Es reicht hier daran zu erinnern, dass Julius Caesar am 10. Januar 49 v.Chr., also einige Tage nach Ciceros Rückkehr, den *Rubico* mit seinen Truppen überschritt und nach Rom marschierte. Pompeius verließ Rom am 17. Januar; Mitte März führte er sein Heer nach Griechenland.

18 Eigentlich war es den Statthaltern gesetzlich verboten, während ihrer Amtszeit ihre Provinz zu verlassen: Eine *lex Iulia de provinciis praetoriis* aus dem Jahre 100 v.Chr. enthielt dieses Verbot; die einzige Ausnahme war die Abwesenheit *rei publicae causa*. Vgl. dazu Dio Cass. 43,25; A. Lintott, The Constitution of the Roman Republic, Oxford 1999, 102.

19 A. Lintott, The *leges de repetundis* and Associate Measures under the Republic, ZRG RA 98 (1981) 162-201.

Missbrauch des *imperium* zu unterbinden: *lex Calpurnia, lex Iunia, lex Bembina, lex Servilia Caeponis, lex Servilia Glauciae, lex Porcia, lex iudicaria* des Livius Drusus, *lex Cornelia* ... In diese Reihe der öffentlichen *legislatio* fügt sich die *lex Iulia* aus dem Jahre 59 v.Chr. ein.

Dieses Gesetz wird in den Quellen meistens als *lex Iulia de pecuniis repetundis* zitiert; es liegt nahe, dass diese *lex* von Julius Caesar eingebracht wurde.[20] Die *lex Iulia* gehörte zu jenem regen Gesetzgebungsprogramm, durch das Caesar die politischen Spannungen in der römischen Republik glätten wollte.[21] Es war das letzte große republikanische Gesetz gegen Korruption der höchsten Magistrate; spätere Ergänzungen und Korrekturen erfolgten dann in Form von *Senatus Consulta*.[22] Die Kommentare der klassischen römischen Juristen zu diesem Gesetz sind im Digestentitel D. 48,11 überliefert. Bei der Auslegung muss man jedoch darauf achten, dass diese Juristenschriften etwa hundertfünfzig oder zweihundert Jahre später entstanden sind. Dazu kommt, dass die Selektion (welche Fragmente überhaupt in die Digesten Aufnahme fanden) im 6. Jh. n.Chr. von den Kompilatoren Justinians getroffen wurde. Die Überlieferungsgeschichte mahnt also zur Vorsicht. Lintott rekonstruiert deshalb den mutmaßlichen Inhalt überwiegend aus den zeitgenössischen literarischen Quellen.[23] Es steht fest, dass sich das Gesetz gegen die Bestechung von Magistraten und Unterschlagung öffentlicher Gelder wendet: Erpressung, Annahme von Bestechungen usw. wird mit der Kapitalstrafe bedroht.[24]

Es lohnt sich hier, doch den gesetzlichen Tatbestand kurz zu zitieren (D. 48,11,1 pr. Marcianus 14 institutionum): *Lex Iulia repetundarum pertinet ad eas pecunias, quas quis in magistratu potestate curatione legatione vel quo alio officio munere ministeriove publico cepit, vel cum ex cohorte cuius eorum est.* Die *lex Iulia* über den Missbrauch der Amtsgewalt (*repetundae* kann als magistratische Handlung „in Übertretung seiner Amtspflicht durch Erpressung, Bestechung oder unerlaubte Geschenkannahme“ gedeutet werden[25]) bezieht sich auf jedwede Gelder (*pecunia*), die durch sein Amt in die Verwaltung oder sonstwie in die Obhut des Magistrats gelangten. Es wird in mehreren Quellen überliefert, dass diese *lex* ausdrücklich auch die Art und Weise der Abrechnung (bzw. deren technische Ausführung) mit den öffentlichen Geldern regelte. Es ging vor allem darum, der höchsten Ebene der provinzialen Verwaltung Restriktionen aufzuerlegen.[26] Deshalb schrieb die *lex Iulia* vor, dass der scheidende Statthalter vor dem Verlassen ihrer Provinz seine Abrechnungen zweimal kopieren und in zwei verschiedenen Städten der betroffenen Provinz zur Verwahrung hinterlassen solle.[27]

20 Roman Statutes Nr. 55; vgl. dazu auch Z. Yavetz, Julius Caesar and his Public Image, London 1983, 108-109; C. Williamson, The Laws of the Roman People. Public Law in the Expansion and Decline of the Roman Republic, Ann Arbor 2005, 378, 384 und 400-401.

21 Das Hauptinteresse der Historiker gilt eher einer anderen Norm aus dieser Periode: Die *lex Iulia de bonis cedendis*, vgl. dazu Williamson 2005: 378-379; M.W. Frederiksen, Caesar, Cicero and the Problem of Debt, JRS 56 (1966) 128-141.

22 Lintott 1981: 202.

23 Lintott 1981: 207.

24 D. 48,11,3 Macer 1 public.; D. 48,11,4 pr. Venuleius Saturninus 3 public. iudic.

25 H. Heumann / E. Seckel, Handlexikon zu den Quellen des römischen Rechts, Graz 1958.

26 Vgl. Lintott 1999: 160; Williamson 2005: 384.

27 Die Anfertigung der Abrechnung und Hinterlegung in Rom war schon immer verlangt; s. dazu Kunkel 1995: 106ff.

Es ist evident, dass die *lex Iulia* im Jahre 59 v.Chr. die Hinterlegung der Abrechnungen in zwei verschiedenen Städten der betroffenen Provinz deshalb vorschrieb, um Korruption, Unterschlagung oder ungetreue Verwaltung öffentlicher Gelder zu unterbinden. Nicht nur den zentralen Organen der *res publica* (des römischen Staates), sondern auch den führenden lokalen Amtsträgern der Provinz, d.h. der provinzialen Bevölkerung, sollte die Möglichkeit zur Einsicht und zur Überprüfung der Verwendung der öffentlichen Gelder gewährt werden. Gerade Ciceros berühmte Reden gegen Verres, den korrupten Statthalter der Provinz Sicilia, bieten Paradebeispiele dafür, dass die provinziale Bevölkerung diese Möglichkeit bei großen Missbräuchen auch nutzte. Es ist bekannt, dass Verres nach Ablauf seiner Amtszeit in Rom verklagt wurde, wobei die Provinzialen für ihre Sache Cicero als Ankläger gewinnen konnten. In diesen Gerichtsreden betreffen lange Ausführungen die mutmaßlichen Unregelmäßigkeiten und Fälschungen in Verres' Geschäftsbüchern.

Bei der Prüfung der öffentlichen Abrechnungen ging es aber nicht nur um Geld, sondern auch um Ehre und strafrechtliche Verantwortung. Wie oben bereits erwähnt, wurden schwerwiegende Arten der Korruption mit der Kapitalstrafe bedroht. Aber nicht nur die *condemnatio* hatte fatale Folgen, sondern bereits durch eine Anklage ging die *dignitas* – die allgemeine soziale Wertschätzung der Person – verloren.[28]

Die gesetzlich vorgeschriebene Rechenschaftspflicht und die dabei erforderliche Genauigkeit waren Cicero wohl bewusst. Er selbst bezieht sich andernorts darauf mit den Worten: „Meine Abrechnungen habe ich sofort der Staatskasse vorgelegt, wie dein Gesetz es vorschreibt; das war der einzige Punkt, in dem ich dein Gesetz befolgt habe. Wenn du die Abrechnung prüfst, dann kannst du feststellen, dass niemand so viel von seiner Bildung gehabt hat wie ich. Sie ist so sachkundig und überlegt aufgesetzt, dass sich der Schreiber bei der Staatskasse, der sie übernahm, mit der linken Hand die Stirne rieb, als er alles abgeschrieben hatte, und vor sich hinmurmelte: ‚Wahrhaftig, die Abrechnung ist klar – und das Geld flöten.' Mit diesen Worten (ich zweifle nicht daran) kannst du ihn, wenn er sich schon anschickt, den Triumphwagen zu besteigen, noch zurückhalten."[29] An anderer Stelle verweist er darauf, dass der Statthalter die wichtigen Daten seines Amtsjahres in *tabulae publicae* festhalten musste: „... es sind Akten vorhanden, es gibt amtliche Protokolle; widerlege mich, wenn ich lüge; verlies die Aussagen der Zeugen; zeige, dass man in den Prozessen gegen diese Leute außer dem Gift des Oppianicus irgendeinen Vorwurf erhoben hat, nicht nur zur Anschuldigung, sondern auch nur um der Beschimpfung willen."[30] Über die Gestaltung der „Bürokratie" der statthalterlichen Kanzlei stehen uns aus der republikanischen Zeit nur wenige Quellen zur Verfügung; der Prinzipat ist besser belegt.[31]

Diese gesetzliche Pflicht wurde bei Ciceros überstürzten Abreise aus der Provinz Kilikien zu locker gehandhabt. Zweifelsohne hat er einige Abrechnungen angefertigt, aber

28 Vgl. dazu etwa Mouritsen 2001: 128ff. Zum Verhältnis zwischen *amicitia, virtus* und *dignitas* s. auch A. Wilcox, The Gift of Correspondence in Classical Rome: Friendship in Cicero's 'Ad familiares'and Seneca's 'Moral Epistles', Wisconsin 2012, 65ff.

29 Cicero gegen Piso 61; Übersetzung M. Fuhrmann, Marcus Tullius Cicero, Die Gerichtsreden II, Lateinisch-deutsch, Darmstadt 1997, 387.

30 Cic. Cluent. 62 (Rede für Cluentius Habitus), Fuhrmann 1997: 427.

31 Kunkel 1995: 106-107 verweist vor allem auf Cic. Cluent. 62 (auch hier zitiert), dann auf Festus s.v. *tablinum*; Cic. Verr. 2,1,98f., Cic. Pis. 61, Cic. ad Fam. 5,20, Cic. Att. 6,7,2, Plut. Cato min. 17,3 und Liv. 38,55,11f.

er hat es unterlassen, seine Version (wie allgemein üblich) mit seinem Amtskollegen, dem Quästor L. Mescinius Rufus, abzuklären. Wie oben bereits erwähnt, traf die persönliche Haftung für die Staatsfinanzen nicht nur den Statthalter, sondern auch den Quästor an seiner Seite. Gewiss steht es mit dem Prinzip der Kollegialität im Zusammenhang, das die republikanische Amtsführung Roms in jeder Hinsicht beherrschte.[32] Cicero reiste also ab – und stellte damit seinen Kollegen vor vollendete Tatsachen.

Die dadurch entstandene Situation dürfte L. Mescinius Rufus sehr unangenehm gewesen sein. Er wollte jedenfalls seine Pflicht gewissenhaft erfüllen: Er nahm sich Zeit und Mühe zur Überprüfung der von Cicero hinterlassenen Geschäftsbücher. Aus dem oben zitierten Brief geht hervor, dass er die Korrektheit von Ciceros Dokumentation in manchen (nicht zu vernachlässigenden) Details bestritt. Es ging dabei um keine geringe Summen: Zweimal ist ein Eintrag von 100.000 Sesterzen und einmal einer von 2.200.000 Sesterzen erwähnt.

Um das Gewicht dieser Summen auch für den heutigen Leser verständlich zu machen, reicht es hier darauf zu verweisen, dass der Jahressold eines Legionärs damals etwa um 900 Sesterzen lag. In Vertragsurkunden aus Puteoli aus dem 1. Jh. n.Chr. erfährt man, dass eine ganze Schiffsladung Getreide auf 20.000 Sesterzen geschätzt wurde.[33]

Cicero war sich wohl dessen bewusst, dass die Abrechnungen eine heikle Sache waren – er wollte sich dieser Pflicht sicherlich nie ganz entziehen. Die politisch delikate Situation schildert er selbst sehr vorsichtig in einem anderen Brief, der um diese Zeit entstanden ist (Cic. Att. 6,6(7),2): „Ich habe meinem Quästor Mescinius den Auftrag gegeben, in Laodicea zu warten, um so, wie es das julische Gesetz vorschreibt, die Abrechnungen bei zwei Gemeinden hinterlegen zu können. Der Kinder wegen will ich nach Rhodos, von dort möglichst bald nach Athen, wenn auch die Passatwinde dafür recht ungünstig sind. Aber ich möchte durchaus noch unter den jetzigen Beamten heim, deren Entgegenkommen ich bei dem Dankfest erfahren habe. Doch schicke mir bitte einen Brief entgegen, ob Du es aus politischen Gründen für richtig hältst, wenn ich noch etwas verziehe.“ Dieses Schreiben wurde in der Stadt Tarsos im Juli des Jahres 50 v.Chr. verfasst und ist an seinen Freund Atticus adressiert. Man erfährt daraus, dass Cicero bereits seit Juli dieses Jahres unterwegs war: Er verließ Kilikien, um mehrere griechische Ortschaften aufzusuchen. Cicero befasst sich bereits hier mit dem Problem seiner Rechnungsbücher bezüglich Kilikien. Er betont, dass sein Quästor Mescinius Rufus auf seinen ausdrücklichen Befehl noch in der Provinz verweilte. Er habe ihm aufgetragen, in Laodicea zu bleiben und sich um die Hinterlassung der Abrechnungen in zwei Provinzstädten gemäß der *lex Iulia* zu kümmern. Dieser Brief eröffnet einen Blick auf seine Motive: Er wollte „unter den jetzigen Magistraten“, also noch in der Amtszeit der scheidenden Kollegen, in der Nähe von Rom sein – wohl um auf den Machtwechsel Einfluss zu nehmen. Atticus stand ihm so nahe, dass er seine Sorgen mit ihm offen teilte.

---

32 Die Kollegialität diente nicht bloß zur Kontrolle; man kann darin kaum eine Verfassungskontrolle im modernen Sinne sehen, worauf bereits Lintott 1999: 100-101 hingewiesen hat. Es ging eher darum, dass im Falle der Abwesenheit oder Behinderung eines Magistrats sein Kollege die Amtsführung, die Ausübung des *imperium* übernehmen sollte.

33 TPSulp. 79 (15. März 40), s. dazu É. Jakab, Horrea, sûretés et commerce maritime dans les archives des Sulpicii, in J. Hallebeek / M. Schermaier / R. Fiori / E. Metzger, J.-P. Coriat (Hgg.), Inter cives necnon peregrinos: Essays in honour of Boudewijn Sirks, Göttingen 2014, 331-350.

III. Rationes

Vor dem weiteren Aufrollen des Sachverhalts werfen wir einen Blick darauf, wie solche Abrechnungen damals ausgesehen haben. Bereits der oben geschilderte Sachverhalt legt es nahe, dass die Führung der Rechnungsbücher strengen Regeln unterlag, damit die Buchführung nicht gefälscht und die Einträge nicht im Nachhinein gelöscht oder geändert werden konnten.

In Ciceros Brief findet man immer wieder technische Begriffe aus der Buchführung; diese erinnern an die aus dokumentarischen und literarischen Texten wohlbekannte Terminologie der *rationes*. Es reicht hier auf einige Wendungen hinzuweisen: *litteras esse adlatas, rationes ex provincia,* sich durch *litterae obligare, sestertia ferre, quid si mihi expensa ista HS c tulisses*. Bekanntlich waren die Einnahmen und Ausgaben in der antiken Buchführung nicht getrennt.[34]

Labeo hebt hervor, dass die *rationes* Geschäftsvorgänge erfassen, die im wechselseitigen Geben und Nehmen, Kreditieren, sich Verpflichten und Erfüllen bestehen. Er betont weiterhin, dass allein durch die bloße Bezahlung einer Schuld noch keine Abrechnung entstehe. Juristisch relevant waren insbesondere die Abrechnungen der Bankiers, weil diese im Prozess bekanntgegeben werden mussten."[35]

Die umfassenden *rationes*, die etwa zur Monats- oder Jahresabrechnung die „Reinschrift" lieferten, wurden aufgrund von kleinen Notizen, sogenannten *ad hoc*-Listen (*provisoria*) zusammengestellt. Neben den großen Übersichtslisten fertigte man auch kürzere, spezielle Listen an, die etwa die Vermögensbewegungen einzelner Personen oder gewisser Produkte dokumentierten.

Mustert man Texte mit Abrechnungen aus dem römischen Ägypten durch, kommt man bald zu dem Schluss, dass es kein festes System oder typisches Formular gab. Am besten zeigen die großen „Übersichtslisten" oder „Geschäftsbücher", die sich auf einen Gesamtbetrieb (etwa einer Bank, eines Haushalts oder eben einer Provinz) konzentrieren, wie die Einträge ausgesehen haben dürften. Sie wurden zwar chronologisch, aber sonst ziemlich unsystematisch geführt. Es lassen sich jedoch gewisse Trends beobachten, deren kurze Übersicht zum besseren Verständnis Ciceros Abrechnungen beitragen kann.[36] Die Abrechnungen Ciceros als Statthalter der Provinz Kilikien dürften am ehesten denen einer gut geführten Bank nahestehen. Es sind kaum Papyri oder Holztäfelchen mit Abrechnungen der Statthalter überliefert, aber es sind *rationes* aus verschiedenen Gebieten der Privatwirtschaft bekannt. Diese können als Indizien dafür dienen, wie die öffentlichen Abrechnungen (darunter auch jene Ciceros) ausgesehen haben dürften.

BGU XIV 2431 (Herakl., 1. Jh. v.Chr.) ist ein vollständig erhaltenes Stück aus dem Geschäftsbuch einer Bank; das Dokument überliefert eine bemerkenswert gegliederte Auf-

---

34 Vgl. D. W. Rathbone, Economic Rationalism and Rural Society in Third-Century A.D. Egypt. The Heroninos Archive and the Appianus Estate, Cambridge 1991, 333; A. Bürge, Fiktion und Wirklichkeit: Soziale und rechtliche Strukturen des römischen Bankwesens, ZRG RA 104 (1987) 509ff.; R. M. Thilo, Der Codex accepti et expensi im Römischen Recht, Göttingen 1980, 68.

35 D. 2,13,6,3 Ulp. 4 ed.

36 Vgl. die Untersuchungen von R.S. Bagnall, The Kellis Agricultural Account Book (P.Kell. IV Gr. 96), Oxford 1997, 25ff.; F. Mitthof / A. Papathomas, Das Archiv des ἐλαιουργός Sambas: Unterhaltszahlungen in Öl an die Bediensteten eines Gutes (Arsinoites; 6. Jh.n.Chr.), ZPE 103 (1994) 53ff.

stellung über Geldeinnahmen. Am Anfang steht die Herkunft der Einzahlungen mit dem Gesamtbetrag:

Φεβίχεως σειτωνίων β̣ Βχ
καταγωγίου ρδ
(γίνονται) Βψδ, (ὧν) τρα(πέζῃ)
Φαμενὼ(θ) ᾱ φ, λ̣̄ ϡμ, Φαρμοῦ(θι) κγ̄ ϡκη,
Μ(ε)χ(εὶρ) κε̄ ξδ, Μ(εσορὴ) λ̄ σοβ, (γίνονται) ᾿Βψδ
vac.
παράτιμον ο̣λ̣( ) ἀπὸ̣ ἀ̣ργ(υρίου) ἀργ(υρίου) υι, (ὧν) τρα(πέζῃ)
Μ(εσορὴ) λ̄ σοη, Ἐπεὶφ ιβ ρκ, ιϛ̄ ιβ, (γίνονται) υι
vac.
Τρύφωνος τιμὴν οἴνου τῶν ἐν Ταλῇ `κ̣(ατοίκων)´ ἀργ(υρίου) υ (ὧν) τρα(πέζῃ)
Φαμε(νὼθ) λ̄ ξ, Φαρμο(ῦθι) κγ̄ ρ, Μ(ε)χ(εὶρ) κε̄ π, Μ(εσορὴ) λ̄ π,
Ἐπεὶφ ιβ π, (γίνονται) υ
vac.
Ὡρίωνος τιμὴν οἴνου ἀργ(υρίου) ᾿Βωοθ, (ὧν) τρα(πέζῃ)
Χοιὰχ κε̄ χϙϛ, Μ(εσ)ο(ρὴ) κϛ̄ ω, Φαμε(νὼθ) ᾱ τϙβ, λ̄ τκη,
Φαρμοῦ(θι) κγ̄ τοε, διὰ Πάτρωνος ρ, (γίνονται) υοε
Μ(ε)χ(εὶρ) κε̄ ϙϛ, Με(σορὴ) λ̄ ξδ, (γίνονται) ᾿Βωνα

„(1) aus (dem Dorf[37]) Phebichis[38], Spesen 2 (?): 2.600; …
„(8) von Tryphon für den Preis des Weines von den Katöken in Tale: 400 Silberdrachmen; …"
„(11) von Horion für den Preis des Weines: 2.879 Silberdrachmen …"

Nach jedem Einnahmeposten folgt ein Überblick über die Einzahlungen, monatlich eingetragen (3. 6. 8. 11), etwa:

„die der Bank (in folgenden Raten gezahlt worden sind):
(4) Phamenoth 1. — 500; 30. — 940; Pharmouthi 23. — 928;
(5) Mecheir 25. — 64; Mesore 30. — 272; (insgesamt) — 2.704",

usw. Der Herausgeber deutet den monatlichen Überblick als detaillierte Aufstellung über den Ausgangsbetrag der Einnahmen. Es ist jedoch auch denkbar, dass es sich hier bereits um Ausgaben handelt, die aus den Einnahmen abgebucht und einem hier namentlich nicht erwähnten Bankier (wohl einem ständigen Geschäftspartner) gezahlt worden sind. Die noch einmal addierte Gesamtsumme würde eher zu der zweiten Variante (Auszahlung) passen.[39] Für die antike Buchführungstechnik ist es außerdem typisch, dass die Gesamtmenge, worüber abgerechnet wird, in der ersten Zeile als Ausgangspunkt angeführt wird.[40] Dieser Aufbau folgt aus dem antiken Rechenwesen: Der Rechenvorgang wurde nicht in der Rech-

37 Als Personenname nicht belegt, daher stellt bereits der Herausgeber auf die Deutung als Ortschaft ab, vgl. W. M. Brashear, Kommentar zu Z. 1, S. 118.
38 Zu Bankiers in Phebichis s. R. Bogaert, Les documents bancaires de l'Égypte gréco-romaine et byzantine, Ancient Society 31 (2001) 176.
39 P.Oxy. VI 985 (2. Hälfte des 1. Jhs.) zeigt eine ähnliche Struktur.
40 Vgl. etwa P.Mich. XV 741 über Wein.

nungsliste, sondern auf dem *abacus* vollzogen.[41] Die Ausgangszahl ist der jeweils aktuelle Bestand, danach werden die einzelnen Ausgaben angeführt, zusammengerechnet und von der Ausgangszahl abgezogen.[42] Für die vorliegende Untersuchung sind jedoch die Mitwirkung eines Bankhauses und die korrespondierenden, nach einzelnen Einnahmequellen geführten Eintragungen von Interesse.

TPSulp. 94-95, von Giuseppe Camodeca unter dem Titel *Rationum fragmenta* geführt,[43] sind von ihrem Aufbau her mit den mutmaßlichen Aufstellungen des Cicero vergleichbar. Es handelt sich wohl auch hier um Eintragungen im Geschäftsbuch.[44]

TPSulp. 94 (3. Juni 42)

[---] comparem [---]
a[b C(aio)] Sulpicio F[austo id quod in]fra scriptum est:
C(aio) Caecina Largo C(aio) Cestio Gallo cos., III nonas Iunias, [E]unuo Amaranti Ti(berii)
Claudi Caesaris Augusti Germanici ser(vi) Hyacinthiani vicario HS I))).

TPSulp. 95 (9. Juli 42)

[---C(aio) Caecina Largo, C(aio) Caestio co(n)s(ulibus)]
[III non(as) Iunias, E]unuo Amaranthi vicario HS I))). (vac.) C(aio) Cae[cina Largo]
[C(aio) Ces]tio co(n)s(ulibus), VII [i]dus Iulias, Thallo Phori vicario HS ((I)) ((I)) I)).

TPSulp. 94, Z. 4 deutet darauf hin, dass die Fragmente aus dem Geschäftsbuch[45] des Caius Sulpicius Faustus[46] stammen. Der anschließende Posten beginnt mit der Datierung nach den Konsuln, dann folgt ein Name im Dativ und ein Betrag. Die chronologisch geführten Täfelchen dokumentieren die Auszahlungen aus der Bankkasse an einzelne Personen. Der Dativ (etwa *Eunuo Amaranthi vicario HS I)))*[47] macht deutlich, dass Eunus und Thallus[48] die Empfänger der hohen Auszahlungen waren. Aus der „Übersichtsliste" des Geschäftsbuches lässt sich nicht mehr entscheiden, ob die Zahlungen *obligandi* oder *solvendi causa* getätigt wurden.[49] Es sind jedenfalls verschiedene Varianten denkbar: Überweisung eines Dritten durch die Bank, Auszahlung aus der eigenen Einlage oder schließlich aus der Kasse der Bank, also Kreditgewährung. Es werden hier jedoch weder die *causa* der Zahlung noch

---

41 Vgl. dazu Thilo 1980: 65ff.

42 Zum üblichen Aufbau der Aufstellungen vgl. H. Harrauer, Kommentar zu P.Prag. II 180, S. 149; L. Bandi, I conti privati nei papiri dell'Egitto greco-romano, Aegyptus 17 (1937) 375ff.

43 Vgl. G. Camodeca, Tabulae Pompeianae Sulpiciorum. Edizione critica dell'archivio puteolano dei Sulpicii I-II, Roma 1999, 205f.

44 Vgl. dazu K. Verboven, L'organisation des affaires financière des C. Sulpicii de Pouzzoles, Cahiers du Centre Gustave-Glotz 11 (2000) 162, 165.

45 Camodeca 1999: 205 stellt auf *codex rationum* ab.

46 Zur Person vgl. J.G. Wolf, Der neue pompejanische Urkundenfund. Zu Camodecas 'Edizione critica dell'archivio puteolano dei Sulpici', ZRG RA 118 (2001) 80f.

47 TPSulp. 95, Z. 2.

48 Zur wirtschaftlichen Rolle und zum sozialen Gewicht der Freigelassenen in Puteoli s. J. D'Arms, Commerce and Social Standing in Ancient Rome, Cambridge 1981, 123ff.

49 Anders Camodeca 1999: 205, der auf *credendi causa* abstellt.

Sicherheiten (Bürgschaft oder Pfand) vermerkt,[50] was eher für eine Auszahlung *solvendi causa* spricht.[51]

Zusammenfassend ist noch einmal zu betonen, dass die Geschäftsbücher und Abrechnungen eine bunte Vielfalt der Techniken der Buchhaltung zeigen. Die Einnahmen und Ausgaben werden grundsätzlich nicht getrennt, eine doppelte Buchführung ist ebenfalls unbekannt. Vielmehr werden bei beträchtlichen Einnahmen einzelne Kolumnen gebildet, die den Verbrauch des Betrages und die Ausgaben davon unmittelbar auflisten. Dadurch entsteht ein einigermaßen nach Sachen und Personen gegliedertes, in kleine geschlossene Einheiten aufgeteiltes System, das Übersichts- und Einzelabrechnungen frei mischt und vor allem einem schnellen Inventar dient. Die verschiedenen Arten der Buchführung sind kaum definierbar, weil die Modelle von den antiken Schreibern nicht auseinandergehalten werden.[52]

Die antike Buchführung will vor allem „Bestandsaufnahmen" herstellen, welche die regelmäßige Kontrolle des Betriebs ermöglichen. Aus diesem Konzept lässt sich die Anordnung nach Sach- oder Personengruppen, Wirtschaftszweigen, Produkten und ähnlichem bzw. das starke Bestreben nach ständiger Bilanz ableiten. Bei Einnahmen und Ausgaben, Schulden und Rückzahlungen wird konsequent versucht, zum jeweiligen Posten auch die korrespondierende Buchung einzutragen. Auf dieser Weise bleibt die Übersicht über Leistungen und Gegenleistungen auch in einem unsystematisch geführten „Geschäftsbuch" möglich. Wenn man von einem Geschäftsbuch spricht, ist darunter keineswegs ein festgebundener Band zu verstehen. Im römischen Ägypten waren die „Geschäftsbücher" vielmehr Sammlungen von *grammata*, von kleinen Schriftstücken, die etwa in den großen landwirtschaftlichen Betrieben monatlich oder jährlich zu einer Übersichtsliste zusammengetragen wurden.[53]

Es ist im Schrifttum umstritten, wie solche Belege der antiken Buchführung zu bewerten sind. Früher glaubte man, in den Quellen die Technik der modernen Buchführung zu erkennen.[54] Diese Auffassung wurde in der neueren Forschung widerlegt: Die Autoren be-

50 In den Papyri finden wir hingegen zahlreiche Beispiele dafür, dass der Vertragsgrund und die Sicherheiten in der Eintragung im Bankbuch erscheinen, vgl. beispielsweise P.Lips. I 10 mit ausführlichem Kommentar von L. Mitteis, Leipzig 1906. Für eine ähnliche Praxis in Rom s. P. Gröschler, Die tabellae-Urkunden aus den pompeianischen und herkulanensischen Urkundenfunden, Berlin 1997, 278ff.

51 In diesem Sinne bereits Wolf 2001: 83, jedoch mit anderen Argumenten.

52 Diese Natur der graeco-ägyptischen Geschäftsbücher lässt gegen Gröschlers logisch aufgebaute, reine Kategorien (*codex accepti et expensi, rationes* und *codex rationum*) Bedenken aufkommen, vgl. Gröschler 1997: 258ff.

53 Vgl. etwa Rathbone 1991: 335 mit tabellarischer Übersicht über alle erhaltenen Monatsrechnungen im Heroneinos-Archiv. Ähnlich auch der schon oben angeführte BGU XIV 2431 (Herakl., 1. Jh. v.Chr.) oder die Meldungen von Bankdiagraphai P.Ross.Georg. II 18 (Faijum, 140) und 36 (Faijum, 2. Jh.). Die Liste könnte man noch lange weiterführen; vgl. jetzt auch A. Jördens, in diesem Band. Zur *bibliotheke enkteseon* s. kürzlich A. Papathomas, Kommentar zu P.Heid. VII 397, S. 86ff. mit weiterer Literatur; auch R. Bogaert, Les opérations des banques de l'Égypte romaine, Ancient Society 30 (2000) 259ff.; und A. Jördens, Nochmals zur Bibliotheke Enkteseon, in G. Thür (Hg.), Symposion 2009. Vorträge zur griechischen und hellenistischen Rechtsgeschichte, Wien 2010, 277-290.

54 S. etwa F. Preisigke, Girowesen im griechischen Ägypten, Strassburg 1910, 62ff.; M. Voigt, Über die Bankiers, die Buchführung und die Litteralobligation der Römer, Leipzig 1887, 529-535; Th. Niemeyer, Bespr. von: M. Voigt, Ueber die Bankiers, die Buchführung und die Litteralobligation der Römer, ZRG RA 11 (1890) 312-326.

tonen die Einfachheit der antiken Buchführungen und lehnen jede Gleichsetzung mit den modernen Techniken ab: „Graeco-Roman bookkeeping was exceedingly rudimentary, essentially restricted to a listing of receipts and expenditures, from which it was impossible to determine the profitability.“[55] Im jüngeren Schrifttum wird eher betont: „simpler accounting systems were and are quite adequate for economically rational management of relatively uncomplicated economic enterprises; simple accounts do not necessarily indicate a simple economic mentality.“[56]

Die Auszüge aus den Rechnungsbüchern, die von Einnahmen und Ausgaben berichten, können auch für den Juristen wertvolle Informationen vermitteln. Es ist von Interesse, wie die einzelnen Einträge in den Geschäftsbüchern dokumentiert wurden. Die vorliegende Untersuchung strebt keineswegs ein vollständiges Panorama des Quellenbestandes an. Es wird vielmehr nach buchhalterischen Techniken gesucht, die den selbstverständlichen praktischen Hintergrund der Rechenschaftspflicht der Magistrate bildeten. Sie gehören zum historischen, wirtschaftlichen und sozialen Kontext und können zum richtigen Verständnis unserer Quelle beitragen.[57]

Auch die Schriften der klassischen römischen Juristen vermitteln gewisse Informationen über die Gestaltung der professionellen Abrechnungen. Insbesondere der Titel D. 2, 13 (*De edendo*) enthält solche Details. Das prätorische Edikt hat bestimmt, dass die Bankiers die Abrechnungen unter Hinzufügung von Tag und Konsul bekanntgeben sollen.[58] Die Auszüge aus den Geschäftsbüchern dienen vor Gericht als authentische Beweise über Geldtransaktionen. Der Prätor verlangt, dass die aktuelle Kopie mit dem Namen des Adressaten, aber besonders mit einer präzisen Datierung aus dem Bankbuch kopiert wird. Die Voranstellung von Tag und Konsul war ein gemeinsames Merkmal der Abrechnungen. Ulpian bespricht in D. 2,13,4 pr. einen Fall, wo eine der Prozessparteien die Korrektheit des Auszugs aus dem Geschäftsbuch bestritt. Der Jurist legte fest, dass der Kunde einen Anspruch darauf habe, dass er in seinem Interesse diese authentische Kopie aus dem Geschäftsbuch (das den Charakter eines öffentlichen Archivs hatte) erhält. Die Bankiers führten für Privatpersonen individuelle Rechnungsbücher, deshalb wurden sie vom Prätor gezwungen, ihre Abrechnungen in einem eventuellen Prozess vorzulegen.[59] In einem laufenden Prozess war es auch von Relevanz, welche Bank – und aus welcher Entfernung – zur Information zu Beweiszwecken gezwungen werden konnte.[60] Die Rechnungslegung war nicht nur über öffentliche

---

55 M.I. Finley, The Ancient Economy², London 1985, 181; G.E.M. de SteCroix, Greek and Roman Accounting, in A.C. Littleton - B.S. Yamey (Hgg.), Studies in the History of Accounting, London 1956, 14-74; R.C. Duncan-Jones, The Economy of the Roman Empire², Cambridge 1982, 39ff. Daraus hat man übrigens oft den Schluss gezogen, dass auch die antike Wirtschaft in einem primitiven Zustand verharrte.

56 Rathbone 1991: 332f.; J. Andreau, Modernité économique et statut des manieurs d'argent, MEFRA 97 (1985) 373-410.

57 S. bereits Thilo 1980: 60 ff.; s. auch G. Minaud, La comptabilité à Rom. Essai d'histoire économique sur la penseé comptable commerciale et privée dans le monde antique romain, Lausanne 2005 mit weiterer Literatur.

58 D. 2,13,4 pr. Ulp. 4 ed.

59 D. 2,13,4,1 Ulp. 4 ed.

60 D. 2,13,5. S. dazu auch D. 2,13,6 pr. Ulp.

Gelder, sondern auch in privatrechtlichen Rechtsverhältnissen von zentraler Bedeutung (D. 2,13,9 pr. Paulus 3 ed.).[61]

Die prätorischen Vorschriften über die Buchführung zeigen, welche Voraussetzungen eine korrekte Abrechnung erfüllen musste. In einem eventuellen Rechtsstreit, etwa wenn der Statthalter wegen Mängel in der Abrechnung angeklagt wird, müssen die Geldtransaktionen aus dem Geschäftsbuch restlos rekonstruierbar sein. Im staatlichen Kontext geht es dabei vor allem darum, wer als Zahlungsempfänger und Zahlender eingetragen ist, und aus welchem Rechtsgrund (*causa*) die Einnahmen und Ausgaben erfolgten. Die Personen (Amtsträger), welche die Abrechnungen der Magistrate überprüften, konnten die Einträge im Geschäftsbuch mit den korrespondierenden Einträgen in den Geschäftsbüchern der betroffenen Personen vergleichen. Zur Korrektheit der *rationes* gehörte also eine vielseitige Übereinstimmung mit parallel (privat oder staatlich) geführten Abrechnungen.[62]

IV. Cicero und Rufus

Gerade in diesem Punkt beanstandete Rufus eine Diskrepanz. Aus Ciceros Versuch, die Sache zu klären, kann man Rückschlüsse auf die Beschwerden des Rufus ziehen. Einerseits bittet Cicero ihn, wegen einer ‚lächerlichen Summe' von 100.000 Sesterzen keine Schwierigkeiten zu machen. Er sollte ein Auge zudrücken und ignorieren, dass die Verwendung dieser Summe nicht geklärt sei. Als Scherz schreibt er ihm, dass er aus dieser *causa* wohl keine Vollstreckung gegen ihn anstreben wolle! Es ist nicht klar, wohin dieses Geld wirklich geflossen ist. Die Ungewissheit ergibt sich auch daraus, dass die Abbuchung dieser Summe bloß durch einen Privatbrief vereinbart worden war.[63] In Ciceros privatem Geschäftsverkehr finden sich oft Hinweise darauf, dass Geldtransaktionen – Anweisungen, Aufträge – informell, durch bloße Andeutungen angebahnt, und dann getreu ausgeführt wurden.[64]

Problematischer scheint die Abrechnung über die 2.200.000 Sesterzen, die man kaum als eine ‚lächerliche Summe' abtun kann. Cicero behauptet, dass er diesen Betrag bei den *publicani* in Ephesos in Verwahrung gab, und dort soll das Geld später von Pompeius beschlagnahmt worden sein. Liest man jedoch den ersten Teil des Briefes und die parallele

61 Wenn ein Gesellschafter seine Geschäfte arglistig geführt hat, schritt der Prätor nicht aufgrund dieser Ediktklausel ein. Dafür gab es nämlich die Gesellschafterklage. Aber auch den Vormund zwang der Prätor nicht aufgrund dieses Edikts, dem Mündel Abrechnungen bekanntzugeben; vielmehr wurde der Vormund gewöhnlich mit der Vormundschaftsklage zur Bekanntgabe gezwungen.

62 Vgl. dazu H.L.W. Nelson / U. Manthe, Gai Institutiones III 88-181 (Studia Gaiana VIII), Text und Kommentar, Berlin 1999, 196 ff.; Thilo 1980: 55ff.

63 Zum häufigen Gebrauch der *epistula* auch im Geschäftsverkehr s. É. Jakab, Urkunden in Briefform: Chirographum und Epistula im römischen Privatrecht, in U. Yiftach-Firanko (Hg.), The Letter: Law, State, Society and the Epistolary Format in the Ancient World: Proceedings of a Colloquium held at the American Academy in Rome 28-30.9.2008, Wiesbaden 2013, 219-238.

64 Vgl. etwa Cic. Att. 2,4,1: „Mit der Übersendung Serapios Buch hast Du mir einen großen Gefallen getan. Freilich – unter uns darf man es ja wohl sagen – ich verstehe kaum den tausendsten Teil davon. Das Geld dafür habe ich Dir bar auszuzahlen befohlen, damit Du es nicht unter der Rubrik „Geschenke" buchst. Und wo wir nun schon einmal vom Geld reden: siehe doch bitte zu, dass Du, einerlei wie, mit Titinius ins reine kommst. Steht er nicht zu seinen Versprechungen, so bin ich durchaus dafür, die zu teuer entstandenen Gegenstände zurückzugeben, wenn Pomponia damit einverstanden ist ..." (H. Kasten, Marcus Tullius Cicero, Atticus-Briefe, Lateinisch-deutsch, München 1959, 97).

Überlieferung, wird die Rolle der *publicani* in der ganzen Affäre etwas deutlicher. Die *publicani* (Steuerpächter) waren große, kapitalstarke Gesellschafter, die staatliche Aufgaben durch öffentliche Versteigerungen erworben haben; ihr wichtigstes Geschäft war die Eintreibung von Zöllen und Steuern.[65]

Die Millionen, deren Verwendung in den Abrechnungen Ciceros unklar blieb, hatten mit den Unternehmungen der dort tätigen *publicani* zu tun: „Was Volusius angeht, so hat das mit der Abrechnung nichts zu tun. Rechtskundige Männer ... haben mir nämlich auseinandergesetzt, dass der Schuldposten nicht von Valerius auf Volusius hätte übertragen werden können und die Bürgen des Valerius haftbar sind. ... denn das Geld war uns namens des Valerius als Unternehmer überwiesen worden. Was am Gesamtbetrage fehlte, habe ich in der Abrechnung angeführt".[66] Aus dieser Stelle geht hervor, dass Rufus eigentlich nach drei Millionen suchte; Cicero korrigierte (reduzierte) den Betrag auf 1,9 Millionen. Im Hintergrund scheint ein etwas suspektes Geschäft zu stehen, worin auch ein gewisser Volusius (ein Angehöriger von Ciceros Stab) verwickelt war. Aus den verstreuten Daten kann man darauf schließen, dass dieser Volusius in der Provinz Abgaben gepachtet hatte. Besser gesagt, er wirkte als „Strohmann" für einen Unternehmer namens Valerius mit, weil jener – aus welchem Grund immer – den Vertrag nicht im eigenen Namen abschließen konnte oder wollte. Cicero und sein Stab schienen genau Bescheid gewusst zu haben ... Jener Valerius handelte nämlich während des ganzen Geschäftsablaufs als „Stellvertreter" des Volusius. Er war es auch, der die Geldtransaktionen *mancipis nomine* (im Namen des Ersteigerers, des *manceps*) unternahm.[67] Der Vertrag mit dem Staat wurde – wie üblich – mit hohen dinglichen und persönlichen Sicherungen abgeschlossen. Aus den Abrechnungen zeigte sich aber bald, dass die Kontrahenten (wohl Valerius) mit 1.900.000 Sesterzen in Verzug geraten sind – und dieser Betrag fehlte in den Staatseinnahmen. Valerius wollte dafür jedoch nicht einstehen; er verwies vielmehr auf Volusius, der im Vertrag mit dem Staat als Kontrahent aufgetreten war. Der Fall wurde in der statthalterlichen Kanzlei mehrmals diskutiert. Die *iuris periti* waren sich dann darüber einig, dass nicht Volusius (der Strohmann), sondern eher die Bürgen haftbar gemacht werden sollten. Diese Bürgen waren aber zwei Männer aus Ciceros Stab, die sich damals – etwas naiv, wohl wegen des Kameraden – zu den Bürgschaftsstipulationen hatten überreden lassen. Würde eine Klage gegen sie eingebracht, hätten sie eine so hohe Summe keineswegs leisten können. Das heißt aber, dass gegen sie die Vollstreckung mit all ihren vermögens- und personenrechtlichen Folgen eingeleitet worden wäre.[68]

Offenbar wollte Cicero seine Leute nicht „opfern"; die *amicitia* und die damit verbundene *dignitas* waren in den höheren Klassen der römischen Gesellschaft moralisch allge-

65 Zur Tätigkeit der *publicani* s. U. Malmendier, Societas publicanorum. Staatliche Wirtschaftsaktivitäten in den Händen privater Unternehmen (= Forschungen zum Römischen Recht 49), Köln 2002, 221ff.

66 Cic. ad Fam. 5,20,3: *De Volusio quod scribis, non est id rationum; docuerunt enim me periti homines ... ad Volusium traferri nomen a Valerio non potuisse, praedes Valerianos teneri – neque id erat HS XXX ut scribis, sed HS XIX – erat enim curata nobis pecunia Valeri mancipis nomine; ex qua reliquum quod erat, in rationibus rettuli.*

67 Zur Versteigerung s. etwa A. Mateo, Manceps, redemptor, publicanus. Contribución al estudio de los contratistas públicos en Roma, Santander 1999.

68 Schon die Forderung wesentlich kleinerer Beträge hätte Cicero ruinieren können; s. etwa Cic. Att. 15,21(20), 4.

mein verpflichtend.[69] Die Mitglieder seines Stabes standen unter seiner *potestas* und waren dadurch auch mit seiner *dignitas* verbunden. Dies bedeutete – der *patria potestas* ähnlich – nicht nur eine Befehlsgewalt über diese Personen, sondern auch die Verpflichtung, sie öffentlich zu beschützen.[70] Wahrscheinlich deshalb hat Cicero beschlossen, diesen (beträchtlichen) Betrag aus seinem „Etat", aus der ihm zur Verwaltung stehenden (öffentlichen) „Kasse" abzuschreiben. Diese suspekte Buchung stach dem L. Mescinius Rufus bei der Überprüfung der Abrechnungen ins Auge.

69 Aristot. NE 1155a. Zur Rolle der Freundschaft in der antiken Gesellschaft und Wirtschaft vgl. D. Nörr, Mandatum, fides, amicitia, in Sh. Nishimura (Hg.), Mandatum und Verwandtes, Berlin 1993, 13-14 (= Historiae iuris antiqui III, T.J. Chiusi, W. Kaiser, H.-D. Spengler Hgg., Goldbach 2003, 1933-1934); K. Verboven, The Economy of Friends, Aspects of Amicitia and Patronage in the Late Republic, Bruxelles 2002.

70 S. etwa D. 2,13,9,4 Paul. 3 ed.

Verres' Books: Documentary Proof in Cicero's *Verrines*

Miklós Könczöl, Budapest

Introduction

In 71 BC, the representatives of the Sicilians initiated a legal procedure (*quaestio de repetundis*) against Caius Verres, who had held (between 73 and 71) the post of governor (*propraetor*) in the province. He notoriously used his power to extort money from the people of Sicily, individuals as well as communities, and in addition to enrich his private art collection with a number of precious works he took from temples and wealthy families. The Sicilians soon approached Marcus Tullius Cicero, previously (in 75) *proquaestor* in the province, to plead on their behalf. Accepting their request and winning, against Quintus Caecilius Niger, a close ally of Verres, the right to prosecute, Cicero started to collect evidence on Verres' activity in Sicily in general, and on the individual transactions in particular. After a good deal of strategic moves concerning the timing of the trial, the first hearing finally took place in August 70,[1] where Cicero could finally deliver his first speech against Verres. In that speech, he opted for an unusual strategy, and not only gave a summary of the events in question, but also started to marshal the evidence he was going to discuss further in the following sessions.

Facing the massive body of proof, and having failed to secure a friendly jury for himself, Verres found it wiser to go into exile (to Massilia) after the first days of the trial. Having thus won the case for the Sicilians, Cicero nevertheless decided to publish the material he gathered in the form of a series of five speeches (the *actio secunda in Verrem*), together with his speech against Caecilius (the *divinatio in Caecilium*) and the one he actually gave before the court (the *actio prima in Verrem*). He may have done so for several reasons. First, he may have felt the need actually to argue his case against the influential Verres, to convince a broader audience that his claims were well-founded indeed. Second, he may have used the opportunity to showcase his rhetorical and legal skills. Knowing Cicero's habit of publishing, sometimes in heavily edited form, the speeches he delivered, one is tempted to think that he had planned to publish the texts anyway, and Verres' premature departure only gave him the extra possibility of laying out the material he found most convincing on the one hand, and perhaps most useful didactically on the other,[2] also making some modifications on the speech of the first *actio*.

---

1 In July 70, Quintus Hortensius Hortalus and Quintus Caecilius Metellus were elected consuls for the next year, with Marcus Caecilius Metellus becoming *praetor* in charge of extortion cases. Thus, Verres could hope for a much more favourable setting for the continuation of his trial if he succeeded to extend the procedure beyond the end of the year.

2 Cicero's insistence on keeping the form of judicial speeches with all the usual elements (*exordium, peroratio,* summaries of the arguments made, direct addresses to the judges and the defendant, etc.)

The structure of the speeches[3] is the following. In the *Divinatio*, Cicero focuses on two issues: the justification of his role as accuser, and the comparison between Caecilius and himself in terms of their capability of pleading against Verres. Accordingly, we find no account of the facts in the speech, apart from some references to the motives of the Sicilians' choice, and insinuation against Caecilius with reference to him being personally involved in Verres' affairs. In the *Actio prima*, Cicero first warns the judges of the defendant's attempt to extend the trial to the following year, to have the case decided by a different court. For that reason, Cicero explains, there is no time for a proper speech, and he needs to start to prove his case without delay. The fictitious *Actio secunda* falls into five parts, published as five books, each with a different focus. The first book (*De praetura urbana*) deals with Verres' offices (*quaestor, legatus, praetor urbanus*) before going to Sicily, through a few examples of his misuse of power. The second one (*De praetura Siciliensi*) then gives an overview of his activity as *propraetor*, especially in the fields of private and criminal adjudication, the appointment of officials, collecting money for his own statue, and his relationship with the *publicani.* The third, and longest, part (*De re frumentaria*) is about the actual extortion committed by Verres in connection with the grain tax. Here, the series of figures help the audience to see the *propraetor*'s actions as parts of a planned and systematic crime against the people of the province. The fourth speech (*De signis*) gives an account of Verres' 'acquisitions' of works of art, first enumerating the cases in which the property of individuals was taken, then those concerning communities and sacred places. In the last piece (*De suppliciis*), Cicero comes to Verres' abuses of his *imperium* in military as well as civic affairs. These complete both the portrayal of Verres' character and the political assessment of his activity.

While the arrangement of the evidence as we have it may be overly artificial and not reflect actual forensic practice, the material itself seems genuine in the sense that Cicero only published what he actually collected to ground his case against Verres, without inventing or forging additional evidence in the absence of the defendant.[4] Hence, the *Verrines* have always attracted considerable attention as an incomparably valuable source of information on both the way provincial administration, financial management and co-operation worked in practice, and the forms and objects of art collection in Rome.

Classical scholarship in the last decade has examined the speeches from various angles. Cicero's text has been used as a source on the practice of Roman lawyers[5] and administration in the provinces.[6] Cicero's use of numbers and figures has been scrutinised, both from a formal[7] and a substantive[8] perspective. In terms of rhetoric, the doctrinal sources of the

makes the impression that he also wanted the text to be useful for students of rhetoric. On the popularity of the *Verrines* as model speeches, see Tempest (2016, pp. 70–71).

3 On Cicero's rhetorical use of *dispositio* in the Verrines, see Tempest (2007).

4 See Frazel (2004) and Gurd (2010, pp. 81–82). That said, Cicero seems to have used the material with some licence (see e.g. Steel, 2004), especially in terms of the numbers, see most recently Steel (2007) and Cioffi (2011).

5 Lehne-Gstreinthaler (2016).

6 Pfuntner (2015).

7 Cuomo (2011).

Verrines,[9] as well as aspects of Cicero's performance[10] have been discussed. The present paper seeks to contribute to that latter field.

In what follows, I am going to look at Cicero's use of Verres' accounts as documentary proof. I shall do so by first looking at the text of the *actio secunda*, and the characterisation of the defendant in particular. Then I turn to the rhetorical doctrine of 'non-technical proof' (*pisteis atechnoi*), using Aristotle's *Rhetoric* and Cicero's own rhetorical works for comparison. Such a contrast, I hope, furthers our understanding of Cicero's rhetorical strategy on the one hand, and the possible functions of non-technical proof in rhetorical argumentation on the other.

Cicero's Use of Verres' Books

In Roman literary sources, bookkeeping sometimes appears as one of the characteristics of a *bonus et diligens paterfamilias*.[11] Considered from a moral perspective, dishonesty or negligence often begin with one's failure to make accounts, the absence of which may be intended to make investigations more difficult. That latter insight occurs repeatedly in Cicero's speeches against Verres. Verres' failure to submit his accounts as *praetor*, as well as his delay in submitting them as a *legatus* and the lapidary manner in which he accounted for his finances as *quaestor*, reflect negatively on his character. That, of course, can be discounted as mere rhetoric, similarly to the opposite moves we find in Cicero's characterisation of his own efforts to get access to Verres' and others' private accounts and to gather relevant information from these and from other sources. He emphasises his own *diligentia* already in the first speech (I.11.32–33).[12]

Yet Cicero goes further and claims that Verres was, apparently, not incapable of keeping records or paying attention to detail in general. Rather, the gaps in his books are due to his efforts not to leave any trace of his unlawful businesses – Cicero is happy to point out that these were all in vain. Coming thus to accounts as 'non-technical proof', to use Aristotle's rhetorical terminology, we see that Cicero is well aware of the role they can play in persuasion, firstly by grasping the attention of the audience. They are, he states, part of the 'action' in the case before the court, as opposed to mere narration (I.10.28–29). Beyond arousing attention, accounts can prove transactions having been made. In that respect, we see Cicero following Aristotle's advice once again, emphasising or downplaying the importance and credibility of accounts, according to his persuasive aims.

All the above methods can be well observed in practice in a passage where Cicero discusses tablets recording receipts and expenses in connection with paintings (*tabulae pictae*) and

8 Cioffi (2011).

9 Frazel (2009).

10 See Gurd (2010) on Cicero's act of rewriting his speech as compared to Verres' rewriting of his account entries, and Tempest (2016) on Cicero's considerations on and practice of performance.

11 An interesting example is Plautus' *Mostellaria*, a play where the ways of spending money are not only in the focus of the plot but also used to distinguish the moral qualities of the characters.

12 I use the text of Klotz's (1923) edition. Roman numerals in the references indicate the speeches of the *Actio secunda*.

statues. It will be not contested, he states, that Verres has had a remarkable collection of works of art, which he claims he has paid for. Cicero now challenges him to show the corresponding entries in his books: 'Show me just one you bought in your books or those of your father: then you have won' (I.23.61: *unum ostende in tabulis aut tuis aut patris tui emptum esse: vicisti*).

Here, Verres could clear himself of the charges by just showing an entry in his records, Cicero implies. Yet from the same passage, we also learn something Cicero too finds weird. Verres tells that some time ago he gave up keeping records. Cicero carefully enumerates the possibilities: it may be the case that someone just does not keep records at all. It may also happen that someone who did not keep records before, starts to do so at a certain point. Yet the opposite, keeping records and then stopping it needs an explanation. Cicero seems sceptical about the truth of Verres' claim, and later mentions various reasons why existing records cannot be accessed. A later commentary, however, the so-called *Scholia Sangallensia*, tells us that keeping records went out of fashion, as Romans realised it may be dangerous for them: 'The custom was for every individual to set down a day-by-day household account (*domestica ratio*) for his entire life, in which would appear what he had laid aside from his revenues, from interest charged, from profit, on what day, and any expenses or losses. But once everyone began to be convicted by their own *tabulae* as a result of the confiscation of the records of accused persons (*obsignandis litteris reorum*), this entire ancient practice came to an end, even to the present day.'[13] What speaks for Cicero's version, though, is that the degree of organisation in Verres' various businesses must have made some sort of bookkeeping necessary.

Cicero also tells us about his difficulties in obtaining the accounts of Verres' partners. When trying to gather information on the affairs of a *societas publicanorum* in Sicily, he writes, he tried to get hold of the archives of the former officers: 'for I knew that it was the habit of *magistri* who had to keep records, that on handing down the books to the new *magister*, they see it fit to keep a copy for themselves' (II.74.182: *sciebam enim hanc magistrorum qui tabulas haberent consuetudinem esse, ut, cum tabulas novo magistro traderent, exempla litterarum ipsi habere non nollent)*. Apparently, Lucius Vibius did not expect any inquest, and Cicero could find two letters, in which Lucius Canuleius let other members of the association know about goods exported from Syracusae. A meagre harvest, Cicero admits, but at least something he can bring before the court, *quasi exempli causa*, as a proof that people closely related to Verres have exported goods collected in Sicily on a large scale during his praetorship (ibid. 183).

In other passages, too, we see Cicero using other people's records to supplement what is missing from those of Verres. He even tells him that only an idiot would think that not

13 Ps.-Asc., In act. II l. 1 § 60, quoted by Butler (2002, p. 43): *Moris autem fuit unumquemque domesticam rationem sibi totius vitae suae per dies singulos scribere, [in] quo appareret quid quisque de reditibus suis, quid de arte fenore lucrove seposuisset quo die, et quid item sumptus damnive fecisset. Sed postquam obsignandis litteris reorum ex suis quisque tabulis damnari coepit, ad nostram memoriam tota haec vetus consuetudo cessavit* (238.21-26 Stangel).

entering something into his own books may be sufficient to save him from charges on the one hand and from being convicted on the other. Speaking of money Verres gave to Quintus and Gnaeus Postumus Curtius, he exclaims: 'Of what use was it to you, not to enter it among your expenses? did you think that you would be pleading based exclusively on your accounts?' (I.39.102: *quid proderat tibi te expensum illis non tulisse? an tuis solis tabulis te causam dicturum existimasti?*). Other parties to the transactions, Cicero explains, may well have the sums concerned in their books, even indicating the legal title (*nomen*). Such a thing might, of course, be dangerous for the others as well. Cicero tells the audience about the problem faced by those who were forced to bribe Verres and then did not know how to call it in their book entries (I.41.106).

That Verres and those cooperating with him sometimes tried to hide or destroy evidence has been clear for Cicero. In the case of the *publicani*, for instance, after his surprise visit to Vibius, he did not have any chance to collect further documents referring to the exports from members of the society. Yet there were the wax tablets with their accounts, the *tabulae accepti et expensi*, which they just could not destroy. On these, Cicero could expect to find payments by people who had to borrow money from Verres' close friend, Carpinatius, to be able to bribe Verres. Knowing the dates from other sources (mainly the testimonies of those who were requested to pay for a favourable judgment or something else), Cicero knew what to look for, and he actually found the entries within the respective time frames: 'with not only the consuls' names but also the months corresponding' (II.76.186: *non solum consulibus verum etiam mensibus convenire*). These payments, however, were made for a certain Gaius Verrucius, son of Gaius, rather than Verres. What was curious about that, Cicero explains in a dramatic fashion, was the corrections made on the wax tablets: 'up to the second R, the letters were intact: all the others were written over an erasure (*in litura*)' (ibid. 187: *sic tamen ut usque ad alterum R litterae constarent integrae, reliquae omnes essent in litura*). After Carpinatius could not tell Cicero who exactly Verrucius was, Cicero had him brought before the new praetor, Metellus, then had exact transcripts of the tablets made, indicating the letters as well as the deletions, and sealed by 'most respected men' (ibid. 188–189, and 190: *haec omnia summa cura et diligentia recognita et collata et ab hominibus honestissimis obsignata sunt*).

In the case of the ship Verres had made by the Mamertini, Cicero practically has no financial documents to use as evidence, apart from the testimony of the envoys from Messana. Verres, he anticipates, will respond that he actually paid for the ship–Cicero is quick to highlight that such a private purchase would be illegal in itself. Verres could then point out that there is no trace of any relevant transaction in the Messanian accounts. To that, Cicero says that such works do not necessarily entail payments: the Capitolium itself was built by the citizens who worked for free. Moreover, he finds a number of entries in their books that seem to be based on fictitious labour contracts (*operum locationes falsas atque inanis*). And finally, he adds, if it is an argument that the Mamertini did not have the payment on their books, then the same goes for Verres himself: he should be able to produce written evidence for having paid for the ship himself (V.18–19.47–48).

A final example may be the use of accounts by Cicero in connection with Verres' collection of the grain tax and his additional purchases of grain. Here, the illegitimate move was that after letting the *decumani* collect more grain than stated in their contracts, he stole the grain, then took the public funds from which he should have bought an additional amount of grain for Rome (*frumentum imperatum*) at a set price, and deposited part of it with the *societas publicanorum* at an interest, paying either nothing to the cities or inventing various titles for deductions. Finally, being allowed to buy a further amount (*frumentum aestimatum*) of wheat and barley for himself and his household, he did not accept the grain offered by the cities, but let them pay for it, and set a price considerably higher than what the grain was worth on the market. It is that latter circumstance that Cicero proves with the help of farmer's records, explaining that 'it is not the setting of the price or the three denarii that make for the crime, but how the grain price was related to the set price' (III.82.189: *non ex aestimatione neque ex ternis denariis pendere crimen, sed ex coniunctione annonae atque aestimationis*).

Documentary Proof in Rhetorical Doctrine

In the above overview I have repeatedly referred to the Aristotelian doctrine of 'non-technical' proof. In Book I of his *Rhetoric*, Aristotle makes a distinction between 'technical' and 'non-technical' proof (1355b 35–39), the former comprising sources of persuasion speakers have to invent themselves (*ēthos, pathos* and *logos*), and the latter referring to documentary proof that is ready for use by the speaker. What makes the second group relevant for rhetoric is the question of how to make use of such documents in one's argument, channeling these into the construction of technical proof.[14]

Discussing non-technical proof within the judicial branch of rhetoric, towards the end of Book I, Aristotle distinguishes five kinds of documents: laws, witness testimonies, contracts, slave testimonies, and oaths. For each of these, he gives different sets of topics for constructing arguments. In the case of laws, the primary way of dealing with these is by amplifying or downplaying their relevance and importance. For witnesses, the main question is that of credibility, that is, a testimony that is favourable for one's case needs to be presented as reliable, while in the contrary case the reliability of the document needs to be questioned. Furthermore, Aristotle distinguishes between testimonies concerning the case and testimonies concerning someone's character (1376a 25). Contracts are somehow between laws and testimonies, as both their importance and credibility can be addressed in a speech (1376b 2–5. 15–17). The discussion of the topics relevant for slave testimonies lacks the balance characteristic of the previous types of proof: Aristotle apparently disapproves of that kind of testimony due to his view that torture cannot be expected to result in reliable accounts of the facts. Even more interesting is the use of oaths in persuasion since here the balance is between giving and taking an oath, or refusing to do so (cf. 1377a 29–b 3). In the two last cases, Aristotle's words make the impression that slave testimonies and oaths are not regarded as proofs in the substantive sense (that is, referring to the facts of the case), but rather as procedural means of shedding positive or negative light on oneself or the opponent.

14 Cf. Carey (1994) 96.

In his rhetorical writings, Cicero seems much less concerned with that part of the rhetorical tradition.[15] In some works, he does not discuss non-technical proof at all. In others, he is quite concise on the topic. In the *De oratore,* his longest rhetorical treatise, he comments on the vast difference between school rhetoric and forensic practice, pointing out that the former does not prepare the student for the latter. In school, he argues, only easy cases are analysed, while 'in the forum, wills, evidence, contracts, covenants, stipulations, relationship by blood, by affinity, decrees, opinions of lawyers, and even the lives and characters of those concerned in the cause, are all to be investigated' (2.24.100: *at vero in foro tabulae testimonia, pacta conventa stipulationes, cognationes adfinitates, decreta responsa, vita denique eorum, qui in causa versantur, tota cognoscenda est*; trans. J. S. Watson). That might be read as a list of non-technical proof, somewhat in the vein of Aristotle, yet even that remark is embedded into a sketch of the theory of rhetorical issues (*staseis*), with no specific topics for documentary proof.

In the *Partitiones oratoriae,* a more systematic overview of school rhetoric, two types of arguments are distinguished under the heading of *inventio,* external and internal. The former are exemplified by testimonies (*remota ... ut testimonia*, 2.6), which are then divided into divine and human. For human testimonies, their credibility rests on 'authority, intention, free or forced speech', while their examples are 'writings, contracts, promises, oaths and questionings' (ibid.: *humanum, quod spectatur ex auctoritate et ex voluntate et ex oratione aut libera aut expressa: in quo insunt scripta, pacta, promissa, iurata, quaesita*).

Finally, in the *Topica,* the discussion of non-technical (*artis expers*) proof (which, as Cicero notes, only takes place for the sake of completeness) is similarly focused on the concept of testimony (*in testimonio posita est*). However, here we find an even broader understanding of *testimonium*, defined as 'everything that is taken from something external to bring about persuasion' (19.73: *testimonium autem nunc dicimus omne quod ab aliqua re externa sumitur ad faciendam fidem*). Among the various types of evidence mentioned here, one of the Aristotelian types is alluded to (forced testimonies, 20.74), but the emphasis is not on its procedural role but the source of its credibility.

From the perspective of rhetorical theory, Verres' accounts certainly fall within the field of 'non-technical' proof. In Aristotelian terms, these books would most probably qualify as 'testimonies', albeit somewhat unusual ones, as they stem from the defendant himself. More importantly, that classification would mean that the key issue for the speaker is their credibility. Cicero's own theoretical approach, it seems, would lead to the same result with even less doubt, given his umbrella class of 'testimony', which roughly equals to 'external' or 'non-technical' proof. For him, too, credibility would be key when composing an argument based on accounts.

15 On the differences between Aristotle's and Cicero's understanding of non-technical proof in general, see Schütrumpf (1994, pp. 101–105). On the relationship of Cicero to the Aristotelian tradition see Guérin (2006).

Thus, comparing Aristotle's and Cicero's discussions on non-technical proof, we see that while they concur in much of their findings, the two approaches are clearly different. Aristotle, in his *Rhetoric*, gives the corresponding sets of topics for each type of proof, distinguishing the arguments useful for the one party from those for the other. Cicero, in turn, brackets the classification according to types of documents, and focuses on the topics instead. In the *Topica* that is hardly surprising, since he urges speakers (lawyers) to try to approach legal cases through the topics rather than legal categories. Yet even in the *Partitiones oratoriae*, where we see the traces of a more rigorous classificatory approach, the emphasis is on the general means of analysis, as in the case of *De oratore*, where the list of sources of evidence only serves to highlight the importance of an analytic method.

Conclusion

Looking at Cicero's use of Verres' books as evidence in the *Verrines*, we have seen that these are linked rhetorically to the characters of the defendant as well as the accuser, thus contributing to technical proof from *ēthos*. An interesting point to note here is that in addition to the actual entries of the books, their absence and later modifications are also constructed as proof by Cicero. In terms of Verres, even the occasional lack of systematic bookkeeping is depicted as part of a greater system, one of organised crime. In terms of Cicero, the story told is about his equally systematic efforts to gather and recover the evidence, against the malicious moves of Verres and his collaborators. His *diligentia* thus comprises both perseverance and organisedness, which is contrasted with the apparent sloppiness of Verres, revealed through Cicero's investigations as mere deceit.

In terms of theory, we have seen that both Aristotle and Cicero identify credibility as the key issue when dealing with 'testimonies', the class of non-technical proof that would cover Verres' books. In the speeches, credibility is for the most part simply assumed: book entries *qua* book entries are depicted as reliable.[16] It is against this background that Verres' omissions and deletions become meaningful for Cicero's argument. On the one hand, they indirectly prove that Verres had something to conceal. On the other hand, they provide space for Cicero's reconstructions, which thus gain in credibility.

It seems, then, that Cicero's remark in the *De oratore*, opposing forensic practice to school rhetoric, actually corresponds to his use of documentary proof in the *Verrines* in the sense that he does not deal with the issue of credibility directly (as suggested by the systematic discussion of relevant topics in Aristotle's *Rhetoric*). Rather, he constructs his proof through embedding the documents in a narrative frame, which connects the power of the documentary evidence to that of arguments from character.

16 On the issue of reliability in the case of *tabulae*, see Meyer (2004, esp. p. 219).

Bibliography

Butler, Shane (2002). *The Hand of Cicero*. London and New York: Routledge.

Carey, Christopher (1994). 'Artless Proofs' in Aristotle and the Orators. *BICS* 39: 95–106.

Cioffi, Robert L. (2011). Fuzzy Math: The Place of Numerical Evidence in Cicero *In Verrem* 3.116. *Mnemosyne* 64: 645–652.

Cuomo, Serafina (2011). All the Proconsul's Men: Cicero, Verres, and Account-keeping. In: Roselli, A. (ed.) *L'insegnamento delle techno nelle culture antiche: Atti del convegno, Ercolano, 23–24 marzo 2009.* Pisa: Fabrizio Serra. 165–188.

Frazel, Thomas D. (2004). The Composition and Circulation of Cicero's *In Verrem. Classical Quarterly n. s.* 54: 128–142.

Frazel, Thomas D. (2009). *The Rhetoric of Cicero's 'In Verrem'.* Berlin: Vandenhoeck & Ruprecht.

Guérin, Charles (2006). Cicero as User and Critic of Traditional Rhetorical Patterns: Structural Authority from *De inuentione* to *De oratore.* In: Galewicz, Cezary (ed.). *Texts of Power, the Power of the Text: Readings in Textual Authority Across History and Cultures.* Kraków: Homini. 61–85.

Gurd, Sean (2010). Verres and the Scene of Rewriting. *Phoenix* 64.1–2: 80–101.

Klotz, Alfred (1923). *M. Tulli Ciceronis scripta quae manserunt omnia.* Lipsiae et Berolini: Teubner.

Lehne-Gstreinthaler, Christine (2016). 'Jurists in the Shadows': The Everyday Business of the Jurists of Cicero's Time. In: DuPlessis, Paul J. (ed.). *Cicero's Law: Rethinking Roman Law of the Late Republic.* Edinburgh: Edinburgh University Press. 88–99.

Meyer, Elizabeth A. (2004). *Legitimacy and Law in the Roman World:* Tabulae *in Roman Belief and Practice.* Cambridge: Cambridge University Press.

Pfuntner, Laura (2015). Cooperation and Conflict between Governor and *poleis* in the *Verrines. Phoenix* 69.3–4: 355–375.

Schütrumpf, Eckart (1994). Non-Logical Means of Persuasion in Aristotle's *Rhetoric* and Cicero's *De oratore.* In: Fortenbaugh, William W. and Mirhady, David C. (eds.) *Peripatetic Rhetoric after Aristotle.* New Brunswick, NJ and London: Transaction Publishers. 95–110.

Steel, Catherine (2004) Being Economical with the Truth: What Really Happened at Lampsacus? In: Powell, J. and Patterson, J. (eds.). *Cicero the Advocate.* Oxford: Oxford University Press. 233–251.

Steel, Catherine (2007). The Rhetoric of the *de Frumento.* In: Prag, J. R. W. (ed.). *Sicilia nutria plebis Romanae: Rhetoric, Law, and Taxation in Cicero's Verrines.* London: Institute of Classical Studies. 37–48.

Tempest, Kathryn (2016). Staging a Prosecution: Aspects of Performance in Cicero's *Verrines.* In: Kremmydas, C., Powell, J., and Rubinstein, L. (eds.). *Profession and Performance: Aspects of Oratory in the Graeco-Roman World.* London: Institute of Classical Studies. 41–72.

Tempest, Kathryn (2007). Cicero and the Art of *dispositio:* The Structure of the *Verrines. Leeds International Classical Studies* 6.02: 1–25.

Index of Sources

Cuneiform Sources

Not included are the cuneiform tablets from Emar discussed by Fleming.

Ancient Authors and Works

Legal Texts

Linear B Tablets

Inscriptions

Papyri and Ostraca

Other